Sami Uljas & Andreas Dorn (eds)

Crossroads VI:
Between Egyptian Linguistics and Philology

Lingua Aegyptia

Studia Monographica

Herausgegeben von

Frank Kammerzell, Gerald Moers und Kai Widmaier

Band 30

Institut für Archäologie
Humboldt Universität
Berlin

Widmaier Verlag
Hamburg

Institut für Ägyptologie
Universität Wien
Wien

Crossroads VI

Between Egyptian Linguistics and Philology

edited by

Sami Uljas & Andreas Dorn

Widmaier Verlag · Hamburg
2024

Titelaufnahme:
Sami Uljas & Andreas Dorn (eds),
Crossroads VI:
Between Egyptian Linguistics and Philology,
Hamburg: Widmaier Verlag, 2024
(Lingua Aegyptia – Studia Monographica; Bd. 30)
ISSN 0946-8641
ISBN (paperback) 978-3-943955-30-9
DOI: https://doi.org/10.37011/studmon.30

Gedruckt auf säurefreiem, archivierfähigem Papier.

Druck und Verarbeitung: Hubert & Co., Göttingen
Printed in Germany

www.widmaier-verlag.de

CONTENTS

Preface

This volume brings together a collection of papers presented at the Sixth International Conference of Egyptian Grammar (Crossroads VI) held at Uppsala, Sweden, in the early days of 2020. The Crossroad(s) tradition, initiated in 1986, was reignited in 2009 after a sixteen-year hiatus, and since then conferences bringing together specialists on Egyptian linguistics have taken place at regular intervals. The organisers of the present event sought to bring a new element to the tradition and to address a novel issue or, it might be said, a problem that has emerged in Egyptological language- and textual studies over the last two decades or so. In the preface to the 2009 Crossroads proceedings, the organisers of that symposium emphasised how research on Ancient Egyptian had moved closer to general linguistics.[1] They expressed the hope that the relationship between the two would soon become reciprocal, with students of Egyptian providing data and ideas to general linguists rather than merely applying and appropriating the latter's theories and models. After fifteen years, it is fair to say that this solemn hope has been realised. Egyptological linguists habitually converse with their colleagues in general linguistics, and Egyptian material has been made accessible and utilisable to linguists who do not happen to be Egyptologists as well. Simply put, Egyptological linguistics has become part of general linguistics, and cooperation between the two research strands has begun to bear fruit.

Yet whilst having acquired a new audience outside of Egyptology, it seems that Egyptian linguists have simultaneously begun to lose another one within the subject. It is nowadays common – correctly or not, and often with at least some overlap in between – to classify scholars working with Egyptian textual material as either "linguists" or "philologists". In the bygone days of our science, there was no such division: Early luminaries of Egyptian text research such as Adolf Erman, Kurt Sethe, or Sir Alan Gardiner were all both first-class philologists as well as linguists. However, after 202 years of study, a split has emerged. The "linguists" focus on the language itself and are sometimes less involved with – and consequently informed of – the advances made by their "philologist" colleagues whose primary interest lies in the historical, ideational, and broadly cultural analysis of texts. Conversely, the "philologists" are understandably reluctant to burrow into the "linguists'" sometimes highly technical discussions, whose contribution and application to their own work is not necessarily always immediately apparent to them. Linguistic research is not, of course, a mere aid to philological analysis (e.g., a means of obtaining better translations) any more than philology should automatically be assumed to feed into linguistic understanding. Moreover, advances in theoretical and analytic sophistication within any area of scholarly investigation usually result in an increase in specialisation and even exclusiveness, which is arguably what has happened within Egyptological language- and textual studies regardless of orientations. Nevertheless, all researchers studying ancient Egyptian texts are, of course, using and working with exactly the same mate-

1 Müller, Matthias & Sami Uljas (eds). *Proceedings of the Fourth International Conference on Egyptian Grammar (Crossroads IV). Basel, March 19–22, 2009*. Göttingen; (*Lingua Aegyptia* 17).

Sami Uljas & Andreas Dorn (eds), *Crossroads VI. Between Egyptian Linguistics and Philology*, vii–x
DOI: https://doi.org/10.37011/studmon.30.00

rial. Against this, and the traditions and history of such studies noted, diminishing mutual discourse between the two research traditions is not desirable. There is also a more global issue involved here. Egyptology is a small subject within the constantly evolving field of Humanities, where cooperation between sub-disciplines is crucial not only for the sake of maintaining a public image, but also securing the increasingly important access to external funding for research.

The Uppsala conference was organised against this background. It was the second Crossroads gathering with a specific theme: *Between Egyptian Linguistics and Philology*.[2] Rather than to be another "Conference on Egyptian grammar", its idea was to provide a *table ronde* for discussions between researchers interested in the linguistic side of Egyptian and those engaged primarily in the philological study of texts. The participants invited were asked to include an element in their contributions that could help establish more common ground and dialogue between these two increasingly divergent strands of investigation. It was hoped that the Conference might provide not only a one-off forum for addressing these issues, but perhaps also serve as impetus for scholars to continue searching ways in which their work might serve the wider audience of Egyptological textual research beyond their immediate target group.

In prefaces to conference proceedings it is almost *de rigueur* to state that the aims and aspirations of the event were fulfilled to the complete satisfaction of all concerned. Alas, this was not entirely the case with the present symposium. A rather large number of researchers invited declined the summons to participate and/or to submit a paper, and some seem to have found it difficult to explicitly address the main theme of the conference in their contributions. This perhaps serves to corroborate the intuition of the organisers that a certain sense of unity and common cause is waning. It seems that more work is required before the emergent cracks within Egyptological textual studies can be smoothed over and that one conference between the people concerned, however well-intended, is not enough.

That said, the Uppsala symposium nevertheless provided an arena for vibrant discussions on Ancient Egyptian texts and language, as the contributions to the present volume demonstrate. The studies included here, written by leading specialists, discuss a wide variety of linguistic and philological phenomena that present a panorama of the status quo in the field and illustrate the extraordinary range of topics of investigation.

In his paper tackling the thorny question of Egyptian negations, **Marc Brose** suggests that the earlier language possessed a negative pattern *n* + "circumstantial" *sḏm-f* expressive of negative continuous action and thus differing from the more common *n sḏm-n-f*, analysed as semantically negative habitual. **Gaëlle Chantrain** provides an overview of how negative emotions were expressed in (Late) Egyptian single lexemes or compound expressions, both of which are employed metaphorically to describe the abstract concepts of feelings and emotion. **Mark Collier**'s discussion of Late Egyptian WH-questions fo-

2 The first thematic Crossroads conference, "Crossroads V: Whence and Whither? Egyptian-Coptic Linguistics in Comparative Perspectives" took place in February 17–20 2016 at Berlin: see Werning, Daniel. 2018. *Proceedings of the Fifth International Conference on Egyptian-Coptic Linguistics (Crossroads V). Berlin, February 17–20, 2016*. Hamburg; (*Lingua Aegyptia* 25).

cuses on the non-canonical cases where an interrogative word serves as the direct subject or object of a verb. These are analysed as pragmatically laden skeptical questions that challenge the addressee either to provide information for a sufficient response contrary to the negative expectations of the speaker, or to accept that no such response is possible. **Roberto Díaz-Hernández** scrutinises New Kingdom witnesses of Middle Egyptian literary works, arguing that the "Late-Egyptianisms" identifiable in this corpus of material result from diglossia between the Post-Classical form of Middle Egyptian and the contemporary form of the language. **Hans-Werner Fischer-Elfert**'s paper is a discussion of two Roman Period writing boards containing collections of verbs of motion in late hieratic script. These enigmatic texts are suggested to have served as pedagogic aids in teaching future priests the contemporary and ancient vocabulary of their native language that reveal a high degree of understanding of semantic and grammatical categories. **So Miyagawa** and **Heike Behlmer** investigate the use of Biblical quotations in the Coptic idiom of St Shenute of Atripe and his disciple Besa. The authors propose a new methodology based on isolating so-called Quotative Index Phrases (QIP) in text in order to identify quotations also when these are not explicitly marked as such or display extensive modification of the original. Coptic is also the subject of **Matthias Müller**'s contribution discussing locative adverbial clauses of the type "where X is/goes to/comes from" etc. He shows that instead of interrogatives such as *where/whence*, etc., Coptic used an appositive construction with the word "place" followed by a definite-marked relative clause to express such meanings. **Elsa Oréal** returns to the difficult topic of the Earlier Egyptian element *in*, used to code a pragmatically marked nominal actor of a Cleft Sentence and the agent of a passive or non-finite verb. She suggests a diachronic explanation to this polyfunctionality and proposes that the original function of *in* was that of an agentive marker and that its use in Clefts arose from its re-employment as an introducer of extra-posed topics rather than foci, with the "focalising" flavour deriving from word order. **Joachim Quack**'s article is an earnest attempt to answer the question of whether Demotic and linguistic studies can have a mutually beneficial and reciprocal relationship. By means of a critical examination of a number of key works by other authors along with a range of test cases from Demotic texts, he ultimately answers the question in the affirmative. **Chris Reintges** delves into the intricacies of Old Egyptian datival possessive sentences of the type X *n*-Y "X (is) to Y" > Y has X. Through a careful dissection of the data, he demonstrates that the possessive interpretation in fact derives from the animate status of the possessor Y but wanes or disappears with inanimate dative-marked noun phrases. The paper by **Nathalie Sojic** takes a close look into the layout and graphics of New Kingdom epistolary documents and highlights a series of conscious devices and techniques used by the scribes to enhance and enrich the text with subtle additional layers of meaning. Finally, **Jean Winand** describes verbal and lexical suppletion in (mostly Late) Egyptian. Focussing on a number of case studies such as the variance between the roots *šm* and *ḥn* "go" and *hꜣi* and *ẖr* "fall" in different verb forms and over time, he shows that suppletion was a widespread phenomenon in Egyptian that, moreover, often had a central role in historical grammar.

Of the above colleagues, Marc Brose, Mark Collier, and Chris Reintges were unable to attend the conference in person but sent in their contributions in a written form. Conversely, papers read but not included in the present volume include those by **Roland Enmarch** (Liverpool), "New paradigms and chaos: Incorporating the insights of linguistics into the interpretation of Middle Egyptian pessimistic literary texts"; **Roman Gundacker** (Vienna), "Analysing Egyptian royal names – a challenge at the crossroads of syntax, semantics, morphology and historical phonology"; **Stéphane Polis** (Liège) & **Eitan Grossman** (Jerusalem), "Expecting the unexpected. Rules and exceptions in Late Egyptian", and **Sami Uljas** (Uppsala), "The seven most important things that the linguists ever gave us".

In view of the merging of Egyptological and general linguistics as well as the avowedly interdisciplinary aims of the conference, the contributors to the present volume were asked to equip their Egyptian examples with linguistic glosses, following the modified Leipzig glossing rules suggested by Di Biase-Dyson, Kammerzell & Werning in the proceedings of the 2009 Crossroads.[3] Glossing is still a relatively novel method in Egyptology, and although the study just named did introduce an (partial) inventory of glosses for the use of fellow researchers, no strict rules concerning their application have yet been established. Consequently, the contributions to the present volume diverge widely in the ways in which they use glosses, with some authors meticulously dividing up expressions along morphemic boundaries and others adopting a more summary way of division. In many cases also no strict one-to-one correspondence between divisions made in Egyptian and glosses is maintained. Uniformity here would, of course, be desirable, but it is scarcely attainable yet. The editors decided ultimately to dispense with demands to this effect inasmuch as enforcing strict rules here would have required an impossible degree of micro-managing and persuasion.

This volume has been longer in the making than expected. The conference was held only a few weeks before the Covid-19 pandemic and the following travel bans, lockdowns, etc. rendered such events impossible. This may be deemed a stroke of luck, but the restrictions during 2020–22 often hampered contributors' access to libraries and other essential resources, which in many cases caused considerable delays in submitting papers.

We would like to tender our most heartfelt thanks to C.E. Gernandts Stiftelse, whose generous financial support made possible both the conference itself and the publication of its printed proceedings, as well as to Frank Kammerzell, Gerald Moers, and Kai Widmaier of Widmaier Verlag, who kindly typeset the contributions. We would also like to thank all the contributors as well as the following friends and colleagues who offered their help in preparing this volume: Fredrik Hagen (Copenhagen), Hanna Jenni (Basel), Anne Landborg (Uppsala), Julianna Paksi (Liège), and Luigi Prada (Uppsala).

Uppsala, January 2024 Sami Uljas & Andreas Dorn

---

3 Di Biase-Dyson, Camilla, Frank Kammerzell & Daniel Werning. 2009. Glossing Ancient Egyptian. Suggestions for adapting the Leipzig Glossing Rules, in: Müller, Matthias & Sami Uljas (eds). *Proceedings of the Fourth International Conference on Egyptian Grammar (Crossroads IV). Basel, March 19–22, 2009*. Göttingen; (*Lingua Aegyptia* 17), 343–66.

The 'Newest Rule of Gunn'?, or: Is there a Negative Construction *n sḏm=f* with a Present/Imperfective *sḏm=f* Form?

Marc Brose[1]

Abstract

In the majority of the recent grammars of Middle Egyptian/Earlier Egyptian there is no negative construction *n sḏm=f* containing a present/imperfective *sḏm=f* form. This article discusses the question whether such a negative construction might be attestable — a question which can only be understood by revisiting the complicated research history. After an overview of the relevant steps of research history a list of several instances is offered where the negative construction *n sḏm=f* with a present/imperfective *sḏm=f* form and present/imperfective function could be assumed, and also the problems emerging in connection with them are named. Furthermore, it will be shown that the verb form in question might be identified with the circumstantial *sḏm=f*/*jrı͗=f*, not with the Second Tense *jrr=f*. At the end the semantics of the negative construction are discussed and how it differs from the *n sḏm.n=f* construction. The conclusion is that *n sḏm=f* expresses negative continuous action, in direct opposition to *n sḏm.n=f* expressing negative habitual action.

Introduction

It sometimes happens that grammarians or general linguists come up with questions that philologists had not contemplated before because such questions did not matter in their daily work, where they try to create practical grammatical rules rather than ones that are supposed to fulfil advanced theoretical concepts introduced from outside, as general linguists and grammarians may sometimes do. One such question is whether negative constructions of the shape *n sḏm=f* containing a present/imperfective *sḏm=f* form and expressing present/imperfective meaning had existed in Earlier Egyptian. In the majority of recent grammars, no example for such a construction is quoted. Also, from a philological perspective there is no need for such a pattern because the *n sḏm.n=f* includes

1 Ägyptologisches Institut, Universität Leipzig; E-Mail: <marcbrose[at]yahoo.de>. I grant my thanks to the editors who gave me the chance to publish this article, although I could not participate in the conference. I again owe thanks to Sami Uljas for some useful comments and improving my English style, and last but not least Juliane Stein and Ann-Katrin Gill (both Leipzig) for a final style check.

Sami Uljas & Andreas Dorn (eds), *Crossroads VI. Between Egyptian Linguistics and Philology*, 1–26
DOI: https://doi.org/10.37011/studmon.30.01

all required functions of expressing 'present/imperfective' situations. Yet if one takes a deeper look in the research history, the problem becomes evident, for in older grammars there are, in fact, some corresponding instances quoted. One can therefore say that the question did not arise from the textual evidence but from the ongoing progress in research and continuous change in the linguistic description of Egyptian, which results in new or alternating definitions of syntactic functions of forms and constructions and their semantic oppositions.

The present article is structured as follows: At first an overview of the roots of the problem is given, starting from the 'Studies in Egyptian Syntax' by Gunn and his famous – or notorious – 'Gunn's Rule' through its modifications by Gardiner, Gilula, Polotsky and Hannig, to its current shape in recent grammars (section 1). In the second part a list of diverse attestations is offered where the identification of the *sḏm=f*-form as 'present/imperfective' is debatable. It is also discussed whether the form may be the 'circumstantial' form *sḏm=f*/*jri͗=f* or the 'nominal' form showing reduplication, *jrr=f*, and finally what its basic meaning might be and how it might differ on the semantic level from the *n sḏm.n=f* construction (section 2).[2]

1 Emergence of the Problem

1.1 Gunn's Rule

The starting point of the discussion is the so-called 'Gunn's Rule' (or: 'Rule of Gunn'). In 1924, Battiscombe Gunn published his 'Studies in Egyptian Syntax',[3] whose one part consisted of several studies about negated verbal forms. Gunn drew attention to a curious and counterintuitive phenomenon,[4] which became later known as 'Gunn's Rule'. He noted that the negation of the *sḏm.n=f* form did not normally carry a negative past or perfect meaning like in the affirmative usage, but rather a kind of present tense or imperfect value, often expressing negated customs, abilities and timeless generalizations, and also progressive actions, valid for all time positions.[5] Compare the following examples:

(1) Eloquent Peasant B1, 256 (old) = 287 (new) [Gunn (1924: 111)] [Tenseless]

n	*rḫ.n.tw*	*wnn.t*	*m*	*jb*
NEG	know.PRF.PASS	exist.PIA.SG.F	in/at	heart

'One perceives not what may be in the heart.'[6]

---

2 This article only discusses negative main clause patterns of the verbal system with negative particles *n* (and *nn*). Other kinds of negation, like the ones with the auxiliary *tm* or the type *n…js* are not relevant here.

3 Gunn (1924).

4 But this is not unique; cf. Werning (2008: 278 with footnote 46) noting some other languages where the negative perfect form has unexpected imperfect(ive) meaning.

5 Gunn (1924: 118).

6 The given translations in the examples are normally those of the quoted authors (but sometimes modernized).

(2) Ptahhotep, §§13+16 [Gunn (1924: 113)] [Present tense]
rꜣ gr n mdwi̯.n=f …
mouth be_silent.STAT.3.SG.M NEG speak.PRF=3SG.M
jb tm.w n sḫꜣ.n=f sf
heart finish.STAT.3SG.M NEG recall.PRF=3SG.M yesterday
'The mouth is silent, and does not speak … the mind is closed, and does not recall the past.'

(3) pWestcar 12,3 [Gunn (1924: 112)] [Past tense]
wn.jn=s ḥr dbn tꜣ ꜥ.t
AUX.CNSV.PST=3SG.F on.CVB.PRS encircle.INF ART chamber
n gmi̯.n=s bw jrr.w st jm
NEG find.PRF=3SG.F place do.PIP.SG.M DO.3PL/COLL there.ADV
'She went round the room, and (while doing so) she was not finding (could not find?) the place wherein it was being done.'

In connection with this, Gunn added several forms and constructions with present and imperfective value as affirmative correlatives, including bare *sḏm=f*, *jw=f sḏm=f*, *jr sḏm=f*, *sḏm.ḫr=f*, imperfective participle and the stative conjugation. He further noticed that the negative opposite of *sḏm.n=f* with simple past or (present/past) perfect meaning was normally *n sḏm=f*, e.g.:[7]

(4) Urk. IV, 132–133 [Gunn (1924: 94)]
rdi̯.n=f … jri̯.n=f … n gmi̯.tw … n ꜥwn=j …
let:PRF=3SG.M make:PRF.3SG.M NEG find:IPRF.PASS[8] NEG rob:IPRF=1SG
'He let … he made … one did not find … I did not rob …'

Furthermore, this was not the only function of the negative *n sḏm=f* construction. Gunn also noted the expression of tenseless, present and future/optative meaning,[9] e.g.:

(5) Sinuhe, B 259–260 [Gunn (1924: 99)] [Present tense]
n mdwi̯=k dm.t(w) rn=f
NEG speak.IPRF=2SG pronounce.IPRF.PASS name=3SG.M
'You are not speaking, (although) your name is pronounced.'

(6) Ptahhotep, §55 [Gunn (1924: 100)] [Tenseless; 'gnomic']
n jni̯.tw ḏr.w ḥmw.t
NEG bring.IPRF.PASS limit craft/art
'The limits of art cannot be reached.'

---

7 Gunn (1924: 93–97).
8 For there was only one indicative *sḏm=f*-form with 'imperfect' meaning in the discourse in the early 1920s, such *sḏm=f* forms are glossed as 'IPRF' in the examples quoted from Gunn.
9 Gunn (1924: 97–105).

(7) Urk. IV, 415.8 [Gunn (1924: 103)] [optative]

n	*sk*	*rn=f*	*ḏt*
NEG	perish.IPRF	name=3SG.M	eternity.ADVZ

‘May his name not perish forever.’

However, he tried to explain such cases as special uses of the past negation:

(a) the present as result of the inceptive force of the past, i.e. *n mdwi̯=k* ‘he didn’t start speaking’ → ‘he does not speak/is not speaking now’;

(b) the tenseless use as ‘gnomic’, as it appears in Classical Greek, where the past tense form of the perfective aspect (the ‘aorist’) is often used to express general statements, the so-called ‘gnomic aorist’;

(c) the optative as non-indicative, volitive usage as it can also be found at the perfect form of Semitic languages (see infra).

Gunn also quoted a single instance with the reduplicated *jrr=f* form:

(8) Eloquent Peasant, B1, 121 (old) = 152 (new) [Gunn (1924: 105)]

n	*jrr=k*	*st*	*n*	*jrr*	*st*	*zf*
NEG	do.IPRF.MOD	DO.3PL/COLL	NEG	do.IPRF.MOD	DO.3PL/COLL	kind_one

‘If you did not do it, the kind man would not do it.’

At the end of his ‘Studies’, Gunn generalized his observations and put them in the following crossover scheme,[10] which became later known as ‘Gunn’s Rule’,[11] and is even today taught in courses of Middle Egyptian for beginners:

Tense	Affirmative	Negative
‘he heard’	*sḏm.n=f*	*n sḏm=f*
‘he hears’	*sḏm=f*	*n sḏm.n=f*

Finally, he left it to the colleagues to find an answer to this strange phenomenon.

At this point some further additions should be made. Gunn’s generalization is not the last consequence of his observations, because they only apply to the affirmative and negative *sḏm.n=f* and their direct counterparts, i.e. *n sḏm=f* with past/perfect meaning and affirmative *sḏm=f* with present/imperfective meaning (as in *jw sḏm=f*). However, he also mentioned evidence for negative *n sḏm=f* with optative meaning, which he explained as special optative use of the past/perfect form as it is attested in Arabic or Assyrian.[12] Gunn also introduced a specialized negation for the future, *nn sḏm=f*[13], whereas the affirmative optative and future were both expressed by simple *sḏm=f*. The reason for his doing so is

10 Gunn (1924: 198).

11 As Gardiner (1962: 33) noted, the term was either created by Kurt Sethe (in German: ‘Gunn’sche Regel’) or at least was frequently used by him and so became very common in informal discourse.

12 Gunn (1924: 103–06). Gunn’s analogy is not perfect, because the usual affirmative past/perfect form of Egyptian, the *sḏm.n=f* form, cannot express the optative, as the Arabic perfect *qatala* or the Assyrian *iprus* (usually in the specific shape *liprus* with optative particle *lū*) can do.

13 Gunn (1924: 119–126).

that in the contemporary discourse of Egyptian grammar there existed only one indicative *sḏm=f*-form ('imperfect') with a broad semantic range that covered past, present, future tense, optative mood and also nuances like 'can, may' and so on. The only other 'normal' *sḏm=f* form (that means without any special marker like *n*, *jn* etc.), the reduplicated *jrr=f*, was viewed as a form carrying a special modal force ('emphatic'), but with almost the same semantic range as the indicative form. Hence the full scheme for all slots was as follows:

Tense/Mood	Affirmative	Negative
'he heard'	*sḏm.n=f*	*n sḏm=f*
'he hears'	*sḏm=f*	*n sḏm.n=f*
'he will hear'	*sḏm=f*	*nn sḏm=f*
'he should/might hear' (optative)	*sḏm=f*	*n sḏm=f*
'he can hear', 'he hears in general' (for all tenses)	*sḏm=f*	*n sḏm.n=f*

But as mentioned above, this was just a broad generalization that Gunn formulated at the end of the 'Studies'. It was, however, subsequently transferred into grammatical discourse and is still used by philologists – and also by beginners – at least as a mnemonic aid.[14]

1.2 Modifications by Gardiner

Only some years after the publication of the 'Studies', Alan Gardiner made some modifications to Gunn's model. First of all, he reclassified the two *sḏm=f* forms as 'perfective' (*jri͗=f*) and 'imperfective' (*jrr=f*). Secondly, he restricted the semantic definition of the *n sḏm.n=f* as expressing '*characterizations*, *statements of custom*, and *generalizations* of all kinds', adding that 'The true *modus operandi* of *n sḏm.n=f* becomes clear when we realize that the best way of confirming a generalization is to assert the absence of any invalidating incident'. His general definition conforms to what general linguists today call 'habitual', namely 'to deny the occurrence of an action throughout the course of a more or less prolonged period'.[15] Yet the opposite part of the 'habitual aspect', which general linguists call the 'continuous/progressive aspect', seen e.g. in English *he is hearing* (as opposed to the

14 The term 'Gunn's Rule' (or: 'Rule of Gunn', 'Gunn'sche Regel') did not appear in grammars of the following decades, cf. Erman (⁴1928), Gardiner (1927 & ³1957), De Buck (1952) or Lefebvre (²1955), and also in the prominent monography of Satzinger (1968) on negative constructions. Also recent grammars rarely mention it; see section 1.5 below. That underlines its prominence as informal 'philological' rule, not as a fully accepted grammatical one.

15 Gardiner (1927: 332–33, §418) = (³1957: 332–33, §418). Cf. the definition of 'habitual aspect' (as part of the imperfective super-aspect) by Comrie (1998: 27–28): 'The feature that is common to all habituals, whether or not they are also iterative, is that they describe a situation which is characteristic of an extended period of time, so extended in fact that the situation referred to is viewed not as an incidental property of the moment, but, precisely, as a characteristic feature of a whole period.'

habitual *he hears*) was not accepted as a function of *n sḏm.n=f*.[16] In Gardiner's model the affirmative correlatives of *n sḏm-n=f* are all the forms and constructions with included habitual meaning like the reduplicated *jrr=f*-form (the 'imperfective *sḏm=f*'), the *jw=f sḏm=f* (with 'perfective *sḏm=f*'!), the imperfective participle and also the stative conjugation.[17]

Otherwise, in his overview to the *n sḏm=f* construction,[18] Gardiner still viewed its function of referring to present occurrences (without a concrete distinction between 'general' and 'incidental') as normal rather than as a special use of the past negation as Gunn did. But if such an example seemed to be best rendered as 'he cannot', Gardiner argued that it might be a miswriting of the *sḏm.n=f* form, as in:

(9) Ptahhotep, §55 [Gardiner ([3]1957: 376, §455.4)] [see above ex. 6)]

n	*jni̯.tw*	*ḏr.w*	*ḥmw.t*
NEG	bring.PFV.PASS	limit	craft/art

'The limit of the art cannot be attained.'

An alternative would be – again – a reading as past event: 'he has not, *or* never, heard', i.e. a special rendering of the past function.

Further examples of present occurrences may be:

(10) Dialogue between a man and his soul, 5 [= Gardiner ([3]1957: 376, §455.2)]

n	*mdwi̯*	*b3=j*	*ḥnᶜ=j*
NEG	talk.PFV	ba/soul=1SG	with=1SG

'My soul does not speak with me.'

(11) Dialogue between a man and his soul, 115–116 [Gardiner ([3]1957: 376, §455.2); also quoted by Gunn (1924: 99)]

n	*sḫ3.t(w)*	*sf*
NEG	remember.PFV.PASS	yesterday

n	*jri̯.t(w)*	*n*	*jri̯*	*m*	*t3*	*3.t*
NEG	do.PFV.PASS	DAT	do.PPA.SG.M	in/at	ART	moment

'Yesterday is not remembered, the helper is not helped (lit. one does not do to the doer) at this moment.'

1.3 Modifications by Polotsky and Gilula

Crucial modifications to the Gunn-Gardiner analysis of the negative constructions were made by Hans Jakob Polotsky and Mordechai Gilula. When Polotsky published his theory of the Second Tenses in 1944, he rearranged the *sḏm=f* paradigm in a not yet seen manner:[19]

16 Compare Gardiner's statement 'the absence of any invalidating incident' and the definition of the continuous aspect by Comrie (1998: 33): 'imperfectivity that is not occasioned by habituality'. This refers to its characteristic feature as 'the incident property of the moment' (p. 28; mentioned in the definition of habituality).

17 Gardiner (1927: 332, §418) = ([3]1957: 332, §418).

18 Gardiner (1927: 375–76, §455) = ([3]1957: 375–76, §455).

19 Polotsky (1944: 93).

Tense	Predicative form	Concrete relative form	Abstract relative form (= Second tense)
'Passé'	*ḥz.n=f*	*ḥz.n=f*	*ḥz.n=f*
'Temps indefini'	*ḥzz=f* (sic) [meant to be *ḥz=f*]	*ḥzz(.w)=f*	*ḥzz=f*
'Futur (Prospectif)'	*ḥz=f*	*ḥz.y=f*	*ḥz=f*

Polotsky was one of the first to accept Gunn's proposal of the existence of specialized prospective verbal forms,[20] and probably the first to proclaim a concrete prospective *sḏm=f*.[21] It took decades before the theory of the Second Tenses and also the prospective *sḏm=f* form (also under the name 'subjunctive') became accepted.[22] It was in 1970, in a review to Helmut Satzinger's monograph on the negative constructions in Earlier Egyptian, when Gilula, under the influence of Polotsky's theory,[23] restricted the phenomenon known as 'Gunn's Rule' to the so called *circumstantial forms*, i.e. the forms used to form circumstantial clauses or main clauses in connection with main clause marking particles like *jw*. He did so, because he argued that the constructions with bare negative particle *n* with the observable crossover semantics worked only as negative correlative of those circumstantial forms. He also limited *n sḏm=f* as negation of the past, without function of negative present (i.e. negative present action!). Moreover, he removed the negative future/optative value of *n sḏm=f* from the discussion, and in his model, it became part of the functional range of the prospective *sḏm=f* form like *nn sḏm=f*.[24]

In Polotsky's final version of the theory of the Second Tenses, the general scheme of 'Gunn's Rule' looks as follows:[25]

Aspect	Affirmative		Negative
'Accompli'	*jw sḏm.n=f*	↘ ↗	*n sḏm=f*
'Inaccompli'	*jw=f sḏm=f*	↗ ↘	*n sḏm.n=f*

20 Gunn (1924: 1–44).

21 Gunn (1924: 45–65) discussed the construction *jn* NN / *ntf sḏm=f*, but he only allocated prospective function to it. Apart from that Gunn was the first to proclaim a prospective verbal form at all, the 'prospective relative form', but he did not classify it as a 'normal' *sḏm=f* form. As Gunn (p. 1 n. 2) noted, the term 'prospective' was suggested by Gardiner to him. Gunn himself preferred at first 'future'. For the term 'prospective' and its origin see Polotsky (1964: 270 n. 2).

22 The history of research of the verbal forms running in the recent discourse under 'prospective', 'subjunctive' and 'future' is very complicated, see Hutter (2017: 76–83, 95–103) and Depyudt (1993), but this debate is insubstantial to the present issue.

23 Especially the statements in the 'Egyptian tenses'; Polotsky (1965).

24 Gilula (1970: 207); for the prospective/subjunctive *sḏm=f* in contemporary publications see also Polotsky (1964: 271–72); Satzinger (1968: 39, §§57–58).

25 Polotsky (1976: 44, §4.1.1) [there without crossing arrows]. This stands *pars pro toto* for several schemes depending on the lexical verb class (transitive, verbs of movement) and the *genus verbi* (active, passive)!

Polotsky also replaced the terms referring to tenses by terms referring to aspects.[26] And, finally, he was the first who proclaimed that the *sḏm=f* form in the *jw=f sḏm=f* construction was not the same as in the *n sḏm=f* construction, after after having compared the verbal stems of mutable verbs like *rḏi̯* and *mꜣꜣ*, which show in the first paradigm the stems *ḏi̯* and *mꜣꜣ*, and the stems *rḏi̯* and *mꜣ* in the second.[27] The second stem corresponds to the independent narrative usage of the *sḏm=f* in Old Egyptian autobiographical texts. Polotsky brought them together and so proposed a new form, with the following features: 'verbale' ('verbal') on the syntactical level, i.e. it did not need any particle or auxiliary to work as predicate of the main clause, and 'factive' ('factual') on the semantical level, i.e. with mainly past meaning and sometimes present meaning under special conditions.[28] In recent discourse this form is usually termed 'past *sḏm=f*', 'indicative *sḏm=f*', 'perfective *sḏm=f*' or 'momentanous *sḏm=f*'.[29] As a result, Polotsky finally disrupted 'Gunn's Rule' and its crossover semantics, as the following scheme demonstrates:[30]

Aspect	Affirmative	Negative
Accompli	*jw sḏm.n=f*	*n sḏm=f* / *rḏi̯=f* / *mꜣ=f*
Factive	*sḏm=f* / *rḏi̯=f* / *mꜣ=f*	
Inaccompli	*jw=f sḏm=f* / *ḏi̯=f* / *mꜣꜣ=f*	*n-sḏm.n=f*

1.4 The 'Neue Gunn'sche Regel' ('New Rule of Gunn') by Hannig

Some years after Polotsky's efforts Rainer Hannig tried to 'save' the old 'Gunn's Rule' – with a unique form *sḏm=f* (!) – by an alternative explanation based on the aspectual values of the corresponding *sḏm.n=f* and *sḏm=f* forms, under comparison with the evidence in Russian.[31] He stated that in Russian, when forms with perfective aspect value are used, it is expressed that the action cannot be initiated or performed in total, and when forms with imperfective aspect value are negated, it signals only a simple negation of the action. Then he transferred this evidence to Egyptian: Here *n sḏm.n=f* – the negated perfective aspect – shows the inability to initiate an action or perform it in total, and *n sḏm=f* – the negated imperfective aspect – is used for simple negation of the action. These semantics are valid for all time positions (past, present, future), and that *n sḏm=f* shows past meaning in most of the evidence is a pure incidence. Hannig's linear scheme for his 'Neue Gunn'sche Regel' ('New Rule of Gunn') looks as follows:[32]

26 Polotsky did not make any comment about the semantic value of *n sḏm.n=f* as overall negative *inaccompli* (like Gunn's negative present) or as specialized negative habitual (as Gardiner did).

27 Satzinger (1968: 8, §12) had already suggested that, but he did not proclaim a new form.

28 Polotsky (1976: 45–46, §4.1.5). See also Polotsky (1964: 272–75), where he had already discussed ideas of a separate 'indicative' *sḏm=f*.

29 See Hutter (2017: 19–26, 284–85, Table III:1).

30 The scheme is not presented in Polotsky (1976) but was drawn by the author of this article.

31 Hannig (1984).

32 Hannig (1984: 68).

Aspect	Affirmative	Negative
Perfective	*jw sḏm.n=f* →	*n sḏm.n=f*
Imperfective	*jw=f sḏm=f* →	*n sḏm=f*

Here *n sḏm=f* means 'he did not/does not/will not hear', and *n sḏm.n=f* 'he could not/cannot hear', 'he was/is/will be disabled to hear', and also 'he did not/does not/will not hear in general'. So the assumed crossover semantics that come forth in translations to English, French or German would only be a phantom resulting from a transfer from an aspect-prominent language to tense-prominent languages.

1.5 'Gunn's Rule' in recent grammars of Middle Egyptian

Hannig's 'New Rule of Gunn' was not successful,[33] and Polotsky's approach carried the day. It is found in most recent grammars of Middle Egyptian, although the way in which it is presented is not uniform. The standard is the following:[34]

- *n sḏm=f* with past/perfective etc. *sḏm=f* shows usually past meaning and sometimes, under special conditions, present meaning (see infra section 2.1–2).
- *n sḏm.n=f* functions as negative present/habitual.

If the term 'Gunn's Rule' is mentioned at all, it is used as a kind of mnemonic aid,[35] and sometimes its prominence in the history of research is noted.[36]

Some Grammars make several additions to the standard model. Ockinga and Beylage include the 'negative continuous/progressive' value, denoting the concrete present ('here and now') as a further function of *n sḏm.n=f*;[37] e.g.:

(12) Eloquent Peasent, B2, 113–114 [Beylage (2018: 415)]

mk	*wj*	*ḥr*	*spr*	*n=k*
Attn	Sbj.1Sg	on.Cvb.Prs	plead.Inf	Dat=2Sg.m

n	*sḏm.n=k*	*st*
Neg	hear.Prf=2Sg.m	Do.3Pl/Coll

'Behold, I am pleading you, but you do not pay attention to it.'

Borghouts mentions, as e.g. Edel, Westendorf, Satzinger and Allen did long before (but mainly for Old Egyptian and Medical Texts with a specialized scientific style),[38] that *n sḏm.n=f* could sometimes show the meaning of a 'simple' negative past/perfect,[39] e.g.:

33 See also the discussion in Brose (2017: 27–35, esp. 27–29).

34 E.g. Malaise & Winand (1999: 397–401, §§634–40); Schenkel (2012: 243–44); Werning (2015: 73, §46.4).

35 E.g. Graefe (⁶2001: 80–81, §35.5; 161, §63).

36 Malaise & Winand (1999: 396–97, §633); Werning (2015: 73–74, §46.4).

37 Ockinga (2005: 79–80, §136a); Beylage (2018: 415).

38 Edel (1955/64: 255–56, §§542, 544); Westendorf (1962: 172, §§241.2–3); Satzinger (1968: 18–20, §§27–29); Allen (1984: 293, §435).

39 Borghouts (2010: 248–49, §68b).

(13) CT II 33g (B1C) [Borghouts (2010: 248, §68b)]

n	*gmi̯.n(=j)*	*bw*	*ꜥḥꜥ=j*	*jm*
NEG	find.PRF=1SG	place	stand.FUT=1SG	there.ADV

'I did not (ever) find a place so that I might stand on it.'[40]

Further, Allen (second edition of 'Middle Egyptian') quotes again a possible example for a negative construction with circumstantial *sḏm=f* and with general meaning (which Gunn formerly explained as special function of the past reference and which Gardiner excluded):[41]

(14) Ptahhotep, §348–349 [Allen (²2010: 279, §20.15)]

n	*jni̯.tw*	*ḥtp.t*	*r*	*dmj*
NEG	bring.IPFV.PASS	contentment	to	harbor
jw	*jni̯.tw*	*ꜥq.wwn*		*ꜣq*
MCM	bring.IPFV.PASS	close_friendsexist.IPFV		disaster

'Contentment is not brought to harbor, and close friends are brought when there is a disaster.'

Otherwise, and following the standard model, Daniel Werning rates the peripheral functions of *n sḏm.n=f* as negative past/perfect and *n sḏm=f* as negative present as 'nicht sicher belegt'.[42]

Not all recent grammars follow the standard. The grammars of Allen (third edition) and Maderna-Sieben advocate a pan-*sḏm=f* approach, which more or less leads back to Gunn and where 'Gunn's Rule' is not only a mnemonic aid, but a full functional grammatical rule.[43] Another approach is a wider functional range of the 'factual' *sḏm=f* introduced by Polotsky and found in the grammars of Zonhoven and Jenni, where it includes diverse present/general meanings like the NN *sḏm=f* construction (both) or the *jw=f sḏm=f* construction (only Jenni). Jenni views the *sḏm=f* as a form expressing past tense at an earlier language stage, whose semantic range was subsequently widened, but the negative *n sḏm=f* preserved the archaic function as negative past.[44] In Zonhoven's grammar the form is said to have a general factual value denoting past and present events, and sometimes this holds for the negative construction too.[45] As an example, Zonhoven quotes ex. 10 from above: *n mdwi̯ bꜣ=j ḥnꜥ=j* 'My soul does not speak with me.' [his translation: 'mein Ba spricht nicht (mehr) mit mir']. Furthermore, in both grammars, the *n sḏm.n=f* is said to function only as negative habitual.[46]

---

40 Borghouts does not explain why it cannot mean negation of ability 'I could not find any place etc.', which fits well in the context.

41 Allen (²2010: 279, §20.15).

42 Werning (2015: 73, §46.4). Because of the restricted length of this article a detailed discussion of the *n sḏm.n=f* construction and its semantic range need to be ignored here.

43 Allen (³2014: 256–58, §17.11; 277–79, §18.13); Maderna-Sieben (2016: 237, §27.1.1); but only the latter draws the well-known crossover scheme and uses the term 'Gunn'sche Regel'.

44 Jenni (2010: 237–38, §22.3.1).

45 Zonhoven (2000: 109, §43.C.2).

46 Zonhoven (2000: 123, §49.B.2); Jenni (2010: 238, §22.3.2).

Finally, and as mentioned above, Gunn’s Rule is still well established in the informal discourse and also in the academical education of the Egyptian language.

Now, following the standard model, a new question arises: When the *n sḏm=f* construction does not show past/perfective meaning but a present/imperfective one, how can this be explained?

2 Debatable attestations of *n sḏm=f* with present/imperfective meaning

The following section will show that there are more attestations of this value than one would expect at first sight, but not all examples are equally clear and might be explained as specific subfunctions of the past/perfective *sḏm=f*. The attestations are arranged according to the specific functions. These are in detail:

2.1 *n sḏm=f* denoting a present state

Gunn had already quoted a lot of examples where *n sḏm=f* denoted a present state, almost always with state verbs like adjectives and *rẖ* ‘know’, which express their affirmative present tense usually with a stative, cp.:

(15) pWestcar 9,1/3 [Gunn (1924: 98)]

jw=k	*rẖ.tj* …	*n*	*rẖ=j* …
MCM=2SG.M	know.STAT.2SG.M	NEG	know.IPFV?=1SG

‘You know … I don’t know …’

(16) CT V, 223f–g B1C [Gunn (1924: 97); there quoting the old edition: Textes rel. 1, C/72]

‘I know you, I know your names [*jw=j rẖ.kw ṯn rẖ.kw rn.w=ṯn*]

n	*mwt=j*	*n*	*šwꜣ=j*	*n*	*šp=j*
NEG	die.IPFV?=1SG	NEG	be_destitute.IPFV?=1SG	NEG	e_blind.IPFV?=1SG

n	*jd=j*
NEG	be_deaf.IPFV?=1SG

I am not dead, I am not destitute, I am not blind, and I am not deaf.”

But it was also Gunn who explained such instances with the resultative effect of the past/perfect negation which can be easily derived from the inceptive meaning of the root, e.g. *n mwt=j* ‘I have not died’ → ‘I am not dead’, *n šp=j* ‘I have not become blind’ → ‘I am not blind’, *rẖ=j* ‘I have not become aware-of’ → ‘I do not know’ and so on. This was accepted by Gardiner[47] and is common in the grammatical discourse until today.[48] That is, such attestations can easily be explained as special usage of the past/perfective *sḏm=f*.[49]

---

47 Gardiner (^{3}1957: 376, §455.2).

48 E. g. Malaise & Winand (1999: 397–98, §635); Beylage (2018: 388).

49 The examples quoted by Satzinger (1968: 7, §9) for negative circumstantial clauses with present meaning belong here.

2.2 *n sḏm=f* denoting a statement of a general, customary action

Sometimes *n sḏm=f* seems to denote a general statement or the lack of ability, as *n sḏm.n=f* normally does. It is not surprising that such instances are often found in instructions. Two examples have already been quoted above, i.e.:

(17) Ptahhotep, §55 [see above ex. 6 = 9]

n	*jni̯.tw*	*ḏr.w*	*ḥmw.t*
NEG	bring.IPFV?.PASS	limit	craft/art

'The limit of the art cannot be attained.'

(18) Ptahhotep, §348–349 [see above ex. 14]

n	*jni̯.tw*	*ḥtp.t*	*r*	*dmj*
NEG	bring.IPFV?.PASS	contentment	to	harbor
jw	*jni̯.tw*	*ꜥq.w*	*wn*	*ꜣq*
MCM	bring.IPFV?.PASS	close_friends	exist.IPFV	disaster

'Contentment is not brought to harbor, and close friends are brought when there is a disaster.'

Another example would be:

(19) Ptahhotep, §348 [L2] [Gunn (1924: 100)]

n	*jni̯.tw*	*ḥtp*	*m*	*ḏrḏrj*
NEG	fetch.IPFV?.PASS	comfort	from	stranger

'One cannot obtain comfort from a stranger.'

And once variation between *n sḏm=f* and *n sḏm.n=f* occurs:

(20) pPetersburg 1116A [Merikare], rt. 93 [= rt. 9,1] [Gunn (1924: 101)]

n	*qn.n=f*	*n*	*gr*	*qn.tw=f*
NEG	conquer.PRF=3SG.M	NEG	also:ADV	conquer.IPFV?.PASS=3SG.M

'He (the Asiatic) does not conquer, yet he cannot be conquered.'

Gardiner argued that in such instances the verbal forms might show miswriting, i.e. *jn<.n>.tw* or *qn.<n>.tw*.[50] Support for this explanation might come from the fact that the last strong consonant of the root (*jni̯*, *qn*) is *n*, and it is not impossible that the writer forgot one *n*. For *jni̯* there is also the option to read just *jni̯.n.tw* because the writing 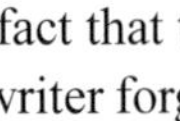 permits that reading.

Recent grammars do not usually mention instances like those above. The reason is not obvious at first sight. Again, it was Gunn who found a way to explain them as further special usage of the past/perfect(ive) meaning.[51] When he quoted such instances, he used the term 'gnomic' to describe this function. This term is frequently applied to the use of forms denoting past tense, the perfect or the perfective aspect, to express general statements, like the aorist in Classical Greek. Here one may also compare e.g. German where one finds statements of general value like 'Es ist noch kein Meister vom Himmel gefallen.' (with

50 Gardiner ([3]1957: 376, §455.4).
51 Gunn (1924: 100–01).

present perfect), which is more or less equivalent to 'Ein Meister fällt nicht vom Himmel.' (with simple present). Also, in English such statements would be understandable (though not very common): 'No master has ever fallen from sky.', 'Not once a master fell from sky.' or 'Masters have not (yet) fallen from the sky.'[52] And so, in accordance with the contexts, the Egyptian statements could be read, i.e.:

- ex. 17: 'The limit of the art has not (yet) been attained.'
- ex. 18: 'Contentment has not (yet) been brought to harbor.'
- ex. 19: 'One has never/not (yet) obtained comfort from a stranger.'
- ex. 20: 'He does not conquer, yet he has never/not yet been conquered.'[53]

So, the *sḏm=f* form in such instances may be the past/perfective *sḏm=f*.[54] However, what Gunn did not consider was the affirmative correspondent of such statements. Here two constructions are very common, one with the Second Tense, the 'imperfective' *sḏm=f*/ *jrr=f*, and one with the *jw(=f) sḏm=f*/*jri̯=f* construction with 'circumstantial' *sḏm=f*;[55] cf.:

(21) Ptahhotep, §349 (L2) [Gardiner (^{3}1957: 352, §440.1)]

jnn.tw	*m*	*ꜥq*	*wn*	*ꜣḫ.w*
fetch.IPFV.PASS	in/at	friend	exist.IPFV	trouble

'One has recourse to an intimate when there is trouble.'
The witness P has instead *jw jni̯.tw*.

(22) Ptahhotep, §55 (P) [Gardiner (^{3}1957: 385, §462)]
'Eloquence is more hidden than the emerald,

jw	*gmi̯.t(w)=s*	*m-ꜥ*	*ḥm.wt*	*ḥr*	*bn.wt*
MCM	find.IPFV.PASS=3SG.F	with	handmaiden.PL	on	millstone.PL

(but) it is found with handmaidens at (their) mill-stones.'
The witness L2 has *jw gmm.tw* (!), which is not a regular usage of the *jrr=f* form.

In Gardiner's classification the form after *jw* is the 'perfective' *sḏm=f* (with a broader semantic range than the recent past/perfective *sḏm=f*), but in more recent analyses its TAM-value is viewed as present/imperfective. So, there seems to be the option that in the negative construction the *sḏm=f* form may also be one of the imperfectives. But that is not the final word, because there may be attestations for the gnomic use of the past/perfective *sḏm=f*, too; e.g.:

---

52 The example from German is that of the author of this article. Other languages where such gnomic statements are commonly performed by forms expressing past tense or perfect/perfective aspect are Semitic languages, see e.g. Brose (2019: 45–46, ex. 42; 55–56, ex. 63; 66, ex. 89; 72, ex. 98; 79–80, ex. 116) for the earlier West Semitic languages.

53 This kind of reading is optional for all instances quoted by Gunn (1924: 99–100)!

54 One grammar in which this function is noted is Malaise & Winand (1999: 398, §635).

55 See Gardiner (^{3}1957: 352–53, §440.1; 385–86, §§462–63).

(23) Sinuhe B 66 [also cited by Gardiner (^{3}1957: 367, §450.2, note 7)]

Sinuhe says in praising the king:

mri̯	*sw*	*nʾ.t=f*	*r*	*ḥꜥ(.w)<=sn>*
love.PFV	DO.3SG.M	city=3SG.M	than	body=3PL

'His city loves (< has ever loved) him more as itself.'[56]

For a 'present/imperfective' form one would expect *jw mri̯=f* or *mrr=f*![57]

So, it cannot be determined with certainty whether the verb form in the instances of *n sḏm=f* with general/gnomic value is a present/imperfect form or in fact the past/perfective *sḏm=f*. What is needed for a definite decision is an instance with a significant mutable verb like *rḏi̯* or *mꜢꜢ*. But the most adequate solution would be to assume an idiomatic distribution: Past/perfective *n sḏm=f* expresses gnomic statements (the event did never happen in the past and it is not expected that it happens now or anytime in the future), and *n sḏm.n=f* expresses habitual statements (the event does usually not happen, but sometimes it has happened in the past, perhaps happens anywhere in the present and there is still the chance that it can happen in the future). And in correspondent affirmative statements *jw=f jri̯=f* (imperfective) / *jrr=f* express the habitual statements and *jri̯=f* (Perfective) the gnomic ones.

2.3 *n sḏm=f* denoting a non-general, present/imperfective meaning

The most secure way to proof the existence of a present/imperfective *sḏm=f* form in the *n sḏm=f* construction would be to find instances where not general, customary actions are expressed, but rather incidental actions.[58] That was not excluded by Gardiner, but Gunn explained it as special usage of the past meaning of *n sḏm=f*, and such cases are not mentioned in modern grammars.

Three examples have already been quoted above:

(24) Sinuhe B 259–260 [see above ex. 5; also cited by Gardiner (^{3}1957: 376, §455.2, note 2)]

n	*mdwi̯=k*	*dm.t(w)*	*rn=f*
NEG	speak.IPFV?=2SG	pronounce.IPFV.PASS	name=3SG.M

'You are not speaking, (although) your name is pronounced.'

---

56 The example fully quoted by Gardiner is Adm. 102 = Lamentation of Khakheperreseneb, BM EA 4645, rt. 11: *rḏi̯.tw mꜢꜥ.t <r>-rw.tj* 'Truth is cast outside.'; but it is in its context easily to understand as past: 'The land is in trouble … Truth was cast outside. Chaos is in the hall (now).'

57 See Gardiner (^{3}1957: 367, §450.2), where no *jw* is positioned before the verb.

58 An ideal example would not only show incidental action but would also have a highly significant mutual verb for distinguishing the different verbal forms. But there is no verb that fulfils these conditions, not even *rḏi̯*, which can also show the stem *ḏi̯* in the past/perfective *sḏm=f*; see Borghouts (2010: 200, §55.b.2, with reference Beni Hassan I, pl. XXVI, l. 122 [Tomb 3]).

(25) Dialogue between a man and his soul, 5 [see above ex. 10]

n	*mdwi̯*	*bꜣ=j*	*ḥnꜥ=j*
NEG	talk.IPFV?	ba=1SG	with=1SG

'My soul does not speak with me.'

(26) Dialogue between a man and his soul, 115–116 [see above ex. 11]

n	*sḫꜣ.t(w)*	*sf*
NEG	remember.IPFV?.PASS	yesterday

n	*jri̯.t(w)*	*n*	*jri̯*	*m*	*tꜣ*	*ꜣ.t*
NEG	do.IPFV?.PASS	DAT	do.PPA.SG.M	in/at	ART	moment

'Yesterday is not remembered, the helper is not helped at this moment.'

However, in ex. 24 and 25 the context allows an interpretation of the form as past/perfective. In ex. 24 Sinuhe has prostrated before the king and is silent while the king holds his speech. He has not yet said a word. So the king might also conclude: 'You did not speak when your name was pronounced (i.e. some minutes ago until now).' In ex. 25 the man expresses his desperation. Before the quoted sentence he had said: 'That is too much for me today.', and then he could have continued: 'My ba did not talk to me (i.e. when I had the need of talking).' But in ex. 26 this is not as easy: *sḫꜣ.tw* may belong to the group of verbs like *rḫ* and *mwt* (see above chap. 2.1), whose past negation has a resultative meaning 'it has not come to be remembered' → 'it is not remembered'. Also, Gunn pointed out that in such instances the resultative meaning of the inceptive use of the root might be present.[59] But regarding the second clause with *jri.tw*, the adverbial phrase *m tꜣ ꜣ.t* 'at the moment/now' signals a real present meaning, and that supports the assessment as a present/imperfective form. An interpretation such as 'it came not into performance' or the like → 'it is not made' sounds very strange.

The following examples come from medical texts:

(27) pEbers 106,3–5 (case 863a) [also quoted by Westendorf (1962: 148, §212.2a), here in more detail]

jr	*wpi̯=k*	*ꜥꜣ.t*	*n.t*	*ḥꜥ.w …*
if.COND	isolate.SBJV=2SG.M	swelling	GEN.SG.F	flesh

gmm=k	*sj*	*mj*	*jnm*	*n*	*ḥꜥ.w=f*	*gs.t(j)*
find.IPFV=2SG.M	DO.3SG.F	like	skin	GEN.SG.M	flesh=3SG.M	tan=STAT.3SG.F

n	*šmi=s*	*jwi̯{t}=s*	*ḥr*	*ḏbꜥ.w=k*
NEG	go.IPFV?=3SG.F	come=IPFV(?)=3SG.F	with	finger.PL=2SG.M

wp.w-ḥr	*smn*
except	stay_firm.INF

'If you locate a swelling of the flesh … (and) you find it like the skin of his (= the patient's) flesh, being like tanned (?), (and) it (i.e. the swelling) does not go and come (i.e. deform) under your fingers but stays solid (…, then you should say …).'

59 Gunn (1924: 97–98). See above section 1.1 and 2.1.

(28) pEbers 48,3–4 (case 252) [also quoted by Gunn (1924: 99), here in more detail]

jr	*ḏꜣ*	*tp*	*n*	*z*	*ḥr=k*	*wꜣḥ=k*
if.COND	shake.SBJV	head	GEN.SG.M	man	OBLV=2SG.M	lay.IPFV=2SG.M

ḏr.t=k	*ḥr*	*tp=f*	*n*	*šni̯=f*	*sj*
hand=2SG.M	on	head=3SG.M	NEG	suffer.IPFV?=3SG.M	DO.3SG.F

'If a man's head shakes, you are to lay your hand upon his head, without his suffering from it (lit. 'while he is not suffering from it [i.e. the laying down of the hand]').'

Both cases show on the surface a negative construction functioning on the syntactic level as clause of circumstance, but indicate present/imperfective value, not the expected past value.[60] Given the context, it does not make good sense to analyse them as a kind of past/perfective, as Gunn tried to do, but Westendorf did not.[61]

Further debatable examples can be found in the Admonitions:[62]

(29) Admonitions 3,6–7 [also quoted by Gunn (1924: 102), here in more detail]

jw	*ms*	*qd.w*	*ꜥq.w*	*m*	*ꜥḥw.tj.w*
MCM	PTCL.MOD	builder.PL	enter.STAT.3PL	as	field-worker.PL

wn.w	*m*	*dp.t-nṯr*	*nḥb [...]*
exist.PPA.PL.M	in	god's_ship	yoke.STAT.3.PL

n	*ms*	*ḫdi̯.tw*	*r*	*[Kp]nj*	*mjn*
NEG	PTCL.MOD	sail_north.IPFV?.PASS	to	Byblos.TN	today

'O, yet, builders have been trained (lit. have entered) as field-workers, those who were (before) in the god's ship are (now) yoked […]. And yet (as consequence), no one sails north (any longer) to [Byb]los today.'

Here the context with the adverb *mjn* 'today' supports the assumption that the negative construction might express the incident present tense, and the verb form is a present/imperfective form. Nevertheless, in his recent commentary, Roland Enmarch translates the clause with perfect ('no one has travelled north'), without any comment.[63] But the context suggests that the cancelled travel to Byblos is a consequence of the sailors having been taken from the ship for some menial labour or the like. So, in my opinion, the present tense makes more sense.[64] The following example is similar:

---

60 Gunn (1924: 99) lists further instances from the Coffin Texts (or 'textes religieuses', as their name was in the contemporary discourse, after the former main edition of Pierre Lacau), but all of them could be easily explained as negative future.

61 Westendorf (1962: 148, §212.2a).

62 S. Uljas (personal communication) mentioned that the Text of the Admonitions of Ipuwer should better be avoided for the argumentation because of its most probable 'post-classical' dating in the 18th Dynasty. There is in fact a vigorous debate about the dating of that composition. The author of this article follows the contributions by Enmarch (2008: 18–24), van Seters (2013: 589–93) and Stauder (2013: 463–67) who argue for a 'late classical' date between the late 12th dynasty and the advanced 2nd Intermediate Period.

63 Enmarch (2008: 87–88).

64 A further Spanish translation of Rosell (2015: 18) has also the present tense: 'Hoy nadie **navega** al norte hacia Biblos.' Malaise & Winand (1999: 417, §665) interpret this passage as general/gnomic

(30) Admonitions 9,5–6 [also quoted by Gunn (1924: 102), but here in more detail]
'Look, he who (normally) does not have dependents is (now) the possessor of subordinates. He who was (before) a […] is (now) one who is able to undertake his errands himself.

mṯn	*qn.w*	*n.w*	*tꜣ*
ATTN.PL	strong_one.PL	GEN.PL.M	country

n	*smj[=sn]*	*sẖr.w*	*n(.w)*	*rḫ.yt*	*wꜣi̯.w*	*r ꜣq*
NEG	report.IPFV?=3PL	plan.PL	GEN.PL.M	commons	be_far.STAT.3PL	to perish.INF

mṯn	*ḥmw.w*	*nb(.w)*	*n*	*bꜣk=sn*
ATTN.PL	craftsman.PL	every.PL.M	NEG	work.IPFV?=3SG.M

sšwꜣ	*ḫft.jw*	*tꜣ*	*ḥmw.t=f*
impoverish.IPFV?/FUT?	enemy.PL	country	craft=3SG.M

Look, the strong (men) of the country, they do not report (any longer) the plans of the commons, (for) they have come to ruin.
Look, all the craftsmen, they do not work (any longer), (and) the enemies of the country are impoverishing its crafts (or: so that the enemies can impoverish …).'

Again, Enmarch translates mechanically as past: 'they have not reported' and 'they have (ceased) to work', without any comment.[65] His translation suggests that he thought, as Gunn had done (see section 1.1 and 2.1), that it is in fact the past negation, but with specific scope on the inceptive action, showing the value of an ongoing negative state in the present as a result of the past event. Another example may be:

(31) Admonitions 2,12–13 [also noted by Gunn (1924: 102), but without translation]
'It means destruction of the land, since one says:

m	*dgs*	*ꜥꜣ*	*mk*	*sj*	*<m>*	*šn.w*
do_not.IMP	tread.ADVZ	here.ADV	ATTN	SUB.3SG.F	as	net

mk	*ḫnd.tw*	*sḫt*	*mj*	*rm*
ATTN	tread.IPFV.PASS	trap	like	fish

n	*tni̯*	*sw*	*snḏ.w*	*m-ꜥ*	*ḥr.y<t>*	*jb*
NEG	distinguish.IPFV?	DO.3SG.M	fearsome_one	from	terror	heart

Do not tread here. Look, it is a net. Look, one treads the trap as fish (would do it). (And) the fearful one cannot distinguish because of the terror of (its) heart.'

Enmarch translates the negative clause as follows: 'the fearful man could not distinguish',[66] i.e. as past. However, here the interpretation as 'gnomic usage' makes also good sense ('not (once) has distinguished'). But as it is shown, not all examples succumb to such an explanation. The last example from that text may be:

---

use of the past/perfective *sḏm=f*, but restricted to intransitive verbs and passive forms.

65 Enmarch (2008: 150). Cp. again Rosell (2015: 26): 'Mira, los poderosos de la tierra no **son informados** del estado de los súbitos, (que) ha caído en ruinas. Mira, todos los artesanos no (están) en sus trabajos (y) los enemigos de la tierra **echan** a perder a su artesania.' with present tense.

66 Enmarch (2008: 81). Cp. again Rosell (2015: 17): '(…) El hombre temeroso no (**puede**) distinguir por el miedo del corazón.' with present tense.

(32) Admonitions 2.3 [also noted by Gunn (1924: 102) but without translation]

jw	*ms*	*ḥꜥpj*	*ḥr*	*ḥwi̯(.t)*	*n*	*skꜣ.tw*	*n=f*
MCM	PTCL	Hapi	on.CVB.PRS	flow.INF	NEG	plough.PASS.IPFV?	DAT=3SG.M

z-nb	*ḥr(-ḏd)*	*n*	*rḫ=n*	*ḫpr.t*	*ḫt*	*tꜣ*
every_man	saying	NEG	know.PFV=1PL	become.PIA.SG.F	through	country

‘O, yet the Inundation rises (but) no one ploughs for himself; every man says, ‘We do not know what happens throughout the land’ (Transl. by Enmarch 2008: 73).

Here Enmarch translated with present as well, but he emends the verbal form from *n skꜣ.tw* to *n skꜣ<.n>.tw*. He says: ‘The emendation *skꜣ<.n>:tw* is required by sense: ploughing only happens after the inundation.’ That can only mean, that in his view a present/imperfective negation is needed, not a past/perfective negation.[67] On the other side this emendation seems to be justified because of several other sentences of similar shape and meaning but using *n sḏm.n=f* in the surrounding sections, e.g.:

(33) Admonitions 2,5

jw	*ms*	*ḥm.w*	*jr.j*	*jb.w=sn*	*snm.w*
MCM	PTCL	servant.PL	thereof	heart.PL=3PL	be_sad.STAT.3PL.M

n	*snsn.n*	*sr.w*	*rmṯ=sn*	*nḥm.w*
NEG	associate.PRF	official.PL	people=3PL	rejoice.PIA.PL.M

‘O, yet the servants thereof, their hearts are saddened; officials do not associate with their people, who cry out (?).’ (Transl. by Enmarch 2008: 74)

So ex. 32 seems to be more doubtful than ex. 29–30.[68]

The next example is an early one from the 4th Dynasty:

(34) Urk. I 16,16–17 [also quoted by Edel (1955/64: 570, §1095)]

sꜣ-nswt	NN	*jri=f*	*[jmj.t-pr(?)]*	*ꜥnḫ*	*ḥr*	*rd.wj=f(j)*
prince	PN	make:IPFV=3SG.M	testament	live:STAT.3SG.M	on	foot.DU=3SG.M

ny	*mn=f*	*jḫ.t*
NEG	suffer:IPFV?=3SG.M	thing

‘(Regnal Year XY …): The prince NN, he is making [a testament (?) (or the like)], being alive on his feet, without suffering on anything.’

Here *ny mn=f* can be interpreted as circumstantial present ‘while he is not suffering’, indicating that the prince was not suffering on a disease when he was making the document. Alternatively, *ny mn=f* may be circumstantial past/perfect ‘without having got any disease (and now still suffering on it)’ if the prince had to prove that he had never had a disease in the past which could lead to physical or psychological restrictions in the present.[69]

67 Cp. again Rosell (2015: 16), who does not emend, but without any comment.

68 Gardiner ([3]1957: 376, §455.2, note 3) noted one further passage from the Admonitions, Adm. 1,2, but it is too fragmentary to quote.

69 Edel (1955/64: 570, §1095) assessed the circumstantial clause of *ny mn=f* as clause of present circumstance, not more. Simon Schweitzer (2005: 189, §450) identified the form as past/perfective but translated as (relative) present circumstance (!): ‘als er auf seinen beiden Beinen lebte und an keiner Sache litt’.

The last example is also ambiguous:

(35) Dialogue between a man and his soul, 76–80 [compare Gunn (1924: 99), who quoted it, but not at length]
The soul tells a story about an unlucky commoner: '... Finally, he (= the commoner) sits down and speaks with broken/sad voice:

n	*rmi̯=j*	*tfꜣ*	*msi̯.t*					
NEG	weep=IPFV?=1SG	DEM.SG.F	give_birth:PPA.SG.F					
nn	*n=s*	*pri̯.t*	*m*	*jmn.t*	*r*	*k.t*	*ḥr*	*tꜣ*
NEG	DAT=3SG.F	come_forth:INF	from	west	to	other:SG.F	on	earth
mḥi̯.y=j	*ḥr*	*ms.w=s*	*sd.w*	*m*	*swḥ.t*			
care_for:SBJV=1SG	on	child:PL=3SG.F	break:PPA.PL.M	in	egg			
mꜣ.w	*ḥr*	*n*	*Ḫntj*	*n*	*ꜥnḫ.t=sn*			
see:PPA.PL.M	face	GEN.SG.M	Khenti:DN	NEG	live:FUT.PRF=3PL			

'I do/did not weep for that (woman of mine) having born (my children). For her there is no return from the west (= the netherworld) to another (existence?) on earth. I will care for her children who got broken in the egg, who saw the face of Khenti (= the crocodile god) before they could have come into life (or: who had not yet even lived).'

The context allows three interpretations: (a) The man might have said: '(In the past) I did not weep for her (and do not do so now)' or (b): '(Now, in the situation when I am speaking) I do not weep (any longer) for her (because her death lies long ago in the past)'.[70] A future reading is also an option: (c): 'I shall not weep (any longer) for her ... I will care for her children ...'.[71]

To sum up: There is a good number of attestations (exx. 26–30, maybe ex. 32) of the negative construction *n sḏm=f* which shows present/imperfective meaning and cannot be well explained as special usage of the construction *n sḏm=f* with regular past/perfective value or as negative prospective/optative. Consequently, it is likely that a negative construction *n sḏm=f*, containing a present/imperfective *sḏm=f* form and showing present/imperfective value, actually existed.

2.4 Circumstantial *sḏm=f*/*jri̯=f* or Second Tense *jrr=f*?

There remains the question, which kind of *sḏm=f* form with present/imperfective meaning is used in the suggested negative construction: the circumstantial *jri̯=f* or the Second Tense *jrr=f*. At first glance the verb stems of the forms in exx. 26 (*jri̯.tw*), 28 (*šni̯=f*) and 29 (*ḫdi̯.tw*) would seem to suggest the circumstantial form *jri̯=f*.[72] However, there are, in fact,

---

70 So Malaise & Winand (1999: 131, §194, ex. 276): "Je ne pleure pas ...". Gardiner (^{3}1957: 376, §455.2, note 2) cited it as example for negative present, too.

71 See Allen (2011: 72–73) with comment and bibliography. He himself decided to classify the construction as the past negative.

72 Werning (2008: 278) also suggested that the verb form might be the circumstantial *sḏm=f* but based on another example; see infra ex. 38.

some instances where *jrr=f* seems to appear in the *n sḏm=f* construction. In recent research the general debate continues over whether circumstantial forms or the Second Tenses are used in negative constructions with simple *n*.[73] However, all supposed instances with *jrr=f* are doubtful. One example was cited above:

(36) Eloquent Peasant, B1, 121 [(old) = 152 (new)] [see above ex. 8, but here in another shape; cp. Gardiner (³1957: 359, §445.1) and Borghouts (2010: 235, §64.e)]
n *jrr=k* *st* *n* *jrr=s* *<s>t*
NEG do.IPFV DO=3PL/COLL NEG do.IPFV DO.3PL/COLL
'(If) you did not do it, she would not do it.'

The other witness R 23,2 (new = 158 old) has *[...] nn jri͗=s sw* instead, i.e. the common Middle Egyptian negative future construction. However, both written forms in B1 have , which can be read as *jrr* as well as *jri͗* in that manuscript! So there are two other options: (a) to read *n jri͗(.w)=k* and *n jr(.w)=s*, i.e. an attestation of the archaic negative construction *n sḏm.w=f* (= the prospective form) corresponding to the younger construction *nn sḏm=f*;[74] (b) in accordance with the argumentation in this article to read *n jri͗=k* and *n jri͗=s* as *n* + circumstantial *sḏm=f* (?).[75]

Another example may be:

(37) PT 722c–d[T] (Spell 412) [quoted by Edel (1955: 231, §496), and Satzinger (1968: 15, §20)]
n *sw3͗3͗* *rd=k* *n* *š3͗ss* *nm.t=k*
NEG pass.IPFV? foot=2SG.M NEG cross.IPFV?=2SG.M walk=2SG.M
n *ḫnd=k* *ḥr* *ḥw3͗.t* *Wsjr*
NEG tread.IPFV?=2SG.M on decay Osiris
'Your foot shall not pass, your walk shall not cross, you shall not tread on the decay of Osiris.'

But an interpretation of the first two verbal forms as prospective passive (i.e. the *sḏmm=f* form) and of the third as prospective active also makes sense here in the given context; see the recent translation by J. Allen: 'Your foot will not be bypassed, your stride will not be traversed, and you will not step on Osiris' decay.'[76]

Also, the following example might be of relevance here:

73 See e.g. Schenkel (2009: 48–49), who prefers circumstantial forms, based on the Coffin Texts' evidence of written forms of the verbs II. gem. in the *sḏm.n=f* form; and Depuydt (2011: 501, 505), who opts for Second Tenses, based on the prospective forms *sḏm.w=f* and *sḏmm=f*, which are in Depuydt's view Second Tenses in general. This discussion started with Polotsky (1957), who had identified forms after *n* as Second Tenses, but became more complicated after Polotsky (1976: 44–45, §4.1.5) had introduced the 'factual' *sḏm=f*, also appearing with *n*, as verbal form.

74 See Brose (2009: 19–21), where I argued for that option.

75 The second option was not mentioned by me in Brose (2009: 19–21).

76 Allen (2005: 86, T228); see also Brose (2009: 18–19).

(38) PT 323a-b^{W} (Spell 260) [quoted by Werning (2008: 278) and Brose (2017: 33)]

bw.t *Wnjs* *pw* *šꜣs* *m* *kk.w*
abomination Unis.RN COP walk_around.INF in darkness
n *mꜣꜣ=f* *sẖd.w*
NEG see.IPFV=3SG.M turn_upside_down.PPP.PL.M
'It is Unis' abomination to walk around in darkness, without being able to see those who are upside down.'

However, the form *mꜣꜣ=f* is unrevealing, because the verbal stem *mꜣꜣ* appears in the circumstantial form as well as in the Second Tense. Furthermore, the second clause can be read as future: 'It is Unis' abomination to walk around in darkness. He shall not see those who are upside-down.' (with prospective form *mꜣꜣ=f*!).[77]

Satzinger also mentions several instances for the verb *wnn*, but there the general problem is that a writing *n wnn=f* () can always be read as *n wn.n=f*.[78] A final example is quoted by J. Borghouts:

(39) pRamesseum II, rt. 4.2 [Borghouts (2010: 235, §64e)]

pẖꜣ *pḥ*
be_perspicacious.PPA.SG.M attain.PIA.SG.M
n *jrr=f* *js* *ḥmw.y* *wẖꜣ-sw*
NEG do.IPFV=3SG.M FOCZ craft/art fool (lit. 'the foolish-is-he')
'The perspicacious one (is) one who succeeds; he does at least not practice the art of the fool.'

However, Borghouts overlooked that this is an example with the negation *n ... js*, which is regularly used for Second Tenses,[79] and not of the simple negation with *n*. The only thing that seems odd is the lack of any marker of a required adverbial phrase, i.e. something like <*m*> *ḥmw.y* with a preposition. It is also conceivable that the composer of the text intended to put concrete emphasis on the direct object and used the negated Second Tense, but this would be very unusual.[80]

It might now be concluded that the *sḏm=f* form in the present/imperfective negative construction *n sḏm=f* is rather the circumstantial *sḏm=f*/*jri͗=f* and not the Second Tense *jrr=f*.

---

77 See Allen (1984: 217, §333) & (2005: 47, W 170); and the translation of that passage by D. Topmann for the TLA.

78 Satzinger (1968: 15, §21).

79 See Polotsky (1976: 46–47, §4.2).

80 There is still the problem that the broader context of the passage has lacunas and is quite uncertain in details; see the edition of the text in Barns (1956: pls. 7–9), and several translations by Brunner (1988: 194) = (1991: 194), Vernus (2001: 234), Quirke (2004: 188), and P. Dils for the TLA; the passage/sentence in question has either been omitted in the translation or has been translated with many question marks.

2.5 Basic meaning of present/imperfective *n sḏm=f* and semantic difference relating to *n sḏm.n=f*

The final question concerns the semantics of the *n sḏm=f* construction and the difference between it and *n sḏm.n=f*. In section 2.3 above the crucial function of *n sḏm=f* was defined to be that of expressing incidental actions. If one looks at examples 26–30 it also becomes clear that, in contrast to *n sḏm.n=f*, the idea of general or customary actions is not present and seems to be excluded by context. One can thus conclude that the basic meaning of the present/imperfective *n sḏm=f* construction is in fact the expression of the continuous/progressive aspect, whose characteristic feature is 'the incident property of the moment',[81] i.e. an action denoting a 'here and now' situation. Its difference vis-à-vis *n sḏm.n=f* turns out to be the common binary opposition between continuous and habitual aspect (as sublevel aspects of the imperfective super-aspect [so in Semitic languages] or of the present super-tense [so in English]). There is also no objection to sometimes translating *n sḏm.n=f* as negative continuous, cf.:

- above ex. 12: *mk wj ḥr spr n=k n sḏm.n=k st* 'Behold, I am pleading you, but you do not pay [perhaps better: you refuse to pay?] attention to it.'

Compare it with the following, similar example, but with the negative continuous *nn sw ḥr sḏm*:

(40) Shipwrecked Sailor 73–75:

jw	*mdwi̯=k*	*n=j*		
MCM	talk.IPFV=2SG.M	DAT=1SG		
nn	*wj*	*ḥr*	*sḏm*	*st*
NEG	SBJ.1SG	on.CVB.PRS	listen.INF	DO.3PL/COLL

'You're talking to me, (but) I do not listen to it.'[82]

At this point, it should be remembered that the habitual aspect is the unmarked partner in the opposition and the continuous aspect the marked partner, so that a construction denoting habitual aspect can also be used for the 'junior partner' when the semantic specification is not expressed. Here one may compare English, where 'he does not speak' can be used for: 'he does not speak now' (continuous/progressive) or 'he does not speak every day between 6 and 7 pm' (habitual/iterative) and also for 'he does not speak in general/he is unable to speak' (habitual/general). However, 'he is not speaking' can only be used for the first.[83] This would also correspond to the affirmative side, where *jw=f sḏm=f* can express both habitual and continuous action, but *jw=f ḥr sḏm* only continuous action (with

---

81 See Comrie (1998: 28).

82 That is the one single instance of the negated *jw=f ḥr sḏm* construction cited in the grammars!

83 The continuous meaning seems to be obvious when the *n sḏm.n=f* construction is used as negative counterpart of the pseudo-verbal construction *jw=f ḥr sḏm*. For such instances Vernus (1990) argued that *jw=f ḥr sḏm* had undergone a yet further expansion of meaning from progressive to habitual, as is common at later stages of Egyptian but quite uncommon in Middle Egyptian of the 12th Dynasty, whereas *n sḏm.n=f* had preserved its habitual force and had not expanded its semantic range. This argument is no longer necessary.

an expansion to the habitual aspect in the later stages of the language). That may also be the reason why *n jri̯=f* with present/imperfective meaning is so rarely attested: There was normally no real need for it. Its usage was only feasible if two conditions were fulfilled: (1) there must be an overarching context where it could be embedded as clause of circumstance or as statement of consequence; and (2) the nuance 'cannot hear'/'do not hear in general' must be excluded.[84] As consequence I dare to draw a general scheme for affirmative and negative actions in Old and Middle Egyptian, which lacks any regularity or linearity, and thus there is no actual 'Newest Rule of Gunn' mentioned in the title:

<table>
<tr><th>Tense/Aspect</th><th>Affirmative</th><th>Negative</th></tr>
<tr><td>Perfect</td><td>(jw) sḏm.n=f</td><td rowspan="2">n jri̯=f / rḏi=f [a]</td></tr>
<tr><td>Past/Perfective</td><td>jri̯=f / rḏi̯=f</td></tr>
<tr><td>Habitual (optional: including continuous actions)</td><td>jw(=f) jri̯=f / ḏi̯=f</td><td>n sḏm.n=f</td></tr>
<tr><td>Continuous (specific; excluding habitual actions)</td><td>jw=f ḥr sḏm</td><td>n jri̯=f / ḏi=f [b]</td></tr>
</table>

a As noted above (sec. 1.5 with footnote 38), there are a few examples appearing in Pyramid Texts and scientific Medical Texts (with a specialized style) where *n sḏm.n=f* shows an archaic usage expressing perfect action.

b As noted above (ex. 40) there is also one single instance of the negated *jw=f ḥr sḏm* in a Middle Egyptian text.

3 Summary

The article started with the statement that the negative construction *n sḏm=f* shows a widespread semantic range on the surface, denoting past actions, present states and actions, general statements and disabilities and also the negative optative. On the other side the negative construction *n sḏm.n=f* has counterintuitively not past or perfect meaning but that of a negative present or habitual as negative counterpart of one of the main functions of the simple *sḏm=f*, and the indicative *n sḏm=f* has almost exclusively past/perfect meaning as counterpart of simple *sḏm.n=f*. This system is known today in informal discourse and academic education as 'Gunn's Rule'. Later on, scholars divided the graphemic form *sḏm=f* into several morphological forms, and so 'Gunn's Rule' was reduced in its range by removing all future/modal forms from the discussion. On the other hand, they explained some functions of *n sḏm=f* – the expression of situations of present state and present actions and also general ('gnomic') statements – as special subfunctions of the 'indicative'/ 'past'/'perfective' *sḏm=f*, denying the function 'continuous/progressive present' (= 'here and now'). Philologists usually read instances where such a function can be assumed as past or a special function that can be derived from the basic past meaning, or try to reinterpret the context so that the assigned basic meaning fits again. Nevertheless, this article has demonstrated that instances in Old and Middle Egyptian of the negative construction *n sḏm=f* exist, where the context indicates a continuous present and which cannot really

84 For the second condition compare above ex. 26, 29, 30 and 40, where the ability to act is existent but the supposed actor is not willing to act.

be explained as past or a resultative/gnomic meaning. Furthermore, it has been shown that the *sḏm=f* form in this construction is probably the circumstantial *sḏm=f/jri̯=f* and not the Second Tense *jrr=f*. Finally, it was deduced that the basic meaning of this *n sḏm=f* construction was to express negative continuous action and that the semantic difference between *n sḏm=f* and *n sḏm.n=f* conformed to the general linguistic opposition between continuous/progressive and habitual aspect. Accordingly, 'Gunn's Rule' is finally dead, and philologists should use it only as a mnemonic aid that has a complicated and tricky grammatical background.

Glossing Abbreviations

1/2/3	$1^{st}/2^{nd}/3^{rd}$ person	F	Feminine	PL	Plural
ADV	Adverb	FOCZ	Focalizer	PN	Personal Name
ADVZ	Adverbialization	FUT	Future	PPA	Participle, perfective active
ART	Definite article	GEN	Genitive marker	PPP	Participle, perfective passive
ATTN	Attention marker	IMP	Imperative	PRF	Perfect
AUX	Auxiliary	INF	Infinitive	PRS	Present
CNSV	Consecutive	IPRF	Imperfect	PRV	Perfective
COLL	Collective	IPFV	Imperfective	PST	Past
COND	Conditional	M	Masculine	PTCL	Particle
COP	Copula	MCM	Main clause marker	RN	Royal name
CVB	Converb	MOD	Modal	SBJ	Subject
DAT	Dative marker	NEG	Negation (marker)	SBJV	Subjunctive
DEM	Demonstrative	OBLV	Obligative	SG	Singular
DN	Divine name	PASS	Passive	STAT	Stative conjugation
DO	Direct object	PIA	Participle, imperfective active	TN	Toponym
DU	Dual				
		PIP	Participle, imperfective passive		

Bibliography

Allen, James P. 1984. *The Inflection of the Verb in the Pyramid Texts*. Malibu; Bibliotheca Aegyptia 2.

Allen, James P. 2005. *The Ancient Egyptian Pyramid Texts*. Leiden & Boston; SBL Writings from the Ancient World 23.

Allen, James P. ^{2}2010. *Middle Egyptian. An Introduction to the Language and Culture of Hieroglyphs, Second Edition, Revised*. Cambridge.

Allen, James P. 2011. *The Debate between a Man and His Soul. A Masterpiece of Ancient Egyptian Literature*. Leiden & Boston; Culture & History of the Ancient Near East 44.

Allen, James P. ^{3}2014. *Middle Egyptian. An Introduction to the Language and Culture of Hieroglyphs, Third Edition, Revised and Reorganized, with a New Analysis of the Verbal System*, Cambridge.

Barns, John. 1956. *Five Ramesseum Papyri*. Oxford.

Beylage, Peter. 2018. *Middle Egyptian*. Winona Lake; Languages of the Ancient Near East 9.

Borghouts, Joris F. 2010. *Egyptian. An Introduction to the Writing and Language of the Middle Kingdom. Part I: Grammar, Syntax and Indexes*. Leuven; Egyptologische Uitgaven 24/1.

Brose, Marc. 2009. 'Verbaler Gebrauch des „abstrakt-relativischen" Präsens *jrr=f*?', *Göttinger Miszellen* 223, 17–25.

Brose, Marc. 2017. 'Das ägyptische Verb und der ägyptisch-semitische Sprachvergleich', *Lingua Aegyptia* 25, 1–40.

Brose, Marc. 2019. *Perfekt, Pseudopartizip, Stativ. Die afroasiatische Suffixkonjugation in sprachvergleichender Perspektive.* Wiesbaden; Abhandlungen für die Kunde des Morgenlandes 117.

Brunner, Helmut. 1988. *Altägyptische Weisheit. Lehren für das Leben.* Zurich & Munich.

Brunner, Helmut. 1991. *Die Weisheitsbücher der Ägypter. Lehren für das Leben*, Zurich & Munich.

Comrie, Bernard. 1998. *Aspect. An Introduction to the Study of Verbal Aspect and Related Problems*, Tenth printing. Cambridge.

De Buck, Adriaan. 1952. *Grammaire élémentaire du Moyen Égyptien.* Leiden.

Depuydt, Leo. 1993. 'A History of Research on the Prospective *sḏm.f* Forms in Middle Egyptian', *Journal of the American Research Center in Egypt* 30, 11–31.

Depuydt, Leo. 2011. 'Zu Lehr- und Lernbarkeit des ägyptischen Verbs. Wie viele typisch Mittelägyptische *sḏm=f*-Formen gibt es eigentlich? Neun!', in: Alexandra Verbovsek, Burkard Backes & Catherine Jones (eds), *Methodik und Didaktik in der Ägyptologie. Herausforderungen eines kulturwissenschaftlichen Paradigmenwechsels in den Altertumswissenschaften.* Munich; Ägyptologie und Kulturwissenschaft 4, 481–508.

Edel, Elmar. 1955/64. *Altägyptische Grammatik*, 2 vols. Rome; Analecta Orientalia 34/39.

Enmarch, Roland. 2008. *A World Upturned. Commentary on and Analysis of The Dialogue of Ipuwer and the Lord of the All.* Oxford & New York.

Erman, Adolf. [4]1928. *Ägyptische Grammatik, Vierte, völlig umgestaltete Auflage.* Berlin; Porta Linguarum Orientalium 15.

Gardiner, Alan H. 1927. *Egyptian Grammar. Being an Introduction to the Study of Hieroglyphs.* Oxford.

Gardiner, Alan H. [3]1957. *Egyptian Grammar. Being an Introduction to the Study of Hieroglyphs, Third edition, Revised.* Oxford.

Gardiner, Alan H. 1962. *My Working Years* [without location].

Gilula, Mordechai. 1970. Review to Satzinger (1968), *Journal of Egyptian Archaeology* 56, 205–14.

Graefe, Erhart. [6]2001. *Mittelägyptisch. Grammatik für Anfänger, 6. verbesserte und teilweise veränderte Auflage.* Wiesbaden.

Gunn, Battiscombe. 1924. *Studies in Egyptian Syntax*, Paris.

Hannig, Rainer. 1984. 'Die Neue Gunnsche Regel', in: Friedrich Junge (ed.), *Studien zu Sprache und Religion Ägyptens, zu Ehren von Wolfhart Westendorf, überreicht von seinen Freunden und Schülern*, vol. 1. Göttingen, 63–70.

Hutter, Kristina. 2017. *Das sḏm=f-Paradigma im Mittelägyptischen.* Hamburg; Lingua Aegyptia Studia Monographica 18.

Jenni, Hanna. 2010. *Lehrbuch der klassisch-ägyptischen Sprache.* Basel.

Lefebvre, Gustave. [2]1955. *Grammaire de l'Égyptien classique, 2e édition, revue et corrigée avec la colloboration de Serge Sauneron.* Cairo; Bibliothèque d'Étude 12.

Maderna-Sieben, Claudia. 2016. *Mittelägyptische Grammatik für Anfänger. Ein ausführliches Kompendium für den Unterricht.* Berlin.

Malaise, Michel & Winand, Jean. 1999. *Grammaire raisonnée de l'égyptien classique.* Liège; Aegyptiaca Leodiensia 6.

Ockinga, Boyo. [2]2005. *Mittelägyptische Grundgrammatik, Zweite, überarbeitete Auflage.* Mainz.

Polotsky, Hans Jakob. 1944. *Études de syntaxe copte.* Cairo (reprinted: Hans Jacob Polotsky, *Collected Papers.* Jerusalem 1971, 102–207).

Polotsky, Hans Jakob. 1957. 'The "Emphatic" *śḏm.n.f* Form', *Revue d'Égyptologie* 11, 109–117 (reprinted: H. J. Polotsky, *Collected Papers.* Jerusalem 1971, 43–51).

Polotsky, Hans Jakob. 1964. 'Ägyptische Verbalformen und ihre Vokalisation', *Orientalia N.S.* 33, 267–85 [reprinted: H. J. Polotsky. *Collected Papers.* Jerusalem 1971, 52–90].

Polotsky, Hans Jakob. 1965. 'Egyptian Tenses', in: *The Israel Academy of Sciences and Humanities* Vol. II, No. 5, 1–26 [reprinted: H. J. Polotsky. *Collected Papers.* Jerusalem 1971, 71–96].

Polotsky, Hans Jakob. 1976. 'Les transposition du verbe en égyptien classique'; in: *Israel Oriental Studies* 6, 1–50 [reprinted: Hans Jakob Polotsky, *Scripta Posteriora on Egyptian and Coptic.* Göttingen 2007; Lingua Aegyptia Studia Monographica 7, 55–104].

Quirke, Stephen. 2004. *Egyptian Literature 1800BC, Questions and Readings*. London; Golden House Publications 2.

Rosell, Pablo Martín. 2015. *Las Admoniciones de Ipuwer. Literatura política y sociedad en el Reino Medio egipcio*. Oxford; BAR International Series 2752.

Satzinger, Helmut. 1968. *Die negativen Konstruktionen im Alt- und Mittelägyptischen.* Berlin; Münchner Ägyptologische Studien 12.

Schenkel, Wolfgang. 2009. 'Prädikatives und abstrakt-relativisches *śčm.n=f.* Beobachtungen an den Verben II. gem. und ult. n im Korpus der Sargtexte', in: Gideon Goldenberg & Ariel Shisha-Halevy (eds), *Egyptian, Semitic and General Grammar. Workshop in Memory of H .J. Polotsky (8–12 July 2001)*. Jerusalem, 42–60.

Schenkel, Wolfgang. 2012. *Einführung in die klassisch-ägyptische Sprache und Schrift*, Tübingen.

Schweitzer, Simon. 2005. *Schrift und Sprache der 4. Dynastie*. Wiesbaden; Menes 3.

van Seters, John. 2013. 'Dating the Admonitions of Ipuwer and Biblical Narrative Texts', in: Gerald Moers et al. (eds), *Dating Egyptian Literary Texts.* Hamburg; Lingua Aegyptia Studia Monographica 13, 589–96.

Stauder, Andréas. 2013. *Linguistic Dating of Middle Egyptian Literary Texts.* Hamburg; Lingue Aegyptia Studia Monographica 12.

Vernus, Pascal. 1990. 'La date du *Paysan Eloquent*', in: Sarah Israelit-Groll (ed.), *Studies in Egyptology, Presented to Miriam Lichtheim*, vol. II. Jerusalem, 1033–47.

Vernus, Pascal. 2001. *Sagesses de l'Égypte pharaonique* [without location].

Werning, Daniel A. 2008. 'Aspect vs. relative tense, and the typological classification of the Ancient Egyptian *sḏm.n=f*', *Lingua Aegyptia* 16, 261–92.

Werning, Daniel A. 2015. *Einführung in die hieroglyphisch-ägyptische Schrift und Sprache. Propädeutikum mit Zeichen und Vokabellektionen, Übungen und Übeungshinweisen*, 3. verbesserte Ausgabe. Berlin [<https://edoc.hu-berlin.de/handle/18452/14302>; DOI: 10.18452/13650].

Westendorf, Wolfhart. 1962. *Grammatik der medizinischen Texte*. Berlin; Grundriss der Medizin der Alten Ägypter VIII.

Zonhoven, Louis. 2000. *Mittelägyptische Grammatik. Eine praktische Einführung in die ägyptische Sprache und die Hieroglyphenschrift*. Leiden.

Internet Resources

TLA = Thesaurus Linguae Aegyptiae, <http://aaew.bbaw.de/tla> [last update: October 31th, 2014; last accessed: July 4th, 2020].

Sadness, Anxiety and Other Broken Hearts

The Expression of Negative Emotions in Ancient Egyptian

Gaëlle Chantrain[1]

0 Introduction

Aims and general structure

This article aims at providing an overview of negative emotion expression in Ancient Egyptian, through the prism of figurative language. The general structure is as follows: after a brief introduction of the topic, the theoretical framework applied and the presentation of the corpus, the first section of the article is dedicated to lexical-level linguistic actualizations of conceptual metaphors – mostly metaphors and metonymies. These are divided in two categories: 1) single lexemes with metaphor-induced co-lexification[2] and 2) compound expressions. The second section of the article deals with the concept of 'false friend' metaphors, which are a major challenge in metaphor translation. The term, introduced here for the first time, refers to metaphorical expressions which, when translated literally in the target language, do correspond to an existing metaphorical expression but do not convey the same meaning as in the source language.

What is emotion?

The theoretical definition of emotion, feeling and temperament used in this paper is based on the framework established by Scherer,[3] developed and adapted to the case of Ancient Egyptian by Di Biase-Dyson & Chantrain.[4] Scherer defines an emotion as 'an organism's affective response to specific situations' (e.g. loss, danger, etc.) and, as such, to be distinguished from a feeling, which is 'the subjective emotional experience component of emotion'.[5] An emotion is moreover a 'bounded event' in the life of an individual, which

---

1 University of Louvain. Contact: gaelle.chantrain@uclouvain.be. Most of the research work for this article was conducted when I was still employed by the F.R.S-FNRS and the University of Liège.

2 François (2008) first proposed this term. He defines it as "the linking of two senses by a single lexeme in synchrony (*strict* co-lexification) or in diachrony (*loose* co-lexification)" (François 2008: 171). I chose to adopt it in this study because it allows to express the three steps in the metaphor-induced semantic evolution continuum of a lexeme: metaphorical use, polysemy and semantic change.

3 Scherer (2005, 2009, 2013).

4 Di Biase-Dyson & Chantrain (2022: 604).

5 Scherer (2013: 25).

Sami Uljas & Andreas Dorn (eds), *Crossroads VI. Between Egyptian Linguistics and Philology*, 27–61
DOI: https://doi.org/10.37011/studmon.30.02

involves an appraisal of the event and consecutive mental and somatic changes leading to expression and reaction.[6] An emotion is thus characterized as transient, momentary, while mood and character, by opposition, are characterized as more lasting. In Ancient Egyptian as in other world languages, 'many lexical units describing emotion are additionally used to portray the temperament of a person, what Scherer[7] calls an *affect disposition*'. The latter describes 'the tendency of a person to experience certain moods more frequently or to be prone to react with certain types of emotions' and they may also influence emotion regulation.[8] The co-lexification of an emotion and the temperament characterized by this dominant emotion (e.g. anger and choleric) is thus very well attested in Egyptian.

How is emotion expressed in Egyptian? Conceptual metaphor theory and its actualization in the language.

Figurative language is a constant element in the expression of abstract concepts across cultures and languages.[9] Ancient Egyptian makes of course no exception[10] and emotion expression relies on it to a great degree. The theoretical framework used in this study is primarily the conceptual metaphor theory (CMT).[11] This theory makes the distinction between the use of metaphorical transfer on the conceptual level, as a transdomain mapping between a source and a target domain (e.g. SAD IS DOWN) and the actualization of this mapping in a specific language (e.g. in French 'avoir le moral dans les chaussettes' lit. 'having the mood in the socks' = feeling sad, discouraged, depressed). In Egyptian, on top of the linguistic dimension, can also be added the visual one. SAD IS DOWN will thus be actualized in the classifiers  or , for example. The first expresses the semantic feature *down* through body language (sited position and falling arms), and the second through the categories SMALLNESS/NEGATIVITY expressed by .

On the linguistic level, the conceptual metaphor can be actualized in a lexical unit – single lexeme or compound expression – and/or it can be expressed through an entire text passage. In the frame of this study, I will limit myself to the first case, the lexical level.

Source domains of emotion expression

A prominent source domain in metaphors expressing emotion is the domain of sensory perception,[12] but it is not the only one. While walking through the emotional landscape of ancient Egyptians, one realizes quickly that some of the variety of conceptual metaphors attested is rich but also corresponds to a well-defined taxonomy. Indeed, just as concepts,

6 Frijda and Scherer (2009); Scherer (2013: 24–25); Bender (2009: 300).
7 Scherer (2005: 705).
8 The detail of affective phenomena description by Scherer is given in Di Biase-Dyson & Chantrain (2022: 625, note 3).
9 Sweetser (1990); Traugott & Dasher (2001: 95).
10 Di Biase-Dyson (2018); Steinbach-Eicke (2019).
11 Lakoff & Johnsson (2001).
12 Di Biase-Dyson & Chantrain (2022).

even abstract ones,[13] can be organized in more or less detailed categories inspired by natural taxonomies (subordinate, basic, superordinate), conceptual paths can be hierarchized in the same way. In the case of EMOTION expression and similarly abstract concepts such as COGNITION or VOLITION, the standard cross-domain mapping is CONCRETE → ABSTRACT. Under this general direction, several cross-linguistically well-documented paths are actualized in Egyptian, both on the linguistic and the visual levels. This observation is particularly interesting because it adds a consequent historical depth to the validation of the conceptual metaphor theory as well as further data exploitable for cross-linguistic comparison. Going back to the idea of a taxonomy of conceptual metaphors, on the most general level, one finds MIND AS BODY[14] and THE SOCIAL WORLD IS THE PHYSICAL WORLD[15] as central in emotion expression. Directly under these general paths, one can identify a variety of other paths that apply to Egyptian as well. I will limit my description for now to the superordinate level. Further levels will be added in the conclusion, based on the findings.

- EMOTION IS PHYSICAL EXPERIENCE, including sensory perception[16]
- EMOTION IS PHYSICAL STATE
- EMOTION IS NON-QUIETNESS (including PHYSICAL ACTIVITY[17] and SOUND[18])
- EMOTION IS THE EFFECT OF AN EMOTION.

Conceptual metaphors are found in the text corpus in several forms of linguistic realizations,[19] ranging from the lexical to the textual level. Visual metaphors or visual metaphor markers are also well-represented. Both linguistic and visual dimensions of figurative language are discussed in the present study, through the following scenarios:

- a lexeme is used metaphorically, with or without semantic change;
- the metaphor is conveyed through a compound expression;
- a metaphor is actualized on the visual level through classifiers;
- a specific classifier works as a metaphor marker;
- running through larger text extracts (including several elements from the lower levels).

Negative emotions: an overview of emotion categorization

Under the label 'negative emotions' are considered a large range of emotions, feelings, moods and temperaments. They are all situated in the spectrum of three primary emotions ANGER, SADNESS and FEAR. These primary emotions generate a network of related negative/afflictive emotions whose number and classification varies according to the different stu-

---

13 Chantrain (2021).

14 Sweetser (1990); Barsalou (1999); Traugott & Dasher (2001: 95); Casasanto & Gijssels (2015).

15 Kövecses 2010: 255; Di Biase-Dyson (2018).

16 Koptjevskaja-Tamm (2015); Steinbach-Eicke (2019); Vanhove & Hamid (2019); Di Biase-Dyson & Chantrain (2022).

17 Vanhove (2008).

18 Di Biase-Dyson & Chantrain (2022: 608–09).

19 In the broad sense, according to the MIPVU criteria: including direct, implicit, personification, similes. Cf. Steen & al. (2010) and http://www.vismet.org/metcor/documentation/MIPVU.html.

dies in emotion theory. For the needs of current study, four emotion categorization systems were taken as reference: the HUMAINE proposal for Emotion annotation and Representation in Language (HUMAINE-EARL),[20] Parrott's[21] taxonomy, the Geneva Emotion Wheel (GEW)[22] and the Plutchik wheel.[23]

The HUMAINE-EARL proposal identifies 48 emotions distributed in 10 categories. Negative emotions are distributed into 5 main categories, among which 3 of them correspond to my 3 pivot notions: ANGER, SADNESS and FEAR. In the HUMAINE-EARL categorization, these notions correspond respectively to the categories *negative and forceful*; *negative and passive*; *negative and not in control*. To these, the HUMAINE-EARL adds two other categories: *negative thoughts* and *agitation*. I chose not to retain them because, after comparison with other categorization systems, they appear to be an unnecessary distinction. *Frustration* is listed in the category *negative thoughts* but it will be treated here as being in the semantic spectrum of ANGER, which is confirmed by the lexical data and overlaps with Parrott's classification (under the label *bitterness*). As for the category *agitation*, it covers stress, shock and tension, which I recategorized here under to the category *not in control*, based on the classification of Parrott (see category FEAR).

Table 1: Emotion categorization based on the HUMAINE-EARL proposal.

		Negative emotions		
Negative and forceful	*Negative and not in control*	*Negative thoughts*	*Negative and passive*	*Agitation*
Anger Annoyance Contempt Disgust Irritation	Anxiety Embarrassment Fear Helplessness Powerlessness Worry	Pride Doubt Envy Frustration Guilt Shame	Boredom Despair Disappointment Hurt Sadness	Stress Shock Tension
		Positive emotions		
Positive and lively	*Caring*	*Positive thoughts*	*Positive and quiet*	*Reactive*
Amusement Delight Elation Excitement Happiness Joy Pleasure	Affection Empathy Friendliness Love	Courage Hope Humility Satisfaction Trust	Calmness Contentment Relaxation Relief Serenity	Interest Politeness Surprise

20 Douglas-Cowie, Cox at al. https://web.archive.org/web/20080410193636/http://emotion-research.net/projects/humaine/earl/proposal . The work started with EARL and later evolved into the EmotionML : https://www.w3.org/TR/emotionml/#ref-emotion-xg (Schröder et al. 2011).

21 Parrott (2001).

22 Scherer et al. (2013).

23 Plutchik (1980).

Parrott[24] divides the emotional domain into three main categories: primary emotion, secondary emotion and tertiary emotion. ANGER, SADNESS and FEAR belong to the first category. The related emotions that will be treated in this study belong to the secondary or tertiary emotion category.

These three primary emotions also shape the left half of the Geneva Emotion Wheel (GEW). Its structure partially overlaps with Parrot's categories. However, no less than 20 emotions are listed as basic, which encompasses both *primary emotion* and *secondary emotion* (with a few divergences).

Table 2: Categorization of emotions according to Parrott (2001).

Primary emotion	Secondary emotion	Tertiary emotion
LOVE	Affection	Adoration, fondness, liking, attraction, caring, tenderness, compassion, sentimentality
	Lust	Desire, passion, infatuation
	Longing	longing
JOY	Cheerfulness	Amusement, bliss, gaiety, glee, jolliness, joviality, joy, delight, enjoyment, gladness, happiness, jubilation, elation, satisfaction, ecstasy, euphoria
	Zest	Enthusiasm, zeal, excitement, thrill, exhilaration
	Contentment	Pleasure
	Pride	Triumph
	Optimism	Eagerness, hope
	Enthrallment	Enthrallment, rapture
	Relief	relief
SURPRISE	Surprise	Amazement, astonishment
ANGER	Irritability	Aggravation, agitation, annoyance, grouchy
	Exasperation	Frustration
	Rage	Anger, outrage, fury, wrath, hostility, ferocity, bitterness, hatred, scorn, spite, vengefulness, dislike, resentment
	Disgust	Revulsion, contempt, loathing
	Envy	jealousy
	Torment	torment

24 This categorization is based on the study by Shaver et al. (1987: 1067) in which a tree-structured representation of emotion categorization was proposed.

SADNESS	Suffering	Agony, anguish, hurt
	Sadness	Depression, despair, gloom, glumness, unhappiness, grief, sorrow, woe, misery, melancholy
	Disappointment	Dismay, displeasure
	Shame	Guilt, regret, remorse
	Neglect	Alienation, defeatism, dejection, embarrassment, homesickness, humiliation, insecurity, insult, isolation, loneliness, rejection
	Sympathy	Pity, mono no aware, sympathy
FEAR	Horror	Alarm, shock, fear, fright, horror, terror, panic, hysteria, mortification
	Nervousness	Anxiety, uneasiness, apprehension, worry, distress, dread

Finally, the Plutchik wheel is still a reference in emotion theory and inspired more recent works such as the GEW. Plutchik lists eight primary emotions: JOY, TRUST, FEAR, SURPRISE, SADNESS, DISGUST, ANGER, ANTICIPATION. Other emotions are associated to these eight primary ones with the same colour code but with a variation in intensity. The intensity of the colour corresponds to the intensity of the emotion (e.g. the primary emotion ANGER declines itself into the intense emotion *rage* and the mild emotion *annoyance*). These emotions are then combined into dyads, which correspond to feelings composed of two emotions. He distinguishes primary dyads (emotions that are one petal apart, e.g. love = joy + trust), secondary dyads (two petals apart, e.g. despair = sadness + fear), tertiary dyads (three petals apart, e.g. pessimism = sadness + anticipation). Finally, opposite emotions are situated four petals apart (e.g. sadness vs joy).

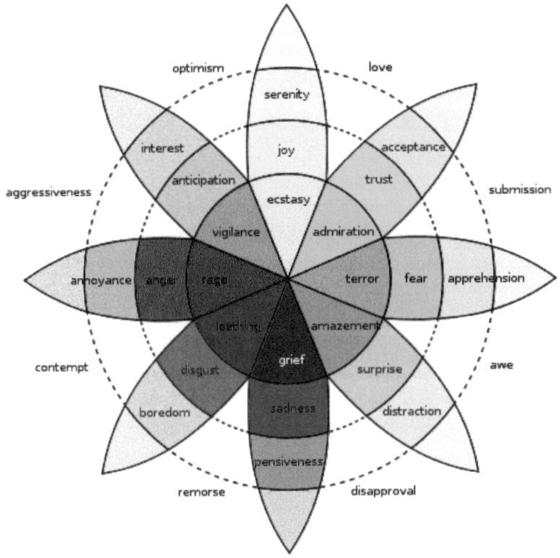

Fig. 1: Plutchik wheel (image: Wiki commons).

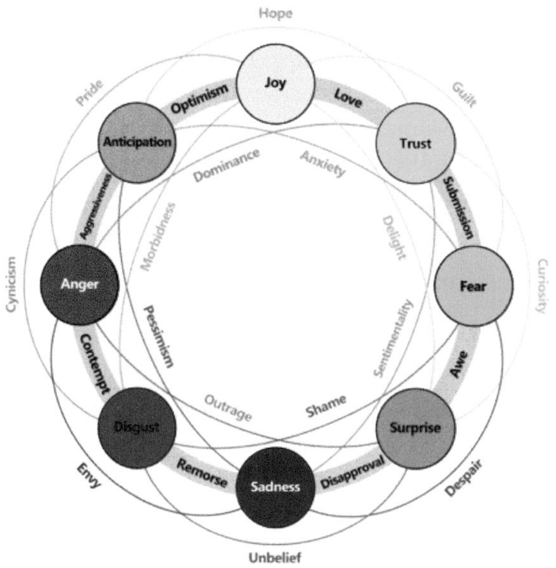

Fig. 2: Dyads of the Plutchik wheel (image: Wiki commons).

Some of the non-primary emotions lie at the intersection of several primary categories, to which they borrow their defining features. As an example, *frustration* lies at the intersection of ANGER and SADNESS. Indeed, in the EARL, it appears under negative thoughts, here recategorized as sadness, while its parasynonym *irritation* lies under the category *negative and forceful*, together with ANGER. *Irritation* thus appears as being closer to the pole ANGER, while *frustration* is closer to the pole SADNESS of the continuum. Worth is mentioning that not all negative emotions included in the wheel are found in pre-Coptic Egyptian. For example, shame and guilt do not seem to be lexicalized before the Coptic period, or if so, very scarcely.

The primary negative emotions ANGER and FEAR are not treated here. I chose to focus on the related non-primary emotions of *irritation/frustration* and *anxiety* respectively. In the same line, SADNESS is rather addressed through the related secondary emotions of *disappointment, discouragement, weariness, despair* and *depression. Compassion/empathy* (*sympathy* in Parrot) is also related to SADNESS but borrows feature to positive emotions since it partially overlaps with the category *caring* (EARL). Indeed, it is characterized as a form of sadness felt for someone else's condition and that involves a feeling of care for one's peers. It lies thus at the intersection between afflictive and positive emotions since it involves a part of suffering but is inspired by a positive and altruistic feeling. As for *anxiety*, unlike *fear* which is a direct response to a threat, it is based on projections into the future and apprehension of danger or unpleasant events to be faced.[25] Anxiety is shown in psychology studies to be tightly related to sadness and depression, which is reflected in the texts.

25 Edna B. Foa et al. in Evan D. et al. (2017: 190).

Corpus and tools

The corpus considered is made of the texts from the *Thesaurus Linguae Aegyptiae* (*TLA*)[26] and *Ramses.*[27] For the big picture, I considered the data from the Old Kingdom to the Ptolemaic Period. Most of the examples discussed in the article though are from New Kingdom, Third Intermediate Period and Late Period texts. Data have been cross-checked with the *Wörterbuch* and the Hannig dictionary.[28]

1 Lexemes and compound expressions

This section presents a sample of some lexemes expressing negative/afflictive emotions as a result of metaphor-induced polysemy. The list of lexemes and expressions treated here is not exhaustive but is meant to give an overview of the main cases encountered in the Egyptian lexicon. The examples are divided in two categories: 1) lexemes that can be used by themselves or in combination with body parts (most often the heart, *jb* or *ḥꜣtj*) to convey an emotional meaning; 2) others conveying an emotional meaning only when part of idiomatic expressions (for example with *jb* and/or *ḥꜣty*). In this case, the components of the expression cannot be used independently to express the emotional meaning. The distribution of compound expressions in diachrony shows a clear increase of their use from the New Kingdom onwards, especially at the Ramesside period. This of course can be a partially biased observation due to the unbalanced ratio of sources between periods in the corpus. Nevertheless, it does say something about the language evolution and its growing tendency toward an analytic rather than synthetic functioning.

The lexemes and expressions analysed have been grouped by conceptual path: the metaphorical expressions with a similar source domain have been analysed together.

The expressions with *jb/ḥꜣty* are framed in a series of symmetries: quiet vs. motion/action/speech; inside vs outside (of the body-container); weak vs strong and sick vs healthy.

1.1 Emotion is physical experience (> emotion is sensory perception)

As already mentioned in the introduction, sensory perception is a major source domain in emotion conceptualization. In the scope of afflictive emotions, taste appears to be primary and the idea of 'bitterness', or, perhaps more generally of 'bad/strong taste' is associated to irritation and frustration. Two lexemes mainly represent this category: *dḥr* and *jkn.*[29]

dḥr (Wb 5, 482.14–483.4): frustration is bitterness

The verb *dḥr*, which translates as 'to be bitter' first appears in medical and magical texts from the Second Intermediate Period (SIP). In rare cases, it is used metaphorically

26 https://aaew.bbaw.de/tla/index.html. Last accessed on October 21, 2021.

27 http://ramses.ulg.ac.be (link to the beta version). I sincerely thank the directors of the project for granting me access to the entire dataset. Last accessed on October 21, 2021.

28 Hannig (2006).

29 For a more developed commentary about *dḥr*, *bnr* and *nḏm*, see Di Biase-Dyson & Chantrain (2022).

in relation to people's temperaments or emotions, as it is the case in *The Teachings of Ptahhotep* (§305):

Ex. 1 *jw=f* *dḥr=f* *ḫnms* *bnr*
BS=3SG.M be_bitter:IPFV=3SG.M friend sweet
'He makes the kind (lit. sweet) friend frustrated (lit. bitter)' P. BM EA 10509, 4, 16 (L2)[30]

More often, *dḥr* rather applies to the way of interacting. Indeed, in the New Kingdom, *dḥr* is used attributively to describe unpleasant talk, especially in contrast to *bnr* and *nḏm*:

Ex. 2. *j-ḏd* *pꜣ* *nḏm* *jw=f* (*ḥr*) *ḏd* *pꜣ* *dḥ{ꜣj}<r>*
say:IMP ART:M.SG sweet SBRD=3SG.M (on) say ART:M.SGbitter
'Say what is pleasant (lit. sweet) when he says something unpleasant (lit. bitter).' (Ani, P. Boulaq 4, 22,7)

Ex. 3. [*bn*] *tp.j(w)t-r'* *bnj* *bn* *st* *dḥrj*
NEG utterance-F.PL sweet NEG 3PL bitter
'Your utterances are [neither] sweet nor are they bitter'. (Letter of Hori, P. Anastasi I, 5, 2–3)

jkn (*Wb* 1.140. 4–5): FRUSTRATION IS 'BAD TASTE'

The lexeme *jkn* is overall rarely attested and, as far as sources can tell, appears exclusively in *The Teachings of Amenemope*. The usual translation of *jkn* as 'to be bitter' is based on its parasynonymic relation with *dḥr*. Both lexemes are used as antonyms for *bnr* and *nḏm*, expressing 'sweetness'.[31]

In *Amenemope*, an example associates *bnr* (sweet, pleasant) to *jkn* (bitter, unpleasant, frustrated), both lexemes being used in a metaphorical way. It illustrates the contrast between the form and the content of speech, highlights the lack of sincerity of the speaker, who speaks out of repressed anger (here figuratively realized as 'fire'). Moreover, in a metaphorical way, it shows that, the further from the surface the body part is in the body, the truer the emotion. This passage thus also illustrates the metaphor BODY AS A CONTAINER, in addition to EMOTION IS PHYSICAL EXPERIENCE.

Ex. 4 *sp.ty=f* *bnr* *ns.t=f* *jkn* *tꜣ* *ẖ.t*
lip:F.DU=3SG.M sweet tongue:3SG.M bitter ART:F.SG body-F
rkḥ.tw *m* *ẖ.t=f*
burn:STAT in body-F=3SG.M
'His lips are sweet, but his tongue is bitter. The fire burns in his body' (Amenemope, P. BM 10474, 13.6)

30 The causative *sdḥr* 'to make bitter' is attested in the parallel version of P. BM EA 10371+10435, a.7 (L1): *jw=f sdḥr=f* *ḫnms* [*bnr*] 'He makes the kind (lit. sweet) friend angry (lit. bitter).'

31 Laisney (2007: 130).

The idea expressed by *jkn* seems to be the one of a strong taste in general, rather unpleasant. The association of *jkn* with the idea of HEAT/FIRE might also be a clue for a possible translation as 'piquant, spicy', rather than 'bitter'. However, *jkn* might also refer to the taste of something harmful, poisonous (a strong taste that indicates that some aliments have gone bad, for example).

Indeed, the association of dangerous things with the concept of ANGER (and, by extension, *frustration/irritation*) is well attested cross-culturally,[32] including in Egyptian. Just to quote a few examples, the path ANGER IS A DANGEROUS ANIMAL is actualized on the visual level by *ḳnd* 'to be angry' (*Wb* 5, 56.16–57.12) with the classifier of the baboon; *ꜣd* 'to be angry' (*Wb* 1, 24.12–15) with the classifier of the crocodile. In the same line, the path ANGER IS HEAT is represented for example by *šmm* 'the hot one', which designates an aggressive or impetuous person (*Wb* 4, 469.1–3). This lexeme is usually written with the classifier [HEAT/FIRE], sometimes in association with [NEGATIVITY] or [ENEMY/DEATH].

Most attestations of *jkn* take the classifier (G37), except for one (P. Stockholm MM 18416, 2, 9–*Amenemope* (= P. BM 10474 10,18–14,5)) which takes the group (D20-A24). This latter case is interesting and suggests a possible connection between the semantic of *jkn* and the domain of SMELL, but also the pole ANGER. Indeed, the classifier is found with lexemes from the following categories: [NOSE AND ACTIONS OF THE NOSE; HUMIDITY; RETAINING, LETTING BURST SOMETHING][33]. The group (D20-A24) is otherwise attested as the normal group of classifiers for *tpj* 'to breath'[34] and is also attested once for two negative emotions *ḳnd* 'to be furious' and *ḥḏn* 'to be outraged'. Finally, one attestation of *ršw.t* 'joy' in a lacuna is also written with this group. The idea of 'outburst', of 'internal pressure' might in my opinion constitute the key to the understanding of the use of in this context. Indeed, OUTBURST is commonly used cross-culturally in joy and anger conceptualization,[35] which would both confirm this semantic value for the classifier and explain its use in some specific contexts in relation to intense emotions such as joy and anger.

1.2 EMOTION IS PHYSICAL STATE

States affecting the physical body are often used to describe mental states. Sickness as physical suffering, is a very common way of conceptualizing afflictive emotions and states of mind, in Egyptian and in many world languages. Similarly, physical weakness is used to express discouragement.

---

32 Lakoff (1997: 382 sqq).

33 Based on the *Ramses* data. Last accessed Oct. 21, 2021.

34 Note that *tpj* might be a case that supports the hypothesis of the colexification of smell and taste by the same lexeme. Indeed, the lexeme *tpj*, is listed in Ramses as meaning both 'to smell'/'to atem' and 'to spit', co-lexifying actions of the nose and the mouth. However, there is no token available for this entry.

35 *Ibidem*.

1.2.1 EMPATHY IS SICKNESS AND SUFFERING

m(ḥ)r ḥ3ty/mḥr n ḥ3ty (*Wb* 2, 95.1–15) and *šnj ḥ3ty* (*Wb* 4, 494.15–18): SADNESS IS SICKNESS/SUFFERING OF THE HEART

The path followed with *m(ḥ)r ḥ3ty* goes from physical sickness to psychological prostration, sadness. In the same line of ideas, the expression *šnj ḥ3ty* (lit. 'the heart suffers') is also attested. In example 6, *šnj* as mental suffering echoes the actual physical suffering of Seth.

The two compound expressions *m(ḥ)r ḥ3ty* and *šnj ḥ3ty* have in common to express shared sadness, sadness for the suffering of someone else. In other words, compassion/ empathy. Empathy is described in terms of embodied suffering, with SICKNESS as source domain.

Ex. 5 *jw ḥ3ty n pr-ʿ3 ʿ,w,s mr n=f*
MCM heart of pharaoh life, prosperity, health sick for=3SG.M
r-jḳr sp-sn
excellently twice
'And the heart of Pharaoh, l.p.h. was very sad for him' (Two Brothers, P. Orbiney, 16, 6 = *LES* 26, 6)

Ex. 6 *ʿš n ḥmty=ṯ*
shout:IMP to harpoon=2SG.F
sfḫ jm=j
get_off:IMP from=1SG
jnk p3y=k sn n mw.t 3s.t
1SG POSS:M.SG=2SG.M brother of mother-F Isis-F
wn.jn=s ḥr šnn ḥ3ty=s n=f r-jḳr zp-sn
CJVB:CNSV=3SG.F on suffer:INF heart=3SG.F to=3SG.M excellently twice
zp-sn
twice
'Tell your harpoon to get off me, I (Seth) am your uterine brother, Isis! Then she felt for him an immense sadness' (Horus & Seth, P. Chester Beatty 1, 9, 5)

Another lexeme that might illustrate the path MENTAL STATE IS PHYSICAL STATE, with PHYSICAL SUFFERING as source domain is *jnd* (*Wb* 1, 102.16). The possibility of physical sickness or injury as primary meaning of *jnd* is evoked in the *Wb*., followed by the *TLA*. The examples of *jnd* with a clear physical meaning are rare to non-existent in the present corpus. However, other examples were brought to my attention[36] and confirm a physical meaning of *jnd* as well as its belonging to the SADNESS category, at least to some extent. A point worth highlighting here though is that some examples in medical context are interesting in several respects. Indeed, the meaning of *physical suffering*, which could appear as an obvious choice at first cannot always be clearly established. The reason for this is that the magical dimension of these texts is salient and disease or injuries are closely

36 See Jenkins (2022).

associated with manifestations of anger or frustration of gods and demons[37] and/or with personified elements (e.g. fire). In other words, the difference might sometimes be difficult to establish in spells of protection between an exhortation for the beneficiary of the spell not to be sick/injured and for the supernatural entity likely to cause the disease/injury not to become angry/frustrated and actually cause it. For example, in pBM EA 10059, 11.9: *m jnd zp-sn* is translated in the *TLA* as 'Don't be sick, don't be sick' but might also likely be an exhortation not to cause arm and therefore to be translated as 'don't be vexed, don't be vexed'. A similar example is found in a *Spell against Burns* from pLeiden I 348[38]: *m jnd=f m jnd=f m jr mw ḥwꜣ,* which is translated as 'Don't vex him, don't vex him, don't make foul water'. Finally, one will note that, in some contexts, *jnd* seems to express frustration/irritation rather than sadness. Its semantics thus seems to be situated at the intersection between the fields covered by *mḥr ḥꜣty* and *šnj ḥꜣty* on the one hand and *dḥr* and *jkn* on the other hand. *jnd* shares with the first two the meaning of *empathy* in some contexts[39], for example when associated to *jb*; and it shares with the two others the expression of *frustration*, or even *irritation*. It is thus situated on a continuum between the poles ANGER and SADNESS and moves closer to one or the other depending on its use in context.

1.2.2 DEPRESSION IS DECOMPOSITION

ḥwꜣ ḥꜣty (*Wb* 3, 50.6–16): DEPRESSION IS A DECOMPOSING HEART

In the tale of the Two brothers, several metaphors based on the path EMOTION IS PHYSICAL STATE are used for the expression of SADNESS and related negative emotions. We have just seen *m(ḥ)r ḥꜣty*, in example 5, another one is *ḥwꜣ ḥꜣty* 'the heart decomposes', attested earlier in the text.

Ex. 7 *jw ḥꜣty=f (ḥr) ḥwꜣ r-jkr zp-sn m-sꜣ nꜣ*
MCM heart=3SG.F (on) decompose:INF excellently twice after ART.PL
ʿḥʿ.w m-dj=f m-mnt 
blame-PL with=3SG.M daily
'Because his heart was really decomposing (getting sad) because of the blames he was receiving daily' (P. Orbiney, 11, 1–2 = *LES* 20, 15)

The idea conceptualized through the image of decomposition, is the slow fading away of someone's good mood or happiness because of an undermining situation (in the present case, the repeated blames addressed to the chief of the launderers).

37 Di Biase-Dyson, *Religious thought and figurative language – some case studies from Egypt*, communication given at the *Language, Semantics and Cognition* conference (Yale University, April 2021).
38 pLeiden I 348, v° III, 4 (*Ramses* id 5207).
39 Jenkins (2022), ex. 10.

1.2.3 GLOOM/DISCOURAGEMENT IS LACK OF PHYSICAL ENERGY

bgj ḥ3ty (*Wb* 1, 431.2–11): GLOOM IS A TIRED HEART

The expression written *bgs ḥ3ty*, only found in the *Doomed Prince*, is most likely to be interpreted as *bgj ḥ3ty*. It appears in the well-known passage where the young prince wants a dog, despite the prophecy. Retaining the *bgs* hypothesis, the literal translation would be 'so that his heart will not revolt', which would then likely refer to the fact of being upset. However, the classifiers suggest rather a lack of activity. In this case, *bgj* appears as a more likely interpretation, since the group  is the one usually used to classify this lexeme.

Ex. 8 *jmj* *jṯ.tw* *n=f* *wꜥ* *ktkt* *šrj,* [*tm*] {*bgs*} <*bgj*>
give:IMP take:PASS to=3SG.M one springer little, NEG be_tired
ḥ3ty=f 
heart:3SG.M
'Have brought to him a little dog (lit: 'little hopping thing'), so that he (his heart) will not be sad anymore' (Doomed Prince, P. Harris 500, v° 4, 10 = *LES* 2, 9)

The lexeme *bgj* can also be used by itself to refer to both physical and psychological state of tiredness/weakness. Furthermore, it takes in some contexts the negative connotation of *laziness*, as illustrated in example 9.

Ex. 9 *s3w* *tw* *jmj=k* *bgj* 
watch:IMP 2SG not_be:IMP=2SG.M be_tired:INF
'Watch yourself! Don't be lazy' (P. Anastasi 4, 13, 10 = *LEM* 49, 16)

bdš ḥ3ty (*Wb* 1, 487.15–23): HELPLESSNESS IS A TIRED HEART

The compound expression *bdš ḥ3ty* expresses psychological discouragement in terms of physical tiredness. This expression appears in military context and seems mostly restricted to royal inscriptions in *Égyptien de Tradition* from the New Kingdom onwards.

Ex. 10 *ḥ3ty.w* *bdš*(*.w*)  *m* *ẖ.wt=sn* *n* *snḏ*[*=i*]
heart-PL be_tired:STAT in body-F.PL=3PL because fear[=1SG]
'Their (= the enemies) hearts were discouraged in their bodies because of the fear of me' (Qadesh (K1), §135)

ẖsj jb/ḥ3ty (*Wb* 3, 398–399.10): HELPLESSNESS IS A WEAK HEART

Finally, another construction *ẖsj jb/ḥ3ty* also expresses discouragement, or cowardness. There too, it seems to be attested mostly in royal inscriptions.

Ex. 11 *wn.jn=f* *ḥr* *bdš* *jb=f* *ẖs*(*.w*) *snḏ.t* *ꜥ3.t*
CJVB.CNSV=3SG.M on tired:INF heart=3SG.M be_weak:STAT fear-F great-F
ꜥḳ.tj *m* *ḥꜥ.w=f* 
enter:STAT in limb-PL=3SG.M
'He (Menen) was discouraged, his heart was miserable and a great fear had entered his body' (Qadesh poem §207, P. Sallier 3, 5, 4)

In this example, *jb ẖs(.w)* is reinforced by the verb *bdš* 'to be tired, discouraged', in this case used on its own.

1.2.4 Other physical states used for emotion expression

ft jb/ḥ3ty (*Wb* 1, 580.8–13): WEARINESS IS A DISGUSTED HEART

Physical sensation of disgust is here used as source domain to express the feeling of 'being weary'. Both expressions with *jb* and *ḥ3ty* are attested from the early 19th dynasty. The expression *ft jb/ḥ3ty* expresses extreme mental tiredness and discouragement, to the point of disgust.[40] Note that, in the first example, the classifier of the tongue (F20) is added to (A2). The first one visually reflects the source domain SENSORY PERCEPTION > TASTE, while the second one, as superordinate classifier for INGESTION/SPEECH/EMOTION/COGNITION, encompasses both source and target domains of the metaphor.[41]

Ex. 12 *ḥ3ty=j*	*ft*	*m*	*ḏd*	*mtr.t*
heart=1SG	be-disgusted:STAT	in	say:INF	testimony-F

'My heart is weary of teaching' (P. Sallier 1, 7, 10 = *LEM* 85, 8)

Ex. 13 *jr*	*jry=k*	*7*	*rnp.wt*	*n*	*wḫ3=f,*
COND	do:SBJV=2SG.M	7	year-F.PL	of	search:INF=3SG.M
m -dj	*ft*	*ḥ3ty=k*			
PROH-CAUS	be_disgusted:SBJV	heart=2SG.M			

'Even if you spend seven years looking for it, may your heart not get discouraged' (P. Orbiney, 8, 5 = *LES* 18, 1)

1.3 Emotion is non-quietness

1.3.1 EMOTION IS MOTION

One common way of expressing a large range of negative emotions is to use MOTION (most often of the heart) as source domain. Motion is used in opposition with quietness (*gr*), which stands both for absence of sound and of movement. This relation is thus partially asymmetrical since the semantics of *gr* covers two fields and thus involves two series of possible antonyms.[42]

1.3.1.1 SADNESS IS (MOTION) DOWN

sh3 ḥ3ty (*Wb* 4, 207.2–5): OUTRAGE IS CAUSING (THE HEART) TO GO DOWN

The verb *sh3j* is the causative form of the verb *h3j* whose primary meaning is 'to go down' and, later on, evolved into meaning 'to fall'. The primary meaning of *sh3j* was thus 'to cause to go down' or 'to cause to fall' (*Wb* 4, 206.10–15). In the New Kingdom, *sh3j*

40 This might be somehow similar to the modern concept of 'burn out'.

41 This 'agglutinative' classification strategy is very common in the New Kingdom (Chantrain, in press).

42 Di Biase-Dyson & Chantrain (2022).

adopted the metaphorical meaning ‘to act in a downgrading way’, ‘to cheat’, ‘to lie’.[43] It seems that the causative form with *s*- then became exclusively affected to the metaphorical meaning, while the primary meaning ‘making go down’ (the actual motion) became then assumed by the so-called *new causative* construction [*rdj* (= do, make) + *h3j*]. A compound expression *sh3j ḥ3ty*, which means ‘causing the heart to go down/to fall’ is also attested. It conveys the meaning of ‘fooling someone’ and causing disappointment. The case of *sh3j* clearly illustrates the conceptual paths EMOTION IS MOTION and NEGATIVE IS DOWN.[44] It falls under the non-primary emotion *outrage*. On the classifier level, two changes can be seen: instead of the initial classifier 𓂻 reflecting the source domain MOTION, most attestations take the classifier 𓂽, which works here as metaphor marker (ex. 14).[45] In addition to this, three attestations take yet another classifier, 𓅪, instead of 𓂻 (see ex. 15) and as an alternative to 𓂽. In this case, the classifier has thus been adapted to the target domain: 𓅪 (SMALLNESS/NEGATIVITY) is used instead of 𓂻 (MOTION).

Ex. 14 *jr* *ptr=k* *ky* *jw=f* *ḥr* *sh3* 𓊃𓉔𓅯𓂽
COND see:SBJV=2SG.M other SBRD=3SG.M on go_down:INF
j.jr=k *sw3* *n=f* *m-w3w*
THMZ=2SG.M pass:INF to=3SG.M away
‘If you see another committing fraud, you should go away from him’ (*Amenemope*, P. BM 10474, 18, 6–7)

Ex. 15 *j.jr=tw* *m* *ḏd=ṯ*
THMZ=IMPRS in say=2SG.F
One will act only according to what you said
bn *sh3<=j>* 𓊃𓉔𓅯𓅪𓏪 *h3ty=t* *m* *ḏd(.t)* *nb.t*
NEG CAUS-go_down=1SG heart=2SG.F in word(-F) every-F
j.jr.t<=j> *spr* *r=ṯ*
to:do=1SG reach:INF to=2SG.F
‘I will not fool your heart with any word until I join you’ (Letter to a departed wife, O. Louvre N698, v° 21)

43 Winand (2018: 130, 132).

44 Lakoff & Johnson (2003: 15–16). Symmetrically, positive emotions are linked to the fact of being up, which is sometimes expressed visually in the spellings in Egyptian, for example, with the classifier of the exulting man 𓀠 (A28).

45 Chantrain (2021; in press) argues that the classifier 𓂽 works as metaphor marker in specific genres – mostly wisdom texts and oracular texts (see also Chantrain & Di Biase-Dyson: 2017). This usage of 𓂽 is attested between the end of the NK and the LP. Besides this usage, it also stands for the conceptual category BACKWARD/REROUTED MOTION. The reason for the choice of this classifier as marker of a metaphorical meaning may appear somewhat obscure at first glance. Indeed, it is not always motivated by a contiguity relation toward the meaning of the lexeme: the classifier 𓂽 is also used as distinctive classification for other verbs than motion verbs when used metaphorically. It is here argued though that the choice of the classifier is thus in this case not motivated by the semantics of the lexeme itself, but by the very concept of METAPHOR AS ‘REROUTED’ WORDS and thoughts.

However, in ex. 16, the classifier (MOTION) is exceptionally maintained, even though the meaning is also metaphorical.

Ex. 16 *r-ḏd sḥꜣ=k m pꜣ ḥḏ ẖr m wꜥ*
COMP CAUS-go_down=2SG.M in ART:M.SG money say in one
'you cheated with money – they said to one another' (Tomb Robberies, P. BM 10052, v° 8, 9 = K*RI* 786, 7)

Finally, one should note that another expression, *hꜣj jb/ḥꜣty* 'the heart goes down', with the heart as agent, is attested too, but does not refer to a negative emotion. It is rather the idea of 'calming down' that is conveyed in this case through the image of the heart going down, going back to its right place.

1.3.1.2 ANXIETY IS REPEATED MOTION

Repeated motion of the heart inside the body

pẖr jb/ḥꜣty (*Wb* 1, 544.14): CONCERN IS THE HEART TURNING TO SOMEONE and ANXIETY IS THE HEART MOVING AROUND

To my knowledge, the first example below from the Love Songs, is the only one that features *pẖr* in the sense of 'overthinking', conceptualized as REPEATED MOTION, as the heart running around in someone's body (*pẖr m-ẖnw ẖ.t*). This reference to restless thoughts describes very accurately one of the main symptoms of anxiety. Admittedly, this example is somewhat problematic since the subject of *pẖr* is in a lacuna. However, the reconstruction is likely and based on the high number of personifications of the heart present in the text as well as on the use of the adverbial complement of location *m-ẖnw ẖ.t*.

Ex. 17 *jr jry=j ꜣ.t n tm mꜣꜣ=s*
COND do:SBJV=1SG moment-F of NEG see:INF=3SG.F
[jb/ḥꜣty]=j ḥr pẖr m-ẖnw ẖ.t
heart=1SG on turn_around:INF inside body-F
'If I spend one moment without seeing her, my [heart] is moving around in my body' (O. DeM 1266 + O. CG 25218, 26)

Other examples show that *pẖr ḥꜣty* or *pẖr jb* can express concern or interest toward a person or an affair.

Ex. 18 *nfr ꜣms-jb sꜣ pẖr=f ḥꜣty m-sꜣ jt=f*
perfect concern son turn_around:REL=3SG.M heart after father=3SG.M
'Perfect is the concern of a son who cares about his father' (Abydos, Great dedicatory inscription of Ramses II, 30 = K*RI* II)

In example 19, the constructions *jb pẖr* and *ḥꜣty m-sꜣ* are used symmetrically, which highlights their semantic proximity. Indeed, the expression *ḥꜣty m-sꜣ*, treated below in section 1.3.4., expresses extreme care or concern.

Ex. 19 *jb=j* *pẖr.w* *n* *nty* *wrd* *ḥꜣty* *m-sꜣ*
heart=1SG turn_around:STAT to REL:M.SG tired:PTCP heart after
jt=j *mꜣʿ*
father=1SG true
'my *jb*-heart is concerned about the one who is tired, my *ḥꜣty*-heart cares about my true father' (Abydos Stela of Seti I for Ramses I, x+18)

pẖr ḥꜣty can also mean 'to divert the attention of someone' (toward something else), or, in the same spirit, 'to put someone in the right mood'. Such case occurs in amuletic and oracular texts, as a way of protecting the beneficiary of the text:

Ex. 20 *jw=j* *(r)* *pẖr* *ḥꜣty* *n* *ns-sw-ẖnsw* *tꜣy*
fut=1SG FUT turn_around:INF heart of name ART:F.SG
šrj.t *n* *tꜣ-ḥn.t-ḏḥwty*
daughter-F of name
jw bn jw=s (r) jr.t md.t nb.t bjn.t r pꜣy-nḏm pꜣ šrj n ꜣs.t-m-ꜣẖ-bjt
'I will divert the attention of *ns-sw-ẖnsw*, the daughter of *tꜣ-ḥn.t-ḏḥwty*, and she will not say anything bad against *pꜣy-nḏm*, the son of *ꜣs.t-m-ꜣẖ-bjt*' (Nesikhenesu, T. CGC 46891, l. 36)

Cases like *pẖr ḥꜣty* show well the importance of looking at all attestations and their context. A same metaphorical path may indeed result in expressing slightly different ideas and therefore being translated differently. The *TLA*[46] (lemma 62010 and 854241) and the *Wörterbuch*[47] for example do not mention the link with anxiety (*pẖr ḥꜣty m-ẖnw*) but they do list focus switch related meanings: 'driving away someone's attention', 'being inclined toward someone (else)'or 'caring for'.

ṯjṯj n ḥꜣty (*Wb* 5, 357.7–9): ANXIETY IS A TROTTING HEART

The meaning of the expression *ṯjṯj n ḥꜣty* refers to an anxious state, to running thoughts. The classifier is used here again in its function of metaphor marker, as previously seen for the verb *sḥꜣj*.[48] The spelling with the reduplicated *ṯꜣ*-bird in example 21 is exceptional: besides its phonetic value, it may as well play a role on an iconicity level. Indeed, this spelling might refer to ANXIETY AS NON-QUIETNESS OF THE HEART in two ways: MOTION *VS* QUIET and LOUD *VS* QUIET. An anxious heart would then be a wandering and loud heart, if one assumes that the spelling is somewhat onomatopoeic.[49] This conceptual path may thus be seen as expressed through a double metonymy: the expression of worry as its symptoms – a faster heart rate and louder, stronger heartbeats.

---

46 *pẖr ḥꜣty* (lemma 62010) and *pẖr jb* (lemma 854241).

47 *Wb* 1, 544.14–545.3.

48 The usual classifier is (D54). The use of (D55) is possibly also conferring a negative nuance of 'wrong doing', which appears to be part of the semantic features assumed by this classifier, judging by the list of lemmas with which it appears (Chantrain, *in preparation*).

49 This interpretation might be conforted by an attestation of *ṯjṯj* in pBoulaq 4 (18, 6) written with the classifier (A17).

Ex. 21 *jw=n* (*r*) *šd=f* *r* *n3* *tjtj* *n* *ḥ3ty* 
FUT=1PL FUT protect=3SG.M against ART:PL trot:INF of heart
'We will protect him from the peregrinations of heart" (P. Berlin P. 3059, 52)

Both expressions *tjtj n ḥ3ty* and *pẖr jb/ḥ3ty m ẖnw* thus describe a state of anxiety, of concern. They have in common the fact of conceptualizing this emotional state in terms of 1) repeated motion, which reflects the obsessive character of the thoughts and 2) introspection, or even rumination, which is expressed through the location of the heart inside the body.

1.3.1.3 EMOTIONAL DETACHMENT IS CENTRIFUGAL MOTION

Centrifugal motion of the heart (source oriented)

ṯmḥ ḥ3ty (*Wb* 5, 369.2): ANNOYANCE IS A HEART TURNING AWAY

Ex. 22 *wnn=f* (*ḥr*) *dj.t* *ẖnnw* *m* *pr=f*
when=3SG.M (on) give:INF trouble in house=3SG.M
jw *ḥ3ty.w* (*ḥr*) *tmḥ* 
CORD heart-PL on turn_away:INF
'When he (the Akh-spirit) places trouble within a house, the hearts turn away'
(Ani, P. Boulaq 4, 22, 3)

The expression *ṯmḥ ḥ3ty* seems to refer to annoyance, to the fact of taking distance from someone consecutively to an argument. However, it is a bit hard to assess with certainty since this is the only attestation of *ṯmḥ ḥ3ty* found in the corpus, except for a parallel version of *Ani* (P. Louvre E 30144). There seems to be no similar construction with *jb*.

rwj ḥ3ty (*Wb* 2, 406.2–407.4): WEARINESS IS A HEART GOING OUT

This expression refers to a kind of depressive attitude which has for result a lack of dedication to tasks and duties. Literally, the attention (the *ḥ3ty* here) moves away. This meaning is obtained through the association of *rwj ḥ3ty* with the lexeme *gḥ/g3ḥ*. This lexeme is attested only a few times in the New Kingdom, as a verb[50] and as a noun.[51] The translations given are the ones of 'being tired/weary' and 'tiredness/exhaustion, weariness'.

Ex. 23 *rwj* *sw* *p3y=j* *ḥ3ty* *m* *gḥ=f*
go_away:PFV 3SG.M POSS:M.SG=1SG heart in exhaustion=3SG.M
w3ḥ.n=j *m3w.t=j*
offer:PFV=1SG refrain-F=1SG
'My heart moved itself away in its weariness after I have performed my refrain'
(Harpist, TT 194, F 10)

50 Ramses id: gAH_1002_5706.
51 TLA id: 856733.

1.3.1.4 LACK OF CONTROL IS CENTRIFUGAL MOTION (TARGET ORIENTED)

Centrifugal motion of the heart (target oriented)

jb/ḥ3ty m-s3 (*Wb* 1, 59.10–60.11): WORRY IS A HEART BEING/PLACED AFTER STH.

In the first example, from the P. Harris 500, the 'sister' is concerned about the sincerity of her lover's feelings. Her thoughts are focused on him and everything that relates to him, to the point of becoming an obsession.

Ex. 24 *sn* *mry{.t}* *jb=j* *m-s3* *mrw.t=k*
brother love:PTCP heart=1SG after love-F=2SG.M
ḳm3yt *n=k* *nb*
create:PTCP for=2SG.M every
'Brother, my beloved, I worry about your love (my heart is after your love) and everything that was created for you' (Love Songs, P. Harris 500, r° 4, 2)

A related expression is *rdj jb/ḥ3ty m-s3*, which is based on a target-oriented centrifugal transfer action (the heart is moved from the owner's body to another location).

In the following example, the potential worries are about how works are performed in the tombs of the royal children.

Ex. 25 *twj* *ḥr* *b3k* *m-sšr* *zp-sn*
PRS-1SG PRS= work:INF excellently twice
mnẖ *zp-sn* *m* *jr* *nfr* *m* *jr* *mnẖ*
efficient twice in do:INF perfect in do:INF efficient
m-dy *dj.t* *p3y=j* *nb* *ḥ3ty=f* *m-s3=w*
proh:CAUS give:SBJV POSS:M.SG=1SG lord heart=3SG.M after=3PL
y3 *twj* *ḥr* *b3k* *r-jḳr* *zp-sn*
EXLM PRS-1SG PRS= work:INF excellently twice
'I work really excellently and perfectly, acting well and efficiently.
Do not let my lord worry about them (= the tombs of the royal children)
Indeed, I work really excellently!' (O. OIC 16991, v° 4–5)
Ramses III – letter

jb/ḥ3ty m-s3 has usually a rather negative meaning 'to worry' or 'to care', but excessively. The positive meaning 'to be interested in', 'to invest oneself into' is rather expressed by the expression *rdj jb m* 'to put the heart into something'.

Ex. 26 *jmy* *jb=k* *r* *sš.w* *r-wr* *sp-sn*
give:IMP heart=2SG.M to writing-PL very-greatly twice
'Have great interest in writings' (O. Gardiner 2, 2)

tfj ḥ3ty/jb (*Wb* 5, 297.11–298.10): AGITATION IS A HEART THAT JUMPS OUT

In the first example, obsessed with her love for the 'brother', the 'sister' feels agitated, restless and goes out at night to see him, despite the prohibition. She acts irrationally, oblivious of social conventions.

Ex. 27 *tf* *jb=j* *r* *pr* *r* *rdj.t* *gmḥ=j*
jump:PFV heart=1SG to go_out:INF for give:INF see:SBJV=1SG
sn *m* *pꜣ* *grḥ*
brother in ART:M.SG night
'My heart jumped to the point of going out to let me see the brother tonight' (Love Songs, P. Chester Beatty I, v° C4, 5–6)

In the second example, it is the young scribe's lack of dedication to its duties that his stressed. The lemma is here spelled *tftf*, which appears to be derived from *tfj* (*Wb* 5, 300.7).

Ex. 28 *jb=k* *tftf* *ḥꜣty=k* *mḥy*
heart=2SG.M jump:STAT heart=2SG.M fly_away:STAT
'(I have been told that you gave up writing and that you lost yourself in pleasures) Your heart jumped out, your heart flew away' (Advice to an idle scribe, P. Turin A, v° 1, 5 = *LEM* 121, 14)

A heart that is jumping out is thus a way to express a restless attitude or a lack of commitment, of dedication. In both cases, the expression denotes an impulsive and unreasonable attitude, based and emotional impulse instead of rationality.

1.3.1.5 IMPATIENCE IS FAST MOTION

ꜣs-jb (Wb 1, 20.1–6): IMPATIENCE IS A FAST HEART

Ex. 29 *nn* *ꜣs-jb* *šw* *m* *ḫrw.w=f*
not_existant fast-heart free from enemy-PL=3SG.M
'There is no impatient free of enemies' (O. Michaelides 16, 6–7)

A fast heart conceptualizes impatience, thus an affect disposition rather than a transient emotion. The expression *ꜣs-jb* refers to a kind of personal behaviour that interferes with peaceful, cordial relations to others, as opposed to a thorough, quiet and balanced way of dealing with tasks and people.

This is confirmed by the symmetry with the patient and pondered behaviour expressed two lines below, by the verb *gr* (to be quiet). This example perfectly illustrates the fact that *gr* can express quietness on two levels: absence of sound and absence of movement.

Ex. 30 *nn* *kꜣ* *wšm=tw* *n=f* *md.t*
not_existant think:PTCP question:SUBJ=IMPRS for=3SG.M speech-F
jr *gr=k* *ḫpr* *n=k* *pḥ.wj*
COND be_silent:SBJV=2SG.M become:SBJV for=2SG.M limit
'There is no thinking man whose words are questioned(?).[52] If you stay quiet, you will get your way' (O. Michaelides 16, 7)

Note that the classifiers in Ex. 29 also reflect the idea of both MOTION (D54) and INTERACTION/OPPOSITION (Z9).

52 The meaning of *wšm* is unclear.

1.3.2 EMOTION IS ACTION

1.3.2.1 The heart as agent

1.3.2.1.1 Centripetal action (source oriented): WORRY IS TAKING IN

ṯꜣ ḥꜣty sḫr.w (*Wb* 1, 150.12–13): WORRY IS A HEART THAT TAKES MATTERS

The idea conveyed by this expression is the one of worrying about a situation, and perhaps take responsibility for it. It seems to be attested only in Wenamun for the present corpus. One finds here the conceptual metaphor THINKING IS OBJECT MANIPULATION,[53] with the sub-path TAKING INSIDE THE MIND IS TAKING INSIDE THE BODY.

Ex. 31

jw=f	(*ḥr*)	*dj.t*	*jn.tw*	*n=j*	*tꜣ-n.t-njw.t*	*wꜥ.t*
BS=3SG.M	on	give:INF	bring:PFV.PASS	to=1SG	name	one-F

ḥs.t	*n*	*km.t*	*jw=s*	*m-dj=f*
singer-F	of	Egypt-F	SBRD=3SG.F	with=3SG.M

r-ḏd	*ḥsy*	*n=f*
COMP	sing:IMP	for=3SG.M

m-dj	*ṯꜣy* 	*ḥꜣty=f*	*sḫr.w*
PROH-CAUS	take:SBJV	heart=3SG.M	plan-PL

'He made brought to me *tꜣ-n.t-njw.t*, a singer who was with him and said: 'Sing for him! Do not let his heart take matters' (do not let him worry)' (Wenamun, P. Moscow 120, 2, 69 = *LES* 74, 6)

This expression is conceptually linked to another one: *tꜣ ḫ.t m ḥꜣty* 'the thing in the heart', which designates the object of worry, of concern (i.e. the matter that was taken by the heart). Their common idea is INTROSPECTION/RUMINATION.

Ex. 32

mntn	*tꜣ*	*ḫ.t*	*nty*	*m*	*ḥꜣty=j*
2PL	ART:F.SG	thing-F	REL	in	heart=1SG

jw=j	(*ḥr*)	*hꜣb*	*r*	*rdj.t*	*ꜥm=tn*	*nꜣy=tn*	*rmṯ.w*
CORD	on	send:INF	to	give:INF	know:SBJV=2PL	POSS.PL=2PL	people

ꜥnḫ	*wḏꜣ*	*snb*
live:STAT	be_wealthy:STAT	be_healthy:STAT

m dy.t	*ḥꜣty=tn*	*m-sꜣ=w*
PROH-CAUS	heart=2SG.PL	after=PL

'You are the matter which is in my heart. I wrote to inform you that your men are alive, wealthy and healthy. Do not worry about them' (P. Genève D 407, v° 15–16 = *LRL* 16, 5)

1.3.2.2 The heart as patient

This section deals with various actions undergone by the heart. Two main categories have been distinguished: the actions that the protagonists inflict to their own heart, and the ones inflicted to someone else's heart.

---

53 Lakoff (2014: 1).

1.3.2.2.1 NEGATIVE EMOTION IS VIOLENT ACTION

nḥm jb (*Wb* 2, 295.12–297.4) and *tfj jb* (*Wb* 5, 297.11–298.10): HELPLESSNESS IS A HEART TAKEN AWAY

Taking away the heart of someone conceptualizes the fact of causing despair and self-control – or even identity – loss. The concept of deprivation, of non-wholeness, seems to be central in this metaphor. This expression is regularly used in royal ideology texts, in battle scenes. The heart is seen as the keeper of the individual's personality and strength and its metaphorical removal corresponds to a major trauma and its consequences on someone's behaviour.

Ex. 33	*mšꜥ.w*	*wpwty.w*	*n.w*	*tꜣ*	*nb*	*jb=sn*	*tfi(.w)*
	envoy-PL	messenger-PL	of-PL	land	every	heart=3PL	remove:STAT
	nḥm(.w)						
	take_away:STAT						

'As for the envoys and messengers of every land, their heart was removed and taken away' (Medinet Habu 28, 39 = K*RI* V, 24, 1)

In this category are listed other expressions that conceptualize emotional affliction as physical concrete impact of a violent action. This action can affect the patient by modifying the heart's physical integrity as if it were an entire body. The actions undergone by the enemies' heart modify their body posture and their agency potential (from up to down and from standing to lying: *ḥdb jb/ḥꜣty* and *dẖ jb*/*ḥꜣty*) and compromise their physical integrity (*ḥḏ jb/ḥꜣty*)

In the first two examples, a parallel is clearly made between the physical prostration of the enemies and their emotional distress.

ḥdb jb (*Wb* 3, 205.8–17) and *dẖ jb* (*Wb* 5, 483–484.8): DESPAIR IS AN OVERTHROWN HEART

Ex. 34	*ḥdb.n=k*	*jb.w*	*sṯty.w*
	lay:PFV=2SG.M	heart-PL	Asiatic-PL

'You have prostrated the hearts of the Asiatics' (Medinet Habu, K*RI* V, 34, 3)

Ex. 35	*dẖ.n=f*	*jb.w*	*mšwš*				
	overthrow:PFV	heart-PL	asiatic				
	nꜣy.w	*nẖt-ꜥ.w*	*smꜣ*	*m*	*ḫfꜥ[=f]*	*m*	*ḏnḥ.w*
	POSS:PL	hero-PL	kill:STAT	in	fist=3SG.M	in	captive-PL
	r-ḥꜣ.t	*ssm.wt*					
	before	horse-F.PL					

'He has overthrown the hearts of the Asiatics, their heroes are slain in [his] grasp or are captives before his horses' (Medinet Habu, K*RI* V, 45, 4)

ḥḏ jb/ḥ3ty (*Wb* 3, 212–213.16): UNFAITHFULNESS IS A BROKEN HEART

The second expression, *ḥḏ-jb,* conceptualises a break in someone's line of conduct that leads to unfaithful actions. It can take different nuances of meaning, depending whether it applies to the subject's own heart or to someone else's heart. The case of *ḥḏ-jb* is treated in detail in section 2.

1.4 EMOTION AS EFFECT OF THE EMOTION

1.4.1 Emotion as physical effect of the emotion

Another way of conceptualizing emotions in Egyptian is their description as the physical manifestation of this emotion. The intensity criterion in this case seems to be playing a predominant role. In both cases below, this intensity is highlighted by a reduplication pattern 1) in the structure of the lemma itself (*nyny*) or 2) in the expression of the instrument, the medium, conveying the emotional manifestation (*m jr.tj*).

nyny ḥ3ty (*Wb* 203, 8–13): DESPAIR IS AN IMPLORING HEART

This expression of emotional distress, of despair, is related to a form of supplication prayer (*Wb* 2, 203.7).[54] Rather than transient sadness, *nyny* suggests a lasting or recurring feeling. In contrast with the expressions seen before, this form of sadness is not interiorised but clearly and loudly expressed. The interaction/externalization feature contained in *nyny* 'to implore' makes the difference with the next expression *rmj.t jb m jr.tj*. Indeed, while the two expressions share the feature intensity, the second one does not involve a recipient. Furthermore, in *nyny ḥ3ty*, an attempt is made at regaining control on the situation.[55]

Ex. 36 *ḥ3ty=s* (*ḥr*) *nyny* 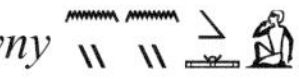
heart=3SG.F on implore:INF
jw=s *ʿḥʿ.tw* <*ḥr*> *sp.t* <*n*> *p3* *ym*
SBRD=3SG.F stand:STAT on shore-F of ART:M.SG sea
jw=s (*ḥr*) *nyny* *rʿ* *nb* *zp-sn* 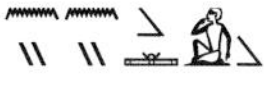
CORD=3SG.F on implore:INF day every twice
'Her (Isis) heart implores, while she is standing on the seashore. Her heart implores every single day' (P. Boulaq 6, r° II, 1)

rmj.t jb m jr.tj (*Wb* 2, 417.11–13): GRIEF IS A HEART THAT CRIES WITH TWO EYES

The meaning of this expression is very clear, it is a simple case of personification with effect of an emotion standing for the emotion itself. The adverbial complement *m jr.tj*

54 As already suggested by Koenig (1981) in his edition of P. Boulaq 6 (1981: 19, 135). He makes the parallel with 'faire le geste *nyny*', an imploration gesture. Some confusion exists in dictionaries databases (both TLA and Ramses) as for the number of entries and their respective token distribution (*Wb* II 203, 8–13; Hannig 2006: 415; Ramses nyny_1010_67805 and nyny_1001_3569; TLA id 80180).

55 DESPAIR is categorized under *not in control* in the HUMAINE-EARL categorization.

'with two eyes' makes explicit the intensity of the emotion (in a similar way as *zp-sn*) and thus refers to deep sadness, despair.

Ex. 37 *jb=j* (*ḥr*) *rmj.t* *m* *ir.ty*
heart=1SG on cry:INF in eye-F.DU
'My heart cries with two eyes' (O. Turin N57380, r° 4)

1.4.2 EMOTION AS PSYCHOLOGICAL EFFECT OF THE EMOTION

1.4.2.1 EMOTION IS IGNORANCE

ẖm + *jb* (*Wb* 3, 278.5–280.5): AGITATION IS AN IGNORANT HEART and NEGLECT IS AN IGNORED HEART

Emotional reactions are framed in an opposition with rational, conscious, reactions. The heart, as centre of both emotions and reason, is described as being ignorant of the latter when its owner becomes a slave to their emotions, oblivious of the constraints of contextual circumstances and social conventions. The cross-domain mapping attested here is a bit different since it does not follow the path CONCRETE ABSTRACT seen in the other examples. It results too from a personification of the heart and is based on transfer from COGNITION to EMOTION, in other words, from an abstract domain to another.[56]

Ex. 38 *ẖm* *tw* *jb=j* *r-jḳr*
be_ignorant:PTCP 2SG.M heart=1SG excellently
'You are really ignorant, my heart' (P. Chester Beatty I, v° C2, 7)

Worth is also mentioning that besides the expression *ẖm* + *jb* 'the heart is ignorant', with *jb* as subject of *ẖm* means 'to act foolishly', another one is attested, featuring *jb* as object of *ẖm* ('to ignore the heart'). The latter has a totally different meaning, since it refers to an unfaithful, dishonest or hypocrite attitude. Purposely ignoring one's own heart is ignoring, dismissing, one's own moral principles, in other words, acting in a way that is not in line with one's own values or thoughts.[57] This expression is semantically close to *ḥḏ jb/ḥ3ty* 'to break the heart' when applied to someone's own heart. This case is developed below in section 2.

Ex. 39 *ẖm=k* *jb=k* *r* *ꜥnḫ*
be_ignorant:PFV=2SG.M heart=2SG.M to swear:INF
'you ignored you heart at the time of taking the oath' (O. DeM 1595, 2)
19-20 dyn. – teaching

56 This is attested elsewhere in Egyptian, for example in the metaphorical use of *rḫ* 'to know' as referring to carnal knowledge, sometimes with the classifier variation (D53) in addition to (Y1), which reflects the figurative meaning (see for example *Truth and Falsehood*, P. BM 10682, r° 4, 5 = *LES* 32, 5).

57 Chantrain (2023).

2 'False friends' metaphors

2.1 *ḥḏ jb/ḥꜣty* (*Wb* 3, 212–213.16) 'to break the heart'

Another example of the necessity of a philological analysis in semantic studies is that a thorough reading of the cotext and context can help identifying 'false friends' metaphors hidden in texts and that keep fooling our dictionaries and databases.

The expression *ḥḏ ḥꜣty/jb* appears in the Love Songs and is regularly translated literally as 'He cannot break my heart'. This Egyptian expression is usually understood as having the same meaning as its literal English translation: sadness caused by love misfortune. Their semantics is indeed very close in the context of the Love Songs, but, looking at attestations in other texts, one can see that the Egyptian *ḥḏ ḥꜣty/jb* carries a specific semantic feature that English does not have: *unfaithfulness*. This unfaithfulness can be toward someone else (= to break someone else's heart), for example while cheating on someone in a love context, but it can also be a form of unfaithfulness toward oneself: betraying one's own values/principles (= break one's own heart). In other words, in this specific case, even if the conceptual mapping seems similar to the one in the target language,[58] the meanings of the two expressions do not overlap completely. 'Breaking the heart' in Egyptian thus seems to also refer to the fact of breaking a line of conduct, a behavioural pattern based on moral values, whether it is in the faithfulness toward someone else or toward yourself and your principles.

Meaning 1: OFFENDING SOMEONE IS TO BREAK SOMEONE'S HEART

The meaning of *ḥḏ jb/ḥꜣty* when applied to the heart of someone else is explicitly expressed in the passage of the Love Songs from P. Harris 500: *ʿḏꜣ=f wj <m> ky ḏd gm=f kt.t* 'he cheated on me; he found another one'.

The use of *ḥḏ ḥꜣty* echoes the compound word *pꜣ ḥḏ-jb* in line 5.11 of the same text. This compound is translated as 'intrigue, offense' in the Hannig dictionary,[59] which is a quite accurate translation since it reflects the idea of *unfaithfulness* by hiding something from someone else and by acting against their interest.

Ex. 40 *bw gr jb=j*
NEG be_silent:PFV heart=1SG
hꜣb=f n[=j] wpwtj ꜣs {=j} rd.wj m ʿḳ
send:PFV=3SG.M to=1SG messenger fast foot-M.DU in enter:INF
ḥr pr.t
on go_out:INF
r ḏd n=j ʿḏꜣ=f wj <m> ky ḏd
to say:INF to=1SG cheat:PFV=3SG.M 1SG in other say:INF

58 In this case the target language is English, but the same conceptualization is well-attested cross-linguistically. Kövecses (2000: 27) refers to LOVE IS A UNITY OF PARTS as the central metaphor of LOVE.

59 Hannig (2006: 619; [22498]).

gm=f *kt.t* *sy* *ḥr* *g3g3w* *n* *ḥr=f*
find:PFV=3SG.M other-F 3SG.F on be_astonished:INF of face=3SG.M
jḫ *rf* ***p3*** ***ḥḏ-jb*** *n* *{ky}* *<k.t>* *ḥr* *ḫpp*
Q thus ART:M.SG break-heart of other-F on alienate:INF
'My heart is not quiet,
He sent to me a fast messenger going back and forth
To tell me that he cheated on me, in other words, that he found another one
She is in admiration of him
So, what? The **offense** caused by another one is taking me…' (Love songs, P. Harris 500, r° 5, 8–12)

A few lines above though, the 'sister' was still affirming about the brother 'he cannot break my heart' and evoking her status of favourite, which, as the rest of the text shows, was not meant to last.

Ex. 41 *dj=f* *wj* *m* *tpy.t* *n* *nfr.wt*
give:PFV=3SG.M 1SG in first-F of beautiful_one-F:PL
bw ***ḥḏ=f*** ***p3y=j*** ***ḥ3ty***
NEG break:PFV=3SG.M POSS:M.SG=1SG heart
j.dj=j *ḥr=j* *ḥr* *p3* *sb3* *n* *bnr*
give:THMZ=1SG face=1SG on ART:M.SG door of outside
mk *sn* *(ḥr)* *jy.t* *n=j*
ATTN 3PL on come:INF to=1SG
'He placed me as the first of the beautiful ones
He cannot break my heart
It is toward the outside door that I turn my attention
See, the brother is coming to me'

Meaning 2: TAKING OUTRAGE IS TO BREAK YOUR OWN HEART

The next example illustrates the semantics of *ḥḏ jb* when the agent affecting the integrity of the heart is its own owner. Translated here as 'do not take offense', *ḥḏ jb* conveys the idea of breaking with the usual line of behaviour and/or getting emotionally affected by someone else's action. In the *Wb* (213), this use of *ḥḏ jb/ḥ3ty* is indeed listed with the translation 'sein eigenes Herz kränken' which corresponds to the meaning 2 'to fool oneself', 'to take offense'. This idea conveyed by *ḥḏ jb/ḥ3ty* seems to enter the scope of the emotion OUTRAGE established by Plutchik

Ex. 42 *whn* *n3y=k* *ṯnr.w*
overturn:IMP POSS:PL=2SG.M resentment-PL
tm *bi3.t=k* *ḳnd* *{r}* *wp=k*
NEG character-f=2SG.M angry open:INF=2SG.M
m-jrj ***ḥḏy*** ***jb*** *ḥr* *ḏs=k*
PROH-do break:INF heart on self=2SG.M

pnꜥ=f *ḥs.t=f* *ꜣs*
turn_upside_down:SBJV=3SG.M favour-F=3SG.M quickly
m-sꜣ *wnw.t=f* *nḥꜣ.t*
after hour-F=3SG.M terrible-F
'Dispel your resentments,
So that your angry character will not condemn you
Do not take offense (lit: break your own heart)
He will change his mind quickly after his terrible moment' (Ani, P. Boulaq 4, 22, 9)

The general path actualised by *ḥḏ jb/ḥꜣty* is thus MORAL INTEGRITY IS PHYSICAL INTEGRITY, derived itself from the superordinate path MIND AS BODY.

2.2 *nn wn ḥꜣty m ẖ.t*: 'there is no heart in your body' and *jwty jb* 'to be heartless'

Other candidates to the 'false friend' metaphor status are the Egyptian expressions that translate literally as 'to be heartless'. The fact of being heartless refers to someone insensitive in the target language[60] and thus belongs to the domain EMOTION. However, the construction has a different meaning in Egyptian: heartlessness does not refer to a lack of emotional sensitivity but to a lack of consciousness, of rationality. It usually translates in context as 'to be foolish', 'to be irrational', 'to act stupidly'. Being heartless in Egyptian thus expresses a hiatus between the actual person's attitude in a given situation and a socially acceptable way of behaving. Interestingly, rather than expressing a lack of emotion, heartlessness is Egyptian expresses exactly the opposite since the rational reason for the grounded behaviour of the subject to be affected is often overwhelming emotions. The meaning of the expressions *nn wn ḥꜣty m ẖ.t=k* and *sw m jwty jb=f*[61] are thus not the equivalent of the English expression 'to be heartless' or of the French one 'être sans coeur' but rather corresponds to 'being out of one's mind'. It is clearly the cognitive dimension of *jb* and *ḥꜣty* that is stressed here rather than the emotional one.

The first example below comes from the corpus of Miscellanies. In this text, the profession of soldier is compared to the one of scribe: all the disadvantages of the first with respect to the latter are highlighted. The conclusion reached here is that wanting to be a soldier with all the disadvantages of the condition is such a foolish idea when you can be a scribe and have a much higher social status and a comfortable life.

Ex. 43 *jw=tw* *r* *ḫrp=k*
fut=IMPRS FUT beat:INF=2SG.M
nn.wn ***ḥꜣty*** ***m*** ***ẖ.t=k***
not_existant heart in body-F=2SG.M
jr *n=k* *tꜣy* *jꜣw.t* *sr*
do:IMP for=2SG.M DEM:F.SG function-F magistrate

60 I am here talking about the specific case of English. This might of course vary according to the target language of the translation.
61 The semantics of this expression is close to *ḫm jb/ḥꜣty* (cf. supra).

nḏm *ꜥšꜣ* *ḫ.wt* *pꜣy=k* *gstj*
sweet numerous thing-F.PL POSS:M.SG=2SG.M tablet
tꜣy=k *ꜥr.t* *ḏmꜥ*
POSS:F.SG=2SG scroll-F papyrus
'One will beat you!
Are you out of you mind? (lit: there is no heart in your body)
Work as for you in this function of magistrate
Your tablet and your papyrus scroll are full of sweet things!'
(P. Anastasi 5, 10, 8–11, 1 = *LEM* 61, 6–7)

Example 44 comes from the Love Songs and illustrates a recurring theme of this corpus: the lack of control experienced by the lovers on their own feelings and the resulting behaviours. The situation described here by the sister is the fight of reason against passion: her 'rational' heart is irritated by the loss of control that she is experiencing. The love feelings that the brother inspires her have a hold on her, which is expressed here by *jṯt wj mrw.t=f* 'his love captured me', a clear actualization of the metaphor TO MAKE FALL IN LOVE IS TO CAPTURE. Somewhat funnily, the sister's heart (*jb*) is in this passage itself described as having no heart (*jb*), as being out of its mind.

Ex. 44 *mk* ***jb=j*** ***ḥḏn*** *<m>* *sḫꜣ=f*
ATTN heart=1SG be_furious in remember=3SG.M
jṯt *wj* *mrw.t=f*
capture:PFV 1SG love-F=3SG.M
mk *sw* ***m*** ***jwty*** ***jb**=f*
ATTN 3SG.M in NEG.REL-M.SG heart=3SG.M
jw *swt* *jw=j* *mj-ḳd=f*
CORD but SBRD=1SG like=3SG.M
'See, my heart is irritated while remembering it
His love captured me
See, he is acting foolishly (lit: heartless)
But I am like him' (P. Chester Beatty I, v° C2, 1)

4 Conclusions

The figurative language of negative emotions is expressed through a very large panel of lexemes and metaphorical expressions. They have in common to be based on the general MIND AS BODY metaphor. This superordinate level path is declined in more precise ones according to this schema in the negative/afflictive emotion domain:

- EMOTION IS PHYSICAL EXPERIENCE
  - EMOTION IS SENSORY PERCEPTION
    - FRUSTRATION IS BITTERNESS
    - FRUSTRATION IS 'BAD TASTE'

- EMOTION IS PHYSICAL STATE
    - EMPATHY IS SICKNESS AND SUFFERING
    - DEPRESSION IS DECOMPOSITION
        - DEPRESSION IS A DECOMPOSING HEART
    - GLOOM/DISCOURAGEMENT IS LACK OF PHYSICAL ENERGY
        - GLOOM IS A TIRED HEART
        - HELPLESSNESS IS A TIRED HEART
        - HELPLESSNESS IS A WEAK HEART
    - WEARINESS IS A DISGUSTED HEART
- EMOTION IS NON-QUIETNESS
    - EMOTION IS MOTION
        - SADNESS IS (MOTION) DOWN
            - OUTRAGE IS TO CAUSE (THE HEART) TO GO DOWN
        - ANXIETY IS REPEATED MOTION
            - CONCERN IS THE HEART TURNING TO SOMEONE
            - ANXIETY IS THE HEART MOVING AROUND
            - ANXIETY IS A TROTTING HEART
        - EMOTIONAL DETACHMENT IS CENTRIFUGAL MOTION (SOURCE ORIENTED)
            - ANNOYANCE IS A HEART THAT TURNS AWAY
            - INDIFFERENCE IS A HEART THAT TURNS AWAY
            - WEARINESS IS A HEART GOING OUT
        - LACK OF CONTROL IS CENTRIFUGAL MOTION (TARGET ORIENTED)
            - WORRY IS A HEART BEING AFTER STH.
            - AGITATION IS A HEART THAT JUMPS OUT
        - IMPATIENCE IS FAST MOTION
            - IMPATIENCE IS A FAST HEART
    - EMOTION IS ACTION
        - WORRY IS TAKING IN
            - WORRY IS A HEART THAT TAKES MATTERS
        - NEGATIVE EMOTION IS VIOLENT ACTION
            - HELPLESSNESS IS A HEART TAKEN AWAY
            - HELPLESSNESS IS AN OVERTHROWN HEART
            - OUTRAGE IS A BROKEN HEART
    - EMOTION IS (LOUD) SOUND
- EMOTION AS EFFECT OF THE EMOTION
    - EMOTION AS PHYSICAL EFFECT OF THE EMOTION
        - DESPAIR IS AN IMPLORING HEART
        - GRIEF IS A HEART THAT CRIES WITH TWO EYES
    - EMOTION AS PSYCHOLOGICAL EFFECT OF THE EMOTION
        - EMOTION IS IGNORANCE
            - AGITATION IS AN IGNORANT HEART
            - NEGLECT IS AN IGNORED HEART

BODILY EXPERIENCE and LACK OF QUIETNESS – whether it is actualized in sound, motion or action – are thus central in the expression of negative emotions in Egyptian. They all express emotions, feelings, moods or characters related to the primary emotions of ANGER, SADNESS and FEAR.

When looking at the data distribution in diachrony, one can see a clear increase in metaphor usage in the New Kingdom, with a peak in the Ramesside Period. This is tight to two observations that deal with two different levels in lexicon organization. The first observation is a high number of lexemes that colexify at least one metaphorical meaning in addition to their primary meaning. This highlights the important role of metaphor-induced colexification in the semantic evolution of the Egyptian lexicon. The second observation is a clear increase in the usage of compound expressions involving body parts, especially *jb* and *ḥ3ty*. This may be influenced by several factors. First of all, as always, due precaution must be taken given the uneven distribution of the corpus, with a higher number of texts available for the New Kingdom. Besides this obvious statement, this development might also be related to the tendency of the language to become more analytic in its functioning. Indeed, in Late Egyptian, besides this statement being clearly observable for grammatical constructions, the lexicon also tends to increasingly develop on the basis of compound expressions. Without surprise, texts with literary qualities display a much higher number of metaphors.

Compound expressions based on a personification of the heart are very frequent in emotion expression. The heart can assume different semantic roles: agent, patient or experiencer. When the heart is an agent, it denotes a lack of control of its owner; when it is a patient, there are two main cases: 1) the heart is affected by its own owner, which reflects a break in personal behaviour patterns and/or a hiatus between moral values and actual behaviour; 2) the heart is affected by someone else, which refers to negative emotions triggered by someone else's behaviour. Finally, the heart can be an experiencer and be described as feeling the emotion instead of its owner.

Ancient Egyptian data add a diachronic depth to the validation of the conceptual metaphor theory. Indeed, despite the temporal and cultural gaps, a great majority of conceptual paths represented in Egyptian are well attested cross-linguistically. The linguistic actualization of these paths does vary to some extent from a language to another since it is influenced by the general background and environment of the speakers: natural environment, climate, culture, epoch, technology, etc. An important nuance to add to the picture comes with the concept of 'false friends' metaphors introduced here. Indeed, a linguistic expression that appears as the exact translation of one known in another language, their semantics does not necessarily overlap (completely).

An adapted table of the different negative emotions based on the comparison between the different categorisations and the actualisation of these emotions in the Ancient Egyptian lexicon can be presented as follows in table 3. The categories in grey are the negative or ambivalent emotions attested elsewhere in the Egyptian lexicon[62] but were not treated in this study.

62 The examples given in the table are not exhaustive.

Table 3: Adapted table of negative emotions and distribution of the Egyptian lexemes and expressions by category.

<table>
<tr><th colspan="3">Negative emotions</th></tr>
<tr><td>Negative and forceful
ANGER</td><td>Negative and passive
SADNESS</td><td>Negative and not in control
FEAR</td></tr>
<tr><td>Anger
ꜣd, ḳnd

Annoyance
ṯmḥ ḥꜣty

Contempt
(ANGER ∩ DISGUST)
sẖrj-ꜥ (Wb 4, 271.1–3)

Disgust
ft jb/ḥꜣty

Irritation
jkn</td><td>Grief
rmj.t jb m jr.tj

Gloom
bgj ḥꜣty

Weariness
rwj ḥꜣty

Depression
ḥwꜣ ḥꜣty

Empathy (SADNESS ∩ LOVE)
mḥr ḥꜣty
šnj ḥꜣty
jnd</td><td>Anxiety/ restlessness/agitation
ṯṯj n ḥꜣty
pẖr jb/ḥꜣty
tfj ḥꜣty
ẖm jb (subj)
nn wn ḥꜣy m ẖ.t
jwtj jb

Worry
jb/ḥꜣty m-sꜣ
ṯꜣ ḥꜣty sẖr.w
pẖr jb/ḥꜣty

Fear
snḏ, ḥrj.t

Terror
bꜣ m ḏr.t[a]</td></tr>
<tr><td colspan="2">Frustration
dḥr
jnd

Outrage (followed with disappointment)
ḥḏ jb/ḥꜣty
shꜣj ḥꜣty (Wb 4, 207.2–5)

Neglect
ẖm ḥꜣty (obj.)

Envy/greed
ꜥwn-jb (Wb 1, 172.12–13)
skn (Wb 4, 318.9–10)</td><td></td></tr>
<tr><td>Pride
(ANGER ∩ JOY)
wmt-jb (Wb 1, 306.13)</td><td colspan="2">Despair
nyny ḥꜣty

Helplessness/Powerlessness
bdš ḥꜣty
ẖsj ḥꜣty
nḥm jb
tfj jb
ḏḥ jb</td></tr>
</table>

a Hori, P. Anastasi 1, 24, 1. The expression of 'having the ba in the hand' might refer to the ba being about to leave its place (the body) and fly away because of a deadly fear (Renaud Pietri's suggestion in a personal communication; October 18, 2021). This interpretation of extreme fear, already suggested by Fischer-Elfert, is confirmed by the bodily reactions described in the direct cotext : *ṯꜣ {ḥr}=k pꜣ ḏnn; ḏꜣḏꜣ=k šnrf* 'a shiver takes possession of you, your hair is standing on end'. The later illustrate the path EMOTION IS THE EFFECT ON AN EMOTION. This expression likely falls under the primary emotion FEAR, with enhanced intensity, which corresponds to *terror* (see Plutchik wheel).

Bibliography

Catricala Bution, Denise & Muglia-Wechsler, Larissa. 2016. 'Dependência emocional: uma revisão sistemática da literatura', *Estudos Interdisciplinares em Psicologia* 7, 77–101 (doi: 10.5433/2236-6407.2016v7n1p77).

Casasanto, Daniel & Gijssels, Tom. 2015. 'What makes a metaphor an embodied metaphor?', *Linguistics Vanguard* 1, 327–37 (doi: https://doi.org/10.1515/lingvan-2014-1015).

Chantrain, Gaëlle. 2014. 'The use of classifiers in the New Kingdom. A global reorganization of the classifiers system?', *Lingua Aegyptia* 22, 39–59.

Chantrain, Gaëlle. 2018. 'Semantic changes in Ancient Egyptian. Some case studies', in: Kahlbacher, Andrea & Elisa Priglinger (eds). *Proceedings from the International Congress for Young Egyptologists, Vienna, 15-19 September 2015*. Vienna; Contributions to the Archaeology of Egypt, Nubia and the Levant 6, 149–59.

Chantrain, Gaëlle. 2021. 'Classification strategies from the end of the Ramesside Period until the Late Period: a living system', in: *Zeitschrift für Ägyptische Sprache und Altertumskunde* 148, 1–15.

Chantrain, Gaëlle. 2023. 'Ignorance and forgetfulness in Late Egyptian and Classical Egyptian from the New Kingdom until the 26th dynasty. A lexical study', *Lingua Aegyptia* 31, 53–90.

Chantrain, Gaëlle. *in press*. 'Metaphor-induced lexical semantic evolution and classification strategies in Ancient Egyptian', in: Chantrain, Gaëlle (ed.). *Language Semantics and Cognition in Ancient Egypt and Beyond*. Yale Egyptological Studies (25 pp.).

Chantrain, Gaëlle & Di Biase-Dyson, Camilla. 2017. 'Making a case for multidimensionality in Ramesside figurative language', in: Werning, Daniel (ed.). *Proceedings of the Fifth International Conference on Egyptian-Coptic Linguistics (Crossroads V) Berlin, February 17–20, 2016*. Hamburg; *Lingua Aegyptia* 25, 41–66.

Di Biase-Dyson, Camilla. 2018. 'The figurative network. Tracking the use of metaphorical language for "hot" and "cold" in Ramesside literary texts', in: Kubisch, Sabine & Ute Rummel (eds). *The Ramesside Period in Egypt: Studies into Cultural and Historical Processes of the 19th and 20th Dynasties, Proceedings of the International Symposium held at Heidelberg, 5th to 7th June, 2015*. Berlin; Sonderschriften des Deutschen Archäologischen Instituts, Abteilung Kairo 41, 33–44.

Di Biase-Dyson, Camilla and Chantrain, Gaëlle. 2022. 'Metaphors of sensory experience in Ancient Egyptian texts: Emotion, personality and social interaction', in: Neumann, Kiersten & Allison Thomason (eds). *The Routledge Handbook of the Senses in the Ancient Near East*. London, 603–35.

Douglas-Cowie, Cox. et al. HUMAINE proposal for EARL: https://web.archive.org/web/20080410193636/ http://emotion-research.net/projects/humaine/earl/proposal.

Evans, Dwight & al. (eds). 2017. *Treating and Preventing Adolescent Mental Health Disorders: What We Know and What We Don't Know* (2nd ed.). Oxford DOI : 10.1093/med-psych/9780199928163.001.0001

Faulkner, Raymond. 2002 [1962]. *A Concise Dictionary of Middle Egyptian*. Oxford.

François, Alexandre. 2008. 'Semantic maps and the typology of colexification. Intertwining polysemous networks across languages', in: Vanhove, Martine (ed.). *From Polysemy to Semantic Change*. Amsterdam/Philadelphia; Studies in Language Companion Series 106, 163–215.

DZA = Digitales Zettelarchiv. aaew.bbaw.de/tla/servlet/DzaIdx?u=gast&f=0&l=0.

Frijda, Nico & Scherer, Klaus. 2009. 'Emotion definition (psychological perspectives)', in: Sander, David & Klaus Scherer (eds). *Oxford Companion to Emotion and the Affective Sciences*. Oxford, 142–43.

Gardiner, Alan. 1935. *Hieratic Papyri in the British Museum, Third Series. Chester Beatty Gift*. London.

Gibbs, Raymond. 2006. 'Metaphor interpretation as embodied simulation', *Mind and Language* 21, 434–58.

Givón, Talmy. 1986. 'Prototypes: Between Plato and Wittgenstein', in: Craig, Colette (ed.). *Noun Classes and Categorization. Proceedings of a Symposium on Categorization and Noun Classification, Eugene, Oregon, October 1983*. Amsterdam/Philadelphia; Typological Studies in Language 7, 77–102.

Goldwasser, Orly. 1995. *From Icon to Metaphor. Studies in the Semiotics of the Hieroglyphs*. Fribourg & Göttingen; Orbis Biblicus et Orientalis 142.

Goldwasser, Orly. 2002, *Prophets, Lovers and Giraffes. Wor(l)d Classification in Ancient Egypt; With an Appendix by Matthias Müller*. Wiesbaden; GOF IV 38/3 = Classification and Categorization in Ancient Egypt 3.

Goldwasser, Orly & Grinevald, Colette. 2012. 'What are determinatives good for?', in: Grossmann, Eitan, Stéphane Polis & Jean Winand (eds). *Lexical Semantics in Ancient Egyptian*. Hamburg; Lingua Aegyptia Studia Monographica 9, 17–53.

Goossens, Louis. 1990. 'Metaphtonymy. The interaction of metaphor and metonymy in expressions for linguistic action', *Cognitive Linguistics* 1, 323–40.

Hannig, Rainer. 2006. *Großes Handwörterbuch Ägyptisch-Deutsch (2800 – 950 v. Chr.)*. Mainz.

Jenkins, Madeline. 2022. 'On the Semantics of *jnd*. A lexical-semantic analysis of the 'sadness' lexeme *jnd*', *Lingua Aegyptia* 30, 171–200.

Koenig, Yvan. 1981. *Le Papyrus Boulaq 6: transcription, traduction et commentaire*. Cairo.

Kövecses, Zoltan. 2000. *Metaphor and Emotion*. New York & Cambridge.

Kövecses, Zoltan. 2005. *Metaphor in Culture: Universality and Variation*. Cambridge.

Kövecses, Zoltan. 2010. *Metaphor. A Practical Introduction* (2nd ed.). Oxford.

Kövecses, Zoltan & Radden, Günter. 1999. 'Towards a theory of metonymy', in: Panther, Klaus-Uwe & Günter Radden (eds). *Metonymy in Language and Thought*. Amsterdam; Human Cognitive Processing 4, 17–60.

K*RI* = Kitchen, Kenneth 1969–1990. *Ramesside Inscriptions. Historical and Biographical*. 8 Volumes. Oxford.

Laisney, Vincent. 2007. *L'Enseignement d'Aménémopé*. Rome; Studia Pohl Series Maior 19.

Lakoff, George & Johnson, Mark. 2003 [1980]. *Metaphors We Live By*. London.

Lakoff, George. 2014. 'Mapping the brain's metaphor circuitry: Metaphorical thought in everyday reason', *Frontiers in Human Neuroscience* (doi: 10.3389/fnhum.2014.00958).

LEM = Gardiner, Alan. 1937. *Late Egyptian Miscellanies*. Brussels; Bibliotheca Aegyptiaca 7.

LES = Gardiner, Alan. 1932. *Late Egyptian Stories*. Brussels; Bibliotheca Aegyptiaca 1.

Lincke, Elise-Sophie. 2011. *Die Prinzipien der Klassifizierung im Altägyptischen*. Wiesbaden; GOF IV/38 = Classification and Categorization in Ancient Egypt 6.

Lincke, Elise-Sophie & Kammerzell, Frank. 2012. 'Egyptian classifiers at the interface of lexical semantics and pragmatics', in: Grossman, Eitan, Stéphane Polis & Jean Winand (eds). *Lexical Semantics in Ancient Egyptian*. Hamburg; Lingua Aegyptia Studia Monographica 9, 55–112.

Majid, Asifa & Levinson, Stephen. 2011. 'The senses in language and culture, *The Senses and Society* 6, 5–18.

Malaise, Michel & Winand, Jean. 1999. *Grammaire raisonnée de l'égyptien classique*. Liège; Ægyptiaca Leodiensia 6.

Mathieu, Bernard. 2008. *La poésie amoureuse de l'égypte ancienne. Recherches sur un genre littéraire au Nouvel Empire*. Cairo; Bibliothèque d'Étude 115.

Meier, Brian & Robinson, Michael. 2004. 'Why the sunny side is up: Associations between affect and vertical position', *Psychological Science* 15, 243–47.

Meier, Brian, Robinson, Michael, Crawford, Elizabeth & Ahlvers, Whitney. 2007. 'When "light" and "dark" thoughts become light and dark responses: Affect biases brightness judgments', *Emotion* 7, 366–76.

Niemeier, Susanne. 2003. 'Straight from the heart – Metonymic and metaphorical explorations', in: Barcelona, Antonio (ed.). *Metaphor and Metonymy at the Crossroads: A Cognitive Perspective.* Berlin/New-York, 195–213.

Nyord, Rune. 2009. "Taking phenomenology to heart. Some heuristic remarks on studying ancient Egyptian embodied experience'," in: Nyord, Rune & Annette Kjølby (eds). *Being in Ancient Egypt. Thoughts on Agency, Materiality and Cognition.* Oxford; British Archaeological Reports, BAR International Series 2019, 63–74.

Parrott, W. Gerrod. 2001. *Emotions in Social Psychology. Key Readings in Social Psychology.* Philadelphia.

Plutchik, Robert. 1980. 'A general psychoevolutionary theory of emotion', in: Plutchik, Robert & Henry Kellerman (eds). *Theory of Emotion.* New York, 3–33.

Polis, Stéphane & Rosmorduc, Serge. 2015. 'The hieroglyphic sign functions: suggestions for a revised taxonomy', in: Amstutz, Hans, Andreas Dorn, Matthias Müller, Miriam Ronsdorf & Sami Uljas (eds). *Fuzzy Boundaries: Festschrift für Antonio Loprieno 1.* Hamburg, 149–74.

Ramsès = *Ramses Online.* http://ramses.ulg.ac.be/.

Rosch, Eleanor. 1978. 'Principles of Categorization', In: Rosch, Eleanor & Barbara Lloyd. (eds). *Cognition and Categorization.* London, 28–49.

Scherer, Klaus. 2005. 'What are emotions? And how can they be measured?', *Social Science Information* 44, 695–729.

Scherer, Klaus. 2009. 'The dynamic architecture of emotion: Evidence for the component process model', *Cognition and Emotion* 23, 1307–51.

Scherer, Klaus. 2013. 'Measuring the meaning of emotion words: A domain-specific componential approach', in: Fontaine, Johnny, Klaus Scherer & Cristiana Soriano (eds). *Components of Emotional Meaning: A Sourcebook.* Oxford, 7–30.

Scherer, Klaus, Shuman, Vera, Fontaine Johnny & Soriano, Cristiana. 2013. 'The GRID meets the Wheel: Assessing emotional feeling via self-report', in: Fontaine, Johnny, Klaus Scherer & Cristiana Soriano (eds). *Components of Emotional Meaning: A Sourcebook.* Oxford, 281–98.

Schröder Marc, Baggia Paolo, Burkhardt Felix, Pelachaud Catherine, Peter Christian, Zovato Enrico. 2011. 'EmotionML – An upcoming standard for representing emotions and related states. In: D'Mello Sidney, Arthur Graesser, Björn Schuller & Jean-Claude Martin (eds). *Affective Computing and Intelligent Interaction. ACII 2011.* Berlin/Heidelberg; Lecture Notes in Computer Science 6974 (https://doi.org/10.1007/978-3-642-24600-5_35).

Shaver, Philipp, Schwartz, Judith, Kirson, Donald & O'Connor, Gary. 1987. 'Emotion knowledge: Further exploration of a prototype approach', *Journal of Personality and Social Psychology* 52, 1061–86.

Steen, Gerard, Dorst, Aletta, Herrmann, Berenike, Kaal, Anna, Krennmayr, Tina & Pasma, Trijntje. 2010. *A Method for Linguistic Metaphor Identification.* Amsterdam; Converging Evidence in Language and Communication Research 14.

TLA = *Thesaurus Linguae Aegyptiae.* http://aaew.bbaw.de.

Toro Rueda, María. 2003. *Das Herz in der ägyptischen Literatur des zweiten Jahrtausends v. Chr. Untersuchungen zu Idiomatik und Metaphorik von Ausdrücken mit jb und ḥꜣtj*, PhD Dissertation, Georg-August-Universität Göttingen.

Traugott, Elizabeth & Dasher, Richard. 2001. *Regularity in Semantic Change.* Cambridge; Cambridge Studies in Linguistics 97.

Urk. IV = Sethe, Kurt. 1906–1909. *Urkunden der 18. Dynastie IV. Band I–IV (Heft 1–16).* Leipzig; Urkunden des ägyptischen Altertums IV & Helck, Wolfgang. 1955–1958. *Urkunden der 18. Dynastie IV.* Heft 17–22. Berlin.

Wagner, Andreas. 2017. 'Emotionen in Text, Sprache und materialen Bildern. Eine Skizze aus Sicht der Metaphernanalyse', in: Kipfer, Sara (ed.). *Visualising Emotions in the Ancient Near East*. Fribourg/ Göttingen; Orbis Biblicus et Orientalis 285, 207–18.

Wb. = Erman, Adolf & Grapow, Hermann. 1971 [1926–1931]. *Wörterbuch der ägyptischen Sprache I–V*. Berlin.

Winand, Jean. 1992. *Etudes de néo-égyptien. La morphologie verbale.* Liège; Ægyptiaca Leodiensia 2.

Winand, Jean. 2016. 'Dialects in pre-Coptic Egyptian. With a special attention to Late Egyptian', *Lingua Aegyptia* 23, 229–59.

Winand, Jean. 2018. 'Words of thieves', in: Cromwell, Jennifer & Eitan Grossmann (eds). *Scribal Repertoires in Egypt from the New Kingdom to the Early Islamic Period*. Oxford, 127–52.

Challenging Questions in Late Egyptian

Mark Collier

One of the primary interfaces between grammatical/linguistic and philological approaches to the study of the Ancient Egyptian language and its surviving textual sources is the tailored, nuanced, enriched meaning which comes from reading a passage in its original co(n)text. Of course, this is an area which presents considerable challenge in trying to understand the contextualized expressions of an ancient dead language from our own inherently historicized cultural and cognitive perspective.

For my case study, I would like to look more from the grammatical/linguistic point of view at a distinction in content-question form and the associated meaning distinction between these forms.[1] If we look specifically at content-questions questioning the participant expressed by the direct object of a verb, then two constructional formats can be found in Late Egyptian, here illustrated by two examples from *Horus & Seth*.

1. The canonical question format is the use of the pseudo-cleft focus construction[2] positioning the question-word (Q-word) *ỉḫ* in initial focus position followed by a defined relative clause in which the question-word is either resumed in the direct object position by a resumptive pronoun or by gap within the relative clause depending on the tense construction used (as standard in Late Egyptian relative clauses). In example 1, the resumptive pronoun *=f* appears in direct object position within the defined third future relative clause:

1 I am grateful to Andreas Dorn and Sami Uljas, the organisers of the conference, for inviting me to contribute a paper to the published proceedings even though I was unable to attend the conference itself. I should note from the outset that this paper was written during the initial COVID-19 pandemic in the UK, including lockdown and consequent restrictions of access to resources. Not least with those restrictions in mind, I would also like to thank Stèphane Polis for sending me a *Ramsès* search on examples of *ỉḫ* and *nym*, which has helped me to consolidate and expand my existing example set. Thanks also to my Egyptological colleagues at Liverpool not then on leave (Violaine Chauvet, Roland Enmarch, Marina Escolano Poveda, Glenn Godenho, Steven Snape and Silvia Zago), with whom I discussed my work for this paper at the first online Liverpool Egyptological Seminar in July 2020; their questions and feedback were particularly useful.

2 This is part of a broader canonical strategy of using isolating constructions (nominal sentence and focus constructions) for content questions with *ỉḫ*. The pseudo-cleft construction is, of course, essentially a grammaticalized derivative of the nominal sentence construction.

Sami Uljas & Andreas Dorn (eds), *Crossroads VI. Between Egyptian Linguistics and Philology*, 63–84
DOI: https://doi.org/10.37011/studmon.30.03

Ex. 1. *Horus & Seth* 16, 3: [= *LES* 59, 15][3]

ỉḫ	*pꜣ*	*nty*	*ỉw=tw*	*r*	*ỉr=f*	*n swtḫ*
what	DET:M.SG	REL	FUT=IMPRS	FUT	do.INF=it	for Seth

What can be done for Seth?

2. There is also another, non-canonical,[4] and rather under-investigated, constructional format in which the Q-word *ỉḫ* appears *in-situ* as the direct object of the verb and the tense appears in its ordinary form without relativization:

Ex. 2. *Horus & Seth* 5, 12 [= *LES* 43, 15]:

ỉw=t	*dỉt*	*n=ỉ*	*ỉḫ*
FUT=you.F.SG	give.INF	to=me	what

What can you give me?

Whilst there is a general Egyptological understanding of key elements of the meaning or use of the canonical pseudo-cleft question, I am unaware of a clear formulation or proposal for the meaning or use of the non-canonical question format as a whole, beyond proposals (discussed briefly below) to read certain specific examples of the non-canonical questions as rhetorical questions. So, the issue for this paper is: what is the meaning of the alternative constructional format in which the question-word *ỉḫ* is positioned directly as the direct object of the verb and the verbal tense is the ordinary tense form (here the third future tense)? To flag up for the reader where the discussion will go: in essence, I will propose that the pseudo-cleft question format is the format typically used for questions seeking information from the addressee (the prototypical type of question), whereas the non-canonical *in-situ* question format is typically found used for sceptical questions of challenge/confirmation aimed more at influencing the addressee towards the questioner's point of view.

In order to constrain this paper to article-length, the primary discussion is limited to the specific construction types illustrated by examples 1 and 2: content-questions with the most common simplex question-word *ỉḫ* 'what' either linked to, or directly placed in, direct object position in relation to a verb. The account is then briefly extended to subject position in relation to a verb. Content-questions with other grammatical positionings of *ỉḫ* are not discussed (for example, the common *ỉḫ pꜣy=f sḏm* form of content-question), nor content-questions with other question words, with the exception of a brief discussion

3 Glossing is restricted to illustrating the main issue at hand and not to cited extensions to examples. Certain standard Egyptological tense designations (in abbreviation) are used for convenience: SQNT 'sequential' and TRMN 'terminative'.

4 'Non-canonical' in the sense deployed e.g. by Dayal (2016: 4, and in more detail: chapter 9). In English, non-canonical content questions with *in-situ* question word are usually discussed from the point of view of their echo or repair properties such as seeking clarification of what has previously been said or incredulous response, but there are also uses with sceptical tone on the question word which overlap with the attested Late Egyptian use discussed here. It is unknown whether the Late Egyptian forms had echo usages and I do not discuss this here. Similarly, I do not discuss the role of intonation in distinguishing usages of questions.

of questions with *nym* where *nym* is either linked to or directly placed as the subject of a tensed verbal construction.[5]

The state of play

In the standard grammars of Late Egyptian, the variety of content-question forms are usually listed, but without attempts to differentiate meaning. Just two examples. In the Černý & Groll grammar, section 61.7 inventories 'interrogative sentence patterns containing the interrogative particle *ỉḫ*, "what?",' starting with '*ỉḫ* as direct object of the third future formation' and going through other uses: as subject, in a 'dative' expression, in the nominal sentence, and the 'nominal cleft sentence', but without suggesting distinctions of meaning.[6] In Neveu's more recent grammar, chapter 43 (= Appendix 1: interrogative syntagms) is given over to an inventory of question forms. Section 43.3 goes through the deployment of *ỉḫ* in nominal sentences (43.3.1.1), cleft sentences (43.3.1.2) and then what is termed 'verbal sentences' (section 43.3.1.3) with sub-divisions with *ỉḫ* as subject, direct object and object of a preposition, but again without providing distinctions of meaning.[7]

In the research literature, the most detailed investigation of questions in Late Egyptian is in Sweeney's investigation of the pragmatic factors, primarily speech acts, in Late Ramesside letter-writing.[8] Chapter 3 centres on questions and presents a wealth of data and discussion for the deployment of questions and the use of interrogative forms in questions and for other speech acts (such as indirect requests and complaints). Within this discussion, Sweeney has sections focusing in on rhetorical questions.[9] She notes explicitly that 'Rhetorical questions are not associated with any specific verb form or sentence patterns'[10] and illustrates this clearly from her example set. However, within her discussion, she includes the *ỉry=ỉ ỉḫ r=k* 'what have I done to you' type question and (referring back to earlier work by Groll), she notes that 'certain questions whose direct object is *jḫ* may be rhetorical.'[11]

So far as I am aware, this link between certain examples of direct-object-*ỉḫ* questions and rhetorical question usage is the only distinctive meaning association which has been suggested for certain specific examples of questions of the direct-object-*ỉḫ* question type. However, I will argue below that these possible rhetorical question usages of questions with direct-object *ỉḫ* exemplify end-scale closure of the question (as presented by the

5 In like manner, I will minimise my references to issues of direct mention and try to avoid tangential discussion. I concentrate my examples on documentary and literary Late Egyptian texts.

6 Černý & Groll (1993: 557–58).

7 Neveu (2015: 226–31).

8 Sweeney (2001). It is important to note that a number of the examples considered below come from literary texts, which Sweeney (2001: 15) explicitly rules out from her dataset on entirely appropriate grounds for her topic at hand and so the question form looked at here is not as prominent in her dataset.

9 See particularly Sweeney (2001: 101, 106–08, 141–47).

10 Sweeney (2001: 106).

11 Sweeney (2001: 108 n. 64) and compare Groll (1995: 48), where the term 'exclamatory' is used.

questioner), whilst other examples regularly have negative expectations and attempt to manipulate the addressee towards the questioner's point of view, but do not close off the question to the same degree or to the degree required for this particular rhetorical-question usage.

I will first discuss in brief (and incompletely) the canonical pseudo-cleft question before turning to the non-canonical *in-situ* question type.

Pseudo-cleft questions with *ỉḫ* linked to the verbal direct object position

Pseudo-cleft constructions with *ỉḫ* will not be considered here in detail, just certain relevant properties.[12] As already noted, in the pseudo-cleft construction, the question-word *ỉḫ* is expressed in the initial focus position in the construction followed by a defined/determined relative clause in which the question-word is linked, in the specific examples considered here, to the direct object position.[13]

In terms of meaning, although question-forms can be used in a variety of ways, the pseudo-cleft questions with *ỉḫ* (linked to the direct object position of the verb) can be used close to the prototype for questions; that is, the standard speech act model for questioning:[14] the act of the questioner seeking information from the interlocutor, information which the questioner most typically wants to know, but lacks, and which the questioner believes the addressee can provide.[15] In ex. 1, Ptah's question comes immediately after Horus is crowned king, so Ptah raises the issue of what is to be done with Seth, his rival for the throne. Pre-Horakhty gives a direct answer to this, providing the information that Seth is to stay with Pre-Horakhty and to thunder in the sky and to be feared, thus providing the information Ptah requested. More pertinently for the discussion here, Egyptologists have long recognised that there is a presuppositional dimension here in the use of the pseudo-cleft question:[16] that the question takes for granted, or presupposes, that something should/can be done for Seth and seeks information on what that something is.

---

12 E.g. issues of form are not discussed, particularly the relationship with the nominal sentence. It is, though, worth noting that simplex *ỉḫ* itself is invariant in form and gender-number marking, but is compatible not only with a masculine singular defined relative clause but also with feminine singular (e.g. *Horus & Seth* 9, 11) and common plural (e.g. O. DeM 126, 3) defined relative clauses. When in a phrase with a noun ('what kind of'; linked by *m/n*), then it is that noun which controls agreement with the following definite article of the defined relative clause (masculine singular: *Horus & Seth* 11, 9–10; feminine singular: P. BM EA 10052 (vso) 14, 18 (= ex. 18 below); common plural: P. BM EA 10052 (rto) 5, 9–10).

13 Cf. Neveu (2015: 195–96).

14 See, for example, Levinson (2012: 15) on the prototype and then allowing for other question uses to radiate away from this prototype along various dimensions.

15 For more details, see, for example, Levinson (2012: 14–15), Dayal (2016: 1–5), Sweeney (2001: 102–03).

16 Cf. conveniently Neveu (2015: 195) using the term 'theme'.

In the case of example 1, *ꞽḫ* is in combination with the (light-)verb *ꞽr* and questions the ontological category of ACTIVITY or SITUATION,[17] as indicated also by Pre-Horakhty's answer. More typically, however, *ꞽḫ* questions the ontological category of THINGS as indicated in the following example:

Ex. 3. P. Mayer A (vso) 9, 11:

Karbaal relates that Montusankh had asked 2 thieves:

ꞽḫ	*pꜣ*	*ꞽn=tn*	*ꞽm*
what	DET:M.SG	bring.PST.REL=you.PL	there

What did you take away from there?
What is it that you took away from there?

This question has the propositional presupposition:[18]

You took something from there

Notice that there is also a standard existential presupposition on the question word itself that a positive value for the information interrogated by the question word can be returned in a truthful answer:

There is something which you took from there

Formal semantic treatments of the meaning of questions standardly invoke such an existential presupposition as part of an approach formalising meaning within the set of possible propositional answers and the constraints thereon.[19] This will be of relevance when I turn to non-canonical *ꞽḫ* questions.

It is important to note that pseudo-cleft questions of this form are not always used close to the prototype of information-seeking use and that the format, with its presuppositions, can be used in a variety of ways. This is illustrated by an example from the intricate dialogue between Tjekerbaal and Wenamum over the provision of timber for the bark of Amun-Re in *Wenamun*. Tjekerbaal is responding to Wenamun's argument that just as Tjekerbaal's ancestors provided the timber, so should Tjekerbaal (despite Wenamun's lack of formal letters, a ship, or means of payment). Tjekerbaal has just noted that Wenamun needs to pay and points out that his ancestors did indeed supply timber for the bark of Amun-Re king of the gods, but that this was only after payment had been received in the warehouses of Byblos. Tjekerbaal then concludes with the following pseudo-cleft question:

---

17 Late Egyptian, like the preponderance of languages, does not have a specific pro-verb Q-word and so uses the combination of *ꞽḫ* with the verb *ꞽr* for this usage. I note that this usage is well-represented in the examples of the direct-object *ꞽḫ*-questions which I look at below.

18 Here I follow standard usage in pragmatics in deploying a propositional presupposition with a variable (expressed by 'something' in the informal presentation here), rather than distinguishing a constituent as theme or similar as often found in the Egyptological literature (again, conveniently as an instance: Neveu [2015: 195]).

19 Cf. Dayal (2016: 13, 51–52), including her discussion there of 'nothing' answers, as well as Dayal (2016: 53) for the interpretation of the Q-word as an existential quantifier in her baseline theory.

Ex. 4. *Wenamun* 2, 8: [= *LES* 68, 1]

ntk, ỉḫ	*pꜣ*	*ỉn=k*	*n=ỉ,*	*gr*	*ỉnk*	
you what	DET:M.SG	bring.PST.REL=you	to=me	also	me	

You, what have you brought for me, for my part?'

Tjekerbaal here flouts (or, if the reader prefers, is written to flout)[20] the sincerity condition for the typical speech act of questioning. He knows that Wenamun has not brought what is needed = payment.[21] However, adopting the pretence/position of asking what Wenamun has brought (the pretence of him wanting to know) grounds the question in Tjekerbaal's argument for what should be the arrangement:[22] once Wenamun pays, Tjekerbaal will provide the timber. Wenamun does not in fact answer at this point in the text. However, an answer truthful to actual context, recognising Wenamun's lack of resource, would imply (without further address of Tjekerbaal's argument) agreement that Tjekerbaal should not undertake the task. In this way Tjekerbaal drives home his view of the inappropriateness of the actual situation of Wenamun turning up without the necessary payment and thus of Wenamun's attempts to persuade Tjekerbaal to undertake the task without providing payment.

As will become clear from the following, there is a degree of overlap here with my proposal for direct-object-*ỉḫ* questions, particularly in the implied answer 'nothing'.[23] However, whereas non-canonical *in-situ* questions involve a sceptical challenge as to whether or not the addressee can provide a suitable response, the pseudo-cleft question here implicates no issue to be resolved of 'whether or not' Wenamun has brought payment. Wenamun has not brought sufficient payment and both parties know this and it is part of the common background of this particular act of questioning.

Questions with *ỉḫ* directly positioned as the verbal direct object

I will first outline my proposal for reading questions with *ỉḫ* directly positioned as the verbal direct object (direct-object-*ỉḫ* questions) before considering illustrative examples:

- An existential presupposition for the value of the question word is not invoked or is suspended:[24] from the questioner's point of view, there is a question as to whether or

20 I will just concentrate on the dialogic situations presented in the textual sources and not engage with issues such as the role of writing and the writer.

21 For resumé of the different suggestions for interpreting this 'payment', see Sweeney (2001: 208 n. 104). I will stick to 'payment' here for convenience.

22 That is, the existential presupposition for the Q-word holds directly within Tjekerbaal's perspective of how the situation should be, rather than in (his view of) the actual situation.

23 Cf. Sweeney (2001: 208): 'At first sight, one might interpret the utterance above as a rhetorical question, intended to embarrass Wenamun, but in fact it is part of Tjekerbaal's negotiations to ensure that payment will be forthcoming.'

24 In the LES seminar, Roland Enmarch raised the issue of definiteness within the pseudo-cleft construction as marked by the definite article/determiner before the relative clause, which correlates nicely with the standard expectation of existential presupposition of the expression in focus. By contrast, then, the Q-word in the non-canonical question can be thought of as being

not there is, in fact, something (some value of the variable-under-question x) such that a direct propositional answer (sharing the same polarity as the question) can be provided by the addressee, which will satisfy the questioner. In the case of *Horus & Seth* 5, 12 (ex. 2 above), reading Nemty's question in this way has the meaning that Nemty does not presuppose that the old woman will be able to give him something of sufficient value that he will ferry her across to the island in the middle; rather, he leaves this open.

- As a consequence, the question covers both a negative polarity propositional zone[25] (where the old woman/Isis cannot give him something sufficient) and a positive polarity propositional zone (where the old woman/Isis can give him something sufficient). For the question in *Horus & Seth* 5, 12, as I will discuss below, this is reflected directly in the two responses which the old woman/Isis provides.
- The range of possible values for the question word constitutes a sufficiency-scale which runs from a low-end value of total exclusion ('nothing') as the end-scale within the negative zone of possible non-sufficient values through a(n idealised) threshold into the positive zone with sufficient values.
- However, these two zones and the sufficiency-scale are not treated equally by the questioner. The questioner adopts the disposition of doubt or scepticism towards possible answers/the proposition under question and thus has expectations that the likely answer lies in the negative zone, including the end-scale value of 'nothing'. The more sceptical the stance of the questioner, the more likely that this doubt will drive the expected value for the question-word down towards 'nothing'. That is, the more sceptical the stance of the questioner, the more closed the question becomes, centred on the end-scale value of 'nothing' and can often be captured in translating the question word into English as 'what (if anything)' or 'what (on earth)' and the like.[26]
- Through deploying the question, the questioner presents a challenge to the addressee either to provide a sufficient answer contrary to the negative expectations of the questioner or to confirm those negative expectations and to acquiesce or align them with the negative expectations of the questioner.[27]

These are the aspects of reading direct-object-*iḫ* questions concentrated on in this paper. As evidence for this, we can look at the actual responses recorded in Late Egyptian texts (both fictional and non-fictional) and also any supporting evidence which the questioner supplies to back up their negative expectations.

It will likely strike the reader when looking at the examples discussed below that these questions often lend themselves to emotive dispositions on the part of the questioner such as surprise, incredulity, exasperation, dismay, indignation and the like, but this will not be

used indefinitely. As a kind of indefinite pronoun, it shows the same form of total exclusion under negation which I have noted for indefinite pronouns in Late Egyptian in Collier (submitted).

25 That is, negative in relation to the polarity of the question. The examples of this type of question treated here have positive polarity in the question.

26 Cf. Dayal (2016: 51) on the overt suspension of the existential presupposition in such English questions.

27 Cf. the use of the terms 'open question' versus 'confirmation question' in Fiengo (2007: 10–12, 44, 53–55, 61–63, 75).

investigated here. In like manner, questions of this form typically involve conversational risks and threats (particularly face-threats), something which would certainly repay detailed investigation, but again is not undertaken here.[28]

Horus & Seth 5, 12

I will now take a look in more detail at the direct-object-*ỉḫ* question in *Horus & Seth*, 5,12 and its responses. First the question:

Ex. 5 = Ex 2. *Horus & Seth* 5, 12 [= *LES* 43, 15–16]

Isis has approached Nemty disguised as an old woman, who wants to be ferried over to the island-in-the-middle to see her son. Nemty insists that he has been told not to ferry any woman over. The old woman=Isis says that was just in reference to Isis. Then Nemty asks:

ỉw=t	*dỉt*	*n=ỉ*	*ỉḫ*	*ḏꜣy.tw=t r pꜣ ỉw ḥry-ỉb*
FUT=you.F.SG	give.INF	to=me	what	
What can you give me,				so you will be ferried to the Isle in the Middle?
What (if anything) can you give me				

Taken as a sceptical question, this indicates Nemty's challenge as to whether the old woman before him (Isis) can or cannot give him something sufficient to entice him to ferry her across to the island-in-the-middle, given that he has been instructed not to ferry any woman across (although Isis as the old woman has already defused some of that by stressing that the instruction applied to Isis specifically).

The threshold for this sufficient value is indicated explicitly in this example by the accompanying purpose clause. That is, Nemty indicates doubt that the old woman=Isis can give him something sufficient to overcome this threshold and for him then to ferry her across. His question presents a challenge to the old woman=Isis to see whether or not she can supply a sufficient answer (contrary to the negative expectations of the questioner) or to acquiesce and to confirm the negative expectations of the questioner, Nemty.

Here we have direct evidence for this meaning of the question (as put by Nemty) from the answers which the old woman=Isis provides and Nemty's reaction to them. Her first answer is a direct answer supplying a proposal with a specific value for what she can give Nemty in the same direct-object position as the question-word *ỉḫ* in the original question:

Ex. 6. *Horus & Seth* 5, 13 [= *LES* 43, 16]:

ỉw=ỉ	*dỉt*	*n=k*	*tꜣy*	*wḫꜣt*
FUT=I	give.INF	to=you.M.SG	DEM.F.SG	cake
I can give you this cake.				

Nemty dismisses this, making clear reference to it being an insufficient offer in context on the part of the old woman=Isis:[29]

28 Cf. the discussion in Levinson (2012: 19–25) of an 'economy of information in conversation' and his discussion of 'Carnaps' (value of information exchanged) and 'Goffmans' (social value, including costs).

29 This section is included to support the discussion and is not glossed.

Ex. 7. *Horus & Seth* 5, 13–14 [= *LES* 44, 1–3]:

ỉw=s (r) ỉẖ n=ỉ tꜣy=t wẖꜣt

But what is your cake (worth) to me?[30]

ỉ-ỉr=ỉ ḏꜣy=t r pꜣ ỉw ḥry-ỉb ỉw ḏd.tw n=ỉ m-ỉr ḏꜣy st-ḥmt nb r-ḏbꜣ tꜣy=t wẖꜣt

I am to ferry you to the Isle in the Middle — even though I was told not to ferry any woman — (just) in exchange for your cake!

Nemty's response clearly indicates that the offer of the cake by the old woman=Isis does not meet the threshold he has set for a sufficient answer for the question's polarity.

The old woman=Isis then follows this up with an improved offer, a gold seal-ring (again expressed as the direct object), an offer which Nemty accepts:

Ex. 8. *Horus & Seth* 6, 1 [= *LES* 44, 3–4]:

ỉw=ỉ	*dỉt*	*n=k*	*pꜣ*	*ẖtm*	*n*	*nbw*	*nty*	*m*	*drt(=ỉ)*
FUT=I	give.INF	to=you.M.SG	DEM.M.SG	seal	of	gold	REL	on	hand(=my)

I can give you the gold seal-ring which is on my hand.

Nemty expresses his acceptance through the demand:

Ex. 9. *Horus & Seth* 6, 1 [= *LES* 44, 4]:

ỉmỉ tw pꜣ ẖtm n nbw

Give the gold seal-ring.

This exchange of question and answer can be modelled or visualised in line with the discussion here:[31]

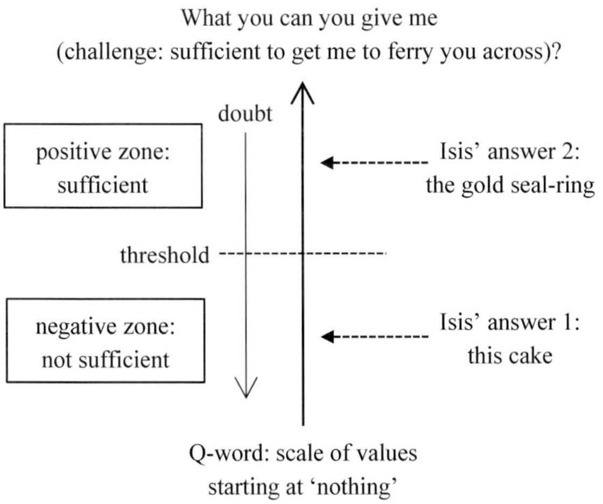

30 An *ỉẖ* question, but with non-verbal pattern, so not discussed here.

31 The visualisation is idealised and organised for clarity. So, for example, the arrows of the answers provided by Isis=the old woman (and their equivalents in other examples below) point at the centre of the zone for visual convenience. There is no attempt to calibrate them more directly against the scale.

As already noted, quite a few examples of this pattern (to be discussed below) focus in more on the negative end of the scale, effectively seeking to exclude the positive zone. This is particularly the case when the doubts of the questioner align with the questioner's wants. However in the case of the question in *Horus & Seth*, 5, 12, Nemty wants to include both the degree to which he is prepared to be obedient to the instructions given to him (which aligns with the negative zone) and (what turns out to be) his greed (which aligns with the positive zone). So, part of the importance of the *Horus & Seth* 5, 12 example is to indicate that this positive zone of answer can be activated and realised with the right answer and so the question does not by necessity expect a direct answer to be restricted to the negative zone, albeit that many examples of the questions certainly focus expectations in the negative zone.

Examples of *ỉry=ỉ ỉḫ r=t* from P. Leiden 371

The most commonly attested example of this type of question is of the following type[32] invoked 4 times in the opening section of the same letter to the dead, a question which more clearly concentrates questioner expectations into, and exploits, the negative zone of expected likely answers:[33]

Ex. 10. P. Leiden 371, rto 1 (with extension), rto 2, rto 4 (with extension), rto 8[34]

ỉr(y)=ỉ	*ỉḫ*	*r=t*
do.PST=I	what	to=you.F.SG

What have I done to you?

---

32 Cf. *Horus & Seth* 9, 4 (*ỉry=ỉ ỉḫ r=t sn(t)=ỉ ꜣst*); O. Ashm. 250, vso 4–5 (*ỉry=ỉ ỉḫ r=k pꜣy=k ḥꜣꜥ r n pꜣy 100 n msḥ r dỉt mwt=ỉ*); O. DeM 326, rto 3 (*ỉry[=ỉ] ỉḫ pꜣy=k hꜣb n=ỉ*), rto 8 (*ỉry=ỉ ỉḫ [...]*); O. DeM 10195, 6 (*ỉrw(=ỉ?) ỉḫ tr*); O. DeM 10248, 3 (*[ỉr]y=ỉ ỉḫ r=k pꜣy [...]*); P. DeM 18, rto 6 (*ỉry=ỉ ỉḫ r=t*); O. IFAO 369, rto 2 (*ỉry=ỉ ỉḫ r=t*); P. Leiden 369, rto 7–8 (*ỉry=ỉ ỉḫ r=tn*); O. Strasbourg H. 44, 1 (*ỉry=f ỉḫ (r?) tꜣy=f nṯrt*).

33 There are other formulations. Sweeney (2001: 108) discusses the example *yꜣ ỉḫ ỉry=ỉ* in P. DeM 4, rto 5, noting that later in the letter the 'the sender explicitly asks the recipient to send him a message explaining what he has done wrong. In this instance, *jḫ ỉry=j* is asked in good faith, and the sender is prepared to admit the possibility that he might have seriously offended the recipient.' A trickier alternative usage is that in pseudo-cleft usage in O. Ashm. 177, rto 2–3 where the writer opens 'As for the matter of the illness which you have been writing to me about,' *ỉḫ pꜣ ỉ-ỉr=ỉ r=tn* 'what is it that I have done to you?' There is insufficient context to demonstrate differences in meaning clearly. This could be an ordinary information-seeking question, though the remainder of the letter perhaps suggests a reading analogous to the *Wenamun* example (ex. 2) perhaps with a context something like: to understand your actions, I would have to presuppose that I have done something to you. But there is no issue here: we both know the answer is 'nothing'.

34 As noted by Gardiner & Sethe (1928: 23), there are orthographic issues with this text, particularly the differentiation of the masculine and feminine seated person (distinguished only by a dot in hieratic). Note their comment in discussing the need to alter the written form of the pronouns in the first example of this construction: 'one is extremely disinclined to correct [*ỉry=t ỉḫ r=ỉ*] to [*ỉry=ỉ ỉḫ r=t*] in the very first line, but the recurrence of the same phrase in ll. 2. 4. 5 (twice). 8 precludes the possibility of doing otherwise. In all the other cases "what I have done against thee?" is a protestation of innocence expecting the answer "nothing!"'

In this letter to his dead wife, the sender opens with his first challenging question, which outlines the predicament quite nicely and provides an expansion indicating the tailored context for the scale of sufficiency and its threshold:[35]

Ex. 11. P. Leiden I 371, rto 1–2:

ỉry=ỉ ỉḫ r=t m btꜣ pꜣ=t ḫpr m pꜣy sḫr bỉn nty tw=ø ỉm=f

What have I done to you (so) wrongfully for you to get into this bad disposition which you are in?

In line with the reading model proposed here, rather than primarily seeking information on what he has done to his wife to merit her behaviour to him, this question challenges the proposition that he has done anything sufficient to merit the wife's actions against him beyond the grave (including the end-scale answer 'nothing') and, with its negative expectations, is seeking to get the wife to acquiesce to this view and to stop affecting him. The opening section concludes with a circumstantial clause which provides a clear statement of what the sender thinks the recipient should acknowledge (where *btꜣ* as direct object of *ỉr* and under scope of negation, 'no wrong', provides the direct correlate for direct-object *ỉḫ* in the question above):[36]

Ex. 12. P. Leiden I 371, rto 3:

ỉw	*bw-ỉr=ỉ*	*btꜣ*	*r=t*
CIRC	NEG-do=I	wrong	to=you.F.SG

whilst I have done no wrong to you.

The bulk of the letter then provides his lengthy account of the numerous ways in which he treated his wife well both during her life and in providing for her proper burial when she died. This is direct evidence for the doubt/scepticism underlying the challenge and drives the expected answer (from the questioner's point of view) firmly into the negative zone, towards the end-point answer 'nothing' (nothing to merit such action on the part of the wife). Visually, this can be depicted:

35 Similarly, in the following example (cf. also O. Ashm. 250, vso 4–5):
Ex. FN1. O. DeM 326, 3–4:
ỉry=ỉ ỉḫ pꜣy=k hꜣb n=ỉ r-ḏd ỉmỉ [ỉ]n.[t]w n=ỉ ꜥqw m-mnt [...] [ỉ]w bwpw=ỉ hꜣb n=k r-ḏd ỉmỉ ỉn.tw n=ỉ ꜥqw [m-mnt]
What have I done for you to write to me saying, 'Send me bread daily!', whereas I have not written to you, saying, 'Send me bread [daily!].'

36 It also correlates nicely with the circumstantial 1st present version of the question contrasting his behaviour with hers, again protesting his innocence:
Ex. FN 2: P. Leiden I 371, rto 5:
ỉw=ỉ ỉr{y=ỉ} ỉḫ r=t
although I have done what against you?

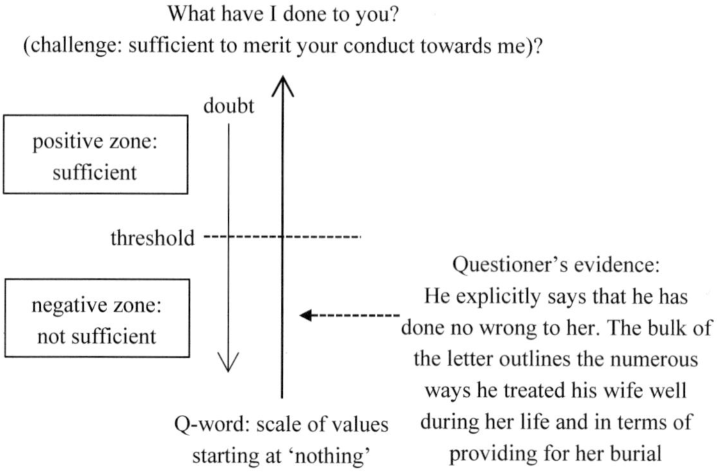
What have I done to you?
(challenge: sufficient to merit your conduct towards me)?
doubt
positive zone:
sufficient
threshold
Questioner's evidence:
He explicitly says that he has done no wrong to her. The bulk of the letter outlines the numerous ways he treated his wife well during her life and in terms of providing for her burial
negative zone:
not sufficient
Q-word: scale of values
starting at 'nothing'

P. Leiden I 371 provides key examples lying behind Sweeney and Groll's note of the tendency for direct-object-*iḫ* questions to be used as rhetorical questions. It should be clear now that this usage reflects the end-scale of negative expectation in the use of this question type, where the expected answer is 'nothing' and the addressee is expected to acquiesce to, and to confirm, this view of things. The example from *Horus & Seth* 5, 12 shows us that the same question format can be used in contexts where a positive response, providing information questioned, can be and is provided, a response which may be deemed sufficient or insufficient by the questioner.

Having indicated the meaning range of direct-object *iḫ* questions in terms of this reading model, a selection of other examples will now be considered more briefly, restricted to examples where the surviving context is sufficiently rich to support the discussion here.

Second person subject *iry=k iḫ* 'what have you done': O. DeM 328 rto, 8–10

Not all of the examples of the past *sḏm=f* of *ir* with direct object *iḫ* are in the first person:

Ex. 13. O. DeM 328, rto 8–10:

O. DeM 328 is a letter clearly responding to a prior directive from the addressee (Maanakhtef) to let Ib work for/with the sender (Pabaki). Pabaki complains that Ib is not performing well, taking all day over bringing a jug of water, and that he has not taken on board a previous quoted piece of guidance/rebuke to him from the addressee:

ir=k	*iḫ*	*pꜣ*	*hrw*
do.PST=you.M.SG	what	DET.M.SG	day

What have you done today?

If read according to the model proposed here, this is not a question seeking an itemisation of the tasks Ib has done, but challenges whether the tasks Ib has done are sufficient against the scale of the obligations he faces ('what should you have done today?'). Pabaki provides direct evidence that Ib has not met the challenge through his case of Ib taking all day over bringing the jug of water and ends his letter 'Look, the sun has set and he is still far off with the jug'. Visually:

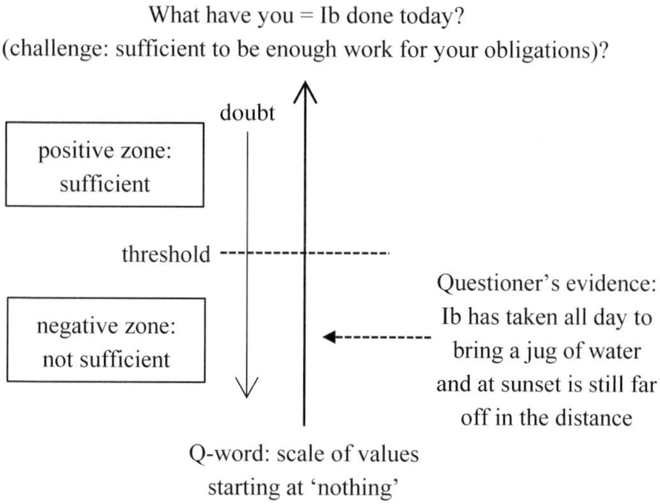

Direct-object-*ỉḫ* question using the sequential: *Horus & Seth*, 7, 8

Horus & Seth supplies an example with the sequential *ỉw=f (ḥr) sḏm* construction:

Ex. 14. *Horus & Seth* 7, 8 [= *LES* 46, 10]:

Seth has been fooled by Isis into undermining his own claim to the throne based on the analogous problem she has put to him in her guise as a beautiful woman (which attracted Seth's attention to her). She tells him the story of her son (=Horus) being cheated out of his cattle (using the pun *ỉȝwt* 'cattle'/'office') by an interloper. Seth then rather ashamedly goes to Pre-Horakhty to confess the story to him. He recounts the story told to him by the beautiful woman=Isis, but his recorded speech in the story is interrupted by Pre-Horakhty's interjected question below, just before the crucial section where Seth's own answer to Isis undermines his case:

ỉw=k	*ḏd*	*n=s*	*ỉḫ*
SQTL=you.M.SG	say.INF	to=her	what

And what did you say to her?
You said what to her? (with exasperated tone)

Rather than simply asking for information about what Seth said next, this can be read as a question challenging under (considerable) doubt whether Seth was able to provide an answer sufficient not to undermine his case (i.e. Pre-Horakhty knows generally what is coming and that it will condemn Seth's case; he just needs to know specifically exactly what Seth said):

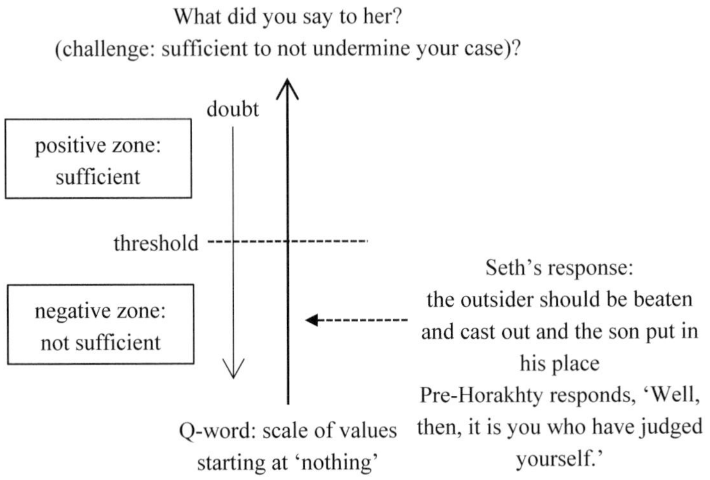
What did you say to her?
(challenge: sufficient to not undermine your case)?
doubt
positive zone: sufficient
threshold
negative zone: not sufficient
Seth's response: the outsider should be beaten and cast out and the son put in his place
Pre-Horakhty responds, 'Well, then, it is you who have judged yourself.'
Q-word: scale of values starting at 'nothing'

Direct-object-*ỉḫ* questions using the third future

An example with the third future *ỉw=f (r) sḏm* has already been discussed above. However, there are two others which repay brief discussion:[37]

Ex. 15. *Khonsuemheb and the Spirit*, von Beckerath's Text A 3, 11–12:[38]

Khonsumheb has promised to provide a new tomb for the spirit. The spirit notes that this has been promised to him 4 times already over the years and asks:

ḫr ỉw=ỉ r ỉrt ỉḫ m nꜣ ỉ-ḏd=k ꜥn

PRT FUT=I FUT do.INF what

So, what (if anything) am I to do with what you've said to me already?

It seems clear that this is a question challenging under doubt whether Khonsuemheb can provide an answer with a sufficient value for the Q-word. Khonsuemeheb attempts to answer this with a number of suggestions, but the Spirit follows this up with a response of his own, which is damaged, but which seems to indicate his continued doubt at this point in the tale:

37 Other exx. of direct-object-*ỉḫ* questions using the third future: *Astarte* 3, y-2–y-1 *(ỉw=ỉ r ỉrt ỉḫ r=sn ỉnk)*; P. DeM 4, rto 7 (*ỉw=ỉ ỉr ỉḫ*). Possible example with subjunctive *sḏm=f*: O. Leipzig 16 [= *HO* pl. 33.2], rto 3 (*ỉry(=ỉ) ỉḫ tꜣy kt nty m-dỉ=ỉ*).

38 Von Beckerath (1992: 98).

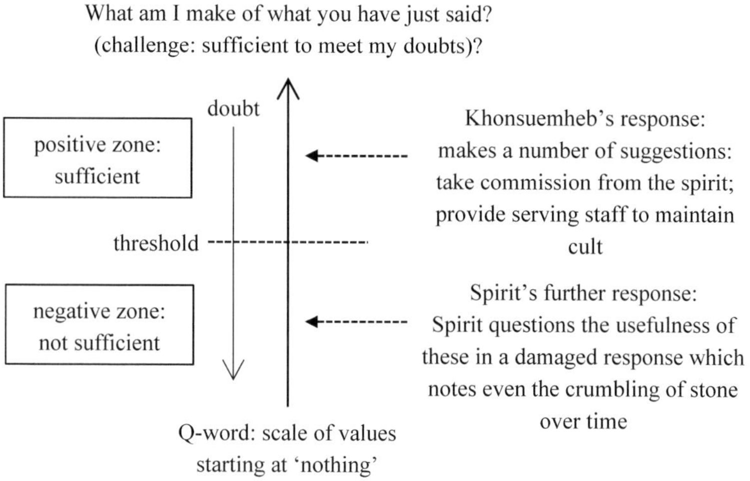
What am I make of what you have just said?
(challenge: sufficient to meet my doubts)?
doubt
positive zone:
sufficient
threshold
negative zone:
not sufficient
Q-word: scale of values
starting at 'nothing'
Khonsuemheb's response:
makes a number of suggestions:
take commission from the spirit;
provide serving staff to maintain
cult
Spirit's further response:
Spirit questions the usefulness of
these in a damaged response which
notes even the crumbling of stone
over time

An example from the tomb robbery papyri illustrates a rather different power dynamic:

Ex. 16. P. BM EA 10052, rto 6,4:

Nesmut[39] has followed the thieves (her brother + 4 thieves, who are separately totalled: Userhatnakht, Sheduskhonsu, Nesamun and her husband Perpatjau) as they are about to divide up the spoils, even though they are rather denigrating (*bḥn* lit. 'bark'; perhaps 'snap at' or 'deride' or similar in English) to her. She asks the following:

ỉw=tn	*wnm*	*ỉḫ*	*m-dỉ=tn*
FUT=you.PL	eat.INF	what	with/from=you.PL

What (if anything) can I 'eat' with/from you?[40]

Rather than use a pseudo-cleft construction, with its presumption that she should/will get something and simply looking for the information as to what, Nesmut uses (or Nesmut is written by the scribe as using) a question which challenges under doubt whether or not, or to what degree, she will be allowed to share or be included in the sharing out of the spoils in some way or other. In terms of the power dynamic here and issues such as face-threat, this would seem to be a reasonable conversational strategy for her to adopt. The immediate response is from her brother: *ḥnw ỉn n=ỉ* 5 *ḫt* 'Go and get 5 wood for me'. Nesmut then continues to relate how the haul was divided up into 4 shares. Although there are different ways to try to understand exactly how this works out (though the 4 shares seem to be those recorded elsewhere in testimonies and to be for the 4 thieves, including her husband, Perpatjau), it would seem, then, that Nesmut is allowed to participate in the division of

39 Nesmut is explicitly named in the unpublished, fragmentary end to page 5, at the end of line 5, 34.

40 The example uses *wnm* 'eat' in the well-attested sense in the tomb robbery texts of 'share in the proceeds from the thefts'.

the spoils, but is not allocated a separate share of her own, although she may share in her husband's share and certainly relates how she spent some of her husband's share.

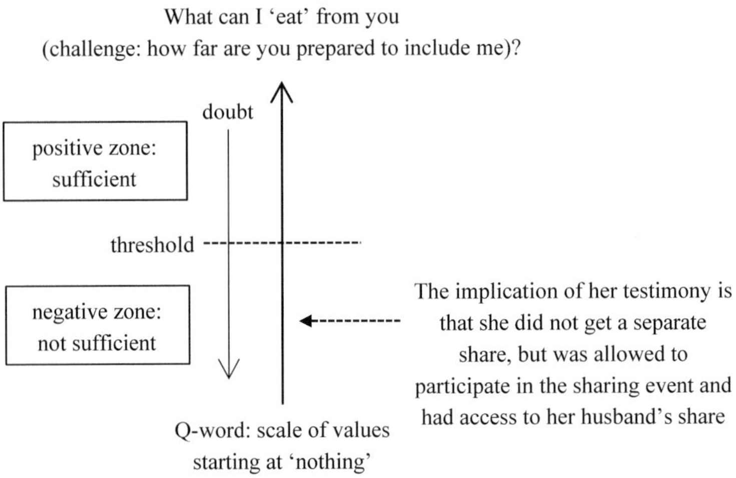
What can I 'eat' from you
(challenge: how far are you prepared to include me)?
doubt
positive zone:
sufficient
threshold
negative zone:
not sufficient
The implication of her testimony is
that she did not get a separate
share, but was allowed to
participate in the sharing event and
had access to her husband's share
Q-word: scale of values
starting at 'nothing'

Direct-object-*ỉḫ* question with the (auxiliarified) first present[41]

Ex. 17 *Horus & Seth* 8, 3 [= *LES* 47, 9]:

Pre-Horakhty and Atum send a message to the Ennead, who have not concluded the issue of whether to crown Horus or Seth king. They challenge them (with the question below) for not having brought things to conclusion and instruct them to crown Horus as king:

tw=tn	*dy*	*ḥms.tỉ*	*ḥr*	*ỉrt*	*ỉḫ*	*m-r-ꜥ*
you.PL	(t)here	sit.STAT-2PL	PRES	do.INF	what	still

What (if anything suitable) are you still there (sat) doing?
You're still (sat) there, but doing what?

41 Similarly (note, all with *ỉrt ỉḫ*: often extensions to a basic first present pattern or location pattern; often with *dy* marking): P. An. 8, 1,1–2 (*tw=k ꜥꜣ ḥr ỉrt ỉḫ m-r-ꜥ*); O. Ashm. 5, rto 7 (*ỉw=k dy ỉrt ỉḫ m pꜣy dmỉ nṯr*); P. An. 5, 11,6 (*tw=k ḥr šmt (r) ỉrt ỉḫ*).

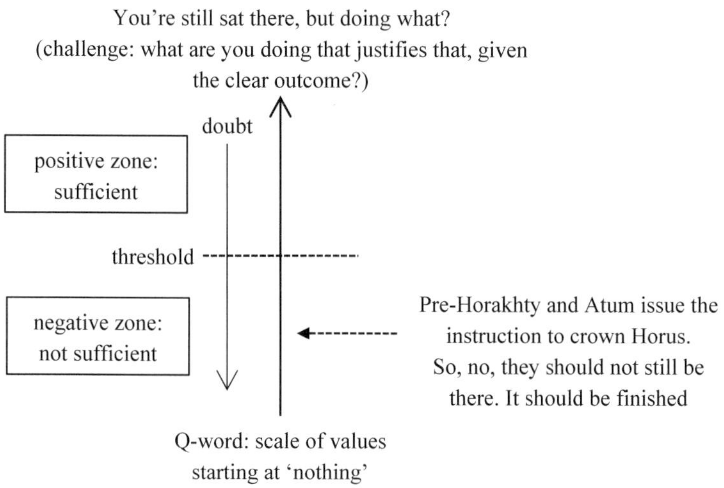
You're still sat there, but doing what?
(challenge: what are you doing that justifies that, given the clear outcome?)
doubt
positive zone: sufficient
threshold
negative zone: not sufficient
Pre-Horakhty and Atum issue the instruction to crown Horus. So, no, they should not still be there. It should be finished
Q-word: scale of values starting at 'nothing'

Extending the account to subject-*ỉḫ* questions

The proposal here for reading direct-object-*ỉḫ* questions can be extended straightforwardly (but here more briefly) to examples where *ỉḫ* occurs as the subject of a verbal tense.

First, though, a quick look at a focus-construction question with *ỉḫ* linked to the subject position of a predication. As noted by Neveu,[42] *ỉḫ* in subject-linked focus occurs with the pseudo-cleft construction (contrast *nym*, discussed briefly below). In the next example here, the predication within the relative clause is non-verbal:

Ex. 18. P. BM EA 10052 14, 18:

The fisherman Panakhtenope is interrogated. He confesses to ferrying a group of thieves over the river and names them. He has denied seeing the load they were carrying and is asked again:

ỉḫ m ꜣtp(t) tꜣ wn (ḥr) nḥbt=w
what as load.F.SG DET.F.SG PST.PTCP (on) shoulders=their
What sort of load was it that was on their shoulders?'

The existential presupposition here is that there was a load on their shoulders that Panakhtenope could see and the question seeks information as to what that was. He responds:

Ex. 19. P. BM EA 10052 14, 18:

wn nꜣy=w ḥnw (ḥr) nḥbt=w *bwpw=ỉ ptr=w*
PST their things (on) shoulders=their
Their things were on their shoulders, but I did not see them.

So, Panakhtemope confirms the presupposition, but claims that he was unable to identify more precisely what the thieves were carrying.

42 Neveu (2015: 228).

In the following examples, all of which show *ỉḫ* with its situational sense, *ỉḫ* occurs directly as the subject of a verbal tense:

Ex. 20. *Wenamun* 2, 66 [= *LES* 73, 16–74, 1]:

Just as he thinks things are going his way now that Tjekerbaal has provided the timber, Wenamun spots 11 ships of the Tjeker, who have been chasing him. He collapses in tears and, after being asked what is up with him, he says:

š3ꜥt ỉḫ ỉy ỉw=ỉ dy ḫ3ꜥ.tw

TRMN what come.INF

How long am I to be abandoned here?

(lit. Until what has come about, with me being abandoned here?)

The sense of dismay in this seems clear enough. This question is not primarily seeking a factual answer as to when he will be able to get home, but is a sceptical question expressing his negative expectations as to when he will be able to get home ('no end in sight'). Wenamun brackets this question, first by pointing out (in a *nn* question) the migratory birds now on their second cycle of returning to Egypt and then by noting (in another *nn* question) those who are coming to detain him once again.

This use of the terminative may be the proper analysis of the following example as well, if the restoration of the initial *r*- of the earlier terminative form is made:[43]

Ex. 21. *Doomed Prince* 4, 12 [= *LES* 2, 12]

The prince writes to his father asking to be let free so that he can live life on his own terms until fate and the god intervene. He begins by asking his father:

(r)-ỉyt ỉḫ ỉw(=ỉ) mỉn3 ḥms.kw

come.TRM what

Until what comes (if anything) am I to stay put here?

The same open-ended sense of negative expectation on the terminus seems clear enough in both examples ('how long', literally 'until what (if anything) comes'). In both there is a sense of 'no obvious end in sight'.

Ex. 22. P. Geneva D407, vso 5–6 [= *LRL* 15, 8–9][44]

Butehamun responds to his father's request that Butehamun should not neglect writing to his father about the welfare of the family back home, by making the following comparison:

ỉr wn ỉḫ ḫpr r=n ỉw=k ꜥḥꜥ.tw

FUT PST what happen.INF to=us

What could happen to us while you are around[45]?

ntk ỉ-ỉr=k h3b n=n ꜥ=k

Rather, it is you who should write to us about how you are!

43 See, for example, Winand (1992: 295 ex. 696), with reference in n. 22 to the analogous *Wenamun* example, my ex. 20 = his ex. 702.

44 For comments on the tense form used in this question, see Wente (1967: 36 note m). Of the options he proposes, the irrealis analysis is the one I prefer (despite issues of the order of the initial grams; it is perhaps worth noting that there is a line change between *ỉr* and *wn*).

45 Cf. Wente (1967: 36 note n). In terms of parallels for the clause with *ꜥḥꜥ*, I would look to the similar circumstantial present clause with *ꜥḥꜥ* in *Horus & Seth* 6, 12–13 and 7, 9, used to reflect the

It seems clear enough that Butehamun is not seeking information on what the kinds of things are which could happen to the family back home. Here the sense of the question is clearly one with negative expectation relative to the scale of things/situations injurious to well-being within the presented reinforcement of social relationships: it is unlikely that anything is going to happen to us, given that we have you to look after us (even from afar) and that we are back at home safe and sound, especially when compared to the greater risks you face on the military expedition into Nubia. So, we want to hear from you about how you are.

A brief section on *nym*

The question word *nym* 'who' usually refers to people (or similarly agentive beings). As such, it can be found in subject-linked or direct-subject position. Here discussion is restricted just to the usage of *nym* in subject-linked or direct subject position in relation to a verbal tense.

The canonical question format for this is the cleft sentence (participial statement) in which *nym* occurs after the particle *m* (not always present)[46] and is primarily followed by the participle form of the verb. This pattern can be found in the more prototypical question function of seeking information:

Ex. 23. *Two Brothers* 4, 10 [= *LES* 14, 1–2]:

The wife has failed in her attempt to seduce the younger brother. She makes herself sick and uses bandages to pretend that she has been assaulted and does not prepare the house for her husband's return. When he returns to find the house in darkness, he asks his wife:

m	*nym*	*mdw*	*m-dỉ=t*
PRT	who	speak.PST.PTCP	with=you.F.SG

Who (was it who) argued with you/abused you?

The wife answers, 'No one has argued with me except your younger brother,' thus supplying the information requested. She then goes on to recount the tale laying the blame on the younger brother.

Of course, examples can be found with a less direct information-seeking usage. In the following, it is possible that the questioner may be flouting the prototypical speech act conditions for information-seeking questions in a similar manner to Tjekerbaal's question to Wenamun used as ex. 4 above.

woman's son being around and hence why the cattle should not go to the stranger. In *Horus & Seth*, 7,9 Seth repeats to Pre-Horakhty that his answer to the problem that the woman was facing was 'Are the cattle to be given to the stranger,' *ỉw pꜣ šrỉ n pꜣ ꜥḥꜣwty ꜥḥꜥ* 'while the man's son is (still) around/alive?'

46 As is well known, *nym* itself is derived from the fusion of the earlier Egyptian cleft-sentence particle *ỉn* followed by the earlier Egyptian question word *m*.

Ex. 24. O. DeM 582, 5–6:

In testimony, Prahotep says his donkey had been left outside by his wife. But when he looked for it, it was gone. He then found his donkey with Kal, loaded with emmer. He asks Kal:

m	*nym*	*ỉ-dỉ*	*n=k*	*pꜣ*	*ꜥꜣ*
PRT	who	give.PST.PTCP	to=you.M.SG	DET.M.SG	donkey

Who (was it who) gave you the donkey?

Perhaps this is a question simply seeking information, but on the other hand Prahotep knows that he did not give the donkey to Kal, nor (from what she told him) did his wife. So, the presupposition ('someone gave you the donkey') may not reflect what he believes, but does reflect the idealised situation for why Kal might have the donkey and perhaps is intended to get Kal to see this as well. Kal responds by giving his own account of finding the donkey all on its own and so still provides information in response to the question.

There are, however, also examples where *nym* is used directly as the subject of a verbal tense. As might be expected from my discussion above, these questions can readily be read as sceptical questions of challenge. Indeed, these examples rather strongly implicate the end-scale of negative expectations and are included by Sweeney as clear examples of rhetorical questions:[47]

Ex 25. P. BM EA 10052 (rto) 3, 17:

Shedsukhonsu's father has attempted to intervene, pointing out that Bukhaaf's gang are taking Shedsukhonsu's share, but still opening him up to punishment. Amenkhau treats the father dismissively as a useless, silly old man and says, 'If you were killed and thrown into the water', then:[48]

ỉw	*nym*	*wḫꜣ=k*
SQNT	who	seek.INF=you.M.SG

Who (if anyone) would look for you?

The question is not seeking information about whoever might look for the father in such circumstances, but to challenge whether anyone would look for him at all, thus putting the father in his place. The implicated answer is clearly that no-one would look for him, because (in Amenkhau's presentation) the father is just not worth it.

---

47 Sweeney (2001: 143–44 exx. 74 & 76). Note that Sweeney's context for P. BM 10052 (rto) 3, 16–17 seems to be drawn from the different mention of a foolish old man in the testimony in 10, 8–9.

48 The tense is glossed as the *ỉw=f ḥr sḏm* construction found in certain apodoses, here termed 'sequential' for convenience. The alternative is to take it as the third future tense (with Sweeney [2001: 144] and Neveu [2015: 233 ex. 84 with n. 509]), but see the roughly contemporary Turin Marriage example below, where the expected *ỉr* before a noun subject appears in the third future tense before *nym*. Whatever the case, it is not to be analysed as a cleft sentence (= participial statement) construction as found in Černý & Groll (1993: 557 ex. 1594).

Ex. 26. P. Turin 2021 + Geneva D409 rto 3, 10:

The adult children are asked about the settlement their father is now making and they agree to it. Before saying that his property is his to dispose of, they are recorded as saying, 'As for what he has done':

ỉr	*nym*	*rẖ*	*mdt*	*ỉm=f*
FUT	who	be-able.INF	speak.INF	with=him

Who (if anyone) could dispute with him?

This question is not seeking information about the identity of (potential) parties who would dispute this, but to challenge whether anyone would dispute with him, with the implicated answer 'no one would dispute with him', thus implicitly including the sons themselves ('not us').

Conclusion

The present paper has made a case for reading non-canonical *ỉẖ* questions (more specifically those where *ỉẖ* is used directly as the direct object or subject) as sceptical questions challenging the addressee either to provide information for a sufficient response contrary to the negative expectations of the speaker or to accept that there is not a sufficient response and to acquiesce and conform to the questioner's point of view (including examples where the expected answer is effectively 'nothing'). Questions with *nym* in direct subject position have also been briefly considered from the same perspective.

Obviously, this is only a part of a much wider interrogative domain that cannot be mapped out in detail here. However, for those familiar with my work, I am in essence treating these non-canonical sceptical *ỉẖ* and *nym* questions as the content-question analogue to polarity-reversal polar questions with *ỉs(t)*.[49] Whereas polarity-reversal polar questions with *ỉs(t)* deploy polar alternatives, the sceptical content-question format deploy scaled alternatives (thus with greater variety) within the polar zones.

Bibliography

Beckerath, Jürgen von. 1992. 'Zur Geschichte von Chonsemḥab und dem Geist', *Zeitschrift für Ägyptische Sprache und Altertumskunde* 119, 90–107.

Černý, Jaroslav and Groll, Sarah Israelit. 1993. *A Late Egyptian Grammar*. 4th edn. Rome; Studia Pohl Series Maior 4.

Collier, Mark. 2014. 'Antiphrastic questions with *ỉst* and *ỉs* in Late Egyptian', in: Eitan Grossman, Stéphane Polis, Andréas Stauder, and Jean Winand (eds). *On Forms and Functions: Studies in Ancient Egyptian Grammar*. Hamburg; Lingua Aegyptia Studia Monographica 15, 7–40.

Collier, Mark. Submitted. 'Polarity sensitivity and bare low-endpoint indefinites in Late Egyptian'. Submitted for publication in the proceedings of the conference 'Negation in Ancient Egyptian', Paris, 11–13 December 2014.

Dayal, Veneeta. 2016. *Questions*. Oxford; Oxford Surveys in Semantics and Pragmatics.

Fleng̃o, Robert. 2007. *Asking Questions. Using Meaningful Structures to Imply Ignorance*. Oxford.

49 Collier (2014).

Gardiner, Alan & Kurt Sethe. 1928. *Egyptian Letters to the Dead Mainly from the Old and Middle Kingdoms*. London

Groll, Sarah. 1995. 'Unconventional use of the system of shifters as a means of signaling the use of different sources: Papyrus Anastasi VIII in the light of the "Standard Theory"', *Lingua Aegyptia* 5, 43–56.

Levinson, Stephen. 2012. 'Interrogative intimations: on a possible social economics of interrogatives', in: Jan P. de Ruiter (ed.). *Questions: Formal, Functional and Interactional Perspectives*. Cambridge; Language, Culture & Cognition 12, 11–32.

Neveu, François. 2015. *The Language of Ramesses: Late Egyptian Grammar*. Translated by Maria Cannata. Oxford. Original French edition 1996.

Sweeney, Deborah. 2001. *Correspondence and Dialogue. Pragmatic Factors in Late Ramesside Letter-writing*. Wiesbaden; Ägypten und Altes Testament 49.

Winand, Jean. 1992. *Études de néo-égyptien, 1. La morphologie verbale*. Liège; Ægyptiaca Leodiensia 2.

Late Egyptian Features Transferred by Shift-Induced Interference in New Kingdom Witnesses of Middle Egyptian Literary Works

'We know that texts cannot be taken at face value
but must be subjected to philological analysis
to ensure quality and accuracy of data.'[1]

Roberto A. Díaz Hernández[2]

1 Introduction

In pursuing the spirit of the last *Crossroads*, the present article endeavours to encourage and reinforce the multidisciplinary dialogue between philology and linguistics in Egyptology. It aims to explain Late Egyptian forms in New Kingdom witnesses of Middle Egyptian literary works as features transferred by shift-induced interference[3] from Late Egyptian into those texts. Schneider has recently published *Language Contact in Ancient Egypt* on the phenomenon of linguistic interference between Egyptian and other Asian and Nubian languages.[4] However, shift-induced interference existed in Ancient Egypt not only between Egyptian and other languages, but also internally between different stages of Egyptian.[5] Copies of texts written in an earlier variety of Egyptian occasionally

---

1 Joseph (2019: 166).

2 I thank Andreas Dorn and Sami Uljas for having invited me to deliver this paper at the conference *Crossroads VI – Between Egyptian Linguistics and Philology*. I am also grateful to Joachim Quack for his suggestion to include here the New Kingdom witnesses of *Sinuhe* and *Ptahhotep* and to the anonymous reviewer for enlightening comments.

3 According to conventional terminology in historical linguistics, 'interference' (note: sing.; from Latin *inter-* 'between' and *ferens* (active participle of *ferre* 'bring') is defined as 'the introduction of foreign elements into the more highly structured domains of language', see Weinreich (1953: 1). In this regard, Thomason and Kaufman (1988: 37–39; see also Thomason 2019: 117) distinguish two basic types of interference: 'borrowing', i.e. 'the incorporation of foreign features into a group's native language by speakers of that language' ($\text{Language}_2 \rightarrow \text{Language}_1$) and 'substratum interference' or 'shift-induced interference' (note: sing.), i.e. the incorporation of features transferred from the shifting speaker's language into the target language caused by his imperfect learning of the latter ($\text{Language}_1 \rightarrow \text{Language}_2$).

4 Schneider (2023: 45–46 and 81–101).

5 I read a paper on this topic, 'Middle Egyptian features in Middle Kingdom witnesses of the Pyramid Texts and Coffin Texts—A case of shift-induced interference' at the international conference *Looking Beyond the Text. Scribal Practices in Ancient Egypt* organized by Margaret Geoga, Aurore Motte and Judith Jurjens at Mainz on 17 May 2023. It will be published in the proceedings of this

Sami Uljas & Andreas Dorn (eds), *Crossroads VI. Between Egyptian Linguistics and Philology*, 85–124
DOI: https://doi.org/10.37011/studmon.30.04

show features transferred from a later variety, for example Late Egyptian features find their way into literary witnesses written in Middle Egyptian as it was learnt and used by New Kingdom scribes as a classical language, i. e. as a model and a standardized written language. For this research work, I chose the following texts (see table 1): *The Tale of Sinuhe* on the Ashmolean Ostracon 1945.40, The *Teaching for Kagemni* in Papyrus Prisse, *The Teaching of Ptahhotep* in Papyrus Prisse and Papyrus BM EA 10509, *The Complaints of Khakheperreseneb* on the Board British Museum EA 5645, *The Prophecies of Neferti* in Papyrus Petersburg 1116, *The Teaching for Merikare* in Papyrus Ermitage 1116 A, *The Teaching of Amenemhat* in Papyri Millingen and Sallier II, *The Teaching of Khety* in Papyri Amherst XIV and Sallier II and on the Board Louvre 693 and *The Admonitions of Ipuwer* in Papyrus Leiden 344 r.

Table 1 | Text corpus

Witness	Literary work	Dating	Section
Ashmolean Mus. Ostracon 1945.40 (AOS)	Sinuhe	19th Dyn.	§ 3.1
Papyrus Prisse (P)	Kagemni	13th–18th Dyn.	§ 3.2.1
Papyrus Prisse (P)	Ptahhotep	13th–18th Dyn.	§ 3.2.1
Papyrus BM EA 10509 (L2)		18th Dyn.	§ 3.2.2
Board British Museum EA 5645 (EA 5645)	Khakheperreseneb	Mid–18th Dyn.	§ 3.3
Papyrus Petersburg 1116 (Pet)	Neferti	Mid–18th Dyn.	§ 3.4
Papyrus Ermitage 1116 A (E)	Merikare	Mid–18th Dyn.	§ 3.5
Papyrus Millingen (M)	Amenemhat	Mid–18th Dyn.	§ 3.6
Papyrus Sallier II (S II)		19th Dyn.	§ 3.6
Papyrus Amherst XIV (A XIV)	Khety	18th Dyn.	§ 3.7
Board Louvre 693 (L 693)		18th Dyn.	§ 3.7
Papyrus Sallier II (S II)		19th Dyn.	§ 3.7
Papyrus Leiden 344 r. (L 344)	Ipuwer	19th Dyn.	§ 3.8

This article has three parts:

1. Explanation of the textual criticism approach used to study Late Egyptian features transferred by shift-induced interference in the texts selected (see §2 below). They are not to be considered mere scribal errors, but rather a kind of 'conceptual variants' (*variantes conceptuelles*).
2. Analysis of the Late Egyptian features identified in the texts selected (see §3 below). Research has shown that Papyrus Prisse contains Late Egyptian features, which means that it does not date from the 12th Dynasty, as traditionally supposed, but rather later than the Middle Kingdom, probably between the 13th–18th Dynasties.[6]

---

conference. I thank the editors, Andreas Dorn and Sami Uljas, for allowing me to share this article with Margaret Geoga before publication.

6 I acknowledge that Prof. Schenkel warned me against the use of Papyrus Prisse for my PhD thesis because he intuitively guessed that it was not a Middle Kingdom manuscript. In fact, he does

3. Discussion on the causes for the use of Late Egyptian features in New Kingdom witnesses of Middle Egyptian literary works and their classification in a table under five categories of interference: graphemic, lexical, morphological, semantic and syntactic features transferred from Late Egyptian into Middle Egyptian (see §4 below).

2 Late Egyptian features transferred by shift-induced interference as 'conceptual variants'

The preserved witnesses of Middle Kingdom literary works are separate and surviving links of a broken chain. They are copies transmitted and altered throughout generations. Regarding their production, three methods of textual transmission are to be considered:[7]

a) Copying from another exemplar (*Vorlage*).
b) Dictation.
c) Memorising.

Errors originating during production of a literary witness can be classified under three categories closely related to the transmission method used:[8]

a) Misreading of a spelling in the *Vorlage*.
b) Phonetic misunderstanding when listening.
c) Wrong reproduction due to the scribe's faulty memory.

These three types of errors can be found in witnesses of Middle Egyptian literary works, that is, they were made when copying *Vorlagen*, dictating to someone copying or relying on one's memory. However, a classification of scribal errors according to the method of transmission is not easy, as shown by Burkard's study on Middle Kingdom teachings.[9] For some errors may be due to different methods of textual transmission, for example:

 (Ptahh. 73, P 5,14)

rn	*=k*	*nfr(.w)*	*m*	*rh̠*	*n(.ỉ)*	*śr.w*
name(M.SG).STPR	=2SG.M	good:STAT-3SG	in:PREP	know:INF	of-M.SG	official(M.PL)

 (Ptahh. 73, L2 2,2–2,3)

rn	*=k*	*nfr(.w)*	*m*	*ꜣh̠.wỉ*	*śr.w*
name(M.SG).STPR	=2SG.M	good:STAT-3SG	in:PREP	influence(M.SG).STC	official(M.PL)

'Your name is good in the opinion (L2: sphere of influence) of the officials'.

not include *The Teaching of Ptahhotep* among the main literary works handed down in Middle Kingdom witnesses (Schenkel 2012²: 20). Late Egyptian features present in Papyrus Prisse confirm Prof. Schenkel's hypothesis.

7 Burkard (1977: 2).

8 Burkard (1977: 3).

9 Burkard (1977: 247).

The replacement of  with  may be either due to a hearing problem given the phonetic similarity of *r* and *ꜣ* or to a misreading because  and  are written similarly in Hieratic.[10]

Changes introduced in a text during transmission can be better explained by means of a descriptive analysis of their forms. To this regard Ragazzoli and Delnero classify text alterations into two types: 'mechanical errors' (*erreurs mécaniques*) and "conceptual variants" (*variantes conceptuelles*).[11] On the one hand, 'mechanical errors' are mostly due to the scribe's incompetence or lack of concentration when copying a text *directly* from another exemplar or when taking down a text dictated to him by someone else. In this case, the scribe would write down the text automatically without trying to understand its grammatical and lexical scope. Mechanical errors can be classified into the following types:[12]

a) Changes in spelling and pronunciation, e.g.:

 (Sin. 10, G 12) *ꜥẖ* instead of 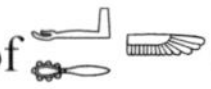 (Sin. 10, R 21) *ꜥẖ* 'fly away'.

 (Sin. 8, AOS 6–7 r.) *śgꜣ[b.w]-ꜥnḫ.w* instead of
 (Sin. 8, R 15) *śḳr-ꜥnḫ(.w)* 'captives'.

b) Changes of grammatical person, e.g.:

 (Sin. 39, AOS 35 r.)

rn *=f*
name(M.SG) =3SG.M

instead of

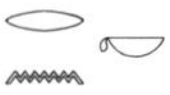 (Sin. 39, B 74 and R 99)

rn *=k*
name(M.SG) =2SG.M

'your (AOS: his) name'.

---

10 Burkard (1977: 10–11).

11 Ragazzoli (2019: 78–79). Strictly speaking, Delnero (2012: 192–95) uses the label 'memory errors', under which he includes omission and addition (Delnero 2012: 196), although he acknowledges (2012: 203) that both can be mechanical when copying or dictating. Ragazzoli (2017: 100–03) labels Delnero's 'memory errors' as 'conceptual variants' which she defines as lexical and grammatical changes *mainly* (*sic*) due to memory processes, although they could originate when copying a text.

12 Cf. Reynolds & Wilson (1991: 222–33) and Delnero (2012: 203).

 (Sin. 46, AOS 44 r.)

č̣t.n	*=ỉ*
say:PST	=1SG

instead of

 (Sin. 46, B 111)

č̣t.n	*=f*
say:PST	=3SG.M

'he (AOS: I) said'.

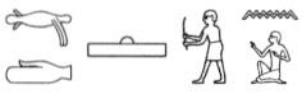 (Sin. 63, AOS 19 v.)

šṭ.n	*=ỉ*
read:PST	=1SG

instead of

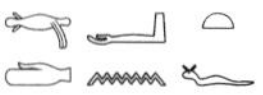 (Sin. 63, B 200)

šṭ.n	*-t(w)*	*=f*
read:PST	=IMPRS	=3SG.M

'One read it (i. e. the message) (AOS: I read)'.

c) Metathesis, e.g.:

 (Sin. 28–29, AOS 24 r.)

n	*w{s}fꜣ{t}*	*-tw*	*n*	*psg*	*-tw*	*m*	*ḥr*	*=ỉ*
NEG	discuss:PST	=IMPRS	NEG	spit:PST	=IMPRS	on:PREP	face(M.SG)	=1SG

'One[13] did not discuss. One did not spit on my face'.

instead of

 (Sin. 28–29, R 64)

n	*[psg]*	*-tw*	*=ỉ*	*n*	*wfꜣ*	*-tw*	*r-ḥr*	*=ỉ*
NEG	spit:PST	=IMPRS	=1SG	NEG	discuss:PST	=IMPRS	about: PREP	=1SG

'One did not spit me. One did not discuss about me'.

13 For the use of *tw* as a simplified noun with the impersonal meaning 'a body, a person (or similar)' i.e. 'one' instead of a passive morpheme see Díaz Hernández (2021a and 2022).

d) Omission of letters, words or sentences, occasionally due to haplography or parablesis, e.g.:

 (Sin. 19, AOS 17 r.)

ḥč<.n>	*tꜣ*
become bright:PST	land(M.SG)

instead of

 (Sin. 19, R 46)

ḥč.n	*tꜣ*
become bright:PST	land(M.SG)

'it was dawn'.

 (Sin. 8, AOS 7 r.)

<nn>	*č̣r.w*
<NEG>	limit(M.PL)

instead of

 (Sin. 8, R 17)

⌜nn	*č̣r⌝.w*
NEG	limit(M.PL)

'without limit'.

 (Sin. 72, B 249; haplography)

ṭh<n>.n	*=ỉ*
<touch:PST>	=1SG

'I touched'.

e) Addition of letters, words and sentences, occasionally due to dittography, e.g.:

 (Sin. 23, AOS 20 r.)

ỉw	*ỉr.n*	*=ỉ*
MCM	do:PST	=1SG

instead of

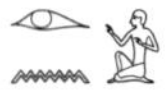 (Sin. 23, R 54) *ỉr.n=ỉ*

ỉr.n	*=ỉ*
do:PST	=1SG

'I did'.

 (Sin. 11, AOS 9 r.; dittography)

{nn}	*nỉś[.n*	*-tw]*
	call: PST	=IMPRS

instead of

 (Sin. 11, R 24) *nỉś.n-tw*

nỉś.n	*-tw*
call: PST	=IMPRS

'(one) called'.

f) Misunderstanding or misreading of the *Vorlage* usually leading to a lexical change or to a new meaning, e.g.:

 (Sin. 50, AOS 51 r.)

ỉb(.w)	*nb(.w)*	*mr{.kw}*
heart(M.PL)	every: ADJ	be sore:STAT-3SG.M

instead of

 (Sin. 50, B 132–133)

ỉb(.w)	*nb*	*mr(.w)*	*n*	*=ỉ*
heart(M.SG)	every: ADJ	be sore:STAT-3SG.M	for:PREP	=1SG

'Every heart was sore for me'.

 (...) (Sin. 54, AOS 57 r.)

ỉw	*{nn}*	*[ỉb]*	*=f (...)*
MCM		[heart(M.SG)]	=3SG.M

instead of

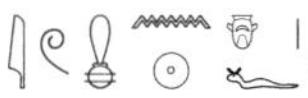 (...) (Sin. 54, B 149) *ỉw mỉn ỉb=f (...)*

ỉw	*mỉn*	*ỉb*	*=f (...)*
MCM	ADV	heart(M.SG)	=3SG.M

'today, his heart (...)'.

On the other hand, 'conceptual variants' are due to the scribe's *active* mindset, frequently by cognitive interference, when trying to make the text comprehensible or to improve on it by the introduction of words and grammar structures, as for example:

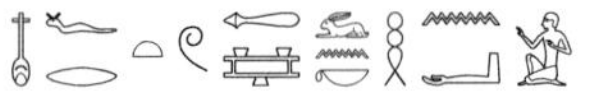 (Sin. 24, AOS 21 r.)

nfr	*tw*	*ꜥꜣ*	***wn***	***=k***	*ḥnꜥ*	*=ỉ*
lucky:ADJ	=2SG.M	ADV	be:PRS	=2SG.M	with:PREP	=1SG

instead of

 (Sin. 24, R 55) *nfr tw ḥnꜥ=ỉ*

nfr	*tw*	*ḥnꜥ*	*=ỉ*
lucky:ADJ	=2SG.M	with:PREP	=1SG

'You are lucky with me (AOS: you are lucky here being with me)'.

Witness AOS inserts the adverb *ꜥꜣ* "here" and the verb form *wn=k* 'being (lit.: while you are)', which modifies the grammatical structure of the text on witness R. According to Ragazzoli, two categories of conceptual variants can be distinguished: grammatical and lexical variations.[14] Features transferred by shift-induced interference from Late Egyptian to Middle Egyptian texts are a third category of conceptual variants, whose study has been disregarded hitherto. Such an interference process implies that New Kingdom scribes were bilingual and interference was due to their imperfect knowledge of Middle Egyptian. In that interference process, Late Egyptian was the source language (L_1) and Middle Egyptian the recipient language (L_2).

In the case of New Kingdom witnesses of Middle Egyptian literary works, once a Late Egyptian feature is transferred into those works, the text remains subject to alteration during its transmission, as can be inferred from the following passage occurring in the Millingen, Sallier I and Sallier II witnesses containing the *Teaching of Amenemhat*:

(...)  (Amenemhat § 5b, M 1, 9–10)

(...) ḳmṯ{.t}	*n.tỉ*	***n***	*śḉm*	*-tw*	*=f*
mourning(F.SG)	REL-M.SG	NEG	hear:PST	=IMPRS	=3SG.M

(...)  (Amenemhat § 5b, S I 1,6)

(...) ḳmṯ{.t}	*ỉw.tỉ*	***{n} bw***	*śḉm*	*-tw*	*=f*
mourning(F.SG)	NEG.REL-M.SG	NEG	hear:PST	=IMPRS	=3SG.M

14 Ragazzoli (2017: 102). I intentionally exclude cases of omission and addition because they can also be considered mechanical errors. Omission and addition errors made unconsciously are hardly distinguishable from those made consciously as conceptual variants. To what extend New Kingdom scribes were conscious of the transfer of Late Egyptian features into Middle Egyptian texts is a controversial question which lies beyond the scope of the present study; cf. the distinction between conscious and unconscious memory errors in Delnero (2012: 200–01).

(...) 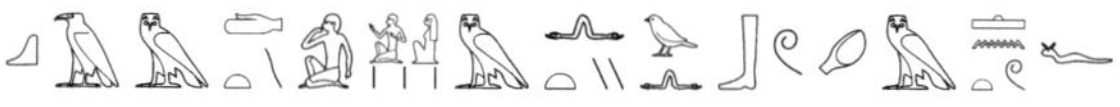 (Amenemhat § 5b, S II 1,7–1,8)

(...) ḳmṯ{.t}	*m*	*ỉw.tỉ*	***{n} bw***	*śčm.**n***	*-tw*	*=f*
mourning(F.SG)	as:PREP	NEG.REL-M.SG	NEG	hear:PST	=IMPRS	=3SG.M

'(...) a mourning which could not be heard (S II: as one which cannot be heard)'.

The mid-Eighteenth Dynasty Papyrus Millinger shows the Middle Egyptian relative pronoun *n.tỉ* before the negative structure *n śčm-tw=f*, which was replaced by Late Egyptian *bw śčm-tw=f* in Sallier I. This grammar structure transferred from Late Egyptian probably took place during the recension of the Middle Egyptian *Vorlage* in Ramesside times in order to make the text more comprehensible to a contemporary audience. Yet, the Late Egyptian version was modified again in the same period by the addition of the preposition *m* before *ỉw.tỉ* and the ending *n* after *śčm*, thus altering the text's meaning.

3 Late Egyptian features in New Kingdom witnesses of Middle Egyptian literary works

3.1 *Sinuhe*: The Ashmolean Ostracon 1945.40 (AOS)

The Tale of Sinuhe survives today in at least 7 papyri and 26 ostraca dating from the Middle Kingdom to the beginning of the 21st dynasty.[15] The story is preserved almost complete in three witnesses: Berlin P 3022 (B) and Berlin 10499 (R) papyri from the Middle Kingdom and the Ashmolean Mus. Ostracon 1945.40 (AOS)[16] from the 19th dynasty. According to Kahl, the Middle Kingdom knew three textual traditions of Sinuhe: one transmitted in B, another one in R and a third β, from which later witnesses originate.[17] Due to the fact that hypothetical witness β is not preserved, Winand has recently pointed out that we can only be sure of the existence of B and R textual traditions. In addition, he suggests that New Kingdom witnesses such as AOS arose from a recension made at the beginning of the 18th dynasty originating mainly in the R-witness, although the B-witness was also used. According to him, the New Kingdom recension served to fix the text by creating a final version which had been changing during the Middle Kingdom due to the oral transmission in performances and to everyday use.[18] This New Kingdom recension preserved in the AOS-witness contains the following features transferred from Late Egyptian by shift-induced interference:

1) Late Egyptian spellings for Middle Egyptian words, e.g.:[19]

 (Sin. 11, AOS 9 r.; Sin. 76, AOS 55 v.) for the particle *ỉśt*.

 (Sin. 67, AOS 33 v.) *wpw* for *wpw-ḥr* (Sin. 67, B 228) "except for".

15 Winand (2014: 223). Kahl counts 6 New Kingdom papyri and 26 ostraca (1998: 383).

16 Barns (1952).

17 Kahl (1998: 388–90).

18 Winand (2014: 236–43).

19 Cf. Kahl (1998: 395).

2) *śt* used as the suffix pronoun *=ś* (f. sg.), e.g.:

(Sin. 58, AOS 69 r.)

mś.w	*=śt*
child(M.PL)	=3SG.F

instead of

(Sin. 58, B 172)

mś.w	*=ś*
child(M.PL)	=3SG.F

'her children'.

(Sin. 58, AOS 69 r.)

sb(ꞽ).w	*=śt*
pass:SBJV	=3SG.F

instead of

(Sin. 58, B 172)

sb(ꞽ)	*=ś*
pass:SBJV	=3SG.F

'may she pass'.

3) The Late Egyptian independent pronoun *mntf* instead of its Middle Egyptian equivalent *ntf* (B 267) 'he':

(Sin. 76, AOS 54 v.)

(...) mntf	*pw*
3SG.M	*pw*-SENT

'It is he'.

4) Omission of the preposition *ḥr* in the pseudoverbal construction attested since the Second Intermediate Period:[20]

(...) (Sin. 11, AOS 10 r.)

(...) ꞽw=f	<*ḥr*>	*mṭ.t*	*{=f}*[21]
SBRD=3SG.M	<on=>	speak:INF	{=3SG.M}

20 Díaz Hernández (2017: 51–53) and Kroeber (1970: 51).

(...)  (Sin. 11, B 2)

(...) ỉw=f	*ḥr*	*mṭ.t*
SBRD=3SG.M	on=	speak:INF

'(...) while he was speaking'.

5) The Present I *tw=ỉ/św ḥr śčm* attested since the 13th dynasty:[22]

(...)  (Sin. 58, AOS 2–3 v.)

(...) śšm.w	*pn*	*n.tï*	*tw=ỉ*	*ỉm*	*=f*
state(M.SG)	DEM:M.SG.	REL-M.SG	PRS=1SG	in:PREP.STPR	=3SG.M

(...) 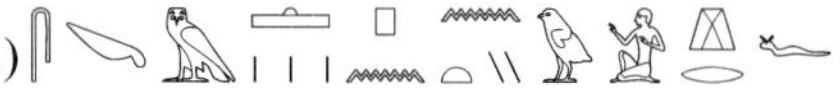 (Sin. 58, B 173–174)

(...) śšm.w	*pn*	*n.tï*	*wỉ*	*ẖr*	*=f*
state(M.SG)	DEM:M.SG.	REL-M.SG	=1SG	in:PREP.STPR	=3SG.M

'(...) the state in (B: under) which I was'.

 (Sin. 73, AOS 45 v.)

⸢tw=ỉ	*mỉ*	*s(.ỉ)⸣*
PRS=1SG	like:PREP	man(M.SG)

 (Sin. 73, B 254)

ỉw=ỉ	*mỉ*	*s(.ỉ)⸣*
MCM=1SG	like:PREP	man(M.SG)

'I was like a man'.

 (Sin. 75, AOS 51 v.)

[m]=k	*tw[=ỉ]*	*m-bꜣḥ*	*[=k]*
ATTN=2SG.M	PRS[=1SG]	before:PREP.STPR	[=2SG.M]

 (Sin. 75, B 263)

m=k	*wỉ*	*m-bꜣḥ*	*=k*
ATTN=2SG.M	=1SG	before:PREP.STPR	=2SG.M

'See, I am before you'.

21 The suffix pronoun *=ỉ* after *ỉw* was emended to *=f* by the scribe in this ostracon, see Koch (1990: 11a, obs. 8a).

22 On the earliest attestation of this structure in the tomb of Seneb-Kay at South Abydos see Cahail (2019: 20–24).

(...)  (Sin. 70, AOS 39 v.; attested only in this witness)[23]

(...) r	*r⌜ç⌝.t*	*rḫ*	*[-tw]*	*r-[n.tï]*	*tw=ỉ*	*⌜ỉy⌝.kw*
to:PREP	let:INF	know:SBJV	[=IMPRS]	COMP	PRS=1SG	come:PERF

'(...) to let it be known that I have come'.

6) The Late Egyptian past *śçm=f*[24] is used instead of the 'narrative' infinitive:

 (Sin. 12, AOS 11 r.)

ỉr	*=ỉ*	*šm.t*	*m*	*ḫnt.yt*
make:PST	=1SG	go:INF	in:PREP	voyage southwards(F.SG)

 (Sin. 12, B 5–6 and R 29)

ỉr.t	*=ỉ*	*šm.t*	*m*	*ḫnt.yt*
make:INF	=1SG	go:INF	in:PREP	voyage southwards(F.SG)

'I made off (B and R: my making off) upstream'.

3.2 *Kagemni* and *Ptahhotep*: Papyrus Prisse (P) and Papyrus BM EA 10509 (L2)

3.2.1 Papyrus Prisse

The Papyrus Prisse contains the end of the *Teaching for Kagemni* and the full text of the *Teaching of Ptahhotep*. The first of these teachings is only known from that papyrus, while the second teaching is also preserved fragmentarily in the Middle Kingdom Papyrus BM EA 10371 + 10435 (L1), the Carnarvon wooden board 1 (C) from the 17th–18th Dynasty and the early New Kingdom Papyrus BM EA 10509 (L2). In addition, some traces of Ptahhotep are attested in four witnesses of the second half of the New Kingdom: Papyrus Turin CG 54014 and ostraca DeM 1232–1234.[25] Witnesses L2 and C follow the textual tradition of the Middle Kingdom witness L1, which is older than P as shown by orthographical, palaeographical and grammatical evidences. Frequent variants between P and the other witnesses confirm that P is based on a different textual tradition.[26] Cases with same textual tradition between L2 and P, but different from L1, are exceptional.

Papyrus Prisse has been dated to the Middle Kingdom on palaeographical and orthographical criteria.[27] On the one hand, Dévaud assigned a late 12th Dynasty date to Papyrus

23 Koch's reading (1990: 70); cf. Barns (1952).

24 Brose (2019: 41–60) has recently argued that the Late Egyptian past *śçm=f* arose morphologically from the Middle Egyptian past *śçm=f* assuming the semantic function of Middle Egyptian *ỉw śçm.n=f*.

25 Hagen (2012: 131–87).

26 Hagen (2012: 134 and 248).

27 Hagen (2012: 142).

Prisse based on an orthographical analysis that places it later than witness L1.[28] On the other hand, the script shows archaising tendencies and the text is written in lines after having been copied from another exemplar in columns as it was usual in the 11th and 12th Dynasties.[29] However, orthographical and palaeographical criteria are not always sound evidence for text dating, for a text may have been copied from another exemplar preserving its archaising handwriting and old spellings, as happens with New Kingdom witnesses of the Kemit written in the hieratic script of the early Middle Kingdom and in archaising columns.[30] Lexical and grammatical features are more reliable for text dating. In this regard the following features in Papyrus Prisse are striking in Middle Egyptian high registers while being characteristic of Late Egyptian and New Kingdom texts, which suggests a later date between the 13th and the 18th Dynasty, and therefore the archaising features have to be considered an instance of fine work by a professional New Kingdom scribe:

1) The possessive adjective *nꜣy=f*:

 (Kagemni, P 2,3)

nꜣy	*=f*	*n*	*ẖrṭ.w*
POSS:PL	=3SG.M	of	children(M.PL)

‘his children’.

In the Middle Kingdom, the possessive adjective occurs predominantly in the ‘communicative register’ of documentary texts.[31] It is attested for the first time in Papyrus Cairo CG 58045/JE 31061, col. 8 dated at the end of the 11th Dynasty. It is noteworthy that the possessive adjective is spelled without an *y* in that instance contrary to its usual spelling with an *y* in later times, as in Papyrus Prisse 2,3.[32] The possessive adjective occurs frequently in documents dating from the end of the 12th Dynasty and the beginning of the 13th Dynasty. It is remarkable that in those texts the possessive adjective *nꜣy=* is attested several times with the word *ẖrṭ.w*, as in Papyrus Prisse 2,3.[33] This means that *nꜣy=f n ẖrṭ.w* in Papyrus Prisse was surely transferred from the communicative register of the documentary texts. Due to the fact that the transfer of features from the ‘communicative register’ into the higher registers of the historical-biographical and literary texts became a usual phenomenon from the 13th Dynasty onwards,[34] the use of the possessive adjective in P, and in another similar literary passage of *The Tale of the Eloquent Peasant* in witness Berlin 3025 (B2),[35]

28 Dévaud (1924: 11). See also Díaz Hernández (2013: 42–43).

29 Burkard (1991: 195).

30 Kaper (2010: 122).

31 On Middle Egyptian registers and text genres see Díaz Hernández (2021b: 13–37).

32 Zöller-Engelhardt (2016: 160 and 163–64).

33 Zöller-Engelhardt (2016: 160) and Brose (2014: 77–79).

34 Díaz Hernández (2017: 51–54).

35 B2 128: *nꜣy=k n spr.(w)t* “your petitions”. Another exceptional structure attested only in these two witnesses is *wn.ỉn* + adjectival sentence (B2, 131–132 and Kagemni P 2, 6–7). See Loprieno, Müller & Uljas (2017: 700–01 and 728–29).

serves to establish a *terminus ante quem non* for P and B2.[36] Neither manuscript could have been written before the 13th Dynasty.[37]

2) Particle *ỉw* as an adverbial converter without a suffix pronoun as a subject + pseudoparticiple:

 (Kagemni, P 1,8–1,9)

ỉr	*św̓r*	*=k*	*ḥnꜥ*	*tẖ.w*	*šsp*	*=k*
COND	drink-SBJV	=2SG.M	with:PREP	drunkard(M.SG)	accept-SBJV	=2SG.M

ỉw	*ỉb*	*=f*	*ḥtp.w*
SBRD	heart(M.SG)	=3SG.M	satisfied-STAT

'If you drink with a drunkard, you should accept when his heart is satisfied'.

According to Allen, *šsp=k* is an emphatic verb form which stresses the subordinate sentence *ỉw ỉb=f ḥtp.w*. He wonders why the particle *ỉw* introduces a subordinate sentence with a pseudoverbal predicate.[38] Following Gardiner and Schenkel, in Middle Egyptian the particle *ỉw* can subordinate sentences with an adverbial or a pseudoverbal predicate if, and only if, it is used with a suffix pronoun as a subject.[39] By contrast, in Late Egyptian *ỉw* without a suffix pronoun serves to subordinate sentences with an adverbial or pseudoverbal predicate. Therefore, the sentence *ỉw ỉb=f ḥtp.w* is to be considered a Late Egyptian feature in P. Indeed Gardiner quotes this passage as an exception to his rule.[40]

3) Omission of the preposition *ḥr* in the pseudoverbal construction:

 (Kagemni, P 1,6)

ỉw	*nfr.t*	*<ḥr>*	*ỉṯn*	*bw-nfr*	*ỉw*	*nh*
MCM	good:PTCP	<on=>	replace:INF	goodness:(M.SG)	MCM	lack:(M.SG)

n(.ỉ)	*ktt*	*<ḥr>*	*ỉṯn*	*wr*
of-M.SG	small:(M.SG)	<on=>	replace:INF	greatness(M.SG)

'What it is good serves for (lit. replaces) goodness. A little bit serves for (lit. replaces) greatness'.

---

36 Indeed, Parkinson (1991: xxvi) suggests that the witness Berlin 3025 (B2) may be later than Berlin 3023 (B1), i.e. B2 was written by the end of the 12th or at the beginning of the 13th Dynasty.

37 Stauder's interpretation of *nꜣy=f n ḫrṭ.w* as carrying a strongly deictic expression (Stauder (2013: 115) is irrelevant for the dating of Papyrus Prisse, for, according to Zöller-Engelhardt (160: footnote 745), the possessive adjective lost quickly its deictic power after the 11th Dynasty and therefore a date for that papyrus in the First Intermediate Period is improbable.

38 Allen (2015: 164).

39 Gardiner (1957: 247, § 323) and Schenkel (2007: 161–65).

40 Gardiner (1957: 248, § 323). He translates that instance as a clause of result: 'take thou (so that) his heart is content'.

Stauder suggests that a hypothetical noun + *śčm* construction is used in this passage of *The Teaching for Kagemni*, as well as in another passage of *The Loyalist Teaching*. In his opinion, the verb form *śčm* may occur without a suffix pronoun in a similar way as the verb form *śčm.nï/w*.[41] However, *śčm.nï/w* is well attested in Middle Kingdom texts, especially after the negative *n*,[42] while the odd structure noun + *śčm* occurs only in the abovementioned cases. From a text-critical point of view, Allen's explanation of passage P 1,6 is more convincing—the scribe omitted twice the pronominal subject after the verb form *ỉṭn*. If this is so, the suffix pronouns *=ś* and *=f* must be emended in order to conform with the gender of the words *nfr.t* and *nh* acting as topicalized subjects.[43] However, there might be here a case of omission of the preposition *ḥr* in a pseudo-verbal construction, as it occasionally happens in New Kingdom witnesses of Middle Egyptian literary works (see § 4 and table 2, below). Both pseudo-verbal constructions (*ỉw nfr.t <ḥr> ỉṭn bw-nfr ỉw* and *nh n(.ỉ) ktt <ḥr> ỉṭn wr*) would have a gnomic meaning, frequent in Middle Egyptian texts from the New Kingdom,[44] instead of a progressive meaning as is usual in Middle Egyptian.

4) The use of  *śt* instead of *śn* (f. pl.) is attested at least once:

 (Ptahh. 274, P 9,6)

ỉw	*čṭ*	*-tw*	*ỉw*	*tr*	*r*	*m*
MCM	say:PRS	=IMPRS	MCM	Q	for:PREP	what:(M.SG)
th	*=f*	*śt*				
contravene:PRS	=3SG.M	=3PL				

 (Ptahh. 274, L2 4,14)

ỉw	*čṭ*	*-tw*	*ỉw*	*tr*	*r*	*m*
MCM	say:PRS	=IMPRS	MCM	Q	for:PREP	what:(M.SG)
ỉr	*=f*	*śt*				
do:PRS	=3SG.M	=3PL				

'One says: "For what purpose does he contravene (L2: do) them (the petitions)?"'

41 Stauder (2013: 101). He states that noun (N) + *śčm* is 'a variation on the more common N *sḏm.n*' and quotes instances used by Edel to explain the use of *śčm.nï/w* with transitive verbs (Edel 1959: 30–34; cf. Stauder 2013: 25–26). Since Stauder acknowledges that Middle Egyptian grammars do not deal with the noun + *śčm.n* construction, the (N) + *śčm* form is consequently left out. The reason for this is that *sčm.n* after a noun is to be considered either the *śčm.n* verb form with omission of the suffix pronoun *=śn* or the *śčm.nï/w* with omission of the weak consonant *ï/w*. In any case, no one (but Stauder) argues for the existence of a noun + *sčm.n* construction—even Junge (2003: 254 (482)), quoted by Stauder to back up his statement, asserts literally: '*n ꜥq.n.j* = *sdm.n* mit Pluralersatzform/Adverbialtranspositor *-j* "sie können nicht eintreten"', which means that noun + *śčm* / *sčm.n* cannot be considered two new grammatical constructions, but rather the corrupted spellings of two well-known grammatical constructions.

42 Gardiner (1957: 397, § 486 Obs. 2).

43 Allen (2015: 163).

44 Allen (2014: 200).

 *śt* refers to the plural word *śpr.(w)t* 'petitions' in the previous sentence (Ptahh. 273). Though Egyptian grammars explain that *śt* can be used instead of *śn* in Middle Egyptian,[45] it is quite remarkable that it occurs instead of *śn* more frequently in Middle Egyptian texts from the New Kingdom than it actually does in Middle Kingdom texts.[46]

5) The ending *.w* of strong verbs used as subjunctive verb forms:

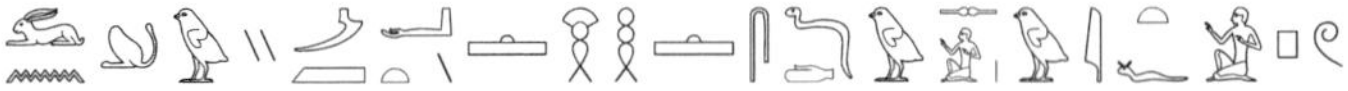 (Ptahh. 97–98, P 6,7)

wn	*pḥ.wï*	*m3ˁ.t*	*w3ḥ*	*=ś*	***čṭ.w***	*s(.ỉ)*
exist:PRS	end:M.SG)	Truth:(F.SG)	endure:SBJV	=3SG.F	say:SBJV	man:(M.SG)

w	*ỉt*	<=ỉ>	*pw*
area:(M.SG)	father:(M.SG)	<=1SG>	*pw*-SENT

 (Ptahh. 97–98, L2 2,9)

wn	*pḥ.t{t}(ï)*	*m3ˁ.t*	*w3ḥ{t}*	*śï*	***čṭ.w***
exist:PRS	strenght:(M.SG).STC	Truth:(F.SG)	permanent:PTCP	=3SG.F	say:SBJV

s(.ỉ)	*(ỉ)ẖ.(w)t*	*ỉt*	*=ỉ*	*pw*
man:(M.SG)	things:(F.PL).STC	father:(M.SG)	=1SG	*pw*-SENT

'If the end exists (L2: If the strength of the Truth exists), Truth will endure (L2: she will be permanent), in order that a man may say: "This is my father's area (L2: things, i.e. heritage)"'.

Though the text in both witnesses is different, the meaning and the spelling of the verb form *čṭ.w* is the same. Ptahhotep states the logical premise of Egyptian thinking that the legitimate richness of a man is his father's property, i.e. his heritage.[47] The two first sentences express a universal truth in Egyptian thinking: as long as truth prevails, there is also an end. That universal truth is the reason that allows a man to claim his father's property (when he dies). If *w* is construed as the Old Kingdom enclitic negation,[48] then the universal truth would be that a man cannot claim his paternal heritage, which is contrary to the Egyptian sense of righteousness.[49] Authors who consider *w* an enclitic negation reject that *w* could be the ending of a subjunctive *śčm=f* because in Middle Egyptian this verb form features an ending *w* only with weak verbs. However, Stauder points out that the subjunctive of strong verbs can occasionally be written with the ending *w* in New Kingdom

45 Gardiner (1957: 46, § 46), Malaise & Winand (1999: 106, § 151), Allen (2014: 62).

46 Stauder (2013: 71), Quack (1992: 37). This issue calls for a deeper study to find out when the use of *śt* for *śn* started to spread in Egyptian texts.

47 Cf. Parkinson (1997[1]: 252).

48 Allen (2014: 176). Stauder (2013: 106 and footnote 157) and Dils' comment in his translation on the website of the *Thesaurus Linguae Aegyptiae*.

49 Hapi-Djefay says about his donations to his funerary priests that they came from his father's property, not from his position as a nomarch (*(ỉ)ẖ.(w)t=ỉ pw n.(ỉ)w pr ỉt=ỉ , n (ỉ)ẖ(w)t ỉś pw pr ḥ3(.tỉ)-ˁ* Asyut I 288, cf. 301).

witnesses of Middle Egyptian literary works,[50] which supports the interpretation of *čṭ.w* as a subjunctive verb form subordinated in a final clause.

6) The early Late Egyptian future *tw=ỉ / św r śčm*:

 (Ptahh. 81–82, P 6,2–6,3)

ḳśn	*pw*	*ḥčč.w*	*ḥwr.w-ỉb*	***tw***	*r*
bad:ADJ.(M.SG)	*pw*-SENT	destroy:PTCP(M.SG)	poor-hearted:(M.SG)	IMPRS	to=

ỉr.t	*n.tt*	*m*	*ỉb*	*=k*
do-INF	REL.F	in:PREP	heart:(M.SG)	=2SG.M

 (Ptahh. 81–82, L2 2,5)

ḳśn	*pw*	*ḥčč.w*	*ḥwr.w-ỉb*	***św***	*r*
bad:ADJ.(M.SG)	*pw*-SENT	destroy:PTCP(M.SG)	poor-hearted:(M.SG)	3SG.M	to=

ỉr.t	*n.tt*	*m*	*ỉb*	*=f*
do-INF	REL.F	in:PREP	heart:(M.SG)	=3SG.M

'A bad person is one who destroys a poor-hearted. One (L2: he) will do what is in your (L2: his) heart'.

This passage has recently been studied by Stauder who suggests a segmentation of the text different from the traditional one.[51] He reads in P *ḳśn pw ḥčč.w ḥwr.w* ***ỉb=tw*** *r ỉr.t n.tt m ỉb=k* instead of Žába's *ḳśn pw ḥčč.w* ***ḥwr.w-ỉb*** *tw r ỉr.t n.tt m ỉb=k*. According to Stauder, the word *ỉb* does not belong to the expression *ḥwr.w-ỉb*,[52] but it is rather the noun *ỉb* 'heart' in the Late Egyptian expression *ỉb* X *r śčm*, which he translates literally 'le cœur de X est porté à écouter (X's heart is inclined to listen)', and he explains the function of *tw* as an indefinite pronoun with the meaning 'on' in French.[53] His explanation of the passage is convoluted and unconvincing, for the expression *ỉb* X *r śčm* is extremely rare and only attested in New Kingdom witnesses,[54] while the function of *tw* as an indefinite pronoun after a noun is not attested in Middle Egyptian,[55] which means that the traditional reading of Ptahhotep 81–82 should be kept.[56] It is noteworthy here that the expression *tw r śčm* is attested only in New Kingdom witnesses of Middle Egyptian literary works and in a

50 Stauder (2013: 71).

51 Stauder (2016 and 2013: 360). Cf. Žába (1956: 23).

52 *Wb.* III 55, 10.

53 Stauder (2016: 781), *Wb.* I 60, 13.

54 See examples in Stauder (2016: 782).

55 Gardiner (1957: 46–47, § 47 Obs.).

56 Panov (2021: 54) points out that *ḥwr.w-ỉb* "poor-hearted" is separated from the dependent pronoun *św* by means of a red point in witness L2. This also speaks for the traditional segmentation of the passage in Papyrus Prisse.

personal name from between the 13th and the 18th Dynasties,[57] a fact that puts the 13th Dynasty as the *terminus ante quem non* for P. Moreover, a comparison of P and L2 shows that a swap of grammatical persons, a common scribal error (see § 2, above), occurred during textual transmission. Pronouns *św* (3rd. sing.) and *=f* (3rd. sing.) appear in L2 instead of the impersonal *tw* ('one') and *=k* (2nd. sing.) in P.

7) The Late Egyptian adverbial sentence:[58]

 (Ptahh. 353–54, P 11,6)

wḥm(.w)	*mṭ.t*	*m3<.t>*	*n*	*śč̣m.n(w)*	*śt*	*r*
repeat:PTCP(M.PL)	matter:(F.SG)	seen:PTCP(F.SG)	NEG	hear:PST	=3SG.F	to:PREP

t3	*m*	*č̣ṭ*	*rś-śt*
land:(M.SG)	NEG	say:ADVZ	ADV

'(Those) who repeat a seen matter, they cannot listen. It (i.e. the seen matter) should be to the earth (free: it must be put aside or ignored). Don't say (it) at all'.

The meaning of this passage must be that it is a waste of time to speak about a well-known affair because everybody knows it. Grammatically, *wḥm* has usually been translated as an imperative: 'Repeat a speech'.[59] The structure *n śč̣m* has been explained by Allen as a negated passive participle ('not heard'), in spite of the omission of the particle *îś* frequently used in that structure,[60] and he reads *n(.î) śt r t3 (...)* considering *n(.î)* as a nisbe expressing a relationship of possession ('it belongs').[61] However, Dils, along with Vernus, suggests that *n śč̣m.n* is a verb form with an omitted subject and the enclitic pronoun *śt* as an object ('one cannot hear it').[62] If this be so, the adverbial complement (*r t3*) remains isolated, which is grammatically unusual. The key to understand P 11,6 is found in the following passage of the same text:

(Ptahh. 482–83, P 14,3)

îr	*pr(.w)*	*m*	*mẖr*	*n*	*ʿḳ.n(w)*	*în*
TOPZ	go:PTCP(M.PL)	from:PREP	storehouse(M.SG)	NEG	come in:PST	AGT

t'	*n(.î)*	*pšš.t*	*ḫnt(i̯)*	*ḥr*	*=f*
bread:(M.SG)	of-M.SG	sharing:(F.SG)	covet:PTCP(M.SG)	for:PREP	=3SG.M

57 Kroeber (1970: 94–96) and Stauder (2013: 363–64).
58 Loprieno, Müller & Uljas (2017: 42–43).
59 Allen (2015: 198).
60 Allen (2014: 155).
61 Allen (2015: 198–99).
62 See Dils' comment in his translation on the website of the *Thesaurus Linguae Aegyptiae*.

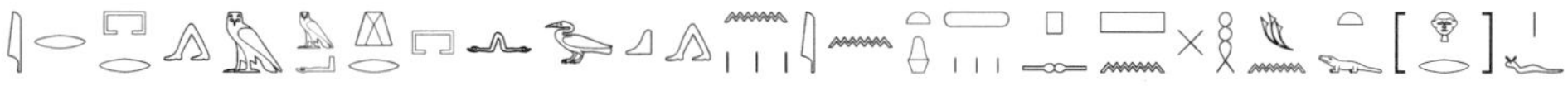

(Ptahh. 482–83, L1 5,9–5,10)

ỉr	*pr(.w)*	*m*	*mẖr*	*n*	*ꜥḳ.**nw***	*ỉn*
TOPZ	go:PTCP(M.PL)	from:PREP	storehouse(M.SG)	NEG	come in:PST	AGT

tꜣ	*pśš{n}*	*ḥnt(i̯)*	*[ḥr]*	*=f*
bread:(M.SG)	shared:PTCP(M.SG)	covet:PTCP(M.SG)	[for:PREP]	=3SG.M

'As for (those) who went out from the storehouse, they cannot come in. It is the bread for sharing (L1: shared bread) which is coveted'.

The Middle Kingdom witness L1 shows *ꜥḳ.nw* for *ꜥḳ.n(w)* in P, which means that the structure used in that passage and in P 11,6 is doubtless *n śčm.nï/w* 'they cannot hear'.[63] The subject of this verb form is expressed by a marked noun topic introduced by the particle *ỉr* in Ptahh. 482–83. By comparison, the subject of the verb form *śčm.n(w)* in P 11,6 must be the active participle *wḥm* used as an unmarked noun topic without any particle. Moreover, it is remarkable in Ptahh. 482–83 that an independent sentence follows the verb form *ꜥḳ.nw*. Similarly, it must be assumed in P 11,6 that the adverbial sentence after *n śčm.n(w)* is syntactically independent. In this case, it is a Late Egyptian adverbial sentence with *śt* as a subject.

3.2.2 Papyrus BM EA 10509 (L2)

As has already been shown when discussing the date of P, Late Egyptian features can be found in L2, for example, the ending *w* in the subjunctive of strong verbs and the early Late Egyptian future with *św*. Another instance of early Late Egyptian future can be found in the same witness:

 (Ptahh. 72, L2 2,2)

tw	*r*	*wfꜣ*	*=f*	*ỉn*	*śčm.yw*
IMPRS	to=	reproach:INF	=3SG.M	AGT	hearer PTCP (M.PL)

 (Ptahh. 72, P. 5,14)

wr	*wfꜣ*	*ỉn*	*śčm.yw*
great: ADJ.	reproach: (M.SG)	AGT	hearer PTCP (M.PL)

He will be reproached (P: Great is the reproach) by the judges (lit.: one will reproach him, particularly, the hearers)'.

Witness P probably preserves the Middle Egyptian version, which obviously underwent a phonetic change (*wr* > *tw r*) during the textual transmission process in L2 altering thus the grammar of the sentence.

---

63 Gardiner (1957: 397, § 486 Obs. 2 and marginal note 7).

In addition, the following Late Egyptian features are attested in L2:

Use of  *śt* instead of *=śn* (f. pl.), e.g.:

 (Ptahh. 49, L2 13)

śçm.t(ỉ)=śt
PTCP.POST-PL

instead of

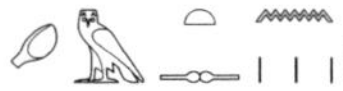 (Ptahh. 49, C 7)

śçm.t(ỉ)=śn
PTCP.POST-PL

'(for them) who will listen'.

Particle *ỉw* as an adverbial converter + *śçm.n=f*:

 (Ptahh. 129, L2 2,15–2,16)

mṭw(ị)	*=k*	*ỉw*	*wšṭ.n*	*=f*	*tw*
SBJV	=2SG.M	SBRD	address:PST	=3SG.M	=2SG.M

 (Ptahh. 129, P 7,1)

mṭw(ị)	*=k*	*ḫft*	*wšṭ*	*=f*	*tw*
SBJV	=2SG.M	in accordance with/when: PREP	address:PRS	=3SG.M	=2SG.M

'You should speak after (P: when) he addressed (P: addresses) you'

In Middle Egyptian, the subordination of the verb form *śçm.n=f* through the adverbial converter *ỉw* is only attested in a letter from Kahun.[64] This is not surprising for the 'communicative register' of documentary texts is characterized by the early use of elements from Late Egyptian. During the transmission of Ptahhotep, *ỉw śçm.n=f* in an adverbial subordination replaced the Middle Egyptian structure *ḫft* + *śçm=f* still preserved in Papyrus Prisse.

3.3 *Khakheperreseneb*: British Museum Board EA 5645 (EA 5645)

The Complaints of Khakheperreseneb survive in two Second Intermediate Period witnesses (Carnarvon Tablets VI and VII)[65] and in two other witnesses from the 18th Dynasty (British Museum Board EA 5645 and an ostracon (G) of uncertain location known today only from a photograph in Gardiner's files at the Griffith Institute).[66] Carnarvon Tablet VI contains

64 Brose (2014: 343, example 15). Schenkel (2007: 185–86).
65 Hagen (2019: 1–32).
66 Parkinson (1997²: 65).

the three first lines of the text preserved on recto of EA 5645, and Carnarvon Tablet VII only the first line plus a continuation of the text missing in the other witnesses. The text of the two tablets is written in Middle Egyptian with no Late Egyptian features. A comparison between Carnarvon Tablet VI and EA 5645 shows differences mainly in the spelling, for example (CT VI, 1) and (CT VI, 3) instead of (EA 5645, 1) and (EA 5645, 2). EA 5645 and Gardiner's ostracon belong to the same textual tradition[67] for they differ from each other only in a few details. The following Late Egyptian features can be identified in EA 5645:

1) New Kingdom spellings for Middle Egyptian words,[68] e.g.:

(EA 5645, 1 v.) for the word *ꜣh* 'misery'.

2) Dittography of *t* in the morpheme *tw*, e.g.:

(EA 5645, 11 r. = G 4) *wn{t}-tw*

wn{t}	*-tw*
neglect:PST	=IMPRS

'one neglected'.

3) Use of *pꜣ* and *nꜣ* as articles:

(EA 5645, 3 v.)

pꜣ	*hrw*
ART.M-SG	day:(M.SG)

'today (lit. the day)'.

In the Middle Kingdom, *pꜣ hrw* is only attested in the 'communicative register' of documentary texts (Heqanakht II 5 r. and Berlin 10063).[69] It occurs in the language of other text genres from the New Kingdom onwards.[70]

(...) (EA 5645, 1 v.)

(...) nꜣ	*n.t{ï}<w>*	*ẖt*	*tꜣ*
ART.PL	REL-M.PL	throughout:PREP	land:(M.SG)

'(...) what (lit.: the which) is throughout the land'.

67 Parkinson (1997²: 66).
68 More instances in Stauder (2013: 163, footnote 373).
69 Stauder (2013: 164–65).
70 Wb. II 499, 11.

Here *nꜣ* occurs as an article of the relative sentence used as a noun. This structure is common in Late Egyptian, but in the Middle Kingdom it occurs only in documentary texts.[71] In the literary works of this period, *pꜣ*, *tꜣ*, *nꜣ* are attested only as demonstratives used as reference words with a deictic meaning before relative forms and sentences.[72]

4) The Late Egyptian past *śč̣m=f*:

 (EA 5645, 10–11 r.)

śhꜣ	*tꜣ*	*ḫpr(.w)*	*m*	*ḥč̣*	*n?*
uproar (M.SG).STC	land(M.SG)	become:RES-3SG.M	as:PREP	destruction(M.SG)	for:PREP?

=ỉ	*ỉr.w*	*m*	*ḥtp(.w)*	***rč̣***	***-tw***	*mꜣꜥ.t*	*<r-> rw.tï*
=1SG	made:PRF-3SGM	in:PREP	rest(M.SG)	put:PST	=IMPRS	Truth(F.SG)	ADV

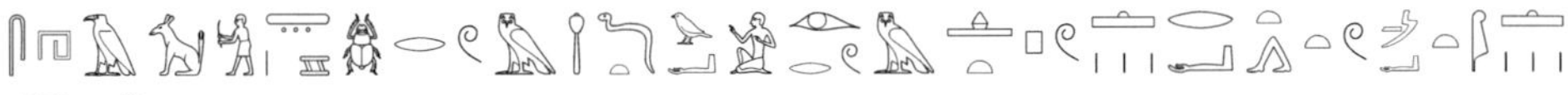
 (G 2–3)

śhꜣ	*tꜣ*	*ḫpr.w*	*m*	*ḥč̣.t*	*=ỉ*
uproar (M.SG).STC	land(M.SG)	become:RES-3SG.M	as:PREP	destroy:INF	=1SG

ỉr.w	*m*	*ḥtp.w*	***rč̣***	***-{t}tw***	*mꜣꜥ.t*	*r-rw.tï*
made:PRF-3SGM	in:PREP	rest(M.SG)	put:PST	=IMPRS	Truth(F.SG)	ADV

'The uproar of the land has become as a (G: my) destruction for (?) me and it has been made a state of rest. Truth was put outside'.

Although the Late Egyptian past *śč̣m=f* is unexpected in *Khakheperreseneb*, (since it is not attested in Middle Egyptian literary works), *rč̣-tw* must be so analysed because the verb *rč̣i̯* shows its usual spelling for the Late Egyptian past *śč̣m=f*, and the past meaning suits the context.[73] It is likely that the narrative infinitive *rč̣.t* was originally present in the Middle Kingdom *Vorlage* instead of the verb form *rč̣-tw*, as the writing with dittography *rč̣.{t}tw* in witness G suggests, which can also be considered a narrative infinitive if the signs 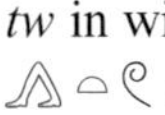 are read as *ỉwt* (the subjunctive form of *ỉwi̯*) 'Having let go the Truth outside'.[74] This assumption is also justified by the fact that New Kingdom scribes used the past *śč̣m=f* to replace the Middle Egyptian narrative infinitive, as attested in the New Kingdom witness AOS of Sinuhe (see §3.1 above).

71 Brose (2014: 69).

72 Cf. Stauder (2013: 164).

73 Stauder (2013: 161–62) suggests that, on semantic grounds, *rč̣-tw* might be a present tense. This is improbable because the verb *rč̣ỉ* is usually spelled  as a predicative present used, for example, after the particle *ỉw* or in a circumstantial sentence, or it is spelled  as an abstract-relative present used, for example, at the beginning of an emphatic construction. Neither of these spellings nor such syntactic uses occur in EA 5645, 10–11 r.

74 Parkinson (1997²: 66).

3.4 *Neferti*: Papyrus Petersburg 1116 (Pet)

The Prophecies of Neferti are preserved in 22 New Kingdom witnesses.[75] The main one is the mid-18th Dynasty Papyrus Petersburg 1116 containing the complete version of *Neferti*. Helck pointed out that Pet follows a different textual tradition from that of the Ramesside ostraca due to occasional omission and addition errors on them.[76] Particularly, the following Late Egyptian features occur in Pet:

1) New Kingdom spellings for Middle Egyptian words, e.g.:[77]

 (Nef. Ij, Pet 6) for  *ꜥš* 'call'.

 (Nef. Vd, Pet 25) for  *šnỉ.t* 'storm cloud'.

 (Nef. VIa, Pet 26) for  *ỉtr.w* 'river'.

 (Nef. VIe, Pet 28) for  *rś.w* 'South wind'.

2) The Ramesside spelling  for the suffix pronoun *=k* (2nd m. sing.) is attested once in Pet:[78]

 (Nef. VIIi, Pet 35)

śčr	*=k*	*ḥr*	*<čṭ>*
spend the night: SBJV	=2SG.M	on:PREP	<say: INF>

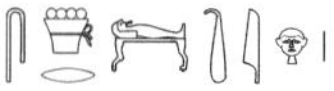 (Nef. VIIi, DeM 1074, 11)

śčr.tỉ ḥr <čṭ>

śčr.tỉ	*ḥr*	*<čṭ>*
spend the night: PRF-2SG	on=	<say: INF>

'You will (DeM 1074: may [pseudoparticiple in desiderative function]) spend the night <saying>'.

3)  *śt* instead of *śn* (f. pl.), e.g.:

(...)  (Nef. VIIIb, Pet 36) *śtr śt*

 (Nef. VIIIb, Vand 2) *[...] śn*

'(...) to respect them'.

---

75 Helck (1970¹: 1–2).

76 Helck (1970¹: 59–60).

77 Stauder (2013: 72–74).

78 Dils and Felber's reading; cf. their translation in *Thesaurus Linguae Aegyptiae*. On the use of that spelling in Ramesside literary and documentary texts, see Polis (2018: 106–08).

4) The word *nꜣ* used as the definite article:

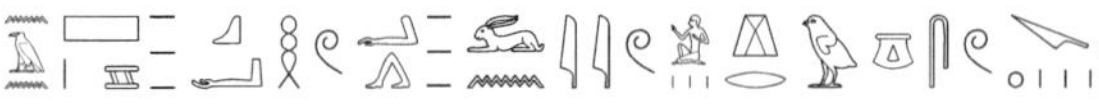 (Nef. VIIa, Pet 30)

nꜣ	*n*	*š(.w)-ḳꜥḥ.w*	*wn.yw*	*ẖr*	*gś.w*
ART.PL	of	fishponds(M.SG)	exist: PTCP-M.PL	under:PREP	animals(M.SG)

'The fishponds which are (full) with prey animals'.

In this passage, *nꜣ n(.ỉ)* has not the deictic meaning of a demonstrative adjective because the lakes are not related to the scope of Neferti. It is used to specify the lakes where fishing was usual, which is why *nꜣ n(.ỉ)* is frequently translated with the definite article in this passage.[79]

5) The early Late Egyptian future with *tw* occurs frequently, e.g.:

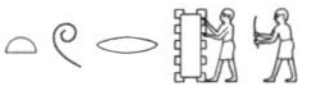 (...) (Nef. XVa, Pet 66 = C25229)[80]

tw	*r*	*ḳṭ (...)*
IMPRS	to=	build:INF

'One will build (...)'.

6–7) Two Late Egyptian features are attested in the following passage: the particle *ptr* with the meaning 'see' instead of the common particle *m=k*[81] and the particle *ỉw* as a circumstantial converter of an adverbial sentence:

 (Nef. VIIId, Pet 38, similar Vand. and C25224)

ptr [...]	*śčm*	*ḥr*	*ỉṭu̯<.t>*	*ỉw*	*gr*	*ẖf<t>-ḥr*
ATTN	hear: PTCP-M.SG	on=	be deaf: INF	SBRD	be silent: PTCP-M.SG	ADV

'See, the hearer is deaf, while the mute takes the lead'.

3.5 *The Teaching for Merikare*: Papyrus Ermitage 1116 A (E)

The main text witness of *The Teaching for Merikare* is the Papyrus Ermitage 1116 A v. (E) from the mid-18th Dynasty and it is partly preserved in two other witnesses from the end of the 18th Dynasty: Papyrus Moskau 4658 (M) and Papyrus Carlsberg VI (C). Some lines are also found on ostracon DM 1476 from the Ramesside period. According to Quack, witness E follows a textual tradition different from the one of M and C.[82] Late Egyptian features can be identified in E, for example:

79 Helck (1970¹: 30), Lichtheim (1975: 141) and Parkinson (1997¹: 136).

80 See other instances in VIb, Pet 27, VIIg and h, Pet 34, VIIIf, Pet 39 and Xh, Pet 48. Cf. Stauder (2013: 363–64).

81 See also Stauder (2013: 102).

82 Quack (1992: 11).

1) Use of  *śt* instead of *=śn* (f. pl.) and *=ś* (f. sg.), e.g.:

(...) 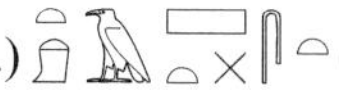 (Merikare E 82, see also E 56[83], E 84 and E 96)

(...) tȝš.t	*=śt*
boundary(M.SG)	=3SG.F

'(...) its (i.e. *nʾ.t* 'the city') boundary'.

2) The adverb *m-m* 'there(in)' first attested in the 18th Dynasty:

 (Merikare E 137, see another evidence in E 87)[84]

śmȝm.n	*=f*	*ẖȝk.w-ỉb*	*m-m*
slay:PST	=3SG.M	traitors(M.PL)	ADV

"It was therein, where he slew the traitors".

3) The expression *r-čȝw.t* 'in return for, in accordance with' common in the 18th Dynasty witnesses:[85]

(...)  (Merikare E 31) *(...) ḥśf=k r-čȝw.t [...]*

(...) ḥśf	*=k*	*r-čȝw.t [...]*
punish:PRS	=2SG.M	in accordance with:PREP

'(... that) you punish in accordance with [...]'.

4) *ḥmw-ỉb* 'with a skilful understanding' unattested before the New Kingdom:[86]

 (Merikare E 32–33) *n ỉy.n-tw ḥȝ ḥmw-ỉb*

n	*ỉy.n*	*-tw*	*ḥȝ*	*ḥmw-ỉb*
NEG	come: PST	=IMPRS	around:PREP	skillful(M.SG)

'One cannot overcome the skilful'.

83 Quack (1992: 37, remark b).

84 Wb. II 2, 17. See also Stauder (2013: 190).

85 Stauder (2013: 190–91).

86 Stauder (2013: 191).

5) At a syntactic level, the only Late Egyptian feature to be identified is the particle *ꞽw* used as an adverbial converter in the following sentence:[87]

 (Merikare E 40)

ḫm	*(ꞽ)ḫ(.w)t*	*pw*	*ḥntï*	*ꞽw*	*n*
be ignorant of:PTCP-M.SG	things(F.PL)	*pw*-SENT	covet:PTCP-M.SG	SBRD	for:PREP

k(y).wy
other:INDF.PL

'A fool is who covets, while others possess something (lit.: while something belongs to others)'.

3.6 *The Teaching of Amenemhat*: Papyri Millingen (M) and Sallier II (S II)

The Teaching of Amenemhat is attested on the walls of the tomb Assiut N13.1,[88] 6 papyri, 3 wooden boards, 1 leather scroll and more than 200 ostraca.[89] The main witness is Papyrus Millingen (M) from the mid-18th Dynasty (now lost).[90] But the text is preserved complete in the 19th Dynasty Papyrus Sallier II (S II), which also contains the *Teaching of Khety* (see §3.7 below). According to Helck, M follows the textual tradition of the Boards Brooklyn I and II produced during Amenhotep's II reign, which are the oldest witnesses containing *The Teaching of Amenemhat*. However, S II did not arise from M, but rather from the wooden board Carnarvon 5 dating from the period of Thutmosis IV.[91] Late Egyptian spellings, morphological and syntactic features can be found in witnesses M and S II, though they are more frequent in S II:

New Kingdom spellings, e.g.:

 (Amenemhat § 7b, M II,3 = S II) for  *ḥw-nï* 'attack'[92].
 (Amenemhat § 5b, M I,10 = similar S II) for *ḳmṭ* 'mourning'[93].

2)  for the suffix pronoun *=k* (2nd m. sing.), e.g.:[94]

 (Amenemhat § 1e, S II 10,2)[95] for 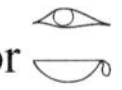 (Amenemhat § 1e, M 1,3)

ꞽr	*=k*
do:PRS	=2SG.M

'you do/make'.

87 Cf. Lichtheim (1975: 100), Quack (1992: 29), Parkinson (1997[1]: 219) and Dils' translation in *Thesaurus Linguae Aegyptiae*.
88 Verhoeven (2013: 143).
89 Adrom (2006: IX–XVII).
90 See the last study on Papyrus Millingen in Geoga (2021).
91 Helck (1969: 100–01).
92 Stauder (2013: 491).
93 Wb. V 40, 6. As often in Late Egyptian, *ḳꜣ* is used for *ḳ*.
94 Junge (2008: 53).
95 See other instances in § 3a, S II 1,4; § 7f, S II 2,3; and § 15i, S II 3,7.

(...)  (Amenemhat § 2c, M 1,4; S II: *m wᶜ.n=k*)

(...) m	*wᶜ*	*=k*
in/when:PREP	be alone:PRS	=2SG.M

'(...) when you are alone'.

3)  (Amenemhat § 5d, S II 1,8; destroyed in M) for the particle *ἰśt*.[96]

4) Use of  *śt* instead of *=śn* (f. pl.) and *=ś* (f. sg.), e.g.:

(...)  (Amenemhat § 2b, S II 1,3 and § 4b, S II, 16)

ḥr	*=śt*
because of:PREP	=3SG.F

'(...) because of it'.

Late Egyptian morphological and syntactic features:

5) The suffix pronoun *=w* (3rd pl.):

(Amenemhat § 5a–b, M 1,9)

śnn.w	*=ἰ*	*ᶜnḫ(.w)*	*psš(.w)*	*=ἰ*	*m*	*r(m)č(.w)*
image(M.PL)	=1SG	live: PTCP-M.SG	partner(M.PL)	=1SG	among:PREP	men(M.PL)

ἰr	***=w***	*n*	*=ἰ*	*ḳmṯ{.t}*
do:PRS	=3PL	for:PREP	=1SG	mourning(F.SG)

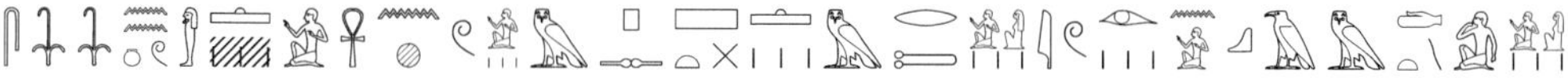

(Amenemhat § 5a–b, S II 1,7)

śnn.w	*=ἰ*	*ᶜnḫ.w*	*m*	*psš.t*	*m*	*r(m)č(.w)*
image(M.PL)	=1SG	live: PTCP-M.SG	as: PREP	partner (M.PL)	among: PREP	men (M.PL)

ἰw	***ἰr***	***=w***	*n*	*=ἰ*	*ḳmṯ{.t}*
MCM	do:PRS	=3PL	for: PREP	=1SG	mourning (F.SG)

M 1,9: 'My living images and my partner men, they make for me a mourning'.

S II 1,7: 'My living images are (lit.: like) partner among men. They make for me a mourning'.

The verb form *ἰr=w* has been frequently translated as an imperative,[97] though it is unsuitable here for syntactic and contextual reasons – the imperative is usually built indepen-

96 Amenemhat § 6e, M II,1 shows the spelling *ἰśw*, which should probably be emended *ἰś<t>w*.

97 Helck (1969: 37), Lichtheim (1975: 136) and Parkinson (1997[1]: 206). See also Dils' comment on this passage in his translation of *The Teaching of Amenemhat* published in *Thesaurus Linguae Aegyptiae*.

dently at the beginning of a sentence without antecedents in Middle Egyptian;[98] besides, the abrupt use of the imperative breaks the narrative sequence of the text, which is about Amenemhat's report on the causes of his death. For these reasons, Westendorf rejected the explanation of *ỉr=w* as an imperative and he considered this verb form as an active participle used as an attribute of *rmč(.w)* or as a predicate of a nominal sentence.[99] However, Westendorf's explanation is not convincing either: on the one hand, if *ỉr=w* is an attribute of *rmč(.w)*, then *psš* must be considered as a stative in the role of the predicate of the sentence, but the sign  (a determinative or the suffix pronoun *=ỉ*) makes clear that *psš* is not a stative, but rather a participle used as a noun; on the other hand, a nominal sentence with a participle as a predicate usually needs the particle *ỉn*, but this does not occur in any witness. In this connection, Blumenthal pointed out that the particle *ỉw* is written before *ỉr=w* in witnesses Sallier I and II. Therefore, for syntactic reasons only, ir may be a verb form accompanied by the Late Egyptian third person plural suffix pronoun *=w*,[100] which refers to *śnn.w=ỉ ꜥnḫ(.w) psš(.w)=ỉ m r(m)č(.w)* used as a topic in M 1,9.[101] In S II 1,7, *śnn.w=ỉ ꜥnḫ(.w) m psš.t m r(m)č(.w)* is an adverbial sentence preceding the one with the particle *ỉw* and the verb form *ỉr=w*.

6) The Late Egyptian pronoun *mntk*:

 (Amenemhat § 14e² + f², S II 3,4: M is lost) *mntk ỉb=k çs=k*

mntk	*ỉb*	*=k*	*ç̣s*	*=k*
2SG.M	heart(M.SG)	=2SG.M	own(M.SG)	=2SG.M

'Your own heart belongs to you (lit.: you are your own heart)'.

7) The negative *bw* instead of *n* (for this instance see also § 2, above):

(...) 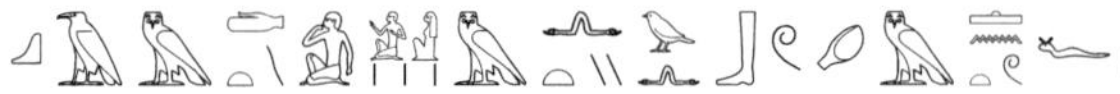 (Amenemhat § 5b, S II 1,7–1,8)

(...) ḳmṭ{.t}	*m*	*ỉw.tỉ*	***{n} bw***	*śç̣m.**n***	*-tw*	*=f*
mourning(F.SG)	as:PREP	NEG.REL-M.SG	NEG	hear:PST	=IMPRS	=3SG.M

(...)  (Amenemhat § 5b, M 1, 9–10)

(...) ḳmṭ{.t}	*n.tỉ*	***n***	*śç̣m*	*-tw*	*=f*
mourning(F.SG)	REL-M.SG	NEG	hear:PST	=IMPRS	=3SG.M

'(...) a mourning which could not be heard (S II: as one which cannot be heard)'.

---

98 Gardiner (1957: 258, §337).

99 Westendorf (1981: 36).

100 Blumenthal (1984: 88, footnote 23).

101 In Schenkel's terminology *śnn.w=ỉ ꜥnḫ(.w) psš(.w)=ỉ m r(m)č(.w)* is a 'Rang-IV-Erweiterung/unmarkiertes substantivisches Topik', see Schenkel (2012¹: 74–75).

M shows the Middle Egyptian variant with the negative structure *n śčm-tw=f*, which was replaced by Late Egyptian *bw śčm.n-tw=f* in S II. The original negative *n* continued to be transmitted as an error in S II.

3.7 *Khety*: Papyrus Amherst XIV (A XIV), Board Louvre 693 (L 693) and Papyrus Sallier II (S II)

The Teaching of Khety is attested since the 18th Dynasty in ten papyri, four wooden boards, more than 280 ostraca and in two graffiti in the tomb Assiut N13.1.[102] The oldest witnesses are Papyrus Amherst XIV (A XIV) and the Board Louvre 693 (L 693) dating from the 18th Dynasty. L 693 does not show any Late Egyptian features although it contains more text than A XIV. Comparison with 19th Dynasty witnesses shows that L 693 stems directly from Middle Kingdom textual tradition because it does not contain any Late Egyptian features. On the contrary, two Late Egyptian features can be found in A XIV:

1) Use of  *śt* instead of *=śn* (f. pl.) and *=ś* (f. sg.), e.g.:

 (Khety § 11,2/2, A XIV 2,4)

k3.(w)t	*=śt*
work(F.PL)	=3PL

'their works'.

2) Omission of the preposition *ḥr* in the pseudoverbal construction:

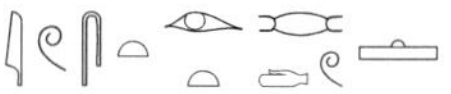 (Khety § 12,2, A XIV 3,2)

ἰw	*=śt*	<*ḥr*>	*ἰr.t*	*ʿṭ.w*
MCM	=3SG.F	<on=>	do: INF	fat(M.SG)

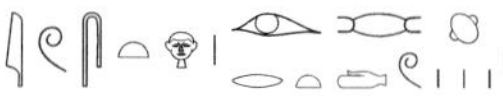 (Khety § 12,2, S II 5,6) *ἰw=śt ḥr ἰr.t ʿṭ.w*

ἰw	*=śt*	*ḥr*	*ἰr.t*	*ʿṭ.w*
MCM	=3SG.F	<on=>	do: INF	fat(M.SG)

'It (i.e. his neck) is making fat (this means, festering)'.

The Ramessid Papyrus Sallier II (S II) is considered the main witness of *The Teaching of Khety* because it is preserved in full. It contains *The Teaching of Amenemhat* (see §3.6, above) and also *The Hymn to Hapi*, and it was copied by the scribe Inena,[103] who also penned *The Teaching of Khety* in Papyrus Anastasi VII (A VII). Both witnesses are charac-

---

102 Jäger (2004: 5) and Widmaier (2013: 506–08). For the textual transmission of this literary work see Helck (1970^2: 152–58).

103 For Inena see Allon & Navratilova (2017: 103–19).

terized by a great number of Late Egyptian features, whether graphemic, morphological or syntactic.

Graphemic features:

1)  for the suffix pronoun *=k* (2nd m. sing.), e.g.:

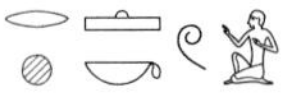 (Khety §22, S II 9,2) for 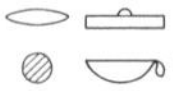 (Louvre 693, 13 v.)

rḫ	*=k*
know:PRS	=2SG.M

'you know'.

2)  (Khety §1,3/1, S II 3,9) for the particle *ỉśt*.

3)  (Khety §20,2, S II 8,7) for the particle *ḥꜣ* 'if only'.

4) Dittography of *t* in the morpheme *tw* and addition of *w* after the ending *t*, especially before suffix pronouns, e.g.:

 (Khety §9,2/2, S II 5,8)

ꜣḥ.t{tw}	*=f*
field(F.PL)	=3SG.M

'his fields'.

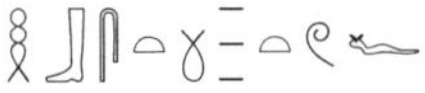 (Khety §9,2/2, S II 5,8)

ḥbs.t{tw}	*=f*
cloth(F.PL)	=3SG.M

'his clothes'.

 (Khety §2,5, S II 4,3) *ś.t{tw}=f*

ś.t{tw}	*=f*
seat(F.SG)	=3SG.M

'his seat'.

Morphological features:

5) *ỉ*-augment in the nominal verb form *ỉ:č̣t=f*:

 (Khety §27,1/1–2 S II, 10,3)

ỉ:č̣t	*{=f}*	*<=k>*	*mỉ*	*ỉ:č̣t*	*=f*	*św*
speak:NMLZ	{=3SG.M}	<=2SG.M >	like:PREP	speak:NMLZ	=3SG.M	3SG.M

'It is as he speaks, how you have to speak'.

6) Use of  *śt* instead of *=śn* (f. pl.) and *=ś* (f. sg.), e.g.:

(...)  (Khety §2,4/1, S II 4,3 and § 3,2, S II 4,5)

(...) ỉm	*=śt*
in:PREP	=3PL

'(...) in it'.

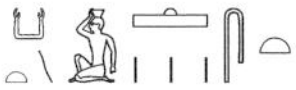 (Khety §7,3, S II 5,5)

kꜣ.(w)t	*=śt*
work(F.PL)	=3PL

'their works'.

7) Use of the definite article *pꜣ*, *tꜣ*, *nꜣ* and the possessive adjective *pꜣy=f*, *tꜣy=f*, *nꜣy=f*, e.g.:

 (Khety §21,3, S II 8,9) (see another instance of *pꜣ* in Khety § 21,4, S II 9,1)

pꜣ	*ỉp.w*
ART:M.SG	payment(M.SG)

'the payment'.

 (Khety §9,6, S II 5,9)

nꜣ	*ỉwy.(w)t*
ART:PL	public place(F.PL)

'the public places'.

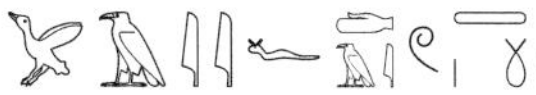 (Khety § 16,4, S II 7,8)

pꜣ	*=f*	*ṯꜣỉ.w*
POSS:M.SG	=3SG.M	linen cloth(PL)

'his linen cloth'.

8) The Late Egyptian pronouns *mntk* and *mntf* instead of *ntk* and *ntf*, e.g.:[104]

 (Khety §21,6/2 S II 9,2)

mntf	*ẖrp.w*
3SG.M	administrator(M.SG)

 (Khety §21,6/2 A VII 4,6)

nt{w}f	*ẖrp.w*
3SG.M	administrator(M.SG)

 (Khety §21,6/2 L 693, 12 v.) *ntf pw ẖrp[...]*

ntf	*pw*	*ẖrp[w ...]*
3SG.M	*pw*-SENT	administrator(M.SG)

'He is the administrator'.

Syntactic features:

9) Omission of *ḥr* in the adverbial sentence:

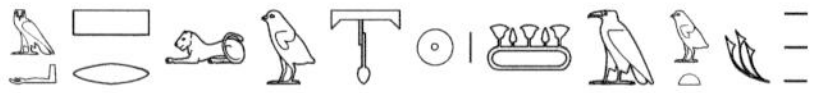 (Khety §12,3/1–2 S II, 6,7)

mšr.w	*<ḥr>*	*š3w.t*
evening(M.SG)	<on:PREP>	coriander(F.SG)

 (Khety §12,3/1–2 A XIV, 3,3)

mšr.w	*ḥr*	*š3w.t*
evening(M.SG)	on:PREP	coriander(F.SG)

'(He passes) the (A XIV: his) evening by the coriander'.

10) Early Late Egyptian future with *tw* and omission of *r*, e.g.:

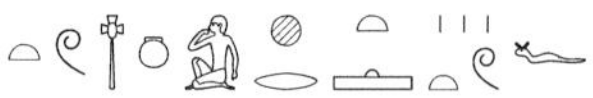 (Khety §3,5 S II, 4,6)[105] *tw <r> nḏ ẖr.t{tw}=f*

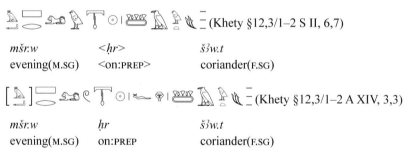

tw	*<r>*	*nḏ*	*ẖr.t{tw}*	*=f*
IMPRS	<to=>	ask:INF	state(F.SG)	=3SG.M

'One will greet him'.

104 See another instance in Khety §24,1 S II 9,7.

105 See another instance in Khety §3,6 S II, 4,6.

11) Particle *ỉw* as an adverbial converter without a suffix pronoun as a subject + an adverbial sentence:

 (Khety §24,2–3 S II, 9,8)

ỉr	*ʿḳ*	*=k*	*ỉw*	*nb{.t}*	*m*	*pr*	*=f*
COND	come:PRS	=2SG.M	CORD	lord(M.SG)	in:PREP	house(M.SG)	=3SG.M
ỉw	*bw<ȝ>*	*ʿ.wỉ*	*=f*	*n*	*ky*	*r-ḥȝt*	*=k*
CORD	be high:PRS	hand(M.DU)	=3SG.M	for:PREP	other:INDF.M.SG.	before:PREP	=2SG.M
ỉw	*ḥms*	*=k*	*čr.t*	*=k*	*m*	*rʾ*	*=k*
MCM	sit:PRS	=2SG.M	hand(F.SG)	=2SG.M	in:PREP	mouth(M.SG)	=2SG.M

'When you come in, being the lord of the house in his house, while his hands are high honouring someone else before you, you should sit with your hand in your mouth'.

12) Negative *bw* + *śčm=f*:

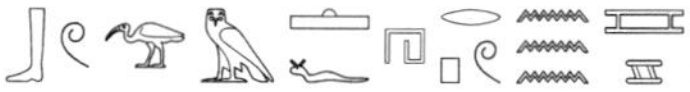 (Khety § 20,1 S II, 8,6)

bw	*gm*	*=f*	*hrp.w*
NEG	find: PRS	=3SG.M	be immersed:STAT-3SG.M

'He does not find anything when he is immersed (under the water)'.

3.8 *Ipuwer*: Papyrus Leiden 344 r. (L 344)

The *Admonitions of Ipuwer* are preserved only in the 19th Dynasty Papyrus Leiden 344 r., where the following Late Egyptian features can be identified:[106]

1) Late Egyptian spellings for words attested in earlier periods, for example:

 (L 344, 3.7) instead of  *ptr* 'what'.
 (L 344, 2.6) instead of  *ỉtr.w* 'river'.
 (L 344, 6.11) instead of 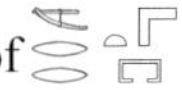 *mrr.t* 'street'.
 (L 344, 12.4; cf. Amenemhat §7b, M II,3 = S II) instead of  *ḥw-nï* 'attack'.
 (L 344, 4.5) *mḥʿ.w* 'flax'.

106 Cf. Gardiner (1909: 2–4), Enmarch (2008: 20–22).

2) Use of  *śt* instead of *=śn* (f. pl.) and *=ś* (f. sg.), e.g.:

 (L 344, 2.6)

(...) ỉm *=śt*
in:PREP =3SG.F

'(...) in it'.

(...)  (L 344, 5.4)

(...) ḥr *=śt*
on:PREP =3SG.F

'(...) on it'.

 (L 344, 5.7)

śmꜣm *=śt*
slay:PRS =3PL

'(Terror) slays them (i.e. the children)'.[107]

3) Dittography of *t* in the morpheme *tw* and addition of *w* after the ending *t* e.g.:

 (L 344, 8.2)

ḥś.t{w} *=f*
favour:INF =3SG.M

'to favour him'.

 (L 344, 9.3)

ỉn.t{w}
carry:INF

'to carry'.

 (L 344, 7.13)

šwy.t{tw} *=f*
shade(F.SG) =3SG.M

'his shade'.

107 See other instances in L 344, 9.5 (*pr=śt* '(who) lends it out') and L 344, 12.1 (*nw(.t)=śt* 'to care them').

4) Late Egyptian features are hardly recognized at a syntactic level in Papyrus Leiden 344. In this regard, it is only remarkable to notice the uncommon use of the particle *ḫr* with particles *kꜣ* and *ỉs*, unattested elsewhere in the Middle Egyptian text corpus:

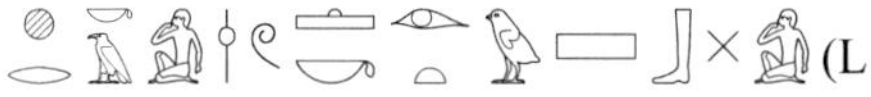 (L 344, 12.14)

ḫr *kꜣ* *wč̣* *=k* *ỉr.t* *wšb*

PTCL PTCL order:SBJV =2SG.M make:INF answer(M.SG)

'And then you should order the making of an answer'.[108]

4 Conclusions

Late Egyptian features in New Kingdom witnesses of Middle Egyptian literary works are a consequence of the situation of diglossia involving the *égyptien de tradition* i.e. the classical variant of Middle Egyptian and Late Egyptian in the New Kingdom. They are the result of a shift-induced interference from Late Egyptian as source language (L_1) into Middle Egyptian as recipient language (L_2) made by New Kingdom scribes. In fact, this phenomenon is already attested in the Second Intermediate Period, when lexical and grammatical features are transferred from Late Egyptian and Middle Kingdom 'communicative register' into the 'commemorative register' of historical-biographical texts and the 'recreative register' of literary texts, as for example: the definite article *pꜣ*, *tꜣ*, *nꜣ*, the pseudoverbal construction without *ḥr*, the First Present *tw=ỉ* / *św ḥr śč̣m* and the Late Egyptian past *śč̣m=f*.[109]

However, a distinction must be emphasized between the two historical cases of shift-induced interference: in the Second Intermediate Period, Middle Egyptian was still spoken at least till the end of the 17th Dynasty and the interference is probably due to stylistic reasons between linguistic registers. On the contrary, Middle Egyptian in New Kingdom literary witnesses was already considered as a classical language to be used only on special occasions following the 'Latinate' pattern according to which a language is first lost in domestic contexts and then restricted to high registers.[110] Though Classical Egyptian was no longer spoken in the New Kingdom, it was used as a standardized written language and it was constantly evolving due to the introduction of Late Egyptian features. Mastery in using and writing classical Egyptian without any kind of Late Egyptian features depended on good learning and training by the New Kingdom scribes.[111] If a Middle Egyptian word or grammar structure was no longer understood or it was considered obsolete during textual transmission, it was replaced by a more common Late Egyptian one, and the text continued to be handed down. It must therefore be stressed that Late Egyptian features were introduced by New Kingdom scribes in order to modernize Middle Egyptian texts. That

108 For this sentence see Stauder (2013: 467), who remarks that the particle *ḫr* can precede any construction in Late Egyptian. *Hr ỉś* occurs in L 344, 3.12.

109 Díaz Hernández (2017: 62–64).

110 Gal (1996: 588).

111 The main reason for shift-induced interference is indeed the imperfect learning of a second language, see Thomason and Kaufman (1988: 39 and 145–46).

is why the replacement of old spellings or grammatical structures by their Late Egyptian equivalents, such as the Middle Egyptian adverbial sentence by the First Present or the negative *n* by *bw*, must be seen as linguistic variants instead of scribal errors.

According to Thomason and Kaufman, 'any linguistic feature can be transferred from any language to any other language'.[112] Indeed, New Kingdom witnesses of Middle Egyptian literary works contain five types of Late Egyptian features: graphemic, lexical, morphological, semantic and syntactic. However, the frequency of Late Egyptian features varies according to the witness: they are scarce on Papyrus Ermitage 1116 A (*Merikare*) and Papyrus Leiden 344 r. (*Ipuwer*), they occur occasionally on Papyrus Prisse (*Kagemni* and *Ptahhotep*), Papyrus BM EA 10509 (*Ptahhotep*), the Board British Museum EA 5645 (*Khakheperreseneb*), Papyrus Petersburg 1116 (*Neferti*) and Papyrus Millingen (*Amenemhat*), whereas they are frequent on the Ahsmolean Ostracon 1945.40 (*Sinuhe*) and on Papyrus Sallier II (*Khety*). Particularly, Late Egyptian features in those texts can be classified according to their typology (figures match those used in table 2, below):

(I) Graphemic and (II) lexical features:

1. Late Egyptian expressions and New Kingdom spellings for words attested in older times.
2. Dittography of *t* in the morpheme *tw* and addition of *w* after the ending *t*.
3.  for the suffix pronoun *=k* (2nd m. sing.)
4.  for the particle *ἰśt*.

(III) Morphological features:

5. The ending *.w* of strong verbs used as subjunctive verb forms.
6. The *ἰ*-augment in nominal verb forms.
7. The Late Egyptian suffix pronoun *=w*.
8.  *śt* used as the suffix pronouns *=ś* (f. sg.) and *=śn* (f. pl.).
9. The Late Egyptian independent pronouns.
10. The definite article *pꜣ*, *tꜣ*, *nꜣ*.
11. The possessive adjective.

(IV) Semantic features:

12. The particle *ptr* with the meaning 'see' instead of the common particle *m=k*.
13. The Late Egyptian past *śc̣m=f*.

(V) Syntactic features:

14. The omission of the preposition *ḥr* in pseudoverbal constructions.
15. The Late Egyptian adverbial sentence.
16. The First Present *tw=ἰ / św ḥr śc̣m*.
17. The early Late Egyptian future *tw=ἰ / św / tw r śc̣m*.
18. The negative structure *bw śc̣m / śc̣m.n=f*.
19. The particle *ἰw* as a circumstantial converter of an adverbial sentence

112 Thomason and Kaufman (1988: 14).

Finally, the existence of Late Egyptian features by shift-induced interference in New Kingdom witnesses of Middle Egyptian literary works should be taken into account when using those texts as sources for linguistic principles or theories in Middle Egyptian grammars and studies. They may readily be used as examples of grammatical structures already attested in Middle Kingdom witnesses with the warning that the source comes from the New Kingdom. Indeed, excellent examples for teaching purposes can be found in the New Kingdom witnesses. But it must be kept in mind that those texts are characterized by the use of Middle Egyptian as a standardized language containing Late Egyptian features.

Table 2 | Typology of the Late Egyptian features in New Kingdom witnesses of Middle Egyptian literary works

	Sin.	Kag./ Ptahh.	Ptahh.	Khakh	Nef.	Mer.	Amenemhat		Khety		Ipuwer
	AOS	P	L2	EA	Pet	E	M	S II	S II	A XIV	L 344
	I.–II. Graphemic and lexical features										
1.	✓				✓	✓	✓	✓	✓		✓
2.				✓					✓		✓
3.					✓		✓	✓	✓		
4.	✓							✓	✓		
III. Morphological features											
5.		✓	✓								
6.									✓		
7.							✓	✓			
8.	✓	✓	✓		✓	✓		✓	✓	✓	✓
9.	✓							✓	✓		
10.				✓	✓				✓		
11.		✓							✓		
IV. Semantic features											
12.					✓						
13.	✓			✓							
V. Syntactic features											
14.	✓	✓							✓	✓	
15.		✓									
16.	✓										
17.		✓	✓		✓				✓		
18.								✓			
19.		✓	✓		✓	✓			✓		

5 Bibliography

Adrom, Faried. 2006. *Die Lehre des Amenemhet*. Brepols; Bibliotheca Aegyptiaca XIX.

Allen, James. 2014. *Middle Egyptian. An Introduction to the Language and Culture of Hieroglyphs*. Cambridge.

Allen, James. 2015. *Middle Egyptian Literature. Eight Literary Works of the Middle Kingdom*. Cambridge.

Allon, Niv and Hana Navratilova. 2017. *Ancient Egyptian Scribes. A Cultural Exploration*. Bloomsbury; Bloomsbury Egyptology.

Barns, John Wintour. 1952. *The Ashmolean Ostracon of Sinuhe*. London & Oxford.

Blumenthal, Elke. 1984. 'Die Lehre des Königs Amenemhet (Teil I)', *Zeitschrift für Ägyptische Sprache und Altertumskunde* 111, 85–107.

Brose, Marc. 2014. *Grammatik der dokumentarischen Texte des Mittleren Reiches*. Hamburg; Lingua Aegyptia Studia Monographica 13.

Brose, Marc. 2019. 'Zur Genese des präteritalen *sḏm=f* des Neuägyptischen', *Lingua Aegyptia* 27, 41–60.

Burkard, Günther. 1977. *Textkritische Untersuchungen zu ägyptischen Weisheitslehren des alten und mittleren Reiches*. Wiesbaden; Ägyptologische Abhandlungen 34.

Burkard, Günther. 1991. 'Die Lehre des Ptahhotep', in: Kaiser, Otto (ed.). *Texte aus der Umwelt des Alten Testaments* III.2. *Weisheitstexte* II. Berlin, 195–221.

Cahail, Kevin. 2019. 'The earliest attestation of the Late Egyptian *tw=j ḥr sḏm* construction in the Second Intermediate Period tomb of Seneb-Kay at South Abydos: evidence of a residence sociolect?', *Revue d'Égyptologie* 69, 15–34.

Clyne, Michael. 1991. *Community Languages. The Australian Experience*. Cambridge.

Delnero, Paul. 2012. 'Memorization and the transmission of Sumerian literary compositions', *Journal of Near Eastern Studies* 71, 189–208.

Dévaud, Eugène. 1924. *L'âge des papyrus égyptiens hiératiques d'après les graphies de certains mots (de la XIIe dynastie à la fin de la XVIIIe dynastie)*. Paris.

Roberto A. Díaz Hernández. 2013. *Tradition und Innovation in der offiziellen Sprache des Mittleren Reiches. Ein strukturalistischer Vergleich der historisch-biographischen mit den literarischen Texten der 1. Zwischenzeit und der 12. Dynastie*. Göttingen; Göttinger Orientforschungen IV 56.

Roberto A. Díaz Hernández. 2017. 'Die Weiterentwicklung der offiziellen Sprache in der 2. Zwischenzeit', *Lingua Aegyptia* 24, 41–65.

Roberto A. Díaz Hernández. 2021a. 'The Man-impersonal *śčm.n-tỉ/tw(=f)* Form in Earlier Egyptian', *Lingua Aegyptia* 29, 37–59.

Roberto A. Díaz Hernández. 2021b. *Libro de ejercicios para la gramática de egipcio clásico*. Alicante.

Roberto A. Díaz Hernández. 2022. 'The Man-impersonal Verb Forms of the Suffix Pronoun Conjugation in Earlier Egyptian', *Lingua Aegyptia* 30, 25–90.

Edel, Elmar. 1959. 'Die Herkunft des neuägyptisch-koptischen Personalsuffixes der 3. Person Plural *-w*', *Zeitschrift für Ägyptische Sprache und Altertumskunde* 84, 17–38.

Enmarch, Roland. 2008. *A World Upturned: Commentary on and Analysis of The Dialogue of Ipuwer*. Oxford.

Erman, Adolf & Hermann Grapow (eds). 1926–1963. *Das Wörterbuch der Ägyptischen Sprache*. Berlin.

Gal, Susan. 1996. 'Language shift', in: Goebl, Hans, Peter Nelde et al. (eds). *Kontaktlinguistik. Contact Linguistics. Linguistique de contact*. Berlin/New York, 586–93.

Gardiner, Alan. 1909. *The Admonitions of an Egyptian Sage from a Hieratic Papyrus in Leiden (Pap. Leiden 344 Recto)*. Leipzig.

Gardiner, Alan. 1957. *Egyptian Grammar. Being an Introduction to the Study of Hieroglyphs*. Oxford.

Geoga, Margaret. 2021 'New insights into Papyrus Millingen and the reception history of The Teaching of Amenemhat', *Journal of Egyptian Archaeology* 107, 225–38.

Griffith, Francis. 1889. *The Inscriptions of Siûṭ and dêr Rîfeh*. London.

Hagen, Fredrik. 2012. *An Ancient Egyptian Literary Text in Context. The Instruction of Ptahhotep*. Leuven/Paris; Orientalia Lovaniensia Analecta 218.

Hagen, Fredrik. 2019. 'New copies of old classics: Early manuscripts of *Khakheperreseneb* and *The Instruction of a Man for His Son*', *Journal of Egyptian Archaeology* 105, 177–208.

Helck, Wolfgang. 1969. *Der Text der „Lehre Amenemhets I. für seinen Sohn"*. Wiesbaden; Kleine Ägyptische Texte.

Helck, Wolfgang. 1970[1]. *Die Prophezeiung des Nfr.tj*. Wiesbaden; Kleine Ägyptische Texte.

Helck, Wolfgang. 1970[2]. *Die Lehre des Dwꜣ-Ḫtjj, Teile I und II*. Wiesbaden; Kleine Ägyptische Texte.

Jäger, Stephan. 2004. *Altägyptische Berufstypologien*. Göttingen; Lingua Aegyptia Studia Monographica 4.

Joseph, Brian. 2019. 'Historical Linguistics in the 50 years since Weinreich, Labov, and Herzog (1968)', in: Boas, Hans & Marc Pierce (eds). *New Directions for Historical Linguistics*. Leiden & Boston; Brill's Studies in Historical Linguistics 9, 153–73.

Junge, Friedrich. 2008. *Einführung in die Grammatik des Neuägyptischen*. Wiesbaden.

Junge, Friedrich. 2003. *Die Lehre Ptahhoteps und die Tugenden der ägyptischen Welt*. Fribourg/Göttingen; Orbis Biblicus et Orientalis 193.

Kahl, Jochem. 1998. 'Es ist vom Anfang bis zum Ende so gekommen, wie es in der Schrift gefunden worden war. Zur Überlieferung der Erzählung des Sinuhe', in: Dietrich, Manfried & Ingo Kottsieper (eds). *"Und Mose schrieb dieses Lied auf". Studien zum Alten Testament und zum Alten Orient. Festschrift für Oswald Loretz zur Vollendung seines 70. Lebensjahres mit Beiträgen von Freunden, Schülern und Kollegen*. Münster; Alter Orient und Altes Testament 250, 383–400.

Kaper, Olaf. 2010. 'A Kemyt Ostracon from Amheida, Dakhleh Oasis', *Bulletin de l'Institut Français d'Archéologie Orientale* 110, 115–26.

Kroeber, Burkhart. 1970. *Die Neuägyptizismen vor der Amarnazeit. Studien zur Entwicklung der ägyptischen Sprache vom Mittleren zum Neuen Reich*. Tübingen.

Lichtheim, Miriam. 1975. *Ancient Egyptian Literature: A Book of Readings I: The Old and Middle Kingdoms*. Berkeley.

Loprieno, Antonio, Matthias Müller & Sami Uljas. 2017. *Non-Verbal Predication in Ancient Egyptian*. Berlin, Boston; The Mouton Companies to Ancient Egyptian.

Malaise, Michel & Winand, Jean. 1999. *Grammaire raisonnée de l'égyptien classique*. Liège; Ægyptiaca Leodiensia 6.

Panov, Maxim. 2021. *The Manuscripts of the Maxims of Ptahhotep*. Novosibirsk.

Parkinson, Richard. 1991. *The Tale of the Eloquent Peasant*. Oxford.

Parkinson, Richard. 1997[1]. *The Tale of Sinuhe and Other Ancient Egyptian Poems 1940–1640 BC*. Oxford; Oxford World's Classics.

Parkinson, Richard. 1997[2]. 'The text of "Khakheperreseneb": New readings of EA 5645, and an unpublished ostracon', *Journal of Egyptian Archaeology* 83, 55–68.

Polis, S. 2018. 'The scribal repertoire of Amennakhte son of Ipuy. Describing variation across Late Egyptian registers', in: Cromwell, Jennifer & Grossman, Eitan (eds). *Scribal Repertoires in Egypt from the New Kingdom to the Early Islamic Period*. Oxford; Oxford Studies in Ancient Documents, 89–126.

Quack, Joachim. 1992. *Studien zur Lehre für Merikare*. Wiesbaden; Göttinger Orientforschungen IV/23.

Ragazzoli, Chloé. 2017. 'Beyond authors and copyists: The role of variation in Ancient Egyptian and New Kingdom literary production', in: Gillen, Todd (ed.). *(Re)productive Traditions in Ancient Egypt. Proceedings of the Conference held at the University of Liège, 6th–8th February 2013*. Liège; Ægyptiaca Leodiensia 10, 95–126.

Ragazzoli, Chloé. 2019. *Scribes: les artisans du texte de l'Égypte ancienne (1550–1000)*. Paris.

Reynolds, Leighton & Nigel Wilson. 1991. *Scribes and Scholars. A Guide to the Transmission of Greek and Latin Literature*. Oxford.

Schenkel, Wolfgang. 2007. 'Die Partikel *ỉw* und die Intuition des Interpreten. Randbemerkungen zu Antonio Loprieno „On fuzzy boundaries in Egyptian syntax"', *Lingua Aegyptia* 15, 161–201.

Schenkel, Wolfgang. 2012[1]. *Tübinger Einführung in die klassisch-ägyptische Sprache und Schrift*. Tübingen.

Schenkel, Wolfgang. 2012[2]. 'Mitteläg yptische Grammatik: von den Texten zu den Texten', *Bibliotheca Orientalis* 69, 13–42.

Schneider, Thomas. 2023. *Language Contact in Ancient Egypt*. Berlin; Einführungen und Quellentexte zur Ägyptologie 16.

Stauder, Andréas. 2013. *Linguistic Dating of Middle Egyptian Literary Texts*. Hamburg; Lingua Aegyptia Studia Monographica 12.

Stauder, Andréas. 2016. 'Ptahhotep 82 P', in: Collombert, Philippe, Dominique Lefèvre, Stéphane Polis & Jean Winand (eds). *Aere Perennius. Mélanges égyptologiques en l'honneur de Pascal Vernus*. Leuven; Orientalia Lovaniensia Analecta 242, 779–810.

Thomason, Sarah. 2019. 'Historical Linguistics since 1968: On some of the causes of linguistic change', in: Boas, Hans & Marc Pierce (eds), *New Directions for Historical Linguistics*. Leiden & Boston; Brill's Studies in Historical Linguistics 9, 110–131.

Thomason, Sarah & Terrence Kaufman. 1988. *Language Contact, Creolization, and Genetic Linguistics*. Berkeley & Los Angeles.

Verhoeven, Ursula. 2013. 'Literatur im Grab – der Sonderfall Assiut', in Moers, Gerald, Kai Widmaier, Antonia Giewekemeyer, Arndt Lümers & Ralf Ernst (eds). *Dating Egyptian Literary Texts*. Hamburg; Lingua Aegyptia Studia Monographica 11, 139–158.

Weinreich, Uriel. 1953. *Languages in Contact. Findings and Problems*. New York.

Westendorf, Wolfhart. 1981. 'Die Menschen als Ebenbilder Pharaos. Bemerkungen zur Lehre des Amenemhet' (Abschnitt V). *Göttinger Miszellen* 46, 33–42.

Widmaier, Kai. 2013. 'Die Lehre des Cheti und ihre Kontexte. Zu Berufen und Berufsbilder im Neuen Reich', in Moers, Gerald, Kai Widmaier, Antonia Giewekemeyer, Arndt Lümers & Ralf Ernst (eds). *Dating Egyptian Literary Texts*. Hamburg; Lingua Aegyptia Studia Monographica 11, 483–557.

Winand, Jean. 2014. 'The *Tale of Sinuhe*. History of a literary text', in: Hays, Harold, Frank Feder & Ludwig Morenz (eds). *Interpretations of Sinuhe*. Leuven; Egyptologische Uitgaven 27, 215–43.

Žába, Zbyněk. 1956. *Les Maximes de Ptaḥḥotep. Prague.*

Zöller-Engelhardt, Monika. 2016. *Sprachwandelprozesse im Ägyptischen: eine funktional-typologische Analyse vom Alt- zum Neuägyptischen*. Wiesbaden.

Semantic Fields in Ancient Egyptian Philology

Verbs of Motion as Explained on Two Roman Period Writing Boards

Hans-Werner Fischer-Elfert[1]

1 Preliminaries

The number of original sources bearing testimony on ancient Egyptian philology and grammar is still rather limited. Exercises on grammatical paradigms such as tenses are known particularly from Demotic and have been edited and commented upon e.g. by Ursula Kaplony-Heckel[2] and most recently by Luigi Prada.[3] A BM hieratic manuscript carrying intralinear translations from Middle to Late Egyptian or early Demotic was identified and interpreted by Joachim Quack.[4] The Onomastika from Tebtunis, dating to the 2nd century CE and edited by Jürgen Osing, with their supralinear *matres lectionis* in Demotic and Old Coptic script, render further information on the contemporary pronunciation of ancient words and entire verb forms from times long past. Annotations on the reading of old titles with so–called honorific transposition in the Copenhagen manuscript of copies of Assiut inscriptions from the First Intermediate Period give an idea of the extensive amount of

---

1 First of all, I would like to express my warmest thanks to the organizers for their kind invitation – and their insistence – to attend this distinguished series of conferences constantly represented by the leading experts on the Egyptian language. As I have never developed any degree of expertise in linguistic matters in general nor in Egyptian ones in particular, I take it as a special honor of having had the chance to present some uninvestigated lexical material in addition to some already ongoing discussions, with a particular focus on the verbs of motion. My thanks also go to Katharina Stegbauer (Leipzig Univ.) and Svenja Damm (Sächsische Akademie der Wissenschaften zu Leipzig) for taking the trouble to turn my handmade transcription of the passages quoted into digital ones. Contrary to what is stated on https://www.schoyencollection.com/papyri–ostraca–collection/hieratic/papyrus–dictionary–ms–189 (accessed August 2020), publication rights of the Schøyen board have been transferred to the present writer by the owner of the Oslo collection, Dr. Martin Schøyen, in March 2015, to whom I render my sincerest thanks. I also feel deeply obliged to Prof. William J. Tait (UCL) for his generosity to make use of his transcription of the Schøyen tablet, which has, no doubt, been extremely helpful. The same applies to Prof. Erhart Graefe from Münster University for sharing his material on and photographs of the TT 34 tablet. – It should also be mentioned that the images of the Schøyen-tablet rt. and vs. and the cut-outs as presented here have been enhanced by means of the *Hierax. Software for Enhancing the Legibility of Papyri* tool: https://hierax.ch/. Since the current whereabouts of the joint tablet from TT 34 remain elusive, I have refrained from including any photographic reproductions of this partner tablet for the time being.

2 Kaplony-Heckel (1974).

3 Prada (2017).

4 Quack (1999).

Sami Uljas & Andreas Dorn (eds), *Crossroads VI. Between Egyptian Linguistics and Philology*, 125–145
DOI: https://doi.org/10.37011/studmon.30.05

study and awareness on the part of the Egyptian priests from the early Roman period of ancient texts and their vocabulary. These Tebtunis-copies include i.a. several sections on Egyptian verbs and nouns, but only these two categories of words. Mixing verbs with nouns in one and the same section seems, as far as I can see, to have been avoided. This differentiation may represent an underlying linguistic categorization. Thus, the question remains if e.g. particles, prepositions or adverb(ial)s such as we would define them were treated likewise in sources now lost or as yet unidentified. Nor is there much evidence on how the priests or philologists may have termed them in every single case, or in what way they may have spoken in a more or less fixed and formal parlance about their own language and its constituents.[5]

The verbs grouped in the Tebtunis-Onomastikon are difficult to ascribe into what one might call semantic, word, or lexical fields, although this is a general problem also with languages less ancient and better accessible than Egyptian. In any case, Jürgen Osing's Tebtunis papyri may offer at least a small part of such a lexical field that covers quite a number of verbs of motion including many ABAB–reduplications like e.g. *bnbn*, *mnmn* et al.[6] Among these are certain entries picked up from the same category as the verbs attested on the two wooden tablets from the same period discussed here.[7] The Tebtunis word lists often arrange members of different semantic fields by mixing them in one and the same section, with the *raison d'être* for such a distribution remaining unclear. Thus, verbs of 'building' and 'burial' stand next to those of 'destroying' right at the fragmentary beginning of the Tebtunis lists. The same phenomenon applies to sections dedicated to nouns, whose members, according to modern criteria, we might attribute to completely different fields.

Much more coherent is the arrangement of verbs of motion as documented on the Oslo wooden tablet in the Martin Schøyen Collection, ms 189, as well as on its partner from TT 34 (Monthemhet). The Schøyen piece measures 16 x 13 cm, whereas the dimensions of its partner from TT 34, due to its being broken into two fragments with no physical join in between, are still unknown to me. In any case, both tablets look as having been smoothed and polished very neatly before being inscribed, perhaps on an additional white plaster now lost.[8] Next to the Oslo piece, the one from TT 34 was found in 1985 by an Egyptian équipe under the direction of S. el-Hegazy in the tomb of Monthemhet, room R 26. The following images and some information concerning the circumstances of its discovery – and subsequent disappearance – I owe to Prof. Graefe who was also generous enough as to hand over this material to me for further study in 2015.[9]

---

5 Fischer-Elfert (2007: 33) on e.g. *ḥw.t* – 'chapter'.

6 Osing (1998a: 80 fn.j) and (1998b: pl. 3 fig. H pass.).

7 Osing (1998), Text, 79–81 and (1998) II, pl. 3 Fragm. H, ll. 7–13.

8 A closer investigation of the Oslo piece is still pending, but as far as we can tell by just looking at the images of both sides as presented here, none of them seems to have been covered with stucco.

9 As the whereabouts of this tablet remain unknown and its publication rights are still unclear, I will refrain from presenting any preview illustrations of their physical state of preservation here. Instead, some specimens of its entries in terms of their hieroglyphic transcription should suffice for the time being. The tablet will hopefully re-surface in the near future.

Fig. 1 | © The Schøyen Collection, MS 189 – Recto

It is the intention of this preview to discuss some of the best–preserved examples of lexical entries both tablets include in their selection of verbs of motion. My study of them is still in its infancy, but certain trends as to their overall criteria of selection and treatment as lemmata as well as sub-lemmata can be discerned already.

First of all, it should be emphasized that each tablet is devoted entirely to verbs belonging to the specific field of motion verbs. They display no mixing up e.g. with verbs or nouns from the field of building, destroying, diseases or the like as practiced in the Tebtunis examples. The common denominator of the verbs is the group of classifiers of human legs moving forward or backward, appearing either as the two walking legs (D54 𓂻 and D55 𓂼) or the single walking leg (D56 𓂾). There is only one example each of the ship–classifier (P1 𓊛) or the road sign (N31 𓈐). Thus, the range of classification of the lemmata is much smaller than the one studied recently by e.g. Sami Uljas,[10] Carlos Gracia Zamacona,[11] or Jean Winand.[12] Even if a snake classifier shows up in one case, it is because the verb in question *h̤f3/h̤fj* denotes a snake–like movement, derived from the noun *h̤f3.w* – 'snake' or *h̤f3.t* – 'female snake; worm'.

10 Uljas (2018).

11 As expounded e.g. in his Paris dissertation (2008) as well as in a number of papers on this particular class of verbs.

12 Winand (2019).

Fig. 2 | © The Schøyen Collection, MS 189 – Verso

In other words, the Oslo item as well as the TT 34 board comprise quite a substantial array of ancient Egyptian *verba movendi* or verbs of motion. Their selection is highly diachronic in nature, and it has to be taken into account that lemmata may be explained by means of 'ancient' as well as 'modern' words at the same time, the latter being roughly contemporary with the period of inscription of the tablets.

On Fig. 3 I have framed the classifiers of ll. x+2–3, particularly the pair of walking legs moving either forward or backward, or of the individual walking leg as displayed on Schøyen tablet ms 189.

It should be noted that we are still far from having the entire set of verbs of motion written down on these two wooden tablets alone. In addition to the two bigger fragments of the TT 34 piece, there are several smaller ones. From a paleographical perspective both can be dated to the 2nd century CE. Both pieces were almost certainly produced by one and the same scribe, which adds to their importance, as the ancient writer was obviously distributing his 'dictionary' entries over a set of at least two of such writing boards.[13] It remains, however, unclear which one was inscribed first and if there was some guiding principle behind (t)his selection of verbs, be it alphabetical, based on semantic similarities,

13 This observation would speak strongly in favor of an archaeological provenance of the Oslo piece from the same tomb as its partner from TT 34.

Fig. 3 | Some of the walking legs classifiers in ll. x+2–3 framed
© The Schøyen Collection, MS 189 – Recto

the age of the words, or their morphological features etc. It will be left to the final edition to demonstrate how many and which verbs of motion in particular have been left uncovered by what remains of these tablets from the Roman Period.

The lemmatization of the *verba explicandi* is presented on both boards along the lines of topicalizing lexical entries or *lemmata* such as *ir-šmꜣ BCD etc. (pw)* or 'As for (the entry/lemma) *šmꜣ*, that means B, C, D etc.'; interspersed with ditto- and *ky-ḏd* -glosses[14].

From a mere aesthetic point of view, the uncial hieratic on both tablets does not suggest to be the work of a scribal student, let alone an absolute beginner. Instead, I would assume both to be the product of a master of his subject, who also intended to lend his copy or copies a well-considered degree of calligraphic dignity. The final product therefore conveys the impression of a lexicographic reference tool, which may have been presented to priestly candidates, with the intent of teaching them contemporary as well as ancient and in some cases even extinct verbs of motion accompanied by their individual meanings in terms of hyponyms. Future priests would have been expected to deal, or even struggle, with a multitude of ancient texts whose grammar and vocabulary differed considerably from their own colloquial Demotic or Old Coptic.[15]

---

14 Whose precise meanings are currently under scrutiny by J.F. Quack (personal communication).

15 We may also refer to the recently edited fragments from the Tebtunis library on pCarlsberg 889 from the 2nd century BC/AD with a 'List of Synonyms' from the domestic as well as priestly space;

From a modern academic perspective, the semantic information provided by documents such as these cannot be overestimated. We get firsthand insight into lexical semantics, which we should consider and even implement in conjunction with our daily text readings and translations, and, above all, our interpretations of Egyptian texts. It is not yet clear to me in every single case what precise stages of the Egyptian language the tablets reflect. There is, however, good reason to believe that this collection covers more than just one stage of Ancient Egyptian, as a substantial number of verbs seem to be quite 'old', if not even old–fashioned or anachronistic (see below).

2 Presentation and discussion of some lexical samples

With these preliminaries in mind, I will now concentrate on two of the best-preserved entries on the Oslo tablet. Since there is no title or heading preserved on either side, we are at a loss to identify the very beginning of this list. According to what we know about the sequence of phonemes included in the Late Egyptian alphabet as reconstructed by Jochem Kahl and Joachim Quack ,[16] it is obvious that no such sequence underlies the arrangement of the lemmata : There is no *halaḥam*-order of phonemes to be observed in the still preserved parts of the Oslo tablet, nor in those of its TT 34 partner.

Both copies, the Oslo one as well as the TT 34 specimen, display one side with fully inscribed lines, whereas some of the lines on their 'reverse' sides are shortened with quite a lot of space left uninscribed. For this reason, I propose to classify them – pro tempore – as recto and verso respectively. The recto of the Schøyen tablet 189 carries x+12 and the verso x+10 lines, whereas the two sides of TT 34 still display x+15 and x+8 lines respectively, amounting to a total of at least x+45 lines.

We can only speculate what the introduction or headline on rt. 1 of both tablets might have been. In this regard I should refer to the general heading *p3-3pd-št3 wḥꜥ-jdn.w*, i.e. 'The secret compendium (?) of explaining difficulties' heading the lists of words in the Tebtunis–Onomastikon I.[17]

Let us now proceed to the verbs of motion themselves. As mentioned already, the lemmata on the Oslo ms. 189 are introduced by the standard topicalizing particle *jr* – 'As for; as far as A is concerned, …":

Schøyen Ms. 189, Recto, displays the following topicalized lemmata:

Töpfer (2020: 119–28) – Techniques of translating 'ancient', i.e. Middle and Late Egyptian, texts in hieratic into 'modern', i.e. demotic, ones can be observed in detail by looking at the so-called *Fundamentals of the Course of the Stars* as edited and studied by von Lieven (2007) and (2010).

16 E.g. Kahl (1991) and Quack (2003a) for the linguistic background of the late 1st millennium BCE Egyptian alphabet; add now Haring (2015) and Fischer-Elfert & Krebernik (2016) for comments on early New Kingdom evidence of this *halaḥam*-sequence. Daniels (2018: 148), however, would prefer to attribute the Egyptian sequence to a 'West Semitic list'.

17 See von Lieven (2007: 258–73) for valuable comments on 'innerägyptische Übersetzungen' and 'Kommentare' in the Nutbook.

- *šmꜣy* (x+2; *Wb* IV 47: 'walk; move around')
- *ptẖẖ* (x+3; *Wb* I 565f. *ptẖ*: tr. 'throw to the ground')
- *ḥwi–tꜣ* (x+4; *Wb* III 48.10–11: without trs.; lit. 'roam a country'; 'high–treason?' in *Sinuhe* story); for details see below;
- *zbzb* (x+5; *Wb* III 434.3–4: 'block a path; enemies')
- *ftft* (x+7; *Wb* I 581.3–6: 'jump; bounce')
- *di̓.t–šnꜥ* (x+10; *Wb* IV 504.5–505.13: 'reject; stop from ...' etc.); here either causative *di̓* in front of a *sḏm=f* form or *di̓.t* as in Tebtunis-Onomastikon I with the meaning like Copt. ϯ ⲙⲛ̄- – 'fight with' (for which see Černý (1976: 179))
- *wḥm–i̓[y.t...]* (x+11; *Wb* I 340–343.15; 'repeat etc.'; here + verb *i̓[y.t...]* – 'come'?)
- *sṯi̓* (x+12; not in *Wb* IV; unclear which entry this refers to).

The only two verbs on the verso to be identified as lemmata and explained by means of sub–lemmata are:

- *ḏfn* (x+4; *Wb* V 571.12 'in unklarem Zusammenhang (NR)'), and
- *i̓sp* (x+9; not in *Wb* I).

The lemmata identifiable on the TT 34 tablet, recto and verso, are as follows:

- *ir-wn-...* (?) (x+7; not in *Wb* I)
- *ir-ꜣhty* (x+13; *Wb* I 117.9: *i̓hi̓* ?)
- *ir–rꜣ-ꜥ-di̓(?) -mkḥꜣ* (vs. x+6):

Fig. 4 | Wooden tablet TT 34 vs. x+6

Out of the total of about a dozen entries, the number of identifiable lemmata on TT34 is only three. These lemmata include subentries with accompanying verbs that represent hyponyms and/or partial synonyms of the higher verbs. Taken together, both tablets contain a total of x+15 lexical entries to be identified as lemmata by means of the topicalizer *jr*. It is hard to tell how many further lemmata one may justly reconstruct given the partial loss of text, particularly on the TT 34 tablet. I would expect at least another five lemmata, especially on the verso of the Oslo tablet. As an explanation of these approximately 15 lemmata, a total of about one hundred verbs of motion and compound expressions of a completely different kind serve as either partial or full *explanata*, which, for lack of space here, I cannot list in their entirety.

The layout of the entries on the verso is again slightly different from the one on the recto (see Fig. 2). It seems that the vast majority of the *ir* + lemma-entries were to be found here at the beginning of lines, with *ḏfn* and *i̓sp* being two exceptions, but some of the lines were left partially uninscribed.

However, it must be emphasized again that we are still far from having the total set of verbs of motion once extant in Ancient Egyptian across the ages. On the contrary, some of the verbs of motion related to the same semantic field may appear in the list more than once in order to explain the individual lemma they are attached to and may, on the other hand, in principle even have formed an independent lemma of their own in places now lost.

Diacritical markings on both tablets:[18]

- *ky-ḏd* – 'different reading and tradition'; on Oslo and TT 34 tablets more precisely 'different, further meaning'; see *Wb* V 625.2 and Coptic ϫⲉⲣⲟ- 'called; (it) means'
- occasionally supralinear glosses consisting of single signs rather than full words as in Tebtunis Onomastikon I
- < – (hieratic) hook – 'ditto'
- x – a supralinear cross-like sign, marking a prosodic unit consisting of /verb + substantive/

The nature of the entries remains unclear in a couple of instances. Explanations and interpretations are often phrased in such a way that – in the case of divergent manuscripts of one and the same composition – various readings are supplied. These variants are explicitly indicated by the term *ky-ḏd* – '*varia lectio*; different tradition'. We encounter this text critical remark every now and then on our tablets, written in its typical Late Period spelling, which looks as if it were to be read *k* + *z* for what is actually to be read *ky-ḏd*. I would like to render *ky-ḏd* in these lists as 'additional meaning'. We should also take into account that, for example, Antef II from the 11th dynasty adds a bilingual list on his Asasif stela of the names or species of his favorite dogs.[19] The translation of their supposedly 'Nubian' (not Berber) names is introduced by the phrase *r-ḏd* – 'to mean (x in Egyptian)'.[20] The phrase *r–ḏd* was still in use e.g. in the so-called *Deutung der Geheimnisse des Rituals für die Abwehr des Bösen* on pBM EA10252 dating to 307/6 BCE.[21]

Fig. 5 | Phonetic *matres lectionis*:
(demot.): /*m*/ < *ỉmw* – 'ship; boat' in *ṯ3nm* < *tnm* – 'to go; lead astray'
© Schøyen Collection, MS 189 rt. 8

Here follow a few illustrations of supralinear glossing of individual entries. It should be noted that the scribe has mostly turned to a *calamus* before adding *matres lectionis*

18 Osing (1998: 40–44).

19 CG 20512; see e.g. https://www.ancient.eu/image/6419/dogs-of-intef-ii/ for an image of the object. For bibliographical details for the stela see Fischer (1980).

20 See Kossmann (2011) for the latest hypothesis as to the linguistic background of the animals' names. I owe this reference to Manfred Krebernik (Jena University).

21 Verhoeven (2001: 75–80).

instead of his brush for the main text. This change of pen is obvious from the fact that the supralinear strokes are much thinner than the entries beneath.

For example, the scribe of the Schøyen tablet felt obliged to annotate his particular spelling of the verb *tnm*, 'to get lost; stray', as *ṯꜣmm* by adding a supralinear hieratic sign for *jmw*, 'boat; ship'. The first *m*-sign was supposed to be supplied with a diacritical, cross-like mark on top of it in order to turn it into /*nm*/, instead of the actually written *m*-owl. The gloss may indicate that only the 'second' *m*-sign is to be pronounced as such, and for this purpose the scribe chose the boat-hieroglyph with its abbreviated reading *m* to make sure which of the two '*m*s' is to be read this way and which one is not.[22] So, what he was striving for is to precisely indicate the root *tnm* – 'to err; go astray; (transit.) lead astray'.

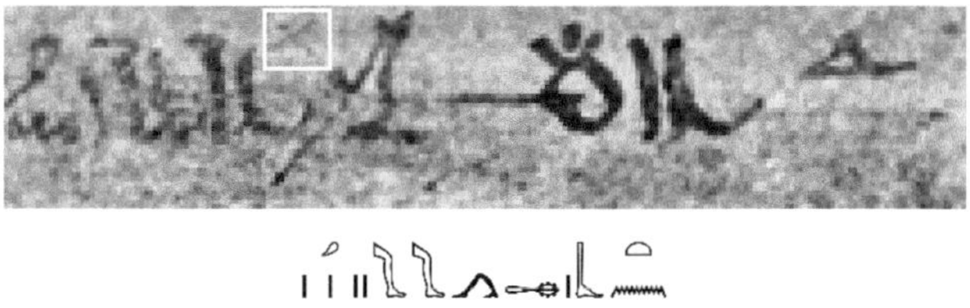

Fig. 6 | Phonetic *matres lectionis*:
Supralinear /x/ for indicating the accent unit in *t/dnbẖ-rd.wy* – 'to lead astray one's feet'
© Schøyen Collection, MS 189 rt. x+9

A cross–shaped prosodic *mater lectionis* represents the supralinear sign already known from the Tebtunis Onomastikon I.[23] In this example, it marks the spot where the two components of the prosodic entity *d/tnbẖ* + *rd.wy* 'lead astray the feet' meet.

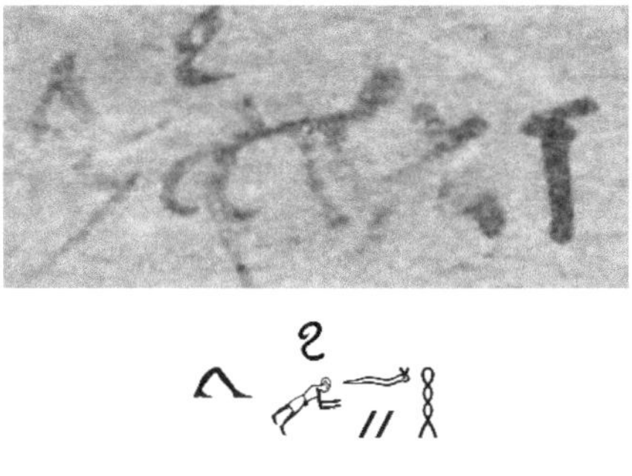

Fig. 7 | Hieratic classifier 'animal hide' taken over from *ḥfꜣ.w* / *ḥfꜣ.t* – 'snake; worm'
to render *ḥfy*(=*f*) – 'to wind; wriggle' – © Schøyen Collection, MS 189 vs. 4

Another interesting case of glossing is the verb *ḥfꜣ* – 'to wind; wriggle', classified by the falling man and spelt *ḥfy* in this case. Its literal meaning supplies the etymon of the words for *ḥfꜣ.w* – 'snake' and its diminutive derivative *ḥfꜣ.t* – 'worm', lit. 'little snake'.[24] The gloss on top of it is, however, not to be read as an indication of its phonology, but of

22 See e.g. Kurth (2010; 155 (14.1.)).

23 See Quack (2013: 228 fn. 18 and 229, with references).

24 See Behrens (1982: part. 18–19).

category: what we see here is the animal skin determinative, whereby reference is made to the substantives related semantically to the verb of motion *ḥfꜣ*.

2.1 The lemma *šmꜣy* – ‘to wander; roam; be a stranger’ etc.

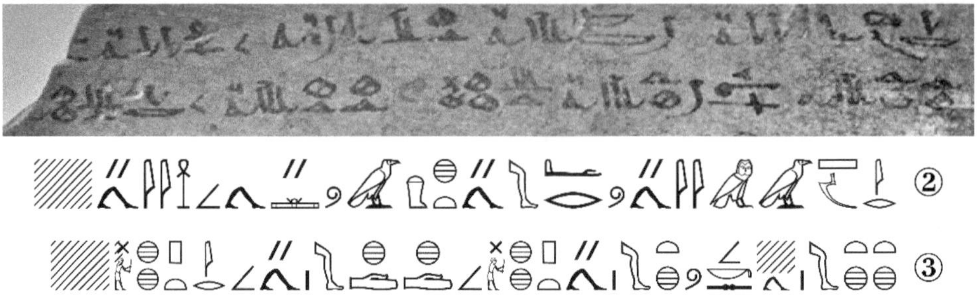

Fig. 8 | Structure of lemmata as displayed by the entry on *šmꜣy* – ‘to roam (the country)’ etc. – © Schøyen Collection, MS 189 rt. x+2–3

x+2: *ỉr-šmꜣy*: ‘As for roaming (the country):’
wʿr – ‘flee’ – *ḫtꜣ* – ‘retreat; repulse; repel’ – < – ‘*ditto*’ – *šny/sny* – ‘[root ?]’ – *ṯḫṯḫ* – ‘confuse’ (Kopt. ⲧⲁϩⲧϩ̄; [Qual.]ⲧⲉϩⲧⲱϩ) – *ky-ḏd* – ‘further meaning’: *wṯḫ* – ‘to flee’ – *pṯḫḫ* – ‘(tr./intr.) cast sth./sb. to the ground’– < – ‘*ditto*’ – *ḫdḫd* – ‘retreat’

Rt. x+2 of the Oslo tablet begins with the topicalized lemma *šmꜣy* – ‘As for roaming (the country), walking around’. This heading is followed by two further verbs of motion *wʿr* – ‘flee’ (*Wb* I 286.8–20) and *ḫtꜣ* – in MEg probably *ḫti* – ‘repel; repulse’ (*Wb* III 342.15–343.4). It is known from elsewhere that *wʿr* refers to ‘fugitives’ (!), ‘fleeing e.g. specifically from work obligations’. The word appears with this meaning e.g. in the register of fugitives from the Great Labour Camp (*ḫnrt-wr*) at Thebes in the 12th–13th dynasties on Brooklyn papyrus 35.1446, where its explanation reads almost like a dictionary entry: *wʿr nn ỉr.t ḥn.t=f* – ‘fugitive, without fulfilling his duties’.[25]

šny or *sny* follow a hook-like check mark meaning ‘ditto’.[26] Both readings are possible, but a corresponding root still remains to be identified. After that, only tiny traces are to be discerned, but at the beginning of x+3 the verb of motion *ṯḫṯḫ* – ‘confuse; be confused’ follows (*Wb* V 328.8–13; Copt. ⲧⲁϩⲧϩ̄; [Qual.]ⲧⲉϩⲧⲱϩ), also attested as *dḫdḫ* in the Tebtunis Onomastikon I. This total reduplication can only be derived from the root *ṯḫ* or *wṯḫ* as a *primae w*-variant.[27]

This, in turn, is followed by the text-critical or philological note *ky-ḏd* – ‘further meaning’. The next explanatory verb or hyponym in line is *wṯḫ* – ‘escape’ (*Wb* I 381.6; Dyn. 18). As for *wṯḫ*, W. Schenkel would narrow down its meaning as follows: ‘… bezieht

25 Hayes (1955: 35; 38; 47–49 and *passim* on *wʿr*). The Egyptians do not seem to have differentiated between ‘fugitives’ on the one hand as defined here and ‘refugees’ on the other hand as we do today.
26 Osing (1998: I, 34); for its incorporation in a Demotic composition see Widmer (2015: 52–4).
27 For primae *w*-verbs, see Otto (1954); with the root *ṯḫ* and its derivatives not covered in his article; Loprieno (1996: 54 with nn. 12–13); Satzinger (2007: 478 for *ḥṯḥt*).

sich meist auf das ungeordnete Davonlaufen der Soldaten feindlicher Truppen (wohl in unwegsames Gelände) …'.[28]

wtḫ in turn is followed by *ptḫḫ* – '(tr. and intr.) cast heavily on the ground' (*Wb* I 565.16–566.3 < simplex *ptḫ*). Our lexicon therefore offers a partial reduplication of the verb *ptḫ* according to the pattern A–B–C–C with intensifying meaning of the simplex.[29] After the check mark or ditto-sign we have *ḫdḫd*, a late and particularly hieratic version of the older verb *ḫtḫt* – 'to retreat' with the leg-classifier either moving forward or backward, also attested transitively (*Wb* III 353.13–354.5).

wꜥr and *wtḫ* – 'be on the run; fugitive';
ḫtꜣ/ḫti – 'retreat; repel';
šny or *sny*, both unclear;
tḫtḫ – qualitative meaning 'be confused'(?);
ptḫḫ – 'hurl sb./sth. to the ground', perhaps also with qualitative meaning 'be cast down to the ground'; see also the following *lemma*;
ḫdḫd/ḫtḫt – 'retreat', similar in meaning with *wꜥr* und *wtḫ*.

Fig. 9 | Semantic potential of the root *šmꜣy*

We may now try to correlate the individual meanings of the hyponyms to *šmꜣy*. The ancient lexicographer seems to have been working on the assumption that adding the semantic potential of the hyponyms listed here would cover the entire spectrum of meanings associated by the topicalized lemma. Provided that the meanings of the verbs of motion explaining the lemma *šmꜣy* given here in the Berlin Wörterbuch are not too wide off the mark, we can venture a preliminary assessment. *šmꜣy* seems to imply physical movement like 'fleeing; retreating; repelling/being repelled; confusing; being confused, hurled to the ground' etc. It is my firm conviction that we are not confronted with a more or less extensive list of synonyms of *šmꜣy*, nor with any of the other lemmata on the tablets from Oslo and TT 34[30]. As for the existence or non–existence of synonymy in general, I here refer to Ullmann (1972: 101–06):[31]

> Reine Synonymie ist … äußerst selten und ein Luxus, den sich die Sprache kaum leisten kann. (...) Einer absoluten Synonymie wirken zwei Kräfte entgegen: Die Unbestimmtheit des Sinns und der Gefühlsbeiklang. Als synonym können nur solche Wörter

---

28 (1977: 277 n. 1).

29 Osing (1976: 296–302); on the meaning of *ptḫ* and *wtḫ* see e.g. Parkinson (2012: 221 and 106 respectively).

30 This is not to deny the possibility of words being glossed by means of supralinear lexical alternatives as discussed briefly by Osing (1998: I 44 (3.)). I frankly admit that I find it quite revealing to come across the term 'synonymie' in C. Zamacoma's Paris dissertation on the verbs of motion in the Coffin Texts only once – on p. 1517 out of 1934 pages all in all – see Zamacona (2008). I may be wrong, but I would take this as a clear, albeit undiscussed, indication of his own conviction that there were no 'real' synonyms among the set of verbs of motion at least in the vast corpus of the Coffin Texts.

31 Ullmann (1972: 101–02).

> gelten, die sich in einem beliebigen Kontext gegeneinander austauschen lassen, ohne daß sich an der erkenntnis- oder gefühlsmäßigen Bedeutung das Geringste ändert.

Following this statement Ullmann quotes e.g. 'leap' and 'jump' as so-called pseudo–synonyms, 'die in einigen Kontexten kongruent und gegeneinander austauschbar sind, in anderen dagegen nicht. … Die Synonymforschung bedient sich verschiedener Methoden, um festzustellen, ob Synonyme austauschbar sind oder nicht. Das Einfachste ist die S u b s t i t u t i o n in unterschiedlichen Kontexten, was nur eine Anwendungsmöglichkeit … ist'.[32] Here he also recommends the search for antonyms, which, as far as Egyptian lexicography is concerned, is still in its infancy, if it has begun at all.

Synonyms may nevertheless be included as well, since the lists draw their examples on a diachronic basis as they contain old lexemes attested in the Old, Middle or New Kingdoms that were no longer in use but are arranged next to more recent ones. Thus, the principle of 'substitution' mentioned by Ullmann may apply to the dropout of e.g. Middle Egyptian verbs and their replacement by e.g. Late Egyptian or Demotic successors[33].

This procedure adopted by the scribe does not guarantee that the hyponyms chosen would add up to the entire range of meanings covered by a lemma such as *šmꜣy*. Nevertheless, there was obviously clear awareness of lexical semantics on the part of the ancient philologist(s) at work while compiling lists like these. *šmꜣy* might be seen to represent the so-called *Archilexem* according to E. Coseriu's structural approach to semantic or lexical fields.[34] Since the two tablets provide a broad range of verbs of motion when taken together, the entry on *šmꜣy* apparently only covers a sub-field of the lexical field 'verbs of motion' by expounding such *sememes* like 'fleeing; retreating, …' etc., as opposed e.g. to sub-fields like 'entering', 'leaving", 'running', and so forth.[35]

As for the morphology of some of the verbs or hyponyms, there seems to be a well-chosen set of verbs based on the root *t̠ḫ* which we have: come across in passing already:

- *t̠ḫt̠ḫ* <*t̠ḫ*
- *wt̠ḫ* < *t̠ḫ*
- *pt̠ḫḫ* <*pt̠ḫ* < *t̠ḫ*
- *ẖdẖd* for *ẖt̠ẖt* as a likely metathesis of *t̠ḫt̠ḫ*.

---

32 Ullmann (1972: 102).

33 This will be one of the main topics in the final study of the tablets.

34 See e.g. Coseriu (1978) and (1970). Verbs heading a lexical or semantic field by covering every single meaning of all its field members Coseriu would classify as an 'Archilexem'. It also remains to be investigated if such an archilexeme of the verbs of motion that was classified as such by the ancient Egyptian philologists existed at all. One might think of *šm*, *prj*, *jj/jwj* and the like as possible candidates, but as long as so–called and much-beloved 'emic' evidence is not available, this issue must remain a moot point.

35 See also Thissen's suggestion for the meaning of the Greek rendering of Seth-Typhon's epithet Σμυ in Plutarch and the ancient author's rendition by ἀναστροφή – 'turning back'. Thissen would like to equate this epithet Σμυ with the Egyptian root *šmꜣ* and its meaning 'wandern, umherirren', and nominally with 'Wanderer, Landfremder'; id. (1993: 248).

It remains to be investigated in depth if *ẖtꜣ* <*ẖtj* also belongs to this assembly. I cannot go into too many details here, but it seems quite obvious that the ancient philologist felt obliged to also draw on a more or less entire *family of words*/*Wortfamilie* in order to explain the range of meanings of *šmꜣy*. The basic root of this family of verbs of motion may be defined as the root *tẖ*. This is then modified by the *primae w* -prefix in the case of *w:tẖ*, by the *p*-prefix and extension of the root *tẖ* to produce *p:tẖ*, and this in turn by way of partial reduplication is then extended further to *p:tẖ:ḫ*.[36] The form *ḫt:ḫt* displays total reduplication of the root *tḫ*, and perhaps also metathesis (?). I would very much doubt whether these parts of the sub-field *šmꜣy* were included for mere reasons of phonemics or stylistics. Instead, I would rather suspect them to reflect the ancient philologist's awareness of the existence of a morphological relationship, or even of a genealogical (af) filiation between the members of the word family based on the root *tẖ*. If so, it seems to bear witness to a high degree of intellectual reflection by the scribe, and, by extension, this degree of linguistic awareness in the early Roman Period will have to be incorporated into future cross-linguistic studies like Trabant's intriguing history of *Sprachdenken* (2002).[37]

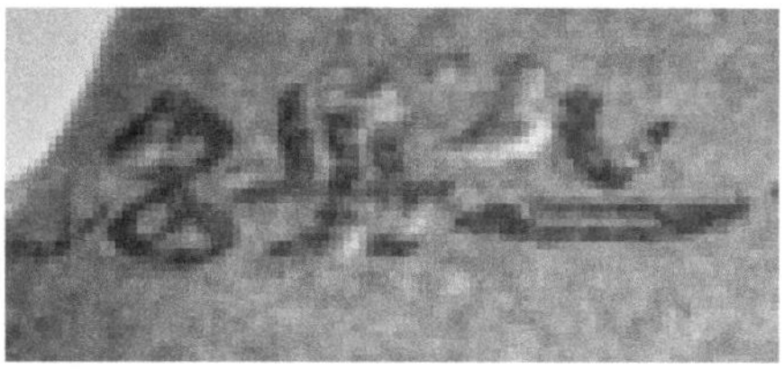

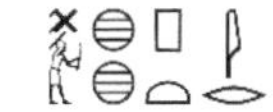

Fig. 10 | The entry *jr ptẖḫ* […] – 'As for: cast (sb./sth.) to the ground […]'
© Schøyen Collection, MS 189 rt. x+3

One of the seven verbs explaining *šmꜣy* was turned into the topic or lemma *ptẖḫ* of its own in the next entry, but what follows next is, unfortunately, lost in a break on the left margin of the tablet. As the beginning of l. x+4 introduces yet another lemma, we have no means of telling what and how many hyponyms were listed in the lacuna at the end of l. x+3.

---

36 See Cauville (1987); see also Gaboda (1992: part. 102–04) with a list of verbs of motion starting with a /p/, without, however, listing *ptẖ(ḫ)*, maybe because it is not classified as such by adding i.a. the  (D55)-glyph.

37 Trabant starts his discussion with Homer, ending up in the 20th century CE, but Egyptology as well as Assyriology, not to mention the Indian branch of early linguistics in the 1st millennium BCE, would have to contribute quite a lot to this kind of research. For the Assyriological part, I should also reference Manfred Krebernik's (2007) illuminating paper on 'Sprachbewußtsein' in the Ancient Near East.

2.2 The lemma *ḥwj-tꜣ* – 'to roam the country' (etc.)

The following lemma *ḥwỉ-tꜣ* we know well from the *Tale of Sinuhe*, interpreted by Feder (2011) as a composite with the meaning 'Hochverrat; high treason'.[38] In terms of its diachrony, *ḥwỉ-tꜣ* first shows up in our documentation in the Old Kingdom, with only a few more attestations in the Middle Kingdom. Apart from *Sinuhe*, it is attested in the *Man Who Was Tired of Life* (the so-called *Lebensmüde*) and at the very end of the unfinished sp. 816 of the Coffin Texts, where Re is asked to *ḥwỉ-tꜣ=k*. The until now last occurrence is pBremner Rhind 4.15, which may also – next e.g. to the Tale of *Sinuhe* – have been known to the philologist(s) of the Oslo tablet.

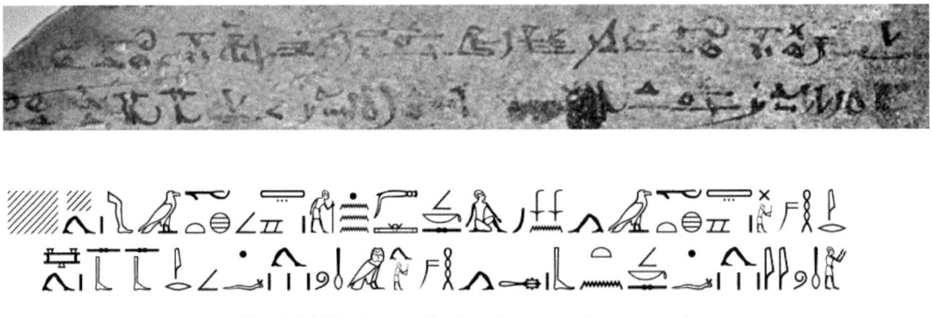

Fig. 11 | The lemma *ḥwj-tꜣ*: 'to roam the country'
© Schøyen Collection, MS 189 rt. x+4–5

x+4: *ỉr ḥwỉ-tꜣ: ẖtỉw nnw ‹ ky-dd mḥw sr-tꜣ ‹ ẖtỉw* [… *dwꜣ(?)*-]

x+4: 'As for *ḥwỉ-tꜣ* – 'roam the country; go into exile(?)': 'retreat'; 'tremble'; ditto; further meaning: 'What permits the Lord of the country to float'; ditto; 'pervade (a country)' [… worship; adore(?)-]

x+5: *ẖrw(?)y=f ky-dd tnbẖ ḥwỉ m ẖrw(?)=f ditto*

x+5: – one's enemies(?)'; ditto; further meaning: 'stray/shiver with fear'; 'beat one's enemy' (?); 'ditto'

The composite *ḥwỉ-tꜣ* is explained in x+4 i.a. by means of *ẖtj(w)*, itself perhaps represented by two slightly different spellings: the first of which is determined by the backwards moving legs and the second by the single walking leg.[39]

This particular entry on *ḥwỉ-tꜣ* is, at least in my view, of utmost importance for its undeniable political implications and impact on the overall interpretation of the *Tale of Sinuhe*. According to the standard dictionaries of Old, Middle and Late(r) Egyptian, the lemma *ḥwỉ-tꜣ* seems to have had some such basic meaning as 'roam the country (for no good purpose)' and with the intent and implication of bringing damage and demolition to it in some way or the other. As shown by the hyponyms added on the Oslo list, there is a strong tinge of political incorrectness attached to *ḥwj-tꜣ* on the part of its perpetrator: 'the

38 Feder (2011); *Wb* V 311.7–12; Meeks (1982: 79.3418); Osing (1998: I 80 n. j), following a reconstruction as proposed by J. Tait).

39 It is not yet clear if the following two walking legs still belong to the hyponym *ẖtj(w)*.

Lord of the country being afloat' is likely to be taken as an allusion to the assassination of Osiris and/or reigning king by getting drowned; more details to that in the final commentary.

Before venturing to suggest an overall interpretation of this lemma, let us first take a look at the set of hyponyms following it.

- *ẖti(w)*: this hyponym is very likely also to be complemented by *tꜣ* – 'country': 'to pervade a country' (*Wb* III 343.5–6).[40] Simple *ẖti* – 'to retreat', according to Osing (1976; 102), is still attested as infinitive ϭⲟⲧⲓ in the Old Coptic magical pBM EA 10808 l. 28.
- *nnw/nini* (*Wb* II 275.2–8) – '(tr.) weary sb.; (intr.) be weary; inert' (Copt. ⲛⲟⲉⲓⲛ, ⲛⲟⲓⲛⲓ, ⲛⲁⲉⲓⲛ, ⲛⲁⲓⲛⲉ, ⲛⲁⲁⲛⲉ – 'move; shuttle; quiver'); 'to be spread over' with reference to the flood, for which D. Meeks kindly refers me to Assmann (1999), 294 (N. 127A, l. 113) and 348 (N. 143 l. 70).
- *mḥw*[41] *sr-tꜣ* – 'to drown the prince of the country; make him float'; *mḥw* intr. 'to drown; be drowned' also tr. 'to drown sb.'; *sr-tꜣ* – 'prince of the country', attested i.a. as an epithet of Osiris; thanks to D. Meeks again for the tr. 'what permits ... to be adrift'.
- *tnbẖ* (*Wb* V 311) with feet walking backwards 'roam about; to tremble (with fear); stray'; attested twice in the Tale of the *Eloquent Peasant* alone: B 128 and B 192. The pig (and hedgehog) determinative does not refer to an 'unclean beast',[42] but rather to the uncoordinated moving around of a pig herd or a hedgehog running around in an allegedly confused manner. This is the way in which Rensi is supposed to move instead of sticking to the rules and guidelines of Ma'at. Even more telling is *Admonitions* 9.2:
  mtn jꜣw.t-nb.t nn s.t r-s.t=s 'Look, every office is out of its place
  mj-jdr tnbẖ nn mnjw=f like a wandering herd without its herdsman.'[43]

Fig. 12 | Semantic potential of the expression *ḥwy-tꜣ*

For the hieratic character *sr/sjrw* – 'prince' (*Hierat. Paläogr.* III, A 11) with an appendix atop its head I can invoke no parallel. A Demotic gloss cannot be excluded, but in the Tebtunis-Onomastika such a gloss seems not to be attested.

If the word *mḥw* chould also be used transitively to mean 'drown sb./sth.' instead of its previously documented intransitive meaning 'to be in the water; drowning', this might then refer to the – violent – act of 'drowning the prince of the country', which would match the political connotation of the lemma *ḥwi-tꜣ*. For *mḥw* as a reversible verb, the subject of which can be both *agens* and *patiens* and which can be connected to Osiris.[44] Vernus quotes, among other things, evidence of the alleged drowning of Osiris, and

40 Dimitri Meeks would also suggest *ẖt-tꜣ* by i.a. referring to A. Gutbub (1973: 313 (f) & personal communication).

41 I owe the reading of the decisive 1st sign in *mḥw* to J.F. Quack.

42 As Parkinson (2012: 106) would have it.

43 Translation and metrics according to R. Enmarch, (2008: 147f.). D. Meeks refers me to Kurth (1998: 255 (141.4) with fn. 9), where the king is said to be the one, 'der im Land-der-Götter umherstreift'.

44 Cf. Vernus (1991: 24–25); see also *Pyr* §766c–d in Vernus (1991: 21 N. 15) and the other documents n. 16–20; 22–23; and 25–43.

suggests that he could not be afflicted in the place 'close to where he was aborted/in which you become immersed':[45] *mḥ*(+ water)*.n=k-ỉm* (*Pyr* §615d). This verse stands in parallel to that in *Pyr* §615b: '..., près de l'endroit où tu a dérivé': *ḏr bw šm.n=k-ỉm*. According to this parallelism, *mḥi* + water classifier also represents a verb of motion, and Vernus cites examples of its transitive use in the Late Period (pBremner-Rhind 3.16 and 9.24).

Since the reading *sr-tꜣ*, 'prince-of-the-country', is beyond doubt, it is crucial to remember the epithet of i.a. Osiris, who may be called a *sr m tꜣ* – 'prince-in-the-country'.[46] An interpretation of the lemma *ḥwi-tꜣ* by, alongside other hyponyms, the syntagma *mḥi-sr-tꜣ* 'The prince of the country drifts off/is drifting away' equals, *in nuce*, a mytho-political description of chaos and would offer itself to serve as a template for the assassination of Amenemhat I in the *Tale of Sinuhe*, hinted at by the very lemma *ḥwi-tꜣ* itself.[47]

In the gap following *ḫtiw* at least one hyponym is missing. Since the first sign of x+5 looks like A 30, the man with his arms raised (*dwꜣ*), the following *ḫrwy=f* may be taken with all due caution as *ḫrwy*, 'his (the king's) enemies', despite the running legs. The verb of motion *ḫr* – 'to fall' + walking legs is the root of the noun *ḫrw* – 'enemy; (lit.) the fallen one/the one to be felled'. In addition, the suffix *=f* speaks in favor of a substantive *ḫrw* at this point. The combination transitive verb + direct object serving as a paradigmatic entry is anything but uncommon in the Tebtunis word lists. The verb *ḫr*, according to Osing, is still attested as the perf. act. part. ϭєр in the approximately contemporary pBM EA 10808.[48]

If Frank Feder is right with his interpretation of *ḥwi-tꜣ* in *Sinuhe* as 'committing high treason', then this might accord well with the traitor's 'worship of his (the prince's/ king's) enemy'.[49]

2.3 The lemma *pẖr-ḥꜣty* on the tablet TT 34

Fig. 13 | The beginning of the entry *pẖr-ḥꜣty* on TT 34 vs. x+4

45 Vernus (1991: 20 –21); Allen (2005: 80).

46 *LGG* VI 421c.

47 For a very sophisticated, yet unmistakable, allusion to the assassination(!) of Amenemhat I in the speech of Ammunenshi to *Sinuhe* see Fischer-Elfert (2006). – The present writer is fully aware of the fact that the previous discussion of *ḥwj-tꜣ* insinuates a substantial knowledge of the *Tale of Sinuhe*, if not in the early Roman Period, at least in the 1st millennium BCE, next to such – alleged – Middle Kingdom 'classics' as The *Teaching of Amenemhat I* and the *Teaching of Khety* as identified in hieratic manuscripts by J.F. Quack (2003b: Saite Period, if not even later) and (2020). As long as not proved otherwise, why not simply assume so? Egyptology is replete with assumptions anyway.

48 Osing (1976b: 62 = l. 6 of the text).

49 For the meaning of *ḥwj-tꜣ* in *Sinuhe* see also Altenmüller (2002: 13), and CT VII 15 r (= sp. 816) (D. Meeks, personal communication). For a less politically susceptible attestation and meaning of *ḥwj-tꜣ* in a biographical inscription from the reign of Djedkare-Isesi see now K.-J. Seyfried (2022), 180 col. 2 and 181 for the translation "nachdem ich das Land seinetwegen bereist hatte".

As a final example, I would like to present a short entry on the writing board found in TT 34 (vs. x+4), namely the lemma or hyperonym *pẖr-ḥ3ty*, literally 'encircle a/the heart', perhaps to be taken more precisely as a metaphor for 'to bewitch/enchant sb.'s heart'.[50] If so, we may here be in front of the Egyptian explanation of what the so-called love spells – in hieratic and demotic – were all about. In that case one should try to reconcile the hyponyms with their preceding entry. Since the original left end margin is missing, further hyponyms may have been part of it.

Unfortunately, the very first hyponym *bꜥ-jb/ḥ3ty* (?) (*Wb* I 446.6), is something of a lexicographical mystery. As for *bꜥ*, L.H. Lesko offers 'to respect'[51] as one entry, with the next one certainly related semantically to this: 'carefully'.

The second hyponym seems to be particularly revealing, since it mentions the *sḫ-sḫm* 'beating the *sḫm*-sistrum".[52] This explanation would imply that the performance of a love-spell was to be accompanied by playing this instrument, which may also be taken as indicating that the spell was to be sung, not just spoken by way of an incantation. The cross-like supralinear sign between the two components *sḫ* and *sḫm* once again characterizes this composite term as an inseparable metrical or prosodic unit, as we already know well from the Tebtunis Onomastikon.

3 The 'Sitz-im-Leben' of the tablets

In closure, some speculations on the *Sitz-im-Leben* of the tablets may be in order. Since the one from TT 34 has a firm archaeological context, with the other one from the Schøyen collection in Oslo displaying the same hand(writing) but no find context, it is likely that both specimens derive from this very tomb. This location may have served, at least in part, as a place of teaching future priests (and philologists!) the vocabulary of their own language in terms of lexical paradigms, arranged according to semantic features of its constituents.[53] The tablets in question would then belong to some such lessons focusing on 'verbs of

50 Love (2016: 55–56 n. 177 and 179–80) on *pẖr-ḥ3ty* and 'binding a woman's heart' and 'mind'.

51 Lesko (1982) 152. Wente (1967: 28y); Caminos (1954: 9).

52 For the two types of sistra in Egypt see D. Elwart (2011: part. 47–50) on the *sḫm*-type.

53 This is why TT 34 would have something in common with the MK tomb Assiut N 13.1 frequented by NK teachers and students for penning their school lessons on walls and pillars alike; see now Verhoeven (2020) for the details. Private tombs of the late SIP in the Asasif, and particularly their forecourts, may have been used for training future scribes by e.g. copying/reproducing parts of well–established literary compositions and other texts. Some of the writing boards discovered during the 1908–1913 Carnarvon excavations in the lower Asasif were actually found either within *rishi*-coffins in tomb chambers or outside the tomb complex proper, left or dropped in its forecourt. The question remains when and exactly where were they inscribed prior to their transfer to the tombs or within its architectural precinct. My thanks go to an anonymous reviewer for this and many other annotations and the following bibliographical references. For the archaeological background of Lord Carnarvon's excavations with regard to wooden tablets see the fine reconstruction established by Manniche (2019: *pass.*); see also Hagen (2013: 85–91) and (2019: 207–08). On education strategies of scribes in ancient Egypt in comparison to the ones in the ancient Near East see Cancik-Kirschbaum & Kahl (2018: 47–69).

motion and their respective meaning(s)', representing different strata of the Egyptian language by mixing synchrony with diachrony. As the Tebtunis Onomastikon I shows quite explicitly, there must have been an awareness of such linguistic entities or categories such as [substantive] and [verb], to mention just these two.[54] Within these different word categories, something like 'semantics' comes into play, with words differing from one another by differentiating sememes. Likewise, there will have been some idea about the concept 'semantics' and of lexical, semantic or word field in the 2nd century CE at the latest.[55] It should also be remembered that the ancient philologist(s) were aware of the fact that verbs related to one another in terms of their morphology, as in the case of *wtḫ*, *ptḫḫ* and *ṯḫṯḫ* etc. or that they could display what we would call today partial or total reduplication of roots. We should not be surprised if lists of verbs related to one another in terms of their morphological properties and all deriving from one and the same root should turn up some day.

At the very end, perhaps a somewhat daring presumption about the existence and practical ways of lexicographical philology in the genuine Egyptian priestly milieu may be offered.[56] Training on the two word-categories [substantive] and [verb] provided in the Tebtunis Onomastikon edited by Jürgen Osing is perfectly in line with what we know about the Hellenistic grammarians and their philology from Alexandria – *ad Aegyptum*. A more or less direct influence of the Alexandrian scholars on their Egyptian colleagues is just one scenario of how the word lists quoted here may have come about.

The Romance philologist and linguist Jürgen Trabant has also pointed out that linguistic categories such as nouns and verbs have been part of the systematic thinking on language and parts of speech since the time of Homer at the latest.[57] The Tebtunis Onomastikon and the wooden tablets from TT 34 date about seven or eight centuries later, but who can tell how long it took the Egyptians to comment on the lexicon of their native tongue? Tiny remnants of yet another onomastikon or lexicon at Halle University and prior to the one from Tebtunis, dating to the early Hellenistic Period, do not yet display any supralinear annotations or glosses.[58] This particular habit of glossing may not have been practiced until the last two centuries before or shortly after the turn of the millennium. Jürgen Trabant's book starts with Homer, Plato and especially with Aristotle's discussion of the nature and function of language in general. In the future, we will have to add the much older Babylonian tradition dealing with the Sumerian language, dating back to the Old Babylonian Period and roughly contemporary with the late Middle Kingdom in Egypt. Linguistics never was an invention of the Greeks or Indians. Instead, it first appeared in Mesopotamia and evolved out of the Babylonian scholarly treatment and analysis of the Sumerian language which became more or less extinct as a spoken language in the Old Babylonian Period.[59] Ancient Egypt, by comparison, followed suit rather late.

---

54 Uljas's (2012) brilliant paper on 'Linguistic consciousness' is probably the best reference on this topic.

55 As Zeidler (1999: 156) would presuppose too: 'Wissen um die Strukturierung ihrer Wortfelder', which I would take as a remarkable comment.

56 Cancik-Kirschbaum & Kahl (2018: 47–69).

57 Trabant (2003).

58 See the present writer's edition of Pap. Hal. Kurth Inv. 33 A–C (2008).

59 See once again Krebernik's paper cited in fn. 37 above.

Bibliography

Abbreviations

CT = de Buck, Adriaan † & Sir Alan H. Gardiner. 1961. *The Egyptian Coffin Texts VII. Texts of Spells 787–1185*. Chicago; The University of Chicago Oriental Institute Publications Volume LXXXVII.

LGG = Leitz, Christian (ed.). *Lexikon der Ägyptischen Götter und Götterbezeichnungen. Vol. I–VII*. Leuven; Orientalia Lovanensia Analecta 110–16.

Pyr = Sethe, Kurth. 1908. *Die Altägyptischen Pyramidentexte nach den Papierabdrücken und Photographien des Berliner Museums Erster Band*. Berlin.

Wb = Erman, Adolf & Hermann Grapow (eds). 1926–1931. *Wörterbuch der Ägyptischen Sprache I–V*. Berlin.

Books and articles

Allen, James. 2005. *The Ancient Egyptian Pyramid Texts*. Atlanta; Writings from the Ancient World 23.

Altenmüller, Hartwig. 2002. 'Die Zeit "'diesseits und jenseits der Todesschwelle"' im Brief Sesostris' I. an Sinuhe'. *Göttinger Miszellen* 188, 9–14.

Behrens, Peter. 1982. 'Das afroasiatische Diminutivmorphem *t* im Ägyptischen'. *Göttinger Miszellen* 57, 17–24.

Caminos, Ricardo A. 1954. *Late Egyptian Miscellanies*. Oxford; Brown Egyptological Studies I.

Cancik-Kirschbaum, Eva & Jochem Kahl. 2018. *Erste Philologien. Archäologie einer Disziplin vom Tigris bis zum Nil. Unter Mitarbeit von Klaus Wagensonner*. Tübingen.

Cauville, Sylvie. 1987. 'Un préfixe en *p* en Égyptien?', *Revue d'Égyptologie* 38, 183–84.

Coseriu, Eugenio. 1970. *Einführung in die strukturelle Betrachtung des Wortschatzes*. Tübingen.

Coseriu, Eugenio. 1978. *Probleme der strukturellen Semantik*. Tübingen.

Daniels, Peter T. 2018. *An Exploration in Writing*. Sheffield.

Elwart, Dorothee. 2011. 'Sistren als Klang des Hathorkultes', in: Meyer-Dietrich, Erika (ed.). *Laut und Leise. Der Gebrauch von Stimme und Klang in historischen Kulturen*. Mainz; Mainzer Historische Kulturwissenschaften 7, 37–59.

Enmarch, Roland. 2008. *A World Upturned. Commentary and Analysis of The Dialogue of Ipuwer and the Lord of All*. Oxford.

Feder, Frank. 2011. 'Ist das "'Erschüttern des Landes"' (*ḥwj tꜣ*) Hochverrat?', in: Feder, Frank, Ludwig Morenz & Günter Vittmann (eds). *Von Theben nach Giza. Festmiszellen für Stefan Grunert zum 65. Geburtstag*. Göttingen; *Göttinger Miszellen* Beihefte 10, 41–47.

Fischer, Henry George. 1980. 'Hundestele', in: *Lexikon der Ägyptologie III*. Wiesbaden, 81–82.

Fischer-Elfert, Hans-Werner. 2006. 'Ammunenshi und die Tagewählerei oder der präsumtive Todestag Amenemhets' I. (Sinuhe B 43–45 und R 5–6)', in: Fischer-Elfert, Hans-Werner & Karola Zibelius-Chen (eds). *Eine Frau von reichlich ägyptischem Verstand. Festschrift für Waltraud Guglielmi zum 60. Geburtstag*. Wiesbaden; Philippika 11, 23–28.

Fischer-Elfert, Hans-Werner. 2007. 'Wort – Vers – Text. Bausteine einer altägyptischen Textologie', in: Wilcke, Claus Wilcke (ed.Hg.), *Das geistige Erfasssen der Welt im Alten Orient. Sprache. Religion, Kultur und Gesellschaft*. Wiesbaden, 27–38.

Fischer-Elfert, Hans-Werner & Manfred Krebernik. 2016. 'Zu den Buchstabennamen auf dem Halaham-Ostrakon aus TT 99 (Grab des Sennefri)', in: *Zeitschrift für Ägyptische Sprache und Altertumskunde* 143, 169–176.

Gaboda, Péter. 1989. 'A p-Prefix in Egyptian'. Budapest; *Studia Aegyptiaca* XII, 93–107.

Gutbub, Adolphe. 1973. *Textes fondamentaux de la théologie de Kom Ombo*. Cairo; Bibliothèque d'Études 47.

Hagen, Fredrik. 2013. 'An Eighteenth Dynasty Writing Board (Ashmolean 1948.91) and The Hymn to the Nile', in: *Journal of the American Research Center in Egypt* 43, 73–91.

Hagen, Fredrik. 2019. 'New Copies of Old Classics: Early Manuscripts of *Khakheperreseneb* and *The Instruction of a Man for His Son*', in: *Journal of Egyptian Archaeology* 105, 177–208.

Haring, Ben. 2015. '*Halaḥam* on an Ostracon of the Early New Kingdom?', in: *Journal of Near Eastern Studies* 74, 189–196.

Hayes, William. 1955. *A Papyrus of the Late Middle Kingdom in the Brooklyn Museum [Papyrus Brooklyn 35.1446]*. New York; Wilbour Monographs V.

Kahl. Jochem. 1991. 'Von *h* bis *ḳ*. Indizien für eine '"alphabetische"' Reihenfolge einkonsonantiger Lautwerte in spätzeitlichen Papyri', in: *Göttinger Miszellen* 122, 33–47.

Kaplony-Heckel, Ursula. 1974. 'Schüler und Schulwesen in der ägyptischen Spätzeit', *Studien zur Altägyptischen Kultur* 1, 227–46.

Kossmann, Maarten. 2011. 'The names of king Antef's dogs', in: Mettouchi, Amina (ed.). *'Parcours berbères'. Mélanges offerts à Paulette Galand-Pernet et Lioned Galand pour leur 90e anniversaire*. Köln; Berber Studies 33, 79–84.

Krebernik, Manfred. 2007. 'Zur Entwicklung des Sprachbewußtseins im Alten Orient', in: Wilcke, Claus (ed.). *Das geistige Erfassen der Welt im Alten Orient. Sprache, Religion, Kultur und Gesellschaft. Sprache, Religion, Kultur und Gesellschaft*. Wiesbaden, 39–61.

Kurth, Dieter. 1998. *Edfou VIII*. Wiesbaden; Die Inschriften des Tempels von Edfu Abteilung I Übersetzungen Band 1.

Kurth, Dieter. 2011. *A Ptolemaic Sign-List. Hieroglyphs Used in the Temples of the Graeco-Roman Period of Egypt and Their Meanings*. Hützel.

Lesko, Leonard. 1982. *A Dictionary of Late Egyptian Vol. I*. Berkeley and Providence.

Loprieno, Antonio. 1995. *Ancient Egyptian. A Linguistic Introduction*. Cambridge.

Love, Edward. 2016. *Code-Switching with the Gods. The Bilingual (Old Coptic-Greek) Spells of PGM IV and their Linguistic, Religious, and Socio-Cultural Context in Late Roman Egypt*. Berlin; *Zeitschrift für Ägyptische Sprache und Altertumskunde* Beihefte 4.

Manniche, Lise. 2019. 'Twelve Carnarvon wWriting Bboards and their Pprovenances', in: *Journal of Egyptian Archaeology* 105, 157–175.

Meeks, Dimitri. 1982. *Année lexicographique. Égypte Ancienne. Tome* 3. Paris.

Osing, Jürgen. 1976a. *Die Nominalbildung des Ägyptischen I–II*. Mainz.

Osing, Jürgen. 1976b. *Der spätägyptische Papyrus BM 10808*. Wiesbaden; Ägyptologische Abhandlungen 33.

Osing, Jürgen. 1998a. *Hieratische Papyri aus Tebtunis I. Text*. Copenhagen; Carsten Niebuhr Institute Publications 17, The Carlsberg Papyri 2.

Osing, Jürgen. 1998b. *Hieratische Papyri aus Tebtunis II. Tafeln*. Copenhagen; Carsten Niebuhr Institute Publications 17, The Carlsberg Papyri 2.

Otto, Eberhard. 1954. 'Die Verba Iae inf. und die ihnen verwandten im Ägyptischen', *Zeitschrift für Ägyptische Sprache und Altertumskunde* 79, 41–52.

Parkinson, Richard. 2012. *The Tale of the Eloquent Peasant: A Readers's Commentary*. Hamburg; Lingua Aegyptia Studia Monographica 10.

Prada, Luigi. 2017. 'Divining grammar and defining foes: Linguistic patterns of Demotic divinatory handbooks (with special reference to P. Cairo CG 50138-41) and a note on the euphemistic use of *ḫft* "'enemy'"', in: Jasnow, Richard & Ghislaine Widmer (eds). *Illuminating Osiris. Egyptological Studies in Honor of Mark Smith*. Atlanta, 277–301.

Quack, Joachim. 1999. 'A new bilingual fragment from the British Museum (Papyrus BM EA 69574)', *Journal of Egyptian Archaeology* 85, 153–64.

Quack, Joachim. 2003a. 'Die spätägyptische Alphabetreihenfolge und das '"südsemitische"' Alphabet', *Lingua Aegyptia* 11, 163–184.

Quack, Joachim F. 2003b. 'Aus einer spätzeitlichen literarischen Sammelhandschrift', *Zeitschrift für Ägyptische Sprache und Altertumskunde* 130, 182–185 & pl. and Taf. XLV.

Quack, Joachim F. 2013. 'Das Dekret des Amun an Isis. Papyrus Kairo CG 58034 + 58028'. In Hallof, Jochen (ed.), *Auf den Spuren des Sobek: Festschrift für Horst Beinlich zum 28.12.2012*. Dettelbach; Studien zu den Ritualszenen altägyptischer Tempel 12, 223–43.

Quack, Joachim F. 2020. 'Eine spätzeitliche Handschrift der Lehre des Cheti (Papyrus Berlin P 14423)', in: Shi–Wei Hsu, Jan Moje & Vincent P.-M. Laisney (eds.), *Ein Kundiger, der in die Gottesworte eingedrungen ist. Festschrift für den Ägyptologen Karl Jansen-Winkeln zum 65. Geburtstag*. Münster; Ägypten und Altes Testament 99, 233–251.

Satzinger, Helmut. 2007. 'Modifizierung ägyptischer Verbalwurzeln durch Reduplikation', *Wiener Zeitschrift für die Kunde des Morgenlandes* 97, 475–89.

Schenkel, Wolfgang. 1977. 'Flüchtling und Flucht aus Arbeitsverhältnissen', in: *Lexikon der Ägyptologie II*. Wiesbaden, 276–77.

Seyfried, Karl-Joachim. 2022. 'Zu den Inschriften aus dem Grab des *Smnḫ-w(j)-Ptḥ rn.f nfr Jtwš* in Saqqara', in: Bußmann, Richard, Ingelore Hafemann, Robert Schiestl & Daniel A. Werning (Hgg.), *Spuren der altägyptischen Gesellschaft. Festschrift für Stephan J. Seidlmayer.* Berlin/Boston; Zeitschrift für ägyptische Sprache und Altertumskunde Beihefte Band 14, 177–195.

Thissen, Heinz Josef. 1993. '… αιγυπτιαξων τη φωνη… Zum Umgang mit der ägyptischen Sprache in der griechisch-römischen Antike', *Zeitschrift für Papyrologie und Epigraphik* 97, 239–52.

Töpfer, Susanne. 2020. 'Fragments of Hieratic Lexical Lists', in: Kim Ryholt (ed.), *Hieratic Texts from Tebtunis Including a Survey of Illustrated pPapyri'*. Copenhagen, CNI Publications 45, The Carlsberg Papyri 15, 113–128.

Trabant, Jürgen. 2003. *Der Garten des Mithridates. Kleine Geschichte des Sprachdenkens*. Munich.

Uljas, Sami. 2012. 'Linguistic consciousness', in Stauder-Porchet, Julie, Andréas Stauder & Willeke Wendrich (eds). *UCLA Encyclopaedia of Egyptology.* accessed online via: http://digital2.library.ucla.edu/ viewItem.do?ark=21198/zz002dn8xd.

Uljas, Sami. 2018. 'Words on the move: Some observations on the lexicalization of kinesis in Earlier Egyptian', *Göttinger Miszellen* 255, 129–37.

Ullmann, Steven. 1972. *Grundzüge der Semantik. Die Bedeutung in sprachwissenschfatlicher Sicht.* 2., unveränderte Auflage. Berlin/New York.

Verhoeven, Ursula. 2001. *Untersuchungen zur späthieratischen Buchschrift*. Leuven; Orientalia Lovanensia Analecta 99.

Verhoeven, Ursula. 2020. *Assiut: Grab N13.1: Dipinti. Zwei Bände*. Wiesbaden;. The Asyut Project 15.

Vernus, Pascal. 1991. 'Le mythe d'un mythe, la prétendu noyade d'Osiris. – De la dérive d'un corps à la dérive du sens'. *Studi di Egittologia e di Antichità Puniche* 9, 19–34.

von Lieven, Alexandra. 2007. *Grundriss des Laufes der Sterne. Das sogenannte Nutbuch.* Copenhagen; CNI Publications 31, The Carlsberg Papyri 8. CNI Publications 31.

von Lieven, Alexandra. 2010. 'Translating the *Fundamentals of the Course of the Stars*', in: Anette Imhausen & Tanja Pommerening (eds.), *Writings of Early Scholars in the Ancient Near East, Egypt, Rome, and Greece*. Berlin, Beiträge zur Altertumskunde 286, 139–150.

Wente, Edward F. 1967. *Late Ramesside Letters*. Chicago; Studies in Ancient Oriental Civilizations 33.

Widmer, Ghislaine. 2015. *Résurrection d'Osiris – Naissance d'Horus. Les papyrus Berlin P.6750 et Berlin P. 8765, témoiganges de la persistence de la tradition sacerdotale dans le Fayoum à l'époque romaine*. Berlin; Ägyptische und Orientalische Papyri und Handschriften des Ägyptischen Museums und Papyrussammlung Berlin 3.

Winand, Jean. 2019. 'Did you say synonyms? The case of *pḥ* and *spr* in Late Egyptian', in Brose, Marc, Peter Dils, Franziska Naether, Lutz Popko & Dietrich Raue (eds). *En Détail. Philologie und Archäologie im Diskurs. Festschrift für Hans-Werner Fischer-Elfert*. Berlin; *Zeitschrift für Ägyptische Sprache und Altertumskunde* Beihefte 7/2, 1235–74.

Zamacona, Carlos . 2008. *Les verbes de movement dans les textes des sarcophages – Étude sémantique.* Paris; Unpublished doctoral dissertation at the École Pratique des Hautes Études.

Zeidler, Jürgen. 1999. 'Der kosmologische Diskurs im alten Ägypten während des Neuen Reiches und der Spätzeit', in Zeller, Dieter (ed.), *Religion im Wandel der Kosmologien*. Frankfurt, 151–62.

Introducing Quotations in Selected Coptic Monastic Writings (Shenoute, *Canon* 6 and Besa)

A Linguistic Analysis[1]

So Miyagawa & Heike Behlmer

1 Quotations in the works of Shenoute and Besa

The monastic writings of two well-known abbots from 4th–5th-century Upper Egypt, Shenoute and Besa, both made frequent use of quotations from the Bible. Although in many cases there is no indication that certain Biblical verses or phrases were quoted, on numerous occasions quotations were prefaced by one of a range of templatic phrases which we call 'Quotative index Phrases' (QIPs). Our inspiration for this term was the term 'Quotative Index' introduced by Tom Güldemann in his work on African languages.[2] This paper builds on Janet Timbie's study of Shenoute's use of QIPs,[3] by integrating results from digital text reuse analyses and comparing Shenoute's usage of QIPs with that of his disciple.

2 Corpus

The current study examines the usage of QIPs in selected writings of Shenoute and the works of his disciple and successor, Besa. As for Shenoute's writings, the corpus consists of the entire remaining *Canon* 6, which is being digitally edited by a project in Göttingen.[4] *Canon* 6, according to the reconstruction of Shenoute's literary corpus by

---

1 This study has been supported by the German Research Foundation (DFG) as part of its Collaborative Research Centre (SFB) 1136 'Education and Religion in Cultures of the Mediterranean and Its Environment from Ancient to Medieval Times and to Classical Islam' (http://www.sfb1136.uni-goettingen.de. Accessed on 17 August 2020) "and by JSPS KAKENHI Grant Numbers JP21K00537, JP20K21975, and JP22H00721. We thank Dr Julien Delhez for his helpful corrections.

2 Güldemann's term indicates a different concept to the case discussed in this paper. See Güldemann (2008: 1–15). Güldemann's quotative index is a means to introduce a quotation in the spoken language such as the verb phrase with a complementizer 'I said that' in English.

3 Timbie typologizes frequently used QIPs (Timbie 2007: 629–30).

4 The project 'Biblical Interpretation and Educational Traditions in Coptic-speaking Egyptian Christianity of Late Antiquity: Shenoute, *Canon* 6' from 2015–2020 was part of the German Research Foundation (DFG)'s Collaborative Research Centre (SFB) 1136 Education and Religion in Cultures of the Mediterranean and Its Environment from Ancient to Medieval Times and to Classical Islam'. The edition is currently in the stage of final revision.

Sami Uljas & Andreas Dorn (eds), *Crossroads VI. Between Egyptian Linguistics and Philology*, 147–157
DOI: https://doi.org/10.37011/studmon.30.06

Stephen Emmel,[5] is one of his nine canons (collections of writings mainly on matters of monastic life and discipline). Besa's works are represented by the two main codices MONB.BA[6] and MONB.BB which have been digitally re-edited with photographs of the original manuscripts.[7]

More specifically, *Canon* 6 encompasses at least five works by Shenoute referred to by their incipits,[8] namely *He Who Sits Upon His Throne*; *Remember, O Brethren*; *Is It Not Written*; *Am I Obliged*; and *People Have Not Understood*. It is likely that more incipits existed in the numerous and extensive lacunae in the attestation of *Canon* 6. The six codices representing this canon are MONB.XF, MONB.XM, MONB.XV, MONB.YJ, MONB.YK, and MONB.XL. While there is little doubt that the first three, and possibly the fourth, are codices of *Canon* 6, the final two are compendiums of works taken from several Canons and Discourses, in particular the last (MONB.XL; the so-called *Florilegium Sinuthianum*[9]). The codices containing the works which comprise *Canon* 6 are scattered across museums and collections in Egypt and several other countries, including Italy, France, the UK, Austria, and the Netherlands, with many pages missing and others severely damaged. Using the 'Virtual Manuscript Room' of the project 'Digital Edition of the Coptic Old Testament' at the Göttingen Academy of Sciences and Humanities,[10] a collaborative research environment which allows the production of digital diplomatic and critical editions and a digital corpus in the TEI XML format,[11] the project team has transcribed these manuscripts from photographs.

Besa's writings, similarly scattered and collected, were transcribed and classified by their editor Karl Heinz Kuhn as *Letters and Sermons*. They are for the most part addressed

---

5 Emmel (2004).

6 The codices originate from the library of Shenoute's monastery (conventionally known as 'White Monastery'). The abbreviation MONB ('Monastero Bianco' = 'White Monastery') goes back to the Corpus dei Manoscritti Copti Letterari project (CMCL; http://www.cmcl.it/. Accessed on 17 August 2020) led by Tito Orlandi (cf. Orlandi 1990).

7 For detailed information on the codices attesting Canon 6, see Emmel (2004: 461–63) for MONB. XF, Emmel (2004: 475–77) for MONB.XM, Emmel (2004: 490) for MONB.XV, Emmel (2004: 472–74) for MONB.XL. For detailed information on the codices attesting Besa's *Letters and Sermons*, see Kuhn 1956: V–XIV and Emmel 2004: 90–3.

8 The contents of these works have been summarized as: (a) 'accusations against Shenoute of excessive force (and his defense)' (*He Who Sits upon His Throne*; *Remember, O Brethren*; *Is It Not Written*), (b) 'Shenoute's illness' (*Remember, O Brethren*, *Is It Not Written*, *Then I Am Not Obliged*), (c) 'affairs of the female community' (*He Who Sits upon His Throne*, *Then I Am Not Obliged*, *People Have Not Understood*), (d) 'monastic rules': Behlmer (2008: 2).

9 Emmel (2004: 111–25).

10 See Behlmer & Feder (2017).

11 Prior to encoding the texts in TEI XML, the *de facto* standard for marking up texts in Digital Humanities, we developed an optical character recognition tool for Coptic (see Miyagawa et al. 2019), which was used to transcribe printed editions. For the linguistic mark-up tools produced by Coptic SCRIPTORIUM (lemmatizer, part-of-speech tagger, syntactic parser, etc.) were used. For the entire pipeline of digitization from manuscript photos to web-based digital text corpora, see Miyagawa et al. (2018).

to the monks and nuns under his authority. In both *Canon* 6 and the writings of Besa a common theme is the call to repentance, expressed in harsh terms.

Overall, the corpus in its current form consists of 49,234 tokens in Shenoute's *Canon* 6 and 60,572 in Besa's works.[12] Hence, our Besa corpus is larger than the Shenoute corpus by about 23%.

3 Methodology

The Göttingen team used the TRACER software developed by the eTRAP research group at the Institute of Computer Science in Göttingen to detect instances of text reuse such as quotations, allusions, and paraphrases.[13] As a case study, we focused on the quotations from the Sahidic translation of the Psalms in the two chosen corpora. Fourteen previously unrecognized quotations were found.[14] These newly identified quotations were analyzed together with the quotations identified by previous studies such as those by Émile Amélineau, Hermann Wiesmann, and Dwight Young for Shenoute, and Karl Heinz Kuhn for Besa.[15]

Both Shenoute and Besa frequently made use of the QIP ⲛⲑⲉ ⲉⲧⲥⲏϩ (*n-t-ʰe et-sêh*)[16] 'in the way which is written' or 'as it is written'.[17] Using an analysis of all incidences of ⲛⲑⲉ ⲉⲧⲥⲏϩ (*n-t-ʰe et-sêh*) in the writings selected as a test case, the present study will discuss the formal characteristics of both authors' use of QIPs.

4 Results and types of the location of QIPs

The phrase ⲛⲑⲉ ⲉⲧⲥⲏϩ (*n-t-ʰe et-sêh*) appears 36 times in Shenoute's *Canon* 6 and 49 times in Besa's *Letters and Sermons*. In syntactic terms, three patterns emerge across both corpora for the use of ⲛⲑⲉ ⲉⲧⲥⲏϩ (*n-t-ʰe et-sêh*), namely pre-posed, inserted, and post-posed, as outlined below.

---

12 Tokens here are almost the same as the morphemes.

13 The doctoral thesis of the group leader Marco Büchler (Büchler 2013) shows the mechanism of TRACER in detail. The significant results produced by TRACER are shown in Büchler et al. (2014). A list of the publication of the eTRAP research group can be found at eTRAP (2015–18).

14 See Miyagawa et al. (forthcoming).

15 While not all the quotations in *Canon* 6 were detected by Amélineau (1907, 1914), Wiesmann (1931, 1952), and Young (2002), almost all the quotations in Besa's *Letters and Sermons* were found by Kuhn (1956).

16 For the transliteration of the Coptic into the Latin alphabet as customary in linguistics, we used the Leipzig-Jerusalem Transliteration Rules (Grossman & Haspelmath 2014).

17 Although both authors also use similar phrases such as ⲕⲁⲧⲁⲑⲉ ⲉⲧⲥⲏϩ (*kata-t-ʰe et-sêh*) 'according to what is written' or ϥⲥⲏϩ (*f-sêh*) 'it is written…' (cf. Timbie 2007: 629), the current paper focuses only on ⲛⲑⲉ ⲉⲧⲥⲏϩ (*n-t-ʰe et-sêh*).

(1) Pre-position of a QIP

a. Target text: Shenoute, *He Who Sits Upon His Throne* (MONB.YJ p. 33)

ⲁⲗⲗⲁ ⲉⲃⲟⲗ ⲣⲱ ϫⲉⲛⲧⲟϥ ⲡⲉⲛⲧⲁϥⲡⲗⲁⲥⲥⲉ ⲛⲛⲉⲩϩⲏⲧ ⲛⲑⲉ ⲉⲧⲥⲏϩ ϩⲛⲛⲉⲯⲁⲗⲙⲟⲥ ϫⲉⲡⲉⲛⲧⲁϥⲡⲗⲁⲥⲥⲉ ⲙⲁⲩⲁⲁϥ ⲛⲛⲉⲩϩⲏⲧ[18]

alla	*e-bol*	*rô*	*če-ntof*	*p-ent-a-f-plasse*
but	DAT-outside	itself	COMP-3SG.M	DEF.SG.M-REL-PST-3SG.M-shape

n-neu-hêt	*n-t-^{h}e*	*et-sêh*	*hn-ne-p^{s}almos*
ACC-POSS.PL:3PL-heart	LOC-DEF.SG.F-way.F	REL-write.STA	in-DEF.PL-Psalm

če-p-ent-a-f-plasse	*mauaa-f*	*n-neu-hêt*
COMP-DEF.SG.M-REL-PST-3SG.M-shape	alone-3SG.M	ACC-POSS.PL:3PL-heart.M

'but because it is he who has shaped their hearts, as it is written in the Psalms: "The one who alone has shaped their hearts" '

b. Source text: Ps 32(33):15[19]

ⲡⲉⲛⲧⲁϥⲡⲗⲁⲥⲥⲉ ⲙⲁⲩⲁⲁϥ ⲛⲛⲉⲩϩⲏⲧ ⲡⲉⲧⲉⲓⲙⲉ ⲉⲛⲉⲩϩⲃⲏⲩⲉ ⲧⲏⲣⲟⲩ

p-ent-a-f-plasse	*mauaa-f*	*n-neu-hêt*
DEF.SG.M-REL-PST-3SG.M-shape	alone-3SG.M	ACC-POSS.PL:3PL-heart

p-et-eime	*e-neu-hbêue*	*têr-ou*
DEF.SG.M-REL-know	DAT-POSS.PL:3PL-work.PL	all-3PL

'The one who alone has shaped their hearts, the one who knows all their works'

The above example is a section from a quotation from Psalms 32:15 which our TRACER analysis newly identified in *Canon* 6, and represents an example of a pre-posed QIP. First, Shenoute quotes Ps 33:15 near-verbatim: ⲁⲗⲗⲁ ⲉⲃⲟⲗ ⲣⲱ ϫⲉⲛⲧⲟϥ ⲡⲉⲛⲧⲁϥⲡⲗⲁⲥⲥⲉ ⲛⲛⲉⲩϩⲏⲧ 'but because it is he who has shaped their hearts' without ⲙⲁⲩⲁⲁϥ (*mauaa-f*) 'he alone'. Then he inserts a QIP ⲛⲑⲉ ⲉⲧⲥⲏϩ (*n-t-^{h}e et-sêh*) 'as it is written' and then quotes Ps 33:15 verbatim: 'the one who himself shaped their hearts' .

(2) Insertion of a QIP

a. Target text: Shenoute, *He Who Sits Upon His Throne* (MONB.YJ p. 33)

ⲡⲣⲱⲙⲉ ⲉϥϭⲱϣⲧ ⲉⲡϩⲟ ⲙⲙⲁⲧⲉ ⲛⲑⲉ ⲉⲧⲥⲏϩ ⲡⲛⲟⲩⲧⲉ ⲉϥϭⲱϣⲧ ⲉⲡϩⲏⲧ [...]

p-rôme	*e-f-côšt*	*e-p-ho*	*mmate*
DEF.SG.M-man.M	CIRC-3SG.M-look	DAT-DEF.SG.M-face.M	very

n-t-^{h}e	*et-sêh*	*p-noute*	*e-f-côšt*
LOC-DEF.SG.F-way.F	REL-write.STA	DEF.SG.M-God.M	CIRC-3SG.M-look

e-p-hêt
DAT-DEF.SG.M-heart.M

'the man looks at the face alone', as it is written, 'it is at the heart that God looks [...]'

---

18 We deleted all the punctuations and diacritics according to the style proposed by the Leipzig-Jerusalem Transliteration Rules. These features will be available in the digital diplomatic editions.

19 The Psalm text is from the base text of the Coptic Old Testament Digital Edition project at the Göttingen Academy of Sciences and Humanities. For the Coptic translation(s) of Psalms, see Nagel (2000, 2022) and Horn (2000). For a general discussion of the use of the Bible in Egyptian monasticism in Late Antiquity, see Behlmer (2016).

b. Source text: 1 Sam 16:7[20]

ⲡⲉϫⲉⲡϫⲟⲉⲓⲥ ⲛⲥⲁⲙⲟⲩⲏⲗ ϫⲉⲙⲡⲉⲣϭⲱϣⲧ ⲉϫⲙⲡⲉϥⲥⲁ ⲟⲩⲇⲉ ⲉϫⲛⲧϭⲟⲧ ⲛⲧⲉϥϣⲓⲏ ϫⲉϥⲣⲥⲟϣϥ ⲛⲁϩⲣⲁⲓ ϫⲉⲛⲑⲉ ⲁⲛ ⲉⲧⲉⲣⲉⲛⲉⲣⲱⲙⲉ ϭⲱϣⲧ ⲉⲡϩⲟ ⲉⲣⲉⲡⲛⲟⲩⲧⲉ ϩⲱⲱϥ ϭⲱϣⲧ ϫⲉⲉⲣⲉⲛⲣⲱⲙⲉ ϭⲱϣⲧ ⲉⲡϩⲟ ⲙⲙⲁⲧⲉ ⲡⲛⲟⲩⲧⲉ ⲇⲉ ⲛⲧⲟϥ ⲉϥϭⲱϣⲧ ⲉⲡϩⲏⲧ

peče-p-čoeis *n-samouêl* *če-mper-côšt*
said-DEF.SG.M-Lord.M DIR-Samuel QUOT-NEG.IMPER-look
ečm-pef-sa *oude* *ečn-t-cot*
upon-POSS.SG.M:3SG.M-beauty.M nor upon-DEF.SG.F-form/size.F
n-tef-šiê *če-f-r-sošf* *nahra-i*
GEN-POSS.SG.F:3SG.M-length QUOT-3SG.M-do-despise.STA before-1SG
če-n-t-^{h}e *an* *etere-ne-rôme* *côšt* *e-p-ho*
COMP-LOC-DEF.SG.F-way.F NEG REL-DEF.PL-man.M look DAT-DEF.SG.M-face.M
ere-p-noute *hôô-f* *côšt* *če-ere-n-rôme* *čôšt*
CIRC-DEF.SG.M-God.M self-3SG.M look COMP-CIRC-DEF.PL-man.M look
e-p-ho *mmate* *p-noute* *de* *ntof*
DAT-DEF.SG.M-face.M very DEF.SG.M-God.M but 3SG.M
e-f-čôšt *e-p-hêt*
CIRC-3SG.M-look DAT-DEF.SG.M-heart.M

'And the Lord said to Samouêl, Look not upon his beauty *nor* upon his stature; for he is despised in my sight; for not as men look at the face, does God look; for men look at the face only *and* God looks rather at the heart'.[21]

The example given above uses a QIP inserted in a quotation from 1 Sam 16:7.

(3) Post-position of a QIP

a. Source text: Shenoute's *Canon* 6 'He Who Sits Upon His Throne' (MONB.XM p. 276)[22]

ϯⲛⲁϫⲟⲟⲥ ⲉⲓⲥⲟⲟⲩⲛ ⲙⲡⲁⲛⲟⲃⲉ ϫⲉⲁⲡⲉⲕϭⲱⲛⲧ ⲧⲁϫⲣⲟ ⲉϩⲣⲁⲓ ⲉϫⲱⲓ ⲁⲛⲉⲕⲟⲣⲅⲏ ⲟⲛ ⲕⲱⲧⲉ ⲉⲣⲟⲓ ⲁⲛⲉⲕϩⲟⲧⲉ ϣⲧⲣⲧⲱⲣⲧ ⲛⲑⲉ ⲉⲧⲥⲏϩ

t^{i}-na-čoo-s *e-i-sooun* *m-pa-nobe*
1SG-FUT-say-3SG.F CIRC-1SG-know ACC-POSS.SG.M:1SG-sin.M
če-a-pek-cônt *tačro* *e-hrai* *ečô-i*
COMP-PST-POSS.SG.M:2SG.M-anger.M be_strengthened DAT-above over-1SG
a-nek-orgê *on* *kôte* *ero-i*
PST-POSS.PL:2SG.M-wrath.F further surround DAT-1SG
a-nek-hote *štrtôr-t* *n-^{t}-he* *et-sêh*
PST-POSS.PL:2SG.M-fear.F trouble-1SG LOC-DEF.SG.M-way.F REL-write.STA

'I will say, knowing my sin, 'Your anger has grown strong over me, and your wrath has surrounded me, your scares have troubled me', as it is written'.

20 Drescher (1970a).
21 Drescher (1970b: 36).
22 This part has a parallel text in MONB.XF pp. 263–64.

b. Source text 1: Ps 87:8

ⲁⲡⲉⲕϭⲱⲛⲧ ⲧⲁϫⲣⲟ ⲉϩⲣⲁⲓ ⲉϫⲱⲓ ⲁⲩⲱ ⲛⲉⲕⲣⲟⲟⲩϣ ⲧⲏⲣⲟⲩ ⲁⲕⲛⲧⲟⲩ ⲉϩⲣⲁⲓ ⲉϫⲱⲓ

a-pek-cônt	*tačro*	*e-hrai*	*ečô-i*
PST-POSS.SG.M:2SG.M-anger.M	be_strengthened	DAT-above	over-1SG

auô	*nek-roouš*	*têr-ou*	*a-k-nt-ou*	*e-hrai*
and	POSS.PL:2SG.M-concern	all-3PL	PST-2SG.M-bring-3PL	DAT-above

ečô-i
over-1SG

'Your anger has grown strong over me, and you brought all your concerns over me'.

b'. Source text 2: Ps 87:17–18

[17]ⲁⲛⲉⲕⲟⲣⲅⲏ ⲉⲓ ⲉϩⲣⲁⲓ ⲉϫⲱⲓ ⲁⲛⲉⲕϩⲟⲧⲉ ϣⲧⲣⲧⲱⲣⲧ [18]ⲁⲩⲕⲱⲧⲉ ⲉⲣⲟⲓ ⲛⲑⲉ ⲛⲛⲓⲙⲟⲟⲩ ⲁⲩⲁⲙⲁϩⲧⲉ ⲙⲙⲟⲓ ϩⲓ ⲟⲩⲥⲟⲡ ⲙⲡⲉϩⲟⲟⲩ ⲧⲏⲣϥ

a-nek-orgê	*ei*	*e-hrai*	*ečô-i*
PST-POSS.PL:2SG.M-wrath.F	come	DAT-above	over-1SG
a-nek-hote	*štrtôr-t*	*a-u-kôte*	*ero-i*
PST-POSS.PL:2SG.M-fear.F	disturb-1SG	PST-3PL-surround	over-1SG
n-t-^{h}*e*	*n-ni-moou*	*a-u-amahte*	*mmo-i*
LOC-DEF.SG.F-way.F	GEN-DEM.DIST.PL-water	PST-3PL-catch	ACC-1SG
hi-ou-sop	*m-pe-hoou*	*têr-f*	
at-INDEF.SG-time	GEN-DEF.SG.M-day.M	all-3SG.M	

'… your wrath has surrounded me. Your scares have troubled me. They have surrounded me like water. They have caught me at once all day long'.

Having pre-positioned ϯⲛⲁϫⲟⲟⲥ ⲉⲓⲥⲟⲟⲩⲛ ⲙⲡⲁⲛⲟⲃⲉ (*t*^{i}*-na-čoo-s e-i-sooun m-pa-nobe*) 'I will say knowing my sin', Shenoute quotes the first half verse of Ps 87:8 verbatim with the complementizer ϫⲉ (*če-*): ⲁⲡⲉⲕϭⲱⲛⲧ ⲧⲁϫⲣⲟ ⲉϩⲣⲁⲓ ⲉϫⲱⲓ (*a-pek-cônt tačro e-hrai ečô-i*) 'your anger has grown strong over me'. This is followed by a quotation from Ps 87:17–18 which is near verbatim, but in which the word order has been changed. Ps 87:17–18 contains four sentences, with two sentences per verse.

Having quoted the past auxiliary and the subject of the first sentence, ⲁⲛⲉⲕⲟⲣⲅⲏ (*a-nek-orgê*) 'your wrath',[23] Shenoute quotes the first half verse of Ps 87:18 ⲁⲩⲕⲱⲧⲉ ⲉⲣⲟⲓ (*a-u kôte ero-i*) 'they have surrounded me' near-verbatim inserting the particle ⲟⲛ (*on*) 'and, further, still, again' and using the subject of the first half verse of Ps 87:17 ⲛⲉⲕⲟⲣⲅⲏ (*nek-orgê*) 'your wrath' instead of the subject pronoun -ⲩ- (*-u-*) 'they'. Thereafter, he quotes the second half of Ps 87:17 verbatim: ⲁⲛⲉⲕϩⲟⲧⲉ ϣⲧⲣⲧⲱⲣⲧ (*a-nek-hote štrtôr-t*) 'your scares have troubled me'. The QIP is post-positioned after the quotation taken from the second half verse of Ps 87:17. It remains unknown whether the writer deliberately chose to mix elements in this way, or whether he was not aware of what he was doing.

A comparison was then made of the ratio of the three different types of ⲛⲑⲉ ⲉⲧⲥⲏϩ (*n-*^{t}*-he et-sêh*) QIP, namely pre-posed, inserted, and post-posed, in the two elements under

23 The possessive article is plural in Coptic and the possessor is the second-person masculine singular.

analysis: Shenoute's *Canon* 6 and Besa's *Letters and Sermons*. The goal of this analysis is to assess the use in which the two authors used Scriptures to prop up their arguments. Findings are presented below.

5 Corpus analysis of location of QIP

As noted above, there are 36 instances of the use of ⲛⲑⲉ ⲉⲧⲥⲏϩ (*n-ᵗ-he et-sêh*) in Shenoute's *Canon* 6, and 49 in Besa's *Letters and Sermons*. These findings were classified into the categories and dimensions illustrated in the two tables below. The two dimensions of these categories are (A) QIP location; and (B) presence or absence of the complementizer ϫⲉ (*če-*). Four possible types are comprised by A: pre-posed, inserted, post-posed, and post-posed/inserted (ambiguous), while (B) is comprised of three types: with ϫⲉ (*če-*), without ϫⲉ (*če-*), and with ⲉⲃⲟⲗ ϫⲉ (*ebol če-*).

Table 1: Distributions of the locations of QIPs in Shenoute's *Canon* 6 and Besa's *Letters and Sermons*

Shenoute's *Canon* 6

	Pre-posed	Inserted	Post-posed	Post-posed/ Inserted[a]
with ϫⲉ (*če-*)	29	0	0	0
without ϫⲉ (*če-*)	0	1	4	1
with ⲉⲃⲟⲗ ϫⲉ (*ebol če-*)	0	0	1	0

Besa's *Letters and Sermons*

	Pre-posed	Inserted	Post-posed	Post-posed/ Inserted[a]
with ϫⲉ (*če-*)	11	0	0	0
without ϫⲉ (*če-*)	0	6	29	2
with ⲉⲃⲟⲗ ϫⲉ (*ebol če-*)	0	0	1	0

a This designates cases where we could not decide whether the QIP is post-posed or inserted.

The complementizer ϫⲉ (*če-*) is always used after a pre-posed QIP by both Shenoute and Besa. Moreover, the complementizer ϫⲉ (*če-*) is absent from all post-posed and inserted QIPs except those with ⲉⲃⲟⲗ ϫⲉ (*ebol če-*). In such cases, ⲉⲃⲟⲗ ϫⲉ (*ebol če-*) is considered a non-complementizer since the clause containing ⲉⲃⲟⲗ ϫⲉ (*ebol če-*) is a reason clause, rather than a typical complement clause, as it signifies the reason for the main clause. The complementizer ϫⲉ- (*če-*) introduces complement clauses including verbs meaning 'say', 'write', 'know', or 'see'; however, it may also have the function of a subordinator of result or purpose, and be used adnominally.[24] All the attestations of ϫⲉ- (*če-*) except for that in

24 There are two possible scenarios of the historical change of ϫⲉ- (*če-*): (i) developed from *r-ḏd* (see examples in Collier 2007: 43–46), (ii) developed from *m-ḏd* (see Example 10 in Stauder

ⲉⲃⲟⲗ ϫⲉ (*ebol če-*) after ⲛⲑⲉ ⲉⲧⲥⲏϩ (*n-t-*^{h}*e et-sêh*) in the corpora at the basis of this paper form complement clauses, not other types of clauses.[25]

The construction of a pre-posed QIP places the actual direct quotation after the QIP with the complementizer ϫⲉ- (*če-*), while the construction for the post-posed QIP places it before the QIP without ϫⲉ- (*če-*). So does the construction for the inserted QIP construction, but with the QIP inserted within the quotation without the complementizer. Hence, in the pre-posed QIP construction the QIP introduces the quotation directly. Then the QIP clarifies that the following clause with ϫⲉ- (*če-*) is a quotation while it indicates the range of the quotation. On the other hand, in the other two types, the QIP implies that the surrounding phrase, clause, or sentence is a quotation without indicating the range of the quotation directly.

The pie charts below illustrate the distributions of the different QIP locations.

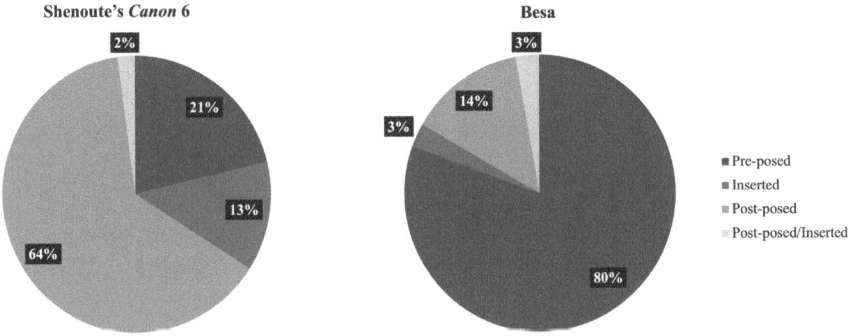

Figure 1 Distributions of the locations of the QIP in Shenoute's *Canon* 6 and Besa's *Letters and Sermons*

It can be seen that Shenoute's *Canon* 6 shows a predominance of post-posed QIPs, while the majority of QIPs in Besa's *Letters and Sermons* are pre-posed. Pre-posed construction accounts for only 21% of Shenoute's use of QIPs, as opposed to 80% in the case of Besa whereas the percentages for post-posed constructions are 64% and 14%, respectively. Although this difference is largely one of style, it demonstrates Shenoute's tendency to use quotations, particularly from Scripture, as part of his direct argument.

Within his use of pre-posed QIPs, Shenoute makes frequent use of the '[near-verbatim quotation] as it is written that [verbatim quotation]' pattern: four instances of this were

---

2014: 468). The process of grammaticalization and semantic conditions which led to *ḏd* being extended to perception verbs is discussed at length by Polis (2009: 344–97), who asserts that the grammaticalization derives from Late Egyptian *r-ḏd* or *m-ḏd* . Phonologically and in terms of diachronic evidence it is well-nigh certain that the origin of ϫⲉ- (*če-*) is *r-ḏd* . See also Allen (2013: 185–86).

25 ⲥⲏϩ (*sêh*) is a stative form of the verb ⲥϩⲁⲓ (*shai*) 'write' with static passive connotation (see Layton 2021: 129) so the complement clause is not a direct object of the verb, rather, it is a juxtaposition of the pro-dropped subject of ⲥⲏϥ (*sêh*). In English, a direct speech or quotation cannot be a that-clause, but in Coptic it can be a ϫⲉ-clause; see Layton (2011: 423–30).

identified in *Canon* 6, as opposed to one in the *Letters and Sermons*. Besa's text corpus analyzed in this study is substantially larger than Shenoute's Canon 6, and he makes more frequent use of pre-posed QIPs in general; nevertheless, Shenoute uses this particular pre-posed construction more often. Example 1(a) demonstrates Shenoute's use of this pattern. In this case, the writer first bases his argument on an adapted and incomplete quotation ⲉⲃⲟⲗ ⲣⲱ ϫⲉⲛⲧⲟϥ ⲡⲉⲛⲧⲁϥⲡⲗⲁⲥⲥⲉ ⲛⲛⲉⲩϩⲏⲧ (*e-bol rô če-ntof p-ent-a-f-plasse*) 'because it is he who has shaped their hearts', after which he uses the QIP ⲛⲑⲉ ⲉⲧⲥⲏϩ (*n-t-^{h}e et-sêh*) 'as it is written' with a complementizer, followed by a complete quotation 'the one who alone has shaped their hearts'. In other words, the incomplete quotation is used without ⲙⲁⲩⲁⲁϥ (*mauaa-f*) 'alone', after which a QIP and complete quotation are used. This practice suggests that Shenoute employed a wider range of rhetoric devises to drive in his point through Scriptural quotations than Besa.

6 Conclusion

Shenoute's use of quotations demonstrates his skill at integrating scriptural selections into his teachings as head of a monastery, someone responsible for the discipline and spiritual welfare of his monks, as Behlmer demonstrated for the first seven pages of MONB.XF.[26] The present research, identifying how Shenoute and Besa made different use of ⲛⲑⲉ ⲉⲧⲥⲏϩ (*n-t-^{h}e et-sêh*), could furnish some support to the argument that Shenoute was, indeed, the more skillful rhetorician. He both uses fewer pre-posed QIPs than Besa (21% vs. 80%), and tends to use a particular pattern when he does so (i.e., an incomplete quotation followed by a pre-posed QIP, complementizer, and verbatim re-quotation). Besa, in contrast, tends to use the single, pre-posed QIP pattern more frequently to clearly signal to his readers that he will be quoting from Scripture. The quantitative analysis undertaken for the present study demonstrates that Shenoute incorporated scriptural passages more deeply into his works than Besa, recontextualizing and integrating the messages of the Bible to support his own educational teachings. Arguably, this particular feature might be an indication that Shenoute was the more skillful rhetorician of the two.

The study has shown how Shenoute mobilized quotations for what appears to be a different range of rhetoric effects. He favored the postposed type, which has a very immediate and forceful effect and probably also required greater processing from the audience inasmuch as such quotations were not immediately signalled. Rather, they were, as it were, built more 'into' his overall rhetoric and were not flagged with a 'pre-warning' as in Besa's case.

References

Amélineau, Émile. 1907. *Œuvres de Schenoudi, texte copte et traduction française*. Vol. 1. Paris.
Amélineau, Émile. 1914. *Œuvres de Schenoudi, texte copte et traduction française*. Vol. 2. Paris.
Allen, James. 2013. *The Ancient Egyptian Language. An Historical Survey*. Cambridge.

26 Behlmer (2017: 327). The first seven pages of MONB.XF are the beginning of *He Who Sits Upon His Throne*, the first work of *Canon* 6.

Behlmer, Heike. 2008. 'Do not believe every word like the fool...! Rhetorical strategies in Shenoute, *Canon* 6', in: Gabra, Gawdat & Hany Takla (eds). *Christianity and Monasticism in Upper Egypt, Vol. 1: Akhmim and Sohag.* Cairo, 1–12.

Behlmer, Heike. 2016. 'Die Bibel im koptischen Mönchtum der Spätantike', in: Peter Gemeinhardt (ed.). *Zwischen Exegese und religiöser Praxis: Heilige Texte von der Spätantike bis zum Klassischen Islam.* Tübingen, 143–76.

Behlmer, Heike. 2017. 'The Use of the Psalms in Shenoute's Tractate *He Who Sits Upon His Throne*', in Brakke, David, Stephen Davis & Stephen Emmel (eds). *From Gnostics to Monastics. Studies in Coptic and Early Christianity in Honor of Bentley Layton.* Leuven; Orientalia Lovaniensia Analecta, 315–30.

Behlmer, Heike & Frank Feder. 2017. 'The complete digital edition and translation of the Coptic Sahidic Old Testament. A new research project at the Göttingen Academy of Sciences and Humanities', *Early Christianity* 8, 97–107.

Büchler, Marco. 2013. *Informationstechnische Aspekte des Historical Text Re-use.* Published doctoral thesis. Universität Leipzig, http://www.qucosa.de/fileadmin/data/qucosa/documents/10851/Dissertation.pdf. Accessed 17 August 2020.

Büchler, Marco, Philip Burns, Martin Müller, Emily Franzini & Greta Franzini. 2014. 'Towards a historical text re-use detection', in: Berry, Michael & Jacob Kogan (eds). *Text Mining, Theory and Applications of Natural Language Processing.* Basel, 221–38.

Collier, Mark. 2007. 'Facts, situations and knowledge acquisition: *gmỉ* with *ỉw* and *r-ḏd* in Late Egyptian', in: Schneider, Thomas & Kasia Szpakowska (eds). *Egyptian Stories: A British Egyptological Tribute to Alan B. Lloyd on the Occasion of His Retirement.* Münster; Alter Orient und Altes Testament 347, 33–46.

Drescher, James. 1970a. *The Coptic (Sahidic) Version of Kingdoms I, II (Samuel I, II) [Textus].* Louvain; Corpus Scriptorum Christianorum Orientalium 313, Scriptores Coptici 35.

Drescher, James. 1970b. *The Coptic (Sahidic) Version of Kingdoms I, II (Samuel I, II) [Versio].* Louvain; Corpus Scriptorum Christianorum Orientalium 314, Scriptores Coptici 36.

Emmel, Stephen. 2004. *Shenoute's Literary Corpus.* 2 vols. Leuven.

eTRAP. 2015–18. 'Output,' https://www.etrap.eu/academic-output/. Accessed 20 October 2021.

Franzini, Greta, Marco Passarotti, Maria Moritz & Marco Büchler. 2018. 'Using and evaluating TRACER for an Index fontium computatus of the Summa contra Gentiles of Thomas Aquinas', in: Elena Cabrio, Alessandro Mazzei & Fabio Tamburini (eds). *Proceedings of the Fifth Italian Conference on Computational Linguistics (CLIC-it 2018): Torino, Italy, December 10–12, 2018,* http://ceur-ws.org/Vol-2253/paper22.pdf. Accessed 03 January 2020.

Grossman, Eitan & Martin Haspelmath. 2014. 'The Leipzig-Jerusalem transliteration of Coptic', in: Grossman, Eitan, Tonio Sebastian Richter & Martin Haspelmath (eds). *Egyptian-Coptic Linguistics in Typological Perspective.* Berlin; Empirical Approaches to Language Typology 55, 145–54.

Horn, Jürgen. 2000. 'Die koptische (sahidische) Überlieferung des alttestamentlichen Psalmenbuches — Versuch einer Gruppierung der Textzeugen für die Herstellung des Textes', in: Aejmelaeus, Anneli & Udo Quast (eds). *Der Septuaginta-Psalter und seine Tochterübersetzungen.* Göttingen; Abhandlungen der Akademie der Wissenschaften in Göttingen, Philologisch-Historische Klasse, Folge 3, 320: Mitteilungen des Septuaginta-Unternehmens 24, 97–106.

Kramer, Ruth. 2012. 'Egyptian', in: Edzard, Lutz (ed.). *Semitic and Afroasiatic: Challenges and Opportunities.* Wiesbaden; Porta Linguarum Orientalium 24, 59–130.

Kuhn, Karl-Heinz. 1956. *Letters and Sermons of Besa.* Louvain; Corpus Scriptorum Christianorum Orientalium 157, Scriptores Coptici 21.

Layton, Bentley. 2011. *A Coptic Grammar: With Chrestomathy and Glossary: Sahidic Dialect.* Third Edition, Revised. Wiesbaden; Porta Linguarum Orientalium 20.

Miyagawa, So, Amir Zeldes, Marco Büchler, Heike Behlmer & Troy Griffitts. 2018. 'Building linguistically and intertextually tagged Coptic corpora with open source tools', in: Chikahiko

Suzuki (ed.), *Proceedings of the 8th Conference of Japanese Association for Digital Humanities*. Tokyo, 139–41.

Miyagawa, So, Kirill Bulert, Marco Büchler & Heike Behlmer. 2019. 'Optical character recognition of typeset Coptic text with neural networks', *Digital Scholarship in the Humanities* 34 (Supplement 1), 135–41.

Miyagawa, So, Marco Büchler & Heike Behlmer. Forthcoming. 'Computational analysis of text reuse/intertextuality: The example of Shenoute Canon 6'. in: Takla, Hany, Stephen Emmel & Maged Mikhail (eds). *Proceedings of the Eleventh International Congress of Coptic Studies*. Leuven; Orientalia Lovaniensia Analecta.

Nagel, Peter. 2000. 'Der sahidische Psalter — seine Erschließung und Erforschung 90 Jahre nach Alfred Rahlfs' Studien zum Text des Septuaginta-Psalters', in: Aejmelaeus, Anneli & Udo Quast (eds). *Der Septuaginta-Psalter und seine Tochterübersetzungen. Symposium in Göttingen 1997*. Göttingen; Abhandlungen der Akademie der Wissenschaften in Göttingen 3/230, Mitteilungen des Septuaginta-Unternehmens 24, 82–96.

Nagel, Peter. 2022. *Der sahidische Psalter. Editio minor nach den Handschriften Ms. Or. 5000 der British Library zu London, Ms. n° 815 der Chester Beatty Library zu Dublin, und Ms. n° 1667 der University of Michigan Library zu Ann Arbor*. Wiesbaden: Harrassowitz; Texte und Studien zur Koptischen Bibel 3.

Polis, Stéphane. 2009. *Étude de la modalité en néo-égyptien*. Unpublished doctoral thesis, Université de Liège.

Stauder, Andréas. 2014. 'A rare change: The degrammaticalization of an inflectional passive marker into an impersonal subject marker', in: Grossman, Eitan, Tonio Sebastian Richter & Martin Haspelmath (eds). *Egyptian-Coptic Linguistics in Typological Perspective*. Berlin; Empirical Approaches to Language Typology 55, 455–532.

Timbie, Janet. 2007. 'Non-canonical scriptural citation in Shenoute', in: Bosson, Nathalie & Anne Boud'hors (eds). *Actes du huitième Congrès international d'études coptes : Paris, 28 juin-3 juillet 2004*. Leuven, 625–34.

Wiesmann, Hermann. 1931. *Sinuthii Archimandritae Vita et Opera Omnia III* (Latin translation). Paris; Corpus Scriptorum Christianorum Orientalium 96, Scriptores Coptici 8.

Wiesmann, Hermann. 1952. *Sinuthii Archimandritae Vita et Opera Omnia IV* (Latin translation). Paris; Corpus Scriptorum Christianorum Orientalium 108, Scriptores Coptici 12.

Young, Dwight. 2002. 'Two Unplaced Fragments From a Copy of Shenute's Sixth Canon', *Göttinger Miszellen* 189, 99–110.

‘Where No Man Has Gone Before …’

Coptic Patterns for Locative Adverbial Clauses

Matthias Müller[1]

Abstract

Locative adverbial clauses of the type ‘Where there is smoke, there is fire’ lead a drab existence in most grammars, not only those of the Coptic language. The present paper aims to describe the Coptic patterns for the first time. Lacking a specific connector, Coptic uses an appositive construction with the word ‘place,’ usually marked as definite, followed by a (restrictive or non-restrictive) relative clause. The use of the locative interrogative ‘where’ is limited to indirect questions.

1 Locative clauses

It is banal but true to say that locative clauses have not received much attention in either linguistic or Coptological cycles. Thompson, Longacre, and Wang devote roughly a third of a page to the issue in Timothy Shopen’s *Language Typology and Syntactic Description.*[2] No Coptic grammar treats this type of clauses explicitly,[3] and even if any of the patterns described below appear in such works, they do so only under very specific circumstances, i.e., in places one would not necessarily look for them. Hence a few general remarks on the type of clauses might serve as an introduction.

To approach the issue, one may draw a list of the basic locative adverbial functions[4] and see whether these can be transferred into adverbial clauses. The core function thereof is arguably the expression of a position in space, i.e., static location as in ‘She is there’. The other most basic spatial notion is direction. However, here one should draw a line between direction towards a goal (‘She goes to town’) versus from a given source (‘She

1 Basel. Due to the Covid pandemic, the present author was forced to abandon writing his actual Crossroads VI contribution *Certain Types of Object Clauses* into a published paper. The editors of this volume were so kind as to accept another paper originally presented at the previous Crossroads conference in Berlin. The author would like to express his gratitude to the participants of the conference in Berlin and their comments during the discussion after the presentation as well as later during the conference. Karsten Schmidtke-Bode/Jena, Jennifer Cromwell/Manchester, Eitan Grossman/Jerusalem, and Sami Uljas/Uppsala provided useful comments to an earlier version of the paper.

2 Thompson, Longacre & Wang (2007: 249).

3 With the exception now of Müller (2021: 502–04).

4 Cf. e.g. Hasselgård (2010: 24–25, 187–217).

Sami Uljas & Andreas Dorn (eds), *Crossroads VI. Between Egyptian Linguistics and Philology*, 159–190
DOI: https://doi.org/10.37011/studmon.30.07

arrives today from Paris'). In addition, direction can be marked via the expression of the path ('A river runs through the valley'). Finally, distance can be expressed as well via spatial adjuncts referring to a spatial extent ('She would walk for miles for that book').

Transferring these functions into locative clauses is relatively straightforward for static location ('... where he is') and the expression of goal- or source-oriented direction ('... wither/where she goes to' vs. '... whence/where she comes from'), and similarly for the expression of path ('where they ran along...'). For the spatial extent one might think of clauses that do not specify spatial extent precisely ('as far as ...') or else do exactly that ('For a stretch of two miles, all houses had been devastated by the storm'). As with spatial adjuncts, the expression of direction is coded primarily by the verbs of motion used, as can be seen in the quoted examples (at least in English). Here, however, two caveats need to be made. One must distinguish the use of locative state of affairs in dependent clauses from those in main clauses. Even if in *'You cannot go where I stand'* a direction towards a goal is expressed, this lies in the main rather than the dependent clause, which expresses a static location instead (*'where I stand'*). A second caveat pertains to distinguishing locative adverbial clauses from complement or relative clauses. In principle, locative clauses can appear in (at least) three environments: as adverbial clauses (e.g. 'Where I lived, no one had ever heard of this'), as relative clauses (as in 'the land where milk and honey flows'), and as argument clauses of certain verbs ('I don't know where she put it').

For a definition of adverbial clauses, I follow Hetterle:[5]

> Adverbial clauses are clausal entities that modify, in a very general sense, a verb phrase or main clause and explicitly express a particular conceptual-semantic concept such as simultaneity, anteriority, causality, conditionality, and the like.

For the present purpose, one will merely have to add the concept of 'space' to the above definition and the class of 'locative clauses' to Hetterle's list of defined individual semantic types.[6] Kortmann included locative adverbial clauses under his residual class of 'others'.[7] So, lest one mix up different concepts, it seems advisable to keep 'space' apart here.

Complement clauses are considered to fill an argument position of a verb.[8] Hence, an example such as *'To bodly go where no man has gone before'* falls out of the scope of the present paper since the direction occupies a locative argument position of the verb *go* instead of modify the state of affairs of the movement; similarly in the above quoted example *'I don't know where she put it'.*

With these definitions, one can weed out examples in which the locative state of affairs modifies only a specific part of a clause, as in *The country where I live is known for its cheese and chocolate*. In such sentences, the locative clause is used as a relative clause modifying a specific NP. However, a certain ambiguity remains since clauses such as *to boldly go where no man has gone before* could be understood as relatives with a zero ante-

---

5 Hetterle (2015: 37–46, with the quote on p. 38).
6 Hetterle (2015: 46–54).
7 Kortmann (1997: 81, 88).
8 Noonan (2007: 52–53).

cedent as in *to boldly go to any place where no man has gone before*. This fuzzy position between adverbial and locative relative clause has probably favoured e.g. the extension of the use of *wo* in Southern German and Swiss German varieties as a general relative particle.[9] Eitan Grossman refers me to the development of Greek ποῦ (originally 'where'), which has taken over a plethora of subordinating functions in Modern Greek.

Thus, the above may be summarised as follows:

- Locative clauses
  - Location in Space 'where p, q'
    German: *Wo ein Genosse ist, da ist die Partei*
    (Where there is a comrade, the party is too).
  - Direction Goal 'whither p, q'
    Whither he looked, clouds darkened the sky.

    Source 'whence p, q'
    Norwegian/Bokmål: *Hvor jeg kommer fra jeg har aldri sett ei svarte svane.*
    (Where I come from, I have never seen a black swan.)

    Path 'along/where p, q'
    German: *Wo wir durchkamen, hatte das Feuer aufgeräumt*
    (Where we came through, the fire had made a clean sweep).
  - Distance 'as far as p, q'/'for ... p, q'
    As far as this river runs, there are no signs of human settlements.
    For the past 10 miles, there were no signs of human settlements.

The first three types of locative clauses above can be expected to appear with a regular (though probably not very high) frequency. Sentences in which a locative clause does focus on the path or the distance are probably not as common.[10]

In addition to the above–mentioned spatial adjunct one might add Universal Concessive Conditionals with spatial reference (henceforth UCC).[11] Similar to the the adverbial patterns above, UCCs can also express a position in space ('Wherever you are...'), a direction towards a goal ('Wherever you go...'), from a source ('Wherever you come from...') or simply the movement ('Wherever you walk') or distance ('How(ever) far ...'). As can be seen from the English examples, the majority of functions are coded with the help of 'wherever'. However, as UCCs are the least grammaticalised category of concessive

9 Thus e.g. Züritüütsch (Swiss German variety of Zurich): *Die wo lüüged, pschyssed au* 'Those who lie deceive as well' (Weber 1948: §§340–44), Bärndütsch (Swiss German variety of Bern): *dä Maa, wo mir geschter hei gseh vorbylouffe* 'the man whom we have seen passing yesterday' (Suter 1992: §§288–91), and Baaseldytsch (Swiss German variety of Basel): *dä Maa, wòn em alles abverheit* 'the man who always fails' (Marti 1985: 235–37). This use intrudes occasionally into the standard variety of certain speakers (*der, wo's nötig hat*).

10 This is, however, no more than a vague impression that cannot, at least at present, be supported by the necessary empirical studies on other languages.

11 Haspelmath & König (1998).

conditionals,[12] one should probably allow for a greater variety of patterns for such expressions in Coptic.

Again, the above may be summarised as follows:

- Universal concessive conditionals
  - Position in Space
    Italian: *Ovunque sei, sto pensendo a te.*
    (Wherever you are, I am thinking of you.)
  - Direction Goal
    German: *Wo auch immer du hingehst, das Problem wird dir folgen.*
    (Wherever you go, that problem will follow you.)

    Source
    French: *D'ou qu'ils viennent, nous devons les aider.*
    (Wherever they come from, we must help them.)

    Path
    Wherever you walk, keep off the lawn!
  - Distance
    How far you may run, they will catch you.

Again, here a certain caveat seems necessary seeing that UCCs often use different patterns depending on their stage of grammaticalisation.[13] German, for instance, can express space position UCCs as *'wo immer p'*, *'wo auch immer p'* or simply by *'wo auch p'*, hence employing different adverbs to distinguish the UCC from the adverbial clause. Similarly, a UCC function can be expressed by employing other adverbs such as *egal* 'regardless, whatever' (e.g. in *'...egal wo du auch pennst'* '...wherever you sleep'). In addition, even an otherwise unmarked pattern, i.e., one formally identical with an adverbial clause, might be open to a generic UCC reading, as in *'Wo Rauch ist, ist auch Feuer'*. It shall be seen below that the same applies in Coptic data as well.

2 Coptic data

Since none of the Coptic grammars contains an entry *Locative adverbial clauses* in their table of contents or index lists, one must search the Scriptures for instances translated as locative clauses in other languages and then study the Coptic forms and constructions that the translators rendered thus. This exercise produces two generic patterns:[14]

- *Patterns with a locative interrogative* and
- *Patterns with a word for place followed by a relative clause.*

One may then consult the Coptic grammars afresh, where constructions with the lexeme ⲙⲁ *ma* 'place' turn out to provide usable data.[15] Yet seeing that grammars still remain more

12 As shown in Müller (2009: 174–76).
13 See again Haspelmath & König (1998).
14 As mentioned in passing in Müller (2012: 153–54).
15 See Layton (2011: §493.43), although for UCCs only.

or less silent on the topic, old-fashioned datamining, i.e., reading through text editions, is the only way to gather data. Further, the existing electronic textual corpora are not yet particularly representative, which explains the somewhat ecletic material base of the present study.

2.1 With locative interrogatives

Although it may appear as rather Eurocentric, addressing the one Coptic pattern similar to the one known from many European languages provides an easy way into the issue. All the examples include the locative interrogative adverb[16] ⲧⲱⲛ *tôn* 'where' in its various dialectal variants (e.g. ᴬⲧⲱ *tô*, ᴸⲧⲟ *to*, ᴮⲑⲱⲛ *tʰôn*):

(1) When the Pharisees objected to Jesus' describing himself as the Light of the World, he answered that his testimony was nevertheless true:

ϫⲉϯⲥⲁⲩⲛⲉ	ϫⲉⲛ̄ⲧⲁⲉⲓ	ⲧⲟ	ⲁⲩⲱ	ⲉⲉⲓⲛⲁⲃⲱⲕ	ⲁⲧⲟ
ce-ti-saune	*ce-nta-(i)-i*	*to*	*auô*	*e-i-na-bôk*	*a-to*
for-1SG-know	that-FOC-PST-1SG-come	where	CON	FOC-1S-FUT-go	to-where

…for I know whence I came and whither I go. (ᴸJohn 8:14)

(2) When a monk tells Cyril that there are five Gospels, the archbishop asks in amazement:

ⲛⲓⲙ	ⲡⲉ	ⲡⲣⲁⲛ	ⲙ̄ⲡⲙⲉϩϯⲟⲩ	ⲛ̄ⲉⲩⲁⲅⲅⲉⲗⲓⲟⲛ	ⲧⲁⲣⲉⲛⲉⲓⲙⲉ
nim	*pe*	*p-ran*	*m-p-meh-tiu*	*n-euaggelion*	*tare-n-ime*
who	COP.M	DF.M-name	of-DF.M-ORD-five	of-gospel	FIN-1PL-know

ϫⲉⲟⲩ{ⲉ}ⲉ̄ⲃⲟⲗ	ⲧⲱⲛ	ⲡⲉ	ⲧⲉⲥⲃⲱ	ⲙ̄ⲡⲉⲭ︦ⲥ︦	ⲧⲉⲛⲉⲓⲙⲉ	ⲉⲣⲟⲥ
ce-u-ebol	*tôn*	*pe*	*te-sbô*	*m-pe-kh(risto)s*	*te-n-ime*	*ero-s*
that-IDF.SG-out	where	COP.M	DF.F-teaching	of-DF.M-Christ	CNJ-1PL-know	OBJ-3MSG

What is the name of the fifth Gospel, so that we know where the teaching of Christ is from and understand it?

(ˢCyril of Jerusalem, *On Mary Theotokos* ed. Budge 1915: 60.29–31)

(3) The Lord urged Israel to repent, for only then would they be saved:

ⲁⲩⲱ	ⲉⲕⲛⲉⲓⲙⲓ	ϫⲉⲉⲕⲧⲱⲛ
auô	*e-k-ne-imi*	*ce-e-k-tôn*
CON	FOC-2MSG-FUT-know	CMP-FOC-2MSG-where

…and realize where you were. (ᶠIs 30:15)

(4) A Gnostic treatise likens the Only-begotten with 'The one who dwells in the Monad which is in the Sêtheus':

ⲧⲁⲓ	ⲉⲛⲧⲁⲥⲉⲓ	ⲉⲃⲟⲗ	ϩⲙ̄ⲡⲙⲁ	ⲉⲛⲧⲉⲥⲉⲛⲁϣϫⲟⲟⲥⲁⲛ
tai	*ent-a-s-i*	*ebol*	*hm-p-ma*	*ente-se-na-š-coo-s=an*
DM.F	REL-PST-3FSG-come	out	in-DF.M-place	REL-3PL-FUT-can-say-3FSG=NEG

ϫⲉⲧⲱⲛ	ⲡⲉ
ce-tôn	*pe*
CMP-where	SE.M

16 From its translation, the lexical status of *tôn* as adverb might appear odd. However, the etymology and syntactic behaviour of *tôn* show that it is not a pronoun and cannot occupy all syntactic positions of NPs.

…which (i.e. the Monad) came from a place of which none will be able to say where it is. ([S]*Acephalous Text* in Cod. Bruce ed. Schmidt & MacDermot 1978: 234.17–19)

(5) The Proverbs ask who it is that suffers from woes and answers with the rhetorical questions as to whether it not be those who linger over wine:

ⲛⲉⲧϣⲓⲛⲉ	ϫⲉⲁⲣⲉⲙ̄ⲙⲁⲛ̄ⲥⲟⲩ	ⲛⲁϩⲱⲡⲉ	ⲧⲱ
n-et-šine	*ce-are-m-ma-n-su*	*na-ḥôpe*	*tô*
DF.PL-REL-ask	that-FOC-DF.PL-place-of-drink	FUT-happen	where

…those who ask where the drinking places is? ([A]Pro 23:30 ed. Böhlig 1958: 118)

(6) Joseph is looking for his brothers near Shechem and asks a man:

ⲁⲓⲕⲱϯ	ⲛⲥⲁⲛⲁⲥⲛⲏⲟⲩ	ⲙⲁⲧⲁⲙⲟⲓ	ϫⲉⲁⲩⲙⲟⲛⲓ	ⲛⲑⲱⲛ
a-i-kôti	*nsa-na-snêu*	*ma-tamo-i*	*ce-a-u-moni*	*n-t^hôn*
FOC-1SG-turn	after-POSS.PL.1SG-brother.PL	IMP-tell-1SG	that-FOC-3PL-pasture	in-where

I am looking for my brothers. Tell me where they pasture! ([B]Gen 37:16)

As can be seen, all these examples share the feature that the locative clause is the argument of a verb of knowlegde (as in 1–3 with ⲥⲁⲩⲛⲉ and ⲉⲙⲓ/ⲓⲙⲓ, both ‘know’) or speech (as in 4 with ϫⲱ ‘say,’ 5 with ϣⲓⲛⲉ ‘ask’ or 6 with ⲧⲁⲙⲟ ‘tell’). One could surmise that the pattern with locative interrogatives was confined to translated (and thus) literary texts. Yet, it can be found also in untranslated texts such as private letters (7) or in Shenute’s writings (8):

(7) An author of a letter reports what he did concerning a certain village-headman. He asks his addressee for help and begs him to go to the place of master Petra:

ⲛⲁⲩ	ϫⲉϣⲁⲣⲉⲡⲕⲱⲙⲏⲕⲁⲑⲏⲕⲏⲥ	ⲉⲓ	ⲧⲱⲛ
nau	*ce-šare-p-kômêkathêkês*	*i*	*tôn*
see.IMP	CMP-AOR-DF.M-village_headman	go	where

ⲉⲙⲟⲛ	ⲡⲣⲱⲥ	ⲡⲙⲁ	ⲁⲇⲉⲗⲫⲏ	ⲡⲣⲱⲥ	ⲡⲙⲁ	ⲛⲁⲡⲁ	ⲃⲁⲛⲉ
emon	*prôs*	*p-ma*	*adelphê*	*prôs*	*p-ma*	*n-apa*	*bane*
verily	after	DF.M-place	N	after	DF.M-place	of-N	N

See where the village-headman will go, whether to the place of Adelphius or the place of Apa Bane. ([S]*P.Ryl.Copt.* 320.11–13)

(8) Shenute speaks about hate among the brethren quoting 1Jn 3:15 (*Who hates his brother is a killer*) and continues:

ⲡⲉⲧⲙⲟⲥⲧⲉ	ⲙⲡⲉϥⲥⲟⲛ	ⲉϥϣⲟⲟⲡ	ϩⲙⲡⲕⲁⲕⲉ
p-et-moste	*m-pe-f-son*	*e-f-šoop*	*hm-p-kake*
DF.M-REL-hate	OBJ-POSS.M-3MSG-brother	FOC-3MSG-be.STA	in-DF.M-dark

ⲁⲩⲱ	ⲉϥⲙⲟⲟϣⲉ	ϩⲙⲡⲕⲁⲕⲉ	ⲉⲛϥⲥⲟⲟⲩⲛⲁⲛ
auô	*e-f-mooše*	*hm-p-kake*	*e-n-f-soun=an*
CON	FOC-3MSG-walk	in-DF.M-dark	DEP-NEG-3MSG-know=NEG

ϫⲉⲉϥⲃⲏⲕ	ⲉⲧⲱⲛ	ϫⲉⲁⲡⲕⲁⲕⲉ	ⲧⲱⲙ	ⲛⲛⲉϥⲃⲁⲗ
ce-e-f-bêk	*e-tôn*	*ce-a-p-kake*	*tôm*	*n-ne-f-bal*
CMP-FOC-3MSG-go.STA	to-where	for-PST-DF.M-dark	shut	OBJ-POSS.PL-3MSG-eye

He who hates his brother dwells in darkness, and in darkness he walks, not knowing where to go since darkness closed his eyes.

([S]Shenute, *Why O Lord* ed. Leipoldt 1908: 124.9–11)

Again, the locative interrogative adverb ⲧⲱⲛ *tôn* 'where' appears in clauses serving as an argument of verbs of perception (ⲛⲁⲩ *nau* 'see' in 7) and knowledge (ⲥⲟⲟⲩⲛ *soun* 'know' in 8). This is the sole syntactic environment where the pattern occurs in the texts examined. Hence, one can formulate the descriptive 'rule' that the appearance of the pattern with a locative interrogative is limited to argument clauses of verbs of perception or of speech acts.

2.2 With a word for a locus plus relative clause

As noted, the second emergent pattern involves the word ^{BSLA}ⲙⲁ *ma*/^{FM}ⲙⲉ *me*[17] 'place' followed by a relative clause. This raises a methodological issue concerning the morpho-syntactic status of the expression, i.e. whether it should be regarded as a still fully lexical word for 'place' or as a grammaticalized element functioning as an adverbial subordinator. Given that—as will be seen shortly—the construction can appear in prepositional phrases and be marked by additional morphemes such as *-ke-* 'other', the first alternative seems more likely. Coptic therefore never fully grammaticalized a pattern for locative adverbials, but employed a locative expression in a flexible way.

The following discussion is subdivided according to the patterns introduced in 1 above, but leaving aside Distance of which no conclusive examples were found.

2.2.1 Static Location/Space Position *('where p, q')*

Basically, the data can be divided from a formal-syntactic perspective into patterns in which the locative clause either appears on its own or is governed by a preposition (such as *hm-p-ma* 'in the place' or *e-p-ma* 'to the place'). Prototypically, the word ⲙⲁ *ma* is marked with the masculine definite article (in Bohairic usually with the long form ⲡⲓ- *pi-* expressing specificity in opposition to generic reference)[18] followed by a relative clause. The following examples have been taken from the major dialects:

(9) The Epistle of James calls for wisdom instead of lies and deceit:

ⲡⲙⲁⲅⲁⲣ	ⲉⲧⲉⲣⲉⲕⲟϩ	ϩⲓϯⲧⲱⲛ	ⲛϩⲏⲧϥ
p-ma=gar	*etere-koh*	*hi-titôn*	*nhêt-f*
DF.M-place=for	REL-jealousy	CON-strife	inside-3MSG

ϥⲙⲙⲟⲟⲩ	ⲛϭⲓⲡⲉϣⲧⲟⲣⲧⲣ	ⲙⲛϩⲱⲃ	ⲛⲓⲙ	ⲉⲑⲟⲟⲩ
f-mmo-u	*nc^hi-pe-štortr*	*mn-hôb*	*nim*	*et-hou*
3MSG-in-3PL	PVS-DF.M-agitation	CON-thing	QU	REL-evil

For where there is jealousy and strife, there is agitation and every evil thing. (^{S}Jam 3:16)

(10) Asked whether a certain place would be dark, the guiding angel responded:

ⲙ̄ⲙⲁⲛ	ϫⲉⲡⲙⲁ	ⲉⲧⲉⲛ̄ⲇⲓⲕⲁⲓⲟⲥ	ϩⲟⲟⲡ	ⲛ̄ϩⲏⲧϥ	ⲙⲛ̄ⲛⲉⲧⲟⲩⲁⲁⲃⲉ	ⲙⲛ̄ⲕⲉⲕⲉ
mman	*ce-p-ma*	*ete-n-dikaios*	*ḫoop*	*nḫet-f*	*mn-n-etuaabe*	*mn-keke*
no	for-DF.M-place	REL-DF.PL-just	be.STA	inside-3MS	CON-DF.PL-holy	NEG-darkness

17 For the sake of convenience, the BSLA form ⲙⲁ *ma* is used to refer to the lexical item in general.
18 Müller (2021: 20–26).

ϩⲟⲟⲡ	ⲙ̄ⲡⲙⲁ	ⲉⲧⲙ̄ⲙⲟ	ⲁⲗⲗⲁ	ⲁⲩϩⲟⲟⲡ	ϩⲛ̄ⲡⲟⲩⲁⲉⲓⲛⲉ	ⲛ̄ⲟⲩⲁⲉⲓϣ	ⲛⲓⲙ
ḫoop	*m-p-ma*	*etmmo*	*alla*	*a-u-ḫoop*	*hn-p-uaine*	*n-uaiš*	*nim*
be.STA	in-DF.M-place	that	but	FOC-3PL-be.STA	in-DF.M-light	in-time	QUA

No! For where the righteous and the saints are, there is no darkness, but they dwell in the light at all time. (^{A}*Apoc. Sophon.* ed. Steindorff 36 2.4–8)

(11) After Jesus had finished his words:

ⲁϥⲓ	ⲁⲃ[ⲁⲗ]	ⲙⲛ̄ⲛⲉϥⲙⲁⲑⲏⲧⲏⲥ	ⲁⲡⲓⲕⲣⲟ	ⲙ̄ⲡⲉⲭⲓⲙⲁ[ⲣ]ⲣⲟⲥ
a-f-i	*abal*	*mn-ne-f-mathêtês*	*a-pi-kro*	*m-pe-khimarros*
PST-3MSG-come	out	CON-POSS.P-3MSG-disciples	to-DF.M-bank	of-DF.M-ravine

ⲙ̄ⲡⲕⲉⲇⲣⲟⲥ	ⲡⲙⲁ	ⲉⲣⲉⲟⲩⲛⲟⲩⲕⲏⲡⲟⲥ	ⲛ̄ϩⲏⲧϥ̄
m-p-kedros	*p-ma*	*ere-un-u-kêpos*	*nhêt-f*
of-DF.M-cedar	DF.M-place	DEP-PTC-IDF.SG-garden	inside-3MSG

ⲁⲡⲙⲁ	ⲛ̄ⲧⲁϥⲃⲱⲕ	ⲁϩⲟⲩⲛ	ⲁⲣⲁϥ	ⲙⲛ̄[ⲛⲉ]ϥⲙⲁⲑⲏⲧⲏⲥ
p-ma	*nt-a-f-bôk*	*ahun*	*ara-f*	*mn-ne-f-mathêtês*
DF.M-place	REL-PST-3MSG-go	into	to-3MSG	CON-POSS.P-3MSG-disciples

When he had said these things, Jesus and the disciples went to the yon bank of the ravine of the Cedar, where there was a garden where he and his disciples went. (^{L}John 18:1)

(12) John Colobus relates that he visited a number of holy places in Jerusalem:

ⲁⲓϩⲱⲗ	ⲟⲛ	ⲉⲡⲓϣⲏⲓ	ⲡⲓⲙⲁ	ⲉⲧⲁⲩϩⲓⲟⲩⲓ̈	ⲛ̇ⲓⲉⲣⲉⲙⲓⲁⲥ
a-i-hôl	*on*	*e-pi-šêi*	*pi-ma*	*et-a-u-hiui*	*n-ieremias*
PST-1SG-go	again	to-DF:S.M-well	DF:S.M-place	REL-PST-3P-throw	OBJ-N

ⲉϧⲣⲏⲓ	ⲉⲣⲟϥ	ⲁⲓϩⲱⲗ	ⲟⲛ	ⲉ̇ⲡⲧⲱⲟⲩ	ⲛⲛⲓϫⲱⲓⲧ
eḫrêi	*ero-f*	*a-i-hôl*	*on*	*e-p-tôu*	*n-ni-côit*
down	to-3MSG	PST-1SG-go	again	to-DF:G.M-mount	of-DF:G.PL-olive

ⲡⲓⲙⲁ	ⲉⲣⲉⲛⲓⲁⲡⲟⲥⲧⲟⲗⲟⲥ	ⲑⲟⲩⲏ̇ⲟⲩⲧ	ⲉⲣⲟϥ	ⲛⲉⲙⲙⲁⲣⲓⲁ̇
pi-ma	*ere-ni-apostolos*	*t^huêut*	*ero-f*	*nem-maria*
DF:S.M-place	DEP-DF:S.PL-apostle	gather.STA	to-3MSG	CON-N

ⲑⲙⲁⲩ	ⲙ̇ⲡϭ︦ⲥ︦
t^h-mau	*m-p-c^h(ôi)s*
DF:G.M-mother	of-DF:S.M-lord

I also went to the well where Jeremiah had been thrown into, and I also went to the Mount of Olives, where the apostles gathered with Mary the mother of the Lord. (^{B}Theodosius of Alexandria, *On the Three Youths of Babylon* ed. de Vis 1929: 136.3–5)

(13) Jesus said that one should not cling onto earthly treasures:

ⲧⲁⲩⲧⲉⲇⲉ	ⲛ̇ⲧⲁϥ	ⲛⲏⲧⲉⲛ	ⲛ̇ϩⲉⲛⲁ̇ϩⲱⲣ	ϩⲛⲙ̄ⲡⲏⲟⲩⲉ̇
taute=de	*ntaf*	*nê-ten*	*n-hen-ahôr*	*hn-m-pêue*
collect.IMP=but	3MSG	for-2PL	in-IDF.PL-treasure.PL	in-DF.PL-heaven

ⲡⲙⲉ	ⲉⲧⲉⲙⲉⲣⲉⲑⲁⲗⲉ	ⲙⲛⲧⲉⲥⲉ	ⲧⲁⲕⲁⲩ
p-me	*ete-mere-t-hale*	*mn-t-ese*	*taka-u*
DF.M-place	REL-NEG.AOR-DF.F-moth	CON-DF.F-moth	destroy-3PL

ⲁⲩⲱ	ⲡⲙⲉ	ⲉⲧⲉⲙⲉⲣⲉⲣⲉϥϫⲓⲟⲩⲉ	ϣⲁϫⲧ	ⲛ̀ϥϫⲓⲟⲩⲉ
auô	*p-me*	*ete-mere-ref-ciue*	*šact*	*n-f-ciue*
CON	DF.M-place	REL-NEG.AOR-AGT-steal	break_in	CNJ-3MSG-steal

But accumulate for yourselves treasures in heaven, where moth and rust do not destroy and where no thief breaks in and steals. ([M]Mt 6:20)

(14) After Timothy's death, Papnute moved on:

ⲁⲓⲙⲟϣⲓ	ⲉ̀ϧⲟⲩⲛ	ⲉ̀ⲡⲓⲧⲱⲟⲩ	ⲉⲧⲥⲁϧⲟⲩⲛ	
a-i-moši	*eḫun*	*e-pi-tôu*	*et-saḫun*	
PST-1SG-walk	into	to-DF:S.M-mountain	REL-inside	
ⲡⲓⲙⲁ	ⲉ̀ⲧⲉⲛⲓⲃⲁⲣⲃⲁⲣⲟⲥ	ⲛ̀ϧⲏⲧϥ	ϧⲉⲛⲡϣⲁϥⲉ	ⲉⲧⲥⲁϧⲟⲩⲛ
pi-ma	*ete-ni-barbaros*	*nḫêt-f*	*ḫen-p-šafe*	*et-saḫun*
DF:S.M-place	REL-DF:G.PL-savage	inside-3MSG	in-DF:G.M-desert	REL-inside

I went on into the inner desert, where the savages are, in the inner wasteland.
([B]Papnute, *Wanderings*, §10 ed. Amélineau 1885)

The difference between relative (ⲉⲧ-) and virtual relative clauses (ⲉ-) following the 'the place' (e.g. 12) can be explained as that between marking the difference between restrictive and non-restrictive relative clauses.[19]

There exists also an alternative pattern, where the locative clause appears within a prepositional phrase that thus does not appear in ante-position. This is mostly encountered after the preposition [SL]ϩⲛ-/[B]ϧⲉⲛ- *hn-/ḫen-* 'in' (exx. 15–16)[20] but also after [SB]ⲉ- *e-* 'to' (17–20):

(15) The sisters of Lazarus sent a message to Jesus that their brother was about to die:

ⲛ̄ⲧⲁⲣⲉϥⲥⲱⲧⲙ̄ⲇⲉ	ϫⲉϥϣⲱⲛⲉ	ⲧⲟⲧⲉⲙⲉⲛ	ⲁϥϭⲱ	ⲛ̄ϩⲟⲟⲩ
ntare-f-sôtm=de	*ce-f-šône*	*tote=men*	*a-f-cʰô*	*n-hou*
TMP-3MSG-hear=yet	CMP-3MSG-be_sick	then=indeed	PST-3MSG-stay	in-day
ⲥⲛⲉⲩ	ϩⲛ̄ⲡⲙⲁ	ⲉⲧϥⲛ̄ϩⲏⲧϥ		
snau	*hn-p-ma*	*et-f-nhêt-f*		
two.M	in-DF.M-place	REL-3MS-inside-3MS		

When he heard that he was sick, he remained where he was for two days. ([L]John 11:6)

(16) Boaz tells Ruth to stay on the field and that he told his people not to molest her. He goes on to tell her that if she felt thirsty, she should go to the vessels:

ⲛⲧⲉⲥⲱ	ϩⲙⲡⲙⲁ	ⲉⲧⲉⲣⲉⲛϣⲏⲣⲉ	ϣⲏⲙ	ⲛⲁⲙⲉϩⲙⲟⲟⲩ	ⲉⲣⲟϥ
nte-ø-sô	*hm-p-ma*	*etere-n-šêre*	*šêm*	*na-meh-mou*	*ero-f*
CNJ-2FSG-drink	in-DF.M-place	REL-DF.PL-son	small	FUT-fill-water	to-3MSG

…and drink where the young men will fill water. ([S]Ru 2:9 ed. Thompson 1911)

(17) A man confessed his sin to Matthew the Poor and told that he enticed a gardener away from the latter's home and wife at night. Then he went on to tell that the Devil had entered him:

19 See Müller (2015) for discussion.

20 For the partial labial assimilation of the nasal see Loprieno & Müller (2012: 119).

ⲁⲓⲧⲱⲟⲩⲛ	ϩⲙⲡⲙⲁ	ⲉϯⲛⲕⲟⲧⲕ	ⲛϩⲏⲧϥ
a-i-tôun	*hm-p-ma*	*et-i-nkotk*	*nhêt-f*
PST-1SG-rise	in-DF.M-place	REL-1SG-lie	inside-3MSG

ⲁⲩⲱ	ⲁⲓⲃⲱⲕ	ⲉⲡⲙⲁ	ⲉⲧⲉⲣⲉⲧⲉⲥϩⲓⲙⲉ	ⲙⲡⲕⲱⲙⲁⲣⲓⲧⲏⲥ	ⲛⲕⲟⲧⲕ	ⲛϩⲏⲧϥ
auô	*a-i-bôk*	*e-p-ma*	*etere-te-shime*	*m-p-kômaritês*	*nkotk*	*nhêt-f*
CON	PST-1S-go	to-DF.M-place	REL-DF.F-woman	of-DF.M-gardener	lie	inside-3MSG

I rose where I slept and I went to where the wife of the gardener slept.

(^S^*Life of Matthew the Poor* ed. Amélineau 1895: 728.1–3)[21]

(18) Frange had tried in vain to visit Mahencnout, but did not meet him. He sent a letter asking him to meet him outside next time:

ⲙ̄ⲙⲟⲛ	ⲁⲛⲟⲕ	ⲣⲱ	ⲁϊⲉⲓ	ⲉϩⲟⲩⲛ	ⲙ̄ⲡⲓϭⲛ̄ⲑⲉ	ⲛ̄ⲉⲓ
mmon	*anok*	*rô*	*a-i-i*	*ehun*	*mp-i-c^{h}n-t-he*	*n-i*
verily	1SG	PTC	PST-1SG-come	into	NEG.PST-1SG-find-DF.F-way	of-come

ⲉⲡⲙⲁ	ⲉⲧⲉⲕⲟⲩⲏϩ	ⲛ̄ϩⲏⲧϥ̄	ⲛ̄ⲧⲁⲁⲡⲁⲛⲧⲁ	ⲉⲧⲉⲕⲙⲛ̄ⲧⲥⲟⲛ
e-p-ma	*ete-k-ûeh*	*nhêt-f*	*nt-a-apanta*	*e-te-k-mnt-son*
to-DF.M-place	REL-2MSG-dwell.STA	inside-3MSG	CNJ-1SG-meet	OBJ-POSS.F-2MSG-ABST-brother

Verily, I came to visit and I could not find the way to enter where you live so as to meet your brotherliness. (^S^*O.Frange* 175.8–13 ed. Boud'hors & Heurtel 2010)

(19) Jesus narrates that the Archangel Michael blesses other angels when they have to descend upon earth, lest the Devil tempts them. He says: *Go in peace*

ⲉⲗⲉⲫϯ	ⲉⲧⲉⲛϣⲙϣⲉ	ⲙⲙⲁϥ	ⲥⲕⲉⲡⲁⲍⲉ	ⲙⲙⲁⲧⲉⲛ	ⲛⲧⲉⲧⲉⲛⲡⲱⲧ	ⲉⲡⲕⲟⲥⲙⲟⲥ
ele-p^{h}-(nu)ti	*ete-n-šmš*	*mma-f*	*skepaze*	*mma-ten*	*nte-ten-pôt*	*e-p-kosmos*
OPT-DF.M-god	REL-1P-serve	OBJ-3MS	protect	OBJ-2P	CNJ-2P-go	to-DF.M-world

ⲉⲡⲙⲉ	ⲉⲧⲉⲛⲁϥⲉⲛϩⲏⲧⲃ	ⲛϫⲉⲡϫⲁⲥⲓϩⲏⲧ	ⲛⲇⲓⲁⲃⲟⲗⲟⲥ
e-p-me	*ete-na-f-enhêt-b*	*nce-p-casihêt*	*n-diabolos*
to-DF.M-place	REL-IPF-3MS-inside-3MS	PVS-DF.M-vain	of-devil

May God, whom we serve, protect you when you enter the profane world where the vain Devil is *(so that you return in peace).*

(^F^*Investiture of Archangel Michael* ed. Müller 1962: 27.15–17)

(20) One day, St Pisenthius beheld a deacon spitting next to the altar with the sacred liturgical objects upon it:

ⲥⲁⲧⲟⲧϥ	ⲁϥⲑⲣⲟⲩⲙⲟⲩϯⲛⲁϥ	ⲉϧⲟⲩⲛ	ϣⲁⲣⲟϥ
satotf	*a-f-t^{h}r-u-muti=na-f*	*eḫun*	*šaro-f*
forthwith	PST-3MSG-CAUS-3PL-call=for-3MSG	into	to-3MSG

21 Some readings have been corrected following Till (1936: 7).

ⲉⲡⲓⲙⲁ	ⲉⲛⲁϥⲉⲣⲏ́ⲥⲓⲭⲁⲍⲉ	ⲛ́ϧⲏⲧϥ
e-pi-ma	*e-na-f-er-êsikhaze*	*nḫêt-f*
to-DF:S.M-place	DEP-PRT-3MSG-AUX-rest	inside-3MSG

Forthwith he had him called in to him where he rested.

(BMoses of Quft, *On Pisenthius* ed. Amélineau 1889: 109 coll.)

As can be seen, the patterns deviate from each other only by their respective dependence from a preposition.

From a semantic point of view, one must discard a number of the above examples, because the majority of them involve appositive rather than adverbial clauses modifying the main clause state of affairs, as required by the initially quoted definition above. Similarly, in (21) below, ‘where the children of Israel dwelled’ in fact serves as an apposition to ‘the land of Goshen’ rather than modifies ‘it did not hail’.

(21) Thunder, hail, and fire falling from the sky destroyed all of Egypt:

ϣⲁⲧⲉⲛⲡⲕⲁϩⲓ	ⲛⲅⲉⲥⲉⲙ	ⲙⲙⲁⲩⲁⲧϥ	ⲡⲓⲙⲁ	ⲉⲛⲁⲩϣⲟⲡ	ⲛϧⲏⲧϥ
šaten-p-kahi	*n-gesem*	*mmauat-f*	*pi-ma*	*e-na-u-šop*	*nḫêt-f*
until-DF:G.M-land	of-N	self-3MSG	DF:S.M-place	REL-PRT-3PL-be.STA	in-3MSG

ⲛϫⲉⲛⲉⲛϣⲏⲣⲓ	ⲙⲡⲓⲥ̅ⲗ̅	ⲙⲡⲉⲡⲓⲁⲗ	ϣⲱⲡⲓ	ⲙⲙⲁⲩ
nce-nen-šêri	*m-p-is(raê)l*	*mpe-pi-al*	*šôpi*	*mmau*
PVS-DF:G.PL-child	of-DF:G.M-N	NEG.PST-DF:S.M-hail	happen	there

Only in the land of Goshen, where the children of Israel dwelled, there was no hail.

(BEx 9:26 ed. de Lagarde 1867)

By contrast, the clause ‘where there is a woman’ in the following example does modify the main clause state of affairs rather than provides additional information concerning an argument of the main clause:

(22) Jesus Sirach elaborates on the effects that women have on men, comparing a woman to possessions of man. Just as the absence of a fence will give others easy opportunity to plunder:

ⲁⲩⲱ	ⲡⲉⲧⲕⲱⲧⲉ	ⲛⲁⲁϣⲁϩⲟⲙ	ⲡⲙⲁ	ⲉⲧⲉⲥϩⲓⲙⲉ	ⲛ̄ϩⲏⲧϥ̄
auô	*p-et-kôte*	*na-ašahom*	*p-ma*	*ete-shime*	*nhêt-f*
CON	DF.M-REL-turn	FUT-sigh	DF.M-place	REL-woman	inside-3MSG

...the one who wanders will groan, where there is a woman.”

(SEccl 36:30 ed. de Lagarde 1883: 171 as 36:33)

This leaves one with examples 9–10, and 15–17 from the above as adverbial clauses, whilst examples 11–14, and 18–20 are better labelled as appositions or complements. Nevertheless, phrasal embedding seems to be irrelevant for the differentiation between the two uses.

The following examples are semantically slightly ambiguous, since the locative clauses are arguments of the main clause verb:

(23) Archellites released his servants from his service since he intended to renounce the world and take residence in a monastery. He told them to go wherever they wish but adjured them by God:

ϫⲉⲕⲁⲥ	ⲛⲛⲉⲧⲛ̄ⲃⲱⲕ	ⲉⲡⲙⲁ	ⲉⲧⲉⲣⲉⲧⲁⲙⲁⲁⲩ	ⲛ̄ϩⲏⲧϥ̄
cekas	*nne-tn-bôk*	*e-p-ma*	*etere-ta-mau*	*nhêt-f*
so_that	NEG.OPT-2PL-go	to-DF.M-place	REL-POSS.F.1SG-mother	inside-3FSG

ϫⲉⲛⲛⲉⲥⲛⲁⲩ	ⲉⲣⲱⲧⲛ̄	ⲛⲥ̄ⲙⲟⲩ
ce-nne-s-nau	*erô-tn*	*n-s-mu*
SO-NEG.OPT-3FSG-see	OBJ-2PL	CNJ-3FSG-die

…that you do not go to where my mother is, lest she see you and die.
(^{S}*Archellites* ed. Drescher 1947: 16.32–33)

(24) As told by God, Abraham arose the next morning, prepared everything, left with Isaac:

ⲁϥⲓ	ⲉ̀ⲡⲓⲙⲁ	ⲉ̀ⲧⲁⲫϯ	ϫⲟⲥ	ⲛⲁϥ
a-f-i	*e-pi-ma*	*et-a-p^{h}-(nu)ti*	*co-s*	*na-f*
PST-3MSG-go	to-DF:S.M-place	REL-PST-DF:G.M-god	say-3FSG	for-3MSG

…and came to where God had told him. (^{B}Gen 22:3 ed. de Lagarde 1867)

(25) Jesus called Lazarus back from the dead and spoke with him. He told him to have no fear but to come out of his tomb and talk. He added further:

ϭⲱϣⲧ̄	ⲉⲡⲙⲁ	ⲉⲛⲉⲕⲛ̄ⲕⲁⲧⲕ̄	ⲛ̄ϩⲏⲧϥ̄
c^{h}ôšt	*e-p-ma*	*e-ne-k-nkatk*	*nhêt-f*
behold.IMP	OBJ-DF.M-place	DEP-PRT-2MSG-lie	inside-3MSG

ϫⲉⲉϥⲙⲉϩ	ⲛ̄ⲓ̈ⲁⲁⲃⲉ	ⲉϥⲗⲟⲙⲥ̄
ce-e-f-meh	*n-iaabe*	*e-f-loms*
for-FOC-3MSG-be_full.STA	with-pus.F	DEP-3MSG-stink.STA

Behold where you lay, for it is full of pus and stinks.
(^{Sf}Athanasius of Alexandria, *On Lazarus* ed. Bernadin 1940: [pl. 8 = 284.21–22])

(26) Eusebius tells his audience that it was Jesus who cast out the demon from the woman's daughter. He then asks:

ⲙⲏⲅⲁⲣ	ⲟⲩⲣⲱⲙⲉ	ⲧⲁⲣⲉϥⲃⲱⲕ	ⲉⲡⲙⲁ	ⲉⲧϥ̄ⲛ̄ϩⲏⲧϥ̄
mê=gar	*u-rôme*	*tare-f-bôk*	*e-p-ma*	*et-f-nhêt-f*
IRP=for	IDF.SG-man	FIN-3MSG-go	to-DF.M-place	REL-3MSG-inside-3MSG

ⲁⲗⲗⲁ	ⲟⲩⲛⲟⲩⲧⲉ	ⲡⲉ	ⲉϥⲙⲟⲩϩ	ⲙ̄ⲙⲁ	ⲛⲓⲙ
alla	*u-nute*	*pe*	*e-f-muh*	*m-ma*	*nim*
but	IDF.SG-god	SE.M	DEP-3MSG-fill	OBJ-place	QU

Is he human so that he might go where he is? Rather he is divine, filling every place.
(^{S}Eusebius of Caesaria, *On the Canaanite Woman* ed. Budge 1910: 142.11–13)

(27) A hermit narrates how he once got severely ill when suddenly a radiant figure appears asking:

ⲙⲁⲧⲁⲙⲟⲓ	ⲉ̀ⲡⲓⲙⲁ	ⲉ̀ⲧⲉⲕϣⲱⲛⲓ	ⲉ̀ⲣⲟϥ
ma-tamo-i	*e-pi-ma*	*ete-k-šôni*	*ero-f*
IMP-inform-1SG	to-DF:S.M-place	REL-2MSG-be_sick	to-3MSG

Show me where it hurts! (^{B}Papnute, *Wanderings*, §8 ed. Amélineau 1885 coll.)

So far, almost all examples have been affirmative, but negated clauses exist as well (see also 13 above):

(28) Shenute speaks against defilement of the souls and says:

ⲡⲙⲁⲅⲁⲣ	ⲉⲧⲉⲣⲉⲡⲉⲡⲛ̅ⲁ̅	ⲉⲧⲟⲩⲁⲁⲃ	ⲛϩⲏⲧϥ	ⲁⲛ
p-ma=gar	*etere-pe-pn(eum)a*	*etuaab*	*nhêt-f*	*an*
DF.M-place=for	REL-DF.M-spirit	holy	inside-3MSG	NEG

ⲉⲣⲉⲙⲛⲧⲁⲥⲉⲃⲏⲥ	ⲛⲓⲙ	[ⲡⲟ]ⲗⲓⲧⲉⲩⲉ	ⲛϩⲉⲧϥ
ere-mnt-asebês	*nim*	*politeue*	*nhêt-f*
FOC-ABST-impious	every	rules	inside-3MSG

ⲡⲙⲁⲇⲉ	ⲉⲧⲉⲣⲉⲡⲉⲡⲛ̅ⲁ̅	ⲉⲧⲟⲩⲁⲁⲃ	ⲛϩⲏⲧϥ	ⲉϥⲙⲙⲁⲩ
p-ma=de	*etere-pe-pn(eum)a*	*etuaab*	*nhêt-f*	*e-f-mmau*
DF.M-place=for	REL-DF.M-spirit	holy	inside-3MSG	FOC-3MSG-there

ⲛϭⲓⲡⲉⲭ̅ⲥ̅
nc^h*i-pekh(risto)s*
PVS-DF.M-Christ

For where the Holy Ghost is not, every impiety rules. Yet, where the Holy Ghost is, there is the Christ. (^{S}Shenute, *I Remember* ed. Amélineau 1914: 331.14–332.2)

To resume the results sofar: The locative clause with 'the place' may or may not be governed by a preposition. The choice of the relative clause pattern is dependent on the need to mark the relative clause as restrictive (relative clause) or non-restrictive (virtual relative clause aka dependent ('circumstantial') in character.[22] The tense-marking of the locative clause is found within the relative clause. Syntactically, all semantically appropriate patterns seem to be allowed, although those expressing stative location predominate due to the semantic nature of the type of adverbial clause.

Yet, not every instance of a clause with the word 'place' followed by a relative clause can and should be regarded as a locative adverbial clause in Coptic:

(29) According to a saying, during Julian the Apostate's Persian campaign, the emperor had sent a demon to the west to bring him news as fast as possible:

ⲛ̀ⲧⲉⲣⲉⲡⲇⲁⲓⲙⲱⲛⲇⲉ	ⲡⲱϩ	ⲉϩⲛ̀ⲙⲁ	ⲉϥϣⲟⲟⲡ	ⲛ̀ϩⲏⲧⲟⲩ
ntere-p-daimôn=de	*pôh*	*e-hn-ma*	*e-f-šoop*	*nhêt-u*
TMP-DF.M-demon=yet	reach	to-IDF.PL-place	DEP-3MSG-be.STA	inside-3PL

ⲛ̀ϭⲓⲟⲩⲙⲟⲛⲁⲭⲟⲥ	ⲁϥϭⲱ	ⲙ̀ⲙⲁⲩ	ⲙ̀ⲙⲏⲧ	ⲛ̀ϩⲟⲟⲩ	ⲙ̀ⲡⲉϥⲕⲓⲙ
nc^h*i-u-monakhos*	*a-f-c*^{h}*ô*	*mmau*	*m-mêt*	*n-hou*	*mpe-f-kim*
PVS-IDF.SG-monk	PST-3MSG-stay	there	in-ten	of-day	NEG.PST-3MSG-move

ⲙ̀ⲡⲉϥϭⲙϭⲟⲙ	ⲉⲙⲟⲟϣⲉ	ⲉⲑⲏ
mpe-f-c^h*mc*^{h}*om*	*e-mooše*	*e-t-hê*
NEG.PST-3MSG-can	to-walk	to-DF.F-front

When the demon reached *places in which/*where* a monk dwelled, he stayed there for ten days, and did not move, nor was he able to proceed further.

(^{S}*ApophPatr* #231 ed. Chaîne 1960: 68)

22 Müller (2015).

In the example above, the use of the plural indefinite article seems to show that this is not an example of an adverbial clause of the type discussed here (i.e. one that could be understood as meaning *reached where a monk dwelled*). Instead, a literal understanding (as *reached places where a monk dwelled*) seems preferable. Similarly, not every instance of ⲡⲙⲁ *p-ma* (i.e. with the singular masculine definite article) plus relative, especially when embedded into a prepositional phrase, should be taken as a locative clause. That is, the expression ⲡⲙⲁ *p-ma* plus relative was not fully grammaticalised as marking locative adverbial clauses only.

2.2.2 Direction goal (⇥ 'whither', 'where to')

As noted in the introduction above, a distinction must be made between examples which mark the goal within their own clausal structure and those with directions marked in the main clause. Thus, the following example (30) is better classified as expressing static location in the adverbial clause even though the semantics of that part of the spell generally express a goal-orientation. Yet this goal-orientation is marked via a spatial preposition:

(30) In a magical spell for success in fishing, the conjurer wishes that Jesus caused the archangel Raphael to collect a mighty catch:

ϫïⲛⲛ̄ϫⲱϥ̄	ⲙ̄ⲡⲕ[ⲁϩ	ϣ]ⲁϫⲱⲃ	ϩⲏⲧ	ⲣⲏⲥ	ⲡⲉⲓⲏϥⲧ	ⲙⲛ̄ⲡⲉⲙⲏⲧ
cinn-cô-f	*m-p-kah*	*ša-cô-b*	*hêt*	*rês*	*p-ieft*	*mn-p-emêt*
from-head-3MSG	as-DF.M-earth	to-head-3MSG	north	south	DF.M-east	DF.M-west

ⲉⲡⲙⲁ	ⲉⲧⲉⲣⲉⲡⲉⲕⲥⲡⲱⲧⲓⲟⲛ	ⲙⲛ̄ⲛⲉⲕⲫⲩⲗⲁⲕⲧ	ⲛⲁϣⲱⲡⲉ	ⲛ̄ϩⲏⲧϥ
e-p-ma	*etere-pe-k-spôtion*	*mn-ne-k-phulakt(êrion)*	*na-šôpe*	*nhêt-f*
to-DF.M-place	REL-POSS.M-2MSG-figure	CON-POSS.P-2MSG-amulet	FUT-be	inside-3MSG

…from end to end of the earth, north, south, east, and west, to where your figure and your amulets will be. ([S]London BL Ms. Or 6795.44–47 ed. Kropp 1931: 33–34)

Clear examples of goal-orientation within the clause are the following:

(31) On the obverse of an ostracon, a list with the names of venerated monks and archimandrites is given. The text on the reverse addresses the Christ and then prays to the Trinity:

ϣⲱⲡⲉ	ⲉⲕ̣[ⲟⲩⲟⲛϩ]	ⲉⲃⲟⲗ	ϩⲙ̄ⲡⲙⲁ	ⲉⲧⲟⲩⲛⲁⲕⲱⲡⲉⲓⲡⲗⲁⲝ	ⲛϩⲏⲧϥ
šôpe	*e-k-uonh*	*ebol*	*hm-p-ma*	*et-u-na-kô-pei-plaks*	*nhêt-f*
happen.IMP	DEP-2MSG-reveal.STA	out	in-DF.M-place	REL-3PL-FUT-DM.M-slab	inside-3MSG

ⲛⲅ̄ⲁⲣⲉϩ	ⲉⲡⲉⲥⲩⲛⲑⲓⲟⲥ	ϣⲏⲙ	ⲡϫⲟⲉⲓⲥ
n-g-areh	*e-pesunthios*	*šêm*	*p-cois*
CNJ-2MSG-guard	OBJ-N	little	DF.M-lord

Make yourself visible where this document will be placed and watch over the little Pesynthios, O Lord. ([S]*P.MoscowCopt.* 93+9.rev. 5–8)

(32) Cyril narrates the story of a rich Jew called Cleopas, who was so gout-ridden that he was neither able to walk nor to mount an animal. His servants carried him around in a litter:

ⲁⲩⲱ	ⲛ̄ⲥⲉϫⲓⲧϥ	ⲉⲡⲙⲁ	ⲉⲧϥ̄ⲟⲩⲱϣⲃⲱⲕ	ⲉⲣⲟϥ
auô	*n-se-cit-f*	*e-p-ma*	*et-f-uš-bôk*	*ero-f*
CON	CNJ-3PL-take-3MSG	to-DF.M-place	REL-3MSG-wish-go	to-3MSG

…and they took him where he wanted to go.

([S]Cyril of Jerusalem, *On the Cross* ed. Budge 1915: 203.23–24)

(33) The archangel Raphael's deeds are narrated in a concise fashion, including the Tobias episode, in which the archangel acted incognito as a guide for Tobias. Then it is said:

ⲁⲩⲱ	ⲡⲙⲁⲟⲛ	ⲛ̄ⲧⲁϥⲃⲱⲕ	ⲉⲣⲟϥ
auô	*p-ma=on*	*nt-a-f-bôk*	*ero-f*
CON	DF.M-place=again	REL-PST-3MSG-go	to-3MSG

ⲁϥⲧⲁⲗϭⲉⲥⲁⲣⲣⲁ	ⲧϣⲉⲉⲣⲉ	ⲛ̄ϩⲣⲁⲅⲟⲩⲏⲗ	ⲁϥⲙⲟⲩⲣ	ⲛ̄ⲁⲥⲙⲟⲇⲁⲓⲟⲥ	ⲡⲣⲉϥϣⲟⲟⲣ
a-f-talc^{h}e-sarra	*t-šeere*	*n-hraguêl*	*a-f-mur*	*n-asmodaios*	*p-ref-šoor*
PST-3MSG-save-N	DF.F-daughter	of-N	PST-3MSG-bind	OBJ-DF.M-N	DF.M-AGT-smite

And again, where he went to, he saved Sara, the daughter of Raguel, and he bound Asmodaios, the smiter. (^{S}John Chrysostom, *On Raphael* ed. Budge 1915: 530.9–11)

(34) The Proverbs state that discipline is a gracious wage for those who use it:

ⲡⲙⲁ	ⲉⲧⲥ̄ⲕⲟⲧⲥ̄	ⲉⲣⲟϥ	ϥⲛⲁⲥⲟⲟⲩⲧⲛ̄
p-ma	*et-s-kot-s*	*ero-f*	*f-na-soutn*
DF.M-place	REL-3FSG-turn-3FSG	to-3MSG	3MSG-FUT-stretch

Where it (discipline) turns to, it (the place) will prosper. (^{S}Pro 17:8 ed. Worrell 1931)

(35) John urges the audience to weep over their deeds and to express their grief over their behaviour:

ϫⲉⲕⲁⲥ	ⲉⲛⲁⲣ̄ⲃⲟⲗ	ⲉⲡⲣⲓⲙⲉ	ⲙⲛ̄ⲡϭⲁϩϭϩ̄	ⲛⲛ̄ⲟⲃϩⲉ
cekas	*e-n-(n)a-r-bol*	*e-p-rime*	*mn-p-c^{h}ahc^{h}h*	*n-n-obhe*
so_that	FOC-1PL-FUT-do-loose	to-DF.M-cry	CON-DF.M-gnash	of-DF.PL-tooth

ϩⲙ̄ⲡⲙⲁ̄	ⲉⲧⲛ̄ⲛⲁⲃⲱⲕ	ⲉⲣⲟϥ
hm-p-ma	*et-n-na-bôk*	*ero-f*
in-DF.M-place	REL-1PL-FUT-go	to-3MSG

…so that we may do away the weeping and the gnashing of teeth in that place whereto we must depart. (^{S}John Nesteutes, *On Repentance & Continence* ed. Budge 1910: 5.28–30)

(36) The Lord tells Moses to forbid the Israelites to follow the practises of the Land of Egypt:

ⲟⲩⲟϩ	ⲛ̀ⲛⲉⲧⲉⲛⲓ̀ⲣⲓ	ⲕⲁⲧⲁⲛⲓⲙⲉⲧⲁⲧⲥⲃⲱ	ⲛ̀ⲧⲉⲡⲕⲁϩⲓ	ⲛ̀ⲭⲁⲛⲁⲁⲛ
uoh	*nne-ten-iri*	*kata-ni-met-at-sbô*	*nte-p-kahi*	*n-k^{h}anaan*
CON	NEG.OPT-2PL-do	like-DF:S.PL-ABST-un-teaching	of-DF:G.M-land	of-N

ⲫⲁⲓ	ⲁ̀ⲛⲟⲕ	ⲉ̀ϯⲛⲁⲉⲛⲑⲏⲛⲟⲩ	ⲉ̀ϧⲟⲩⲛ	ⲉ̀ⲣⲟϥ
p^{h}ai	*anok*	*et-i-na-en-t^{h}ênu*	*eḫun*	*ero-f*
DM.M	1SG	REL-1SG-FUT-bring-2PL	into	to-3MSG

…and you shall not act according to the ignorance of the Land of Canaan wherein I shall bring you. (^{B}Lev 18:3 ed. De Lagarde 1867: 278)

(37) The itinerary of St Paul and the other apostles' journeys included Attalia:

ⲟⲩⲟϩ	ⲉ̀ⲃⲟⲗ	ⲙ̀ⲙⲁⲩ	ⲁⲩⲉⲣϩⲱⲧ	ⲉ̀ⲧⲁⲛϯⲟⲭⲓⲁ̀	ⲡⲓⲙⲁ	ⲉⲧⲁⲩⲧⲏⲓⲧⲟⲩ
uoh	*ebol*	*mmau*	*a-u-er-hôt*	*e-t-antiokhia*	*pi-ma*	*et-a-u-têit-u*
CON	out	there	PST-3PL-do-sail	to-DF:G.F-N	DF:S.M-place	REL-PST-3PL-give-3PL

ⲛϧⲏⲧϥ	ϧⲉⲛⲡⲓϩⲙⲟⲧ	ⲛⲧⲉⲫϯ	ⲉⲡⲓϩⲱⲃ	ⲉⲧⲁⲩϫⲟⲕϥ
nḫêt-f	*ḫen-pi-hmot*	*nte-p^h-(nu)ti*	*e-pi-hôb*	*et-a-u-cok-f*
inside-3MSG	in-DF:S.M-grace	of-DF:G.M-God	to-DF:S.M-thing	REL-PST-3PL-fulfil-3MSG
ⲉⲃⲟⲗ				
ebol				
out				

And from there they sailed to Antioch, where they were recommended to the grace of God for the work that they fulfilled. (^{B}Acts 14:26 ed Horner 1898–1905)

(38) The exiled Israelites prayed to the Lord to take his anger away from them:

ϫⲉⲁⲛⲥⲱϫⲡ	ⲉⲛⲟⲓ	ⲛⲕⲟⲩϫⲓ	ϧⲉⲛⲛⲓⲉⲑⲛⲟⲥ
ce-a-n-sôcp	*e-n-oi*	*n-kuci*	*ḫen-ni-ethnos*
for-PST-1PL-remain	DEP-1PL-be.STA	as-small	in-DF:S.P-people

ⲡⲓⲙⲁ	ⲉⲧⲁⲕϫⲟⲣⲉⲛ	ⲉⲃⲟⲗ	ⲉⲣⲟϥ
pi-ma	*et-a-k-cor-en*	*ebol*	*ero-f*
DF:S.M-place	REL-PST-2MSG-disperse-1PL	out	to-3MSG

…for few are left of us among the peoples where you dispersed us to. (^{B}Bar 2:13)

(39) The Lord says about Shallum, who became king in his father's stead:

ⲫⲏ	ⲉ̀ⲧⲁϥⲓ	ⲉ̀ⲃⲟⲗ	ϧⲉⲛⲡⲁⲓⲙⲁ	ϥ̀ⲛⲁⲧⲁⲥⲑⲟ	ⲉ̀ⲙⲁⲩ	ⲁⲛ	ϫⲉ
p^hê	*et-a-f-i*	*ebol*	*ḫen-pai-ma*	*f-na-tast^{h}o*	*e-mau*	*an*	*ce*
DF:R.M	REL-PST-3MSG-come	out	in-DM.M-place	3MSG-FUT-return	to-there	NEG	then

ⲁⲗⲗⲁ	ϧⲉⲛⲡⲓⲙⲁ	ⲉ̀ⲧⲁⲩⲟⲩⲟⲧⲃⲉϥ	ⲉ̀ⲣⲟϥ	ⲉϥⲉ̀ⲙⲟⲩ	ⲙ̀ⲙⲁⲩ
alla	*ḫen-pi-ma*	*et-a-u-uotbe-f*	*ero-f*	*efe-mu*	*mmau*
but	in-DF:S.M-place	REL-PST-3PL-remove-3MSG	to-3MSG	OPT.3MSG-die	there

ⲟⲩⲟϩ	ⲙ̀ⲛⲉϥⲛⲁⲩ	ⲉ̀ⲡⲁⲓⲕⲁϩⲓ	ϫⲉ
uoh	*nne-f-nau*	*e-pai-kahi*	*ce*
CON	NOPT-3MSG-see	OBJ-DM.M-land	then

He who went away from that place shall return there no more, but where he has been removed to, he shall die and never see that land again. (^{B}Jer 22:11–12 ed. Tattam 1852)

Note that the example from the *Acts* (37) denotes not a real spatial entity but an imagined one, i.e. a grace of God.

Noteworthy are the following examples that differ from the other Bohairic instances by showing the generic article *p^h*- instead of the specifying *pi*-:

(40) Job speaks about the lust for other women and reasons that a fit for passion is uncontrollable. He likens it to a fire that burns on all sides:

ⲫⲙⲁ	ⲉϣⲁϥⲓ	ⲉϫⲱϥ	ϣⲁϥⲧⲁⲕⲟϥ	ⲛⲉⲙⲛⲉϥⲛⲟⲩⲛⲓ
p^h-ma	*e-ša-f-i*	*ecô-f*	*ša-f-tako-f*	*nem-ne-f-nuni*
DF:G.M-place	REL-AOR-3MSG-go	upon-3MSG	AOR-3MSG-destroy-3MSG	CON-POSS.P-3MSG-root

A fire, that burns on all sides, whereupon it goes, it destroys it with its roots. (^{B}Job 31:12 ed. Porcher 1924)

(41) When a man came to the monastery and approached Shenute in order to receive the latter's blessing and a forgiveness for his sins, Shenute told him:

ⲁϫⲉⲡⲉⲕⲛⲟⲃⲓ	ⲙⲡⲉⲙⲑⲟ	ⲉⲃⲟⲗ	ⲛⲟⲩⲟⲛ	ⲛⲓⲃⲉⲛ
a-ce-pe-k-nobi	*mpemt*^{h}*o*	*ebol*	*n-uon*	*niben*
IMP-say-POSS.M-2MSG-sin	before	out	of-one	QU

ⲉⲑⲣⲉⲕϩⲱⲗ	ⲉⲫⲙⲁ	ⲉⲧⲉⲕⲛⲁϩⲱⲗ	ⲉⲣⲟϥ
e-t^h*re-k-hôl*	*e-p*^{h}*-ma*	*ete-k-na-hôl*	*ero-f*
to-CAUS-2MSG-go	to-DF:G.M-place	REL-2MSG-FUT-go	to-3MSG

Declare your sin before everyone so that you may go whither you will go.

(ᴮBesa, *Life of Shenute* §15 ed. Leipoldt 1906: 14.27–28)

This use of the general article might point to an intended UCC-reading ('wherever'); see 2.3.2 below.

As before, not all possible examples are in fact locative adverbial clauses. In (42), the use of *-ke-* 'other' points to *ma* being a lexical rather than a grammatical element.

(42) Aaron is helping a poor debtor and speaks with the rich creditor telling him:

ⲛⲁ	ⲙⲡⲉⲓⲙⲁ	ⲡⲁϣⲏⲣⲉ	ⲧⲁⲣⲟⲩⲛⲁ	ⲛⲁⲕ
na	*m-pei-ma*	*pa-šêre*	*tar-u-na*	*na-k*
do_mercy.IMP	in-DM.M-place	POSS.M.1SG-son	FIN-3PL-do_mercy	for-2MSG

ϩⲙ̄ⲡⲕⲉⲙⲁ	ⲉⲧⲉⲕⲛⲁⲃⲱⲕ	ⲉⲣⲟϥ
hm-p-ke-ma	*ete-k-na-bôk*	*ero-f*
in-DF.M-other-place	REL-2MSG-FUT-go	to-3MSG

Have mercy in this place, my son, so that they will have mercy with you elsewhere where you will go to.

(ˢPapnute, *Life of Aaron* §112 ed. Dijkstra & van der Vliet 2020: 130.18)

Using the same distinction as introduced above, one might weed out examples 36–38 as appositions rather than adverbial clauses. Nevertheless, as with the static location (2.2.1), the function of a locative adverbial clause is to mark the direction towards a goal expressed by a clause headed by *p-ma*, followed by the relative clause containing the goal reference.

2.2.3 Direction source (↦ 'whence', 'from where')

The same necessity to distinguish between clauses with the source of the direction expressed within the adverbial clause ('Nothing moved where the smoke came from') and those in which a direction is expressed in the main clause ('Someone came from where the smoke was') applies here as well. Example (43) below is an instance of the latter since the adverbial clause only expresses a state of affairs taking place somewhere ('...where idols are worshipped'). The source marking appears in the main clause only ('She came from ...') and is therefore best considered as an apposition:

(43) Eusebius says about the Canaanite woman:

ⲁⲥⲉⲓ	ⲉⲃⲟⲗ	ϩⲙ̄ⲡⲙⲁ̄	ⲙ̄ⲡⲗⲓⲃⲉ	ⲙⲛ̄ⲡ̄ⲡⲱϣⲥ̄
a-s-i	*ebol*	*hm-p-ma*	*m-p-libe*	*mn-p-pôšs*
PST-3FSG-come	out	in-DF.M-place	of-DF.M-madness	CON-DF.M-amazement

ⲡⲙⲁ	ⲉⲩϣⲙϣⲉⲉⲓ̈ⲇⲱⲗⲟⲛ	ⲛ̄ϩⲏⲧϥ̄
p-ma	*e-u-šmše-idôlon*	*nhêt-f*
DF.M-place	DEP-3PL-worship-idol	inside-3MSG

She came from the place of madness and folly, where idols are worshipped.

(SEusebius of Caesaria, *On the Canaanite Woman* ed. Budge 1910: 139.28–30)

Conversely, examples (44–50) below are proper locative clauses with reference to the source. Since their number is low, they are all presented together rather than drawing a difference between non-embedded (44–45) and embedded patterns (46–50) as in 2.2.1 above:

(44) A crocodile seized the child of a Nubian man. After Aaron learnt of what happened, he gave a chip of wood to the man, saying with the help of a translator:

ϫⲓⲧⲥ̄	ⲛⲟϫⲥ̄	ⲉⲡⲉⲥⲏⲧ	ⲉⲡⲉⲓⲉⲣⲟ
cit-s	*noc-s*	*e-p-esêt*	*e-p-iero*
take.IMP-3FSG	throw.IMP-3FSG	to-DF.M-floor	to-DF.M-river

ⲡⲙⲁ	ⲛⲧⲁⲡⲙ̄ⲥⲁϩ	ϥⲓ	ⲙⲡⲉⲕϣⲏⲣⲉ	ⲛϩⲏⲧϥ̄
p-ma	*nt-a-p-msah*	*fi*	*m-pe-k-šêre*	*nhêt-f*
DF.M-place	REL-PST-DF.M-crocodile	take	OBJ-POSS.M-2MSG-son	inside-3MSG

Take it and throw it down into the river where the crocodile seized your boy.

(SPapnute, *Life of Apa Aaron* §99 ed. Dijkstra & van der Vliet 2020: 122.24–25)

(45) Jesus says that when an unclean spirit has left a man, it will seek for a resting place, but will not find one. So, it will say to itself:

ⲉⲓⲉ̀ⲧⲁⲥⲑⲟ	ⲉ̀ϧⲟⲩⲛ	ⲉ̀ⲡⲁⲏⲓ	ⲡⲓⲙⲁ	ⲉⲧⲁⲓ̈
eie-na-kto-i	*eḫun*	*e-pa-êi*	*pi-ma*	*et-a-i-i*
OPT.1SG-return	into	to-POSS.M.1SG-house	DF:S.M-place	REL-PST-1SG-come

ⲉ̀ⲃⲟⲗ	ⲛ̀ϧⲏⲧϥ
ebol	*nhêt-f*
out	inside-3MSG

I will return to my house from where I came from. (BMt 12:44 ed. Horner 1898–1905)[23]

(46) Moses narrates how he had turned to God to make supplications for the children of Israel, asking him not to regard their stubbornness, their impieties, and their sins:

ⲙⲏⲡⲟⲧⲉ	ⲛ̄ⲥⲉϫⲟⲟⲥ	ⲛ̄ϭⲓⲛⲉⲧⲟⲩⲏϩ	ϩⲓϫⲛ̄ⲡⲕⲁϩ
mêpote	*n-se-coo-s*	*nchi-n-et-uêh*	*hicn-p-kah*
lest	CNJ-3PL-say-3FSG	PVS-DF.PL-REL-dwell.STA	on-DF.M-earth

ⲙ̄ⲡⲙⲁ	ⲉⲛⲧⲁⲕⲛ̄ⲧⲛ̄	ⲉⲃⲟⲗ	ⲛ̄ϩⲏⲧϥ̄
m-p-ma	*ent-a-k-nt-n*	*ebol*	*nhêt-f*
of-DF.M-place	REL-PST-2MSG-bring-1PL	out	inside-3MSG

…lest the inhabitants of the land where you led us out from say: (a quote follows)

(SDt 9:28 ed. Budge 1912)

23 Note that the Mesokemic version (ed. Schenke) embeds *p-me* into a PP.

(47) A man stole timber from the construction site of the shrine of St Mercurios. Due to the saint's interference, he confessed his theft before the whole city:

ⲁⲩⲱ	ⲁϥⲃⲱⲕ	ⲉⲡⲙⲁ	ⲉⲧⲉⲣⲉⲡϣⲉ	ⲛⲏⲩ	ⲉⲃⲟⲗ	ⲛ̄ϩⲏⲧϥ̄
auô	*a-f-bôk*	*e-p-ma*	*etere-p-še*	*nêu*	*ebol*	*nhêt-f*
CON	PST-3MSG-go	to-DF.M-place	REL-DF.M-wood	come.STA	out	inside-3MSG

And he went to where the wood had come from.

(^S^*Miracle of St Mercurios* ed. Budge 1915: 268.9–10)

(48) A continuation to the previous example:

ⲁϥⲕⲁⲁϥ	ϩⲙ̄ⲡⲙⲁ	ⲛ̄ⲧⲁϥϥⲓⲧϥ̄	ⲛ̄ϩⲏⲧϥ̄
a-f-kaa-f	*hm-p-ma*	*nt-a-f-fit-f*	*nhêt-f*
PST-3MSG-put-3MSG	in-DF.M-place	REL-PST-3MS-carry-3MSG	inside-3MSG

He put it where he had taken it from. (^S^*Miracle of St Mercurios* ed. Budge 1915: 268.12)

(49) Abraham and his people left Egypt together with Lot. Abraham had plenty of livestock and was rich in gold and silver:

ⲟⲩⲟϩ	ⲁϥϣⲉⲛⲁϥ	ⲉ̀ⲡⲓⲙⲁ	ⲉ̀ⲧⲁϥⲓ̀	ⲉ̀ⲃⲟⲗ
uoh	*a-f-še=na-f*	*e-pi-ma*	*et-a-f-I*	*ebol*
CON	PST-3MSG-go=for-3MSG	to-DF:S.M-place	REL-PST-3MSG-come	out

ⲙ̀ⲙⲟϥ	ⲛ̀ϩⲣⲏⲓ	ϩⲓⲡ̀ϣⲁϥⲉ	ϣⲁⲃⲉⲑⲏⲗ	ⲡⲓⲙⲁ
mmo-f	*nhrêi*	*hi-p-šafe*	*ša-bethel*	*pi-ma*
on-DF:G.M-desert	to-N	DF:S.M-place	REL-PRT-POSS.F-3MSG-tent	AUX

ⲉ̀ⲛⲁⲣⲉⲧⲉϥⲥⲕⲩⲛⲏ	ⲭⲏ	ⲙ̀ⲙⲁⲩ	ⲛ̀ϣⲟⲣⲡ	ⲟⲩⲧⲉⲃⲉⲑⲏⲗ	ⲛⲉⲙⲟⲩⲧⲉⲁⲅⲅⲉ	ⲉ̀ⲡⲓⲙⲁ
e-nare-te-f-skynê	*k^{h}ê*	*mmau*	*n-šorp*	*ute-bethel*	*nem-ute-agge*	*e-pi-ma*
in-3MSG	up	there	as-first	between-N	CON-between-N	to-DF:S.M-place

ⲉ̀ⲧⲁϥⲑⲁⲙⲓⲉ̀ⲡⲓⲙⲁⲛⲉⲣϣⲱⲟⲩϣⲓ	ⲙ̀ⲙⲟϥ	ⲛ̀ϣⲟⲣⲡ
et-a-f-t^{h}amie-pi-ma-n-er-šôuši	*mmo-f*	*n-šorp*
REL-PST-3MSG-create-DF:S.M-place-of-do-sacrifice	in-3MSG	as-first

And he journeyed whence he had come into the wilderness as far as Bethel, to the place where his tent had formerly been, between Bethel and Haggai, to the place of the altar that he had made there at first, (and there Abram invoked the name of the Lord).

(^B^Gen 13:3–4 ed. de Lagarde 1867)

(50) Job bewails his fate, wishing that he had never been born at all. He sends his appeal for relief to the Most-high, asking:

ⲭⲁⲧ	ⲛ̀ⲧⲁⲙⲧⲟⲛ	ⲙ̀ⲙⲟⲓ	ⲛ̀ⲟⲩⲕⲟⲩϫⲓ	ⲙ̀ⲡⲁϯϣⲉⲛⲏⲓ	ⲉⲡⲓⲙⲁ
k^{h}a-t	*nt-a-mton*	*mmo-i*	*n-u-kuci*	*mpat-i-še=nê-i*	*e-pi-ma*
let.IMP-1SG	CNJ-1SG-rest	OBJ-1SG	for-IDF.SG-little	NCO-1SG-go=for-1SG	to-DF:S.M-place

ⲉϯⲛⲁⲧⲁⲥⲑⲟⲓⲁⲛϫⲉ	ⲉⲃⲟⲗ	ⲛ̀ϧⲏⲧϥ	ⲉⲡⲓⲙⲁ	ⲛ̀ⲭⲁⲕⲓ
et-i-na-tast^{h}o-i=an=ce	*ebol*	*nẖêt-f*	*e-pi-ma*	*n-k^{h}aki*
REL-1SG-FUT-return-1SG=NEG=then	out	inside-3MSG	to-DF:S.M-place	of-darkness

ⲛⲉⲙⲅⲛⲟⲫⲟⲥ	ⲡⲓⲕⲁϩⲓ	ⲛ̀ⲭⲁⲕⲓ	ϣⲁⲉⲛⲉϩ	ⲡⲓⲙⲁ	ⲉⲧⲉⲙⲙⲟⲛⲟⲩⲱⲓⲛⲓ
nem-gnophos	*pi-kahi*	*n-k^{h}aki*	*ša-eneh*	*pi-ma*	*ete-mmon-uôini*
CON-gloom	DF:S.M-land	of-darkness	until-eternity	DF:S.M-place	REL-NEG-light

ⲙ̀ⲙⲁⲩ	ⲟⲩⲇⲉ	ⲙ̀ⲡⲁⲩⲛⲁⲩ	ⲉⲡⲱⲛϧ	ⲛ̀ⲧⲉⲛⲓⲣⲱⲙⲓ	ⲙⲙⲁⲩ
mmau	*ude*	*mpa-u-nau*	*e-p-ônḫ*	*nte-ni-rômi*	*mmau*
there	nor	NEG.AOR-3PL-see	OBJ-DF:G.M-life	of-DF:G.PL-man	there

Let me rest a little before I go whence I will not return, to a land, dark and gloomy, to a land of perpetual darkness, where there is no light and no human life was seen.

([B]Job 10:20–21 ed. Porcher 1924)

However, examples 44 and 45 can again be left aside inasmuch as the locative clause apparently stands in an appositive relation to the superordinate clause. This leaves one with 46–50, which are all of the embedded subtype. In example 49 it is, however, only the first clause that is of interest because those following it are again appositions. As far as the limited data allow, one may observe that the locative clauses contain the head ⲡⲙⲁ *p-ma*/ ⲡⲓⲙⲁ *pi-ma* 'the place' followed by a relative clause as in the patterns expressing static location (2.2.1).

2.2.4 Direction path (⤳ 'where,' 'along')

Coptic evidence for a locative clause expressing a direction focussing on the path rather than the source or goal as above is difficult to find – presumably because such meaning is generally seldom intended. However, occasional examples do appear, as in the following:

(51) In the future realm of righteousness, only the 'Spirit in the height' will guarantee security, and the people will live in peace, but not in the cities of old. The vision ends with the words:

ⲛⲁⲓⲉⲧⲟⲩ	ⲛⲛⲏ	ⲉⲧϫⲁ	ⲉϫⲉⲛⲙⲁⲩ	ⲛⲓⲃⲓ
naiet-u	*n-nê*	*et-ca*	*ecen-mau*	*nibi*
blessed-3PL	as-DF:R.PL	REL-sow	upon-water	every
ⲡⲙⲉ	ⲉⲧⲉⲣⲉⲧⲁϩⲏ	ϩⲱⲙ	ⲉϫⲱϥ	ⲙ̄ⲛⲡⲓⲱ
p-me	*etere-t-ahê*	*hôm*	*ecô-f*	*mn-p-iô*
DF.M-place	REL-DF.F-cow	tread	upon-3MSG	CON-DF.M-donkey

Blessed are those who sow besides every water, where cow and donkey tread.([F]Is 32:20)

(52) In a vision, Dioscorus sees many of the Egyptian bishops flee rather than attending the Council of Chalcedon. St Athanasius says that their tiaras are to be given to Dioscorus and Macarius. The former refuses them, arguing to be unworthy of them. Then Athanasius says (cf. Rom 5:20):

ⲡⲙⲁ	ⲛⲧⲁⲡⲛⲟⲃⲉ	ⲁϣⲁⲓ	ⲛ̄ϩⲏⲧϥ̄
p-ma	*nt-a-p-nobe*	*ašai*	*nhêt-f*
DF.M-place	REL-PST-DF.M-sin	multiply	OBJ-3MSG
ⲁⲡⲉϩⲙⲟⲧ	ⲉⲣϩⲟⲩⲟ	ⲉⲁϣⲁⲓ	ⲛ̄ϩⲏⲧϥ̄
a-pe-hmot	*er-huo*	*e-ašai*	*nhêt-f*
PST-DF.M-grace	do-more	to-multiply	inside-3MSG

Where the sin multiplied, the grace multiplied further.

([S]Dioscorus of Alexandria, *On Macarius of Tkow* ed. Johnson 1980: 12.16–17)

However, the first example above is again an apposition, while the second example might also be categorized as static location, if one is inclined to consider the multiplication to happen at a given spot only. Nevertheless, one might surmise that a pattern similar to the ones for static (2.2.1), goal (2.2.2) and source (2.2.3) oriented semantics can be expected, i.e., the locative clauses contain the head пма *p-ma*/пima *pi-ma* 'the place' followed by a relative clause.

2.3 Universal concessive conditionals ('wherever')

Turning now to patterns in which the locative adverbial appears in a concessive conditional clause with universal reference ('wherever'), it has been noted that Universal Concessive Conditionals (henceforth UCC) are the least grammaticalised category of Coptic concessive conditionals.[24] Usually, a *free choice* construction[25] consisting of indefinite pronouns or generic nouns plus a quantifier followed by a relative clause is employed. Since the Coptic lexicon does not contain a locative indefinite pronoun, the word ма *ma* is employed here as well.

2.3.1 Static Location/Space Position UCCS *('wherever p, q')*

Even though the expected pattern in Coptic to express an equivalent to 'where + ever' is ^{S}ма нім *ma nim*/ ^{B}маі нівен *mai niben*, i. e. the word 'place' and a universal quantifier followed by a relative clause, examples of this are rather infrequent:

(53) A contract over the sale of a house contains clauses of security at the end:

сорϫ	сϭмϭом
s-orc	*s-c^{h}mc^{h}om*
3FSG-firm.STA	3FSG-be_strong

ауω	свевαιоу	ϩммα	нім	еуναмφαнιζе	ммос	нϩнтч
auô	*s-bebaiu*	*hm-ma*	*nim*	*e-u-na-mphanize*	*mmo-s*	*nhêt-f*
CON	3FSG-guarantee	in-place	QU	DEP-3PL-FUT-show	OBJ-3FSG	inside-3MSG

It is firm, valid, and warranted wherever it will be shown. (^{S}*CPR* IV 26.52–54)

(54) An Egyptian, who had stolen things from a man, is caught in the shrine of St George. Asked whether he would be ready to take a vow in front of the saint, the man answered:

маι	нівен	ѐтекоуаϣч	ϯнαωркнαк	ǹрнϯ	нівен
mai	*niben*	*ete-k-uaš-f*	*ti-na-ôrk=na-k*	*n-rêti*	*niben*
place	QU	REL-2MSG-wish-3MSG	1SG-FUT-VOW=for-2MSG	in-manner	QU

ѐтекоуаϣч
ete-k-uaš-f
REL-2MSG-wish-3MSG

Wherever you wish, I shall vow for you in whichever way you wish.
(^{B}*Miracles of St George* ed. *AM* II 350.16–18)

24 Müller (2009: 174–76).

25 I.e., there is no strictly grammaticalized pattern as with the other types of clauses above.

Occasionally, other quantifying constructions[26] are attested:

(55) Moses reminds the Israelites of the promise of the Lord that if they keep his commandments, he will give them the land and expel all the other peoples:

ⲡⲙⲁ	ⲧⲏⲣϥ̄	ⲉⲧⲉⲣⲉⲧⲧⲁϭⲥⲉ	ⲛ̄ⲛⲉⲧⲛ̄ⲟⲩⲉⲣⲏⲧⲉ	ⲛⲁϣⲱⲡⲉ	ⲛ̄ϩⲏⲧϥ
p-ma	*têr-f*	*etere-t-tac*^{h}*se*	*n-ne-tn-uerête*	*na-šôpe*	*nhêt-f*
DF.M-place	all-3MSG	REL-DF.F-print	of-POSS.P-2PL-foot	FUT-happen	inside-3MSG
ⲉⲩⲛⲁϣⲱⲡⲉ	ⲛ̄ϩⲏⲧⲛ̄				
e-u-na-šôpe	*nhêt-(t)n*				
FOC-3PL-FUT-happen	inside-2PL				

Wherever your footprints will be, shall be yours. (^{S}Dt 11:24 ed. Budge 1912)

Much more common are static location UCCs taking the form of adverbial clauses discussed above, i.e. without the quantifier:

(56) After Naomi suggested to Ruth that she (Ruth) should follow her sister-in-law, turn back to her people and her gods, and leave Naomi, Ruth replies that she had no intent of doing so:

ⲁⲩⲱ	ⲡⲙⲁ	ⲉⲧⲉⲣⲁⲙⲟⲩ	ⲛϩⲏⲧϥ̀	ⲉⲓⲛⲁⲙⲟⲩ	ϩⲱ
auô	*p-ma*	*ete-r-a-mu*	*nhêt-f*	*e-i-na-mu*	*hô-ø*
CON	DF.M-place	REL-2FSG-FUT-die	inside-3MSG	FOC-1SG-FUT-die	also-1SG
ⲛϩⲏⲧϥ	ⲛⲥⲉⲧⲟⲙⲥⲧ	ⲙⲡⲙⲁ	ⲉⲧⲙⲙⲁⲩ		
nhêt-f	*n-se-toms-t*	*m-p-ma*	*etmmau*		
inside-3MSG	CNJ-3PL-bury-1SG	in-DF.M-place	that		

And where(ver) you will die, I will die also and there I will be buried.
(^{S}Ru 2:9 ed. Thompson 1911)

(57) Sarapiôn intends to lead a prostitute to salvation. He visits her and prays to God to save her. When God hears his prayers, the woman prostrates herself at his feet and says weeping:

ⲁⲣⲓⲧⲁⲅⲁⲡⲏ	ⲡⲁⲉⲓⲱⲧ	ⲡⲙⲁ	ⲉⲧⲉⲕⲥⲟⲟⲩⲛ	ϫⲉϯⲛⲁⲟⲩϫⲁⲓ	
ari-t-agapê	*pa-iôt*	*p-ma*	*ete-k-soun*	*ce-ti-na-ucai*	
do.IMP-DF.F-love	POSS.M.1SG-father	DF.M-place	REL-3MSG-know	CMP-1SG-safe	
ⲛ̀ϩⲏⲧϥ̀	ϫⲓⲧ	ⲉⲙⲁⲩ	ⲛ̀ⲧⲁⲡⲛⲟⲩⲧⲉⲅⲁⲣ	ⲧⲛ̄ⲛⲟⲟⲩⲕ	ϣⲁⲣⲟⲓ ⲉⲡⲁⲓ
nhêt-f	*cit-ø*	*e-mau*	*nt-a-p-nute=gar*	*tnnou-k*	*šaro-i e-pai*
inside-3MSG	take.IMP-1SG	to-there	FOC-PST-DF.M-god=for	send-2MSG	to-1SG to-DM.M

Please, my father, where(ver) you know that I will be safe, take me for therefore God has sent you to me. (^{S}*ApophPatr* #240 ed. Chaîne 1960: 73)

(58) The Egyptians tell the Israelites to go and:

ⲙⲁⲑⲟⲩⲉⲧⲧⲟϩⲛⲱⲧⲉⲛ	ⲉⲫⲙⲁ	ⲉⲧⲉⲧⲉⲛⲛⲁϫⲓⲙⲓ
ma-t^h*uet-toh=nô-ten*	*e-p*^{h}*-ma*	*ete-ten-na-cimi*
IMP-collect-straw=for-2PL	to-DF:G.M-place	REL-2PL-FUT-find

26 The Bohairic version of Dt 11:24 shows ⲧⲟⲡⲟⲥ ⲛⲓⲃⲉⲛ.

ⲛⲥⲉⲛⲁϫⲉϫⲉⲃϩⲗⲓⲅⲁⲣⲁⲛ	ⲉⲃⲟⲗ	ϧⲉⲛⲧⲏⲡⲓ	ⲛⲧⲉⲛⲉⲧⲉⲛⲧⲱⲃⲓ
n-se-na-ceceb-hli=gar=an	*evol*	*ḫen-t-êpi*	*nte-ne-ten-tôbi*
NEG-3PL-FUT-reduce-any=for=NEG	out	in-DF:S.F-number	of-POSS.PL-2PL-brick

Collect straw where(ver) you may find it, for nothing of the quota of your bricks will be reduced! (^{B}Ex 5:11 ed. de Lagarde 1867)

Since all the examples above employ a future verbal pattern in the UCC-clause, one might be inclined to consider this as the distinctive marking that separated the adverbial from the UCC use. However, the following eample show that this is not a necessary condition:

(59) Shenute asks how mankind could be human since they have been given a heart of stone:

ⲡⲙⲁⲅⲁⲣ	ⲉⲧⲉⲣⲉⲡⲉⲓϩⲏⲧ	ⲛⲱⲛⲉ	ⲙⲙⲁⲩ	ϥⲙⲙⲁⲩ	ⲛϭⲓⲡⲟⲛⲏⲣⲟⲛ	ⲛⲓⲙ
p-ma=gar	*etere-pei-hêt*	*n-ône*	*mmau*	*f-mmau*	*nc^h^i-ponêron*	*nim*
DF.M-place=for	REL-DM.M-heart	of-stones	there	3MSG-there	PVS-evil	QU

For where(ver) there is a heart of stone, there is everything evil.

(^{S}Shenute, *This Great House* ed. Amélineau 1914: 26.2–3)

Basically, the examined texts show a preference for the same pattern as with the locative adverbial clause, i.e. with the word *ma* 'place' marked as definite and followed by a relative clause. Besides that, the same word *ma* is used with the universal quantifier and followed by a relative clause. However, in view of the low frequency of such examples and the fact that the functions to describe in the following (see 2.3.2) show a slight preference for the quantifier-pattern, it seems better to assume the two to be equally valid variants to express this function.

2.3.2 Direction Goal UCCs (*'to wherever p, q'*)

UCCs expressing goal-oriented direction can be found with the above-mentioned pattern of ⲙⲁ ⲛⲓⲙ *ma nim* plus a relative clause:

(60) The Father blesses each of the apostles. Turning to Philip, he says to him:

ⲙⲁ	ⲛⲓⲙ	[ⲉ]ⲧⲕ̄ⲛⲁⲃⲱⲕ	ⲉⲣⲟϥ	ⲛ̄ⲅ̄ⲛⲁⲧⲁϣⲉⲟⲉⲓϣ	ⲛ̄ϩⲏⲧϥ̄
ma	*nim*	*et-k-na-bôk*	*ero-f*	*n-g-{na}-taše-oiš*	*nhêt-f*
place	QU	REL-2MSG-FUT-go	to-3MGS	CNJ-2MSG-increase-cry	inside-3MSG

ϩⲙ̄[ⲡⲣ]ⲁⲛ	ⲙ̄ⲡⲁⲙⲉⲣⲓⲧ	ⲛ̄ϣⲏⲣⲉ	ⲙⲛ̄ⲡⲉϥⲥ⳨ⲟⲥ	ⲛⲟⲩⲟⲉⲓⲛ
hm-p-ran	*m-pa-merit*	*n-šêre*	*mn-pe-f-s(taur)os*	*n-uoin*
in-DF.M-name	of-POSS.M.1SG-beloved	of-son	CON-POSS.M-3MSG-cross	of-light

[ⲉϥ]ⲛⲁϭⲱ	ⲛⲙ̄ⲙⲁⲕ	ϣⲁⲛⲧⲟⲩⲡⲓⲥⲧⲉⲩⲉ	ⲉⲣⲟⲕ
e-f-na-c^h^ô	*nmma-k*	*šant-u-pisteue*	*ero-k*
FOC-3MSG-FUT-stay	with-2MSG	LIM-3PL-believe	OBJ-3MSG

Wherever[27] you will go and preach in the name of my beloved son and his bright cross, it (the cross) will stay with you until they believe you.

(^{S}*Book of the Resurrection of Jesus Christ* ed. Westerhoff 1999: 160–63)

27 Note that the other variants of the text have ⲡⲟⲗⲓⲥ *polis* 'town' instead of ⲙⲁ *ma* 'place.'

(61) While St Menas is transferred on a ship as a prisoner to the *comes*, the Saviour speaks to him from above, telling the saint to have no fear:

ϫⲉⲁⲛⲟⲕ	ϯϣⲟⲟⲡ	ⲛ̄ⲙ̄ⲙⲁⲕ	ϩⲙ̄ⲙⲁ	ⲛⲓⲙ	ⲉⲧⲟⲩⲛⲁϫⲓⲧⲕ̄	ⲉⲣⲟⲟⲩ
ce-anok	*ti-šoop*	*nmma-k*	*hm-ma*	*nim*	*et-u-na-cit-k*	*ero-u*
for-1SG	1SG-be.STA	with-2MSG	in-place	QU	REL-3PL-FUT-take-2MSG	to-3PL

…for I am with you wherever they will take you.

(^{S}John of Alexandria, *On St Menas* ed. Drescher 1946: 56.a24–27)

Yet here again one encounters the pattern with ⲡⲙⲁ *p-ma* without a quantifier followed by a relative clause:

(62) After Archellites' mother has learned that her son is not dead as feared, but lives in a monastery in Palestine, she decides to go there:

ⲁⲥϫⲓ	ⲛ̄ⲙ̄ⲙⲁⲥ	ⲛϣⲟⲙⲛⲧ	ⲛϩⲙ̄ϩⲁⲗ	ⲉⲩⲧⲁⲓⲏⲩ	ⲛ̄ⲧⲟⲟⲧⲥ̄
a-s-ci	*nmma-s*	*n-šomnt*	*n-hmhal*	*e-u-taiêu*	*ntoot-s*
PST-3FSG-take	with-3FSG	OBJ-three	of-servant	DEP-3PL-honoured.STA	with-3FSG

ⲉⲁⲥϯⲛⲁⲩ	ⲙⲡⲉⲩⲃⲉⲕⲉ	ϩⲱⲥ	ϣⲙⲙⲟ	ⲧⲁⲣⲟⲩϭⲱ
e-a-s-ti=na-u	*m-pe-u-beke*	*hôs*	*šmmo*	*tar-u-c^{h}ô*
DEP-PST-3FSG-give=for-3PL	OBJ-POSS.M-3PL-wage	like	alien	FIN-3PL-remain

ⲉⲩⲡⲣⲟⲥⲕⲁⲣⲧⲏⲣⲓ	ⲉⲣⲟⲥ	ⲁϫⲛϩⲱⲕⲛⲉⲓ	ϩⲙⲡⲙⲁ	ⲉⲧⲥ̄ⲛⲁⲃⲱⲕ	ⲉⲣⲟϥ
e-u-proskartêri	*ero-s*	*acn-hôknei*	*hm-p-ma*	*et-s-na-bôk*	*ero-f*
DEP-3PL-persist	to-3FSG	without-shrink	in-DF.M-place	REL-3FSG-FUT-go	to-3MSG

She took with her three of her servants of good repute and gave them their wages as to strangers so that they would remain in willing attendance upon her wherever she would go. (^{S}*Archellites* ed. Drescher 1947: 24.4–6)

(63) A woman from Samaria travels to the shrine of St Menas. At an overnight stop, an innkeeper, intending to take advantage of her, tries to coax her to sleep not in the inn-room but at his place. She does not see the evil coming and answers to his 'kind' suggestion:

ⲡⲁⲥⲟⲛ	ⲡⲙ[ⲁ]	ⲉⲧⲉⲕⲟⲩⲉϣϫⲓⲧ	ⲉⲣⲟϥ	ϫⲓⲧ
pa-son	*p-ma*	*ete-k-ueš-cit-ø*	*ero-f*	*cit-ø*
POSS.M.1SG-brother	DF.M-place	REL-2MSG-wish-take-1SG	to-3MSG	take.IMP-1SG

ⲉⲩⲙⲁ	ⲉϥⲉⲥⲩⲭⲁⲍⲉ	ϫⲉⲉⲕⲛⲁⲩ	ⲉⲣⲟⲓ	ⲉⲓϣⲱⲛⲉ
e-u-ma	*e-f-esukhaze*	*ce-e-k-nau*	*ero-i*	*e-i-šône*
to-IDF.SG-place	DEP-3MSG-be_quiet	for-FOC-2MSG-see	OBJ-3MSG	DEP-1SG-be_sick

My brother, wherever you intend to take me to, take me to a quiet place, for you see that I am ill. (^{S}*Miracles of St Menas* ed. Drescher 1946: 27.b15–20)

(64) When Sarapion leaves his place to confess the Christ in front of the hegemon, a young servant of his follows him asking what to do with his camels. Sarapion explains that he has no further need of them. Thereupon the lad says:

ⲁⲗⲏⲑⲱⲥ	ⲡⲁⲓⲱⲧ	ⲉ̀ⲑⲟⲩⲁⲃ	ⲁ̀ⲡⲁ	ⲥⲁⲣⲁⲡⲓⲱⲛ
alêthôs	*pa-iôt*	*et^{h}uab*	*apa*	*sarapiôn*
truly	POSS.M.1SG-father	holy	apa	N

ⲡⲓⲙⲁ	ⲉ̀ⲧⲉⲕⲛⲁϣⲉ	ⲛⲁⲕ	ⲉ̀ⲣⲟϥ	ϯⲛⲁⲓ̀	ⲛⲉⲙⲁⲕ	ϩⲱ
pi-ma	*ete-k-na-še*	*na-k*	*ero-f*	*ti-na-i*	*nema-k*	*hô-ø*
DF:S.M-place	REL-2MSG-FUT-go	for-2MSG	to-3MSG	1SG-FUT-go	with-2MSG	also-1SG

Truly, my holy father, the venerable Sarapion, wherever you go, I will go with you too.
(^{B}*Mart. Sarapion* ed. *AM* I 65.1–2)

(65) The miracles of St George quote a section from the saint's martyrdom, where the Saviour appears to him and promises:

ϯⲛⲁⲑⲣⲉϩⲁⲛϣⲫⲏⲣⲓ	ⲛ̀ⲛⲓϣϯ	ϣⲱⲡⲓ	ϧⲉⲛⲡⲓⲙⲁ	ⲉ̀ⲧⲉⲙⲙⲁⲩ
ti-na-t^{h}re-han-šp^{h}êri	*n-ništi*	*šôpi*	*ḫen-pi-ma*	*etemmau*
1SG-FUT-CAUS-IDF.PL-wonder	of-great	happen	in-DF:S.M-place	that

ϧⲉⲛⲡⲓⲙⲁ	ⲉ̀ⲧⲟⲩⲛⲁⲭⲱ	ⲙ̀ⲡⲉⲕⲥⲱⲙⲁ	ⲛ̀ϧⲏⲧϥ
ḫen-pi-ma	*et-u-na-k^{h}ô*	*m-pe-k-sôma*	*nḫêt-f*
in-DF:S.M-place	REL-3PL-FUT-put	OBJ-POSS.M-2MSG-body	inside-3MSG

I will cause great marvels to happen in that place, wherever they will put your body.
(^{B}*Mart. St George of Cappadocia* ed. *AM* II 316.8–10)

The last example above should again be regarded as an apposition.

A similar picture emerges here as with the static location UCC, although with a more even distribution: A pattern with the expression ^{S}ⲙⲁ ⲛⲓⲙ/^{B}ⲙⲁⲓ ⲛⲓⲃⲉⲛ *ma nim/mai niben* 'every place' plus a relative clause co-occurs with one that is identical to that used for locative adverbial clauses, with ^{SB}ⲡⲙⲁ *p-ma* plus relative clause.

2.3.3 Direction Source UCCS *('from wherever p, q')*

So far, no examples of UCCS with indication of the source ('Wherever you are from, you will have heard about….') have been found in the corpus. Seeing that adverbial locative clauses with direction source expression are attested (see 2.2.3 above), this must be due to accidents of preservation. Compared to the situation described above for UCCS of static location (2.3.1) and direction goal (2.3.2), one might expect also here to find both patterns employed, i.e. ^{S}ⲙⲁ ⲛⲓⲙ/^{B}ⲙⲁⲓ ⲛⲓⲃⲉⲛ *ma nim/mai niben* 'every place' plus relative clause and ^{SB}ⲡⲙⲁ *p-ma* plus relative clause.

2.3.4 Direction Path UCCS *('along wherever p, q')*

By contrast to the adverbial clauses in 2.3.3 above, where we had to state the lack of definite examples of that function, the UCC use of them supplies us with at least one possible instance:

(66) The disciples asked Jesus who would be their leader once he left them; he replied:

ⲡⲙⲁ	ⲛ̄ⲧⲁⲧⲉⲧⲛ̄ⲉⲓ	ⲙ̄ⲙⲁⲩ	ⲉⲧⲉⲧⲛⲁⲃⲱⲕ	ϣⲁⲓ̈ⲁⲕⲱⲃⲟⲥ	ⲡⲇⲓⲕⲁⲓⲟⲥ
p-ma	*nt-a-tetn-i*	*mmau*	*e-tetn-(n)a-bôk*	*ša-iakôbos*	*p-dikaios*
DF.M-place	REL-PST-2PL-come	there	FOC-2PL-FUT-go	to-N	DF.M-righteous

ⲡⲁⲉⲓ	ⲛ̄ⲧⲁⲧⲡⲉ	ⲙⲛ̄ⲡⲕⲁϩ	ϣⲱⲡⲉ	ⲉⲧⲃⲏⲏⲧϥ
pai	*nt-a-t-pe*	*mn-p-kah*	*šôpe*	*etbêêt-f*
DM.M	REL-PST-DF.F-heaven	CON-DF.M-earth	happen	because-3MSG

Wherever you come along, you shall go to Jacob the Righteous for whose sake heaven and earth come into being. (^{SL}*EvThom* §12 ed. Layton 1989: 58)

Yet the interpretation of this example hinges on the absence of a directional prepositional phrase (such as 'wherever you have come **to*') and on whether or not the movement is understood as originating from a single locus (as in 'at the very place you come along').

3 Predecessor constructions

As the question of translation-induced development of Coptic grammatical patterns has been recently raised again,[28] it might be useful to investigate whether the construction under examination here had any forerunners in earlier diachronic stages of Egyptian.

Not unexpectedly, the Coptic patterns decribed above go back to similar forerunner patterns. In Demotic, one encounters the word *mꜣꜥ*, the origin of Coptic ⲙⲁ *ma*, which, however, is mostly not used as an adverbial clause, but rather modifies only a part of a sentence instead of serving as an attribute to it as a whole:

(67) When the battlefield was prepared:

pr-ꜥꜣ	*ỉw*	*r-pꜣ-mꜣꜥ*	*mtw-Pꜣ-dỉ-ḫnsw*	*nỉm-f*
Pharaoh	come.STA	to-DF.M-place	REL-N	in-3MSG

Pharaoh came to where Petekhonsu was. (^{D}pKrall 17.16, 2nd cent. BCE)

(68) In an only partly preserved graffito in the Theban mountains, a man asks the Gods:

mtw-w-dỉ	*ḥtp-ỉ*	*n-pꜣ-mꜣꜥ*	*rtw-nꜣy-ỉ-ỉtṱ-w*	*nỉm-f*
CNJ-3PL-give	rest.SBJ-1SG	in-DF.M-place	REL-POSS.PL-1SS-father-PL	in-3MSG
ỉrm-nꜣy-f-sn-w				
CON-POSS.PL-3MSG-brother-PL				

… and that they let me rest where/at the place my ancestors and his^{sic} brothers are. (^{D}grTheben 3548.x+5–7, 4th–1st cent. BCE)

(69) Deities are asked to work in favour of the deceased:

tw-tn	*prỉ-pꜣy-f-bỉ*	*r-tꜣ-p-t*	*r-pꜣ-mꜣꜥ*
give.FUT-2PL	go.SUBJ-POSS.M-3MSG-soul	to-DF.F-heaven-F	to-DF.M-place
nty-mr-f=s			
REL-love-3MSG=3C			

May you let him ascend to the sky where he wishes. (^{D}pRhind I 10.d5, 1st cent. BCE)

In the first example above, the locative clause merely specifies the goal of the movement in the main clause and should be classified as complement of the verb. Similarly, in the second example the position of the deceased ancestors specifies only the location where the man intends to dwell for eternity and should therefore not be regarded as a complement clause either. Closer to what we are looking for would be the third example if read as an

28 Peust (2015: 342–43).

UCC, but the use of the definite article or absence of a quantifier might speak against such an interpretation.

Since the word *mꜣꜥ* 'place' is lexically relatively young (no attestations before the mid-1st millennium BCE), exactly the same pattern is not found in earlier texts. There, a word *bw* 'place' is used instead, which can be followed by relative clauses, relative forms, or virtual relative clauses.

(70) Pharaoh's armies approach the city of Kadesh unaware of the presence of the troops of their foe:

ꜥḥꜥ-n	*bdš-n*	*pꜣ-mšꜥ*	*ntḥtr*	*n-ḥm-f*	*r-ḥꜣ-t-sn*
AUX-PST	be_weak-PST	DF.M-army	chariotry	of-majesty-3MSG	to-front-F-3PL

m-ḫd	*r-bw*	*nty*	*ḥm-f*	*im*
in-move_north.INF	to-place	REL	majesty-3MSG	there

Then his majesty's army and chariotry became discouraged before them (the foes) in their northward progress to where his majesty was.

(^{LE}Kadesh Bulletin §§81–82 ed. Kitchen 1968–90: II 118–19, 13th cent. BCE)

(71) In a magical spell, the god Horus is said to suffer from burns. Help, however, is on its way:

iy	*ꜣs-t*	*nṯr-t*	*r-bw*	*nty*	*nṯr=pn*	*im*
come.PST	N-F	god-F	to-place	REL	god=DM.M	there

Goddess Isis came to where this god was.

(^{ME}P.Leiden I 348 v° iii.3 ed. Borghouts 1971: pl. 17, 13th cent. BCE)

(72) In the diary of a fortress in Nubia the arrival of Nubians is noted for a certain day and that they bartered their commodities. Then it is said:

iw-ø	*ḫnt-ø*	*r-bw*	*iy-n-sn*	*im*	*m-hrw=pn*
PTC-3PL	sail-STA.3PL	to-place	come.PST-3PL	in	in-day=DM.M

And they sailed downstream to where they came from on the same day.

(^{ME}Semnah-Despatch 1.13 [19th cent. BCE], ed. Smither 1945: pl. IIa)

(73) The deceased king is assured:

n	*ḫsf-k*	*m-bw*	*nb*	*šmi-k*	*im*
NEG	adversary-2MSG	in-place	QU	walk.REL-2MSG	in

You will have no adversary wherever you go. (^{OE}PT 365 Pyr. §625c [24th cent. BCE])

However, like the Demotic examples 67–69, none of these instances shows a use of the locative adverbial clause pattern. In examples 70–72, the locative expression is in each case the argument of a verb of movement. In the last example (73), the locative expression either serves as a predicate or as an adverbial expression in an extential sentence (*'You have no enemies, wherever you go'*).

There is obviously a certain gap in the data, since locative clauses are not attested with *mꜣꜥ* nor are examples with *bw* numerous in Late Egyptian. This could be due to accidents of preservation, but locative expressions do seem to have existed in Late Egyptian also in a different guise. Here one finds headless relative clauses with the definite article instead:

(74) The author of a letter accuses a military official for mistreating him, saying that he imposed duties on him but withdrew the necessary manpower. In addition, he requisitioned objects from the author. Other officials, to whom he had turned, gave an order to the military official:

ḫꜣꜥ	*nꜣ-rmṯ-w*	*m-pꜣ-nty=nb*	*st*	*ỉm*
let.IMP	DF.P-man-PL	in-DF.M-REL=QU	3PL	in

Release the people wherever they are!

(^{LE}pAnastasi VI.25 ed. *LEM* 74.8–9, 12th cent. BCE)

(75) God Seth has raped the god Horus, but with help of his mother Isis, Horus managed to make Seth eat lettuce covered with Horus' semen. When they both stood trial, Seth claimed the throne since he had forced himself on Horus. Horus, however, calls Seth's claim a lie and suggests to the divine court:

ỉmỉ	*ꜥš-ṱ*	*n-tꜣ-mtw-t*	*n-stẖ*	*ptr-n*	*pꜣ-nty-ỉw-s-wšb*	*ỉm*
let.IMP	call-one	OBJ-DF.F-semen-F	of-N	see.FUT-1PL	DF.M-REL-OPT-3FS-answer	in

mṱ-ṱ	*ꜥš*	*n-tꜣy-ỉ*	*ỉnk*	*ptr-n*	*pꜣ-nty-ỉw-s-wšby*	*ỉm*
CNJ-one	call	OBJ-POSS.F-1SG	1S	see.FUT-1PL	DF.M-REL-OPT-3FS-answer	in

Have the semen of Seth called, and we will see where it will answer from. Then have my own called, and we will see where it will answer from.

(^{LE}*Horus & Seth* 12.5–6 ed. *LES* 53.10–12, 12th cent. BCE)

Yet again neither of the above examples shows a use of the construction as a locative adverbial clause. The examples cited should suffice to demonstrate that pre-Coptic Egyptian had locative expressions sharing syntactic features with the later pattern, i.e. a word for 'place' followed by a relative clause. One is thus dealing here with a structural pattern that had genuine pre-contact antecedents.

4 Conclusions

Coptic locative adverbial clauses show two patterns: One with a locative interrogative ('where') that is limited to object clauses of verbs of perception and speech, and another making use of the definite word ⲙⲁ *ma* 'place' followed by a relative clause that can be found in all other syntactic environments. Locative adverbial clauses can occur as bare ('where I am …') or as embedded, i.e. within a prepositional phrase ('to where I am'). The majority of examples are clauses of static location ('where she is') whereas the expression of direction towards ('whither they went/where they went to') or from a point of reference ('whence/from where he came.') is less common. Unattested in the examined textual corpora is expression of the path ('wherealong we went') and the distance ('as far as you can'). However, this is probably an accident of preservation rather than a reflection of cognitive limitations as has been suggested for other patterns in earlier literature.[29] The difference between the semantic sub-patterns proposed here is marked within the relative

29 See Brunner-Traut (1974).

clause ('where X is' vs. 'where X went to' vs. 'where X came from'), i.e. the head of the construction is always the same (ⲡⲙⲁ *p-ma*).

Coptic universal concessive conditionals also show a dichotomy of patterns. Here, however, the distinction between the two is not one of syntax but rather of stylistics. A pattern similar to the one used in locative adverbial clauses, i.e. with the word ⲙⲁ *ma* 'place' marked as definite and followed by a relative clause, stands in opposition to another in which the word ⲙⲁ *ma* is used with a universal quantifier followed by a relative clause. Here again, the different semantics are marked only in the relative clause, not on the head.

List of abbreviations (Labels of specific Coptic verbal forms in *Italics*)

The Coptic examples are given as printed in the respective editions. No additional supralineation has been introduced, nor have the ones provided been adjusted. Brackets in the Coptic text indicate restored passages. The system of transliterating Coptic used in this paper should be in most cases self-evident, except perhaps for ϫ = *c* and ϭ = *c*^{h} as well as ⲉⲓ and ⲟⲩ, given simply as *i* and *u* in Coptic words but as digraphs *ei* and *ou* in Greek words. The reason behind this is mainly a practical one, as it allows accounting for and thus aligning the graphemic differences in the respective dialects. Note, however, that this is intended merely as a transciption convention and not as a phonological (and certainly no phonetic) transcript.

The glossing follows a simplified version of that proposed in Grossman & Haspelmath 2015. All Coptic examples are glossed containing a Coptic line, a line with analysed text with morpheme division, a morpheme-by-morpheme glossing line, and a translation. These equal lines (1), (4), (5), and (6) in the glossing proposal of Grossman & Haspelmath (2015: 148–49). Finally, following good papyrological practise, round brackets are used to dissolve abbreviations such as *p-c*^{h}*(ôi)s* for ⲡϭ̅ⲥ̅ rather than pointed parentheses (i.e., *p-c*^{h}*<ôi>s* as in Grossman & Haspelmath 2015: 148). Note also the difference between ⲡⲉ *pe* in the bipartite (glossed as SE) and the tripartite pattern (glossed as COP), following Loprieno, Müller & Uljas 2017.

1,2,3	number
A	Akhmimic dialect
ABST	abstract morpheme
AGT	agentive morpheme
AOR	*Aorist*
AUX	auxiliary
B	Bohairic dialect
CAUS	causative
CMP	complementizer
CMPL	*Completive*
CND	*Conditional*
CNJ	*Conjunctive*
CON	connector
COP	copula
D	Demotic
DF:R	definite
DF:R	definite, generic
DF:S	definite, specific
DF:R	definite, relative clause
DM	demonstrative
DEP	dependent
F	Fayumic dialect
F	female
FIN	*Finalis*
FOC	focus
FUT	future
IDF	indefinite
IMP	imperative

IRP	interrogative particle	PRO	prohibitive
L	Lykopolitan dialect	PROS	prospective
LE	Late Egyptian	PRT	preterite
M	Mesokemic dialect	PST	past (*Perfect I*)
M	masculine	PTC	particle
ME	Middle Egyptian	PVS	post-verbal subject
N	name	QU	quantifier
NCPL	*Negative completive*	REL	relative
NEG	negation	S	Sahidic dialect
OBJ	object	SG	singular
OE	Old Egyptian	SBJ	subjunctive
OPT	*Optative (Futur III)*	SE	subject element
ORD	ordinal	STA	Stative
PL	plural	TMP	*Temporal*
POS	possessive	VOC	vocative

Bibliography

AM I & II = Balestri, Johannes & Henri Hyvernat. 1908 & 1924. *Acta Martyrum* I & II. Paris & Louvain; Corpus Scriptorum Christianorum Orientalium 43 & 86/Scriptores Coptici 3 & 6.

Amélineau, Emile. 1885. 'Voyage d'un moine égyptien dans le desert', *Recueil des Travaux* 6, 166–94.

Amélineau, Emile. 1889. 'Étude sur le Christianisme en Égypte au septième siècle', *Mémoires de l'Institut Égyptien* 2, 261–424 (quoted according to a separate edition with separate pagination).

Amélineau, Emile. 1895. *Monuments pour servir à l'histoire de l'Égypte chrétienne aux IVᵉ et Vᵉ siècles*. Paris; MMAF IV/2.

Amélineau, Emile. 1914. *Œuvres des Schenoudi* II. *Texte copte et traduction française*. Paris.

Bernadin, Joseph Buchanan. 1940. 'The Resurrection of Lazarus'. *The American Journal of Semitic Languages and Literatures* 57, 252–90.

Böhlig, Alexander. 1958. *Der achmimische Proverbientext nach Ms. Berol. Orient. oct. 987* Teil I: *Text und Rekonstruktion der sahidischen Vorlage*, mit einem Beitrag von Hugo Ibscher. Munich; Studien zur Erforschung des christlichen Ägyptens 3.

Borghouts, Joris. 1971. *The Magical Texts of Papyrus Leiden I 348.* Leiden; *OMRO* 51, 1–249.

Boud'hors, Anne & Chantal Heurtel. 2010. *Les ostraca coptes de la TT 29. Autour du moine Frange*, vol. I: *Textes*, Vol. 2: *Index – Planches*. Brussels; Études d'Archéologie Thébaine 3.

Brunner-Traut, Emma. 1974. 'Altägyptische Sprache und Kindersprache: Eine linguistische Anregung', *SAK* 1, 61–81.

Budge, Ernest Alfred Wallis. 1910. *Coptic Homilies in the Dialect of Upper Egypt, from the Papyrus Codex Oriental 5001 in the British Museum*. London; Coptic texts I.

Budge, Ernest Alfred Wallis. 1912. *Coptic Biblical Texts in the Dialect of Upper Egypt, from the Papyrus Codex Oriental 5001 in the British Museum*. London; Coptic Texts II.

Budge, Ernest Alfred Wallis. 1915. *Miscellaneous Coptic Texts in the Dialect of Upper Egypt*. London; Coptic Texts V.

Chaîne, Marius. 1960. *Le manuscrit de la version copte en dialecte sahidique des 'Apophthegmata Patrum'*. Cairo; Bibliothèque d'Études Coptes VI.

CPR IV = Till, Walter. 1958. *Die koptischen Rechtsurkunden der Papyrussammlung der Österreichischen Nationalbibliothek*. Vienna; Corpus Papyrorum Raineri IV.

de Vis, Henri. 1929. *Homélies coptes de la Vaticane* II. Copenhagen; Coptica V.

Dijkstra, Jitse & Jacques van der Vliet. 2020. *The Coptic* Life of Aaron. *Critical Edition, Translation and Commentary.* Leiden & Boston; Supplements to Vigiliae Christianae 155.

Drescher, James. 1946. *Apa Mena. A Selection of Coptic Texts Relating to St Menas*. Cairo; Publications de la Société d'Archéologie Copte: Textes et Documents.

Drescher, James. 1947. *Three Coptic Legends. Hillaria * Archellites * The Seven Sleepers*. Cairo; Suppléments aux Annales du Service des Antiquités de l'Égypte 4.

Grossman, Eitan & Martin Haspelmath. 2015. 'The Leipzig Jerusalem Transliteration of Coptic', in: Grossman, Eitan, Martin Haspelmath & Tonio Sebastian Richter (eds). *Egyptian-Coptic Linguistics in Typological Perspective*. Berlin, Munich & Boston; Empirical Approaches to Language Typology 55, 145–53.

Haspelmath, Martin & Ekkehard König. 1998. 'Concessive Conditionals in the Languages of Europe', in: van der Auwera, Johan (ed.). *Adverbial Constructions in the Languages of Europe*. Berlin & New York; Empirical Approaches to Language Typology, EUROTYP 20:3, 563–640.

Hasselgård, Hilde. 2010. *Adjunct Adverbials in English*. Cambridge; Studies in English Language.

Hetterle, Katja. 2015. *Adverbial Clauses in Cross-Linguistic Perspective*. Berlin & Boston; Trends in Linguistics Studies and Monographs 289.

Horner, George. 1898–1905. *The Coptic Version of the New Testament in the Northern Dialect, Otherwise Called Memphitic & Bohairic, with Introduction, Critical Apparatus & Literal English Translation*, 4 vols., Oxford.

Johnson, Dwight 1980. *A Panegyric on Macarius Bishop of Tkôw Attributed to Dioscorus of Alexandria*. Louvain.; Corpus Scriptorum Christianorum Orientalium 415 & 420/Scriptores Coptici 41 & 42.

Kitchen, Kenneth. 1968–1990. *Ramesside Inscriptions. Historical & Biographical*. Oxford.

Kortmann, Bernd. 1997. *Adverbial Subordination. A Typology and History of Adverbial Subordinators Based on European Languages*. Berlin & New York; Empirical Approaches to Language Typology 18.

Kropp, Angelicus. 1931. *Ausgewählte koptische Zaubertexte* I: *Textpublikation*. Brussels.

de Lagarde, Paul. 1867. *Der Pentateuch koptisch*. Göttingen.

de Lagarde, Paul. 1883. *Aegyptiaca*. Göttingen.

Layton, Bentley. 1989. *Nag Hammadi Codex II,2–7 together with XIII,2*, Brit. Lib Or.4926(1) and P.Oxy. 1, 654, 655* I: *Gospel According to Thomas, Gospel According to Philip, Hypostasis of the Archons, and Indexes*. Leiden, New York, Copenhagen & Cologne; Nag Hammadi Studies XX.

Layton, Bentley. 2011. *A Coptic Grammar, with Chrestomathy & Glossary, Sahidic Dialect* (3rd edition). Wiesbaden; Porta Linguarum Orientalium 20.

Leipoldt, Johannes. 1906. *Sinuthii Vita Bohairice*. Paris; Corpus Scriptorum Christianorum Orientalium 41/Scriptores Coptici 1.

Leipoldt, Johannes. 1908. *Sinuthii Archimandritae Vita et Opera Omnia* IV, *adiuvante W. E. Crum*. Paris; Corpus Scriptorum Christianorum Orientalium 73/Scriptores Coptici 5.

LEM = Gardiner, Alan. 1937. *Late-Egyptian Miscellanies*. Brussels; Bibliotheca Aegyptiaca VII.

LES = Gardiner, Alan. 1932. *Late-Egyptian Stories*. Brussels; Bibliotheca Aegyptiaca I.

Loprieno, Antonio & Matthias Müller. 2012. 'Ancient Egyptian and Coptic', in: Frajzyngier, Zygmunt & Erin Shay (eds). *The Afroasiatic Languages*. Cambridge; Cambridge Language Surveys, 102–44.

Loprieno, Antonio, Matthias Müller & Sami Uljas. 2016. *Non-Verbal Predication in Ancient Egyptian Egyptian*. Berlin; The Mouton Companions to Ancient Egyptian II.

Marti, Werner. 1985. *Berndeutsch-Grammatik für die heutige Mundart zwischen Thun und Jura*. Bern.

Müller, Detlef. 1962. *Die Bücher der Einsetzung der Erzengel Michael und Gabriel*. Louvain; Corpus Scriptorum Christianorum Orientalium 255 & 226/Scriptores Coptici 31 & 32.

Müller, Matthias. 2009. 'Contrast in Coptic I. Concessive Constructions in in Sahidic', *Lingua Aegyptia* 17, 139–82.

Müller, Matthias. 2012. 'Greek connectors in Coptic. A contrastive overview II: Semantically subordinating connectors', *Lingua Aegyptia* 20, 111–64.

Müller, Matthias. 2015. 'Relative Clauses in Later Egyptian', *Lingua Aegyptia* 23, 107–73.

Müller, Matthias. 2021. *Grammatik des Bohairischen*. Hamburg; Lingua Aegyptia Studia Monographica 24.

Peust, Carsten. 2015. Review of Grossman, Polis, Stauder & Winand (eds). *On Forms and Functions*, *Lingua Aegyptia* 23, 339–53.

P.MoscowCopt = P. B. Ернштедт. 1959. *Коптские Тексты государственного музея изобразительных искусств имени А. С. Пушкина*. Moscow & Leningrad.

Porcher, Emile. 1924. *Le Livre de Job: Version copte bohaïrique*. Paris; Patrologia Orientalis XVIII/2, Fasc. 87.

P.Ryl.Copt. = Crum, Walter. 1909. *Catalogue of the Coptic Manuscripts of the John Rylands Library, Manchester*. Manchester & London.

Schmidt, Carl & Violet MacDermot. 1978. *The Books of Jeu and the Untitled Text in the Bruce Codex*. Leiden; Nag Hammadi Studies XIII.

Smither, Paul. 1945. 'The Semnah Despatches', *Journal of Egyptian Archaeology* 31, 3–10.

Steindorff, Georg. 1899. *Die Apokalypse des Elias: Eine unbekannte Apokalypse und Bruchstücke der Sophonias-Apokalypse*. Leipzig; Texte und Untersuchungen zur altchristlichen Literatur NF II/3a.

Suter, Rudolf. 1992. *Baseldeutsch-Grammatik* (3rd revised edition). Basel; Grammatiken und Wörterbücher des Schweizerdeutschen VI.

Tattam, Henri. 1852. *Prophetae maiores in dialecto linguae aegyptiacae memphitica seu coptica* I: *Esaias et Jeremias cum Lamentationes Jeremiae*. Oxford.

Thompson, Herbert. 1911. *A Coptic Palimpsest containing Joshua, Judges, Ruth, Judith and Esther in the Sahidic Dialect*. Oxford.

Thompson, Sandra, Robert Longacre & Shin Wang. 2007. 'Adverbial Clauses', in: Shopen, Timothy (ed.). *Language Typology and Syntactic Description* II: *Complex Constructions* (2nd edition). Cambridge.

Till, Walter. 1936. *Koptische Heiligen- und Martyrerlegenden* II. Rome; Orientalia Christiana Analecta 108.

Weber, Albert. 1948. *Zürichdeutsche Grammatik und Wegweiser zur guten Mundart*. Zürich.

Westerhoff, Matthias. 1999. *Auferstehung und Jenseits im koptischen „Buch der Auferstehung Jesu Christi, unseres Herrn"*. Wiesbaden; Orientalia Biblica et Christiana 11.

Worrell, William H. 1931. *The Proverbs of Solomon in Sahidic Coptic According to the Chicago Manuscript*. Chicago; Oriental Institute Publications 12.

Focus on an Old Topic

A Fresh Look at the Polyfunctionality of *jn*

Elsa Oréal[1]

The morpheme *jn* is well-known for its polyfunctionality in Earlier Egyptian. Its main contexts of use as a free morpheme having scope over a nominal syntagm are the following:

- preposition introducing the nominal referent with the semantic role of agent (or agent-like)[2] in constructions with a marked information structure where the agent bears a contrastive focus:
  - *jn* + agent + *sḏm-f* form with modal semantics
  - *jn* + agent + participle (imperfective or perfective)
- preposition introducing the nominal referent with the semantic role of agent in passive constructions or constructions involving a non-finite form.

Moreover, *jn* is used as a marker with sentential scope in interrogative utterances.[3] A limited use of the particle as a marker of protasis may also be linked to the latter use, in line with a cross-linguistically well attested pattern.

Various earlier studies have aimed at formulating a unifying analysis of this intriguing polyfunctionality. Already in 1988, Antonio Loprieno showed the intricacies of the interplay between syntax, information structure and pragmatics that characterize *jn* in its use as an agentive marker within constructions with a marked word order 'Agent + Predicate'. He also proposed ways of relating other uses of the particle. With a different approach, Chris Reintges's (1998) account is based on the assumption that focus marking is the core function of *jn* in all its uses, in deep syntax if not strictly at the level of information structure. This analysis has a lot of robust arguments, but the author is forced to concede that all contexts where *jn* functions as an agentive particle ultimately derive from a focalizing construction, a step that appears historically debatable. This difficulty is seen and avoided by Tom Güldemann, who in 2014 aimed at exploring the hypothesis of a relationship between the particle *jn* and the quotative verb *j* along a postulated path of verbification.[4] Besides this specific point, Güldemann's approach differs from Reintges 1998 mainly in the proposed origin for *jn*. However, this proposal remains somewhat

---

1 Aoroc, CNRS-PSL, Paris. I would like to thank the reviewers for their careful reading that allowed me to improve substantially the presentation of my arguments.

2 'Agent-like' refers to a participant formally encoded in the same way as a prototypical agent, not to a semantic category of 'less-than-prototypical' agent.

3 Its supposed marginal use as an emphatic assertive particle remains highly dubious, see below.

4 See Schenkel (2017) for a detailed evaluation of this hypothesis.

Sami Uljas & Andreas Dorn (eds), *Crossroads VI. Between Egyptian Linguistics and Philology*, 191–214
DOI: https://doi.org/10.37011/studmon.30.08

vague and linguistically undefined: a 'presentational/identificational marker' appears to put together semantic domains that are not the same, as does the gloss 'it/this/there is', mixing the reconstruction as a kind of deictic copula (indeed, a typological likely source for a focus marker, if this was the function of *jn*), and as an existential copula, which does not fit with the attested role of *jn*. This is probably due to Güldemann's awareness of the place of *jn* within the utterance, which does not favour a deictic origin. Both *js* and *pw*, an earlier and a more recent deictic elements in Earlier Egyptian, never occur in first position. The lack of clarity in this definition as presentative and/or identifying marker also reveals a weak point in the analysis. Within this approach, there remains a difficulty in explaining why such a marker would have its distribution restricted to introducing a referent with an agent or agent-like semantic role. However, this fact is crucial for the understanding of what is marked by *jn* itself in the various constructions where it occurs.[5] Moreover, the account of interrogative *jn* based on such a source appears even less satisfactory than Reintges's, for a presentational particle is not a likely candidate as a source for an interrogative marker. As an identificational copula, *jn* would seem less difficult to connect to interrogation, but other problems arise when one takes into account that *jn* is originally used not in neutral, but in non-canonical questions, as will be seen below.[6]

All approaches acknowledge the relevance of information structure for the understanding of the role played by *jn* in the utterance. However, in the wake of Loprieno's synchronic account, I want to suggest a way out of the confusion between a thematic function (indicating the subject of which the predicate is about) and a use in focalizing context, features that are mixed together in Güldemann's 'presentative/identificational' functions. The reconstructed path of change thus proposes another common source explaining the emergence of other uses of *jn*. According to this historical scenario, *jn* came to acquire its function as a prototypical marker for the semantic role of agent in a source construction where it was used to introduce a topicalized agent. Focalizing semantics obtain only in some of the constructions in which *jn* is used without characterizing *jn* itself. The presence of *jn* as a formative in the paradigm of independent pronouns such as 1s *jnk*, 2ms *jntk* indeed hints at a primary function as a topic marker rather than a focus marker. The proposed explanation also has some bearing on the comparison with Akkadian cognate pronominal forms. A fresh diachronic view at these data thus suggests a closer functional similarity with Egyptian *jn*. The analysis will proceed as follows:

1 Traces of *jn* with a left-extraposed topic
2 From topic marker to agentive preposition in focalizing constructions
3 Postverbal agent in antitopic function
4 Clausal *jn:* topics, conditionals and interrogatives
5 Emphatic affirmative *jn:* a ghost use

---

5 Loprieno (1988).

6 As a focus marker with a deictic origin rather than a verbal expression (as reconstructed in Reintges 1998), the place of *jn* at the beginning of the proposition seems problematic. Moreover, the focus marker *js*, whose deictic origin is much more in line with its syntax and older uses, already plays this role in Older Egyptian. See Oréal (2011).

6 Independent pronouns in Akkadian and in Egyptian
7 The etymology of *jn*
8 Summary

1 Traces of *jn* with a left-extraposed topic

The notion of topic used in this contribution is both formal and functional: it refers to everything that is detached by left extraposition in the utterance, and, pragmatically, 'the matter of current interest which a statement is about and with respect to which a proposition is to be interpreted as relevant'.[7] Within this approach of aboutness topics, a contrastive topic is a topic which, according to the speaker's view, is presented as selected against other possible topics.

Not enough attention has been paid to traces of *jn* + Full Noun used as a left-extraposed topic, although these examples are known and mentioned in the literature.[8] This use is rare and may be considered as recessive already in the *Pyramid Texts*:

(1)	***jn***	*nwt*	*ms-n-s*	*M*	*ḥn*^{c}	*wsjr*
	TOP	Nut	give_birth-ANT-3FS	M	with	Osiris

'As for Nut, she gave birth to M with Osiris' (PT §1428M)

Here the nominal phrase introduced by *jn* has the discourse function of a marked contrastive topic and is resumed in the main clause by a coreferential suffix pronoun. In a variant, the participial statement is used instead:

(2)	***jn***	*nwt*	*ms-t*	*P*	*ḥn*^{c}	*wsjr*
	TOP	Nut	give_birth\PCPL.FV-3FS	P	with	Osiris

'As for Nut, she gave birth to P with Osiris' (PT §1428P)

Does this imply that, both variants having exactly the same meaning, the participial statement and the construction '*jn SN sḏm-n-f*' need to share the same structure, the latter being only the older of the two ?[9] Another possibility is that the two constructions have a very similar, although not identical meaning. An argument in favour of this view lies in the fact that, with the negation, the absence of term focus on the agent marked by *jn* is sometimes made apparent by the choice of the negative pattern. Thus, in the following

---

7 Lambrecht (1994: 119).

8 Allen (1984: §408), while convincingly showing that the constructions with a suffix pronoun coreferential to the topicalized Agent in the main clause are older than the focalizing constructions with participles, considers the *sḏm-n-f* form as a nominal one in a cleft sentence, a syntactic analysis that makes less sense in view of other examples like (7) and (8). He mentions three examples in the *Pyramid Texts:* §644c, §1428e, §1566c.

9 Loprieno (1995: 253) sees this example as a preterital cleft sentence in early form. Kruchten (1996: 58) adopts this diachronic explanation of the difference between the royal dedication formula (name of king and *sḏm-n-f*) and the private one (*jn* A and perfective participle). I would rather suggest that in the royal formula, the name of the king is marked as a salient new topic by anteposition alone before the Anterior *sḏm-n-f* form, while in the private one, exclusive identification of the dedicant really is at stake – hence the use of the participial statement, with or without *jn*.

example, the dislocated agent remains in the same position while the negation *ni* shows up in the main clause:

(3)

jn	*ḥr*	*zꜣ-k*	*ms-n-k*	*ni*	*rḏ-f*	*ppy*	*pn*
TOP	Horus	son-2MS	beget-ANT-2MS	NEG	place\MOD-3MS	Pepi	DEM
tp	*mwt*						
PREP	dead						

'As to Horus, your son whom you have begotten, he shall not place this Pepi at the head of the dead'[10]

This pattern differs from what is expected with a focalizing construction, for with a focalized agent, the following construction appears in order, showing the discontinuous negation *n…js*:

(4)

n	***jn***	*js*	*ppy*	*dbḥ*	*mꜣ-f*	*ṯw*	*m*	*qd-k*	*pw*
NEG	TOP	FOC	Pepi	ask\ PCPL.PFV	see\ SUBJ-3MS	2MS	PREP	form-2MS	DEM
wsjr	*dbḥ*	*mꜣ-f*	*ṯw*	*m*	*qd-k*	*pw*			
Osiris	ask\ PCPL.PFV	see\ SUBJ-3MS	2MS	PREP	form-2MS	DEM			

'It is not Pepi who asked that he may see you in this your form (…), it is Osiris who asked that he may see you in this your form'[11]

In the second part of the passage, one notices that the agent, Osiris, is not preceded by the agentive marker *jn*. Its presence does not seem to be mandatory, a fact that points to its role as having no bearing on focalization itself, but rather at a semantic level (making the semantic role of the participant expressed before the verb explicit), as we shall see below.[12]

In one case, the pronoun *jntsn* of the *jn-* series that integrated the morphem *jn-* at a protohistorical state of the language has the function of a second topic. It is coreferential with the first one, with identificational semantics, as is the case in the usual participial statement focalizing the agent, but with the semantic role of beneficiary marked by the function of the resumptive pronoun in the main clause:

(5)

nṯrw	*nbw (...)*	***jntsn***	*stpp*	*n-sn*	*stpwt-sn*
gods	all	3PL	cut\PASS.PAST	to-3PL	cut-3PL

'All gods (…), (as for) them, one will cut their cuts for them'[13]

10 *Pyramid Texts* §969a.

11 *Pyramid Texts* §1128a–bP.

12 Doret (1991) and Kruchten (1996) explain the omission of *jn* in terms of enunciative involvement of the first-person speaker. However, such an explanation does not fit well with examples from the *Pyramid Texts* where the name of a god is the prominent Agent introduced without *jn* (see the variant §1428eN). It seems more simple to relate this omission to the varying degree of topicality of the participant, a discursive parameter that leaves some freedom of choice to the speaker, but explains why *jn* is mainly omitted before the name of the deceased in examples from the *Coffin Texts*.

13 *Pyramid Texts* §1651cN.

An even more interesting structure appears in the following example where the noun introduced by *jn* is undoubtedly extraposed and resumed in the main clause by the pronoun *swt:*

(6)	***jn***	*jwꜥ-j*	*pw*...	*swt*	*rdi*	*n-j*	*s(y)*
	TOP	heir-1S	DEM	3MS	give\PCPL.PFV	to-1S	it

‘As to this my heir, ...*he* has given it to me’[14]

According to Güldemann, this example shows the original, ‘more basic identificational function’ of *jn.*[15] This is in fact not the case, since the following participial statement is the basic expected pattern where an identifying focus on the agent is expressed. The nominal phrase introduced by *jn* is extraposed and encoding again a contrastive topic.

To sum up, these examples show a recessive use of *jn* in sentences where the extraposed topicalized participant is indexed by a subject suffix pronoun in the following part of the utterance.

Moreover, I propose to analyze the source of the well-attested ‘*jn* + Agent + *sḏm-f*’-construction as a subtype of the same category ‘extraposed topic, main clause’. Since this construction is usually considered as a construction focalizing the agent, which may indeed be its role in synchrony, I shall now turn to the role of *jn* in sentences with a marked information structure where the agent is under focus.

2 From topic marker to agentive preposition in a focalizing construction

There are many arguments in favour of analyzing the polyfunctionality of the particle *jn* as deriving from a basic function as a focus marker.[16] The main one is of course its presence in the participial statement, a construction that has clear focalizing semantics. Güldemann 2014 prefers to highlight features of *jn* that make it akin to a presentational or identificational marker. From a semantic point of view, identification is precisely the basic operation underlying focalization.[17] Accordingly, Güldemann’s presentation of how *jn* is used before a nominal is in fact not very different from that of Reintges, since it replaces the notion of focus by identification. Unfortunately, it misses the crucial point of the difference between the participial statement and the aforementioned construction ‘*jn* + Agent + prospective *sḏm-f* form’.[18] In the latter, the subject suffix pronoun is coreferential with the initial agent. The semantics often show a meaning closer to a marked contrastive topic than a marked focus on the initial agent, resulting in possible glosses as ‘As to N, he has to listen, it is up to him to listen’. In Spell 609 of the *Pyramid Texts* for example, two parallel utterances present supernatural beings who are to play a role in the king’s afterlife. In both cases, the main predicate of the sentence is a modal *sḏm-w-f*:

14 Gardiner (1957: 176).

15 Güldemann (2015: 235–36).

16 Reintges 1998, followed by Jansen-Winkeln (2002: 19), although the latter remains uncommitted as regards the proposed source as a vestigial verbal copula.

17 Robert (1993).

18 Vernus (1990: 55–60).

(7) *snt-k* *spdt* *msṯw-k* *nṯr-dwꜣ(wj)* *ḥmsi-w-k* *jmwt(j)-sn(j)*
sister-2MS Sothis descendant-2MS Morning God sit-MOD-2MS between-3PL
ḥr *st* *wrt* *jr.t* *gs* *psḏ.t(j)*
PREP throne great to\ADJ.F side Ennead
(...)
jn *h<p>nntj* *nḏri-w=f* *ꜥ-k* *jhꜣ-k* *m* *wjꜣ* *rꜥ*
TOP Hpnn.tj sit-MOD-3MS hand-2MS descend-2MS PREP bark Re
'Your sister is Sothis, your descendant is the Morning God, you shall sit between them on the great throne that is on the Two Ennead's side. (…) As to Hpnn.tj, he shall take your hand as you descend in the bark of Re'[19]

In §1707a, the participants introduced in the preceding clause are resumed with a circumstancial function, while in §1709a, the supernatural being is the subject of the modal *nḏri-w=f*. Both share the same discursive status of a topic, not a focus. Accordingly, the informational content of the verbal forms *ḥmsi-w=k* and *nḏri-w=f* is not presupposed as is the case with the participle in the participial statement, but belongs to the comment (or rheme) part of the utterance.

Now if one accepts the proposal that *jn* once had the original function of introducing an extraposed topic to the left of the utterance, it is still necessary to explain its widely attested use in Earlier Egyptian focalizing constructions. In other texts from the corpus of the Pyramid Texts, such as the so-called Cannibal Hymn, the participial statement and the prospective construction with an agent introduced by *jn* may indeed appear to share the same semantic reading as focalizing constructions. A diachronic path from the primary function of *jn* to its latter use may be reconstructed as follows:

Step 1

In the first step of the reconstructible process, *jn* is used as a topic marker with an extraposed agent that is resumed in main clause by a coreferential pronoun. In Earlier Egyptian, this appears to be the case in constructions with a modal *sḏm-f* where initial *jn* + Full Noun Agent, or an independent pronoun, originally encode a contrastive topic, as is the case in the following Old Egyptian example:

(8) ***jn*** *ꜣzḫ* *r-nfr* *jri-f* *sw*
TOP harvest\PCPL well do\MOD-3MS 3MS
'The one who harvest well, he shall do it'[20]

Step 2

Semantically, the contrastive emphasis bearing on the topic introduced by *jn* may have been reanalyzed as a pragmatic focus with maybe only a slight change in prosodic features

19 *Pyramid Texts* §§1707a–1709a.
20 Simpson (1976: figs 5–10, pl. 9–16).

marking the integration of the no longer dislocated agent. From there, the particle *jn* may undergo a reanalysis as marking the initial agent as such.

Step 3

The group *jn* + agent may now extend to nominal, participial constructions where the initial agent is also under focus, without this focus being marked by *jn* itself, but rather by the identificational semantics and word order:

(9) ***jn*** *zꜣ* *snt-f* *jmj-rꜣ-ḥmw-kꜣ* *sn-mrr* *j.jri*
AG son sister-3MS overseer of the ka-priests Sen-merer do\PCPL.PFV
n-f *nw*
to-3MS this
'It is the son of his sister, overseer of the ka-priests Sen-merer who did this for him'[21]

There are other formal features than *jn* that may play a role in characterizing this construction as marked at the level of information structure:

- marked word order: A/S semantic role first
- possibly intonation contour
- nominal predication with identificational semantics, contrastive focus being one possible reading of identification.

Note that other independent pronouns than the *jn*- series may be used in all the focalizing constructions, which is also an argument in favour of *jn* not marking focus in itself. The recessive independent pronouns characterized by a *-t* ending thus are also attested in initial position:

(10) *swt jyi* *r* *wnjs* *ni* *šmi* *wnjs* *r-f*
3MS come\PCPL.PERF PREP Wenis NEG go\NMLZ.PERF Wenis PREP-3MS
'It is him who came against Wenis, Wenis did not go against him'[22]

Moreover, even with a Full Noun agent, the particle *jn* may be omitted in some cases, as seen above. Thus, focus in the participial statement appears to be encoded by the whole construction, word order and possibly intonational contour, but not by the presence of *jn* in itself.

An alternative scenario would involve the reanalysis of a nominal predication with extraposed topic as a sentence with a syntactic order 'subject + predicate', but with an information structure 'focus + presupposition':

21 Hassan (1941: 117, fig. 104, pls 25–27).
22 *Pyramid Texts* §232aW.

(11) '*jn* + Agent, *jri st* + zero copula' > '*jn* Agent *jri st*'
As for A, (he is) who made it 'It is A who made it'

In the latter case, the common semantic feature of contrastive emphasis with the '*jn* A *sḏm-f*' construction would play no role in the use of *jn* in the participial statement

Whatever it may be, both historical scenarios pave the way to a potential reanalysis of a preposition used to introduce an extraposed participant with agent role as a marker of agentivity itself. I shall now turn to other contexts where the agentive preposition resulting from the grammaticalization of a marker introducing the initial agent is extended to a non-initial syntactic position.

3 Postverbal agent in antitopic function

In two main contexts of use, *jn* is used as an agentive preposition introducing a participant in postverbal position. One of them involves the quotative verb *j*. In this marginal but well-attested use, *jn* introduces the nominal agent that is both highly retrievable, in terms of discourse status, and non-contrastive:

(12) *j-t* ***jn*** *jẖm.t*
say\PFV-3FS AG shore
'she said, (namely) the shore'[23]

In the following rare example, *jn* + Full Noun in final position does not follow a verb of saying:[24]

(13) *jr-n-f* *m* *mnw-f* *n* *jtw-f* *m*
make-ANT-3MS PREP monument-3MS to fathers-3MS PREP
bꜣḥ ***jn*** *jḥꜣ*
fore AG Iha
'What he made as his monument for his forefathers, (namely) Iha'[25]

This use has been labeled 'afterthought topic'.[26] However, given the highly formal character of the discourse from which the example derives, an afterthought is perhaps not the likeliest analysis. I suggest to consider *jn* + Noun here and in the preceding example as an antitopic.[27] In discourse, an antitopic may be defined as a highly identifiable term, indexed by a pronominal affix on the verb. It is integrated into the syntax and not dislocated, while

23 CT V 195c.

24 Loprieno (1988) assumes that *jn* + Full Noun expresses a focus, while pronominal forms build on the *jn*- base may serve to topicalization. Formulated with a synchronic viewpoint, his analysis remains highly compatible with the diachronic evolution proposed here.

25 Davies, *Sheikh Saïd*, pl. 29, fr. E.

26 Reintges (1998: 213), referring to Givon (1990: 760).

27 Grossman (2015) analyses the antitopic status of marked postverbal subject in Coptic in a way that is not without connection to the reconstructed historical development of *jn* in proto-Egyptian. However, a crucial difference lies in the mandatory character of the marking in Coptic, a rare typological feature that is not found with *jn*.

an afterthought is dislocated.[28] In terms of information structure, the antitopic is rhematic (fully informative and not given in terms of information structure) rather than contrastive and represents the center of attention. Thus, it can serve to encode an agent that is not already given or presented as such in discourse but rather belongs to the more informative part of the utterance. The same holds true for the following example:

(14)	*smn-s*	*wj*	***jn***	*ꜣst*	*ḥr*	*ꜣkr*
	establish\IMPFV-3FS	1MS	AG	Isis	PREP	earth

‘She establishes me, (namely) Isis, on earth’[29]

From a diachronic point of view, this discourse property could also explain how the group *jn* + agent is used in thetic, all-rhematic passive constructions.[30] In a statement similar to example (9) for the informational content, but formulated with the Old Perfective in an asubjectal construction, the agent role is indeed expressed by a *jn*-phrase in the antitopic position. One may consider it as coreferential with a postverbal pronominal subject with no segmental expression, at least in the source construction of the pattern:

(15)	*jri*	*nw*	***jn***	*jmj-rꜣ-pr*	*ḥm-kꜣ*	*kꜣj*
	do\PFT	DEM	AG	overseer of the house	priest	Kai

‘This was done by the overseer of the house and priest Kai’[31]

In that case, there is no focus on the agent as is the case with the participial statement, where identification of the agent is at stake. Such constructions represent the second main use of agentive *jn* in postverbal position. Here, the verbal form is the third person masculine Old Perfect, originally ambitransitive, whose active or passive reading depends on the expressed participants. The postverbal patient is part of the rheme and there is no participant with the function of topic.[32] The presence of agentive *jn* encodes the semantic role of the following noun phrase. In such a construction, all participants appear to be at the same informational level. This historical scenario makes it unnecessary to posit a former term focus construction as the source of *jn* encoding the agent in asubjectal constructions.[33]

28 Lambrecht (1981: 84–88).

29 Gardiner (1957: 176).

30 I use the term thetic with its classical meaning in information structure linguistic studies as referring to utterances that present a piece of information ‘in one chunk’ and show no topic-comment structure. Their information structure is also sometimes labeled ‘all-new’ or ‘all-rhematic’. See Lambrecht (1987) on the possible interplay between thetic information structure and formal strategies originally dedicated to other linguistic functions.

31 Junker (1929: fig. 51, pl. 36).

32 Alleged examples of the form with a pronominal patient encoded by a suffix pronoun belong to a distinct type of passive (Oréal 2017). The complementarity with the construction ‘pronominal patient + Pseudoparticiple’ does not hold under closer scrutiny, since a full noun patient can in fact occur in the latter if it has a thematic status in discourse.

33 Reintges (1998: 172) postulates a path of emergence for the Agent marker in passive constructions from a former biclausal source construction involving a passive sentence followed by a truncated cleft sentence: ‘P is done, it’s A’ > ‘P is done by A’.

Within the proposed analysis, the incompatibility of agentive *jn* with a suffix pronoun finds a straightforward explanation.[34] In a protohistorical stage of the language, it had indeed combined with the suffix pronoun under its current non initial form *n*. Such is the path of grammaticalization that gave birth to the Anterior *sḏm-n-f* form.[35]

4 Clausal *jn*: topics, conditionals and interrogation

In Earlier Egyptian, left-extraposed topicalization typically goes with another preposed marker with a prepositional origin, namely *jr*. It does not show any affinity with the Agent. A better understanding of the difference between *jn* and *jr* might first come from an analysis of their distinct use for introducing a conditional protasis. Semantically, *jr* appears neutral as to the status of the state of affairs expressed by the protasis:

(16) ***jr*** *pri-f* *m* *sbꜣ* *pw* *jmnt-j* *n-j* *pt*
TOP come_out\NMLZ-3MS PREP gate DEM west-ADJ of-ADJ sky
jni *n-f* *sbꜣ* *pw* *rs-j* *n-j* *pt*
bring\IMP to-3MS gate DEM south-ADJ of-ADJ sky
'If he comes out that gate west of the sky, bring him that gate south of the sky'[36]

This is not the case when *jn* is used before a proposition that has the function of a protasis, much less frequently than *jr*. Thus, in the following example, *jn* introduces a protasis whose informational content is likely to be presented as granted by the speaker:

(17) ***jn*** *mri-ṯn* *ꜥnḫ* *jtmw (...)*
TOP like\NMLZ-2PL live\IMPFV Atum
šzp-ṯn *n-ṯn* *ꜥ* *n* *ppy* *pn*
take\MOD-2PL PREP-2PL hand of Pepi DEM
'If (as I suppose you do) you want that Atum live (...), you shall take to you the hand of this Pepi'[37]

The conditional use of *jr* is well-known and comes as no surprise to the typologist. In a classical paper, John Haiman showed that in many languages there are some formal common features not only between conditionals and topics but also between conditionals

---

34 Reintges (1998: 218–20) interprets this problematic incompatibility of a 'copular verb' as resulting from the fact that suffix pronouns can never receive contrastive focus, but this analysis then conflicts with the fact that *jn* did combine with pronominal endings in the independent, not always focal, paradigm.

35 Werning (2008) is thus right in refuting the analysis of the -*n*-morph in the Anterior form as a result of the integration of agentive *jn*. However, *jn* and *n* ultimately represent distinct results of an evolution involving the same preposition *n*. With a synchronic point of view, Grandet & Mathieu (1991: 148) miss the point that the morpheme -*n* is not a short form of agentive *jn*, but rather *jn* originally is the full form of the preposition *n*.

36 *Pyramid Texts* §1252c–d.

37 *Pyramid Texts* § 879b–880aP.

and interrogatives.[38] Within Güldemann's analysis of *jn* as presentative/identificational marker, this use is better related to a focus on truth-value:

> While I cannot cite a case outside Egyptian where an identificational marker has been recruited to mark this function specifically in questions, it is attested in its affirmative declarative counterpart (…) in several Bantu languages, clause-initial identificational and presentational markers can have scope over an entire clause, which can be paraphrased as 'It is (the case) that ...', and in this use have come to encode predication focus involving in particular truth value-focus.(…) It is thus not far-fetched to hypothesize that a similar process has happened with identificational *jn* in Egyptian – the major difference being that it seems to have been more salient in the interrogative counterpart of the type 'Is it (the case) that ...?[39]

Such an interpretation of interrogative *jn* is thus crucially dependent on the use of sentential *jn* as an emphatic assertive particle. However, it underestimates its highly dubious and marginal character. In order to understand better the way in which the particle *jn* contributes to encoding interrogative force, it is important to recall that its presence is not mandatory. First of all, intonation contour was probably sufficient to mark the utterance as a question in Egyptian. What does interrogative *jn* add in terms of semantics? It is beyond the scope of this paper to analyze the use of *jn* in non-canonical interrogative utterances in all due detail.[40] However, the following observations appear to be relevant to the question of its relationship to topicalization. Not every kind of polar question is in fact marked by *jn*.[41] From a pragmatic point of view, the speech act accomplished with *jn* is indeed not a mere request for information. The state of affairs expressed in the proposition often appears rather as a point considered as given and taken as a common ground by the speaker in order to justify a command or a wish, as shown in the following example:

(18) ***jn*** *wdi-k* *ṯw* *ḥr* *gbt* *nšmt-s* *mj*
INTERR throw\IMPFV-2MS 2MS PREP fish scales-3FS go\IMP
'Are you throwing yourself at the fish and its scales (in the end) ? Go!'[42]

In a caption belonging to a vividly depicted fishing scene, the addressee appears to take too much precaution before going to work. The speaker expresses ironical doubts on his comrade's willingness to come to do real work by using a non-canonical, biased question where no request for information is really at stake. The same is true in the following example:

38 Haiman (1978).
39 Güldemann (2014).
40 Dayan (2016: 268–73).
41 Silverman (1980) illustrates this point abundantly.
42 Steindorff (1913: pls 115 & 117).

(19) ***jn*** *jrr-t* *r-j* *r-gs-ṯ*
INTERR do\PCPL.DEF.PASS-F PREP-1S PREP-2FS
'What about the things done against me at your side ?'[43]

In the context, there is a strong contrast between the questioned situation and the speaker's expectation. Accordingly, the latter is not asking for information but expresses a protest by formulating a biased question.

In accordance with this pragmatic context, the German translation is often 'was soll das,…', the English one 'what does it mean, what about, how come, what is the meaning of…'. However, one should not conclude from the use of a topic marker as a formal means to encode a special type of question that the verb forms following after interrogative *jn* have to be 'nominal' forms. The completed grammaticalization process of the particle involves a larger distribution that makes it able to have scope over a large type of verbal predication. As a sign that the end of the path has been reached, one also finds interrogative *jn* combined with the standard topic marker *jr*, as is the case in the following example:

(20) ***jn*** *jr* *grt* *pꜣ* *jr-t* *bjn-w* *r* *ḥbswt-j*
INTERR TOP PTCL DEM do-INF bad-PL PREP concubine-1s
'What does it mean, concerning this doing bad thigs to my concubine ?'[44]

From a typological point of view, the use of interrogative as conditional clause is widely attested cross-linguistically. After Haiman, Elizabeth Traugott further elaborated on the ability of an interrogative clause to play the role of topic for a following speech act.[45] The *World Lexicon of Grammaticalization* confirms the complex relationship between these domains. It mentions both the well-known pathway of change from question to conditional and, more tentatively, from question to topic:

> The reason for tentatively proposing this pathway is that in a number of languages polar questions can be used in specific contexts to introduce topical constituents.[46]

However, typological studies also evoke a fact that might be crucial for the understanding of Egyptian data, namely that some languages show common formal features shared by conditionals and polar interrogatives even when the conditional marker is not derived from an interrogative one:

> The close relationship between conditionals and polar interrogatives is also observable in languages that grammaticalised their conditional marker from a different domain or where the etymology of this marker is unknown.[47]

43 Gardiner & Sethe (1928: pl. 3).
44 Allen (2002: verso 16).
45 Traugott (1985: 294–95).
46 Kuteva & al. (2019: 354).
47 Haspelmath & al. (2008 : 1014–15).

Jespersen already proposed a model of discourse interaction that explores the motivation for using interrogation as a protasis in a conditional system in German. It is based on dialogue as the source for conditional construction:[48]

A: Scheint die Sonne?
A : Is the sun shining?
B: Ja.
B: Yes.

A: So/Dann gehen wir baden.
A: Then we'll go for a swim.

The historical relevance of such a model has been contested as an example of 'Marker/Structure Fallacy', the idea that 'the sources of markers logically imply the sources of structures'.[49] Taking this objection into account, Van den Nest updates Jespersen's model from a point of view of grammaticalization. His study analyses the pragmatic context for the use of interrogatives as conditional along a line that appears to fit with the Egyptian data concerning *jn*. The crucial point lies in negotiating common ground between the interlocutors:

> By phrasing the antecedent as a polar interrogative, the speaker involves the interlocutor in constructing the hypothetical world.[50]

This study suggests a distinct historical path according to which German thetic declaratives with the verb in first position were in fact remotivated as interrogative. It is thus interesting to note that the path leading to the formal common features between conditionals and interrogatives may involve a more complex explanation than interrogatives simply coming to be used as conditionals. Based on Egyptian data that favour an interpretation of *jn* as being originally a topic marker, I would like to suggest a path for the grammaticalization of polar interrogative where the topic marker is the source for the formal means of encoding (non-canonical) interrogative.[51] Such a proposal is tacitly present in Haiman's study, without being clearly formulated.[52] That conditionals and interrogatives share a semantic common feature that may be subsumed under the notion of topicality has also been formulated in a cognitive linguistics approach:

48 Jespersen (1940: 374).
49 Harris & Campbell (1995: 284).
50 Van den Nest (2010: 115).
51 The main sources identified in the typological literature for the emergence of polar question markers are negation, dubitative markers (perhaps), alternative markers (or) and insubordination of interrogative complementizers (if). See Evans (2007) on this notion.
52 Haiman (1985: 27) points to the fact that questions may be used to introduce a topic.

> The use of conditional *if* in English as an interrogative may be similarly analysed as an instance of metaphoric iconicity. The iconic ground is in this case 'given' or 'topic of a sort', a semantic aspect which is shared by the functions conditional and interrogative.[53]

However, the suggested path from contrastive topic marker to non-canonical interrogative marker needs further qualification. What kind of semantic bridge can relate these uses? In the discourse structure, a contrastive topic is initial and marks a shift in aboutness while establishing a given between speaker and hearer. Establishing this common ground raises the expectation of an apodosis or comment. In the presence of an explicit comment, the topic clause is read as a conditional:

As for p, apodosis > Is p true (as expected), apodosis

Suppressing the apodosis, the topic left alone becomes a biased interrogative speech act:

As for p > Is p true (as expected)?

Thus, if no explicit clause comes as the expected apodosis, the topic clause may be pragmatically interpreted as a question. Thus, according to the context of utterance, the reading of the topic clause can be of more epistemic (condition) or pragmatic (interrogative) sort. The following example illustrates the kind of bridging use that may make the transition from topicalization to interrogative:

(21) ***jn*** *sr* *pj* *jni* *sw*
TOP goose DEM bring\IMP 3MS
'As for this goose, bring it'[54]
'Is it a goose? Bring it'

A medical text also offers a possible interesting example in procedural discourse:

(22) ***jn*** *sꜥq-t* *ni* *qmꜣ-t* *ḥꜥw-f*
TOP enter\PCPL.PFV-FS NEG produce\PCPL.PFV-FS body-3MS
'As for something that was made enter, it is not something that his body produced'[55]

The use of *jn* rather than *jr* here might relate to the fact that *jr* is used in the whole passage as a topic marker introducing each gloss, so that using the *jn*-strategy as a means of encoding a topic allows a better distinction between different kinds of topics in the context.

---

53 De Cuypere (2008: 101).
54 *Pyramid Text* §1224bP.
55 Vernus (1982–1983: 123, example 8).

5 Emphatic affirmative *jn*: a ghost use

In his reference grammar for Old Egyptian, Elmar Edel describes a few cases of *jn* used as a particle putting some emphasis on the affirmative force of the utterance. His clearest example is the following:[56]

(23)

jn	*tr*	*rḫ-wj*	*ṯw*	*jrit*	*mrr-t*
TOP	PTCL	know\PCPL.PFV-DU	2MS	do\INF	like\ PCPL.IMPFV-FS

ḥzz-t	*nb-k*
praise\ PCPL.IMPFV-FS	lord-2MS

jn	*wrš-k*	*sḏr-k*	*ḥr*	*mḥ*	*m*
TOP	spend_day\IPMPFV-2MS	spend_day\IMPFV-2MS	PREP	full\INF	PREP

jrit	*mrr-t*	*ḥzz-t*	*wḏ-t*	*nb-k*
do\INF	like\ PCPL.IMPFV-FS	praise\ PCPL.IMPFV-FS	order\PCPL.IMPFV-FS	lord-2MS

jw	*ḥm-f*	*r*	*jrit*	*sꜣr-w-k*
PTCL	His Majesty	PREP	do\INF	wish-PL-2MS

'If ever you are really able to do what your lord likes and praises, if you spend night and day trying to do what your lord likes and praises, His Majesty will realize your wishes'[57]

The passage of this letter from the king presents a typical conditional system, with a double protasis expressing conditions to be fulfilled for the king to realize his promise of reward (apodosis).[58] There is no need to postulate a distinct assertive meaning of *jn* to explain such a use of the particle. In the same way, the remaining examples are very rare and susceptible of an alternative interpretation, as is the following:

(24)

(j)n	*jrf*	*ni*	*wnm-j*	*ḥs*
TOP	PTCL	NEG	eat\IMPFV-1S	feces

'Is it then not the case that I shall not eat faeces'[59]

Topmann translates this as an assertive utterance.[60] However, her previous references to other interpretations show how this reading is but a semantic effect of non-canonical rhetorical interrogative. As noted by Sweeney, the speaker 'is trying to make [the addressee] agree with him'.[61]

---

56 Edel (1955–1964: 422).

57 Sethe (1933: 129).

58 The other example (Sethe 1933: 61.2) cited by Edel shows the same structure.

59 *Coffin Texts* III 86e (spell 186). The form *n* in this passage has been viewed as the full writing of the preposition *n* with a causal meaning. See Barta (1988: 56).

60 Topmann (2002: 52).

61 Sweeney (1991: 322).

6 Independent pronouns in Akkadian and in Egyptian

Free or independent pronouns represent a well-known potential isogloss between Akkadian and Ancient Egyptian:

	Akkadian 'nominative'		Egyptian independent
1s	*an-ā-ku*		*jnk*
2MS	*atta* <	**an-ta*	*jnt-k*
2FS	*atti* <	**an-ti*	*jnt-ṯ*
3MS	*šū*		*jnt-f*
3FS	*šī*		*jnt-s*

In the Egyptian paradigm, a likely motivation for the emergence and spread of the *jnt* + suffix pronoun may have been the loss of the gender distinction in the second person after the fall of final short vowels. The suffix pronouns were then used to make up for this functional loss in the second person. This process extended to third person by analogy.[62] The first person, unmarked for gender, remained untouched by this evolution. According to such a reconstruction, the first person of the independent pronoun has emerged from the combination of *jn* with the ending that also appears in the Egyptian Old Perfect and in the Akkadian Stative:

**jn-k* >	*jnk*
'as for me'	independent pronoun

Beyond the similarity of forms, there is a well-known mismatch between Akkadian and Egyptian as to the function of the pronouns with *an-/jn-* prefix. However, the function of Akkadian pronouns of the *an*-series is still open to discussion. Huehnergard (2011: 273) mentions the fact that the oblique pronoun *kâta/kâti* often occurs as subject with the nominative *anāku* in Old Babylonian letters. The idea that these pronouns were in fact not originally marked for case lies at hand.[63] Against this, I want to suggest that, similarly to what happens with Egyptian data, their origin and form might also be related to their original discourse function. According to this hypothesis, the so-called nominative of the Akkadian independent personal pronoun may actually represent not a Subject case strictly speaking but rather an emphatic form with contrastive semantics. Such a function appears to show again some possible link to topicalization. Contrastive emphasis indeed appears in a number of examples where the *an-* pronouns are used to encode extraposed topic. Thus, the following examples appear to show an extraposed topic with a verb form in the past:[64]

62 Kammerzell (1991: 192–93). See also Breyer (2003: 25).

63 Hasselbach (2005: 150) also shows that in Sargonic Akkadian the original accusative form had no final *-t*, stating that 'the origin of the forms of independent pronouns with infixed /t/ still requires further study'.

64 All Akkadian examples come from Huehnergard (2011). Gianto (1990: 50–53) illustrates the use of the free pronoun *anāku* as casus pendens in locative and existential sentences.

(25) ***anāku*** *u* ***atta*** *ni-ṣbat*
1s and 2MS 1PL-seize\PAST
'You and I (we) seized'

(26) ***anāku*** *ward-am* *a-mḫur*
1CS servant-ACC 1CS-receive\PAST
'As for me, I received a male servant'

In the first sentence, the extraposed pronouns make explicit the reference of the subject affix. In both examples, the free pronoun has the discourse function of a more or less contrastive topic. The same phenomenon is also found with a Stative form:

(27) ***anāku*** *barī-āku*
1CS be_hungry\STAT-1CS
(who else is hungry in your house) 'As for me, I am hungry'

According to John Huehnergard, examples showing the independent pronoun followed by the Stative should be understood as a casus pendens topicalizing the subject while the Stative ending remains the grammatical subject of the verb. This view has been challenged by Kouwenberg, according to whom the ending on the final verb is not a constituent but a person index.[65] One may discuss the synchronic analysis, but from a diachronic point of view, I believe it is relevant to see it the way John Huehnergard does.

According to grammars, the same pronoun is also found in utterances with a marked focus on the subject in verbal clauses:

(28) ***atta*** *ta-šriq*
2MS 2MS-steal\PAST
'(It is) *you* (who) stole'

As is the case in Ancient Egyptian, the extension of use to encode focus might have also involves prosodic features that remain out of reach.

In nominal predication, another focus marker, -*ma*, needs also be used to encode focus when the *an*- pronoun is used. This fact also points to its primary function as marking the topic:

(29) ***anāku****-ma* *rēʾūm* *mušallimum*
1CS-FOC shepherd bring_peace\PCPL
'*I* am the shepherd who brings peace'

The same focus marker is also used with the third person pronoun when bearing the focus, so that one can assume that focus marking is no more inherent to the first person pronoun than to the pronoun *šu*:

(30) ***šu****-ma* *šarraq*
3MS-FOC be_a_thief\STAT
'*He* himself is a thief'

65 Kouwenberg (2000: 30, n.12)

Thus, only in some cases does the extraposed independent pronoun seem to bear a contrastive focus. If topic marking was the original use of the independent pronouns, what kind of path can one propose to explain such an evolution? Again, semantically, contrastive emphasis appears as a likely bridge between topic use and use in sentences with marked contrastive focus:

Topic > **contrast** > focus

The free pronoun also appears as a subject in verbless clauses at the end of the sentence. In such cases, no emphasis seems to be present. Still, it represents the topic and not the focus or predicate in the clause and is not incompatible with its emergence as a topic, initial or not. Further study is still needed on the Akkadian word order in nominal predication.

7 The etymology of *jn*

Having proposed a path from topic marker to other functions of *jn*, I shall now come back to the question of its possible origin. From a morphological point of view, the relationship between *jr* + topic and the preposition *(j)r*, 'towards, concerning' is transparent. The same relationship may exist between the preposition *n*, 'to' and the full form *jn:*

(31) *jn* *kꜣ*
to ka
'For the ka'[66]

It lies at hand to see in *jn* the former full form of the preposition *n* when placed at the beginning of an utterance.[67] Within the context of the participial statement, the full form *jn* was reanalyzed as marking the agent role while the nominal phrase extraposed to the left was reintegrated within the main nominal clause with zero copula:

(32) *jn* NP *jrr* Ø > *jn* NP *jrr*
TOP NP do\ PCPL COP > AG NP do\ PCPL
'As to NP, it is the one who does' > 'it is NP who does'

After gaining its remotivation as an agentive marker in this source construction, *jn* had its use extended to non-initial position. Semantically, the meaning 'as for, as to' fits perfectly well with the use of *jn* with an extraposed topic.[68]

preposition *n* > *jn* + NP: initial topic marker
preposition *r* > *jr* + NP: initial topic marker

From a historical point of view, *jr* is the main marker of topicalization in Earlier Egyptian. The relationship between the two formations may have been both diachronic and

66 Edel (1955–1964: 757).

67 See also also the king's utterance in Peasant: *jn-mrwt wn-f ḥr ḏd gr* 'In order that he keep talking, be quiet'. I thank an anonymous reviewer for this example.

68 On the relationship between an initial *jn* and the preposition *n*, see Gilula (1976), Barta (1988; 1989) and Fischer (1989).

functional or, alternatively, the explanation could be only diachronic. Thus, the use of *jr* as topic marker would have emerged after the evolution of *jn* from topic marker to agentive preposition in both focal and non-focal constructions took place. The fact that interrogative *jn* is already well-established in Old Egyptian may point to a diachronic relationship between an older and a more recent topic marker. However, even if the relationship between *jn* and *jr* is one of diachronic succession, the semantic profile of each marker may not be identical, thus explaining their respective further development. Thus, the distinct profiles of the source prepositions may be related to the distinct semantics of protasis marked by *jr* and *jn:*

Preposition	Protasis
r, 'towards' direction	conditional *jr:* unspecified viewpoint
n, 'to' direction reaching goal	conditional *jn:* common ground shared with addressee

From a comparative point of view, and going back to the possible cognate in Akkadian, one may now ask whether some corresponding linguistic feature is to be found in this language, as could be expected based on the similarity between Egyptian independent and Akkadian nominative free pronouns. The proposed analysis thus predicts the existence of a topic marker *an(a)* in Akkadian. The Akkadian preposition *an(a)*, 'to, for', whose special meaning 'as regards, with respect to, concerning' is well-attested,[69] is indeed employed with topicalized nominals too.[70] Thus in letters, *ana* may introduce a typical Aboutness topic:

(33) *ana* *amt-im* *ša* *ta-ṭrud-īm*
PREP slave-GEN REL 2FS-send\PAST-1S
'As to the slave whom you sent me'[71]

According to Khan (1984), it is frequent in omen texts such as the following:

(34) *ana* *marṣ-im* *i-balluṭ*
PREP sick-GEN 3MS-live\NPAST
'As for the sick man, he will live'[72]

Moreover, *ana* is part of the particle *aššum*, based on *ana* followed by a form of *šumum*, 'name', that is also used as a particle introducing a topic.[73] The crucial difference between Egyptian and Akkadian, namely the existence of a free morph *jn* used before nouns in the former, thus appears less crucial than is usually assumed when comparing the similar basis of the free pronouns paradigms in both languages.[74] Hence, according to the proposed

69 Von Soden (1965: 48).
70 Von Soden (1995: 204–05).
71 Huehnergard (2011: 261).
72 Khan (1984: 259).
73 Khan (1984: 257–58).
74 Jansen-Winkeln (2002: 18).

reconstruction, the morphology of the Nominative free pronouns would result from the following process:

ana + *-aku* > *an-ā-ku*
an[75] + *-ta* > *an-ta* > *atta*[76]
an + *-ti* > *an-ti* > *atti*

The proposed analysis thus suggests a possible path of emergence for free emphatic pronouns as a preposition *an(a)* meaning 'as to' used to introduce a topic. Such a reconstruction also includes an explanation for the fact that Akkadian has no *jn*-form for the third person, since there is no pronominal ending corresponding to *-ku*, and *-ta*, *-ti*. The unexplained fact that the preposition *ana* does not occur with suffix pronouns could be related to its diachronic position within the history of the language. After combining with clitic pronouns of the older series *-ku*, *-ta*, *-ti*, a new combination with the series of suffix pronouns is not expected to happen. Here one should mention the current discussion within Semitic linguistics about the possible reconstruction of the Akkadian preposition *ana* as **ha-na*.[77] However, this proposal is not without weaknesses.[78] Its relevance needs to be reevaluated in light of the likely stronger relatedness to Ancient Egyptian *jn*. In an Afroasiatic perspective, the question remains open whether common features in Ancient Egyptian and Akkadian only illustrate the parallel emergence of similar forms involving a common preposition and shared personal suffixes or whether they might be interpreted as traces of a previous stage common to both languages. Whatever the answer to this question may be, the long known similarity between free and emphatic pronouns may now be interpreted in a new light.

8 Summary

To sum up the main arguments of this paper, I wanted to show that the hypothesis of an identificational copula or a focus marker is not the best way to account for all the uses of the Egyptian particle *jn*. Güldemann (2015) rightly mentions the common feature shared by the uses of *jn* before a noun in clefts, passive and as a quotative, namely its restriction to introducing a nominal with agentive role.[79] However, he gives no explanation for such a situation, which is not expected if the particle originates as a presentative or

75 Von Soden (1995: §13b) considers the short form *an* to be the result of final vowel loss. According to Hasselbach (2005: 168), it results from an analogy with the preposition *in*.

76 Von Soden (1995: 204) states that the proclitic form of *ana* was easily assimiled to the following consonant.

77 Huehnergard (2006: 16), in the wake of Christian (1924: 159), whose comparative methodology appears generally unsound (see the hypothesis about German preposition '*mit*' related to deictic *n/m* in Semitic). Tonietti (2013: 139–40) tentatively proposes the same hypothesis.

78 Kogan (2015: **li*). To his observations one may add Krebernik (2003: 305) according to whom the hadramitic *h-* found in the preposition meaning 'to' comes from a former **l-* as is also the case with precative *l-*. In that case, the parallel with MSA appears even more precarious.

79 Güldemann (2014: 247–48).

identificational marker. Why would such a particle be restricted to the agent-like semantic role ? However, his statement that 'the referent in the scope of *jn* is prototypically non-topical and in some way salient in pragmatic terms', if restricted to a synchronic approach of its main uses, is indeed compatible with the present analysis, but his study focusses on an incomplete understanding of *jn's* polyfunctionality and diachronic evolution. As a matter of fact, the seminal study by Loprieno (1988) had already brought to light crucial features of the particle as essentially agentive and marking pragmatic prominence but not necessarily focus. In the wake of his analysis, my argumentation proposes that the use of *jn* in focalizing constructions result from the reanalysis of a source construction with extraposed topic. Word order, and not *jn*, initially encodes focalization, with a likely contribution of prosodic features that remain out of reach to philology. The normal VSO word order in Older Egyptian makes the participial statement appear as a marked pattern involving a pragmatic and information structural motivation.

This approach allows for a better understanding of the emergence and evolution of Ancient Egyptian *jn* and Akkadian *an(a)* from a likely common source. Morphologically, it involves a preposition **an(a)*- used, among other functions, to introduce a lexical topic or a pronominal one. Internal changes within the history of each language result in a distinct, more extended polyfunctionality of *jn* in Earlier Egyptian.

Evolution internal to Akkadian:
- preposition
- contrastive free pronouns
- use as topic marker

Evolution internal to Egyptian:
- divergence between preposition *n* and initial *jn*
- contrastive emphatic pronouns
- emergence of agentive *jn* in agent or agent-like initial focus constructions and extension to constructions with postverbal agent
- development of conditional and interrogative *jn* < topic marker *jn*

Focussing on the Semitic preposition **l*-, comparative studies have neglected to consider the possibility that the Egyptian preposition *(j)n* and the Akkadian preposition *an(a)* could be cognates. There is no discussion about the fact that the formal resemblance between the two forms could represent a mere coincidence. However, when one takes into account their partially common use in topicalization and as a base for the free/independent pronouns, this historical hypothesis becomes much more appealing.

As expected, linguistic typology by itself does not provide any answer as regards Egyptian data. However, it surely helps to understand what is at stake in analyzing the formal similarity between interrogation, conditionals and topics. The proposed path of change from topic to interrogative marker does not seem to have been clearly identified in typological literature on source constructions for question markers. However, it is implicitly present in functional and cognitive accounts of the use of interrogatives as conditionals. Thus, Egyptian data may contribute usefully to the typology of strategies used cross-linguistically to encode questions and conditions, as they provide an interesting case for a grammaticalization path from topic to both conditionals and non-canonical questions.

Bibliography

Allen, James P. 1984. *The Inflection of the Verb in the Pyramid Texts*. Malibu; Bibliotheca Aegyptiaca 2.

Allen, James P. 2002. *The Heqanakht Papyri*, New York; PMMA 27.

Barta, Winfred. 1988. '*Jn* als Pleneschreibung der Präposition *n*', *Göttinger Miszellen* 103, 7–11.

Barta, Winfred. 1989. 'Beispiele der Sargtexte für *jn* als Pleneschreibung der Präposition *n*', *Göttinger Miszellen* 107, 55–8.

Breyer, Francis. 2003. 'Der semitische Charakter der Altägyptischen Sprache', *Die Welt des Orients* 33, 7–30.

Christian, Viktor. 1924. 'Die deiktischen Elemente in den semitischen Sprachen nach Herkunft, Anwendung und Verwandtschaft Untersucht', *Wiener Zeitschrift für die Kunde des Morgenlandes* 31, 137–92.

Dayan, Veneeta. 2016. *Questions*. Oxford.

Davies, Norman de G. 1901. *The rock tombs of Sheikh Saïd*. London; ASE 10.

De Cuypere, Ludovic. 2008. *Limiting the Iconic*. Amsterdam/Philadelphia; Iconicity in Language and Literature 6.

Doret, Eric. 1991. 'Cleft-sentence, substitutions et contraintes sémantiques en égyptien de la première phase (V-XVIII Dynastie)', *Lingua Aegyptia* 1, 57–96.

Edel, Elmar. 1955–1964. *Altägyptische Grammatik*. Rome; Analecta Orientalia 34 & 39.

Evans, Nicholas & Honoré Watanabe. 2016. 'The dynamics of insubordination', in: Evans, Nicholas & Honoré Watanabe (eds). *Insubordination*. Amsterdam; Typological Studies in Language 115, 1–38.

Fischer, Henri. 1989. 'Occurrence of jn, agential and dative', *Göttinger Miszellen* 107, 69–75.

Gardiner, Alan. 1957. *Egyptian Grammar* (3rd ed.). Oxford.

Gardiner, Alan & Kurt Sethe. 1928. *Egyptian Letters to the Dead*. London.

Gianto, Agustinus. 1990. *Word Order Variation in the Akkadian of Byblos*. Rome; Studia Pohl 15.

Gilula, Mordechai. 1976. 'Shipwrecked Sailor, lines 184–85', in: Johnson, Janet & Edward Wente (eds). *Studies in Honor of George R. Hughes*. Chicago; Studies in Ancient Oriental Civilizations 39, 75–82.

Grandet, Pierre & Bernard Mathieu. 1991. 'La construction ergative de l'accompli égyptien', in: Curto, Silvio, Anna Maria Donadoni Roveri & Bruno Alberton (eds). *Atti del Sesto Congresso Internazionale di Egittologia* I, Turin, 149–51.

Grossman, Eitan. 2015. 'No case before the verb', in: Grossman, Eitan, Martin Haspelmath, & Tonio Sebastian Richter (eds). *Egyptian-Coptic Linguistics in Typological Perspective*. Berlin/Münich/Boston; Empirical Approaches to Language Typology, 203–25.

Güldemann, Tom. 2015. 'How typology can inform philology: quotative *j(n)* in Earlier Egyptian', in: Grossman, Eitan, Martin Haspelmath, & Tonio Sebastian Richter (eds). *Egyptian-Coptic Linguistics in Typological Perspective*. Berlin/Münich/Boston; Empirical Approaches to Language Typology, 227–60.

Haiman, John. 1978. 'Conditionals are topic', *Language* 54, 564–89.

Harris, Alice & Lyle Campbell. 1995. *Historical Syntax in Cross-Linguistic Perspective*. Cambridge; Cambridge Studies in Linguistics 74.

Hassan, Selim. 1941. *Excavations at Gîza 1931–1932*. Cairo.

Hasselbach, Rebecca. 2005. *Sargonic Akkadian: A Historical and Comparative Study of the Syllabic Texts*. Wiesbaden.

Haspelmath, Martin, Ekkehard König, Wulf Oesterreicher & Wolfgang Raible. 2008. *Language Typology and Language Universals* 2. Berlin ; Handbooks of Linguistics and Communication Science.

Huehnergard, John. 2006. 'Proto-Semitic and Proto-Akkadian', in: Deutscher, Guy & Bert Kouwenberg (eds). *The Akkadian Language in its Semitic Context: Studies in the Akkadian of the Third and Second Millennium BC*. Leiden; Uitgaven van het Nederlands Instituut voor het Nabije Oosten te Leiden, 1–18.

Huehnergard, John. 2011. *A Grammar of Akkadian*. Wynona Lake; Harvard Semitic Museum Studies 45.

Jansen-Winkeln, Karl. 2002. 'Zur Personalpronomina im ägyptischen und semitischen', *Die Welt des Orients* 32, 7–19.

Jespersen, Otto. 1940. *A Modern English Grammar on Historical Principles. Part V: Syntax, Fourth Volume*. Copenhagen.

Junker, Hermann. 1929. *Giza* I. Vienna/Leipzig.

Kammerzell, Frank. 1991. 'Personalpronomen der 3. Person im Semitischen', in: Mendel, Daniela & Ulrike Claudi (eds). *Ägypten im afro-orientalischen Kontext. Aufsätze zur Arhäeologie, Geschichte und Sprache eines unbegrenzten Raumes: Gedenkschrift Peter Behrens*. Cologne; Afrikanistische Arbeitspapiere, 177–203.

Khan, Geoffrey. 1984. *Extraposition and Pronominal Agreement in Semitic Languages*. London.

Kouteva, Tania, Bernd Heine, Bo Hong, Haiping Long, Heiko Narrog & Seongha Rhee. 2019. *World Lexicon of Grammaticalization*. Cambridge.

Kogan, Leonid. 2015. *Genealogical Classification of Semitic: The Lexical Isoglosses*. Boston/Berlin.

Kouwenberg, Bert. 2000. 'Nouns as verbs: The verbal nature of the Akkadian Stative', *Orientalia* Nova Series 69/1, 21–71.

Krebernik, Manfred. 2003. 'Lexikalisches aus Tuttul', in: Marrassini, Paolo (ed.). *Semitic and Assyriological Studies Presented to Pelio Fronzaroli by Pupils and Colleagues*. Wiesbaden, 301–19.

Kruchten, Jean-Marie. 1996. 'Deux cas particuliers de phrase coupée sans l'opérateur énonciatif *IN*', *Journal of Egyptian Archeology* 82, 51–63.

Lambrecht, Knud. 1981. *Topic, Antitopic, and Verb Agreement in Non-Standard French*. Amsterdam.

Lambrecht, Knud.1987. 'Aboutness as a cognitive category: The thetic-categorical distinction revisited', *Proceedings of the Thirteenth Annual Meeting of the Berkeley Linguistics Society*, 366–81.

Lambrecht, Knud.1994. *Information Structure and Sentence Form: Topic, Focus, and the Mental Representations of Discourse Referents*. Cambridge; Cambridge Studies in Linguistics 71.

Loprieno, Antonio. 1988. 'Der ägyptische Satz zwischen Semantik und Pragmatik: die Rolle von jn', *Studien zur Altägyptischen Kultur, Beihefte* 3, 77–98.

Oréal, Elsa. 2011. *Les particules en égyptien ancien. De l'ancien égyptien à l'égyptien classique*. Cairo; Bibliothèque d'Egyptologie 152.

Oréal, Elsa. 2012. 'Discourse markers between grammar and lexicon. Two Ancient Egyptian cases for (de)grammaticalization?', in: Grossman, Eitan, Stéphane Polis & Jean Winand (eds). *Lexical Semantics in Ancient Egyptian*. Hamburg; Lingua Aegyptia Studia Monographica 9, 227–45.

Oréal, Elsa. 2017. 'Nominalizations as a source for verbal morphology. Grammaticalization paths of modality and information structure in Earlier Egyptian', *Lingua Aegyptia* 25, 1–33.

Reintges, Chris. 1998. 'Mapping information structure to syntactic structure: One syntax for jn', *Revue d'Égyptologie* 49, 195–220.

Robert, Stéphane. 1993. 'Structure et sémantique de la focalisation', *Bulletin de la Société de Linguistique de Paris* 88, 25–47.

Schenkel, Wolfgang. 2017. '*ỉn*-/- „sagt" < *ỉ(.ỉ) ỉn*- „sagt(e), nämlich"', *Lingua Aegyptia* 25, 231–79.

Sethe, Kurt. 1933. *Urkunden des Alten Reiches*. Leipzig.

Silverman, David. 1980. *Interrogative Constructions with jn and JN-JW in Old and Middle Egyptian*, Malibu; Bibliotheca Aegyptiaca 1.

Simpson, William. 1976. *The Offering Chapel of Sekhem-Ankh-Ptah in the Museum of Fine Arts, Boston*. Boston.

Steindorff, Georg. 1913. *Das Grab des Ti*. Leipzig.

Sweeney, Deborah. 1991. 'What's a rhetorical question ?', *Lingua Aegyptia* 1, 315–31.

Topmann, Doris. 2002. *Die „Abscheu"-Sprüche der altägyptischen Sargtexte: Untersuchungen zu Textemen und Dialogstrukturen*. Wiesbaden; Göttinger Orientforschungen IV/39.

Traugott, Elizabeth. 1985. 'Conditional markers', in: Haiman, John (ed.). *Iconicity in Syntax*. Amsterdam; Typological Studies in Language 6, 289–307.

Van den Nest, Daan. 2010. '*Should conditionals be emergent*... Asyndetic subordination in German and English as a challenge to grammaticalization research', in: Van Linden, An, Jean-Christophe Verstraete & Kristin Davidse (eds). *Formal Evidence in Grammaticalization Research*. Amsterdam; Typological Studies in Language 94, 94–136.

Vernus, Pascal. 1982–1983. 'Études de philologie et de linguistique (II)', *Revue d'égyptologie* 34, 115–28.

Vernus, Pascal. 1990. *Future at Issue. Tense, Mood and Aspect in Middle Egyptian: Studies in Syntax and Semantics*. New Haven; Yale Egyptological Studies 4.

Von Soden, Wolfram. 1965. *Akkadisches Handwörterbuch. Band* I (A–L). Wiesbaden.

Von Soden, Wolfram. 1995. *Grundriss der akkadischen Grammatik*. Rome; Analecta Orientalia 33.

Werning, Daniel. 2008. 'Aspect vs. relative tense, and the typological classification of the Ancient Egyptian *sḏm.n-f*', *Lingua Aegyptia* 16, 261–92.

Can Demotic Studies and Linguistics Get Together Successfully?

Joachim Friedrich Quack

Demotic studies have a strong paleographical component, and this is fully justified given the challenges in decipherment that manuscripts in the Demotic script often pose. We also have to keep in mind that a very substantial part of the available texts is still unpublished, much more so than for any other phase of the Egyptian language. The ongoing need for first editions strongly shapes the trends of the community, and at the moment scholars are much more focused on decipherment than on linguistic analysis.

There are only a few studies devoted specifically to questions of Demotic grammar; during the last decades it would be rare to find more than one or two per year. Even if we consider that most Egyptologists do not deal with Demotic, this number is surprisingly small. On average, publications devoted to Demotic Egyptian have numbered over 50 per year since the 1970s, and over 100 per year since the 1990s.[1] About 1% of these are devoted primarily to questions of grammar. Clearly, discussions of grammatical questions are not much in favor among demotists. I would also like to back up this statement by another one, less amenable to statistics, namely: in reading editions of Demotic texts, not infrequently my instinctive feeling is that I would have liked the editor to explain more closely his/her understanding of the grammatical construction of the passage in question.

Another point can be validated through statistics alone. There exists a sort of dichotomy between scholars publishing on Demotic grammar and scholars editing Demotic texts. During the last decades, the scholar most productive in publishing articles on Demotic grammar has been Leo Depuydt, with at least twelve articles.[2] In contrast, I could find only one single publication by him which was devoted to the first edition of a text, and that concerned an astrological table of terms with mainly just zodiacal signs, planetary symbols, and numbers.[3]

As far as publications on grammar go, Depuydt is numerically rather closely followed by Janet Johnson from whom I could find ten publications on Demotic grammar,[4] not counting the different editions of her introductory grammar *Thus Wrote ʿOnkhsheshonqy*

1 Depauw (2019: 41–42).

2 Depuydt (1990); (1994b); (2000); (2001); (2002); (2003); (2009); (2010); (2011); (2014); (2015) and (2019). There are others where Demotic material appears as part of a discussion of more large-scale evolutions in the Egyptian language.

3 Depuydt (1994a). Even here, one can note that he probably misread two numbers (col. 3, the last two entries from Sagittarius, as noted by Bohleke (1996: 43–44, with note 155).

4 Johnson (1970); (1973); (1976); (1978); (1981); (1986); (1987); (2004); (2013) and (2017).

Sami Uljas & Andreas Dorn (eds), *Crossroads VI. Between Egyptian Linguistics and Philology*, 215–244
DOI: https://doi.org/10.37011/studmon.30.09

or the second printing of the Demotic Verbal System[5] as different works. Since this list includes such a substantial monograph as the *Demotic Verbal System* which really brought the study of Demotic Egyptian verbal sentences to a new level, she could even be said to easily surpass Depuydt in the domain of publishing on Demotic grammar. She also exceeds him a bit as far as editions of texts are concerned, but not very much, with just two single-edited and one co-authored edition of Demotic texts.[6]

There is at least one scholar, namely Robert Simpson, who has made valuable contributions to Demotic Egyptian grammar (and incidentally done good philological work in them),[7] but as far as I can see, has never published a first edition of any Demotic text. Otherwise we have a few scholars mainly working on editions of Demotic texts but occasionally devoting an article specifically to questions of grammar.[8] Most demotists have never published anything specifically on grammar, even if I know several whose editions display a fine knowledge of the intricacies of grammar.

The only person standing somewhat in between is myself. Counting through the last three decades (which also happens to be almost exactly the number of years since my first publication), I note at least seven publications which can be said to have Demotic grammar as their core question.[9] That is not so much less than Depuydt or Johnson. At the same time, I have published a substantial number of first editions of Demotic texts;[10] and several articles can be cited where I improve readings and translations of older editions either as the main topic of the publication[11] or incidentally in the course of my arguments.[12] I have also discussed questions of the reading of certain Demotic groups[13] and – as one of just a few scholars – analyzed the fundamental structure of Demotic writing.[14]

Still, I would not really classify myself as a demotist, in spite of the Wikipedia entry which indicates me to be an 'Egyptologist and Demotist'.[15] Significantly less than half of my publications have a clear relation to Demotic, and none of my monographs has a major

---

5 The second edition (Johnson 2004b) is set in computer font, and for that reason has a different pagination from the first one (Johnson 1976) written with a typewriter. Since the second edition does not take into account the more recent insights into the specific texts analyzed or the Demotic language in general gained since the appearance of the first one, I prefer to cite from the first edition whose official date gives a truer impression of the position within the history of research.

6 Johnson (1975); (1977).

7 Especially Simpson (1996).

8 Like Widmer (1999) or Collombert (2004). One can also mention Feder (2018) as an article on Demotic grammar by someone who has never delivered a first edition of any Demotic Egyptian text at all.

9 Quack (1991); (1992/93); (1994a); (2000); (2006a); (2006b); (2009a). In principle, also the review Quack (1997/98) can be counted here.

10 Quack (2004); (2006/2007); (2009b); (2010/2011a); (2012); Quack & Ryholt (2019).

11 Quack (1994b); (1999); Quack & Ryholt (2000); Quack (2007).

12 A somewhat extreme example is Quack (1992: 63), where a reading improvement to the demotic Tale of the Amazons 3, 31 is so well hidden in the edition of a Classical Egyptian wisdom text that it is even overlooked in the otherwise extremely careful re-edition by Hoffmann (1995: 58).

13 Quack (2010/11b); (2013).

14 Quack (2014).

15 https://de.wikipedia.org/wiki/Joachim_Friedrich_Quack (accessed July 24, 2020).

focus on Demotic texts. I would consider myself rather simply as an Egyptologist with a philological focus who happens to be taken seriously by specialists for Demotic. I should also stress that I see myself mainly as a philologist, not as a specialist on purely linguistic questions. This point is also likely to come out clearly in this paper.

An interesting test case concerning the interaction between linguists and demotists is the work-notes on Demotic grammar by Ariel Shisha-Halevy.[16] He commented on ten different constructions (as part of an intended whole of 19)[17] where he obviously hoped to have furthered understanding. A reaction to this in the *Demotistische Literaturübersicht* by Heinz-Josef Thissen is worth quoting. Thissen wrote: 'Die Akzeptanz seiner Ergebnisse bei den Demotisten wird nicht einmütig sein, da sich seine Übersetzungen von den bisherigen nicht unterscheiden. Ferner stellt er seine Ergebnisse durch eine Anzahl von Fehlern und Flüchtigkeiten selbst in Frage'.[18] This rather negative evaluation combines two different thrusts. The second one, concerning slips and oversights, has some validity; indeed the whole of the first construction which Shisha-Halevy discusses (a supposed analytic future construction *wn-mtw=y sḏm* 'I have to hear') is based on a misreading in Botti's edition[19] which had already been corrected by Zauzich at the time Shisha-Halevy wrote his article.[20] This fact also demonstrates that it is not easy for scholars coming from a more linguistic background to handle Demotic text publications – important corrections to editions might be hidden somewhere. At least for the documentary texts, this situation has now improved considerably with the relatively recent publication of the 'Berichtigungsliste'.[21]

The first reproach by Thissen, however, is much less justified. Should linguists' analyses only be relevant if they lead to completely new translations? In my opinion, philological work on Egyptian texts has by now reached a level where we can expect to have an approximately correct overall understanding of most (but by no means all!) texts. The challenges for Egyptological linguists nowadays lie less in establishing revolutionary new translations and more in helping with fine-tuning the meaning and elucidating the nuances of the usage made in the texts, where there is still room for considerable improvement.

One more point could be made that is important for the possible reception of linguistic analysis. Shisha-Halevy has a rather concise style, and he presupposes knowledge of quite a lot of specialized linguistic terminology. Such a way of presenting his results does not make it easy for demotists without extra training to understand his main points, and this has certainly contributed to the rather limited positive reception of his paper.[22]

Also instructive is a remark by Martin Stadler concerning Robert Simpson's grammar of the Demotic versions of the Ptolemaic sacerdotal decrees. He voiced problems from the

16 Shisha-Halevy (1989a).

17 The intended second installment never materialized, probably as a result of the rather negative reactions to the first one.

18 Thissen (1990: 147).

19 Botti (1967: 153–54).

20 Zauzich (1972: 94–95).

21 Den Brinker, Muhs & Vleeming (2005).

22 At least I genuinely interacted with it in Quack (1991); (1992/93: 221).

perspective of a translator applying grammar.[23] His core point was Simpson's decision to declare words with very low semantic content as primary bases. At the same time, one can also sense some discomfort of a 'traditional' Egyptologist confronted with the concepts and terminology of modern linguistic studies for which he is not prepared. This should be a healthy warning that anybody writing with a linguistic training about Egyptian language should take the trouble to make oneself understandable to people without special training. Otherwise, one will risk not being understood at all.

If we turn to how Demotic is treated in overall descriptions of the historical development of the Egyptian language, the situation does not look good either. The two currently available modern monographs on the ancient Egyptian language in general by Antonio Loprieno and by James Allen[24] both work from only a second-hand knowledge of Demotic, and have their full share of omissions, inexactitudes and downright errors.[25] The first and so far only published volume of an intended large-scale treatment of diachronic Egyptian grammar undertaken at Basel[26] is better, but also not free of errors.[27] It is also marred by a detail of transcription. For the Demotic examples the authors rely principally on the transliterations and translations done by Günter Vittmann in the TLA. However, Vittmann has the somewhat idiosyncratic habit of transliterating as *j* the sign normally transliterated as *y* by demotists. The Basel team has transformed Vittmann's *j* into *ỉ*, thus creating a direct error, because this is a different sign (with different phonetic implications) in the original texts. While the direct negative impact of this mishandling on the analyses in the book in question is likely to be very limited, it creates an impression of a lack of competence, which could easily have a negative impact on the way this study is received by demotists.

23 Stadler (2003: 108).

24 Loprieno (1995); Allen (2013).

25 It would be somewhat tedious to go here into all the details. I intend to demonstrate the weaknesses of Allen's treatment (concerning not only Demotic) in detail elsewhere.

26 Loprieno, Müller & Uljas (2017).

27 Some random examples: In example 163b (p. 123), the definite article *nꜣ* has been dropped before *ḥm.wt*. In example no. 346a (p. 273) correct the transliteration *ꜥn* into *ꜣn* (the regular orthography of the post-negation in the Mythus Leiden manuscript). To my knowledge, there is no omission of the post-negation in a negated adverbial phrase; delete no. 348 (p. 275) because there *bn* is a writing of the negative marker of existence *mn* (a regular orthography in the Leiden Mythus manuscript); also nos. 349b and 349b (p. 275) are negated existential sentences and in them *ꜥn* is not a writing of a supposed post-negation, but simply the adverb 'again, yet'. On p. 775 it is claimed that there are no negated forms of the adjectival verbs in Demotic, but in reality they are attested, see e.g. *bn nꜣ-sbḳ=k n ms ỉn* 'you are not young" pRylands IX, 6,12; *bn.ỉw nꜣ-ꜥšꜣ sḥm.t bꜣn.t ẖn tꜣ mỉ.t n-rn=s ỉn* "there are not many bad women with the behavior (lit. 'way') mentioned' pInsinger 8, 6. Equally, it is claimed on p. 775f. that occasionally the form with the *nꜣ*-prefix can be used like an infinitive, but both alleged examples are not correct. In Khasheshonqy 25 x+18 the form is *n.bn*, which is not the adjective-verb at all (which would be *nꜣ-bn*), but a special (phonetically conditioned?) form used exclusively in the infinitive. The other case (short texts II #909, vs. 1–2) concerns the writing *nꜣ-nfr* which, due to a phonetic interference between the *n* of the prefix and the first radical *n*, actually occurs quite frequently outside the morphology of the adjectival verbs.

As a next case, I would like to take up some remarks made by Friedrich Junge concerning the Demotic text of the Rosettana and its implications for understanding the hieroglyphic version. Junge claimed that *r wꜣḥ=f sč̣m* (Rosettana d 6) is a second tense, based on a former analysis by Williams.[28] From this he further concluded that the *rč̣i̯.n=f* in the hieroglyphic version was a second tense, even though the Greek version did not show the inversion of words which would normally correspond to a second tense in the Egyptian version. But it should have raised suspicion that a second tense in Demotic should be formed by simply prefixing *r*, while elsewhere the converter of second tenses in Demotic is always written as *i͗:i͗ri̯* or *r:i͗ri̯*. Indeed, a more recent analysis by Simpson has rejected Williams' proposal and it has been stated that forms of this kind are most likely circumstantials.[29] I fully concur with this analysis: the writing of the circumstantial converter as *r*, if not followed directly by a suffix, is frequent in Demotic, and the passage in question comes after several clear circumstantial clauses. Even more so, we can point out the close parallel in Philensis II, d, l. 5 where *i͗w wꜣḥ=f č̣i̯.t* is written and corresponds in the hieroglyphic version to *i͗w rč̣i̯.n=f*, which is most definitely not a second tense, and likely to be an unclassical formation of a circumstantial form introduced by *i͗w*. One can seriously doubt whether such a usage really demonstrates 'that the language layer taken as Middle Egyptian never lost its contact to speech reality', as Junge wants to establish.[30] To me, it should better be considered as an indication that the hieroglyphic version of the plurilingual decrees by no means always strives for (or achieves) conformity with the genuine forms of Classical Egyptian.[31]

Beyond the individual problem, this case has major repercussions insofar as it relates to a question about the relation between the different language versions of the plurilingual decrees. In principle, it is good and desirable that this sort of research is done. While Junge can be criticized for not being critical enough, it has to be acknowledged that he followed what at that time was the opinion of several leading demotists. So, demotists should always be aware that postulates based on insufficient or problematic evidence could potentially lead specialists in other phases of the Egyptian language to erroneous conclusions.

On the other hand, it has to be admitted that attention to grammar and discussion of its limitations on the interpretation of texts is hardly the strong point of most editions of Demotic texts. A typical case can be found in pSaqqara 2 vs., x+1, 20.[32] Preserved is *bn i͗w=y šm ⸢r ḫftḥ⸣ n Ḥw.t-Ḥr n pꜣi͗ nw i͗n i͗w=y r č̣t=s r-ḥr-n [...]*. The editors translate 'I am not going to the *dromos* of Hathor at this hour. I will tell it to the [great men]'. In a note, they explain that they want to understand it as a Present I with the post-negation

---

28 Junge (1987: 50 and 55 note 16), citing Williams (1948: 226). Johnson (1976: 205 note 161) seems to accept Williams' proposal.

29 Simpson (1996: 114). Already Spiegelberg (1922: 93 note 79) understood *r* as writing for *i͗w* in these cases.

30 Junge (1987: 49).

31 For further thoughts on the often problematic language of the hieroglyphic version of these decrees, see Quack (2020–23: 141–142).

32 Smith & Tait (1983: 111, pl. 6–8).

ỉn.[33] The editors claim that with the expression *n pꜣỉ nw* 'at this hour',[34] the negative present would be as appropriate as a negated future. So, they postulate a negated present *bn ỉw=y šm ... ỉn*. However, a negated Present I would obviously require the proclitic personal pronoun *bn tw=y ... ỉn*, and the infinitive *šm* is normally not used in the durative tenses. A different segmentation, understanding the first part as a negated future III, 'I will not go to the dromos of Hathor at this time', and making the *ỉn* into a question marker introducing the next sentence as 'should I tell it before [...]?' would certainly be possible. Altogether, taking elementary questions of morphology more seriously would have helped the philological interpretation of the passage in question.

Also quite instructive is the treatment of a passage in pCarlsberg 448 + PSI Inv. D 54 + pCtYBR 4425(27), Fr. 11, l. 9. In her edition, Rana Sérida gave simply *[t]⸢w⸣=y gmy.ṯ=s ḏd* 'I find that ...'.[35] However, if this were really a Present I, the direct construction of the object would violate the Jernstedt rule. For that reason, it is likely that the conjunctive *[m]⸢tw⸣=y gmy.ṯ=s č̣ṭ* '[and] I will find that' has to be restored.[36] In the same fragment, l. 15, Sérida postulated *⸢mtw=f⸣ wꜥ ẖl n rmt nḏm n sꜥnḫ* 'He is a young person, sweet of nourishment'.[37] This would be a nominal sentence in the third person, where the rule in Demotic Egyptian is that it should be constructed with a copula, not an independent personal pronoun. For that reason, a restoration *[r wn]-mtw=f wꜥ ẖl n rmč nč̣m n sꜥnḫ* '[while] he had a lovely foster son' should be seriously considered.[38] Such cases demonstrate the importance of keeping grammatical possibilities in mind when dealing with fragmentary texts – it can be quite helpful for dealing with the lacunae.

Another case where an interpretation is linguistically problematic was produced by John Ray when discussing a formula *ỉw=w č̣ṭ* used in dream reports.[39] He claimed that there are a few cases in Demotic Egyptian where *ỉw* would still have the old value of indicating an affirmation or an assertion. In favor of his claim, he cited two cases, namely pRylands IX, 18, 8 and Ostracon Hor 17, 5. However, in pRylands IX, 18, 8 the *ỉw* follows the sentence-initial particle *tw(y)-s* 'behold', and it is now well-known that in early Demotic, this particle is followed by a circumstantial clause with most sentence-types.[40] Ostracon Hor 17, 5 is a bit more tricky, but we should note that the *ỉw* stands after *č̣ṭ* and might be nothing more than a phonetic indication of the vowel of the particle ϫⲉ. Also, the reading of the passage is not completely certain from the rather mediocre published photograph.

---

33 Smith & Tait (1983: 121 note da). In the TLA, Vittmann even confounds matters further by proposing that the *ỉn* serves here as a post-negation in a negated Future III. However, that construction is regularly formed without a post-negation.

34 Actually, their translation is somewhat inexact; *n pꜣỉ nw* rather means 'at this time'.

35 Sérida (2014: 24) without commentary.

36 Thus Quack (2018: 482).

37 Sérida (2014: 24) again without commentary.

38 Quack (2018: 482).

39 Ray (1987: 85–86).

40 Shisha-Halevy (1989b: 427).

Overall, we should be wary not to postulate too easily singular exceptions to otherwise clear grammatical rules.[41]

The sometimes insufficient attention to grammar in editions of Demotic texts is certainly also due to the usual way of instruction. At most universities where it is taught at all, the teaching of Demotic is focused on the script and paleographical questions; normally there is comparatively little attention to grammar. Of course, this is also somewhat linked to limited available options concerning teaching grammars. Currently, there is only Janet Johnson's *Thus Wrote 'Onkhsheshonqy* as a published teaching grammar. I see problems with its rather unsystematic presentation of the different topics.[42] Also, the translation exercises leave something to be desired; in particular, several fabricated Demotic sentences do not ring idiomatically true to me at all.[43]

I hope to remedy this situation somewhat in the foreseeable future by finally bringing out a Demotic grammar on which I have been working for many years. It aims at being a systematic coverage of all nuances of the grammar (with enough citations from different original texts to appreciate the nuances of use). It also tries to define, where appropriate, differences in use between the different periods within Demotic, and especially to define typically early and typically late Demotic peculiarities. However, much will depend upon the acceptance of this grammar as a tool for actual teaching, with a resulting more grammatically focused syllabus.

I will now take up some recent linguistic discussions among demotists and check to see the extent to which philological points were correctly integrated into them. A somewhat major bone of contention has arisen concerning the interpretation of the orthography of the second tenses in Setne I. Janet Johnson had originally proposed that this manuscript, in contrast to all other Demotic Egyptian manuscripts, shows a clear differentiation in the written forms. According to her, the form *r:ỉrỉ̭=f sč̣m* was used exclusively for the past tense, whereas *ỉ:ỉrỉ̭=f sč̣m* would be the specific form of the present.[44] However, she did not

---

41 Examples of how not to do things can be found in Stadler (2004: 99–100 and 148–50). There, he postulated the use of *tm* for negating nouns in general, not only infinitives. An unfortunate consequence of his erroneous interpretation concerns Codex Hermopolis x+7, 15, where he reproached Donker van Heel (1990: 77) for not having understood the construction, whereas in reality it is Stadler himself who did not understand the elementary rule that in conditional clauses with a substantival subject the negation *tm* (negating the infinitive) can be placed before the subject. He also postulated unnecessarily a singular attestation of a nominal sentence with an independent third personal pronoun (instead of the regular cases with copula). For a critique see Quack (2005a: 177); Richter (2008: 382–85). The rather cavalier attitude of Stadler to grammar can also be seen in Stadler (2019: 112–13), where he takes a quite unattested construction ***sč̣m.tw sw* 'one hears it' for granted.

42 E.g. Johnson presents the *sč̣m=f*-form in Johnson (1986: 17), but only discusses the suffix *=f* two pages later.

43 A particularly bad example is Johnson (1986: 16, sentence A 2) where something is given in Demotic script which seems to read as *tꜣ sḥm.t wꜥ.t ḥm.t tꜣỉ*. But if this were intended to mean 'the woman is a married wife', it would violate the basic rule that *ḥm.t* 'wife' is never constructed without any expression of social relation.

44 Johnson (1976: 99–101 (with a qualification as 'probably') and 107).

present a detailed analysis of the attested forms. Instead, she cited just one form *r:ỉrị͗=f sčm* which from the context must indeed be understood as a past tense.[45] But that is not quite enough to make a good case, especially as she does not give philological considerations for the totality of attestations of either orthography.[46] Johnson's position seems to be driven mainly by the wish to create order by getting a consistent differentiation in usage between two differently written forms in the same manuscript. Johnson's claim was taken up by Leo Depuydt with rather far-reaching consequences, given that he postulated a clear differentiation between the tenses often hidden behind a seemingly identical orthography.[47]

Since a clear empirical demonstration for this differentiation was not provided by either Johnson or Depuydt, I looked into this question in detail in my study on the Demotic second tenses.[48] Here, I let myself be driven mainly by philological considerations, i.e. first of all the intuitive expectation of which tense would make best sense in its immediate context. The results were quite sobering: while most examples for *r:ỉrị͗=f sčm* (eleven out of a total of 13 attestations) would indeed make sense philologically as a past tense, one (3, 11f.) was not quite certain but more likely present,[49] and at least one case (6, 4) was definitely a present tense. Not only was that analysis required by the context, but even more so by the fact that the sentence did not have any infinitival predicate, only an adverbial one, and thus necessarily had to be from a durative tense.[50] For the other writing *ỉ:ỉrị͗=f sčm* there were merely six attestations. Of these, only two would make most sense as present tenses. By contrast, three were certainly past, and one more was probably so. Overall, the basic result was that the clear majority of all second tenses in Setne I was in the past tense, but that there was no clear-cut functional differentiation between the two possible orthographies. In my opinion, this clear empirical, philology-based approach should have settled matters. The two different writings of the augment in Demotic Egyptian as *r* or *ỉ* in this manuscript should be considered as mere free variants, as they certainly are in so many other cases in Late Egyptian and Demotic.

It is therefore with some surprise that I read the treatment by Steve Vinson of the passages in question.[51] First, he claimed that all other passages in the manuscript attesting the writing *r:ỉrị͗=f sčm*, except 6, 3–4, were clearly past tenses (thus disregarding my remark that also 3, 11 could easily be present tense). He admitted that four attestations of the writings *ỉ:ỉrị͗=f sčm* (all of which I indicated) also had a past tense meaning. This

45 Johnson (1976: 107).

46 One can compare the situation in pMag. LL, where Johnson (1976: 102 note 167) sees *ỉ:ỉrị͗* and *r:ỉrị͗* as free variants.

47 Depuydt (1994b: 56–58). Without discussing the orthography of the demotic forms, his argument was doubted by Kruchten (2000: 58 note 10).

48 Quack (2006b: 252–54).

49 It is indeed the direct answer (with the first person) to a question where the same phrase (just put into the second person) is introduced as *ỉ:ỉrị͗*. Without engaging with my arguments, Vinson (2018: 114) translates it as a past tense.

50 As a matter of fact, already Depuydt (1994b: 56 note 17) admits this point, even though he tries to gloss over the difficulties involved by claiming that, since there was no infinitive in that passage, the distinction between past and present might not apply.

51 Vinson (2010: 467–68).

should have been enough to establish that there was no functional difference between the two orthographies, and Vinson comes close to conceding this point when writing 'the difference in usage or nuance, if any, is unclear to me'.[52] However, somewhat strangely he immediately continues with: 'Possibly our scribe was simply not completely thorough in carrying out his intention to systematize the usage of his own exemplar, which might well have ignored tense distinction constructions completely'.[53] This claim induced him even to a quite tortuous translation '(Yet why else) is it that our existence on earth is (??) forfeit,[54] (but because) of it!' for *ỉ:ỉri̯=w čꜣi̯ pꜣy=n ꜥḥꜥ ḥr pꜣ tꜣ r-č̣bꜣ.ṯ̂=f* (4, 26). An intuitive solution for the tense that is in keeping with the regular meaning of the attested words would rather be 'Because of it our lifetime on earth has been taken away'.[55]

Vinson then proceeds to propose an emendation for the last remaining case, Setne I 6, 3–4. First, he admits that the context seems inconsistent with an analysis as a past tense – which certainly is correct. Somewhat surprisingly, he also claims 'And, if this sentence is specifically marked for the past tense, then – as remarked by Depuydt – it is also anomalous in that it lacks an infinitive in the subject clause, which ought to occur only in the second present'. I do not understand Vinson's logic. Indeed, the fact that in the present tense the predicate of a Demotic second tense (in contrast to Late Egyptian)[56] does not have to be an infinitive but can also be an adverbial expression was well established at the time Vinson wrote his remarks.[57] Respecting the transmitted text should have led to the conclusion that what we have here is a present tense, and hence the supposed graphic differentiation between the two writings does not work.

By contrast, based on his previous assumptions, Vinson finally settled on emending the passage in question to *r:ỉri̯=w <ỉri̯> ṭy ẖn tꜣy ḥw.t n ỉp.t n sẖꜣ nfr* which he proposed, after some discussion, to translate as 'That they <came to be> here in this tomb was (only)

52 Vinson (2010: 467 note 103). Similar is also Vinson (2018: 155 (to 4, 26)) where he discusses the question in more detail, even admitting that the orthography in 4, 26 would seem to violate the rule of the direct object in the durative tenses. He claims that such irregularities 'are not rare, even in Ptolemaic Demotic', based just on Johnson (2004b: 40–44) (corresponding in the first edition to Johnson (1976: 55–65)). But there, several supposed violations are just the result of a wrong analysis, e.g. examples 65a and 65b are future, not present, and in example 68, Johnson has overlooked the initial *tw* and the whole sentence has to be understood as past tense. Vinson disregards the more recent discussions where it has been quite clearly established that these supposed irregularities are typically cases of relative clauses where a construction overtly looking like the present tense serves to replace a relative clause of the aorist, or other special but clearly defined rules (see e.g. Depuydt (1994b: 59–64); Simpson (1996: 151–56); Quack (1997/98: 175–76); Depuydt (2009: 109–11)).

53 Vinson (2010: 467–68 note 103).

54 'To be forfeit' is hardly a correct translation of the passive of the verb *čꜣi̯* 'to take'.

55 Already Johnson (1976: 102 note 167) conceded that, in spite of the orthography *ỉ:ỉri̯* and not *r:ỉri̯*, this passage should be a past tense.

56 However, Junge (2008: 198) indicates one possible case already in pBM EA 10052, 5, 22 (late 20th dynasty), and to Andréas Stauder I owe pBM EA 10052 ro 7, 8 as another example.

57 See e.g. Johnson (1976: 104); Quack (2006: 251). There is one other such construction in the same manuscript (Setne I 6, 13), which Vinson (2018: 128) accepts as it stands without any commentary.

through the craft of a good scribe'.[58] His choice of the specific verb to emend was based on the idea that the omission of one *ỉri̯* of the two directly following each other would be quite conceivable when the scribe had a desire to eliminate a perceived redundancy. However, it can hardly be said to be idiomatically correct Demotic,[59] where expressions for 'to be at a place' are regularly quite different. If there is an intended nuance of settling down in a place, the verb *ḥmsi̯* is typically used (e.g. pRylands IX, 9, 10.11.18). If a more neutral 'being' at a place is meant, the idiomatic choice is *ḫpr* (e.g. pRylands IX 14, 7.10; Khasheshonqi 2, x+2.x+3).

If we stand back and look at Vinson's arguments, the evaluation must be rather negative: he proceeds from an *a priori* assumption that there was a consistent functional distinction between two orthographies that has never been empirically proven, and, as a matter of fact, could not stand up to the hard facts of real attestations in the manuscript.[60] Even more so, Vinson had not only to admit that the scribe would have been very inconsistent in applying this supposed distinction, but he had to propose an emendation of the text just to keep his initial theory within the realm of possibilities – and the specific emendation he proposes is not even correct.

Regrettably, this is by no means the only case where Vinson's new edition of Setne I has to be considered a step back in terms of philological as well as linguistic analysis. An obvious case in point is Setne I 4, 19 where Vinson proposes to emend the text into *č̣i̯=f ỉni̯=w wꜥ ḫrṯ̂*[61] *n šs-nsw <ntỉ> mtw=f ỉ.ỉr-ḫr=f* 'He had a strip of royal linen <that> belonged to him brought up to him', claiming that otherwise in the text possessive *mtw=f* would not be used adnominally.[62] However, he thereby overlooks the most elementary point that in Demotic Egyptian a genuine relative clause cannot follow a semantically undefined noun.[63]

Equally erroneous is Vinson's effort to establish a specific second tense of the future for Setne I 4, 27; 5, 9 and 5, 19.[64] In all three alleged cases, examination of the available photographs clearly shows that the true reading is *ỉw.ỉw=k*, not *ỉ:ỉri̯=k* (the manuscript clearly differentiates the two forms *ỉw=k* and *ỉri̯=k*),[65] and this is simply a Future III. Here there has been insufficient paleographical attention.

58 Vinson (2010: 468).

59 As a matter of fact, Vinson (2010: 468 note 113) quotes only attestations of Sahidic Coptic ⲉⲓⲣⲉ in favor of his interpretation.

60 It is quite symptomatic that Vinson quotes my discussion of the second tenses (Quack (2006)) only once (Vinson (2010: 468 note 103)) and never engages with its arguments.

61 Vinson transliterates *šrṯ*, but the first sign of the word is clearly a *ḫ* with some flaking off of ink in the upper left part.

62 Vinson (2018: 120 and 150).

63 The editor of this volume has pointed out to me the study of Müller (2015: 135–137) which might actually attest some rare cases of genuine relative clauses after undefined nouns. For reasons of space, I cannot discuss the cases in detail; in at least some cases, *r* might in reality be a writing for the circumstantial converter *ỉw*.

64 Vinson (2010: 455–57); taken up in Vinson (2018: 156, 162 and 168).

65 See note 112.

Also Vinson's discussion about a possible intended ambiguity in Setne I 5, 14[66] shows a basic mistake. He thinks that a writing can be understood as *ỉw=s r ꜥny m-šs* 'it will be pleasant indeed' with the infinitive (= Coptic ⲁⲛⲁⲓ) as well as *ỉw=s r ꜥn=y m-šs* 'it will please me indeed' (with a suffix). However, the verb *ꜥn(y)* is intransitive (as is Coptic ⲁⲛⲁⲓ), and so its infinitive can on no account take a suffix as direct object. The first analysis of the passage is the only possible one – as was, by the way, already recognized by Griffith and Thompson more than a hundred years before Vinson's publication.[67]

A completely different, more technical question should also be addressed. In recent years, there has been a rather strong tendency by some scholars in Egyptology to introduce glossing with explicit indication of the grammatical analysis.[68] It is seen as a means to make Egyptian texts more accessible to linguists without special Egyptological training. Also, it has been claimed that glossing, by laying bare the analytical steps of the translation, would help to measure the semantic capacity of the source text and allow one to note where translation intersects with interpretation.[69]

I can understand that glossing might indeed be helpful for non-specialists, although I would advise against over-estimating its contribution. It can render it possible to understand more deeply what Egyptologists mean with their analysis, and thus to incorporate their insights into overarching linguistic models. But glossing is hardly ever a sufficient basis for a general linguist to challenge the interpretation of a specialist in a particular field and, on the other hand, somebody from a closely neighboring field could dissect problematic analyses even without recourse to glossing.[70]

Also for translation issues, glossing should not be considered as a universal remedy. Having to provide an explicit justification for every single word and construction could indeed highlight some of the more blatantly obvious violations of Egyptian grammar still seen quite recently in treatments of Egyptian texts. However, based on actual experience, I rather doubt that making use of linguistic glossing will automatically result in being free of errors. It comes also as a healthy warning that the official glossing list gives grossly wrong, nonexistent forms for the Late Egyptian object pronouns in the 3rd person.[71]

An additional complication is that, in Demotic, many linguistic features are supra-segmental and cannot be easily fixed to any single word in the sentence. The Leipzig rules are so far inadequate to really cover the younger phases of the Egyptian language. Nevertheless, an attempt at glossing is presented for the examples in the last section of this paper.

---

66 Vinson (2018: 212).

67 Griffith & Thompson (1904–1909: volume 1, 28).

68 Di Biase Dyson, Kammerzell & Werning 2009.

69 Di Biase-Dyson (2014: 104).

70 A good example are the shrewd and generally valid remarks by the Coptologist Quecke 1979 in his review of Johnson 1976.

71 Di Biase Dyson, Kammerzell & Werning (2009: 354). I had already pointed out the error concerning the 3rd person in Quack (2001: 172).

After these rather critical remarks concerning previous linguistic discussions, I will conclude by discussing in detail a specific construction where I want to examine in a constructive way if bringing together philology and linguistics is possible. I would like to single out the construction of the verb *ḫ3ᶜ* with a direct object followed by a circumstantial clause and carrying the sense of 'let … be …, allow … to be …'. For a long time, this has not been properly understood. While some quite obvious cases were translated correctly, for others ad hoc solutions of dubious quality have been proposed. Previously, I had briefly indicated a few good examples in a short philological note intended to justify my rendering of certain passages in Demotic wisdom texts.[72] Here I intend to give a fuller discussion based on more substantial documentation. I will structure the material according to the occurrence or non-occurrence of negations in the construction.

Negation in the first part:

m-ỉrỉ	*ḫ3ᶜ=w*	*ỉw=w*	*ršy*	*n.ỉm=tn*
NEG.IMP	let:INF=3PL	SBRD=3PL	rejoice	PREP=2PL

Do not let them rejoice over you. (pBerlin P 13544, l. 23–24)[73]

This passage was translated quite correctly by Zauzich as 'Laß nicht zu, daß sie sich über euch freuen!' in the first edition of the text.

m-ỉrỉ	*ḫ3ᶜ=w*	*ỉw=w*	*šm*	*(n (?))*	*p3*	*šw*
NEG.IMP	let:INF=3PL	SBRD=3PL	go	PREP	ART:M.SG	emptiness

Do not let them become fallow (?) (P. Sorbonne IV no. 155, l. 8–9)[74]

There are some problems in the understanding of the details of this passage, but they do not affect the analysis of the construction as such.

tm	*ḫ3ᶜ*	*s3b3*	*rmṯ-ḫm*	*ỉw=f*	*w3ḥ-sḥn*	*mšᶜ*
NEG	let:INF	impious	man-small:ADJ	SBRD=3SG	command	multitude

Do not let an impious or small man command the multitude. (pInsinger 15, 1)

The interpretation of this sentence has always been quite clear.[75]

Negation in the second part:

ḫ3ᶜ=y	*s*	*ỉw*	*bn*	*ỉw=f*	*čṭ*	*bn*	*ỉw=y*	*sčm*	*[... ỉn (?)]*
let:PFV=1SG	3SG	SBRD	NEG	PRS=3SG	say:INF	NEG	FUT=1SG	hear:INF	[… :NEG (?)]

I did not let him say 'I will not hear [….]' (pSaqqara 2 vs., x+1, 17)

72 Hoffmann & Quack (2018: 424 note ak and 425 note aq).

73 Zauzich (1978).

74 Medini in Chaufray & Wackenier (2016: 61–64); I owe this example to Cary Martin. The edition does not address the two most crucial questions: firstly, whether *šm* can be used at all in the durative tenses, and, secondly, which unwritten preposition should one restore (without comment, *r* is given while I prefer *n*).

75 E.g. Lichtheim (1983: 212); Thissen (1991: 297).

This example is problematic given the fragmentary state of preservation of the original text. I only mention it for the sake of completeness without basing any conclusions upon it. In the first edition of the text, Smith and Tait translated it as 'I left him without his saying "I will listen to … […]"'.[76] Regardless of whether one considers the circumstantial clause as belonging to the construction of the verb *ḫꜣꜥ* (as I do) or as a free adverbial extension (as Smith and Tait do), *bn ỉw=f č̣t* is understood as a present tense.[77] Thus we have to postulate that the post-negation *ỉn* (obligatory in the present tense) would have been placed at the very end of the whole construction, after the quoted speech.

mtw=f	*pꜣ*	*ỉ.ỉri̯*	*č̣i̯.t*	*ḫꜣꜥ=ỉ*	*s(t)*
3SG.M	ART	do:AUX:PTCP	CAUS:INF	let:SBJV=1SG	3PL
ỉw	*bn-pw=ỉ*	*ỉni̯=w*	*r*	*rsỉ*	*ỉrm=ỉ*
SBRD	NEG:PST=1SG	bring:INF=3PL	PREP	south	PREP=1SG

He is the one who made me let them not be brought south with me. (pSpiegelberg 11, 19f)

Spiegelberg in his first edition translates 'Er hat mich veranlaßt, sie zu entlassen, so daß ich sie nicht mit mir nach Süden geführt habe'.[78] Hoffmann gives 'Er (ist es), der bewirkte, daß ich sie zurückließ, ohne daß ich sie mit mir nach Süden geholt hatte';[79] similarly Agut-Labordère and Chauveau 'C'est lui qui m'a poussée à les abandonner au lieu de les emmener vers le sud avec moi'[80] and Stadler 'Er war es, der mich sie zurücklassen ließ, so daß ich sie nicht mit mir nach Süden mitnahm'.[81] These four proposals diverge in details of wording, but are identical in their fundamental analysis. There is, however, a subtle and quite important divergence in meaning between these previous translations and my new analysis. The earlier interpretations assume that the two heroes in question were actively dismissed, i.e. they were present at the royal court and sent away explicitly. Mine, by contrast, assumes that they were not present at the court – as it makes sense since they are local chiefs of places other than Tanis where the royal court is – and consequently did not get invited to join the ceremonial royal travel to Thebes. The insult is still present but less blatant, and that would fit well with the fact that eventually the two heroes in question could be convinced to help the king.

76 Smith & Tait (1983: 129).

77 Morphologically, it would be possible to understand it as a future III, but I fail to see how that would make sense in the passage in question.

78 Spiegelberg (1910: 27 and 78).

79 Hoffmann & Quack (2018: 114).

80 Agut-Labordère & Chauveau (2011: 87).

81 Stadler (2015: 432).

Negation in both parts:

bn-pw(=ỉ)	*ḫꜣꜥ*	*rmč*	*(n)*	*Tꜣy=w-č̣y*	*šꜥ*	*H̱mnw*
NEG:PST=1SG	let:INF	man	(GEN)	El-Hiba	PREP	Hermopolis

ỉw	*bn-pw(=ỉ)*	*ỉni̯.ṯ=f*	*r*	*Ḥr-tj*
SBRD	NEG:PST=1SG	bring:INF=3SG	PREP	Hardai

I did not let a man of El-Hiba as far as Hermopolis not be brought by me[82] to Hardai. (pRylands IX 13, 1).

Griffith translated in his original edition 'I left no man of Teuzoi, as far as Khmûn, until I brought them to Hardai'[83] However, the nuance 'until' is hardly present in the original Demotic text. Vittmann gives 'Ich ließ bis Hermopolis keinen Mann von *Tꜣy=w-ḏj*, den ich nicht nach *Ḥr-dj* gebracht hätte'.[84] This translation is very literal, indeed so literal that the usage of 'ließ' seems to me rather unidiomatic in German. Similarly, Agut-Labordère and Chauveau translate 'Je n'ai laissé aucun homme de Téoudjoï jusqu'à Hermopolis que je n'ai amené à Cynopolis'.[85]

m-ỉri̯	*ḫꜣꜥ*	*sḥm.t*	*n*	*pꜣy=k*	*ꜥ.wỉ*
NEG:IMP	let:INF	woman	PREP:ADJ (?)	POSS:2SG.M	house

ỉw	*bw-ỉri̯=s*	*ỉwr*	*msi̯*
SBRD	NEG:GENER[86]=3SG.F	become.pregnant	give.birth:INF

Do not let a woman in your house not become pregnant and give birth/Do not put a woman into your house who does not become pregnant and give birth. (Khasheshonqy 14, 16)

For this sentence, my two alternative translations[87] diverge strongly from all previous ones. Glanville, in his original edition, gave 'Do not abandon a woman of your household because she has not conceived a child'.[88] Lichtheim translates 'Do not abandon a woman of your household who does not conceive and give birth'.[89] Her rendering shows a difference in analyzing the final *msi̯* as a verb, not a noun, but is identical with Glanville for the crucial section. Thissen gives 'Verstoße nicht eine Frau aus deinem Haus, die nicht schwanger wird und gebiert',[90] obviously following Lichtheim. Dieleman gives 'Do not repudiate a woman from your household who does not become pregnant and give birth', with a more technical (legal) nuance for the verb.[91] Similar is also Ritner who opts for

82 I resort to a passive construction because otherwise it would be difficult to render the text in English.

83 Griffith (1909: vol. 1, 90).

84 Vittmann (1998: 157).

85 Agut-Labordère & Chauveau (2011: 174).

86 The list in Di Biase Dyson, Kammerzell & Werning (2009: 362) recommends NEG-do:PFV for this construction, which does not do justice to its nature as a regular negated generalis.

87 The first one is already given in Hoffmann & Quack (2018: 323 and 424 note ak) with explicit reference to the construction of *ḫꜣꜥ* with a circumstantial clause.

88 Glanville (1955: 35).

89 Lichtheim (1983: 79).

90 Thissen (1991: 264).

91 Dieleman (1998: 19).

'Do not abandon a woman of your house when she does not become pregnant or give birth'.[92] The only difference in analysis compared to Lichtheim and Thissen is that he takes the circumstantial clause as a temporal clause whereas they had understood it as a virtual relative clause. Agut-Labordère and Chauveau translate, also in the same vein 'N'abandonne pas une femme (hors) de ta maison si elle ne peut être enceinte et enfanter'.[93]

In summary, all previous commentators had understood the verb *ḫꜣꜥ* literally as 'leave, abandon' (sometimes with a technical legal implication), and taken the circumstantial clause as a free extension (either a causal clause, a temporal clause, a conditional clause[94] or a virtual relative clause). My first proposed understanding, by contrast, is based on the clearly demonstrated existence of a pattern of the verb with following circumstantial clause with an idiomatic meaning. Some discussion of the philology, or more specifically the respective merits of these suggested translations in the direct context, is perhaps in order.

The woman about whom the saying speaks is clearly not the legal wife of the man in question, as can be seen from the terminology used (*sḥm.t n pꜣy=k ꜥ.wỉ* 'a woman in(to)[95] your house(hold)', not *tꜣy=k ḥm.t* 'your wife'); that excludes most charitable interpretations of the sentence, as well as the option that it is speaking about a legal divorce. In my first interpretation, the man as head of the household is advised not to restrain himself but to have extramarital relations with all female serving staff of the house. While definitely not in accordance with our modern moral standards, such an interpretation would make sense in ancient Egyptian society. One can refer specifically to the Saite-period wisdom text of pBrooklyn 47.218.135, 4, 8f., where the addressee is first advised to love his house and to choose for himself many harem women, and then, in a somewhat broken passage, 'worthy of begetting' can be made out.[96] This passage, in turn, is based on the much older instruction of Prince Hardjedef who advises 'choose for yourself harem women among your people' (§ 7, 1).[97] From the point of view of a male member of the ancient Egyptian elite, there was obviously an interest in having additional options for begetting children who would contribute to enhancing the power of the family.[98] So, however objectionable

---

92 Ritner (2003: 514).

93 Agut-Labordère & Chauveau (2011: 291).

94 The interpretation as a conditional clause, which seems to be implied in the translation of Agut-Labordère & Chauveau (2011: 291), is excluded because a negated conditional clause would have to be *ỉw=s tm ỉwr msỉ̯*.

95 This can only be a preposition, not an indirect annexion ('genitive'), because the annexion with *n* is only possible if the first noun is semantically determined; see Simpson (1996: 68f.).

96 See Quack (1993: 14); Hoffmann & Quack (2018: 267).

97 See also Fischer-Elfert (2009: 121), who accepts the relationship between the two texts but still thinks that the reading 'harem women' is a secondary re-interpretation, and proposes 'work-camp' as the original text in the teaching of Hardjedef; similarly also Grandet (2012: 528 and 531) who proposes to delete the suffix *=k* because it does not make much sense (but it would make sense in my interpretation). In my opinion, the reading 'harem women', which is quite obvious in the transmitted copies, has only been rejected by previous editors (Roccati 1982: 18; Helck 1984: 21) because it would result in a sense so different from modern moral concepts.

98 Indeed, the Teaching of Hardjedef continues directly with *ỉmỉ̯ snḏ=k* 'create respect for you'.

my interpretation may seem to modern eyes, it makes sense in its historical and social context.

However, there is one small but important element that needs more discussion, namely the *n*. All previous translators (myself included) have simply taken it as the element of the indirect annexion ('genitive'). But this interpretation is plainly impossible, because after an undefined noun *ı͗s* (< *ns*) would be used for expressing appurtenance.[99] I have, in the first translation above, tried to interpret it as an adverbial predicate. Adverbial predicates do exist in Demotic, even though they have hardly ever been discussed and certainly need more research. But there would be still another option, namely to understand *n pꜣy=k pr* simply as an adverbial extension. In this case, a possible translation would be 'Do not put a woman into your house who is not able to conceive and give birth', and this example would have to be removed from my documentation about the special construction of *ẖꜣꜥ* with circumstantial clause.[100]

What about the previous interpretations? No-one has ever given an explicit commentary on the meaning they attributed to the sentence in question. Theoretically, I see two possibilities. The first is that the woman in question is just some member of the serving staff who happens to be married but barren. However, then the advice does not make much sense – how would the barrenness of a serving woman be of concern to the master of the household if she was simply married to another man? It hardly seems like a serious reason for firing her, and so the saying, interpreted that way, does not make much sense. The second possibility is that the serving woman is not married, but had (or was forced to have) sexual relations with her master. Then the advice would be not to dismiss her if these sexual relations do not result in offspring. Such an interpretation would be even more extreme than mine, but hardly more probable. Finally, I would also add that, given the metaphorical options inherent in the interpretation of proverbs and pithy statements, the sentence might ultimately also mean that one should use all available economic resources of the household to their fullest productivity.

No negation at all:

[...] šꜥr	*mtw=f*	*ẖꜣꜥ*	*pꜣ*	*č̣bꜣ*	*ı͗⸢w⸣=f*	*šm-ı͗yı̯*
[...] price	CORD.MOD=3SG.M	let:INF	ART:M.SG	retribution	SBRD=3SG.M	come:INF-go:INF

[...] price, and he lets the retribution come and go. (pPhiladelphia E 16335, l. 5.[101])

The lacuna at the beginning of this sentence makes the overall interpretation difficult. In the first edition, Houser-Wegener rendered it as '[...] value, and he placed retaliation which comes and goes'.[102] I am not sure what 'to place retaliation' means, and furthermore it seems problematic to me to understand circumstantial clauses after a semantically defined

99 Quack (in press b). A case in point is pInsinger 32, 20 (cited below) where 'a woman of the royal harem' is expressed as *sḥm.t ı͗s pr ı͗py-nsw*.

100 Most likely, this is ultimately the best solution, taking into account also the parallel in oDeM dem. 1-1, Z. 1-2 and pBerlin P 15709 rt. A. x+1, 10-11.

101 See my German translation in Hoffmann & Quack (2018: 274).

102 Wegner (2010: 344).

noun as relative clauses. Zauzich, by contrast, understood the sentence as '[Und der] Wert davon[103] (?) vertreibt den Rächer, wenn er kommt und geht'.[104] Obviously, he did not see the idiomatic construction here, but understood *ḫꜣꜥ* as a simple verb – even though the supposed 'to drive away (actively)' hardly fits with its normal spectrum of meaning. My proposal certainly makes sense in the overall structure.

ḫꜣꜥ=f pꜣ ḥꜣ.t̠ ỉw=f ḥp ẖn nꜣ ỉwf.w
let:PFV=3SG ART:M.SG heart SBRD=3SG.M hide:RES in ART:PL flesh:PL
ỉw-č̣bꜣ pꜣ č̣nf pꜣy=f n b
because ART:M.SG keep.balance:INF POSS:M.SG=3SG master
He (the god) let the heart be hidden inside the flesh, because of keeping his lord in balance. (pInsinger 4, 18)

In this case, it can be seriously debated if a better translation would not be 'he put the heart, being hidden, inside the flesh'.[105] While there is some difference in the nuances, on its own both interpretations would make sense. Only systematic considerations make me prefer the analysis as an idiomatic construction of the verb, not as a free adverbial extension.[106]

mtw=f pꜣ ntỉ ḫꜣꜥ pꜣ sꜣbꜣ ỉw=f šm-ỉyi̭
3SG.M.FOC: ART:M.SG REL let:INF.FOC ART:M.SG impious SBRB:3SG.M come-go
ỉw mn ꜥ.wỉ-(n)-wꜣḥ
SBRD NEG place-(PGEN)-settle
It is he who lets the impious come and go without a settled place. (pInsinger 29, 10)

Here, the overall interpretation has never been in doubt.[107]

ẖr ḫꜣꜥ=f wr ms wr ỉw=f ꜥnḫ ỉw-č̣bꜣ nꜥ
AOR let3=SG.M great born great SBRD=3SG.M live:RES PREP pity
He lets a great one, born of a great one, live out of pity. (pInsinger 31, 16)

For this sentence, some divergent translations have to be taken into consideration. Lichtheim understood it as 'He lets the great-of-birth be great while he lives because of mercy'.[108] Thissen, probably following her, gave 'er läßt den von vornehmer Abkunft groß

---

103 Zauzich's proposal to understand *mtw=f* as a possessive construction is, I think, only possible if his restoration of the definite article in the lacuna is incorrect.

104 Zauzich (2010/11: 90).

105 Thus Lichtheim (1983: 200) translates 'He placed the heart hidden in the flesh for the right measure of its owner'; Thissen (1991: 285) 'Er hat das Herz versteckt ins Fleisch plaziert, damit sein Besitzer im Gleichgewicht bleibe'; Agut-Labordère & Chauveau 2011, 229 '(Et) il plaça (ainsi) le cœur caché dans les chairs pour la mesure de son maître'.

106 A somewhat similar case is Rosettana 27.

107 See e.g. Lichtheim (1983: 227); Thissen (1991: 313); Agut-Labordère & Chauveau (2011: 262). The only debated point is the reading of the last word which Agut-Labordère & Chauveau (2011: 353 note 135) want to read as *ꜥ.wỉ-mn* 'anchor point' (but in my eyes, the reading of the group for *wꜣḥ* and then the house-determinative seems reasonably clear).

108 Lichtheim (1983: 230).

sein, während er lebt, um der Barmherzigkeit willen'.[109] For these proposals, I see basic problems with the construction; it would be impossible to make a form of *wr* (regardless of whether they understood it as infinitive or qualitative) simply dependent upon *ḫꜣꜥ* without any further morphological element (e.g. ***ḫr ḫꜣꜥ=f wr ms ỉw=f wr*).

The translation by Agut-Labordère and Chauveau, in contrast, agrees with me in recognizing the construction as such: 'Il laisse un fils de famille vivre de la charité'.[110] The difference to my understanding concerns the meaning of the preposition *ỉw-č̣bꜣ* and the agency behind the mercy or pity. Agut-Labordère and Chauveau seem to understand that the well-born man might come to a situation where he is reduced to begging and only receives his sustenance from charitable people. While such an interpretation would certainly make sense, I have reservations concerning the construction of the verb *ꜥnḫ*. 'To live from' would certainly require the preposition *n*. What we have here is, however, the preposition *ỉw-č̣bꜣ* 'because of', and it can hardly introduce anything else than the reason why the person in question is left alive.

ḫꜣꜥ=f	*pꜣ*	*ꜥš-sḥn*	*n*	*na*	*pꜣ*	*tꜣ*
let:PRV	ART:M.SG	affair	PGEN	PL:POSS	ART:M.SG	earth

ỉw=f	*ḥp*	*r.r=w*	*n*	*tm*	*rḫ=f*
SBRD:3SG.F	hide:RES	PDAT=3PL	PDAT	NEG	know:INF=3SG.M

He let the destiny of those on earth be hidden from them in not knowing it. (pInsinger 32, 18)

By contrast, for this sentence there is general agreement among most commentators in its meaning.[111] Only Agut-Labordère and Chauveau adopt a different interpretation in translating 'Il a élaboré le plan pour ceux qui sont sur terre (mais) il leur est caché pour qu'il leur demeure inconnu'.[112] I remain skeptical whether simple *ḫꜣꜥ* could mean 'to elaborate', and there is certainly no reason why one should not simply interpret it as a verb with a following circumstantial clause.

ḫꜣꜥ=f	*tꜣ*	*ḫꜥrꜣ.t*	*na-č̣r.t*	*pꜣ*	*ỉ:ỉri̭*	*ỉni̭.ṯ=s*
let:PRV=3.PL	ART:F.SG	food	PDAT	ART:M.SG	AUX:PTCP	bring:INF=3SG.F

ỉw=s	*wꜣṯ*	*r*	*pꜣ*	*r:(?)ỉni̭=w*	*s*	*n=f*
SBRD=3SG.F	send:RES(?)	PDAT	ART:M.SG	bring:REL=3PL	3SG	PDAT=3SG.M

He let the food at the hand of the one who has brought it be destined (?) for the one to whom it is brought. (pInsinger 32, 19)

The interpretation of this sentence presents several problems. These concern less the basic construction of the verb *ḫꜣꜥ* with a circumstantial clause, but rather the interpretation of *wꜣṯ* and the reading and grammatical analysis of the final part. Lichtheim translates 'He lets the food of the servants be different from that of the masters', with a note that she literally understands 'He lets the food of him who brings it be different from that of him

109 Thissen (1991: 315).

110 Agut-Labordère & Chauveau (2011: 265).

111 See e.g. Lichtheim (1983: 231); Thissen (1991: 316).

112 Agut-Labordère & Chauveau (2011: 267).

to whom one brings it'.[113] Thissen gives a similar translation 'Er hat es gefügt, daß die Nahrung bei dem, der sie bringt, verschieden ist von der Nahrung dessen, dem man sie bringt'.[114] Agut-Labordère and Chauveau also understood the phrase in a similar way by translating 'Il a permis que la nourriture, pour celui qui l'a apporté, soit différente de celle qui lui est apporté (au dieu)'.[115]

First, it should be noted that the supposed element *wṱ* 'different', which is normally understood in this passage, is limited in Demotic to the fixed construction *wṱ* ... *wṱ* ... 'One thing is …, another one …', and that syntactically it is never constructed as a verb. There is another word *wṱ*, which seems to mean 'to be excellent, renowned',[116] and which is currently and quite infelicitously classified under the same lemma in the TLA. If we postulate this verb, we might end with a translation 'he let the food of the one who has brought it be better/more excellent than (that of) the one to whom they have brought it'. While sounding a bit surprising, such a version would still fit in with the general tendency of the Great Demotic Wisdom Book to have a 'paradox' section at the end of each teaching unit. Yet another option, which is the basis of my previous translation,[117] is to analyze *wṱ* as the qualitative of the verb 'to send' with a meaning 'to be destined for'.[118]

ḫꜣꜥ=f	*sḥm.t*	*ỉs*	*pr ỉpy-nsw*	*ỉw*	*wn*	*gꜣ*	*ḥwṱ*	*ḥꜣ.ṱ=s*
let:PRV	woman	POSS	royal harem	SBRD	EXIST	another	man	PREP=3SG.F

He let a woman of the royal harem have another man on her mind. (pInsinger 32, 20)

Lichtheim translates this sentence as 'He lets a woman of the royal harem have another husband'.[119] While the analysis of the construction as such agrees with mine, I have doubts concerning her rendering of the final part that literally means 'there is another male before her'. To me, that sounds more like the thoughts of an erotic affair rather than an official marriage. Also the version by Thissen 'Er hat es gefügt, daß eine Frau den königlichen Harem verläßt, wenn ihr ein anderer Ehemann vorschwebt'[120] is hardly possible, starting with the fact that he used the same word *ḫꜣꜥ* for two different elements of the translation ('gefügt' and 'verläßt'). The rendering by Agut-Labordère and Chauveau as 'Il a permis à une femme appartenant au harem royal d'avoir un autre homme dans son cœur'[121] is almost identical with my interpretation.[122]

---

113 Lichtheim (1983: 231 with note 205).
114 Thissen (1991: 316).
115 Agut-Labordère & Chauveau (2011: 267 and 353 note 150) where they explain that they want to emend the final part into *tꜣ ntỉ ỉnỉ.w {s} n=f*. I suppose that they intend to understand *ỉnỉ.w* as a qualitative, but I do not know of any other attestation where this verb has a qualitative ending in *w*.
116 Attested e.g. Raphia-Decree, l. 13; Harpist 4, 14; perhaps also Mythus Leiden 6, 17.24.25.
117 Hoffmann & Quack (2018: 305).
118 Compare e.g. Khasheshonqy 18, x+25 (see e.g. Hoffmann & Quack 2018: 327).
119 Lichtheim (1983: 231).
120 Thissen (1991: 316).
121 Agut-Labordère & Chauveau (2011: 267).
122 The only difference is that they emend the final word into 'her heart' where the orthography of the original text is clearly 'before her'.

ḫꜣꜥ=f	*pꜣ*	*šmꜥ-ꜥꜣ*	*ỉ:ỉri̯*	*ỉyi̯*	*(n-)bnr*
let:PRV	ART:M.SG	stranger	AUX:PTCP	come:INF	from-outside

ỉw=f	*ꜥnḫ*	*m-ḳṭy*	*pꜣ*	*rmč-(n)-ṭmy*
SBRD=3SG.M	live:INF	like	ART:M.SG	man-(PGEN)-city

He let the stranger, who came from outside, live like a local man. (pInsinger 32, 21)

Previous translations agree with mine.[123]

ỉ:ỉri̯=f	*pḥ*	*r*	*mhw.t*
THMZ=3SG.M	reach	PALL	family

ỉw=f	*(r)*	*ḫꜣꜥ*	*nꜣ*	*sn.w*	*ỉw=w*	*ç̣ç̣y*
FUT=3SG.M	(:FUT)	let:INF	ART.PL	brother	SBRD=3.PL	quarrel:INF

If it (retribution) reaches a family, it will let the brothers quarrel. (pInsinger 34, 7)

Previous translations agree overall with mine.[124] The only serious difference[125] with my interpretation is in the final part, where they suggest a restoration as *ỉw=w (n) ç̣ç̣y*, whereas I take *ç̣ç̣y* here as the verb 'to quarrel'.[126]

ỉ:ỉri̯=f	*pḥ*	*r*	*tš*
THMZ=3SG.M	reach	PALL	district

ỉw=f	*(r)*	*ḫꜣꜥ*	*bn*	*ỉw=f*	*ỉri̯-sḫy*
FUT=3SG.M	(:FUT)	let:INF	evil	SBRD:3SG.M	have-power:INF

If it (retribution) reaches a district, it will let an evil man have power. (pInsinger 34, 9)

Previous translations agree with mine, except that they tend to translate 'the evil one',[127] even though no definite article is present.

ỉ:ỉri̯=f	*pḥ*	*r*	*nꜣ*	*ỉrpy.w*
THMZ=3SG.M	reach	PALL	ART.PL	temple

ỉw=f	*(r)*	*ḫꜣꜥ*	*nꜣ*	*lḫ.w*	*ỉw=w*	*ç̣r*
FUT=3SG.M	(:FUT)	let	ART.PL	fool.PL	SBRD:3PL	strong:RES

If it (retribution) reaches the temples, it will let the fools be strong. (pInsinger 34, 10)

Previous translations agree with mine.[128]

ḫꜣꜥ=w	*pꜣỉ-wn-nꜣ.w*	*ḫpr*	*n.ỉm=w*	*ḥr*	*pꜣ*	*tꜣ*
let:PRV	ART:M.SG+PTCL.PRET	happen:INF	PREP=3PL	PLOC	ART:M.SG	earth

ỉw=f	*ḫpr*	*n.ỉm=w*	*[ḫn ỉmn.ṭ]*	*ꜥn*
SBRD=3SG.M	happen:INF	PREP=3PL	[PLOC west]	again

One let that which had happened to them on earth also happen to them [in the west]. (Setne II, 2, 21)

---

123 Lichtheim (1983: 231); Thissen (1991: 316); Agut-Labordère & Chauveau (2011: 267).

124 Lichtheim (1983: 233), Thissen (1991: 318); Agut-Labordère & Chauveau (2011: 269).

125 A minor difference is that I see the sentences 34, 6–12 all as future, not as present tenses. This is based on the fact that 34, 6 clearly writes a future III construction with nominal subject, and in 34, 7 and 9 the Jernstedt rule is not applied.

126 This is the old *čtčt*; see for the word and its development Quack (2010: 101 to line x+1).

127 Lichtheim (1983: 233); Thissen (1991: 318); Agut-Labordère & Chauveau (2011: 269).

128 Lichtheim (1983: 233); Thissen (1991: 318); Agut-Labordère & Chauveau (2011: 269).

While the sense here is clear enough,[129] the interpretation is somewhat marred by the fact that in 2, 19, in a very similar sentence, *gmi̯* 'to find' is used instead of *ḫȝᶜ*.[130]

sḥm.t	*ỉw*	*mri̯=w*	*s*
woman	SBRD	love:PRS=3PL	3SG

ỉ:ỉri̯=w	*ḫȝᶜ=s*	*ỉw*	*ḫȝᶜ=w*	*s*
THMZ=3PL	let:INF=3SG.F	SBRD	leave:PRV=3PL	3SG

A woman who is loved, she will be left abandoned. (Khasheshonqy 17, 21)

This sentence has been the object of serious disagreements about its interpretation. Jacco Dieleman translated it as 'A woman who is loved; after she is abandoned, one abandons her'. He explains his interpretation in detail, namely that, when a woman is abandoned by her husband, everybody will abandon her, and in this way a divorced woman would become socially isolated.[131] Heinz-Josef Thissen explicitly accepted this interpretation.[132] Robert Ritner renders the sentence as 'A women who is loved, when she is abandoned, she *is* abandoned'.[133] Agut-Labordère and Chauveau rendered the sentence as 'Une femme qui est (heureuse) en amour, c'est quand on la répudie qu'elle est (vraiment) abandonnée'.[134] In my opinion, there is one serious problem with it on a purely philological level (aside from the simple existence of the construction of *ḫȝᶜ* with a circumstantial clause). Why would in such a case the clause 'who is loved' form part of the sentence? If the intended sense really were that a divorced woman is socially shunned, the question of previous love would be irrelevant, and it would be more important to say that she had been married (which in Ancient Egyptian society need not necessarily have been much connected with love). So I propose a different explanation. The saying stresses that, if someone had been deeply in love with a woman, in the case of a separation, the rift would be total. Deep feelings would not just go over to neutrality, but they would rather switch to the opposite.

ḫr	*ḫpr=s*	*n*	*nȝ*	*nčr.w*	*[n]*	*tȝ-mḥy*
AOR	happen=3SG.F	PDAT	ART.PL	god	[PGEN]	Lower.Egypt

ntỉ	*ḫpr*	*n*	*tȝ-šmᶜy*	*r*	*ḫȝᶜ=f*	*n=w*
REL	happen:INF	PLOC	Upper.Egypt	SBRD	let:PRV=3SG.M	PDAT=3PL

tȝy=w	*s.t*	*r-ỉw=s*	*wn*	*r*	*tȝ-mḥy*
POSS.F.SG=3PL	place	SBRD=3SG.F	open:RES	PALL	Lower.Egypt

It happens for the gods of Lower Egypt who are in Upper Egypt, that he let their place be open for them towards Lower Egypt. (Mythus Leiden, 5, 14–16)

---

129 Compare Agut-Labordère & Chauveau (2011: 48).

130 Griffith (1900: 158–59) puts a 'sic' to *ḫȝᶜ* and seems not to have understood the construction. See the discussion in Hoffmann & Quack (2018: 383 note ae). However, it should be said that the supposed *gmi̯* is very faint and barely legible in the published photograph of Griffith (1900: pl. II); it is a little bit clearer in a photograph provided by the BM to the DPDP project.

131 Dieleman (1998: 20).

132 Thissen (2002: 256–57 with note 38).

133 Ritner (2003: 517).

134 Agut-Labordère & Chauveau (2011: 294 and 358 note 69) (which just refers to the previous treatments of Dieleman and mine without explicitly taking a position).

Spiegelberg had serious problems with the interpretation of this sentence because he did not realize the idiomatic construction.[135] In the re-edition by de Cenival, the crucial part is rendered ‘il leur a laissé leur établissement ouvert en Basse Égypte’.[136] This mistranslates the preposition *r* (not *n*), but otherwise captures the construction quite well. By contrast, Antonio Loprieno gives ‘Und in der Tat haben die unterägyptischen Gottheiten, die auch in Oberägypten verehrt werden, ihre ursprüngliche Heimat in Unterägypten’.[137] This is a rather free translation, obviously striving for stylistic elegance, but it completely misses the point, namely that the cultic chapels of the deities in question are architecturally structured with a visual axis to their home country.

[ḫr	*ḫpr=s*	*n*	*nꜣ*	*nčr.w*	*n*	*tꜣ-šmꜥy]*
[AOR	happen =3SG.F	PDAT	ART.PL	god	PGEN	Upper.Egypt]
ntỉ	*ḫpr*	*n*	*tꜣ-mḥy*	*[r*	*ḫꜣꜥ=f*	*n=w*
REL	happen:INF	PLOC	Lower.Egypt	[SBRD	let:PRV=3SG.M	PDAT=3PL

tꜣy=w]	*⸢s.t⸣*	*[r]-ỉw=s*	*wn*	*r*	*tꜣ-šmꜥy*
POSS.F.SG=3PL]	place	SBRD=3SG.F	open:RES	PALL	Upper.Egypt

It happens for the gods of Upper Egypt who are in Lower Egypt, that he let their place be open for them towards Upper Egypt. (Mythus Leiden 5, 1–2)

This sentence, added later in the upper margin of the page and now quite damaged, is obviously just a parallel to the preceding one with a switch in the geography.

ḫꜣꜥ=w	*čꜣčꜣ=t*	*ỉw=f*	*slme*	*ỉw=f*	*gwkwe*
let:FUT=3PL	head=2SG.F	SBRD=3SG.M	lank:RES	SBRD=3SG.M	swell(?):RES

(n)	*tꜣ*	*rỉ.t-ḥrỉ.t*	*[ḥr pꜣy]=t*	*ḥre*	*bn*
(PLOC)	ART:F.SG	side-upper-F.SG	[PREP] [POSS:]2SG.F	face	bad-M.SF

One will let your head be lank (?) and swollen[138] *(?) on the top of your bad face.* (oVienna D 70)

In Zauzich’s original edition, the construction was not recognized. His rendering is ‘Man wird deinen Kopf, der (halb) langhaarig und (halb) kahl an der Oberseite ist, [auf dein] mieses Gesicht werfen’.[139] That is, he assigned the verb *ḫꜣꜥ* the literal meaning ‘to throw, put’ and interpreted the circumstantial clauses as virtual relative clauses referring to *čꜣčꜣ=t*. However, it seems hard to imagine how a head could be thrown upon a face. Brunsch translates ‘Ton épicrâne sera couché par terre, avec ses longs cheveux et (parsemé) de calvitie par-dessus ton visage méchant.’[140] This tries to get rid of the illogical positioning inherent in Zauzich’s version, but hardly does justice to the circumstantial clauses. I

135 Spiegelberg (1917: 20–21).

136 De Cenival (1988: 13).

137 Loprieno (1995: 1051).

138 The identification of *gwkwe* with Coptic ⲕⲱⲕ proposed by Zauzich is impossible, because firstly it would not fit phonetically, and secondly the Coptic ⲕⲱ ⲕⲁϩⲏⲩ ‘naked’ goes back to Demotic *ḫꜣꜥ ḥw(ꜣ)* (see Thissen 2004: 591). I hesitatingly identify the word with Coptic ϭⲱϭ.

139 Zauzich (1991: 137–38).

140 Brunsch (1998–1999: 8 and 15).

have already previously translated this passage in a way that implicitly understands the construction of *ḫꜣꜥ* with a circumstantial clause here.[141] While there remain serious problems with the exact translation of the verbs here, my overall interpretation makes sense.

mtw=k	*ḫꜣꜥ*	*ḥr=f*	*n*	*pꜣ*	*ẖbs*	*ꞽw=f*	*sṯ*	[blank]
CORD.MOD=2SG.M	let:INF	face=3SG.M	PGEN	ART:M.SG	lamp	SBRD=3SG.M	turn:RES	[blank]
mtw=k	*ḫꜣꜥ*	*ḥr=f*	*n*	*pꜣ*	*ꜥlw*	*ꞽw=f*	*sṯ*	[blank]
CORD.MOD=2SG.M	let:INF	face=3SG.M	PGEN	ART:M.SG	boy	SBRD=3SG.M	turn:RES	[blank]
r-ḥr	*pꜣ*	*ẖbs*	*ꞽ.ꞽr=k*	*ḥr*	*smḥ*	*n.ꞽm=f*		
PREP	ART:M.SG	lamp	SBRD=2SG.M	PREP	left	PREP=3SG.M		

And you will let the face of the lamp be turned ..., and you will let the face of the boy be turned ... facing the lamp while you are to his left. (pMag. LL 16, 28f)

In the previous translation by Griffith, 'You put the face of the lamp turned (*blank*). You put the face of the boy turned (*blank*) facing the lamp, you being on his left side'. While the difference is not fundamental, it is obvious that Griffith did not recognize the construction as such, but simply operated with the basic meaning of *ḫꜣꜥ* as 'to put' and a following circumstantial clause. Janet Johnson rendered it as 'you leave the face of the lamp turned …; and you leave the youth's faced turned … facing the lamp you being on his left'.[142] This is closer to my interpretation.

There is one somewhat special case where the circumstantial clause does not simply refer to the direct object as a whole, but only to a compound of it:

ꞽw(=ꞽ)	*r*	*ḫꜣꜥ=t*	*ꞽw*	*pꜣy=t*	*ꜥnẖ*	*nfr*
FUT=1SG	FUT	let:INF=2SG.F	SBRD	POSS=2SG.F	life	good:RES
n-ḥw-r	*nꜣ*	*ẖrd.w*	*č̣r=w*			
PREP	ART:PL	child.PL	all:AUG=3PL			

I will let your life be better than that of all (my other) children.[143] (pRylands IX 9, 15)

Previously, Griffith translated 'I will leave you with thy life good beyond (?) all the girls'. Vittmann understood it in a similar way, but again gave a more literal rendering as 'Ich werde dich (zurück)lassen, indem dein Lebensunterhalt besser ist als der aller Kinder'.[144] None of these two seem to have addressed the possibility that *ḫꜣꜥ* could have here a rectional construction with a circumstantial clause. Both translated the verb simply as 'to leave, to abandon', while understanding the following circumstantial clause as a free expansion on the sentence level.

If we have now established that the precise meaning of the construction of *ḫꜣꜥ* with a direct object and a circumstantial clause is actually 'to let … be in a state …', it seems worthwhile to look where it may differ from the well-known causative construction with

141 Quack (2016: 114).
142 Johnson, in Betz (1986: 222).
143 Compare already my translation in Hoffmann & Quack (2018: 34).
144 Vittmann (1998: 145).

rč̣i̯ + subjunctive *sč̣m=f*. One issue concerns the options of negation. In the traditional causative construction, only the verb *rč̣i̯* can be negated, not the subjunctive *sč̣m=f*. In the construction I have discussed, both elements can be negated. This creates more subtlety. Furthermore, in the construction with *ẖꜣꜥ* and a circumstantial clause, a number of different predicates can be used. There are cases with a qualitative, an existential sentence and even a negated and non-negated past tense. One immediate result is that quite often sentences of this type do not imply mandatory acts, but only the opening up of a possibility (permissive). For example, in the sentence *ỉ:ỉri̯=f pḥ r nꜣ ỉrpy.w ỉw=f (r) ẖꜣꜥ nꜣ lẖ.w ỉw=w č̣r* (pInsinger 34, 10), an even more precise translation might be 'if it (retribution) reaches the temples, it will allow the fools to be strong'. The retribution will not directly empower the fools, but, with the havoc it creates, it will give an opportunity which they would not have had otherwise.

I should also point out that the Coptic conjunction ˢϫⲉⲕⲁⲁⲥ, ᴮϫⲉⲕⲁⲥ 'in order that' with its negative counterpart ᴮⲙⲡⲉⲣϫⲁⲥ[145] 'lest' should also be analyzed as originally an imperative with feminine (generic) object and a following circumstantial clause.[146] This point is of some relevance given that purely synchronic considerations tend to interpret it, at least in some dialects, as a simple Future III rather as a Future II.[147] It also explains why in negated forms, ⲉⲛⲛⲉ⸗ can occur instead of simple ⲛⲛⲉ⸗.[148]

Ultimately, I hope to have shown with this example how linguistic and philological work can successfully interact – even though of course I have to leave it to others to judge the success of my approach. I have tried to single out a case where up to now ad hoc solutions for individual sentences were the rule. A more linguistic approach, looking at the structure of the construction, helps to take the individual attestations out of their singularity and recognize them as part of a larger pattern. This in turn makes it possible to improve translations particularly in those cases where the intended sense is not immediately obvious.

Bibliography

Agut-Labordère, Damien & Michel Chauveau. 2011. *Héros, magiciens et sages oubliés de l'Égypte ancienne: une anthologie de la littérature en égyptien démotique*. Paris.

Allen, James P. 2013. *The Ancient Egyptian Language: An Historical Study*. Cambridge.

Betz, Hans Dieter (ed.). 1986. *The Greek Magical Papyri in Translation: Including the Demotic Spells*. Chicago & London.

Bohleke, Briant. 1996. 'In terms of fate: a survey of the indigenous Egyptian contribution to ancient astrology in light of Papyrus CtYBR inv. 1132(B)', *Studien zur Altägyptischen Kultur* 23, 11–46.

Botti, Giuseppe. 1967. *L'archivio demotico da Deir el-Medineh*. Florence; Catalogo del Museo Egizio di Torino, serie prima - monumenti e testi 1.

---

145 Polotsky (1934: 69).

146 In the examples given by Crum (1939: 764f.) it seems that the rule of Demotic grammar that a circumstantial clause of the non-negated Future III is normally replaced by the conjunctive is still functioning. For Sahidic, see Layton (2004: 282f. §355).

147 Thus Till (1961: 67 §296).

148 Compare Layton (2004: 263 and 265 § 338) who considers the identity of the initial ⲉ as uncertain.

den Brinker, Anna-Dorothee, Brian Muhs & Sven Vleeming (eds). 2005. *A* Berichtigungsliste *of Demotic Documents*. Leuven/Dudley, MA; Studia Demotica 7.

Brunsch, Wolfgang. 1998–1999. 'Un précurseur démotique de Henry de Montherlant: ostracon Vienne numéro D 70', *Revue Roumaine d'Égyptologie* 2–3, 5–18.

de Cenival, Françoise. 1988. *Le mythe de l'œil du soleil: translittération et traduction avec commentaire philologique*. Sommerhausen; Demotische Studien 9.

Chaufray, Marie Pierre & Wackenier, Stéphanie. 2016. *Papyrus de la Sorbonne (P. Sorb. IV) Nos 145–160*. Paris.

Collombert, Philippe. 2004. 'La forme démotique *šꜥ-tw-sḏm-f* (néo-égyptien *(r)-šꜥ-m-ḏr-sḏm-f*)', *Lingua Aegyptia* 12, 21–43.

Crum, Walter Ewing. 1939. *A Coptic Dictionary*. Oxford.

Depauw, Mark. 2019. 'The Demotische Literaturübersicht: a short survey of its development 1968–2002', in: Karl-Theodor Zauzich (ed.). *Akten der 8. Internationalen Konferenz für Demotische Studien: Würzburg 27.-30. August 2002*. Wiesbaden, 41–43.

Depuydt, Leo. 1990. '„*Onchsheshonqy*" 2,13 and 4,1–2: a philological note', in: Sarah Israelit-Groll (ed.). *Studies in Egyptology Presented to Miriam Lichtheim*. Jerusalem, 116–21.

Depuydt, Leo. 1994a. 'A Demotic table of terms', *Enchoria* 21, 1–9.

Depuydt, Leo. 1994b. 'On a late Egyptian and Demotic idiom', *Revue d'Égyptologie* 45, 49–73.

Depuydt, Leo. 2000. 'Demotic script and Demotic grammar: a peculiar case involving *hyn* "some"', *Enchoria* 26, 31–40.

Depuydt, Leo. 2001. 'Demotic script and Demotic grammar (II): dummy prepositions preceding infinitives', *Enchoria* 27, 3–35.

Depuydt, Leo. 2002. 'Eight exotic phenomena of Later Egyptian explained', in: Ryholt, Kim (ed.). *Acts of the Seventh International Conference of Demotic Studies: Copenhagen, 23–27 August 1999*. Copenhagen; CNI Publications 27, 101–29.

Depuydt, Leo. 2003. 'Demotic script and Demotic grammar (III): *R-ḥr.f* "on them" in *Mythus* 18,7', *Enchoria* 28, 7–18.

Depuydt, Leo. 2009. 'Demotic script and Demotic language (IV): consolidation of a new rule of grammar. Differentiating Demotic from Coptic', in: Widmer, Ghislaine & Didier Devauchelle (eds). *Actes du IXe Congrès International des Études Démotiques: Paris, 31 août - 3 septembre 2005*. Cairo ; Bibliothèque d'Étude 147, 103–21.

Depuydt, Leo. 2010. 'The double genitive particle in latest Late Egyptian, Demotic, and Coptic', *Revue d'Égyptologie* 61, 43–75.

Depuydt, Leo. 2014. 'The Demoticity of latest Late Egyptian', in: Depauw, Mark & Yanne Broux (eds). *Acts of the Tenth International Congress of Demotic Studies Leuven, 26-30 August 2008*. Leuven/Paris/Walpole MA; Orientalia Lovaniensia Analecta 231, 27–42.

Depuydt, Leo. 2015. 'The morphology and syntax of a Demotic debt construction', in: Haikal, Fayza (ed.). *Mélanges offerts à Ola el-Aguizy*. Cairo; Bibliothèque d'Étude 164, 101–11.

Depuydt, Leo. 2019. 'Contrastive *jw.jr*, Conditional *jw.jr*, Temporal *jw.jr*. On Separating a Demotic Siamese Triplet', *Chronique d'Égypte* 94, 5–48.

Di Biase-Dyson, Camilla. 2014. 'Multiple dimensions of interpretation: Reassessing the magic brick Berlin ÄMP 15559', *Studien zur Altägyptischen Kultur* 43, 93–107.

Di Biase-Dyson, Camilla, Frank Kammerzell & Daniel Werning. 2009. 'Glossing Ancient Egyptian. Suggestions for adapting the Leipzig Glossing Rules', *Lingua Aegyptia* 17, 343–66.

Dieleman, Jacco. 1998. 'Fear of women? Representations of women in Demotic wisdom texts', *Studien zur Altägyptischen Kultur* 25, 7–46.

Donker van Heel, Koen. 1990. *The Legal Manual of Hermopolis [P. Mattha]. Text and Translation*. Leiden.

Feder, Frank. 2018. 'Das "Zweite Tempus" (*focalizing conversion*) in Temporalisfunktion im Demotischen: die unflektierte Relativform als *Converb*', in: Blöbaum, Anke, Marianne Eaton-Krauss &

Annik Wüthrich (eds). *Pérégrinations avec Erhart Graefe: Festschrift zu seinem 75. Geburtstag.* Münster; Ägypten und Altes Testament 87, 153–59.

Fischer-Elfert, Hans-Werner. 2009. 'Ein neuer Mosaikstein im Hordjedef-Puzzle (§7): (Ostrakon Berlin P. 12383)', in: Kessler, Dieter, Regine Schulz, Martina Ullmann, Alexandra Verbovsek & Stefan J. Wimmer (eds). *Texte - Theben - Tonfragmente: Festschrift für Günter Burkard.* Wiesbaden; Ägypten und Altes Testament 76, 118–27.

Glanville, Stephen. 1955. *The Instructions of 'Onchsheshonqy (British Museum Papyrus 10508) Part I: Introduction, Translation, Notes, and Plates.* London; Catalogue of Demotic Papyri in the British Museum 2.

Grandet, Pierre. 2012. 'Encore une tesselle de la mosaïque de Hordjedef (§ VII): O. Louvre E 32928', in: Zivie-Coche, Christiane & Ivan Guermeur (eds). *«Parcourir l'éternité»: hommages à Jean Yoyotte.* Turnhout ; Bibliothèque de l'École des hautes études, sciences religieuses 156, 527–39.

Griffith, Francis. 1900. *Stories of the High priests of Memphis: the Sethon of Herodotus and the Demotic Tales of Khamuas.* Oxford.

Griffith, Francis & Herbert Thompson 1904–1909. *The Demotic Magical Papyrus of London and Leiden.* London.

Helck, Wolfgang. 1984. *Die Lehre des Djedefhor und die Lehre eines Vaters an seinen Sohn.* Wiesbaden; Kleine ägyptische Texte [8].

Hoffmann, Friedhelm. 1995. *Ägypter und Amazonen: Neubearbeitung zweier demotischer Papyri. P. Vindob. D 6165 und P. Vindob. D 6165 A.* Vienna; Mitteilungen aus der Papyrussammlung der Österreichischen Nationalbibliothek (Papyrus Erzherzog Rainer), Neue Serie 24.

Hoffmann, Friedhelm & Joachim Friedrich Quack 2007. *Anthologie der demotischen Literatur.* Berlin/Münster; Einführungen und Quellentexte zur Ägyptologie 4.

Hoffmann, Friedhelm & Joachim Friedrich Quack 2018. *Anthologie der demotischen Literatur, Zweite, neubearbeitete und erheblich erweiterte Auflage.* Berlin/Münster, Einführungen und Quellentexte zur Ägyptologie 4.

Johnson, Janet. 1970. 'Conditional clauses in ,*Onchsheshonqy*', *Serapis* 2, 22–28.

Johnson, Janet. 1973. 'The Coptic conditional particles *šan* and *ene* in Demotic', *Journal of Near Eastern Studies* 32, 167–69.

Johnson, Janet. 1975. 'The Demotic magical spells of Leiden I 384', *Oudheidkundige mededelingen uit het Rijksmuseum van Oudheden* 56, 29–64.

Johnson, Janet. 1976. *The Demotic Verbal System.* Chicago; Studies in Ancient Oriental Civilization 38.

Johnson, Janet. 1977. 'Louvre E3229: a Demotic magical text', *Enchoria* 7, 55–102.

Johnson, Janet. 1978. *Remarks on Egyptian Verbal Sentences.* Malibu CA; Monographic Journals of the Near East: Afroasiatic Linguistics 5/5.

Johnson, Janet. 1981. 'Demotic nominal sentences', in: Young, Dwight (ed.). *Studies Presented to Hans Jakob Polotsky.* East Gloucester MA, 414–30.

Johnson, Janet. 1986. *Thus Wrote 'Onchsheshonqy: An Introductory Grammar of Demotic.* Chicago; Studies in Ancient Oriental Civilization 45.

Johnson, Janet. 2004a. 'The use of the articles and the Generic in Demotic', in: Vleeming, Sven (ed.). *Aspects of Demotic Lexicography: Acts of the Second International Conference for Demotic Studies, Leiden, 19–21 September 1984.* Leuven; Studia Demotica 1, 41–55.

Johnson, Janet. 2004b. *The Demotic Verbal System.* Second Printing, with Corrections. Chicago; Studies in Ancient Oriental Civilization 38.

Johnson, Janet. 2013. 'R + Infinitive in the *Instructions of 'Onchsheshonqy*', in: Budka, Julia, Roman Gundacker & Gabriele Pieke (eds). *Florilegium Aegyptiacum - eine wissenschaftliche Blütenlese von Schülern und Freunden für Helmut Satzinger zum 75. Geburtstag am 21. Jänner 2013.* Göttingen; Göttinger Miszellen Beihefte 14, 198–206.

Johnson, Janet. 2017. 'Compound nouns, especially abstracts, in Demotic', in: Jasnow, Richard & Ghislaine Widmer (eds). *Illuminating Osiris: Egyptological Studies in Honor of Mark Smith*. Atlanta; Material and Visual Culture of Ancient Egypt 2, 163–71.

Junge, Friedrich. 1987. 'Morphology, sentence form and language history', in: Ray, John (ed.). *Lingua sapientissima: A Seminar in Honour of H. J. Polotsky Organised by the Fitzwilliam Museum, Cambridge and the Faculty of Oriental Studies in 1984*. Cambridge, 47–56.

Junge, Friedrich. 2008. *Neuägyptisch. Einführung in die Grammatik. 3., verbesserte Auflage*. Wiesbaden.

Kruchten, Jean-Marie. 2000. 'Assimilation and dissimilation at work in the late Egyptian verbal system: the verb forms built by means of the auxiliary *ỉrỉ* from the second part of the Nineteenth Dynasty until early Demotic', *Journal of Egyptian Archaeology* 86, 57–65.

Layton, Bentley. 2004. *A Coptic Grammar: Second Edition, Revised and Expanded*. Wiesbaden; Porta Linguarum Orientalium.

Lichtheim, Miriam. 1983. *Late Egyptian Wisdom Literature in the International Context: A Study of Demotic Instructions*. Fribourg/Göttingen; Orbis Biblicus et Orientalis 52.

Loprieno, Antonio. 1995a. *Ancient Egyptian: A Linguistic Introduction*. Cambridge.

Loprieno, Antonio. 1995b. 'Der demotische „Mythos vom Sonnenauge"', in: *Weisheitstexte, Mythen und Epen. Mythen und Epen III*. Gütersloh; Texte aus der Umwelt des Alten Testaments 3 (5). 1038–77.

Loprieno, Antonio, Matthias Müller & Sami Uljas. 2017. *Non-Verbal Predication in Ancient Egyptian*. Berlin/Boston; The Mouton Companions to Ancient Egyptian 2.

Müller, Matthias. 2015. 'Relative clauses in Later Egyptian', *Lingua Aegyptia* 23, 107–173.

Polotsky, Hans Jakob. 1934. Review of Walther Till, Koptische Dialektgrammatik, *Göttingische Gelehrte Anzeigen* 196, 58–67.

Quack, Joachim Friedrich. 1991. 'Die Konstruktion des Infinitivs in der Cleft-Sentence', *Revue d'Égyptologie* 42, 189–207.

Quack, Joachim Friedrich. 1992. *Studien zur Lehre für Merikare*. Wiesbaden; Göttinger Orientforschungen IV/23.

Quack, Joachim Friedrich. 1992/93. 'Grammatische Bemerkungen zu einer Formel der Eheverträge', *Enchoria* 19/20, 221–23.

Quack, Joachim Friedrich. 1993. 'Ein neuer ägyptischer Weisheitstext', *Die Welt des Orients* 24, 5–19.

Quack, Joachim Friedrich. 1994a. 'Bemerkungen zum demotisch-koptischen Temporalis', in: *Acta Demotica. Acts of the Fifth International Conference for Demotists, Pisa, 4th-8th September 1993*. Pisa, 231–37.

Quack, Joachim Friedrich. 1994b. 'Korrekturvorschläge zu einigen demotischen literarischen Texten', *Enchoria* 21, 63–72.

Quack, Joachim Friedrich. 1997/98. 'Review of R. Simpson, Demotic Grammar in the Ptolemaic Sacerdotal Decrees', *Enchoria* 24, 171–77.

Quack, Joachim Friedrich. 1999. 'Weitere Korrekturvorschläge, vorwiegend zu demotischen literarischen Texten', *Enchoria* 25, 39–47.

Quack, Joachim Friedrich. 2000. 'Eine spezielle Bildung des Konditionalis und ihre Bedeutung für die Datierung von Texten', *Enchoria* 26, 84–87.

Quack, Joachim Friedrich. 2004. 'Fragmente memphitischer Religion und Astronomie in semidemotischer Schrift (pBerlin 14402 + pCarlsberg 651 + PSI Inv. D 23)', in: Hoffmann, Friedhelm & Heinz Josef Thissen (eds). *Res severa verum gaudium: Festschrift für Karl-Theodor Zauzich zum 65. Geburtstag am 8. Juni 2004*. Leuven/Dudley MA; Studia Demotica 6, 467–96.

Quack, Joachim Friedrich. 2005a. 'Review of Martin Stadler, Isis, das göttliche Kind und die Weltordnung', *Archiv für Papyrusforschung und verwandte Gebiete* 51, 174–79.

Quack, Joachim Friedrich. 2005b. 'Review of Friedhelm Hoffmann & Heinz-Josef Thissen (eds.), Res severa verum gaudium', *Archiv für Papyrusforschung und verwandte Gebiete* 51, 179–86.

Quack, Joachim Friedrich. 2006a. 'En route vers le copte. Notes sur l'évolution du démotique tardif', *Faites de langues 27, Les langues chamito-sémitiques (afro-asiatiques)*, volume 2, 191–216.

Quack, Joachim Friedrich. 2006b. 'Zu Syntax und Zeitbezug der demotischen zweiten Tempora', *Lingua Aegyptia* 14, 251–62.

Quack, Joachim Friedrich. 2006/2007. 'Ein Setne-Fragment in Marburg', *Enchoria* 30, 71–74, pl. 33.

Quack, Joachim Friedrich. 2007. 'Die Initiation zum Schreiberberuf im Alten Ägypten', *Studien zur Altägyptischen Kultur* 36, 249–95.

Quack, Joachim Friedrich. 2008. 'Demotische magische und divinatorische Texte', in: Janowski, Bernd & Gernot Wilhelm (eds). *Omina, Orakel, Rituale und Beschwörungen*. Gütersloh; Texte aus der Umwelt des Alten Testaments, Neue Folge Band 4, 331–85.

Quack, Joachim Friedrich. 2009a. 'Zum Partizip im Demotischen', *Lingua Aegyptia* 17, 231–58.

Quack, Joachim Friedrich. 2009b. 'Fragmente eines änigmatischen Weisheitstextes (Ex P. Oxy. 79/103). Mit Bemerkungen zu den pythagoräischen Akousmata und der spätägyptischen Weisheitstradition', in: Widmer, Ghislaine & Didier Devauchelle (eds). *Actes du IXe Congrès International des Études Démotiques: Paris, 31 août - 3 septembre 2005*. Cairo; Bibliothèque d'étude 147, 267–98.

Quack, Joachim Friedrich. 2010. 'Aus zwei spätzeitlichen Traumbüchern (Pap. Berlin P. 29009 und 23058)', in: Knuf, Hermann, Christian Leitz & Daniel von Recklinghausen (eds). *Honi soit qui mal y pense: Studien zum pharaonischen, griechisch-römischen und spätantiken Ägypten zu Ehren von Heinz-Josef Thissen*. Leuven; Orientalia Lovaniensia Analecta 194, 99–110.

Quack, Joachim Friedrich. 2010–2011a. 'Ein Fragment eines demotischen ethnographischen Textes (PSI Ins. D 88)', *Enchoria* 32, 81–85.

Quack, Joachim Friedrich. 2010–2011b. 'Zur Lesung der demotischen Gruppe für „links"', *Enchoria* 32, 73–80.

Quack, Joachim Friedrich. 2011. 'Remarks on Egyptian Rituals of Dream-Sending', in: Kousoulis, Panagiotis (ed.). *Ancient Egyptian Demonology: Studies on the Boundaries between the Demonic and the Divine in Egyptian Magic*. Leuven /Paris/Dudley MA; Orientalia Lovaniensia Analecta 175, 129–50.

Quack, Joachim Friedrich. 2012. 'Papyrus Berlin P. 23817: Reste eines semidemotischen Traktats über Tierzucht?', in: Lepper, Verena (ed.). *Forschung in der Papyrussammlung: eine Festgabe für das Neue Museum*. Berlin; Ägyptische und Orientalische Papyri und Handschriften des Ägyptischen Museums und Papyrussammlung Berlin 1, 329–35.

Quack, Joachim Friedrich. 2013. 'Zu einigen demotischen Gruppen umstrittener Lesung oder problematischer Ableitung', in: Vleeming. Sven (ed.). *Aspects of Demotic Orthography: Acts of an International Colloquium Held in Trier, 8 November 2010*. Leuven/Paris/Walpole MA; Studia Demotica 11, 99–116.

Quack, Joachim Friedrich. 2014. 'Bemerkungen zur Struktur der demotischen Schrift und zur Umschrift des Demotischen', in: Depauw, Mark & Yanne Broux (eds). *Acts of the Tenth International Congress of Demotic Studies Leuven, 26-30 August 2008*. Leuven/Paris/Walpole MA; Orientalia Lovaniensia Analecta 231, 207–42.

Quack, Joachim Friedrich. 2016. *Einführung in die altägyptische Literaturgeschichte III: die demotische und gräko-ägyptische Literatur*, Dritte, erneut veränderte Auflage. Berlin/Münster; Einführungen und Quellentexte zur Ägyptologie 3.

Quack, Joachim Friedrich. 2018. 'Psammetich der Eunuch. Wie aus Geschichte Geschichten werden', in: Blöbaum, Anke, Marianne Eaton-Krauss & Annik Wüthrich (eds). *Pérégrinations avec Erhart Graefe: Festschrift zu seinem 75. Geburtstag*. Münster; Ägypten und Altes Testament 87, 475–86.

Quack, Joachim Friedrich. in press a. 'Khasheshonqy', in: W. Wilson (ed.), The Library of Wisdom.

Quack, Joachim Friedrich. in press b. 'Demotic expressions of possession – some working notes', in: Grossman, Eitan & Stéphane Polis (eds). *Possession in Egyptian.*

Quack, Joachim Friedrich. 2020–23. 'Review of von Recklinghausen, Daniel. Die Philensis-Dekrete', *Enchoria* 37, 133–144.

Quack, Joachim Friedrich & Kim Ryholt. 2000. 'Notes on the Setne story P. Carlsberg 207', in: Frandsen, Paul & Kim Ryholt (eds). *The Carlsberg Papyri 3: A Miscellany of Demotic Texts and Studies*. Copenhagen; CNI Publications 22, 141–63.

Quack, Joachim Friedrich & Kim Ryholt. 2019. *The Carlsberg Papyri 11: Demotic Literary Texts from Tebtunis and Beyond*. Copenhagen; CNI Publications 36.

Quecke, Hans. 1979. Review of Johnson 1976. *Orientalia* 48, 435–47.

Ray, John. 1976. *The archive of Ḥor*. London; Texts from Excavations 2.

Ray, John. 1987. 'Phrases used in dream-texts', in: Vleeming, Sven (ed.). *Aspects of Demotic Lexicography: Acts of the Second International Conference for Demotic Studies, Leiden, 19-21 September 1984*. Leuven; Studia Demotica 1, 85–93.

Richter, Tonio Sebastian. 2008. 'Review of Stadler, Martin, Isis, das göttliche Kind und die Weltordnung', *Wiener Zeitschrift für die Kunde des Morgenlandes* 98, 380–86.

Ritner, Robert. 2003. 'Demotic Literature', in: Simpson, William Kelly (ed.). *The Literature of Ancient Egypt: An Anthology of Stories, Instructions, Stelae, Autobiographies, and Poetry*, third ed. New Haven/London, 443–529.

Roccati, Alessandro. 1982. 'Su un passo di Hardjedef', *Journal of Egyptian Archaeology* 68, 16–19.

Sérida, Rana. 2016. *The Carlsberg Papyri 14: A Castration Story from the Tebtunis Temple Library*. Copenhagen; CNI Publications 42.

Shisha-Halevy, Ariel. 1989a. 'Work-notes on Demotic syntax', *Orientalia* 58, 28–60.

Shisha-Halevy, Ariel. 1989b. 'Papyrus Vandier *recto*: an early Demotic literary text?', *Journal of the American Oriental Society* 109, 421–35.

Simpson, Robert. 1996. *Demotic Grammar in the Ptolemaic Sacerdotal Decrees*. Oxford.

Smith, Harry & John Tait 1983. *Saqqâra Demotic Papyri I (P. Dem. Saq. I)*. London; Texts from Excavations 7.

Spiegelberg, Wilhelm. 1910. *Der Sagenkreis des Königs Petubastis: nach dem Strassburger demotischen Papyrus sowie den Wiener und Pariser Bruchstücken*. Leipzig; Demotische Studien 3.

Spiegelberg, Wilhelm. 1917. *Der ägyptische Mythus vom Sonnenauge (Der Papyrus der Tierfabeln — „Kufi") nach dem Leidener demotischen Papyrus I 384*. Strassburg.

Spiegelberg, Wilhelm. 1922. *Der demotische Text der Priesterdekrete von Kanopus und Memphis (Rosettana): mit den hieroglyphischen und griechischen Fassungen und deutscher Übersetzung nebst demotischem Glossar*. Heidelberg.

Spiegelberg, Wilhelm. 1925. *Demotische Grammatik*. Heidelberg.

Stadler, Martin. 2003. *Der Totenpapyrus des Pa-Month (P. Bibl. nat. 149)*. Wiesbaden; Studien zum Altägyptischen Totenbuch 6.

Stadler, Martin. 2004. *Isis, das göttliche Kind und die Weltordnung. Neue religiöse Texte aus dem Fayum nach dem Papyrus Wien D. 12006 recto*. Vienna; Mitteilungen aus der Papyrussammlung der Österreichischen Nationalbibliothek (Papyrus Erzherzog Rainer), Neue Serie 28.

Stadler, Martin. 2015. 'Der Kampf um die Pfründe des Amun (Papyrus Spiegelberg)', in: Janowski, Bernd & Daniel Schwemer (eds). *Weisheitstexte, Mythen und Epen*. Gütersloh; Texte aus der Umwelt des Alten Testaments, Neue Folge 8, 418–37.

Stadler, Martin. 2019. 'Review of Wüthrich, Annik, Édition synoptique et traduction des chapitres supplémentaires du Livre des Morts 162 à 167', *Orientalistische Literaturzeitung* 114, 109–14

Thissen, Heinz-Josef. 1990. 'Demotistische Literaturübersicht XVII', *Enchoria* 17, 133–52.

Thissen, Heinz-Josef. 1991. 'Die Lehre des Anchscheschonqi', in: *Weisheitstexte, Mythen und Epen: Weisheitstexte II*. Gütersloh; Texte aus der Umwelt des Alten Testaments 3/2, 251–77.

Thissen, Heinz-Josef. 2002. 'Achmim und die demotische Literatur', in: Egberts, Arno, Brian Muhs & Jacques van der Vliet (eds). *Perspectives on Panopolis: An Egyptian Town from Alexander the Great to the Arab Conquest; Acts from an International Symposium, Held in Leiden on 16, 17 and 18 December 1998*. Leiden/Boston MA/Cologne; Papyrologica Lugduno-Batava 31, 249–60.

Thissen, Heinz-Josef. 2004. '"Wer lebt, dessen Kraut blüht!". Ein Beitrag zu demotischer Intertextualität', in: Hoffmann, Friedhelm & Heinz Josef Thissen (eds). *Res severa verum gaudium:*

Festschrift für Karl-Theodor Zauzich zum 65. Geburtstag am 8. Juni 2004. Leuven/Dudley MA; Studia Demotica 6, 583–94.

Till, Walter. 1961. *Koptische Dialektgrammatik mit Lesestücken und Wörterbuch*. Munich.

Vinson, Steve. 2010. 'Ten notes on the First Tale of Setne Khaemwas', in: Knuf, Hermann, Christian Leitz & Daniel von Recklinghausen (eds). *Honi soit qui mal y pense: Studien zum pharaonischen, griechisch-römischen und spätantiken Ägypten zu Ehren von Heinz-Josef Thissen*. Leuven; Orientalia Lovaniensia Analecta 194. 447–70.

Vinson, Steve. 2018. *The Craft of a Good Scribe: History, Narrative and Meaning in the* First tale of Setne Khaemwas. Leiden/Boston; Harvard Egyptological Studies 3.

Wegner, Jennifer. 2010. 'A fragmentary Demotic cosmology in the Penn Museum', in: Hawass, Zahi & Jennifer Wegner (eds). *Millions of Jubilees: Studies in Honor of David P. Silverman*. Cairo; Supplément aux Annales du Service des Antiquités de l'Egypte 39/2, 337–50.

Widmer, Ghislaine. 1999. 'Emphasizing and non-emphasizing second tenses in the *Myth of the Sun's Eye*', *Journal of Egyptian Archaeology* 85, 165–88.

Williams, Ronald J. 1948. 'On certain verbal forms in Demotic', *Journal of Near Eastern Studies* 7 (4), 223–35.

Zauzich, Karl-Theodor. 1972. 'Korrekturvorschläge zur Publikation des demotischen Archivs von Deir el-Medineh', *Enchoria* 2, 85–95.

Zauzich, Karl-Theodor. 1978. *Demotische Papyri aus den Staatlichen Museen zu Berlin I: Papyri von der Insel Elephantine*. Berlin.

Zauzich, Karl-Theodor. 1991. 'Schmähworte gegen eine Frau', *Enchoria* 18, 135–51.

Zauzich, Karl-Theodor. 2010–2011. 'Die Werke der Götter: ein Nachtrag zu P.Philadelphia E 16335', *Enchoria* 32, 86–100.

Dative Possessive Sentences in Early Egyptian

Chris H. Reintges[1]

1 Introduction

The umbrella theme 'Between Philology and Linguistics' that spearheaded the Sixth Crossroad Conference is a reminder for us all that the modernization of the field has not kept all its promises. The paradigm shift away from the Polotskyan Standard Theory and the opening of the field towards the modern language sciences has not sufficiently fostered more inclusive ways of integrating the theoretical methods of linguistic analysis into the philological-historical study of the extant textual sources. Quite the contrary, an ever-widening gap makes itself felt between Egyptian philology and linguistics. As the two sister disciplines share common ground in their interest in language, grammar and context, the compartmentalization of research in a relatively small academic discipline such as ours is not an inevitable price to pay for scientific progress to be made. Philology can be theoretically informed, presupposing (as seems reasonable) that a broadened understanding of form, meaning and function sheds light on issues relating to text and content structure. Adam Ledgeway (2013) makes a similar point writing that, 'when theory and philological evidence are considered together, the results of traditional philological and linguistic scholarship can be considerably enhanced'.[2]

The study presented here is about variation in the syntax and semantics of dative predicative possession in Early Egyptian.[3] Despite it being a small-scale research, it seeks to contribute to interdisciplinary cross-fertilization in reconnecting philological and linguistic analysis. The organization of the paper is as follows. Section 2 sets the stage for further analysis by presenting some preliminary data and observations. Section 3 briefly reviews major research trends, with particular attention for the liaison between existential, locative and possessive sentences and the different kinds of clausal possession identified in the typological literature. With this background laid out, the study moves on to its central

1 The National Centre for Scientific Research [CNRS], Paris — CNRS/LLF/UMR7110. creintges@linguist-univ-paris-diderot.fr.
I am indebted to Sami Uljas for detailed comments on a previous version of the present paper, which helped me to clarify and develop my arguments. Needless to say, the remaining errors and unclarities are for my own account.
2 Ledgeway (2013: 306).
3 Early Egyptian is understood here as the recorded language of the Old Kingdom, the First Intermediate Period, and the Early Middle Kingdom period (Dynasties IV to XI, ca. 2650–1990 BCE). The corpus is linguistically heterogeneous, yet sufficiently large to illustrate the semantic and syntactic diversity of the dative predicative possessive construction.

Sami Uljas & Andreas Dorn (eds), *Crossroads VI. Between Egyptian Linguistics and Philology*, 245–295
DOI: https://doi.org/10.37011/studmon.30.10

objective of constructing a language-particular typology of dative predicative possession. In order to simplify the investigation and keep the study within reasonable bounds, the semantic profile of the predicative possessor as denoting a human or animate referent is kept constant, whereas the possessee in subject position represents the variable element in the construction. Section 4 begins with dative possessive sentences, which have as subject a bare indefinite noun. Leon Stassen (2009) identifies indefinite predicative possession sentences as the possessive prototype crosslinguistically.[4] The Early Egyptian linguistic facts paint a different picture, where this construction type represents an outlier within the system of non-verbal predicative possession. Section 5 takes a look at the rarely occurring type of quantificational possession sentences, in which is possessee is represented by a universally quantified noun phrase of the form bare noun plus attributive quantifier *nb*. As is well known, Early Egyptian is a language without grammaticalized definite article forms. Section 6 explores how linguistic and contextual clues contribute to the definite interpretation of bare nouns and noun phrases. Section 7 deals with demonstrative possession sentences, in which demonstrative pronouns render the modified noun phrase a definite description. Section 8 completes the picture by looking at double possessive sentences – so called because the possessee constituent in subject position is a possessed noun phrase itself. This constructional pattern allows for the possibility of expressing inalienable predicative possession. Finally, Section 9 concludes the paper with final remarks.

2 Setting the stage

Early Egyptian has a well-developed system of non-verbal predicative possession, which has not received as much scholarly interest as it warrants: its importance lies in the fact that the apparently simple syntax hides a lot of semantic complexity. A remarkable exception to this trend is the richly documented monograph about non-verbal predication structures by Antonio Loprieno, Matthias Müller & Sami Uljas (2019), who grouped together a family of adverbial locative sentences that can be used to express possessive meaning as one of their functions.[5] The present investigation broadens the research focus by exploring the predicative dative possessive construction in Early Egyptian (thereby excluding the classical Middle Egyptian variant). To set the stage for subsequent analysis, I will first outline the fine-grained syntactic details and semantic composition of the construction (§2.1). I will then turn to some key initial examples that illustrate the philological and linguistic complexities of the corpus linguistic data (§2.2).

2.1 Syntactic and semantic features of the dative predicative possession construction

Based upon extensive cross-linguistic research, Bernd Heine (1997) demonstrated that all of the world's languages distinguish between nominal possession and predicative pos-

4 Stassen (2009: 28–33).

5 Loprieno, Müller & Uljas (2019: 185–86, 139–41).

session on a morphosyntactic basis.[6] The different structures involved represent different coding strategies with partially overlapping but not identical meanings. This generally suggests that noun phrase-level and predicative/clausal-level possession are derived independently of each other.

In comprising two distinct case-marked noun phrases or their pronominal equivalents (personal pronouns and demonstratives), dative possessive sentences look deceptively simple in terms of their surface syntax, even if there is more syntactic and semantic variation involved than previously thought. The first noun phrase or term (NP_1) is coded as the subject, which is marked by the morphologically null nominative case. The second term (NP_2) is dative case-marked by the indirect-object preposition *n*- 'to, for'.[7] Nominative and dative cases determine not only the syntactic distribution of the two possessive constituents but also define the associated semantic roles. In particular, the referent of the nominative subject is semantically interpreted as the possessee, i.e., the entity that is possessed, controlled, or created by another entity or is the mereological part of a whole. The referent of the dative case-marked noun phrase or dative clitic pronoun, on the other hand, is interpreted as the possessor, i.e., the entity that legally owns or benefits from the possessee, exercises control over it or, alternatively, subsumes individual parts into a common structure.

If no covert auxiliary verb is posited for non-verbal predication, which seems not only ad-hoc but also inconsistent with what we know otherwise of Early Egyptian clause structure, the dative possessor is the only candidate left for the predicate role.[8] Elaborating on this point, it seems reasonable to treat the relational preposition *n*- as a predicative expression in its own right, which takes its complement as the argument of that predicate.[9]

---

6 Heine (1997: 25–29).

7 For the ease of exposition and typological comparison, I will adopt the traditional-grammar notion of dative case-marking as the primary function of the originally goal-oriented preposition (e.g., Edel 1955/1964: 387 §757). This is a simplifying assumption, given that the morphological nominative–accusative case split of Early Egyptian can only be observed in the person–number–gender paradigms of subject and direct object pronouns.

8 This assumption is controversial. Stassen (2009: 49–50 (11)) includes the presence of 'a locative/existential predicate, in the form of a verb with the rough meaning of "to be"' into the definition of locative possession. The omission of the BE-type copula from the surface structure of possessive sentences is analyzed as a zero-encoding strategy, which 'has nothing to do with the encoding of possession as such', but rather relates to the way in which locative and existential sentences are morphologically marked, i.e., whether or not a verbal item must be present to support tense and agreement morphology (Stassen 2009: 79). In regard to the location schema of possession [Y is at X's place > X has, owns Y], Heine (1997: 50–51) notes that there is often 'no, or no obligatory, verbal item corresponding to the notion *is at*' in the syntactic structure expressing the cognitive schema.

9 A priori, this analysis is supported by the unique potential of the prepositional head to serve as a functor, selecting a nominal or pronominal complement as its argument. Huddleston (1984: 336–37) takes issue with this position, arguing that the categorization of prepositions as relation-marking categories is in need of considerable refinement. Although this point is well taken, it does not provide a decisive argument against the predicate-functor analysis of prepositions. Huddleston also raises an important typological point: the classical languages Ancient Greek and Latin have a

Despite this precision, the nominal or pronominal expression in the dative case will be referred to as the predicative possessor. The resulting nominative–dative sequence $NP_{1Possessee/Nominative} > NP_{2Possessor/Dative}$ marks predicative possession and displays the canonical subject–predicate order of non-verbal predicate sentences.

At the semantic plane, the predicative dative construction denotes material possession, beneficiariness and possessor control broadly conceived but can also convey different related senses. Therefore, it does not come as a surprise when some classifications of the data are ambiguous as to the locative, goal-directed, benefactive or possessive connotations of the dative possessive sentence in question.[10] The constructional polysemy at issue here is of a systematic character and reflects a more general but poorly understood trait of predicative (clausal) possession—what Neil Myler (2016) has dubbed the 'Too-Many-Meanings Puzzle'; or, as the author phrases it, 'How can one possession structure have so many different meanings in given language?'.[11]

With the above considerations in mind, the objectives of this research are three-fold. First, to offer some insight into the language-particular classification of non-verbal possession sentences with predicative dative possessors. Second, to identify the factors contributing to constructional polysemy, and third, to shed light on the asymmetric prominence relation between the two possessive constituents. As it happens, the possessee is outranked by the dative possessor on standard prominence scales related to grammatical person, animacy and definiteness. To this one may add that the predicative possessor may be the target of lexical and syntactic strategies for conveying 'emphasis for intensity', as broadly construed of in Andrea Beltrama & Andreas Trotzke's (2019) state-of-the-art article.[12] Conversely, the asymmetric prominence relation between the two possessive constituents is not an all-or-nothing factor. The possessee subject can gain in referential complexity and discourse saliency when it is modified by a demonstrative pronoun or by an internal possessor noun phrase or pronoun, as we shall see later on (§§7–8).

---

rich morphological case system as well as an elaborate system of simple and complex prepositions, which are morphological case assigners. This argues against the conflation of the notions of case and preposition.

10 The goal-directed sense argues in favor of their subsumption under the goal-relational schema [Y exists to/for X > X has, owns Y]. In Heine's (1997: 59–61) classification system, this type of clausal possession expresses the notion of some entity existing for the benefit of another, typically human entity.

11 Myler (2016: 45 (67)).

12 Beltrama & Trotzke (2019: 9–10, endnote 1) borrow the term 'emphasis for intensity' from phonetics, where it refers to the distinctive features of emotive speech, such as the lengthening of the accented vowel (e.g., *John is biiiiiiig!)*. According to the authors, emphasis for intensity must be distinguished from contrastive emphasis in that it gives prominence to linguistic elements not by directly contrasting them to alternatives but rather by selecting them from an upper range of an ordering, providing them with special prominence (Beltrama and Trotzke 2019: 1–2, 8).

2.2 Preliminary data and observations

In order to better grasp the points brought up so far, I will now consider some representative examples of the predicative dative possessor construction. The philological and linguistic analysis of these preliminary data permit a first assessment of the semantic diversity and constructional polysemy of this predicative possession pattern.

The series of interconnected possession sentences given below comes from a libation ritual performed for the sake of the deceased by the name of Horus-hotep. In view of the performative character of the ritual text, the *plurale tantum* noun *mw* 'water' can be identified as the overall discourse topic, which recurs in the initial, medial and final sentence of a thematically coherent paragraph. The first mention of the referent (referent introduction) represents discourse-new information, which corresponds to indefinite descriptions. The articleless bare noun *mw* can be translated as 'some (quantity of) water'.[13] The indefinite predicative possession construction *mw n-Ḥr* '(Some) water for Horus!' is repeated in full in the subsequent sentence. Such verbatim repetitions are not intended to advance the course of action but rather to build up a crescendo of the speaker (the funerary priest) in oral performance.[14] As will be detailed later (§4), dative possessive sentences with indefinite subjects are illocutionary ambiguous: they can be used to express assertive speech acts, which, according to Jerrold Sadock & Arnold M. Zwicky (1985), are 'subject to judgments of truth and falsehood' or they can express directive speech acts (imperatives) that indicate 'the speaker's desire to influence future events' and demand immediate action to be taken by the addressee.[15]

The transition to the following imperative *jm n=f mw n(j)=jt=f Wsjr* 'Give him the water of his father Osiris!' goes together with the demotion of the topic noun *mw* from the subject to the direct object role. But there is also a simultaneously occurring change from the indefinite non-specific reference to the definite specific reference of the topic noun *mw*. The switch in definiteness is prompted by the postmodifying possessor phrase *n(j)=jt=f Wsjr* 'of his father Osiris'. Addressing related problems about (in)definiteness in English possessives, Chris Barker (2000) puts forward an interpretative principle, according to which definiteness is spread, so to speak, from the possessor modifier to the possessed head noun.[16]

The closing sequence of the libation spell involves a major shift from the delocutive third person to the interlocutive second person performative structure. The rhetorical turn is indicated by the utterance-initial vocative *h3 Ḥr-ḥtp pn* 'Hey, this Horus-hotep (here)' with the vocative particle *h3*, loosely meaning something like 'hey'.[17] As elucidated by Zwicky (1974), vocatives are direct forms of address that are set off from the associated

13 Liquid-denoting nouns like *water* can be classified as mass nouns, which are only inflectable for singular number. However, as observed by Corbett (2019: 81–82), exceptional cases of *pluralia tantia* liquid nouns are attested in Nilotic languages.

14 Reintges (2011: 39–44).

15 Sadock & Zwicky (1985: 160).

16 Barker (2000: 213 (6)).

17 Edel (1955/1966: 434 §865) characterizes the vocative particle *h3* as '*schallstark*' ('strongly sonic'), whose function is to awaken the deceased pharaoh.

sentence by a special intonation break. Vocatives in utterance-initial position are used as calls designed to catch the addressee's attention. Vocatives in utterance-final position, on the other hand, function as summons and accentuate the contact between the speaker and her interlocutor.[18] In conveying familiarity and identifiability, vocatively used noun phrases can only be interpreted as definite descriptions.[19] This holds particularly true for the vocative use of proper names, which are inherently definite descriptions. This raises a question as to why the proper name *Ḥr-ḥtp* that follows the vocative particle *hꜣ* is marked definite by the determiner demonstrative masculine singular *pn* 'this (over here)'. The semantically redundant use of the demonstrative article is only apparently so, and in fact stresses the spatial proximity between the speaker (the ritual performer) and the addressee (the defunct). It may also carry connotations of formality, politeness and honorificity in a respectful address pattern. The use of the vocative for direct address is closely tied to the immediate situation in which the interlocutors' interaction is embedded.

The double possessive sentences *mw=k n=k* 'Your water (belongs) to you(rself)!' and *qbḥ(-w)=k n=k* 'Your libation (belongs) to you(rself)!' are formally parallel to plain dative possessive sentences like *mw n-Ḥr* 'Some water for Horus!' but differ from them in one crucial respect. Rather than expressing a single possessee–possessor relationship, they express two kinds of possessive relationships – one between the pronominally possessed noun phrases *mw=k* 'your water' and *qbḥ(-w)=k* 'your libation' and another between them and the pronominal dative possessor *n=k* 'to you(rself)'. In being related to the provision of water supply, the possessive relation at the phrasal and the clausal level is both alienable and temporary. As for topic management in oral-performative contexts more generally, it looks as if the multiple occurrences of the topic noun *mw* is not so much motivated by considerations of discourse cohesion and coherence but rather reflects the movement up a cline of increasing cognitive accessibility of the topic referent – a process for which Talmy Givón (1978) has coined the term 'definitization'.[20]

(1) Series of dative possessive sentences with increasing topic (referent) accessibility

mw	*n-*	*Ḥr*
water.M.PL	to-	Horus
mw	*n-*	*Ḥr*
water.M.PL	to-	Horus

jm	*n=f*	*mw*	*n(j)=*	*jt=f*	*Wsjr*
give.IMP.M.SG	to=CL.3M.SG	water.M.PL	LINK.M.SG=	father.M.SG=POSS.3M.SG	Osiris

hꜣ	*Ḥr-ḥtp*	*pn*	*mw=k*	*n=k*
VOC	Hor-hotep	DEM.M.SG	water.M.PL=POSS.2M.SG	to=CL.2M.SG

18 Zwicky (1974: 787–88, 799 footnote 2).

19 See Hill (2007: 2084); Bernstein (2008: 226–28); Arsenijević (2019: 426) and others. According to Hill (2007: 2087), the selectional relation of the vocative marker and the following definite noun phrase accounts for the obligatory specificity and familiarity reading of vocative forms of direct address. Lyons (1999: 152–53) takes issue with the position that the definiteness status of vocative proper names carries over to the vocative forms of common nouns, arguing that common noun vocatives are not consistently definite or indefinite.

20 Givón (1978: 315–16).

qbḥ(-w)=k *n=k*
libate_water(-GER.M.SG)=POSS.2M.SG to=CL.2M.SG
'(Some) water for Horus! (Some) water for Horus! Give him the water of his father Osiris! Oh Horus-hotep (here), your water (belongs) to you(rself)! Your libation (belongs) to you(rself)!'[21]

In an effort to restrict the recipient–benefactive–possessive polysemy of the construction, Loprieno, Müller & Uljas propose that dative possessive sentences are used 'to express alienable possession, i.e. ownership in the restricted juridical-ethical sense as well as all kinds of temporary and momentary but not inalienable possession for which the adnominal direct genitive is used instead (e.g. *ỉb=f* "his heart")'.[22] In other words, predicative/clausal possession is semantically constrained in ways that possessive relations within a complex noun phrase are not. This account is intuitively plausible and has some crosslinguistic support.[23] However, as we are about to see, there is language-internal and typological evidence that defies an all-too-neat alienability split in predicative possession contexts. Such borderline cases can be found in double possessive sentences, which have an alienably or inalienably possessed noun phrase as their subject. As pointed out by Ilja A. Seržant (2016), the alienability splits that surface in the environment of adnominal possession cover some of the same ground as the basic lexical dichotomy between non-relational and relational nouns in the nominal lexicon.[24] Non-relational nouns constitute an open class of common nouns, whose members are referentially autonomous expressions. This is another way of saying that referent identification can be achieved without additional descriptive content. When a non-relational noun is combined with another common noun in a genitive relation, the resulting complex noun phrase admits a broad range of semantic relations between the head noun and the possessive modifier. As a result, contextual cues and pragmatic inferencing must be relied on in order to filter out the most plausible

21 Coffin Text VII 34g–i/T1C [Spell 833] (De Buck 1961: 34). The text poses only minor philological difficulties. One of these has to do with the ideographic writing of the suppletive imperative form *jm* 'give!', which is determined by the hieroglyph of the forearm holding a conical bread loaf in the palm of the hand (Gardiner 1957: 454, sign-list D 37). Another difficulty is posed by the rendering of the vocative particle *h3* with the determinative of the legs walking (Gardiner 1957: 457 sign-list D 54), which thus looks as the imperative form of directed motion verb *h3.ỉ* 'to descend'. This spelling does not appear to be particularly common (Edel 1955/1966: 294–95 §§607–08). But this may simply be a copyist's error, considering that the standard spelling of the vocative particle without a determinative is attested in the original Pyramid Text: *h3 Mrjj-n(j)-Rᶜ pj mw=k n=k bᶜḥ=k n=k* 'Hey, this (King) Meri-ni-Re (here), your water (belongs) to you. Your inundation (belongs) to you' (*Pyr.* §774a/M [Spell 424] (Sethe 1908: 424) [MFW med 3] (Pierre-Croisiau 2019, pl. 7).

22 Loprieno, Müller & Uljas (2019: 185).

23 Mosel (1982: 42–46) makes the same point for possessive sentences in Tolai (or Kuanua), a Melanesian language spoken in the Gazelle Peninsula, East New Britain province, in Papua New Guinee. Inalienable possessive relations cannot be expressed by means of an alienability grammar. Instead, the language resorts to existential sentences to express kinship and part–whole relations at the clausal level: *I have three brothers* ~ *My three brothers exist.*

24 Seržant (2016: 147–48).

interpretation of the relevant possessive relationship.[25] Relational nouns, on the other hand, constitute a closed lexical class of referentially dependent expressions that require 'saturation' by a possessor argument for their semantic completeness. To identify the referent of a relational noun, we first need to know the identity of the possessor.[26] Typical examples of this noun class are body-part expressions, consanguineous (sharing common ancestors) and affinal kin-denoting nouns and spatial concept nouns.[27]

Double possessive sentences are semantically versatile and crosscut the alienability splits in possessive noun phrases. This possessive pattern can be used for inalienable predicative possession, as will be illustrated with the case of predicative body-part possession. However seemingly odd it may appear at first blush, the mereological relation between parts and wholes of the body can be construed as a subject–predicate statement. But this option arises as the consequence of a particular conceptualization of body-part possession, in which anatomical parts are cognized as severable from and re-attachable to the body. The construal of body-part partitioning is embedded in a culture-specific context of mortuary rituals. As pointed out by Jan Assmann (1998), the concept of the dismemberment of the corpse signifies the 'initial state of want' at the onset of the ritual performance, which is dedicated to recovery of the dismembered body parts (*restitutio ad integrum*), the revivification of the body and eventually the reversal from death to life.[28] The following passage from the Pyramid Texts features the ritual reunion of the dismembered body-parts. The transition from the mythical precedent to performative enactment is indicated by a narrative shift from interlocutive to delocutive structure without, however, involving a change in temporal location and attendant thematic break. The utterance-final vocative *Wsjr* 'Osiris' serves as a summon and maintains or emphasizes the already established relationship with the addressee. By using the direct address form, the mythical precedent is temporally anchored to the immediate situation context, which is a prerequisite for independent assertive force. It looks as though the borders between the past and the present are surmounted in ritual practice, with the result that the mythical precedent and the mortuary ritual are enacted at the location and time of the utterance. From an anthropological linguistic perspective, it makes a lot of sense to encode the reattachment of dismembered limbs as a bona fide predicative possessive construction. All things considered, the possibility of having inalienable predicative possession in double possessive sentences is contingent on two conditions: firstly, that the noun phrase-internal possessive relation is inalienable, and secondly, that the internal and the external dative possessor are co-referential (referring to the same referent). In the case at hand, the possessive pronoun on the body part noun is doubled, so to speak, by the external pronominal dative possessor.

25 See, among others, Lichtenberk, Vaid & Chen (2011: 669–71); O'Conner, Maling & Skarabela (2013: 112–20).

26 See Barker (2000: 215–17, 2011: 1111–12) and Löbner (2011: 285–86) for an overview of the main issues.

27 Heine (1997: 10–12).

28 Assmann (1998: 137–38).

(2) Series of double possessive sentences with predicative body-part possession

jb=k *n=k* *Wsjr*
heart.M.SG=POSS.2M.SG to=cl.2M.SG Osiris
rd–w(j)=k *n=k* *Wsjr*
leg–M.DU=POSS.2M.SG to=cl.2M.SG Osiris
ᶜ=k *n=k* *Wsjr*
arm.M.SG=POSS2M.SG to=cl.2M.SG Osiris
jb *n(j)=* *Wnjs* *n=f* *ḏs=f*
heart.M.SG LINK.M.SG= Unas to=CL.3M.SG REFLEX=POSS.3M.SG
rd–w(j)=f *n=f* *ḏs=f*
leg–M.DU=POSS.3M.SG to=CL.3M.SG REFLEX=POSS.3M.SG
ᶜ=f *n=f* *ḏs=f*
arm.M.SG=POSS.3M.SG to=CL.3M.SG REFLEX=POSS.3M.SG

'Your heart (belongs) to you to you(rself), Osiris. Your two legs (belong) to you(rself), Osiris. Your arm (belongs) to you(rself), Osiris. The heart of (King) Unas (belongs) to him himself. His two legs (belong) to him himself. His arm (belongs) to him himself.'[29]

Apart from evidencing the existence of inalienable predicative possession, there is another conspicuous feature of the double possessive sentences to be discussed here. This feature is the modification of the pronominal dative possessor *n=f* 'to him' by the emphatic reflexive *ḏs=f* 'himself'.[30] Ekkehard König (1991) argues that emphatic reflexives are focus particles, with one piece of evidence being that they occupy the same positions that are also available to focus particles.[31] Furthermore, the syntactic distribution of these emphatics is correlated with their semantic role. Head-bound reflexives are often of the same form as non-head bound (adverbial) ones but differ from them in terms of scope taking. Non-head bound emphatic reflexives take scope over the entire sentence, whereas head-bound reflexives only take narrow scope and identify the referent of the focus constituent as 'the most salient entity or 'centre' in the relevant context'.[32] In this way a contrast is set up between the focus and the non-focus part of the sentence. When this theory is applied to the case at hand, we may characterize the import of the head-bound body reflexive *ḏs=f* in terms of prominence marking. I find myself in agreement with Ken Safir (1996) that the combination of personal pronouns with emphatic reflexives does not

29 *Pyr.* §364a–b/W [Spell 267] (Sethe 1908: 190). In the philological commentary, Sethe (1962: 83–84) proposes that the genitive linker-marked construction *jb n(j)=Wnjs* 'the heart of (King) Unas' represents the original version. In line with this suggestion, Allen (2005: 48) translates this passage as follows: 'Unis has his own heart, Unis has his own legs, Unis has his own arms'. In later work (Allen 2017: 64 §8.3, 337), the author assumes a consistent speaker oriented viewpoint in the original version of the Unas Pyramid Texts: '*I have *my own mind, *I have *my own legs, *I have *my own arms'.

30 Borghouts (2010: 104 §26.b) deliberates the possibility of a semantic differentiation between body reflexives *ḏs=* 'self' and *ḏt=* 'own'.

31 König (1991: 87–89).

32 König (1991: 91).

create a new type of anaphor but rather conveys the same type of emphasis for intensity as the combination of head-bound reflexives and full noun phrases. It also suggests, as argued in this article, that these emphatics may but need not be subject oriented.[33]

Although the argument is difficult to summarize briefly, there may be a typological parallel between predicative body-part possession in Early Egyptian and the grammar of body-part partitioning in Ewe [Gbe cluster of the Kwa branch of Niger-Congo, spoken in southeastern Ghana, Togo and Benin], as insightfully described by Felix Ameka (1986). In contrast to previous generalizations about alienability splits, possessive linker constructions in Ewe are used for alienably possessed noun phrases as well as for anatomical parts and other meronyms. By contrast, the direct juxtaposition of the possessee and the possessor constituent is restricted to terms for spatial orientation, kinship and other social relations.[34] The language also has a body-part possessor ascension construction at its disposal, in which the body part term is encoded as the subject and the body-part possessor as a prepositional dative-oblique phrase.[35] Ameka explains these findings via a culture-specific conceptualization of body-part possession, in which the possessor of the body exerts control over its individual parts and can do things or have things done to them.[36] Shifting attention back to Early Egyptian, one could posit that just as in the case of Ewe, body parts and other meronyms can be alienably possessed. Alternatively, one could argue that alienability splits in adnominal and predicative possession are morphosyntactically neutralized.

A linguistically oriented philology holds the promise of shedding new light on longstanding conundrums. The ancient invocation offering formula *pr-t ẖrw n-* lends itself for sample treatment. While I cannot provide a full argument for my claims here, I will briefly sketch a tentative analysis of this conventionalized formula as a dative possessive sentence. The variable part of the formula is represented by the predicative dative possessor, which identifies the proper name and titles of the defunct beneficiary. The collocationally fixed expression *pr-t ẖrw* in subject position can properly be analyzed as a free (headless) participial relative clause. Free relative clauses are those clauses that have the relative antecedent implied rather than overtly expressed. The nominal reference of headless participial relatives and their distribution as arguments in the main clause follows from the nominal features of the participle itself. Jamal Ouhalla (2004) offers a comparative syntactic analysis of Semitic relative clauses, in which this relativization strategy is analyzed as a case of internal clause nominalization. Under this analysis, the nominalized verb (participle, gerund or *masdar*—in the Arab grammatical tradition) lacks tense (though not aspect) and assigns genitive case to its complement.[37]

33 Safir (1996: 533 footnote 4).
34 Ameka (1996: 789–802).
35 Ameka (1996: 812–23).
36 Ameka (1996: 812) further notes that body-part possession in Ewe is 'similar to the relationship between, for example, the owner of a basket and the basket'.
37 Ouhalla (2004: 297–99).

As for the internal syntax of the *pr-t ḫrw* construction, I make the reasonable, but not yet tested assumption that the perfective active participle *pr* 'coming' and the deverbal noun *ḫrw* 'voice, invocation' form an indivisible construct state unit. The linearly adjacent nominal constituent *ḫrw* receives genitive case from the construct state-marked participle. Construct state morphology can trigger the elision of the feminine gender suffix *-t* (*pr-t ḫrw* → *pr ḫrw*), with the result that the participial head appears in its uninflected masculine singular form. If this much can be agreed upon, the semantic role of the genitive case-marked noun phrase *ḫrw* still remains to be explained. In effect, the claim here is that it is neither the subject of the participle verb nor the adjoined construct-state possessor. Rather, this is a remarkable use of the genitive case that involves no possession at all and has a causative meaning. Furthermore, the genitive case-marked causer meets a selectional requirement of telic movement verbs, which require a prepositional complement for their semantic completeness. As a final step in the argumentation, the headless participial clause involves subject relativization, which leaves a phonologically invisible but syntactically interpretable gap in the subject position. The resulting structure would look like [$_{\text{RC}}$ [$_{\text{participle}}$ *pr-t* ~ *pr*] __ [$_{\text{Causer}}$ *ḫrw*]]] (where '__' indicates the relative subject gap) and can approximately be rendered as 'what comes forth on account of the invocation (lit. 'voice')'.[38]

With the issues of internal syntax in place, I will now briefly discuss the semantics of the *pr-t ḫrw* construction. Following research by Pauline Jacobson (1995), Alexander Grosu & Fred Landman (1998), Ivano Caponigro (2021), and Louisa Sadler & Maris Camilleri (2018), the headless participial relative clause can be classified as a maximal free relative. Free relative clauses of such kind are characterized by three interrelated properties.[39] The first property is the definiteness property, meaning that free relatives can

---

38 I noticed one example where the invocation offering formula is recast in a headed participial relative clause in which an adverbial locative position is relativized. The relative gap in the complement position of the locative preposition *m* triggers the selection of the long form allomorph *jm* in exactly the same way as the corresponding resumptive pronoun. Of special interest is the presence of the imperfective active masculine singular participle *prr*, which agrees in gender and number with the external relative head *bw* 'place'. In connection with the aforegoing discussion, it should furthermore be observed that the noun phrase *ḫrw* in post-participle position serves as the subject of the oblique participial relative clause. Unsurprisingly, the dative case-marked noun phrase *n-špst* 'for a noblewoman' serves as the beneficiary.

(i) Recast of the *pr-t ḫrw n-* formula in a headed oblique (locative) participial relative clause

m *bw* *nb*$_i$ [$_{RŠ}$ *prr* *ḫrw* *jm*__$_i$ *n-špst*
in place.M.SG each. M.SG PTCP.IMPERF.ACT.M.SG voice.M.SG in to-noble.F.SG
m [*wp*] *rnpt* tp *rnpt* (…)]
in open.GER.M.SG year.F.SG head.M.SG year.F.SG

'in very place where the voice comes forth for a noble woman on the [opening] of the year, the first day of the year (other festivals)' (Mastaba of Queen Mersyankh III, west room, west wall, architrave inscription (2), Dunham & Simpson 1974: pl. XI, fig. 10).

39 Although the empirical focus of Caponigro's (2021) overview chapter is on Mesoamerican languages, it provides a comprehensive typology of varieties of free relatives and the semantic and syntactic issues involved therein (see, in particular, his discussion on pp. 8–30). Free relatives are sometimes interpreted semantically as singular definite noun phrases and sometimes as universals

be replaced or paraphrased by a definite noun phrase. The second property is referentiality, meaning that the descriptive content of the relative clause suffices for successful referent identification. The third property is the maximizing property itself. Simplifying matters somewhat, free relative clauses of the maximizing kind denote the largest entity that fits the description of the property expressed by the relative clause. What is the maximal largest entity denoted by this kind of free relative? According to Jacobson, maximal free relatives come close in meaning to plural definites, but the notion of a maximal plural entity is relativized with respect to a particular context.[40] Depending on the context, this may be a singular atomic entity or a plural entity, whereby the latter results from forming a group by joining together several atomic entities.[41] In the case at hand, we can safely assume that the maximal entity referred to by the participial relative clause is a plural entity. It is further specified by the exhaustively listed provisions, which minimally include the generic food and drink items *t* 'bread' and *ḥnqt* 'beer', respectively.[42] (Here and hereafter the boundaries of the relative clause are indicated by square brackets.)

(3) The invocation offering formula *pr-t ẖrw n-* as a dative possessive sentence

a. *pr* *ẖrw* *n=f* *n-s3* *njswt*
come.PTCP.PERF.ACT.M.SG voice.M.SG to=3M.SG to-son.M.SG king.M.SG
Mnw-ẖꜥ=f *rꜥ* *nb*
Min-khaf day.M.SG every.M.SG
'What comes forth on account of the invocation (belongs) to him, the prince Min-khaf on a daily basis'.[43]

a'. Free subject participle relative: $[_{RC}\ [_{participle}$ *pr-t ~ pr*$]$ __ $[_{Causer}$ *ẖrw*$]]]$

From historical-linguistic perspective, the invocation offering formula is of special interest as it bears on the issue of the antiquity of the dative predicative possession construction.

(Jacobson 1995: 465–71; Grosu & Landman 1998: 155–62). The status of indefinite free relatives is more controversial. Caponigro (2001) argues that indefinite free relatives in Italian require a special licensing context, i.e., they are only possible in the complement position of the auxiliary verb *essere* 'to be'. But the distribution of indefinite free relatives differs crosslinguistically. Sadler & Camilleri (2018: 146–53) argue in detail that indefinite free relative clauses in Maltese are not only permissible in the complement position of existential verbs and non-verbal locative possessive constructions, as expected, but they can also be found with perception verbs (*find*, *look for*, *seek*), transfer verbs (*give*, *bring*, *buy*) as well as with verbs of appearance (*appear*, *arrive*, *occur*).

40 Jacobson (1995: 472–73).

41 See Sadler & Camilleri (2018: 163–65) for a more detailed discussion of the maximizing property including illustrative examples from Maltese.

42 Allen (2000: 358 §24.10).

43 Coffin of Min-khaf (east side, 1st column) (Smith 1933, pl. 21). In reference to the above example, Schweitzer (2005: 143 §314) notes that: '*Eine zweifache Verwendung der Präposition [i.e. n-] ermöglicht eine Betonung des präpositionellen Bestandteils*' ('a repeated use of the preposition permits emphasis on the prepositional component'). Whatever this is supposed to mean exactly, it is clear that the dative-marked noun phrase *ns3 njswt Mnwẖꜥ=f* 'to the prince Min-khaf' has been extraposed to the right. In English, right-dislocated definite noun phrases and proper names are anticipated by cataphoric pronouns, which have the character of an afterthought. In an example like 'They're excellent company, the Smiths', the right-dislocated NP 'the Smiths' disambiguates

From a broader socio-cultural perspective, the *pr-t ẖrw* construction testifies to the sense of alienable possession as legal ownership, which is connected to the juridical and practical subtext of regulating the expenditure for commodities and services.

The significance of the dative predicative possession construction has not gone unnoticed in the linguistic and historical–comparative literature. The Indo-Europeanist Émile Benveniste saw in this possessive pattern a prima facie piece of evidence for the metonymic transfer of the *dativus commodi* ('beneficiary dative') to the domain of predicative possession: 'Now the same construction with the dative *n=* indicates possession: *nbw n=j* 'gold [is] to–me (*n=j*) = I have gold'.[44] Benveniste's finding has found its way into the typological study of predicative possession.[45] But due to the paucity of interlinear glossed examples, efforts to profile non-verbal predicative possession in Early Egyptian have not been met with success. By combining theory with data, the present case-study attempts to rectify this gap in knowledge.

3 Predicative possession in grammar and cognition

Without being an exhaustive overview, this section addresses some key topics and research problems surrounding the typological split between *habere* and *non-habere* languages (from the Latin verb *habere* 'to have'). In the *World Atlas of Language Structures Online* [WALS], Stassen (2013) examines the crosslinguistic distribution of morphosyntactically distinct types of predicative possessive constructions. Out of a total sample of 240 languages, 63 languages, that is slightly more than a quarter (26.25%), resort to a transitive possession verb to encode possessive relationships. In *habere*-languages, the possessor and possessee terms are aligned with the grammatical subject and direct object role, respectively. The WALS sample also contains 48 non-*habere* languages, that is less than a quarter (20%), in which the possessee is promoted to grammatical subject, whereas the possessor surfaces as the locative, genitive, dative or oblique term of a non-verbal predication sentence. Clearly, Early Egyptian belongs to the latter type of non-*habere* languages. The complex relation between existential, locative and possessive sentences has been a major research hotspot for several decades. For reason of space, I will concentrate on the so-called localist hypothesis of predicative possession, according to which the

---

the reference of the personal pronoun *they*. But it can only do so when the Smith family has been mentioned earlier in the discourse (Huddleston 1984: 451–52).

44 Benveniste (1966: 202) '*Or la même construction avec le datif n= indique la possession: nb n=j « or (est) à moi = j'ai de l'or »*'. This observation was inspired by Westendorf's (1953) work on the 'passive theory'. Although this does not diminish the value of Benveniste's discovery, the (reconstructed) model sentence is not entirely felicitous from a discourse-pragmatic and cultural perspective, depicting a financial transaction. The bare indefinite noun *nbw* 'gold' is a non-countable mass noun, which, according to Ter Meulen (1981: 106), has the semantics of a proper names of an abstract entity, a metallic substance as it were. As evidenced by the libation text just examined, dative possessive sentences have mass nouns like *mw* 'water' as possessees. Yet, mass noun reference is generally more abstract than count noun reference—a point to which I will return later (see below §5).

45 For instance, Heine (1997: 190) and Stassen (2009: 321–22).

concept of the possessor amounts to [+human, +animate] location (§3.1). The main objective of linguistic typology is to study grammatical variation across languages with a view to establishing the limits of this variation and seeking explanations for it. Stassen (2009) presents the most recent account of typological diversity in predicative possession (§3.2). Also included is some background about in/definiteness and specificity, as these notions are relevant to the classification of nominal possessum categories and to the construction of a language-specific typology of predicative possession constructions with dative possessors (§3.3).

3.1 The localist theory of predicative possession

Despite its manifold liaisons with the social and cultural practices of a particular speech community, possession embodies, in Heine's own words, 'a universal domain, that is, any human language can be expected to have conventionalized expressions for it'.[46] The universality of grammatical categories of possession is uncontroversial but many problems remain to be solved. One hotly debated issue is the possibility of a unified treatment of locational, existential and possessive predication. John Lyons (1967) has put forward an early formulation of the locative theory of possession, according to which predicative possession sentences have an underlying locative syntax. From a Cognitive Grammar perspective, Ronald W. Langacker (1995) has influentially argued that when predicative possession is conceptualized as a spatial metaphor, the possessor term represents a point of orientation or 'landmark'.[47] The notion of spatial grounding can be sharpened by assuming with Eve Clark (1978) that the landmark which provides cognitive access to the possessor 'is simply an animate place'. The correlatedness of existence, location and possessive predication can be explained by capitalizing on the fact that the possessee 'is located in space, just as the object designed in existential or locative sentences'.[48] Table 1 further illustrates the points just raised.

Table 1. The locative syntax of predicative possession

	POSSESSEE (NP1)	POSSESSOR (NP_2)
Grammatical Role	Subject	Predicate
Semantic Role	Theme	Goal, Recipient, Beneficiary, Possessor
Spatial Orientation	[± animate] located	[+animate] / [+human] location

The localist theory of predicative possession is supported by the crosslinguistic evidence, which shows that predicative possessive constructions in many of the world's languages are locative-existential sentences at the synchronic level and/or are historically derived from such sentences. This leads Suzanne Kemmer (2003) to the conclusion that location

46 Heine (1997: 1).
47 Langacker (1995: 66–68).
48 Clark (1978: 89). The underlining for emphasis is in the original text.

and possession are cognitively closely related categories, with location representing the more basic category:[49]

> Given that we can compare and analyze the relation between the two meanings, and show a plausible link between them, it makes sense to hypothesize that the two categories frequently share the same forms of expression precisely because they are notions that are seen to be similar by humans. At the same time, the fact that some languages treat these same two semantic categories quite differently shows that they are conceptually differentiable.

The picture becomes more complicated when languages with morphosyntactically distinct constructions for location and possession are taken into consideration.[50] Languages of such kind are interesting because the semantic relation between the locatum and location does not stand on equal footing with the possessee–possessor relation. Frantisek Lichtenberk (2003) posits that the possessor is 'conceptually more basic' than the beneficiary.[51] Surprising, though, as this hypothesis may seem at first blush, it is corroborated by the historical-comparative evidence. In the evolution of the Oceanic possessive classifier systems, the erstwhile purely possessive-marking classifiers enlarged their semantic spectrum to include a beneficiary function. Accordingly, the beneficiary connotation is derivative on the possessor sense.[52] I find myself in agreement with Hansjakob Seiler's (2001) middle-ground position that 'while it is true that local and other constructions are drawn upon for the purpose of representing possessive relations, it is also true that after completion of such a shift the resulting expressions no longer are purely local etc. but express something new, called possession'.[53]

3.2 Parameters of crosslinguistic variation

There is little room for doubt that the localist theory of predicative possession is in need of refinement. As it turns out, the concept of spatial proximity does not cover the attested patterns of variation in predicative/clausal possession more generally and the typological split between *habere* and non-*habere* languages more specifically. Other criteria than locality must be factored in for systematic comparison to be carried out. Stassen's typology of predicative possession is based on two binary-valued parameters. The first parameter is

49 Kemmer (2003: 91).

50 Payne (2009) argues that possession is more than location. Empirical support for this claim comes from the opposition between the auxiliary verbs *tii* 'to be at' and *ata* 'to have' in Maa (Maasai) [Eastern Nilotic, Nilo–Saharan]. The auxiliary *ata* can only be used in predicative possessive constructions, whereas the auxiliary *tii* can also appear in existential and locative sentences. In accordance with Pāṇini's Principle, the more specific item must be inserted first, thereby blocking the insertion of the less specific competitor. Given the morphological rule competition, possessive sentences in Maa fall outside the locative paradigm of predicative possession.

51 Lichtenberk (2002: 441).

52 See Lichtenberk (2002: 445–48) and Lichtenberk, Vaid & Chen (2011: 667–69) for further details on the diachronic process.

53 Seiler (2001: 27).

[±CONTROL] and concerns the asymmetric control relation between the possessee and the possessor. The second parameter is [±PERMANENT CONTACT] and concerns the temporality or duration of the possessive relation. With the parameter space thus reduced, 'a prototypical case of possession is characterized by the presence of two entities (the possessor and the possessee) such that a) the possessor and the possessee are in some relatively enduring relation, and b) the possessor exerts control over the possessee (and is therefore typically human)'.[54] The positive or negative value of the two parameters delineate four basic types of predicative possession. These are the only types needed for the construction of the crosslinguistic typology, cf. Table 2.

Table 2. Parameterization of different kinds of predicative possession[55]

Possession relation	[CONTROL]	[PERMANENT CONTACT]
Alienable	+	+
Inalienable	–	+
Temporary	+	–
Abstract	–	–

The construal of alienable possession as ownership (*João has an apartment*) is deeply rooted in a cultural bias, which tends to assimilate the grammatical expression of possession to the legal conception of property rights in western societies.[56] The invocation offering formula *pr-t ḫrw n-*, which could be identified as a dative possessive sentence, bears witness to the sense of ownership (i.e., the possession and control of resources and services) in an ancient non-western society. Inalienable possession (*João has a son*) describes a more intimate SON-of relation without necessarily implying control. At the same time, kinship and interpersonal relations that structure social networks are cross-culturally perceived as eminently time-stable.[57] The same raison d'être applies to body-

54 Stassen (2009: 15 (20)).

55 Adapted from Stassen (2009: 17 (21)).

56 Keen (2013: 187–88).

57 Heine (1997: 34). Attempts in the typological literature to unify the categories of alienable and inalienable possession are faced with non-trivial challenges when the two possessive categories are distinguished on a morphosyntactic basis, with the clearest evidence coming from adnominal possession. Heine (1997: 172) notes a typological tendency for inalienably possessed nouns to require less morphological marking than alienably possessed ones. For instance, in the Western-Oceanic language Manam (Papua New Guinea), there is a basic division of possessive nominal constructions into the so-called direct and the indirect possessive. In the indirect possessive pattern, the same set of possessor-indexing suffixes is attached to a possessive classifier noun. The point of interest here is that the direct possessive is primarily used for inalienably possessed nouns, e.g. *tamá-gu* [father-1SG.POSS] 'my father', while the indirect possessive pairs up with alienably possessed nouns, e.g. *ʔúsi né-gu* [loincloth POSS.CLF-1SG.POSS] 'my loincloth' (Lichtenberk, Vaid & Chen 2011: 661–63). A similar picture emerges for Lakota [Siouan, North/South Dakota]. Possessive pronominal affixes are directly attached to the possessee head noun in cases of inalienable possession, e.g. *ni-c'iye* (2SG-elder + brother) 'your elder brother'. When the possessee is an alienably possessed noun, the possessive affixes are first attached to the linkage marker *t'a*

part possession (*A dog has four legs and a tail*) and mereological relations (*The mountain has a top*), but here a caveat is in order. As exemplified by the case of predicative body-part possession in Ewe and Early Egyptian, the relation between anatomical parts and wholes can be construed of in terms of alienable possession. Temporal possession (*Watch out! That guy has a knife*) is instantaneous. The possessor's control over a potentially harmful object lies at the centre of interest, while the question of legal ownership is beside the point. Abstract possession denotes transient states of the possessor beyond his or her control, such as disease possession (*João has a cold*) or the possession of a mental state (*If a person has a lot of fear and anxiety*). In having a negative value for the [±CONTROL] and the [±PERMANENT CONTACT] parameter, this type of predicative possession is maximally different from alienable, inalienable and temporary possession.[58] Another way to look at this feature combination would be to say that abstract possession is a semantic extension of possession, which falls outside the parameter space of Stassen's typology.

3.3 A taxonomy of nominal possessum categories

As a general critique, Stassen's restrictive approach to predicative possession may be apt to handle large-scale typological samples but it is less so to fully capture the morphosyntactic and semantic diversity of the possessive system in individual languages. Classifying languages according to a particular typological class runs into problems when the language in question has more than one strategy at its disposal to encode predicative possession. As argued in detail by Myler, this is not the only methodological concern that arises.[59] With an eye to constructing a descriptively adequate typology of Early Egyptian dative possessive sentences, I would like to raise two further points. The first point is that the meaning of sentences is compositionally derived from the meaning of their components taken separately and from the way in which they are combined structurally. In predicative possession sentences, the possessee in subject position and the dative possessor in predicative position are noun phrases with independent reference or personal pronouns and demonstratives with anaphoric or exophoric reference. The second point is that the semantic content or the reference type of the possessee constituent distinguishes one type of dative possessive predication from another one, which opens a window to an understanding of constructional polysemy and of the Too-Many-Meanings Puzzle.

As far as the possessee is concerned, everything goes, whereas the dative possessor is by comparison semantically more constrained.[60] With these initial considerations in mind,

---

and the resulting linker + possessive pronoun compound is then prefixed to the head noun, e.g. *mi-t'a-šúŋka kiŋ* (1SG-PRT-dog the) 'my dog' (Lyons 1999: 127). Nichols (1992: 116–23) proposes that the alienability split follows from the closer morphosyntactic bonding between the possessee and the possessor modifier in a possessive noun phrase without having semantic import. This cannot be the whole story, as inalienable nouns are usually relational, requiring saturation by a possessor argument.

58 Heine (1997: 34–35) and Stassen (2009: 19–20).

59 Myler (2016: 83–98).

60 Although limits of space prevent me from entering into further details, I would like to make two interrelated observations. First, there are attested examples where the dative case-marked noun

I will now proceed to develop a language-specific classification system, which is based upon a comprehensive, though not exhaustive, taxonomy of nominal possessum categories and which captures the attested patterns of variation in dative predicative possession constructions.

To this end, several general important concepts of nominal denotation types will be introduced. In particular, I will rely on Irene Heim's (1982) model of 'File Change Semantics', in which the pragmatically enriched meaning of a sentence is modeled as an update function over contexts. In this model, indefinite noun phrases are used to introduce discourse referents into a discourse, with the 'Novelty Condition' amounting to the opening of a new discourse file. Definite noun phrases, on the other hand, pick out an already familiar discourse entity, which either has been introduced in the previous discourse or whose identity can be recovered from the conversational common ground, i.e., the set of assumptions shared by the speaker and the addressee. The 'Familiarity Condition' can thus be likened to the updating of an already existing discourse file.[61] Specificity represents another dimension of contextual meaning that is critical to reference disambiguation. In Mürvet Enç's (1991) theory, the discourse relation relevant for definite noun phrases and personal pronouns is the identity relation. By contrast, specificity involves a weaker kind of discourse linking, in which the intended referent stands in a recoverable relation to some contextually salient entity. The contextual salience of a discourse referent can be enhanced when the sentence is pragmatically enriched by other elements in the context so as to facilitate the identification of that referent. As will be discussed later on (§6), the auxiliary verb *jw* is an illustrative case in point for such a pragmatic enrichment.

---

phrase or pronoun do not denote a prototypical possessor, which is human, animate or otherwise ranking high on the nominal hierarchy. Second, with non-prototypical inanimate possessors, the prominence relation between the possessee and the possessor appears to be reversed. This is not necessarily a problem for the current theory, since prominence reversal and non-prototypical possessorhood block a standard possessive interpretation. An illustrative case in point is shown below.

(i) Dative possessive sentences with pronominal possessee and inanimate dative possessor

jw=k	*sṯ*	*n-*	*tf*	*m*	*rꜣ*	*n(j)*	*Rᶜ*
AUX=2M.SG	PCL	to-	saliva.M.SG	in	mouth.M.SG	LINK.M.SG	Re

'You, too, (belong) to the saliva with the mouth of Re'. (Coffin Text VII 421c/B2Bo [Spell1101] (de Buck 1961: 421)

As noted by Schenkel (2007: 192), the second-position clitic *sṯ* cannot be identified with the subordinating complementizer *jsṯ* 'while', which must always be placed in clause-first position. But the absolute clause-initial position is already taken by the auxiliary verb *jw*. Following Oréal (2011: 181–87), this must be a case of the additive focus particle *(j)sṯ* 'also, too'. The associate of the focus particle is the second person singular masculine subject pronoun *=k*, which encliticizes to the auxiliary *jw*. As is well known, first and second person pronouns are ranked higher than third person pronouns and full noun phrases on a scale of topicality or discourse prominence. Accordingly, the pronominal possessee is more salient than the substance-denoting mass noun *tf*. Leitz (1996: 388) is undecided on whether it should be identified with the serpent's venom or its saliva. The latter interpretation (as saliva) makes good sense for the adverbially modified subject noun phrase *tf m rꜣ n(j) Rᶜ* 'the saliva in the mouth of Re'. But the substance noun *tf* can also mean venom, as seen in: *tf=k ḥfꜣw pr(-w) m jr[t][=k]* 'Your venom of a serpent has come from [your eye]' (*Pyr.* § 1077/P [P/A/E 33] (Berger-el Naggar, Leclant, Mathieu & Pierre-Croisiau 2010, pl. 9]).

61 Heim (1982, chap. 3).

4 Indefinite predicative possession sentences

With the exception of the numeral *w*ᶜ 'one', Early Egyptian lacks indefinite determiners and uses the 'bare' form of the noun to express indefinite status. Possessive constructions with bare indefinites have a limited syntactic distribution and mainly occur in out-of-the-blue contexts. These are contexts which entail the absence of a previous discourse or of a pragmatically salient shared situation. We have already seen an example of an indefinite predicative possession sentence in an out-of-the-blue context (see above §2, example (1)). The dative possessive sentence *mw n-Ḥr* '(Some) water for Horus!' appears in the opening of a thematically coherent paragraph, which by definition is uttered out of the blue. In view of the fact that the possessive predicate is a proper name (Horus), this cannot be an all-new sentence, in which all constituents are discourse-new.

To create a coherent database and avoid complicating the classification system, Stassen's research concentrates on possessive constructions with indefinite possessees. On a more general level, the question arises as to the place of definite predicative possession within the crosslinguistic typology.[62] There are further limits of the empirical domain, which, in my opinion, are not very well motivated. Of the four basic types of predicative possession only alienable possession is considered. Additionally, the possessee and the possessor must be plain noun phrases without determiners and modifiers. Last but not least, the rigidity of the classification system also leads to wrong predications about the canonicity of the possessive construction in question. This particularly holds true for the case of indefinite possession sentences, which occur less frequently in the Early Egyptian documentation than is predicted under Stassen's approach. This may be due to somewhat exceptional character of this possessive pattern, which is closely related to existential sentences (§4.1) and which is ambiguous at the speech-act level (§4.2). The elusive semantic contours of indefinite dative possession makes it an unlikely candidate for a possessive prototype.

4.1 The intersection of indefinite predicative possession and existential sentences

Existential and possessive sentences have a similar syntax with an indefinite noun phrase in subject position. The two indefinite subject constructions have a presentational function denoting the appearance of some new entity into the world of discourse. But while existential sentences assert the objective or conceptual reality of the novel discourse referent, indefinite possession sentences simply presuppose but do not assert its existence and subsequently relate it to another already familiar referent. The general assertion of existence in existential sentences proper has a structural correlate in the presence of a copular verb.

62 Stassen (2009: 28–33). The contrast between indefinite and definite predicative possession is related to the topicality status of the possessee and the possessor noun phrases. Only those instances of predicative possession structures are considered, 'in which THE POSSESSOR NP HAS THE STATUS OF TOPIC, and is marked as such by whichever formal means the language has for this' [Emphasis in the text](Stassen 2009: 30). The argument for excluding quantificational possession sentences is that this type of predicative possession departs from canonical strategies for the encoding of possessive relationships. With numerical expressions, for instance, identificational statements are crosslinguistically common: *John has four brothers* → *John's brothers are four*.

There is a typological generalization, first noted by Louise McNally (2011), according to which existential sentences do not always contain a copular verb, but if they have one, it often is a verb like English *be* or a transitive possessive verb like *have*, but hardly ever a copular verb that literary means *exist*.[63] In Early Egyptian existential sentences, the copular verb *wnn* 'to be' predicates the property of existence of its subject. No such existential predication needs to be expressed in indefinite predicative possession sentences, which are grammatical as they are without an auxiliary verb. Below given is an existential polar question, in which the focus marker *jn* targets the truth value of the existential sentence *wn rm-w* '(there) is fish'. Taking up an earlier analysis of this proclitic particle as a vestigial copula (Reintges 1998), the sequence interrogative/focus marker *jn* > auxiliary verb *jw* > copular verb *wn* represents a tripartite auxiliary clitic cluster.[64]

(4) Interrogative existential sentence with paired auxiliary verbs *jw* and *wn*

jn	*jw*	*wn*	*rm-w*
FOC	AUX	be.PFV	fish-M.PL

'Is (there) fish (lit. are (there) fishes)?'[65]

The combination of the two auxiliaries represents a typologically atypical feature of Early Egyptian existential sentences, which can, however, be explained in terms of a division of labor. The existential verb *wn* asserts the existence of the indefinite plural subject *rm-w* 'fish(es)', while the auxiliary *jw* links the existential utterance to the immediate situation context.

4.2 The illocutionary opacity of indefinite possession sentences

Based upon a sizeable data collection, Loprieno, Müller & Uljas were able to corroborate that 'bare' adverbial locative sentences (i.e., those not preceded by an auxiliary, interjection or a subordinating conjunction) are not as marginally attested as previously thought. Pragmatically, such root clause constructions stand out in carrying out 'desiderative, directive, exhortative, or promissive speech acts'. Indefinite dative possessive sentences are singled out as being of special interest because they used to express 'exclamative utterances expressing the speaker's subjective feelings (surprise, elation, etc.) with respect to the states of affairs whose actuality is presupposed in the speech context'.[66] Despite its initial appeal, there are problems with the proposed analysis. To begin with, exclamative illocutionary force lacks a morphosyntactic correlate, while the prosodic factors being involved are not demonstrable for a dead language. For this reason, the exclamative and mirative connotations that are posited are heavily reliant on contextual interpretation, as the authors themselves admit.[67]

---

63 McNally (2011: 1831).

64 Reintges (1998: 198–204).

65 Tomb of Zau in Deir el Gebrâwi, South Wall, West Side, 3rd register from above (de Garis Davies 1902, pl. 4). See also Edel (1955/1964: 499 §979A) for a brief discussion of this example.

66 Loprieno, Müller & Uljas (2019: 141–43).

67 Loprieno, Müller & Uljas (2019: 145).

Before we dive in deeper into this issue, let us take a step back and briefly touch on some findings in the relevant literature. The universality of exclamatives as a speech act category in its own right is nowadays widely accepted by many researchers. Sadock & Zwicky, for instance, hold that declarative and exclamative clauses present the proposition that they denote as being true but differ from each other in their communicative intent. Declarative clauses are intended to be informative, whereas exclamatives are intended to be expressive, underscoring the speaker's 'strong emotional reaction to what he takes to be a fact'.[68] Raffaella Zanuttini & Paul Portner (2003) focus on the compositional semantics of exclamative clauses, which can be identified as such by three criterial properties.[69] The first property is the presupposition of factivity. Exclamatives are factive in that the truth of their propositional content is presupposed. This provides a straightforward explanation for why exclamative clauses can only be embedded under factive knowledge verbs like *to know*, which imply the truth of the embedded proposition (*Mary knows how very cute he is* vs. **Mary thinks how very cute he is*). The second property is a conventional scalar implicature that the propositional content is located at the 'extreme end of some contextually given scale'. This is where the emotive content and the speaker orientedness of exclamative clauses come into play. The third property is the unavailability of exclamatives in response to a previous question. For obvious reasons, it is not possible to obtain grammaticality judgements on acceptable and non-acceptable sentences in a historical language, considering that the absence of a construction in a particular context may just be an accidental gap rather than a proof of ungrammaticality. With the exception of the second property (which is semantically based), the pervasiveness of the first and the third diagnostic property is not verifiable unless some new evidence emerges that confirms or disconfirms Zanuttini & Portner's claims. Against this background, the main points of divergence with the exclamative analysis are the following two. Firstly, indefinite possession sentences can be used as declarative statements that make a factual assertion. As far as I can see, the indefinite possession sentence below is devoid of any expressive content and overtones of counterexpectation. If anything, the possession of longevity combined with elite status is completely aligned with cultural expectations.

(5) Indefinite possession sentence with declarative illocution

jꜣw	*nfr*	*n=s*	*ẖr*	*nṯr*
age.M.SG	be_beautiful(PTCP.M.SG)	to=CL.3F.SG	under	god.M.SG
ꜥꜣ				
be_great(PTCP.M.SG)				

"A beautiful old age (belongs) to her under the Great God."[70]

68 Sadock & Zwicky (1985 : 162).

69 Zanuttini & Portner (2003: 46–49).

70 Mastaba of Queen Mersyankh III, Main Room, West Wall, architrave inscription (1), Dunham & Simpson (1974: pl. VII, fig.7). Dows & Simpson (1974: 13–14) provide an overall accurate transcription of the passage (*ỉꜣwtỉ nfr n.s ẖr nṯr-ꜥꜣ*) but the structure and content are not correctly analyzed, as evident from the translation 'when she has become old'.

Secondly, illocutionary ambiguity typically arises between declarative and directive speech acts rather than between declaratives and exclamatives. The potential ambiguity can often (but not always) be resolved by contextual clues. The issues that are at play are exemplified by the following Pyramid Text passage, which features the deceased king as the speaker. The descriptive content of the two-word sentence *ẖt n(=j)* 'Something (to eat) for me!' expresses an alienable possession relation between the indefinite pronoun *ẖt* 'something' and the first person singular possessor *n(=j)* 'for me'. The indefinite possession sentence is verbatim repeated four times. Each reiteration is accompanied by an utterance-final vocative phrase (*sšm* 'O butcher', *jm(y) jrt R*^{c} 'O you who (is) in the eye of Re', *wjꜣ* ^{c}*q jm(y) jrt nṯr* 'oh you who enters the bark which (is) in the eye of Re'), which thus represents the variable component in the otherwise formulaic structure. The first person–second person singular interpersonal structure carries over to the subsequent imperative clauses ^{c}*bꜣ mw* 'Serve up water!' and *rkḥ sḏꜣt* 'Light a fire!'. Taken together, the indefinite predicative possession and the thereupon following imperative sentences constitute items on a 'To-do List'. This is reminiscent to the Portner's (2007) theory of directive speech-acts as 'To-do Lists', which make a different contribution to the discourse rather than just adding a new proposition to it. In particular, such 'To-do Lists' assign to each speech participant a set of properties. Imperatives differ from other directive constructions insofar as the set of properties is confined to the addressee.[71]

(6) Indefinite possession sentence with directive illocution

ẖt *n(=j)* *sšm*
thing.F.SG for=1SG butcher.M.SG
ẖt *n(=j)* *sšm*
thing.F.SG for=1SG butcher.M.SG
ẖt *<n(=j)>* [$_{RC}$ *jm(-y)* *jrt* *R*^{c}]
thing.F.SG for=1SG in–NMNLZR.M.SG eye.F.SG Re
ẖt *n(=j)* [$_{RC}$ *wjꜣ* ^{c}*q*
thing.F.SG for=1SG bark.M.SG enter (PTCP.M.SG)
[$_{RC}$ *jm(-y)* *jrt* *nṯr*]]
in–NMNLZR.M.SG eye.F.SG god.M.SG
wdpw ^{c}*bꜣ* *mw* *rkḥ* *sḏꜣt*
attendant.M.SG serve.IMP.SG water.M.PL light.IMP.SG fire.F.SG
"Something (to eat) for me, butcher! Something (to eat) for me, butcher! Something (to eat) <for me>, you who (is) in the eye of Re! Something (to eat) for me, you who enters the bark (of Re), which (is) in the eye of the God! Attendant, serve up water! Light a fire!"[72]

71 Portner (2007: 357–59). For Aikhenvald (2010: 128–33), imperative clauses are temporally anchored to the time of the utterance with a brief extension into the future. The futurate orientation of imperatives is rooted in the necessity or deontic modality of the requested future action. But this position is controversial. Portner (2007: 381) argues that imperatives are not modal clauses. Rather, deontic modality and imperativity relate to two different components of the discourse: 'Modality relates to Common Ground and imperatives to the To-Do List, and neither should be reduced to the other'.

72 *Pyr.* §124a–c/W [Spell 207] (Sethe 1908: 71). The change from utterance-final vocatives, which function as summons, and utterance-initial vocatives, which function as calls, is noteworthy but

I will briefly touch upon the non-specific interpretation of the bare indefinite noun *ḫt* as an existential quantifier pronoun 'something'. It is well known from the semantic literature that sentences with indefinite nouns are often ambiguous between a presuppositional reading, where the speaker does not find the appropriate value for the novel discourse referent, and a non-presuppositional reading, where the speaker has no such referent in mind. Janet Dean Fodor & Ivan Sag (1982) provide a useful list of indicators favoring a specific or a non-specific reading of indefinites.[73] As a rule of thumb, it can be said that the more descriptive content an indefinite nominal has the more likely it is for it to be interpreted specifically. As is relevant to the topic at hand, there is also a connection with speech act types. Klaus von Heusinger (2011) makes the interesting observation that imperatives and other directive speech acts only admit the non-presuppositional reading of indefinites.[74] In indefinite possession sentences with a directive speech act reading, it can safely be assumed that the indefinite possessee in subject position is interpreted as a non-specific indefinite or as a free choice item.[75]

With this digression out of the way, let us return to the illocutionary opacity of dative possessive sentences with indefinite subjects. Prima facie, the variant *ḫt n-nb-w* 'Something (to eat) for the Lords' is interpretable as a declarative statement or as a directive speech act. One way to address this problem would be to say that the indefinite possession sentence is asymmetrically coordinated with the agentless passive sentence *jd(-w) ꜣḫt n-Ḥr Nḫn* 'the horizon is censed for Horus of Nekhen', which marks the opening of the ritual spell. In asyndetic clause coordination, both conjuncts must be 'clausal' in the broadest sense, including predicate coordination.[76] Moreover, the linear order of the coordinated clauses reflects the temporal sequence of events and often implies a cause-effect relationship.[77] In

---

cannot be addressed in this paper. There are two more occurrences of the plain indefinite possession construction *ḫt n(=j) sšm* in the Pyramid Texts, viz. (i) *ṯḥnn-t(j) ṯḥnn-t(j) jḫt n(=j) sšm-w* 'There should be rejoicing. There should be rejoicing. Something (to eat) for me, butchers!'(*Pyr.* §561d/T) (Sethe 1908: 289) and (ii) *jḫt n(=j) sšm jḫt n(=j) jwn* 'Something (to eat) for me, butcher! Something (to eat) for me, pillar!' (*Pyr.* §571a/T) (Sethe 1908: 294). Intriguingly, the Unas version of *Pyr.* §124a–b has almost verbatim been preserved in the main text of a Middle Kingdom limestone stele, which is attributed to an individual called Nehy. The text runs as follows: *ḫt n(=j) sšm ḫt n(=j) sšm ḫt n(=j) jm(-y) jrt Rꜥ ḫt n(=j) wjꜣ ꜥq m* (for *jm(-y)*) *jrt nṯr* 'Something (to eat) for me, butcher! Something (to eat) for me, butcher! Something (to eat) <for me>, you who (is) in the eye of Re! Something (to eat) for me, you who enters the bark (of Re), which (is) in the eye of the God!' (stele Cairo CG 20520 Inscription d, 28–29) (Lange and Schäfer 1908:119). The Middle Kingdom version is philologically interesting for the two following reasons. On the one hand, it is proof for the scribal omission of the dative clitic first person singular *n(=j)* in *sšm ḫt <n(=j)> jm(-y) jrt Rꜥ*. On the other hand, it is evidence for the atypical graphic reversal of the perfective active participle *ꜥq* 'entering' and the nominal direct object *wjꜣ* 'bark'. Franke (2003: 115) and Hays (2012: 105) offer a detailed discussion of the transmission process.

73 Fodor & Sag (1982: 365–78).

74 von Heusinger (2011: 1030).

75 To be sure, this does not solve the philological problem that the standard translation of *ḫt* as 'meal' is solely based on the accompanying bread and beer determinative for food provisions (Gardiner 1957: 531, sign-list X2). Here I propose that there is only a single lexical item, viz. the generic noun *ḫt* 'thing', which refers to some indeterminate or non-specified object.

76 Haspelmath (2007: 7–8).

77 See Reintges (2010: 216–17) for asymmetric clause coordination in Coptic.

the above coordinate structure, it is not particularly evident that the situation described in the first sentence (the burning of incense) is temporally or causally related the situation described in the second sentence (the tendering of foodstuffs). It rather looks as if the relevant link between the two clausal conjuncts lies in the contrastive topicalization of the dative beneficiaries *n-Ḥr* 'for Horus' and *n-nb-w* 'to the Lords'.[78] Although an asyndetic coordination analysis strikes me as perfectly natural, an alternative analysis in terms of mixed illocutionary acts (assertion > directive speech act) cannot a priori be excluded. And so, the problem of illocutionary fuzziness is real.

(7) Indefinite possession sentence with possible declarative or directive illocution

jd(-w)	*ꜣḫt*	*n-*	*Ḥr*	*Nḫn*	*ḫt*	*n- nb-w*
cense(-PASS$_1$)	horizon.F.SG	for-	Horus	Nekhen	thing.F.SG	for- lord–M.PL

'The horizon is censed for Horus of Nekhen. Something (to eat) (belongs) to the Lords!'[79]

Illocutionary ambiguities disappear in embedded clause contexts. The issue of illocutionary force in lexically selected complement clauses is less controversial for directive speech acts, which generally are banned from embedded clause contexts.[80] Earlier on in this paper (§2), the ancient invocation offering formula *pr-t ḫrw n-* was analyzed as a dative possessive sentence with a maximizing free relative clause in subject position. Despite its early attestation and fixed syntax, the construction can be embedded into an adverbial purpose or result clause. The purpose clause itself is introduced by the compound complementizer *n-mrwt* 'so that' when the outcome is positive.

(8) Embedded *pr-t ḫrw n-* construction with declarative illocution

jr(=j)	*nw*	*n- jt(=j)*	*n- sn-w(=j)*	
make.PFV=1SG	DEM.PL	for father.M.SG=POSS.1SG	for- brother-M.PL=POSS.1SG	
n-mrwt	[$_{RC}$ *pr*	*ḫrw*]	*n=sn*	*ḥnʿ(=j)*
for-love.F.SG	come.PTCP.PERF.ACT.M.SG	voice.M.SG	to=3PL	with=1SG
m	*jšt(=j)*			
from	thing.F.SG(=POSS.1SG)			

'I made this for my father and my brothers such that an invocation offering ('what comes out on account of the voice') (would be) (allocated) to them and me together from my property'.[81]

78 In her analysis of English ditransitive constructions, Goldberg (1995: 150) proposes that 'actions which are performed for the benefit of a person are understood as objects that are transferred to that person'. The point of interest here is that the external possessor analysis ties in nicely with the predicatively used dative possessor, which can also be conceptualized as the beneficiary without exerting control of the transfer process.

79 *Pyr.* §296a/W [Spell 255] (Sethe 1908: 159). Allen's (2017: 330–31) reconstruction *ḫt n.(j) nbw* 'A meal for me, lords!' is not very well supported by the context.

80 Sadock & Zwicky (1985: 174). However, Portner (2007: 357) calls attention to the fact that imperative clauses in Korean are embeddable under verbs that express orders, requests, suggestions and advice.

81 Urkunden I 206: 14–15 (Sethe 1933: 206).

Portner (2018) argues that purposive complementizers incorporate into their semantics a causal connotation 'because x wants and intends p', with the variable x being bound by the matrix clause subject.[82] The intentional reading of these complementizers often goes together with the selection of the subjunctive mood in the adverbial purpose clause. The indefinite reading of free relatives does not come as a free rider but needs a special licensing context (see above footnote 39). Although this point requires further clarification, it stands to reason that subjunctive complementation furnishes such a context.

5 Quantificational predicative possession sentences

Quantificational predicative possession sentences are those which have a universally quantified noun phrase as their subject. Traditionally, the quantifier word *nb* is analyzed as an attributive modifier that relies on being adjacent to the modified noun. The adjectival analysis accommodates the agreement behavior of the universal quantifier, whose inflected forms vary according to the gender and number to the preceding head noun. It fares less well in accounting for the distributional differences with adjectival participles, bearing in mind that the quantifier *nb* can never stand on its own as an independent nominal argument. The complementary distribution with demonstrative pronouns provides suggestive evidence that it is a determiner-like element itself. Considering how understudied quantificational phenomena are in Egyptological linguistics, the observations and comments that follow can only be seen as a prelude to future inquiry.[83] As for its typological classification, Early Egyptian belongs to a group of languages that possess but one universal quantifier.[84] In this connection, David Gil (1995) notes that such singleton quantifiers are of the collective *all* NP type, which represents a semantic primitive.[85] Distributive quantifiers of the '*every* NP' type are semantically more complex in combining the quantificational force of a universal quantifier with an extra semantic component pertaining to distributivity.[86] The postnominal universal quantifier *nb* is ambiguous between a collective, a distributive and a negative polarity/free choice reading. The latter interpretation can only be found in negative and modal contexts and will not be considered any further. As predicted by Gil's generalization, the collective reading of the quantifier emerges as the default with singular number nouns, whereas the distributive reading is bound to the notion of semantic plurality.

82 Portner (2018: 108).

83 Edel (1955/1964: 151 §349).

84 As a working hypothesis, the quantificational determiner *nb* can only be combined with bare indefinites, whereas the universal adverbial quantifier *r-ḏr=* 'entirely, completely' must be selected in those contexts in which the head noun is a definite or a possessive description. As pointed out by Haspelmath (1995: 368–69), the adverbial quantifier *r-ḏr=* is not part of the noun phrase that it quantifies over. Rather, the relation between the two constituents is anaphoric, with the possessive pronoun on the adverbial quantifier being co-referential with the quantified noun phrase.

85 Gil (1995: 330).

86 Gil (1995: 322–26).

5.1 Mass-quantificational predicative possession sentences

Besides markedness considerations, the collective and the distributional readings of universally quantified noun phrases are to large extent predictable from the descriptive content of the head noun. This brings me to briefly touch upon the partitioning of the nominal lexicon into countable and uncountable nouns. Examples of countable common nouns are *student, book, lemon,* and *idea,* which refer to concrete individuals, objects or abstract concepts. Such nouns have a sortal semantics, specifying enumerable sets of individuals and objects that are properly individuated. Examples for non-countable common nouns are *water, gold, wood* and *health,* which refer to liquids, substances, materials and physical or mental states. Such nouns have cumulative reference, which is why they are more precisely labelled as mass nouns.

Tackling the count–mass noun distinction from a typological perspective, Jenny Doetjes (2011) finds that the presence or absence of inflectional number marking is a valid criterion for separating count from mass nouns crosslinguistically.[87] Early Egyptian fits the bill as count nouns readily admit dual and plural inflections, whereas mass nouns can only be inflected for grammatical gender but not for non-singular numbers. Due to their low text frequency, quantificational possession sentences are certainly not the best test-cases to trace the semantic effects of the count–mass division, but the few attested examples give us a small glimpse at the phenomenon. In the single-utterance spell given below, the universally quantified noun phrase *ᶜnẖ nb* 'all life' in subject position displays the collective reading of the quantifier *nb*.

(9) Mass-quantificational possession sentence with quantificational temporal adverb *ḏt*

ᶜnẖ	*nb*	*n-*	*Mrjj-Rᶜ*	*pn*	*ḏt*
life.M.SG	every.M.SG	to-	Mery-Re	DEM.M.SG	forever

'All life (belongs) to this (King) Mery-Re (here) forever'.[88]

Another conspicuous feature of the above sentence is the universal temporal adverb *ḏt* 'forever', which takes wide scope over the entire sentence, thereby including the quantificational NP *ᶜnẖ nb* 'all life' in its domain. The resulting reading is one in which the possessive predication is spread out over an infinite period of time.[89]

5.2 Count-quantificational predicative possession sentences

Count-quantificational predicative possession sentences are difficult to come by, but one of the rare examples is presented below. It comes from a bucolic scenery, in which the

87 Doetjes (2011: 2562).

88 *Pyr.* §1352/P [Spell 552]. The reading *ᶜnẖ nb* can be found in the facsimile of [P/V/S 41] in Berger-el Naggar, Leclant, Mathieu & Pierre-Croisiau (2010, pl. 21) re-edition of the Pyramid Text.

89 When determining a mass noun, the definite article *the* can assume a hidden maximality interpretation. The minimal sentence pair *the bread is moldy* vs. *all the bread is moldy* asserts that the totality of the bread as a substance has become rancid. The universal quantifier *all* in pre-article position reinforces the maximality interpretation that is inherent to definite mass nouns (Higginbotham 1994: 474–75).

deceased king benefits indirectly from a chain of food supply that originates in the Nile's delta marshes. All products brought forth by Sakhet, the Lady of the Marshes, belong to her son Ḥāb, the personification of fishing and fowling, who joins the deceased for supper. Despite the overall transparent content and context, the crucial text passage *jr(-w)-t nb Sḫt n-sꜣ=s Ḥꜣb* 'every product ("what is made") by the Lady of the Marshes (belongs) to her son Bird-catch' is fraught with philological and linguistic problems, which will be addressed in turn.

Akin to invocation offering formula *pr-t ḫrw n-*, the possessee subject is represented by a headless participial relative clause. This time, however, the free relative is formed with a perfective passive participle *jr(-w)-t* 'what is produced', which I propose to render by the generic noun 'product'. The placement of the universal quantifier *nb* between the passive participle *jr(-w)-t* and the construct-state possessor *Sḫt* is not necessarily a syntactic anomaly, considering that demonstrative pronouns and quantifiers are the modifiers closest to the head noun, while attributive or possessive modifiers are further removed from it.[90] I will be brief about the mismatch between the feminine gender of the passive participle *jr(-w)-t* and the masculine gender of the quantifier *nb*. In a statistical study on nominal concord in Old Egyptian, Gunnar Sperveslage (2010) concludes that the attributive universal quantifier *nb* agrees with the head noun in feminine gender and plural masculine number in only 15,5% of all Pyramid Text attestations.[91] Accordingly, the non-agreeing cases must be considered the paradigmatic ones. An alternative way to look at the agreement mismatch would be to say that the masculine singular form of the quantifier does not literally express [+male] gender but rather indicates the absence of gender values, which corresponds to neuter gender in many languages.

(10) Count-quantificational predicative possession sentence with free relative clause

a. *jr(-w)-t* *nb* *Sḫt* *n-* *sꜣ=s*
make(–PASS$_1$)–PTCP.F.SG every.M.SG marsh.F.SG for- son.M.SG=POSS.3F.SG
Ḥꜣb
bird-catch.M.SG
wnm *Nfr-kꜣ-Rꜥ* *ḥnꜥ=f* *m* *hrw* *pn*
eat.PFV Nefer-ka-Re with=3M.SG on day.M.SG DEM.M.SG

"Every product ('what is made') by the Lady of the Marsh (belongs) to her son Bird-catch. (King) Nefer-ka-Re will dine with him today."[92]

a'. Free passive participle relative: [$_{RC}$ [$_{pass.\ participle}$ *jr(-w)-t* __ *nb* [$_{possessor/agent}$ *Sḫt*]]]

Jacobson notes that free relative clauses 'at times seem to be singular definites and at times universals' and explains this ambiguity in terms of their maximizing semantics.[93] To elaborate, if the maximal entity equals only one atomic entity, then the free relative

90 Cf. Edel (1955/1964: 154 §§355–56).

91 Sperveslage (2010: 229–31). *Pyr.* §555d is classified as a standard non-agreeing case on p. 233 (Appendix).

92 *Pyr.* §555d–e/N (Sethe 1908: 285). Allen (2005: 74) mistook the quantifier *nb* as the common noun *nb* 'Lord': '[Whatever the Lord of the Marsh might make is for] its [son] Birdcatch'.

93 Jacobson (1995: 468).

will be interpreted as a singular definite noun phrase. On the other hand, if it comprises several such atomic entities, the maximal entity will be interpreted as universal. But then one might wonder how the passive participial relative clause is interpreted as an universal in the absence of plural morphology. In the Old Egyptian record, the feminine plural marker -*wt* is not attested for attributive participles and the quantifier *nb*.[94] Neither is there evidence for verbal plurality, bearing in mind that the passive participle *jr(-w)-t* appears in its perfective aspect form.[95] This leads me to suggest that the headless participial relative clause has the denotation of a singular count noun and imposes a distributive 'every, each' reading on the universal quantifier *nb*.

6 Definite predicative possession sentences

As noted before (§4), a shortcoming of Stassen's restrictive typology is that possessive constructions with definite possessees are not taken account of, although this type of possessive pattern is relatively well attested. The analysis of definite predicative possession is closely related to the question of definiteness marking crosslinguistically. Early Egyptian belongs to a group of languages that lack grammaticalized article forms.[96] As a result, articleless bare nouns can be interpreted as either indefinite or as definite descriptions. This raises an important issue as to how to distinguish the referential status of a nominal expression (i.e., its indefiniteness or definiteness) in the absence of the relevant morphological distinctions. The extensive literature on this subject is replete with remarks about the interplay between linguistic and contextual factors in the resolution of referential ambiguities. This section focuses on three environments that prompt a definite reading of the bare possessee nominal without taking recourse to possessive pronouns and demonstrative forms. These are (i) the immediate situation context (§6.1), (ii) the modificational relative clause context (§6.2) and (iii) the topic continuity in discourse context (§6.3).

94 Sperveslage (2010: 226–29). This statement needs to be further qualified. There is no problem in analyzing the ending -*j.t* as an allomorph of the feminine plural inflection -*w.t*.

95 According to Schenkel (1965), the selection of perfective and imperfective participles is correlated with the singular or plural number of the passive agent. For conceptual reasons, it would be desirable to incorporate verbal plurality directly into the semantics of imperfectivity, but a more detailed discussion would take us too far afield.

96 In Dryer's (2013) typological overview of article systems, 216 languages out of a total sample of 620 languages are identified as having morphologically distinctive definite articles, that is more than one third (35%). A smaller group of 198 languages lacks definite article forms, that is slightly less than one third (32%) of the sample. As for the geographical distribution, languages with definite article systems are particularly common in Western Europe with the notable exception of Slavic languages. Outside of the European continent articleless languages are well attested in the Pacific and in a wide belt across central Africa but not in the southern parts of the continent. Languages with definite article systems but with bare noun indefinites are not particularly common in Asia and South America. Lyons (1999: 48–49) furthermore observes that definiteness marking by means of non-demonstrative articles often emerges an area-linguistic feature.

6.1 The immediate situation context

The immediate situation context is a particular kind of discourse situation in which the speaker and the addressee are located within the same physical environment as the entity they are referring to. This is the relevant pragmatic environment in which definite articles can be used felicitously in those languages that have them.[97] By analogy, this is also where bare nouns have a definite reading in articleless languages. The immediate situation context is well documented in the collection of workmen's speeches and exclamations in the daily life scenes of Old Kingdom elite tombs. Albeit not being an authentic replication of the colloquial language, the '*Reden und Rufe*' genre (after Adolf Erman's 1919 original study) can be considered a unique linguistic register.[98] The following speech caption appears on top of a clap-netting of waterfowl scene. It encompasses two paratactic sentences with different illocutionary forces. The initial imperative sentence *jṯ r=k* 'Pull right now!' instructs the addressee to close a net of honking wild ducks in one fell swoop. The auxiliary-headed definite predicative possession sentence *jw ḥ(ꜣ)b n=k* 'The bird catch (is up) to you' is uttered with emphasis, drawing the addressee's attention to the captured waterbirds in his perceptual field.

(11) Auxiliary-headed definite possession sentence with bare possessee noun

jṯ	*r=k*	[$_{RC}$ *nt(j)*__	*ḥnꜥ(=j)*]
pull.IMP.SG	PCL=2M.SG	COMP.REL.M.SG	with=1SG

jw	*ḥ(ꜣ)b*	*n=k*
AUX	bird-catch.M.SG	to=2M.SG

'Pull right now, my comrade (the one with me)! The bird-catch (is up) to you'.[99]

A conspicuous feature of the above definite predicative possession sentence is the presence of the auxiliary verb *jw*, which anchors the utterance to the immediate situation context and signals the 'directing' intention of the speaker. In this way, the entity in the perceptual field that the speaker is focusing on becomes readily identifiable for the addressee.[100]

---

97 Lyons (1999: 3–4).

98 Motte (2017: 308). Elsewhere (Reintges 2011: 9–12) I draw a connection between such codified forms of spoken discourse and the oral-poetic linguistic mode of Pyramid Text discourse.

99 Tomb of Ptah-hotep at Saqqara, South Wall, East Half (Quibell 1898, pl. 32). Erman's (1919: 37) translation '*zieh, mein Genosse, es ist ein Fang für dich*' ('Pull, my comrade, there is a catch for you') and his nota bene '*das heißt: was wir heut dem Herrn fangen, bekommen wir ja selbst zu essen*' ('that is: whatever we catch for the lord today, we will get to eat ourselves') accentuates the possessive sense of the *jw*–headed sentence, which is however translated as an existential. Erman (1919: 37 footnote 6) further notes the non-canonical position of the predicative dative clitic *n=k* 'to you' to the left of the subject expression *ḥ(ꜣ)b*, which diverges from the expected clause-second position of clitic pronouns. The non-application of pronominal dative shift is made possible by the accentuation of the dative clitic in sentence-final position (for further details see Reintges 2016: 67–70).

100 There are many aspects on auxiliary-headed adverbial sentences that I would like to comment on and explore in further details. Due to space consideration, I shall focus on some key aspects and refer the interested reader to Loprieno, Müller & Uljas' (2019: 153–57) for a more comprehensive treatment. First of all, the deictic motion verb *jw* and the homophonous auxiliary represents a

The utterances of commoners in the daily life scenes are presented as spontaneous speech, including conversational, casual and colloquial speech. However, this should not distract from the fact that the '*Reden und Rufe*' display a tendency towards formulaic language use, with little room for linguistic creativity and stylistic variation. The speech caption presented below, which, like the preceding one, appears on top of a clap-netting of water-birds scene, is structured in a parallel way and combines a directive and a declarative speech-act. The imperative sentence *wn=ṯn r=s* 'Hurry up to it (the clap-net)!' expresses the 'topos of haste' and underscores the urgency of the task at hand, which requires all hands on deck.[101] The dative possessive sentence *jw ḥ(ꜣ)b nfr jm <n-> kꜣ* 'The nice bird-catch (over) there (belongs) to the Double (of)' is not a direct continuation of the imperative but rather refers to a third party (the deceased tomb owner) benefiting from the waterfowl catching. The not-so-bare possessee noun phrase *ḥ(ꜣ)b nfr jm* 'the nice bird-catch over there' can only be interpreted as an immediate situation definite description. But this interpretation is not brought about by noun phrase-internal modification but rather originates in the anchoring and directing role of the auxiliary verb *jw*. Apart from signaling a positive attitude on part of the speaker, evaluative adjectives like *nfr* 'beautiful, wonderful, nice' do not have sufficient semantic weight to contribute to ambiguity resolution.[102] The distal locative adverb *jm* '(over) there' expresses a by comparison weaker notion of spatial grounding than the auxiliary *jw*.[103]

(12) Auxiliary-headed definite possession sentence with not-so-bare possessee

wn	*=ṯ<n>*	*r=s*
hurry.IMP	=CL.2PL	to=3F.SG

jw	*ḥ(ꜣ)b*	*nfr*	*jm*	*<n->*	*kꜣ*	[…]
AUX	bird-catch.M.SG	be_nice(-PTCP.ACT.M.SG)	there	to	Double.M.SG	

'Hurry up, you (guys) towards it (the clap-net)! The nice bird-catch (over) there (belongs) to the Double (of) […]'.[104]

---

complex case of grammaticalization. The lexical source verb indicates movement towards the deictic center. The lexical verb and the auxiliary *jw* differ syntactically from each other in that the latter resists clausal embedding. The restriction of the auxiliary to main sentences may have initiated a further grammaticalization process into declarative marker.

101 Motte (2017: 305).

102 Evaluative adjectives are organized in antonymic pairs such as *good–bad*, *beautiful–ugly*, for which no external comparison class is necessary. It is the speaker's positive or negative attitude towards the referent that determines the use of such subjective-comment adjectives. See Kotowski (2016: 48–52) for concise survey of the literature.

103 Edel (1955/1964: 89–90 §202) calls attention to the fact that the nisbe form *jm(–y)* can replace distal demonstratives and mentions in this connection the honorific use of *bꜣk jm(-y)* 'the servant over there' as the self-referring designation of a socially inferior writer of a letter to his superior.

104 Tomb of Shepsi-pu-Min/Kheni at Akhmim, Chapel, North wall west of the shrine (scene C), 1st register (Kanawati 1981, fig. 22, pl. 6b). In the *Reden und Rufe* genre, the collective noun *ḥꜣb* 'bird-catch' is often used near-synonymously with the term *kꜣ* '(food) supply'. Thus, compare: *wḥꜥ pw jw kꜣ n-Zzj* "oh fowler, the (food) supply (belongs) to Zezi" vs. *jw ḥꜣb n-ꜥ=k wḥꜥ pw* 'The bird-catch (belongs) to your arm, fowler' (Mastaba of Ankh-ma-Hor, 2nd room, Western wall) (Badawy 1978, fig.33). Erman (1919: 37) proposes a literal translation of the latter sentence as:

In being anchored to the immediate situation, the possessive relation is presented as episodic. Dative possessive sentences with immediate situation definites do not fit very well into Stassen's classification and correspond only approximately to the category of temporary alienable possession.

6.2 The modificational relative clause context

If the analysis developed so far is on the right track, one would not expect the aspecto-temporal auxiliary *jw* to be selected in non-episodic contexts, in which the relation between the possessee and the possessor is perceived as temporally continuous. As far as I can see, this prediction is borne out by the evidence. The contrast between episodic and non-episodic possessive sentences is exemplified by the below Pyramid Text passage. In announcing the (re)entrance of the main protagonist on stage, the motion verb sentence *jj r=f Wnjs pn* 'Here comes indeed (King) Unas' has a presentational flavor. This interpretative effect is brought about by the present tense form of the movement verb *jj* 'to go/come', which has an egophoric component and indicates a trajectory towards the location of the speaker. From recent work by Jim Wood & Raffaella Zanuttini (2023), I adopt the idea that the present tense specification requires that the movement on that trajectory is 'still ongoing while the speaker is speaking'.[105] In contrast to the paragraph-initial presentative construction, the following definite predicative possession sentence *jmn-tj-w jm(-y)-w tꜣ n-Wnjs pn* 'the Westerners, who are on earth, (belong) to (King) Unas' conveys a non-episodic present tense interpretation. This is then a case of a gnomic present tense stating a general truth. The relation between the possessee and the possessor holds at all times, including the time of the utterance.

(13) Definite possession sentence with plural-inflected head noun plus relative clause

jj *r=f* *Wnjs* *pn* *ḫwrr* *psḏt*
come.PFV PCL=3M.SG Unas DEM.M.SG fledging.M.SG ennead.F.SG
ꜣḫ [RC *j-ḫm* sk]
spirit.M.SG AUG–not.know(–PTCP.M.SG) destroy.INF
jmn-tj-w [RC *jm(-y)-w* *tꜣ*] *n-* *Wnjs* *pn*
west-NMNLZR-M.PL in(-NMNLZR)-M.PL earth.M.SG to- Unas DEM.M.SG
'Here comes indeed (King) Unas, the Ennead's fledging, a spirit being that cannot

'*es ist ein Fang für deine Hand, Vogelfänger*' ('it is a catch for your hand, fowler') but does not further comment on the conspicuous use of the compound preposition *n-ꜥ=k* en lieu of the dative clitic *n=k*. It would not be unreasonable to assume that the expression *n-ꜥ=k* is a hitherto unattested variant of the compound preposition *m-ꜥ=k* 'through your arm', which is used here to underscore the aspect of physical control in alienable possession. Given that *kꜣ* in the sense of food supply can be used interchangeably with *ḥꜣb*, it stands to reason that the two collective nouns are not used simultaneously as the possessee and the dative possessor, respectively. Kanawati (1981: 26) translates the dative possessive construction as an existential sentence: 'There is a fine catch here for the ka of…', while I understand the not-so-bare NP *ḥ(ꜣ)b nfr jm* 'the nice bird-catch over there' as an immediate situation definite.

105 Wood & Zanuttini (2023: 573 footnote 11).

be destroyed (lit. who does not know destroying). The Westerners, who are on earth, (belong) to this (King) Unas here'.[106]

The possessee *jmn-tj-w* is not a bare noun but a noun bearing plural number morphology. If the gnomic present tense reference blocks the selection of the auxiliary *jw*, how is the possessee's definite status to be explained? As pointed out by several researchers, plural count nouns that denote nationalities, countries or regions are often interpreted generically as kind-referring rather than individual-referring expressions.[107] But now observe that the plural definite refers a particular kind of inhabitants, namely those that occupy the western regions of Egypt. As noted by Klaus von Heusinger, restrictive relative clauses with lengthy descriptions impose a specific-definite interpretation on the head of the relative construction. The specificity bias is even more pronounced in non-restrictive relatives.[108] The locative relative clause *jm(-y)-w tꜣ* 'who are on earth' is clearly of the non-restrictive kind but still provides further information about the intended referent of the relative head. This seems to block a generic interpretation of the bare plural noun *jmn-tj-w*, which can only be interpreted as a specific definite.

6.3 The topic continuity context

There is another pragmatic context for definite resolution, which has not been discussed so far. This is the topic continuity in discourse context in which the definite reference of a bare noun rests upon a second-mention basis. This definiteness context is not very well documented since lexical noun phrases are rarely used as anaphors. That said, the following passage from a serpent incantation can cogently be interpreted in this way. For the sake of argument, I consider the hapax legomenon *nẖj* to designate a species of smaller-sized poisonous serpentes.

(14) Definite possession sentence with identical first and second mention noun

ṯbwt	*Ḥr*	*ẖnd-t(j)*	*nẖj*
sandal.F.SG	Horus	tread–STAT.3F	poisonous_snake.M.SG

nẖj	*n-*	*Ḥr*	*ẖrd*	*nẖn*
poisonous_snake.M.SG	for	Horus	child.M.SG	be_infant(PTCP.ACT.M.SG)

[$_{RC}$ *dbꜥ=f*	*m*	*rꜣ=f*]
finger.M.SG=POSS.3M.SG	in	mouth.M.SG=POSS.3M.SG

'The sandal of Horus has trodden upon a (poisonous) *Nekhi* snake. The *Nekhi*

106 *Pyr.* §§164c–d/W [Spell 218] (Sethe 1908: 92). The interpretational difficulty of this passage lies in the epithet *ẖwrr psḏt*. Sethe (1962 vol. I 64–65) speculates that the epithet *ẖwrr* designates an importuning property of young calves when they are thirsty for milk. Allen (2005: 34) and Hays (2012: 350) render *ẖwrr* as 'fledging, new-born', which makes good sense in the present context. See Sethe (1962 vol. I 72) for the interpretation of the locative relative clause *jm(-y)-w tꜣ* 'who are on earth' as '„im Lande", d.h. in Ägypten' ("'in the country", i.e. in Egypt').

107 Cf. Huddleston (1984: 249, 255) and Lyons (1999: 181–82).

108 von Heusinger (2011: 1030).

snake (belongs) to Horus, the infant child whose (is) his finger in his mouth'.[109]

The first and second mention of the topic referent *nḫj* are anaphorically linked to each other, forming what one might call a referential chain. In lines with Heim's Novelty and Familiarity conditions, the first mention of a noun is indefinite and all subsequent references to this noun are definite. The second mention of the referent *nḫj* occurs in the successive dative predicative possession clause *nḫj n-Ḥr ẖrd nḫn* 'the *Nekhi* snake (belongs) to Horus, the infant child' and is only interpretable as a familiar topic definite. The possessee–possessor relation is difficult to classify but seems to indicate momentaneous possession with strong implications of possessor control. On a final note it should be mentioned that the change from direct object to subject is consistent with the observation made by Tanya Reinhart (1981), according to which familiar topics are preferably encoded as sentence subjects.[110]

7 Demonstrative predicative possession sentences

In an articleless language like Early Egyptian, definiteness as such may be reflected in other ways by using demonstratives or possessives. The interpretative effects of demonstrative and possessive modification are comparable insofar as they render the referent of the modified noun phrase pragmatically more prominent. On the other hand, demonstrative and double possessor predicative possession constructions are different from each other both syntactically and semantically, which is why they are best discussed separately in two successive sections. This section concentrates on demonstrative predicative possession sentences, in which the possessee in subject position is not a bare noun but a fully-fledged determiner phrase with a demonstrative article form.

Before we look at the actual data, there is an important point to highlight here and that is the relevant conditions for demonstrative and definite semantics. The universality of demonstrative systems has led one researcher to the conclude that 'definiteness exists in some form in all languages'.[111] To be sure, an important fact about demonstrative noun phrases is their definite reference status. However, if definite and demonstrative possessees were interchangeable in their referential use, the relevant constructions containing them would constitute a single class of definite possession sentences. Despite its initial appeal, such an unifying treatment is open to challenge. In particular, it falls short of accounting for the semantically contrastive behavior of the two types of definites, which also has a structural correlate in the absence and presence, respectively, of an overt determiner. Dorothy Ahn (2019) tackles these thorny issues from a novel perspective. The main tenet of her proposal is that demonstrative articles and pronouns have an extra layer of meaning

109 *Pyr.* §663b–c/T [Spell 378] (Sethe 1908: 364). Leitz (1996: 385, 426) analyses *nḫỉ n Ḥr* as a possessive noun phrase '*die nḫỉ Schlange des Horus*' ('the *nḫỉ* serpent of Horus'). This strikes me as contradictory: the child Horus has accidently trodden upon a poisonous snake and is subsequently presented as its 'owner'.

110 Reinhart (1981: 62).

111 Lyons (1999: 107).

on top of their definite reference. Regardless of their semantic complexity, demonstrative noun phrases have discourse referents that are contextually less salient than the referents of definite noun phrases, which are already part of the shared common ground. In other words, demonstrative noun phrases and demonstrative pronouns prefer non-topical discourse referents.[112]With this much about exophoric deixis in place, I will first look at the distributional behavior of demonstrative noun phrases and pronouns in the immediate situation context (§7.1). Demonstrative predicative possession sentences are sensitive to information structure, with topic-prominent possessees occurring in the topmost position of the sentence, i.e., outside of the dative possessive kernel sentence (§7.2).

7.1 Demonstrative noun phrases and pronouns in the immediate situation context

Early Egyptian has an elaborate demonstrative system, which is organized around a two-way proximal/distal contrast. Although further research on this domain is warranted, it can be said that the demonstrative pronoun series *pn*/*tn*/*nn* and *pw*/*tw*/*nw* '*this* NP (over here)' express proximal spatial deixis (vicinity to the speaker), whereas the series *pf*/*tf*/*nf* '*that* NP (over there)' marks distal deixis (distance from the speaker).[113] In terms of their syntactic distribution, demonstrative forms have a deictic use as postnominal determiners or an anaphoric use as third person pronouns. Unsurprisingly, demonstrative noun phrases and pronouns are permissible in the immediate situation context, which is the basic context for exophoric deixis.

In general, it looks as if dative possessive sentences with demonstrative possessee noun phrases are outnumbered by the corresponding constructions with demonstrative pronouns. This impressionistic statement needs to be tested against a much larger dataset to determine whether definite predicative possession sentences with bare possessees dominate the scene in immediate situation contexts – and if so, why? One of the rare examples can be found in the dialogue exchange between a father and a son in a caption on top of a boat-building scene. Following up on the father's directive [-A:] *jn n=n šs-w* 'Bring us (the) cords!', the son's response [-B:] *m(j) n=k šs pn* 'Look, this cord (here) (belongs) to you' is uttered on passing on the issued rope. In view of the performativity of the utterance, it makes sense to analyze the uninflected form *m*, which separates the vocative phrase *j jt(=j)* 'O (my) father' from the dative clitic *n=k* 'for you', as an instance of the addressee-oriented particle *m(j)* 'look'. As demonstrated through detailed analysis

112 To be more precise, Ahn (2019, chapter 4) argues that there are actually two properties that distinguish demonstratives from anaphoric pronouns and definite descriptions. Firstly, they allow exophoric uses where an entity present in the immediate situation is referred to. Secondly, they allow generic readings with relative clauses. The two defining properties of demonstrative terms can be subsumed under the broader category of non-familiarity, given that 'an exophoric use or a generic relative clause do not require that the referent be familiar in the context' (Ahn 2019: 128).

113 See Edel (1955/1964: 83–87 §§ 181–93) for an overview of the Early Egyptian demonstrative system and the proximal/distal distinction. The demonstrative system is diachronically unstable. For example, the demonstrative series *pꜣ*/*tꜣ*/*nꜣ* is only marginally attested in the Early Egyptian sources but subsequently gains a momentum and develops into the tripartite definite article system of later Egyptian (Edel 1955/1964: 87–88 §§194–95).

by Elsa Oréal (2011), this interactional particle can take noun phrases or clauses as complements.[114] In turn-taking (-A:, -B:) responses, such as the one presented below, it is used in its back-channeling and feedback-giving function, which is copiously attested in the '*Reden und Rufe*' genre. The word order Presentative particle *m(j)* > Dative clitic *n=k* > Demonstrative noun phrase *šs pn* arises as a consequence of pronominal object shift. During this syntactic reordering process, the dative clitic pronoun undergoes enclisis to the clause-initial element—the sentence-initial particle *m(j)* in the case at hand.

(15) Demonstrative predicative possession sentence with presentative particle *m(j)*

-A:	*j*	*Sbk-qꜣj*	*jn*	*n=n*	*šs–w*	
	VOC	Sobek-qai	bring.IMP	for=1PL	cord–M.PL	
	"Oh Sobek-qai, bring us (the) cords!"					
-B:	*j*	*jt(=j)*	*m(j)*	*n=k*	*šs*	*pn*
	VOC	father.M.SG=POSS.1SG	PRESENT.PCL	for=2M.SG	cord.M.SG	DEM.M.SG
	'O my father, look, this cord (here)(belongs) to you'.[115]					

It is a long-standing and somewhat puzzling observation that the demonstrative pronouns *nn*, *nw* and *nf*, despite their plural morphology, trigger singular masculine agreement.[116] The number mismatch is a good indication that these exclusively anaphoric demonstratives are collective plurals describing a group of entities as a single unit. Consider, in this regard, the following example an auxiliary-headed dative possessive sentence *jw nn n(=j)* 'This (group of fowl) (belongs) to me'. The demonstrative pronoun possessee *nn* in post-auxiliary position refers exophorically to a party of broken-winged geese. The monological utterance of the speaking individual is framed as a dialogue with the field goddess Sakhet, who is revered as *ḥnwt(=j)* 'My Mistress'. Access to the exophoric context must be overly marked by the auxiliary verb *jw*, which, as we have seen previously, encodes the spatial and temporal coordinates of the utterance. The dative clitic pronoun first person singular *n(=j)* 'to me' in predicative position carries the notions of possessor control and beneficiariness.

---

114 Cf. Oréal (2011: 300–304). The presentative particle *m(j)* bears some resemblance with the presentative word *Ecco* in Standard Italian, which tolerates a wide range of syntactic constituents in the particle-adjacent position. It stands to reason that *m(j)* like *Ecco* is a portmanteau morpheme, expressing the spatial and temporal coordinates of the presentative clause as well as having inherent present tense reference (for further details, see Woods & Zanuttini 2023: 595–97).

115 Mastaba of Ptah-hotep, South Wall, East Half (Quibell 1898, pl. 32). Quibell (1898: 29) translates the son's reply as follows: 'O father, here is this rope for thee'. Edel (1955/1964: 297 §611) analyzes the uninflected form *m* an instance of the suppletive imperative form *(j)m* 'Take!' and renders the utterance accordingly as: *j jtjj jm nk šs pn* '*oh mein Vater, nimm dir diesen Strick!*'('O my father, take this cord for you!'). From a philologist's standpoint, this interpretation is impeccable, especially when the orthographic details are taken into account. That said, it should not be overlooked that the register of the *Reden and Rufe* displays a somewhat fluid orthography. As noted by Edel himself (1955/1964: 298–299 §614), the suppletive imperative *(j)m* 'Take!' and the uninflected interjection *m(j)* 'Behold' can erroneously take the determinative of the forearm with a hand holding a conical or a rounded loaf of bread (Gardiner 1957: 454, sign-list D37). This paves the way for a new reading of this admittedly difficult passage as a demonstrative predicative possession construction with a presentational function.

116 For relevant data and discussion, see Edel (1955/1964: 88–89 §§196–98).

(16) Demonstrative possession sentence with the collective plural pronoun *nn*

jw	*nn*	*n(=j)*	*Sẖt*	*ḥnwt(=j)*
AUX	DEM.PL	to=1SG	marsh.F.SG	mistress.F.SG=POSS1.SG

'This (group of fowl) (belongs) to me, Sakhet, My Mistress'.[117]

The use of proximal/distal demonstrative pronouns has the advantage that a certain amount of vagueness is acceptable. Conversely, as pointed out by Ahn, anaphorically used demonstratives can only replace third person pronouns when exophoric deixis is crucial for referent tracking.[118]

7.2 Two kinds of topic-marking construction for prominent possessees

A little noticed fact about demonstrative possession sentences is their syntactically marked status. The modification of the possessee by a demonstrative article and a postnominal possessor phrase produces a referentially 'heavy' nominal constituent, which is no longer permissible in the subject position. Such prominent possessees must instead be attached high in the structure, i.e. outside of the subject–predicate core. The concern here is with two topic-marking constructions, in which the elevated position of the topic-prominent possessee can be diagnosed by its relative placement with respect to the auxiliary verb *jw*. A robust generalization about the syntax of auxiliary verbs is their complementary distribution with subordinating conjunctions. In previous work, I present a structural explanation for this co-occurrence restriction, in which the auxiliary and the subordinator compete for the same position.[119] In the cartographic syntax of Luigi Rizzi (1997), this is the Force head position, which encodes information about illocutionary force and syntactic dependencies.[120] In linearly preceding the auxiliary verb *jw*, the topic-prominent possessee must occupy an even higher position.

One topic marking construction is 'gapped' topicalization, an example of which is shown below. Reinhart posits a semantic restriction on the topic–comment split that is prompted by discourse pragmatics: the content of the comment clause should be interpretable as an inherent property of the topic referent.[121] Ellen Prince (1998) raises a closely related point when she writes: 'topicalization triggers an inference on part of the hearer that the entity represented by the initial NP stand in a salient (…) relation to some entity

117 Tomb of Ti, Chapel, Northern Wall, Western part, 3rd register from above (Steindorff 1913, pl. 117; Junker 1943: 45, fig. 12). Erman (1919: 39) correctly identified the dative possessive structure of the speech caption but did not consider the possibility that the dative preposition *n-* is a defectively written first person singular dative pronoun *n(=j)*: '*dies gehört dem Felde, meine Herrin*' ('That belongs to the field, My Mistress'). Junker (1943: 44–48) analyzed the toponym *sẖt* 'marsh, the Delta' as a nisbe-formation *sẖt(-j)* 'he who dwells in the marshes', which carries an autoreferential denotation: '*Das da ist für den Sumpfbewohner, das heißt, für mich*' ('That (over there) is for the marsh-lander, which means for me').

118 Ahn (2019: 158–59, 169).

119 Reintges (2016: 52–53).

120 Rizzi (1997: 283–85).

121 Reinhart (1981: 63–64).

or entities already evoked in the discourse model'.[122] Now this appears to be the case, as the demonstrative possessive phrase *t wᶜb pw n(j)=Wsjr* 'this pure bread of Osiris' stands in a possessive relation with the dative possessor *n-Zzj jmꜣḫ-w* 'to the revered Zezi'. The anaphoric linkage between the topic and the comment clause is marked by a phonologically invisible gap (indicated as $\_\__i$) in the subject position (whence the label 'gapped' topicalization).

(17) The gapped topicalization construction of topic-prominent possessees

a. *t* *wᶜb* *pw* *n(j)=* *Wsjr*
bread.M.SG be_pure(-PTCP.ACT.M.SG) DEM.M.SG LINK.M.SG= Osiris
jw $\_\__i$ *n-* *Zzj* *jmꜣḫ-w*
AUX to- Zezi revere-PASS$_1$(-PTCP.M.SG)
'That pure bread (i.e. food) of Osiris, (it) (belongs) to revered Zezi'.[123]

a'. $[_{\text{Topic}}$ *t wᶜb pw n(j)=Wsjr*$]_i$ $[_{\text{Gapped subject clause}}$ *jw* $\_\__i$ *n-Zzj*]]

Alice Davison (1984) advances a scale of syntactic markedness in which gapped topicalization occupies the top-ranking position. The reason is that 'an extra constituent must be matched with something within the clause'.[124] This topic-making construction is opposed to the corresponding pragmatically neutral declarative sentence.[125] But how come that gapped topicalization can be used felicitously in discourse-initial contexts? At the beginning of the interaction, there is simply not enough common ground that would allow the addressee to draw inferences about the upcoming discourse topic.[126] The situation at hand is different since an individual utterance does not represent a complete discourse but a just one piece of it. In an attempt to resolve this conundrum, I propose here that gapped topicalization is a compromise strategy used to balance two conflicting constraints. In preferring contextually less salient referents, demonstrative noun phrases on their own do not lend themselves as left-dislocated topic expressions. But additional modification by a

---

122 Prince (1998: 293).

123 Tomb of ᶜAnkh-mᶜa-Hor at Saqqara, Third Room, East Wall, 2nd register from above (Badawy 1978, fig. 37, pl. 49). The use of the bread sign *t* as an ideogram is rare (Gardiner 1957: 531 sign-list X1). The fact that the standard orthography with the bread loaf (Gardiner 1957: 531, sign-list X2) as a determinative is attested in the fourth register (*t wᶜb pw n(j)=Jnpw* 'this pure food (lit. bread) of Anubis') points in the direction of a simple scribal error. The analysis of the gapped topic construction posed considerable difficulties for previous interpreters of this speech caption. Erman's (1919: 33) translation '*diese reine Speise des Osiris, es gehört dem Sesi*' ('This pure food of Osiris, it belongs to Sesi') accords with my understanding of this passage. Lüddeckens (1943: 20) treats the demonstrative possessive noun phrase *t wᶜb pw n(j) Wsjr* as a bipartite nominal sentence, with the proximal demonstrative *pw* functioning as a pronominal subject: '*Das ist das reine Brot des Osiris*' ('This is the pure bread of Osiris'). The auxiliary *jw* headed comment clause is analyzed as an impersonal construction *jw n-Zzj jmꜣḫw* '*es ist für Ssj, den Ehrwürdigen*' ('it is for the venerable *Ssj*'). Edel (1955/1964: 467 §919a) interprets this sentence as a personal pronoun sentences with omission (*pro*-drop) of the subject pronoun in post-auxiliary *jw* position: '*es gehört dem Zzj*' ('it belongs to *Zzj*').

124 Davison (1984: 820).

125 Davison (1984: 807–09).

126 Prince (1998: 293–95).

nominal possessor makes the resulting constituent referentially too heavy such as to be admissible as an unmarked sentence topic in the subject position. The way out is to relocate the topic-prominent possessee *t wꜥb pw n(j)=Wsjr* in the roof top position of the possessive sentence, which thus becomes a more parsimonious expression.

'Aboutness shift' topicalization is another topic-marking construction, in which a lengthy and difficult to process constituent is directly merged into the topmost position of the sentence. In the below given example, the aboutness topic *jr sn-nw n(j) ꜣḥt sṯꜣt 2 pw n(j) pr ḫrw n(j)t mwt(=j)* (...) *Bbj* 'As for that other one of the two arouras belonging to the invocation offering of my mother (...) Bebi' is coded as a directional prepositional phrase. Due to its prepositional phrase format [prepositional head *jr*] + [noun complement]), the aboutness shift topic could not possibly have originated in the subject position, which only hosts categorially nominal constituents and their pronominal counterparts. All the same, the anaphoric link between the aboutness topic and the possessive sentence expressing the comment is established via a resumptive clitic pronoun that does not copy the prepositional head.

(18) The Aboutness topicalization construction of topic-prominent possessees

a. [*jr* *sn-nw* *n(j)* *ꜣḥt* *sṯꜣt* 2 *pw*
as.for second.M.SG LINK.M.SG field.F.SG aroura.F.SG 2 DEM.M.SG
n(j)= *pr* *ḫrw* *n(j)t=*
LINK.M.SG come.PTCP.PERF.ACT.M.SG voice.M.SG LINK.F.SG
mwt(=j) *rḫt* *njswt* *Bbj*]$_i$
mother.F.SG(=POSS.1SG) acquaintance.F.SG king.M.SG Bebi
jw *=f*$_i$ *n-* *sn* *ḏt* *ḥm–kꜣ*
AUX=CL.3M.SG for brother.M.SG estate.F.SG priest.M.SG–Double.M.SG
K(ꜣ)(=j)-m-nfrt
Kai-em-neferet

'As for that other one of the two arouras belonging to the invocation offering of my mother, the royal acquaintance Bebi, it (is allotted) to the co-proprietor of the estate, the funerary priest Kai-em-neferet'.[127]

a'. [$_{\text{Aboutness-shift Topic}}$ *jr sn-nw n(j) ꜣḥt sṯꜣt* 2 *pw* (…)]$_i$ [$_{\text{Comment Clause}}$ *jw=f*$_i$ *n-sn ḏt* (…)]]

Aboutness topicalization has a special discourse function. Valentina Bianchi & Mara Frascarelli (2010) argue that it is used to present a new discourse topic or to reintroduce a pre-established one, as in the above sentence. In effectuating a change in the common

127 Testament deed of Tjenti [Cairo JE 57139: 61–66 = Urkunden I 164:17–65:1 (Sethe 1933: 164–65)]. As first noted by Baer (1956: 116 footnote 10), the reduplicated ordinal number *sn-nw* (...) *sn-nw* is used in the passage under consideration as an identity-of-sense anaphora 'the one ... the other'. The first instance appears in an identical Aboutness-shift topic construction *jr jgr sn-nw n(j) ꜣḥt sṯꜣt* 2 (...) *jw=f n-ḥmt(=j) rḫt njswt Tp-m-nfrt* 'As for the one of the two arouras (...) it belongs to my wife, the royal acquaintance Tep-m-Neferet' [Urkunden I 163: 14–15 (Sethe 1933: 163)]. The measure noun *sṯꜣt* controls the masculine gender of both the demonstrative pronoun *pw* and the subject pronoun *=f* 'it'. Moreno García (2007: 126–36) discusses the legal connotations of title *sn-ḏt* in funerary service-related dispositions.

ground, this topic-marking construction is restricted to main clause environments.[128] The different coding of the anaphoric relation between the topic-prominent possessee and the comment clause argue for two separate derivations. According to Reinhart (1983), gapped topicalization involves a displacement process that leaves behind a gap in the subject position. This contrasts with the aboutness topicalization, in which the topic constituent has never been part of the comment clause but is attached high in the structure from the start.[129] All the same, I will make the simplifying assumption that the topic-prominent possessee ends up in the rooftop position of the sentence from where it precedes the auxiliary verb *jw*, but this point needs fine-tuning in future research.

8 Double predicative possessive sentences

The final section before the conclusions completes the classification by including double predicative possessive sentences. In this type of dative predicative possession, the possessee is modified by a possessor noun phrase or a possessive pronoun. The resulting construction is formally parallel to plain possessive sentences, albeit with the important difference that two rather than a single possessive relationship is entertained. One relation is internal possession in which the possessee and the possessor are contained within the same noun phrase. The other relation is external possession which pertains to the predicative dative possession. In combining adnominal and clausal possession, the double possessive construction is particularly interesting from a language-specific and a typological perspective. Two factors can be singled out that contribute to the polysemy of the construction. The first factor is the alienability split in the encoding of internal possession. As pointed out above (§2), the contrast between alienable and inalienable possessability covers some of the same ground as the two-way distinction between non-relational and relational nouns. One has to be careful, though, not to conflate (in)alienability and nominal relationality or to subsume one category under the other. The second factor is the disjoint or conjoint reference between the internal and the external possessor. In the disjoint reference case, the two possessors have different referents in the discourse, while they refer to the same referent in the conjoint case. The latter co-reference case includes the case of pronominal possessor indexing, in which the possessive pronoun on the possessee noun phrase is clitic-doubled by the predicative dative clitic. One such example has been discussed before (*mw=k n=k* 'Your water (belongs) to you(rself)!'; see above §2, example (1)).

8.1 Double predicative possessive sentences with alienably possessed noun phrases

The discussion that follows below focuses on double predicative possessive sentences, in which the possessee in subject position is alienably possessed and the external predicative

128 Bianchi & Frascarelli (2010: 54–56).
129 Reinhart (1983: 82–86).

possession is of the alienable type as well. Alienable possessive agreement with disjoined referenced possessors appears to be the standard scheme for this possessive construction. A garden-variety instance is found in the running title of a scene depicting a procession of offering bearer. The possessee head noun *t* 'bread' in absolute clause-initial position is modified attributively by the evaluative adjective *wᶜb* 'sacred' and possessively by the genitive case-marked possessor *n(j)=pr Ptḥ* 'of the House of Ptah'. Here the adjectival attribute is the closest modifier to the head, while the possessor is the outer modifier of the possessive noun phrase as a whole. The postmodifying possessor is not a possessor in the strict sense – a semantic role that is not entailed by toponyms like *pr Ptḥ*, which refers to the Great Temple of Ptah at Memphis as a repository of food provisions.[130] Rather, the internal possession relation is a spatial relation of provenance. The external possessor is the dative proper name *n-Mmj* 'to Memi', which denotes the deceased tomb owner as the beneficiary possessor of the depicted food supply. According to the situation context, the procession of offering bearers is ongoing at the time of the utterance. But there is an implicit presupposition that there will be other occasions in the future. The dative possessive sentence is therefore ambiguous between an episodic and a habitual present tense reading. The contrast between episodic and habitual present tense sentences is prompted by the nonappearance of the auxiliary *jw*.

(19) Double possessive sentence with disjoint-referenced internal and external possessor and attendant alienable predicative possession interpretation

t	*wᶜb*	*n(j)=*	*pr*	*Ptḥ*
bread.M.SG	be_sacred (PTCP.ACT.M.SG)	LINK.M.SG=	temple.M.SG	Ptah
n–	*Mmj*			
to–	Memi			

'The sacred bread (supply) of the Temple of Ptah (belongs) to Memi'.[131]

In the absence of pragmatic enrichment by means of auxiliary support or by exophoric deictic reference, the definite reference of the possessive noun phrase *t wᶜb n(j)=pr Ptḥ* must reside in the semantics of internal possession and can therefore be accounted for in compositional terms. Attributive modification cannot be the relevant factor, considering, as we have done previously (§6.1), that positive evaluation adjectives like *nfr* 'beautiful' and *wᶜb* 'sacred' are semantically too light as to permit successful referent identification. This leaves use with the disambiguating potential of possessive modification. Barker advances an interpretative principle adopted here, according to which 'a noun phrase containing a possessor phrase is definite (indefinite) just in case the possessor phrase is definite (indefinite)'.[132] In denoting an iconic landmark, the adjoined possessor *n(j)=pr Ptḥ* is inherently definite and identifiable and familiar in the same way as toponyms like *the White House*, *the Champs Elysée* or *the Vatican*.

130 Cf. Lüddeckens (1943: 20–21).

131 Tomb of Kagemni at Saqqara, Room II, Wall C, 1st register, Inscription 88 (von Bissing 1911: 16 and pl. 1a).

132 Barker (2000: 213 (6)).

We will now look at more complex double possessives sentences, which display alienability splits as well as a mixture of disjoint and conjoint reference properties. The following passage from an apotropaic text comprises two almost-identical instances of this construction. The first instance has as its subject the nested possessive noun phrase *t n(j)=jt=k* 'the bread of your father'. The adjoined possessor *n(j)=jt=k* itself is an inalienable possessive noun phrase formed from the kinship relational noun *jt* 'father'. The relational possessor argument is the 2nd person singular masculine pronoun *=k*, which is subsequently identified with the vocative proper noun *Jkj-nhjj* '(O) Iki-nekhi (snake)'. As an aside, it should be noted that the utterance-final vocative serves to consolidate the relation between the speaking performer and the addressed serpent adversary, which does no harm to him. But while the possessive and the dative clitic pronoun *n=k* 'to you(self)' are co-indexed with one another, the entire possessive noun phrase *t n(j)=jt=k* is disjoint-referenced with it. The resulting interpretation is one in which both the internal and the external possession relation is of the alienable type, without the inalienably possessed possessor interfering in it.

The double possessive sentence that follows can best be analyzed as containing the attributive apposition [*ntk n(j)=jt=k*] 'yours (and) your father's'. The apposition has the structure of an asyndetic noun coordination, with the prosodically independent pronoun second person singular masculine *ntk* serving as the first conjunct, and the second-mention possessor phrase *n(j)=jt=k* serving as the second conjunct. As noted by Rodney Huddleston, John Payne & Peter Peterson (2002), appositions are like coordinate constructions in that they are not syntactically dependent on a head but differ from them in that they are semantically related to what the authors call their 'anchor'.[133] The anchor of the appositional coordination is represented by the enclitic possessive pronoun *=k* on the possessee head noun *t*. As with the previous sentence, the alienably possessed possessee *t=k* 'your bread' is disjoint-referenced with the predicative dative clitic *n=k* and the external possessee–possessor relation is an alienable one. Although this point requires future study, the appositional construction coordination functions as a noun modifier providing additional information about the anchor, which in the case at hand is included in its denotation. On this understanding, the bread rations allotted to the addressee are further specified as being in one part of his own and in one part of his father's. (The ampersand & represents the phonologically null coordinating conjunction.)

(20) Double possessive sentence with disjoint- and conjoint-referenced external possessor and attendant alienable predicative possession interpretation

a. *t*	*n(j)=*	*jt=k*	*n=k*	*Jkj-nhjj*
bread.M.SG	LINK.M.SG	father.M.SG=POSS.2M.SG	to=2M.SG	Iki-nekhi

'The bread of your father (belongs) to you, (oh) Iki-nekhi snake'.[134]

---

133 Huddleston, Payne & Peterson (2002: 1350–56 §5.1).

134 Pyr. §242a/W [Spell 238] (Sethe 1908: 134). Allen's (2005: 18) rendition of the serpent's name *Jkj-nhjj* as 'whose attack has missed' strikes me as plausible but a comment on the internal structure of the proper name would have been welcome. Sethe (1962 vol. I 216) puts forward an analysis of the first dative possessive sentence as containing two asyndetically coordinated dative

a'. nested possessor noun phrase $[_{\text{Possessee}}$ *t* $[_{\text{Linker}}$ *n(j)=*$][_{\text{Possessor1}}$ *jt* $[_{\text{Possessor 2}}$ *=k*]]]]

b. *t=k* [*ntk* *n(j)=* *jt=k*]
bread.M.SG=POSS.2M.SG INDEP.PRON.2.M.SG LINK.M.SG father.M.SG=POSS.2M.SG
n=k *Jkj-nhjj*
to=2M.SG Iki-nekhi
'Your bread – your own (and) (that) of your father – (belongs) to you(rself), (Oh) Iki-nekhi'.[135]

b'. Appositional coordinated noun phrase: $[_{\&P}$ *ntk* $[_{\&'}$ [&] [*n(j)=jt=k*]]]

To summarize, when the possessee constituent in its entirety is an alienable possessed noun phrase, the resulting possessive relation is one of alienable possession. The alienable possession meaning is orthogonal to the disjoint/conjoint reference relation between the internal and the external possessor.

8.2 Double predicative possessive sentences with inalienably possessed noun phrases

As we are about to see, the disjoint and conjoint reference of the internal and the external possessor has semantic effects that go beyond the difference between non-identifying and identifying relationships. In essence, these effects concern the unavailability or availability of an inalienable possessive interpretation at the predicate level. The first case to consider is a double possessive sentence with an inalienably possessed noun phrase, in which such an interpretation is barred. The following speech caption from a clap-netting of waterfowl scene features the contrast between a double and a plain dative possessive sentence, which are uttered by the speaker towards his fellow fowler. I do not have much to say about the goal-directed sense of the locative possessive construction *jw ḥ(ꜣ)b jr=k* 'the bird catch (is) towards you', except that it illustrates the affinity between dative case-marked beneficiaries/possessors and goal case-marked recipients/possessors. It also showcases the limited amount of syntactic variation in a fixed formulaic construction, in which the auxiliary *jw* anchors the possessive statement to the immediate situation context and the bare singular subject *ḥ(ꜣ)b* in that construction is interpreted as a definite description.

At first blush, the preceding double possessive sentence *ḥr=k n(=j) r-ḏr=k* 'your face (belongs) to me entirely' looks like a bona fide example of predicative body-part possession. On closer inspection, it appears that that this cannot possibly be the case. Based on

possessors *n-jt=k* and *n=k*: '*Dein eigenes Brot gehört deinem Vater und dir, o 'Jkj-nhjj*' ('Your own bread belongs to your father and to you, O *'Jkj-nhjj*'). Leitz (1996: 408) adopts Sethe's translation without further comment. However, the expected word order would be one in which the dative clitic *n=k* preceded the dative noun phrase *n-jt=k* in linear order. Allen (2017: 281) offers an improved understanding of this elusive passage: 'The bread of your father is for you, you whose attack has missed!'.

135 Pyr. §242b/W [Spell 238] (Sethe 1908: 134). Borghouts (2010: 340–341 §96.d) suggests that independent pronouns can be supplied with the genitive linkage maker *n(j)=* to function as possessive pronouns. The geminated nasal may then undergo an optionally applying degemination process. This gives rise to a form that is identical to the corresponding independent pronoun: *n(j)=ntk* → *nntk* → *ntk* 'yours'.

the knowledge of biological facts and the interactive context, a literal interpretation, in which the addressee's head comes into the speaker's possession, is simply nonsensical. Accordingly, a non-literal reading of the dative possessive sentence must be assumed, in which the body-part term *ḥr* 'face' has a metonymic extension, allowing it to refer to something more abstract—in this case supposedly the mental state of alertness needed to perform the task ahead. This hypothesis is compatible with the fact that the universal quantificational adverb *r-ḏr=k* 'entirely', which is co-indexed with the internal pronominal possessor, can be interpreted as quantifying over the body part *ḥr=k* or rather the attentive state of mind metaphorically expressed by it.

(21) Double possessive sentence with disjoint-referenced internal and external possessor and no inalienable predicative possession interpretation

j *wḥꜥ* *pw* *ḥr=k* *n(=j)*
VOC fowler.M.SG DEM.M.SG face.M.SG=POSS2.M.SG to=1SG
r-ḏr=k *jw* *ḥ(ꜣ)b* *jr=k*
PREP–entire=POSS.2M.SG AUX catch.M.SG toward=2M.SG
'O (you) fowler (over here), your every attention (lit. your entire face) (belongs) to me. The bird catch (is) towards you!'[136]

The main point to be noted is that the metonymic interpretation of body-part possession has a grammatical basis in the disjoint reference of the internal and external possessor. To see that this is the relevant condition, it should be recalled that body-part possession in the literal sense requires a culture-specific concept of the reattachment of dismembered limbs that is bound to the context of mortuary rituals. Crucially, though, in order for this interpretation to arise, the internal body-part possessor must be coreferential with the external dative possessor. The first section of the ritual text, which contains the mythical precedent, is reproduced here for convenience (see above §2, example (2)).

(22) Double possessive sentence with conjoint-referenced internal and external possessor and attendant predicative body-part possession interpretation

jb=k *n=k* *Wsjr*
heart.M.SG=POSS.2M.SG to=cl.2M.SG Osiris
rd–w(j)=k *n=k* *Wsjr*
leg–M.DU=POSS.2M.SG to=cl.2M.SG Osiris
ꜥ=k *n=k* *Wsjr*
arm.M.SG=POSS2M.SG to=cl.2M.SG Osiris
'Your heart (belongs) to you to you(rself), Osiris. Your two legs (belong) to you(rself), Osiris. Your arm (belongs) to you(rself), Osiris'.[137]

---

136 Tomb of Nefer-Seshem-Ptah at Saqqara, Second Room, East Wall, 3rd register from above (Capart 1907, pls. 86 88; Lloyd, Spencer & El-Khouli 2005: 18, pls. 16, 36). Erman (1919: 36–37) interprets the double possessive sentence *ḥr=k n(=j) r–ḏr=k* as a directive speech act: '(*Wende*) *du ganz dein Gesicht zu mir*' ('(Turn) your face entirely to me'). However, there is no evidence for an elided imperative at the level of syntax and content structure.

137 *Pyr.* §364b/W [Spell 267] (Sethe 1908: 190). See above §2, example (2).

The final example presented here is of special interest for the purpose of this section, since it represents a needle in the haystack case of predicative kinship possession. The inverted word order dative possessor–subject possessee *n=j sꜣ=j* 'to me (belongs) my son' is the result of pronominal object shift, during which the dative clitic pronoun crosses the subject noun phrase. The resulting possessive construction is embedded within the matrix sentence *ḥw ꜣ*.[138] As noted by Oréal, the modal auxiliary *ḥw* and the restrictive focus particle *ꜣ* 'only' form an indivisible morphosyntactic and semantic unit that undergoes univerbation (*ḥw* + *ꜣ* → *ḥꜣ*) diachronically.[139] In terms of information structure, the enclitic *ꜣ* focuses on the constituent which it is linearly adjacent to and takes wide scope over it. In the case at hand, the focused constituent is the embedded double possessive sentence as a whole. This analysis can be taken one step further by comparing the Early Egyptian *ḥw ꜣ* construction with if-only conditionals in English, which also appear without a consequent clause. Noriko Akatsuka (1986) argues that the if-only wish construction represents an elliptical conditional sentence, where the content of the unexpressed consequent clause is contextually recoverable.[140] Barbara Dancygier & Eve Sweetser (2005) offer a mono-clausal analysis of the pattern as a wish-expressing non-conditional form.[141] By using if-only clauses, the speaker communicates her negative epistemic stance towards the state of affairs described, which is seen not merely as contrary to fact time but as 'impossible yet desirable'.[142]

(23) Double possessive sentence with conjoint-referenced internal and external possessor and attendant predicative kinship possession interpretation

ḥw	*ꜣ*	*n=j*	*sꜣ=j*
AUX	PCL	for=1.SG	son.M.SG=POSS.1SG

'If only a son of mine (belonged) to me!'[143]

König raises an interesting point about the semantic contribution of the restrictive focus particle *only*, which is to characterize the alternative scenario described by the if-only conditional as being minimally different from the real world.[144] The evaluation of the difference between the possible world imagined by the speaker and the real world as it exists at utterance time is responsible for the interpretation of such sentences as modest wishes that are easily fulfillable. It is a delicate matter to decide whether the same connotation is present in the above example of predicative kinship possession, in which (in my understanding) the counterfactual interpretation prevails. For now the issue must be left open.

A final puzzling aspect of predicative kinship possession is the referential status of the pronominally possessed relational noun *sꜣ=j*, which should only be interpretable as a definite description 'my son'. But matters are not that simple. The principal difficulty lies

138 Oréal (2011: 51).
139 For further details, see Oréal (2011: 49–55).
140 Akatsuka (1986: 336–39).
141 Dancygier & Sweetser (2005: 217–19).
142 Dancygier & Sweetser (2005: 218).
143 Coffin Text III 334d/S1C [Spell 245] (de Buck 1947: 334).
144 König (1991: 108).

in the fact that the individual that entertains a SON-of relation with the speaker exists in his or her possible world. This favors an alternative interpretation of the kinship possessee *sꜣ=j* as an indefinite partitive possessive noun phrase 'a son of mine'. In a related context, Barker (1998) notes that the acceptability of the indefinite partitive 'a mother of mine' in 'I wouldn't want a mother of mine living in a neighborhood like this' largely rests upon the counterfactual modality of the sentence, which allows for a 'consideration of all possible mothers'.[145] But contrary-to-factness is also a basic component of the *ḥw ꜣ* wish construction in Early Egyptian.

As can be seen from Table 3 below, the disjoint/conjoint reference is one of the most salient opposition within double possessive sentences, which crisscrosses the alienability contrast. It must therefore be the case that the two factors operate independently of each other. The availability of inalienable predicative possession in this construction type is a remarkable and somewhat unexpected finding of this section. It should be kept in mind, though, that inalienable predicative possession depends on a number of factors, including a body-part or kinship possessee and the conjoint reference between the internal and the external possessor.

Table 3. Alienability splits and disjoint/conjoint reference in double possessive sentences

Possessee type	Disjoint reference	Conjoint reference	Predicative possession type
Alienably possessed	+	–	Alienable possession
Alienably possessed	–	+	Alienable possession
Inalienably possessed	+	–	Metaphorical possession
Inalienably possessed	–	+	Inalienable possession

Disjointed referenced body-part possessors, on the other hand, express a metaphorical kind of possessive relationship, which does not fit into Stassen's classification.

9 Concluding remarks

This study can be seen as a plea for a new philology that is informed by grammatical theory and crosslinguistic typology alike, without however losing sight of the complexity of the linguistic evidence. The dative predicative possessive construction in Early Egyptian showcases the productivity of the combination of philological and linguistic approaches when analyzing ancient languages. Dative possessive sentences look deceptively simple in terms of their surface structure but disclose a considerable amount of structural and semantic diversity on closer inspection. This type of non-verbal possessive predication thus showcases constructional polysemy and Neil Myler's 'Too-Many-Meanings Puzzle' in a particularly enlightening way. The summarizing table below presents an overview of the language-particular classification of predicative possessive types. Particular attention is given to presence or absence of an initial auxiliary or presentative particle and the interpretive effects obtained.

145 Barker (1998: 705 footnote 5).

Table 4. A possessee-governed typology of Early Egyptian dative possessive sentences

Possessee type	Auxiliary/particle	Episodic reading	Generic reading
Bare indefinite NP	–	+	–
Universally quantified NP	–	–	+
Immediate-situation definite	+	+	–
Second-mention definite	–	–	+
Demonstrative NP	+	+	–
Possessed NP	–	–	+
Demonstrative possessed NP	+	+	(+)

Stassen's rigid classification system picks out only one dative possessive type, indefinite predicative possession, which is only marginally attested and, for this reason alone, makes an unlikely candidate for a possessive prototype. On top of that, dative possessive sentences with singular bare nouns display the special property of being auxiliaryless and yet being linked to the immediate situation context. A more fine-grained classification system that is based on the lexical content and the referential properties of the possessee in subject position does justice to the subtleties of the language facts and also reveals an interesting correlation between the presence between auxiliary-headed dative possessive sentences and the episodic interpretation of the possessee–possessor relationship that is described. Referentially heavy demonstrative possessive noun phrases are not permissible as canonical subjects but must be located in the rooftop of the possessive sentence. The topic marking of prominent possessees goes together with the selection of the auxiliary verb *jw* but it seems to me that a non-episodic interpretation of the possessive predication is not excluded.

By way of concluding this article, I would like to bring up two desiderata for further research. The first desideratum would be to move beyond prototypical possessive relationships (ownership, beneficiariness, asymmetric control relations) and prototypical possessor categories (human possessors). Non-human possessors, in which the possessee outranks the possessor on the animacy, definiteness or person hierarchy are attested and produce non-possessive interpretations. The second desideratum would be to revisit the coding split between the juxtaposition of the possessor to the possessee and the alternative possessive linker *n(j)=* strategy and to see whether it can or cannot be aligned with the semantic contrast between alienable and inalienable possession. One should not a priori dismiss the possibility that the alienability contrasts lack a morphosyntactic correlate in adnominal and predicative possession. If this turns out to be the case, the Early Egyptian possessive system can better be described without recourse to alienability at all.

Texts consulted

Berger-el Naggar, Catherine, Jean Leclant, Bernard Mathieu & Isabelle Pierre-Croisiau. 2010. *Les textes de la pyramide de Pépy Ier*, 2 vols, 2nd edition. Cairo; Mémoires de l'Institut français de l'archéologie orientale 118/1–2.

von Bissing, Friedrich. 1911. *Die Mastaba des Gem-ni-Kai*, volume II. Berlin.

de Buck, Adriaan. 1947. *The Egyptian Coffin Texts III. Texts of Spells 164–267.* Chicago; Oriental Institute Publication 64.

de Buck, Adriaan. 1961. *The Egyptian Coffin Texts VII. Texts of Spells 787–1185.* Chicago; Oriental Institute Publication 87.

Badawy, Alexander. 1978. *The Tomb of Nyhetep-Ptah at Giza and the Tomb of ᶜAnkhmᶜahor at Saqqara.* Berkeley/Los Angeles/London.

Capart, Jean. 1907. *Une rue des tombeaux à Saqqarah*, volume II: plates. Brussels.

Dunham, Dows & William Kelly Simpson. 1974. *The Mastaba of Mersyankh III* [G 7530–7540]. Boston; Giza Mastabas 1.

de Garis Davies, Norman. 1902. *The Rock Tombs of Deir El Gebrâwi, 2 vols. Volume 2: Tomb of Zau and Tombs of the Northern Group.* London; Egypt Exploration Society, Archaeological Survey Memoir 12.

Kanawati, Naguib. 1981. *The Rock Tombs of El-Hawawish. The Cemetery of Akhmim*, 2 vols., Volume 2. Sydney.

Lange, Hans. & Heinrich Schäfer. 1908. *Grab- und Denksteine des Mittleren Reiches im Museum von Kairo – No. 20001–20780*, Vol. II. Text zu No. 20400–20780. Berlin.

Lloyd, Alan, Jeffrey Spencer & Ali El-Khouli. 2005. *Saqqâra Tombs III: The Mastaba of Neferseshem-ptah.* London.

Quibell, James. 1898. *The Ramesseum and the Tomb of Ptah-hetep.* London.

Pierre-Croisiau, Isabelle. 2019. *Les textes de la pyramide de Mérenrê*, 2 vols. Cairo; Mémoires de l'Institut français de l'archéologie orientale 140.

Sethe, Kurt. 1908. *Die altaegyptischen Pyramidentexte. Nach den Papierabdrücken und Photographien des Berliner Museums neu herausgegeben und erläutert. Erster Band. Text, erste Hälfte, Spruch 1–468* (Pyr. 1–905). Leipzig [Reprint Hildesheim 2001].

Sethe, Kurt. 1910. *Die altaegyptischen Pyramidentexte. Nach den Papierabdrücken und Photographien des Berliner Museums neu herausgegeben und erläutert. Zweiter Band. Text, zweite Hälfte, Spruch 469–714* (Pyr. 906–2217). Leipzig [Reprint Hildesheim 2001].

Sethe, Kurt. 1933. *Urkunden des Alten Reiches.* Leipzig.

Smith, Stevenson. 1933. 'The coffin of *Prince* Min-Khaf', *Journal of Egyptian Archaeology* 19(3/4), 150–59.

Steindorff, Georg. 1913. *Das Grab des Ti (in 143 Lichtdrucktafeln und 20 Blättern).* Leipzig.

Bibliography

Ahn, Dorothy. 2019. *The Determinacy Scale: A Competition Mechanism for Anaphoric Expressions.* Ph.D. Dissertation, Harvard University. Available online at https://dash.harvard.edu/handle/1/42029564 (Accessed 29/11/2023)

Aikhenvald, Alexandra. 2010. *Imperatives and Commands.* Oxford.

Akatsuka, Noriko. 1986. 'Conditionals are discourse-bound', in: Closs Traugott, Elizabeth, Alice ter Meulen, Judy Snitzer Reilly & Charles A. Ferguson (eds). *On Conditionals.* Cambridge, 333–51.

Ameka, Felix. 1996. 'Body parts in Ewe grammar', in: Chappell, Hilary & William McGregor (eds). *The Grammar of Inalienability: A Typological Perspective on Body Part Terms and the Part–Whole Relation.* Berlin; Empirical Approaches to Language Typology 44, 783–840.

Arsenijević, Boban. 2019. 'Serbo-Croatian split vocatives: Class change via lexicalization', *Linguistic Inquiry* 50(2), 425–38.

Allen, James. 2005. *The Ancient Egyptian Pyramid Texts.* Atlanta; Writings from the Ancient World/ Society of Biblical Literature 23.

Allen, James. 2000. *Middle Egyptian: An Introduction to the Language and Culture of Hieroglyphs.* Cambridge.

Allen, James. 2017. *A Grammar of the Ancient Egyptian Pyramid Texts, Volume 1: Unis*. Winona Lake, Indiana; Languages of the Ancient Near East 7.

Assmann, Jan. 1989. 'Death and innovation in the funerary religion of Ancient Egypt', in: Kelly Simpson, William (ed.). *Religion and Philosophy in Ancient Egypt*. New Haven, Connecticut; Yale Egyptological Studies 3, 135–59.

Baer, Klaus. 1956. 'A note on Egyptian units of area in the Old Kingdom', *Journal of Near Eastern Studies* 15(2), 113–17.

Barker, Chris. 1998. 'Partitives, double genitives and Anti-Uniqueness', *Natural Language and Linguistic Theory* 16(4), 679–717.

Barker, Chris. 2000. 'Definite possessors and the Novelty Condition', *Theoretical Linguistics* 26(3), 211–17.

Barker, Chris. 2011. 'Possessives and relational nouns', in: von Heusinger, Klaus, Claudia Maienborn & Paul Portner (eds). *Semantics: An International Handbook of Natural Language Meaning*. 3 vols. Volume 2. Göttingen; Handbooks of Linguistics and Communication Sciences 33(2), 1109–30.

Beltrama, Andrea & Andreas Trotzke. 2019. 'Conveying emphasis for intensity: Lexical and syntactic strategies', *Language and Linguistics Compass* 13(7) – e12343.

Benveniste, Émile. 1966. '« Être » et « avoir » dans leurs fonctions linguistiques', in: Émile Benveniste, *Problèmes de la linguistique générale*. Paris, 187–207.

Bernstein, Judy. 2008. 'English *th-* forms', in: Høeg Müller, Henrik & Alex Klinge (eds). *Essays on Nominal Determination: From Morphology to Discourse Management*. Amsterdam/Philadelphia; Studies in Language Companion Series 99, 213–32.

Bianchi, Valentina & Mara Frascarelli. 2010. 'Is topic a root phenomenon?', *Iberia* 2(1), 43–88.

Caponigro, Ivano. 2001. 'On the semantics of indefinite free relatives', in: van Koppen, Marjo, Joanna Sio & Mark de Vos (eds). *Proceedings of ConSOLE X*. Leiden, 49–62.

Caponigro, Ivano. 2021. 'Introducing headless relative clauses and the findings from Mesoamerican languages', in: Caponigro, Ivano, Harold Torrence & Roberto Zavala Maldonado (eds). *Headless Relative Clauses in Mesoamerican Languages*. New York, 1–50.

Clark, Eve. 1978. 'Locationals: existential, locative, and possessive constructions', in: Greenberg, Joseph, Charles Ferguson & Edith Moravcsik (eds). *Universals of Human Language*. 4 vols., Volume. 4: *Syntax*. Stanford, 85–126.

Corbett, Greville. 2019. 'Plurale tantum nouns and the theory of features: A typology of nouns with non-canonical number properties', *Morphology* 29, 51–108.

Grosu, Alexander & Fred Landman. 1998. 'Strange relatives of the third kind', *Natural Language Semantics* 6(2), 125–70.

Dancygier, Barbara & Eve Sweetser. 2005. *Mental Spaces in Grammar: Conditional Constructions*. New York; Cambridge Studies in Linguistics 108.

Davison, Alice. 1984. 'Syntactic markedness and the definition of sentence topic', *Language* 60(4), 797–846.

Doetjes, Jenny. 2011. 'Count/mass distinction across languages', in: von Heusinger, Klaus, Claudia Maienborn & Paul Portner (eds). *Semantics: An International Handbook of Natural Language Meaning*. 3 vols. Volume 3. Göttingen; Handbooks of Linguistics and Communication Sciences 33(3), 2559–80.

Dryer Matthew. 2013. 'Definite articles', in: Dryer, Matthew & Martin Haspelmath (eds). *The World Atlas of Language Structures Online*. Leipzig. Available online at http://wals.info/chapter/37 (Accessed 25/10/2023).

Edel, Elmar. 1955/1964. *Altägyptische Grammatik*. Rome; Analecta Orientalia 34/39.

Enç, Mürvet. 1991. 'The semantics of specificity', *Linguistic Inquiry* 22(1), 1–25.

Erman, Adolf. 1919. *Reden, Rufe und Lieder auf Gräberbildern des Alten Reiches*. Berlin; Abhandlungen der Preußischen Akademie der Wissenschaften Jahrgang 1918; Philosophisch-Historische Klasse 15.

Fodor, Janet Dean & Ivan Sag. 1982. 'Referential and quantificational indefinites', *Linguistics and Philosophy* 5(3), 355–98.

Franke, Detlef. 2003.'Middle Kingdom hymns and other sundry religious texts – An inventory', in Meyer, Sibylle (ed.). *Egypt – Temple of the Whole World: Studies in Honour of Jan Assmann.* Leiden; Numen Book Series 97, 95–135.

Gardiner, Alan. 1957. *Egyptian Grammar. Being an Introduction to the Study of Hieroglyphs.* Oxford.

Gil, David. 1995. 'Universal quantifiers and distributivity', in: Bach, Emmon, Eloise Jelinek, Angelika Kratzer & Barbara H. Partee (eds). *Quantification in Natural Languages*, Dordrecht/Boston; Studies in Linguistics and Philosophy 54, 321–62.

Givón, Talmy. 1978. 'Definiteness and referentiality', in: Greenberg, Joseph, Charles Ferguson & Edith Moravcsik (eds). *Universals of Human Language.* 4 vols., Volume. 4: *Syntax.* Stanford, California, 291–330.

Goldberg, Adele. 1995. *Constructions: A Construction Grammar Perspective to Argument Structure.* Chicago.

Haspelmath, Martin. 1995. 'Diachronic sources of "all" and "every"', in: Bach, Emmon, Eloise Jelinek, Angelika Kratzer & Barbara Partee (eds). *Quantification in Natural Languages*, Dordrecht/Boston; Studies in Linguistics and Philosophy 54, 363–82.

Haspelmath, Martin. 2007. 'Coordination', in: Shopen, Timothy (ed.). *Language Typology and Syntactic Description*, 2nd Edition, vol. II: *Complex Constructions.* Cambridge, 1–51.

Hays, Harold. 2012. *The Organization of the Pyramid Texts: Typology and Disposition.* Leiden; Probleme der Ägyptologie 31.

Heim, Irene. (1982). *The Semantics of Definite and Indefinite Noun Phrases.* Ph.D. Dissertation, Massachusetts Institute of Technology. Available online at https://semanticsarchive.net/Archive/jA2YTJmN/Heim%20Dissertation%20with%20Hyperlinks.pdf (Accessed 25/10/2023).

Heine, Bernd. 1997. *Possession: Cognitive Sources, Forces, and Grammaticalization.* Cambridge; Cambridge Studies in Linguistics 83.

von Heusinger, Klaus. 2011. 'Specificity', in: von Heusinger, Klaus, Claudia Maienborn & Paul Portner (eds). *Semantics: An International Handbook of Natural Language Meaning.* 3 vols. Volume 2. Göttingen; Handbooks of Linguistics and Communication Sciences 33(2), 1025–58.

Higginbotham, James. 1994. 'Mass and count quantifiers', *Linguistics and Philosophy* 17(5), 447–80.

Huddleston, Rodney. 1984. *Introduction to the Grammar of English.* Cambridge; Cambridge Textbooks in Linguistics.

Huddleston, Rodney, John Payne & Peter Peterson. 2002. 'Coordination and supplementation', in Huddleston, Rodney & Geoffrey Pullum (eds). *The Cambridge Grammar of the English Language.* Cambridge, 1273–1362.

Jacobson, Pauline. 1995. 'On the quantificational force of English free relatives', in: Bach, Emmon, Eloise Jelinek, Angelika Kratzer & Barbara Partee (eds). *Quantification in Natural Languages.* Dordrecht/Boston; Studies in Linguistics and Philosophy 54, 451–86.

Junker, Herman 1943. *Zu einigen Reden und Rufen auf Grabbildern des Alten Reiches.* Vienna/Leipzig; Sitzungsberichte der Akademie der Wissenschaften in Wien, Philosophisch-Historische Klasse 221 vol. 5.

Keen, Ian. 2013. 'The language of possession: Three case studies', *Language in Society* 42(2), 187–214.

Kemmer, Suzanne. 2003. 'Human cognition and the elaboration of events: Some universal conceptual categories', in: Tomasello, Michael (ed.), *The New Psychology of Language: Cognitive and Functional Approaches to Language Structure.* 2 vols., Volume 2. Mahwah, New Jersey, 89–118.

König, Ekkehard. 1991. *The Meaning of Focus Particles: A Comparative Perspective.* Abingdon-on-Thames; Theoretical Linguistics Series.

Kotowski, Sven. 2016. *Adjectival Modification and Order Restrictions: The Influence of Temporariness on Prenominal Word Order.* Berlin/Boston; Studia Grammatica 80.

Langacker, Ronald. 1995. 'Possession and possessive constructions', in: Taylor, John & Robert MacLaury (eds). *Language and the Cognitive Construal of the World.* Berlin; Trends in Linguistics Studies and Monographs 82, 51–79.

Ledgeway, Adam. 2013. 'Testing linguistic theory and variation to their limits: The case of Romance', *Corpus* 12, 271–317. Available online at https://journals.openedition.org/corpus/2408?lang=en (Accessed 25/10/2023).

Leitz, Christian. 1996. 'Die Schlangensprüche in den Pyramidentexten', *Orientalia* 65(4), 381–417.

Lichtenberk, Frantisek. 2002. 'The possessive–benefactive connection', *Oceanic Linguistics* 41(2), 439–74.

Lichtenberk, Frantiser, Jyotsna Vaid & Hsin-Chin Chen. 2011. 'On the interpretation of alienable vs. inalienable possession: A psycholinguistic investigation', *Cognitive Linguistics* 12(4), 659–89.

Löbner, Sebastian. 2011. 'Concept types and determination', *Journal of Semantics* 28(3), 279–333.

Loprieno, Antonio, Matthias Müller & Sami Uljas. 2019. *Non-Verbal Predication in Ancient Egyptian.* Berlin/Boston; The Mouton Companion to Ancient Egyptian 2.

Lüddeckens, Erich. 1943. 'Untersuchungen über religiösen Gehalt, Sprache und Form der ägyptischen Totenklagen', *Mitteilungen des Deutschen Instituts für ägyptische Altertumskunde in Kairo* 11 (1–2), 1–188.

Lyons, Christopher. 1999. *Definiteness.* Cambridge.

Lyons, John. 1967. 'A note on possessive, existential and locative sentences', *Foundations of Language* 3(4), 390–96.

McNally, Louise. 2011. 'Existential sentences', in: von Heusinger, Klaus, Claudia Maienborn, & Paul Portner (eds). *Semantics: An International Handbook of Natural Language Meaning.* 3 vol., vol. 2. Berlin/Boston; Handbook of Linguistics and Communication Science 33(2), 1829–48.

Moreno García, Juan Carlos. 2007. 'A new Old Kingdom inscription from Giza (CGC 57163) and the problem of *sn-ḏt* in Pharaonic Third Millennium Society', *Journal of Egyptian Archaeology* 93, 117–36.

Mosel, Ulrike. 1982. 'Possessive constructions in Tolai', *Arbeiten des Kölner Universalien-Projekts* [*akup*] 44, Cologne: University of Cologne, Department of Linguistics, Available online at https://d-nb.info/1059470578/34 (Accessed 01/11/2023).

Motte, Aurore. 2017. 'Reden und Rufe, a neglected genre? Towards a definition of the speech captions in private tombs', *Bulletin de l'Institut français de l'archéologie orientale*, 293–317.

Myler, Neil. 2016. *Building and Interpreting Possession Sentences.* Cambridge, Massachusetts.

Nichols, Johanna. 1992. *Linguistic Diversity in Space and Time.* Chicago.

O'Connor, Catherine, Joan Maling & Barbara Skarabela. 2013. 'Nominal categories and the expression of possession: A crosslinguistic study of probabilistic tendencies and categorical constraints', in: Börjars, Kersti, David Denison & Alan Scott (eds). *Morphosyntactic Categories and the Expression of Possession, Amsterdam/Philadelphia; Linguistics Today 199, 89–121.*

Oréal, Elsa. 2011. *Les particules en égyptien ancien: De l'ancien égyptien à l'égyptien classique*, Cairo; Bibliothèque d'étude 152.

Ouhalla, Jamal. 2004. 'Semitic relatives', *Linguistic Inquiry* 35(2), 288–300.

Payne, Doris. 2009. 'Is possession mere location? Contrary evidence from Maa', in: McGregor, William (ed.). *The Expression of Possession.* Berlin; The Expression of Cognitive Categories 2, 107–42.

Portner, Paul. 2007. 'Imperatives and modals', *Natural Language Semantics* 15(4), 351–83.

Portner, Paul. 2018. *Mood.* Oxford; Oxford Surveys in Semantics and Pragmatics.

Prince, Ellen. 1998. 'On the limits of syntax, with reference to left-dislocation and topicalization', in: Culicover, Peter & Louise McNally (eds). *The Limits of Syntax*, San Diego, California; Syntax and Semantics 29, 281–302.

Reinhart, Tanya. 1981. 'Pragmatics and linguistics: An analysis of sentence topics', *Philosophica* 27(1), 53–94.

Reinhart, Tanya. 1983. *Anaphora and Semantic Interpretation*, London/Sydney; Routledge Library Editions: Semantics and Semiology 12.

Reintges, Chris. 1998. 'Mapping information structure to syntactic structure: One syntax for *jn*', *Revue d'Égyptologie* 49, 195–220.

Reintges, Chris. 2010. 'Coordination, converbs and clause chaining in Coptic Egyptian: Typology and structural analysis', in: Brill, Isabelle (ed.). *Clause Linking and Clause Hierarchy: Syntax and Pragmatics.* Amsterdam/Philadelphia; Studies in Language Companion Series 121, 203–65.

Reintges, Chris. 2011. 'The oral-compositional form of Pyramid Text discourse', in: Hagen, Fredrik, John Johnston, Wendy Monkhouse, Kathryn Piquette, John Tait & Martin Worthington (eds). *Narratives of Egypt and the Ancient Near East: Literary and Linguistic Approaches*. Louvain; Orientalia Lovaniensa Analecta 189, 3–54.

Reintges, Chris. 2016. 'Marked and unmarked word orders, verbal inflection and the cartography of Early Egyptian sentence structures', in: Allen, James, Mark Collier & Andréas Stauder (eds). *Coping with Obscurity: The Brown Workshop on Earlier Egyptian Grammar*. Atlanta; Wilbour Studies in Egyptology and Assyriology 4, 45–95.

Rizzi, Luigi. 1997. 'The fine structure of the left periphery', in: Haegeman, Liliane (ed.). *Elements of Grammar: Handbook of Generative Syntax.* Dordrecht; Kluwer International Handbooks of Linguistics 1, 281–337.

Sadler, Louisa & Maris Camilleri. 2018. 'Free relatives in Maltese', *Brill's Journal of Afroasiatic Languages and Linguistics* 10(1), 115–59.

Sadock, Jerrold & Arnold Zwicky. 1985. 'Speech act distinctions in syntax', in: Shopen, Timothy (ed.). *Language Typology and Syntactic Description vol. 1: Clause Structure.* Cambridge, 155–96.

Safir, Ken. 1996. 'The semantic atoms of anaphora', *Natural Language and Linguistic Theory* 14(3), 545–89.

Schenkel, Wolfgang. 1965. '"Singularisches" und "pluralisches" Partizip', *Mitteilungen des Deutschen Archäologischen Instituts* 20, 110–14.

Schenkel, Wolfgang. 2007. 'Die Partikel *iw* und die Intuition des Interpreten: Randbemerkungen zu Antonio Loprieno "On fuzzy boundaries in Egyptian syntax"', *Lingua Aegyptia* 15, 161–201.

Schweitzer, Simon. 2005. *Schrift und Sprache der 4. Dynastie*. Wiesbaden; Menes, Studien zur Kultur und Sprache der ägyptischen Frühzeit und des Alten Reiches 3.

Seiler, Hansjakob. 2001. 'The operational basis of possession: A dimensional approach revisited', in: Baron, Irène, Michael Herslund & Finn Sørensen (eds). *Dimensions of Possession.* Amsterdam/Philadelphia; Typological Studies in Language 47, 27–40.

Sethe, Kurt. 1962. *Übersetzung und Kommentar zu den altägyptischen Pyramidentexten vol. 1: Spruch 213–260*. Hamburg.

Sperveslage, Gunnar. 2010. 'Das Kongruenzverhalten von Adjektiven im Altägyptischen', *Lingua Aegyptia* 18, 217–51.

Stassen, Leon. 2009. *Predicative Possession.* Oxford.

Stassen, Leon. 2013. 'Predicative possession', in: Dryer, Matthew & Martin Haspelmath (eds). *The World Atlas of Language Structures Online*. Leipzig. Available online at http://wals.info/chapter/117 (Accessed 25/10/2023).

Ter Meulen, Alice. 1981. 'An intensional logic for mass terms', *Philosophical Studies* 40(1), 105–25.

Westendorf, Wolfhart. 1953. 'Vom Passiv zum Aktiv: Entwicklungstendenzen der altägyptischen Sprache', *Mitteilungen des Instituts für Orientforschung* 1, 227–32.

Wood, Jim & Rafaella Zanuttini. 2023. 'The syntax of English presentatives', *Language* 99(3), 563–602.

Zanuttini, Raffaella & Paul Portner. 2003. 'Exclamative clauses: At the syntax–semantics interface', *Language* 79(1), 39–81.

Zwicky, Arnold. 1974. 'Hey, Whatsyourname!', in: LaGaly, Michael, Robert Allen Fox & Anthony Bruck (eds). *Papers from the Tenth Regional Meeting of the Chicago Linguistics Society*. Chicago, 787–801.

Layout and Graphics in New Kingdom Epistolary Documents

Some Considerations

Nathalie Sojic[1]

Introduction

In the New Kingdom, as in other periods of Egyptian history, documents were written on a variety of media and in a variety of formats. They could be arranged in a rigorous or thoughtful layout, or they could appear to follow no particular organization. The handwriting might be loose or formal, and the texts may be adorned with a paratext or be associated with another text. Some practices appear to be based on collective norms, while others are clearly incidental or idiosyncratic.

Research devoted to the media, layout and graphics of Egyptian texts (especially those written on easily accessible materials such as papyrus or ostraca[2]) is surprisingly scarce[3] in spite of the perspectives that such studies offer.[4] These non-textual components are part of the written culture. Studying them allows us to gauge the cultural and social practices that constitute the intellectual and physical background of a text, endowing it with one or

1 I am indebted to the anonymous reviewer who corrected and improved my English. Remaining errors are, of course, mine. I also warmly thank Aurore Motte (Mainz–Liège) for her careful proofreading and suggestions on a draft version of this paper.

2 Unlike monuments or steles, for example, such texts were not intended as permanent: see Vernus (2010–2011: 21–22 and n. 2).

3 A recently published collective work by Carlig, Lescuyer, Motte & Sojic (2020) aims to begin filling this gap. Devoted to paratextual signs in Egyptian texts from the Old Kingdom to the Byzantine period, the book brings together, in a comparative approach, 17 contributions from specialists from various disciplines. It provides a panorama of the use of these signs and the effects of layout in documents of various languages (ancient Egyptian, Latin, Greek) and using different writing systems (hieroglyphic, hieratic, demotic, Coptic, Greek, Latin). For an overview of this subject in Egyptology, see, in that book, the contributions of Winand, Enmarch, Motte & Sojic, which also include the previous bibliography. To these may be added the works of Rößler-Köhler (1984–1985) (on the use of white space in a book of the dead, P. MMA 35.9.20) and (1990) (on the formal division of P. Jumilhac), von Bomhard (1998) discussing, among other things, abbreviations and signs in the margins of the text, and Ragazzoli's study of the structuring of texts within the *Miscellanea* (Ragazzoli 2019: 62–68).

4 Gasse (1992: 56).

Sami Uljas & Andreas Dorn (eds), *Crossroads VI. Between Egyptian Linguistics and Philology*, 297–326
DOI: https://doi.org/10.37011/studmon.30.11

more layers of particular meaning.[5] What do these practices mean? What circumstances could have led a scribe to make a choice among the possibilities available to him (choice of medium, layout, ink color, etc.)? Is it possible to determine what motivated this/these choice(s)?

The present article offers some considerations concerning the epistolary documents of the New Kingdom, a corpus whose formal heterogeneity has not yet been the subject of any in-depth study despite its richness. This study is more particularly devoted to the graphics and layout effects observed in these documents, starting from the postulate that the form of the message can in itself be meaningful. The first section (§1) provides a state of the art of the research on the layout and graphics of texts, followed by a brief description of the corpus under examination (§2). In the third section (§3), I present the theoretical approach of this study, which allows considering the heterogeneity observed in the letters in terms of variation. I then proceed to the analysis of the sources (§4). The fifth and last section (§5) takes stock of the contribution of this study.

1 State of the art

In philological works, the writing medium and layout of documents are mostly treated as simple carriers and organizers of the text.[6] Very occasionally,[7] editions provide us with material descriptions of the objects, which inform us about their dimensions, the general state of conservation, the ink used, the traces of folding, or even indicate the presence of paratext (punctuation, corrections, glosses, etc.).[8] However, there is still no extensive and systematic study entirely and exclusively devoted to the layout of written sources.[9] This observation applies to all categories of documents from the Pharaonic period preserved on easily manageable media. Letters are an exception insofar as we have three brief syntheses[10] that aim to reconstitute '*the way in which the scribe proceeded when writing them*'.[11] Focusing on epistolary material on papyri, these studies have shown that the scroll was

5 On the question of the meaningful use of writing media, see Vernus (2010–2011: 21–22, and n. 9–10).

6 Vernus (2010–2011: 21).

7 Burkard, Goecke-Bauer & Wimmer's (2002) review of the literature on hieratic ostraca lists the contributions and shortcomings of these works, without emphasizing, however, the eminently sketchy character of the descriptions of the material aspect of the texts.

8 They are usually subordinated to the study of the text.

9 See n. 2 above. Goedicke (1964) proposes a diplomatic study of the documents of the Old Kingdom, essentially on non-manageable supports (steles, walls). Concerning manuscripts, we owe to N. Halleux a little-known study of the layout of Egyptian papyri: Halleux (1986). Quirke (2004: 26–27) and Eyre (2013: 41–54) deliver a short synthesis that also focuses on papyri. For a more conceptual introduction, see Assmann (1994). Černý's (1952) study, meanwhile, provides technical information regarding the design and format of papyrus sheets, ink compositions, and so on, the application of which can be glimpsed in museum work, such as restoration.

10 James (1962) for the Middle Kingdom; Černý (1939a) and Bakir (1970) for the New Kingdom.

11 Černý (1939a: xvii) The section on *LRL* formatting runs from p. xvii to p. xx.

almost always[12] placed vertically[13] on the scribe's lap, and he unrolled it downwards as he wrote. The text runs in cursive script from the left to the right,[14] perpendicular to the direction of the fibers. The folding was first done vertically, until it becomes a thin strip which is then folded lenghtwise two or three times. It is also noted that at the time of the New Kingdom, the average size of a sheet of papyrus was 11 cm in width and 21–22 or 40–42 cm in length. With the exception of the address added after folding, the organization of the text block[15] is treated *a silentio*.[16] The letters on ostraca have received less attention. Lacking an address because they were usually intended for intra-communal communication,[17] the stone or pottery chips were chosen according to the estimated space for the message to be written. They could be very small when limited to a simple note[18] and they were sometimes inscribed on the front *and* back.[19] The use of limestone chips was very popular among the workers in the village of Deir el-Medina, who found them on the building sites in the Western Theban area.[20] Pottery sherds were also extensively used as a writing medium, for they were an easily accessible material.

As we will see, the epistolary documents actually present a much more heterogeneous form than these descriptions suggest.

2 Corpus

The New Kingdom epistolary documents constitute a set of documents written on papyrus and ostraca as well as on tablets. This dossier includes private and official correspondence, as well as exercises, models, literary letters, and drafts. The published material currently amounts to about 550 documents,[21] to which I will be adding 165 items that are currently in process of editing.[22] Most of the material dates to the 19th and 20th dynasties (1295–1069 ACN), the number of witnesses for the 18th dynasty (1539–1295 ACN) hardly exceeding twenty. A division according to the medium reveals that the scribes of the 19th dynasty

12 Only one exception is mentioned in *ibid.*, p. xx, P. BM 10375.

13 This vertical format is applicable also for literary letters, see Ragazzoli (2019: 107–10) about the texts of the *Miscellanea.*

14 The vast majority of these documents come from Deir el-Medineh: Wente (1990: 2).

15 On this concept, see Halleux (1986: 77) '*un bloc d'écriture homogène fait de lignes identiques, strictement alignées à droite (point de départ de la lecture), plus souplement à gauche ; des marges et un interlignage constant*'.

16 The schematic illustrations of Černý (1939a) and Bakir (1970) suggest that the text block ran evenly from the right margin to the left margin, discontinuously from the top to the bottom of the sheet, and that the top and bottom margins were slightly wider than the right and left margins.

17 Wente (1990: 5).

18 Bakir (1970: 22–23).

19 Bakir (1970: 22–23).

20 Bakir (1970: 22–23).

21 The survey was based on the reference work of Wente (1990), the *Ramses* database (http://ramses.ulg.ac.be/), and the *Deir el Medina Database* (https://dmd.wepwawet.nl/).

22 To be published in the series *Documents de fouilles de l'Institut français d'archéologie orientale* (DFIFAO).

used mostly ostraca, while those of the 20th dynasty preferred papyrus.[23] The sources stem mainly from two sites: a minority comes from Memphis in Lower Egypt, but more than 90% of the documentation has been found in Deir el-Medina, the village of workmen who built the tombs in the Valley of the Kings and the Valley of the Queens.

In order to highlight the existence of specific layout and graphic practices, I have occasionally used examples from other corpora for comparison, because oppositions discerned within single groups of written material may also occur more broadly between wider textual corpora.

3 Methodology: Graphetics, Marked and Unmarked Forms, and Graphic Registers

The physical appearance of a letter – and more generally, of a text –, whether it be its layout or its graphic design, is conditioned by more or less constraining material and/or cultural factors, notably:

- The time period in question: on easily manageable media,[24] scribes wrote in columns until the end of the Middle Kingdom and then switched to a horizontal arrangement. This change of orientation led to a greater development of page-setting on this type of media;
- The use of the document: greater care and preparation were devoted to the layout of a text intended for display: a book roll, meant to be read, was more neat and pleasant in appearance[25] than a protective amulet enclosed in a case and worn around the neck.
- The media and the instruments of drafting: an official text inscribed in hieroglyphs on a wall required more time of preparation than a text laid down with a brush on an easily manageable medium;
- Practical contingencies: for example, the length of the columns of text in New Kingdom papyrus scrolls corresponds to the space that runs from one knee to the other of the scribe;[26]
- Formatting conventions specific to a given textual genre: for example, medical recipes are regularly divided into small columns within the text area, probably for readability.[27]

Some of these practices regularly interfere with each other. For example, a scribe who copies a literary letter does not necessarily heed the graphic norms associated with the nature of the text (use of literary hieratic, punctuation...) if it is only a simple draft or learning exercise intended to be read only by its writer. On the other hand, these norms

23 On this issue, see Haring (2018).

24 See Vernus (2010–2011).

25 One can also think of the layout of literary texts copied on large pots. These inscribed vases were probably placed in visible places – schools or homes – as models of edification, or for mere entertainment (A. Gasse, personal communication). On this matter, see Ragazzoli (2019: 54–57).

26 Černý (1952: 17).

27 Motte & Sojic (2020: 59, §3.1.1).

can be applied when the training concerns the calligraphy of the text, even if it remains an exercise.

Layout and graphics effects may convey layers of non-linguistic meaning: they tell something about the text to the reader familiar with the uses of layout and graphic conventions, such as, for instance, its content, its intended audience, and its purpose. They can even affect the linguistic content of the text. Graphetics is a discipline stemming from visual semiotics that allows for identifying such possible layers of non-linguistic meaning. In this study it is coupled with a functional approach that defines sets of oppositions in terms of 'marked' and 'unmarked' forms and 'registers' and 'repertoires'.

3.1 Graphetics

At the crossroads of linguistics, visual semiotics, and anthropology lies the study of graphetics. This is a discipline that studies the visual units that make up the appearance of a text, such as its layout, color, the size and appearance of the writing (visual or descriptive graphetics), or the mechanical elements of text production, such as the medium and the writing tool (mechanical or production graphetics).[28] The objective is to identify the effect of these factors to meaning and linguistic content of the text. Graphetics is not interested in individual writings, but in what characterizes the practices of an entire community.[29] It can consider different levels of granularity, from the strokes that make up the letter to the layout of the text on the surface.[30] The minimal graphetical units are visually delimited by the empty spaces. The layers of meaning identified are by nature and by definition non-linguistic, but this does not prevent them from 'coloring' the meaning of a text and influencing its interpretation. Recently proposed[31] as an analytical tool for the study of graphic registers[32] of Egyptian texts, this approach offers interesting possibilities for investigating the variation at work within the graphic representation of texts in a given context (time, place, textual corpus). It allows for a systemic description of graphic variation: the scribe had a repertoire of visual units (as many strokes, signs, writing styles, layout devices, etc.) that he could utilize according to socio-cultural conventions or depending on the particular communicative intention.

Typically, considerations such as these are related to graphetics. It is quite common, for example, for a scribe to have used red ink in an administrative text to write numbers,

28 Meletis (2020: 32–34).

29 Meletis (2020: 34) 'graphetics is necessarily trans-individual'.

30 The study of each of these levels constitutes a sub-discipline within graphetics: Meletis (2020: 39ff).

31 Unpublished paper by Stéphane Polis, 'Registres graphiques, genres littéraires et registres linguistiques : mythes et réalités d'une corrélation entre forme et contenu en hiératique Ramesside', given during the study days *Registres graphiques. Questions sur la scripturalité* égyptienne organized by Florence Albert and Chloé Ragazzoli within the framework of the ÉCRITURES project (see note 36), and held at Sorbonne University on September 6 and 7, 2019. For more theoretical references on this approach, I refer the reader to the article he co-authored with a specialist in visual semiotics: Klinkenberg & Polis (2018).

32 On this notion, see §3.3.

which may be present in large quantities in such documents. This practice, intended to disambiguate the reading of signs used with different meanings (the number '1' is written by means of a small vertical line, which is also used to indicate an ideographic reading of a hieroglyph[33]), is infrequently employed in other corpora. If used in a magical text, for example, it represents a marked usage, as it is statistically restricted in this corpus.

Systematic considering of the graphic appearance of texts sometimes makes it possible to compare sources that have common graphic characteristics. This may further allow insight into habits of individual scribes.

3.2 Marked and Unmarked Forms

To describe layout and graphical variation observed in epistolary documents, I will speak of 'marked' and 'unmarked' layouts and graphics. Unmarked ones are those expected by default, while 'marked' ones are less common alternatives.

For example, when an ostracon bears a text written in a particularly large and careful script, whose dimensions do not seem natural at first sight,[34] one is entitled to wonder whether it was not intended for a form of display. A case point is the as yet unpublished literary ostracon, OL 6227,[35] which bears a titulary of Ramses II written in characters more than 2 cm high. Compared to another ostracon on which this same handwriting appears in a quite average size (ca. 1 cm high),[36] the particular intention of the scribe to produce a document intended for display seems clear. In this case, the use of oversized writing constitutes a marked, potentially meaningful graphic design.

A marked layout stands always in opposition to other practices. It should be noted that the oppositions at work within epistolary documents are not necessarily transferable to another category of documents. Finally, oppositions can also occur at a broader level than within a single category of documents. Comparisons between different corpora thus make it possible to highlight the fact that a practice marked in certain circumstances will have a neutral meaning in another context, as we shall see below (§4.2.3)

3.3 Graphic Registers and Repertoires

I have already introduced the notion of repertoire above (§3.1) when I mentioned the existence of a stock of grapheme units and layout devices from which the scribe chose (or switched into) according to the circumstances to achieve a specific communicative goal. The notion of graphic register[37] allows for a description and interpretation of graphic variation observed in documents. A 'graphic register' is the materialization of a scribe's

33 Malaise & Winand (1999: §34).

34 Gasse (1992: 57) emphasizes the scattered character of these large writings.

35 Edition will appear in Albert, Gasse & Sojic (in press).

36 The height of the average writing varies between 3.1 mm and 1.1 cm: Gasse (1992: 57).

37 An ongoing research project, the ÉCRITURES project, conducted jointly by Sorbonne University (Chloé Ragazzoli) and the French Institute of Oriental Archaeology in Cairo (Florence Albert and Khaled Hassan), deals precisely with the question of graphic registers in the sources of Pharaonic Egypt (https://www.ifao.egnet.net/recherche/operations/op19225/).

choice within the graphic repertoire. It combines material aspects of writing such as the script (e.g., cursive hieroglyphs, documentary hieratic, chancery script), the text disposition, the medium (writing tool or writing surface) and cultural meanings associated with them. Each graphic register has a semiotic value that contributes to the meaning of a text.[38] It refers to a specific context of production or utilization. For instance, a hieroglyphic inscription incised in an ivory tusk along with drawings[39] indicates a magical context. A semi-hieroglyphic text written on a long papyrus roll beside mythological drawings rather evokes a funerary context.

Graphic registers are organized on a gradient scale (or a continuum) running from a high degree of standardization to a little degree of standardization or no standardization at all. The more standardized a script is, the more it is conventional and formal and the less it displays marks of individuality, since scribes used stereotyped forms. Texts written in a standardized graphic register show greater uniformity than documentary texts. Calibration, de-calibration[40] and elaboration[41] constitute three main strategies[42] of formalization used by scribes, through respectively the graphic registers of literary hieratic and chancery writing (see §4.2.1–4.2.3).

The scale of standardization is paralleled by a scale of sacredness.[43] Hieroglyphs carved on monuments, whose design is highly standardized, form a highly sacred script. They materialized god's words in eternity. As such, they were used in canonized texts, namely, texts having a sacred nature. On the other side of the scale, cursive scripts were used to write secular texts with a non-permanent end.

This close correlation between script and the nature of the content is a norm. However, there are cases where the use of a specific graphic register is determined by factors other than the linguistic content of the text, as will be shown.

4 Data analysis

The selected examples illustrate cases where the layout and writing either connote, in a rather obvious way, the text with a particular non-linguistic meaning or interact with it.

4.1 De-calibration[44] of Signs

Using signs that are larger or longer than the rest of the text can be a way for the writer to

38 Ragazzoli (2001).

39 E.g. Louvre E 3614 : https://collections.louvre.fr/ark:/53355/cl010007235.

40 The term, borrowed from Vernus (2020: 25), designates the use of size to highlight certain signs or sequences.

41 This elaboration can result in exaggerated and decorative movements: Gasse (1992: 63).

42 In addition to calibration and elaboration, figurativity is a quality specific to hieroglyphic writing (Vernus 1990a: 44) which has not broken its ties to hieratic completely (Polis 2020: 4). The question of the figurativity of signs in hieratic writing will not be dealt with in this article.

43 Egyptologists are familiar with this correlation, which Jan Assmann has called 'hierotaxis', see Assmann (1987). For a theorization in French, see Vernus (1990a).

44 See n. 39.

draw attention to a specific part of the message,[45] or even to bring out a particular meaning, with the graphic salience reflecting the informational salience of the text.

This phenomenon is regularly observed in letters which begin by a direct address to the recipient of the type *n* NN 'to NN'.[46] In some cases,[47] the preposition *n* (𓈖) at the very beginning of the letter can be drawn two or three times wider than the one used in the body of the message, as if to catch the eye, like on O. Berlin 9895[48] (Fig. 1), or on O. DeM 613[49] (Fig. 2).

The example of P. Leiden I 371 (ÄMS 64),[50] a letter to a deceased woman, illustrates the same practice on papyrus (Fig. 3).

Fig. 1 O. Berlin 9895 © Staatliche Museen zu Berlin – Ägyptisches Museum und Papyrussammlung

Fig. 2 O. DeM 613 © IFAO

45 See for example Delattre & Vanthieghem (2020) for a study of this phenomenon in Coptic, in the correspondence of the monk Frange.

46 Bakir (1970: 51).

47 The following examples are also very clear: O. Berlin 10664 (Fig. 5), O. DeM 440, O. DeM 968, O. DeM 10110, O. DeM 10253, O. DeM 10261, O. Gardiner 5, O. Gardiner 112, O. Turin CG 57077, O. Turin CG 57491. In other cases, it is difficult to ascertain whether the size of the *n* has been deliberately exaggerated, for various reasons (beginning of the sign in a gap, absence of other *n*'s in the text to serve as elements of comparison, etc.).

48 https://dem-online.gwi.uni-muenchen.de/fragment_e.php?id=183.

49 Sauneron (1959: pl. 29).

50 Gardiner & Sethe (1928: pl. vii–viii).

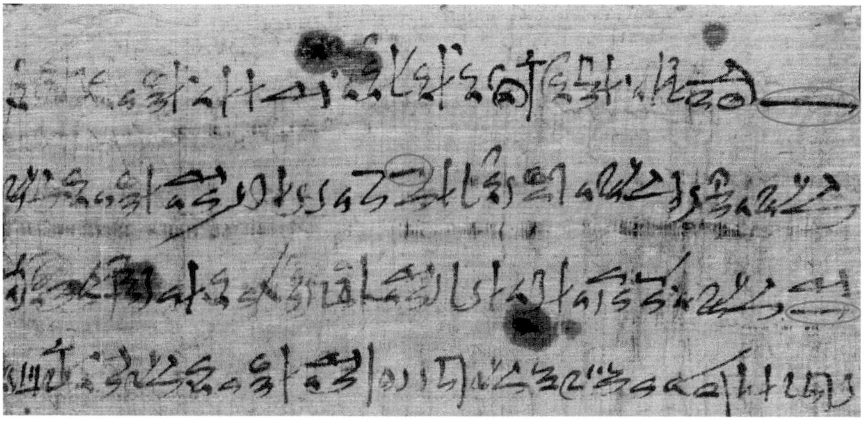

Fig. 3 P. Leiden I 371 (ÄMS 64), detail of ll. 1–4. © Rijksmuseum van Oudheden

This device can also be used when the preposition *n* is not at the beginning of the message, as in O. DeM 10248,1[51] (Fig. 4) and in O. Berlin 10664,1[52] (Fig. 5), which use the formula NN *n* NN.[53] The sign 𓈖 before the mention of the addressee is drawn in a module more stretched than the other *n*'s 𓈖 present in the text.

This practice may have originated in a scribal habit attested as early as the Old Kingdom, of separating by a line the name of the sender and the name of the recipient.[54]

Fig. 4 O. DeM 10248, detail of ll. 1–2 © IFAO

51 Grandet (2010: 355–57).

52 https://dem-online.gwi.uni-muenchen.de/fragment_e.php?id=194.

53 It is not used with the *ḏd* NN *n* NN type formula ('NN says to NN'), for which see Bakir (1970: 48).

54 This may explain why the shifting of the *n* is not attested in the formula *ḏd* NN *n* NN. On this practice, see Bakir (1970: 37–38), who places its origin in the Middle Kingdom. According to him, there are cases where this feature clearly cannot be interpreted as the preposition, but rather as a paratextual mark. In fact, the presence of a vertical bar stroke between the name of the sender and the name of the addressee can be noted as early as the Old Kingdom in Letters to the Dead (which were then written in columns), for example on the Cairo linen in the 6th Dynasty (Gardiner & Sethe 1928: pl. I) or in P. Nag ed-Deir 3737 in the 9th Dynasty (Simpson 1966). At the beginning of the Middle Kingdom (12th Dyn.), the horizontal division line appears in this same corpus (Gardiner & Sethe 1928: pl. VI, n. b). I warmly thank my colleague Aurore Motte for drawing my attention to these cases.

Fig. 5 O. Berlin P 10664 © Staatliche Museen zu Berlin – Ägyptisches Museum und Papyrussammlung

De-calibration can also have a symbolic function. Several epistolary exercises in the category of letters to the vizier show that the signs that make up the dignitary's title in the *incipit* are larger than the signs used in the body of the text. Most of these exercises are written in a so-called 'literary' script, i.e., calibrated and neat (see §4.2.1). In this care for the layout, the large module attributed to the signs in the title of the vizier adds an additional touch of aestheticism or even mannerism, as on O. Cairo GC 25745[55] (Fig. 6).

In case of prestigious titles, the graphic salience perhaps reflects, by a sort of suggested synesthesia, the high social status of the referent. Some epistolary exercises confirm, if need be, that this honorific de-calibration is an intentional process. For example, O. Turin CG 57516[56] (Fig. 7) is small ostracon consisting of three line. The middle one, written in a larger module than the other two, bears the title of the vizier.

OL 1850[57] (Fig. 8) also shows this phenomenon: the title of the vizier, copied in a normal size at the beginning of the letter, has been rewritten below the text, in a more stretched module.

The de-calibration gives the signs a form that recalls the Ramesside chancery script, a sort of hieratic characterized by its monumental dimensions (§4.2.2). It differs, however, in the way it is used within the same document. Ramesside chancery script is a writing style in its own right, used from one end of a text to the other and in a very specific context. By contrast, the groups of signs presented here generally appear either at the beginning or at the end of a text (or section) and simply consist of tracing the signs in a larger module than would naturally be done by hand.

The phenomenon of de-calibration is not peculiar to the epistolary genre. It is also found in other corpora, without it always being possible to determine to what extent its

55 According to Ebgerts (1997: 23–25), the scribe of this text is Djehutymose.

56 López (1984: pl. 170).

57 Sojic (2019: 125).

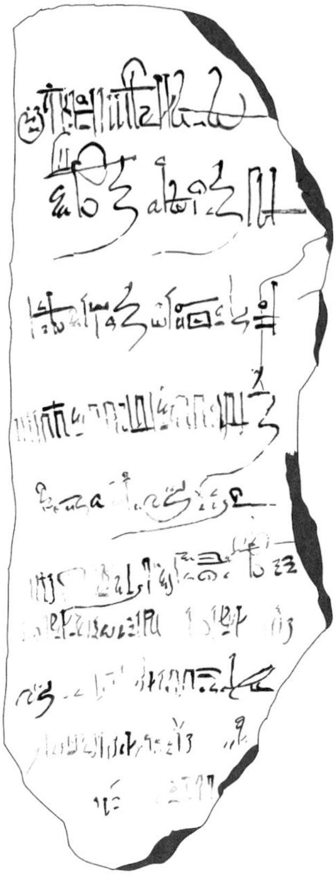

Fig. 6 O. Cairo GC 25745, facsimilé © N. Sojic

Fig. 7 O. Turin CG 57516 © Nicola Dell'Acquila and Federico Taverni, Museo Egizio

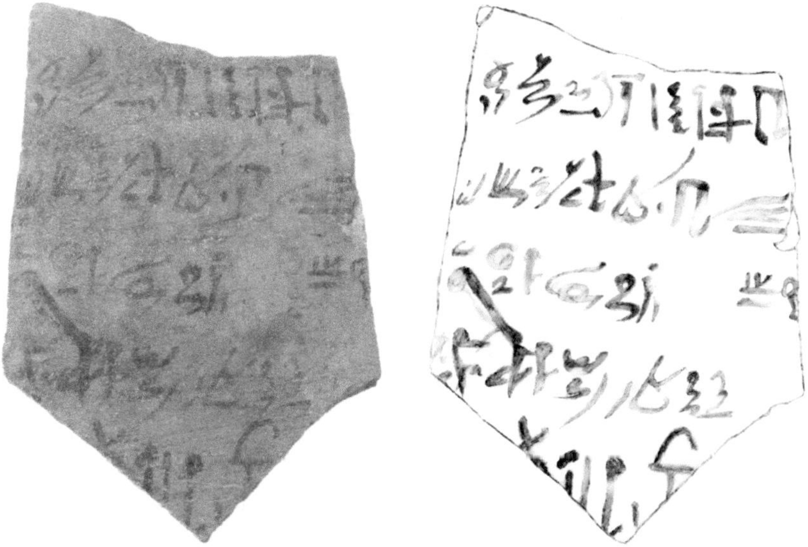

Fig. 8 Photograph and facsimile of OL 1850 © IFAO, N. Sojic

use was intentional or what was the scribe's purpose. A very good example is found in P. Salt 124,[58] a document in which the scribe Amennakht recorded allegations against the foreman Paneb, accused, among other misdeeds, of sleeping with several married women of the village of Deir el-Medineh. Lines 2–4 of column 2 begin with the same verb, *nkꞽ*, 'fornicate' (*Wb* II, 345.3–10). While he generally respects the alignment of the signs at the beginning of the column, Amennakht blithely overflows the tracing of the sign *k* into the right-hand bracket:

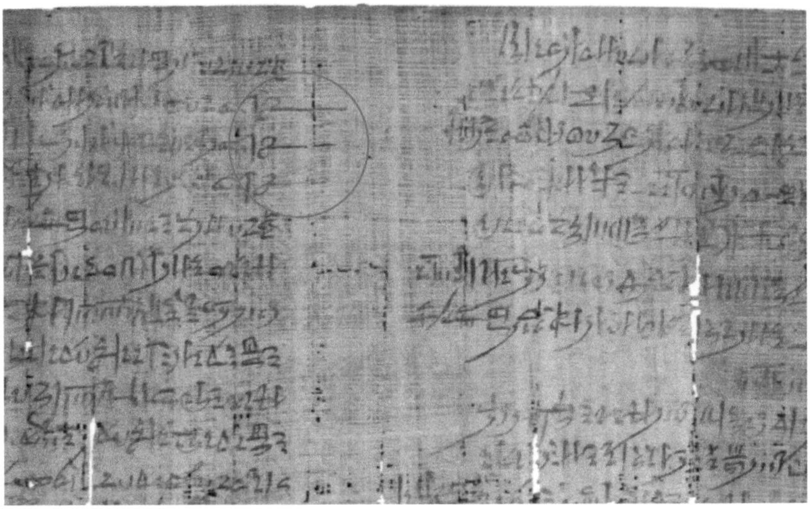

Fig. 9 P. Salt 124, detail of col. 1–2 © Trustees of the British Museum.

The eye of the reader is very quickly attracted to these three long horizontal lines – whose shape is, moreover, reminiscent of a phallus. If all one can say with certainty is that Amennakht got carried away in the drawing of this horizontal line, it is not impossible, however, that he voluntarily exaggerated the size of the sign. One could see it as a humorous stroke playing on the analogy of form, when written in hieratic, between the *k* (𓎡) (circled in blue on the picture) and the 𓂸 (whose shape can be close to that of *k*), or as a reflection of indignation at Paneb's obscenity.

These material observations invite us to define the phenomenon of sign de-calibration as an intentional act that fulfills a function that is sometimes ornamental, sometimes practical, and sometimes symbolic.

4.2 Meaningful Values of Graphic Registers: The Use of Literary and Non-literary Hieratic and Ramesside Chancery Script in Letters

In the New Kingdom, there are several types of hieratic, usually described in terms of 'literary', 'non-literary', and 'chancery script'.[59] These categories can be defined in relation

58 Richard Parkinson, personal communication. The example is reproduced here with his kind permission.

59 Parkinson & Quirke (1995: 27).

to each other in terms of size, organization, and the absence or presence of sign ligatures. The scripts requiring greater effort and application belong to more formal registers. As explained above (§3.3), the more formal and depersonalized a writing is, the more it connotes the text with a form of sacredness or canonicity.

The term 'literary' applies to a writing that has an ordered, regular, and calibrated appearance. The signs are organized in well-ordered squares and have a harmonious height and width. The thickness of the line is also regular. Ligatures are rare and even non-existent.[60]

The term 'non-literary' designates a spontaneous, very cursive writing free of any particular calibration and alignment. There are more ligatures than in literary hieratic writing.

Chancery script is marked by mannerism (stylistic exaggeration) and found in official administrative texts of the Ramesside period. It is characterized by signs written in a larger module than in the previous scripts, sometimes reaching up to 2 cm in height where the average height oscillates between 1 cm and 1.2 cm. The drawing is deliberately exaggerated: one generally observes a stretching in height, sometimes also in width.

The recourse to a given graphic register is not necessarily – even if it is a dominant tendency – ordered by the nature of the text. In the corpus of letters, one finds, by frequency of appearance, non-literary, literary and chancery hieratic regularly without anything in the text indicating that one is dealing with a secular text, a literary work, or a text emanating from the Court. In fact, an examination of the use of these registers in letters, but also in magical texts, illustrates that occasionally the appearance of the layout and graphics of the text constitutes in itself a first message, or that it conveys a particular communicative intention, or even a social meaning.

4.2.1 The Literary Hieratic

The existence of the graphic categories literary/non-literary/chancery is indubitable.[61] This implies that apprentice scribes had to practice each style in order to acquire mastery of a formatted, stereotyped writing, which was depersonalized by nature, and that at least some of them were able to switch from one register to the other when circumstances required it.

Our still relatively limited knowledge of hieratic paleography[62] only rarely gives us the opportunity to verify this assumption. The clues suggesting a learning and use of a calibrated

60 Gasse (1992: 57) uses the term 'organized writing' as opposed to 'disordered' writing.

61 See, *inter alia*, Parkinson (1999: 88–89), Verhoeven (2015: 39–48). The impropriety of the 'literary'/'non-literary' designations is no longer in question: I use them here for the sake of ease. Other denominations have been proposed (e.g., 'organized' *versus* 'disordered' writing, see Gasse 1992), but they have not yet acquired the status of commonly shared official appellations. For my part, I like to speak of 'calibrated', 'decalibrated' and 'spontaneous' writing. The purpose of this article is not to close the debate, nor to replace the terms 'literary', 'chancery' and 'non-literary' by new appellations, but to contribute, as a first step, to a better understanding of scribal practices. Moreover, it is understood that distinctions are to be made within literary writings, see Vernus (2010–2011: 50, n. 85).

62 For a state of the art, see Polis (2020).

graphic register, different from the ordinary writing of the author, are very tenuous.[63] One still hesitates to attribute to the same scribe two different scripts, one literary-formatted and the other non-literary-spontaneous, when these are attested on distinct documents. Rather than speaking of the 'literary hand' or the 'non-literary hand' of e.g. Amennakht, Qenherkhepshef, Hori or Butehamon, one rather describes their handwriting as careful or sloppy depending on the context.[64] Now, if a scribe adopts a completely different layout when switching from a non-literary graphic register to a calibrated register (literary or chancery) thus erasing any personal element in his writing, it is difficult to prove that two anonymous documents were produced by the same scribe unless this occurs within a single text.[65]

The epistolary corpus is of highest interest with regard to this problem. In these documents, the name of the sender, who in most cases can legitimately be assumed to be the scribe,[66] is regularly mentioned. The case of the scribe Maanakhtuf,[67] who lived during the 20th Dynasty, allows us to appreciate the social value attributed to the literary register.[68] Several epistolary documents written by him were discovered in the Valley of the Kings at the place where the remains of workers' huts were brought to light. Among them were a series of letters addressed to the vizier, the discovery of which *in situ* clearly indicates that they are the result of training and not real letters (to which is added the fact that several of them are limited to polite formulas with no real message). These fictitious letters addressed to a high-ranking person are written in a very neat and calibrated handwriting, as can be seen on O. BM EA 50723[69] (Fig. 10).

Two other letters from Maanakhtuf to a private individual have a radically different, much more spontaneous, and less legible appearance. The first, O. Cairo GC 25750[70] (Fig. 11), is addressed to a colleague, the scribe Nebnefer. The writing is not particularly neat:

---

63 The Kemyt copies on ostraca are an example of 'calligraphic' training (I use this adjective for convenience, but improperly in the ancient Egyptian context, to qualify training in careful writing: see Ragazzoli 2019: 69).

64 See Polis (2020: §1.3), for an updated bibliography on methods of identifying scribal hands.

65 On scribes' conscious use of different registers of writing, see especially Ragazzoli (2019: 72). The example she cites of P. Turin B vo. 4, 8 illustrates a change from 'literary' to spontaneous writing in the same text. See also the example of the calendrical tablet given by Vernus (1990b: 49–50), on which the scribe makes use of the literary and the documentary script. I also refer the reader to the cases of O. Strasbourg H 126 and P. Phillipps discussed below. One could argue that two different scribes worked on a single document, but the examples commented below do not fit well with this interpretation (see *infra*).

66 On the so-called 'delegation of writing' (an expression for the fact that a document is written by someone other than the author of the text – e.g. by a relative, a public writer or a secretary) in ancient Egyptian letters, see Bakir (1970: 33–34) and Wente (1990: 6–7). Some ostraca bearing letters fictitiously written in the name of the vizier undoubtedly testify to training to become a secretary in the high administration. On this subject, see Sojic (2019: 126).

67 On this scribe and its written production, see Dorn (2006).

68 See also the case of P. Phillipps below.

69 Demarée (2002: pl. 116).

70 Černý (1935: 77, 91* & pl. XCIV).

Fig. 10 O. BM EA 50723 © Trustees of the British Museum

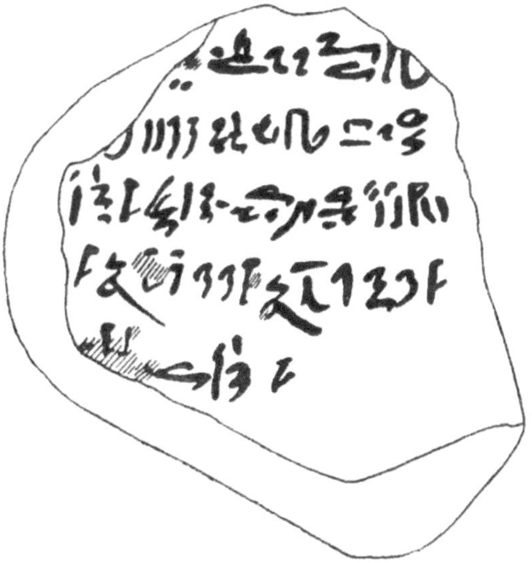

Fig. 11 O. Cairo GC 25750, facsimile from Černý (1935: pl. XCIV)

The second letter, O. Turin CG 57559[71] (Fig. 12), is an epistolary exercise presented as a letter from a vizier to a member of the Tomb institution. The writing is not calibrated:

71 López (1984: pl. 181). It was not possible to obtain a photograph, as the object disappeared from the collection shortly before the publication of the catalog, as reported by López (1984: 43).

Fig. 12 O. Turin CG 57559, from López (1984: pl. 210)

The case of Maanakhtuf allows us to understand his conscious use of literary and non-literary graphic registers, not according to the literary category of the text (we are dealing here with two letters), but according to the status of the person whom he is addressing. Several of these letters to the vizier have no content and are limited to polite formulae. This suggests that the objective of the training, of which these exercises are the fruit, was not only to master the phraseology related to epistolary communication with the vizier, but probably also to practice graphic conventions of an official document, more standardized, and therefore less spontaneous. Through this example, one perceives the social significance, not of the act of writing, but of the graphic appearance of writing. The cases of de-calibration mentioned in §4.1 reflect this same social dimension.

Finally, the literary hieratic is also opposed to the hieratic of the (non-literary) practice on what one could call, following the works of Assmann and Vernus,[72] 'the sacralization scale'. The regular and calibrated appearance of the literary writing makes it a favourite instrument to symbolize a form of canonization[73] within a documentation with nonpermanent end (see §3.3). The opposition literary versus documentary hieratic would be in some way the transfer, on easily manageable media, of the opposition hieroglyphic versus linear hieroglyphs attested on less easily manageable media.[74] Two letters – one on papyrus (P. Phillipps[75]), the other on ostracon (O. Strasbourg H 126) – perfectly testify to

72 See references given in n. 42.

73 This division is not unique to Pharaonic culture. See, for example, M. Beit-Arié's exemplary study of stereotypies and marks of individuality in medieval Hebrew documents: Beit-Arié (1990).

74 Vernus (1990a: 43–45).

75 A photograph of the papyrus is available online on the website of J. Paul Getty Museum without copyright. See the following link: https://www.getty.edu/art/collection/objects/16230/unknown-maker-fragmentary-hieratic-letter-egyptian-1200-1085-bc/.

this symbolic association at work. Both documents contain a long preamble of epistolary formulae before the message itself. These stereotyped preambles are written in literary hieratic, while the rest of the text continues in a much more spontaneous writing (Fig. 13–14):

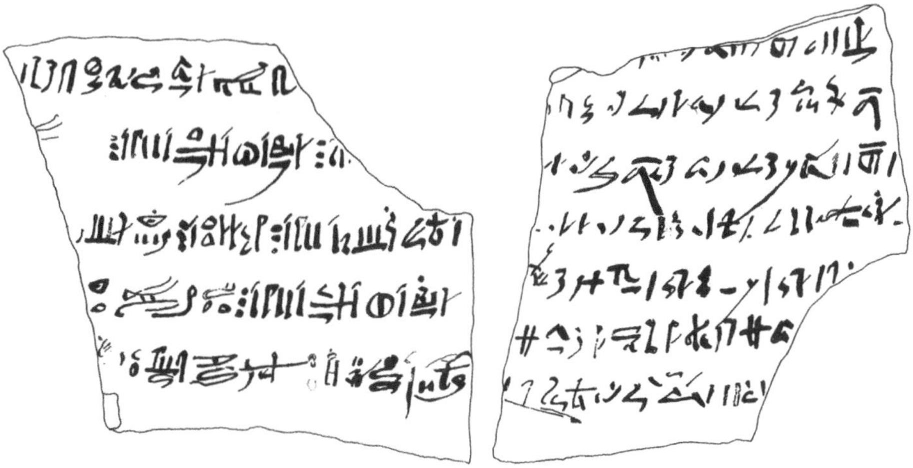

Fig. 13 O. Strasbourg H 126, facsimile from Koenig (1997: pl. 62–63)

O. Strasbourg 126 shows a very localized use of the two graphic registers (literary on the front, non-literary on the back) that perhaps indicate that one is dealing with two distinct letters.[76] However, the example of P. Phillipps confirms that the modification of the writing is not due to a change of scribe but indeed a voluntary and reflected act of one and the same person – namely the famous scribe Butehamon. On the front side of this document, the epistolary formulae, which occupy the upper half of the page, are written in a neat and calibrated handwriting. From the ninth line onwards, Butehamon comes to the message itself and gradually switches to a more spontaneous, much less elegant writing.[77] A link can be established here with the linguistic content: the formal appearance of the writing coincides with a passage displaying conservative and stereotyped uses of language.

4.2.2 The Chancery Hieratic of the Ramesside Period

Used in administrative texts of an official nature, notably royal decrees, the writing known as 'Ramesside chancery script' is characterized by signs with an oversized height and a rather strict arrangement of the squares. This particular script offers the advantage of great legibility, an aspect to which I will return. On an aesthetic and symbolic level, these characteristics along with the near absence of ink refills – the result of a great effort invested in the appearance – give the text a certain pomp and circumstance, thus visually echoing

76 As is the case in the *Deir el-Medina Database*, which offers two entries, one for the front and one for the back, as if they were two separate documents.

77 See Janssen (1991: 90–91) for an illustration.

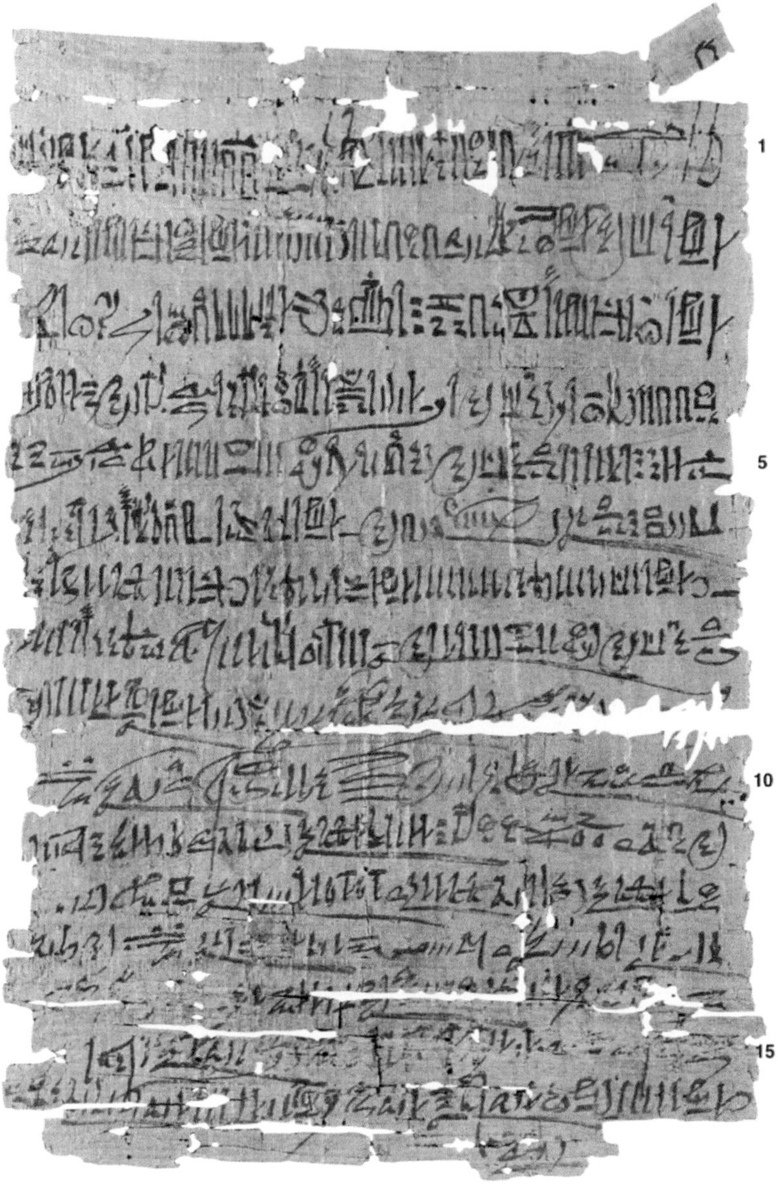

Fig. 14 P. Phillipps

the ceremonial magnificence of the Court. The mere graphic appearance of the text is thus sufficient, independently of its linguistic content, to connote it as a discourse emanating from the supreme authority of the Pharaoh and, through him, of the gods[78] (Fig. 15). In other words, the graphic setting of the text makes its sacredness and authority effective.

78 The work of Pascal Vernus on royal decrees perfectly illustrates the way in which communication from the government conveys, through both content and form, royal propaganda (Vernus 2013a and

Fig. 15 P. Turin CG 1896 © Nicola Dell'Acquila and Federico Taverni, Museo Egizio

It is worth emphasizing here once again the close link between the chancery writing and the person of the Pharaoh.[79] Several ostraca and papyri, most of them unpublished, testify to the training of scribes in this type of writing.[80] The Pharaoh's title is almost always the subject of these exercises, as well as notions that revolve around the royal person, as illustrated by the ostracon O. Turin CG 57506[81] (Fig. 16).

This touches on a cultural, even ideological dimension of writing, manifest in the way in which the person of the Pharaoh is given a personal graphic register. P. Grandet notes here an interesting detail: both in Papyrus Harris I and in other contemporary official texts of a contemporary legal nature written in chancery script, the presence of discursive sequences in which the Pharaoh – supposedly dead at the time of enunciation – expresses himself in the first person singular. The presence of these fictitious speeches has the effect

2013b). The reader will find, in the bibliography of these two articles, references on this subject.

79 Apart from royal decrees, Vernus, *op. cit.*, observes the use of a chancery script in two royal eulogies (P. Chester Beatty I vo, B and P. Turin CG 1882) and in a passage of the *Miscellanea* that includes the titulary of Ramses II (P. Leiden 348 = ÄMS 64). For a more systematic treatment of the use of this graphic register in the *Miscellanea,* see Ragazzoli (2019: 62 & 104–06).

80 At present, it is difficult for me to provide a precise survey of the documents written in chancery hieratic. I have not yet completed the systematic survey; the study is still in progress. Besides the beautiful and famous Ramesside papyri mentioned by Grandet, Vernus and Ragazzoli, one can suspect the existence of a training in this type of writing on some ostraca. Apart from O. Turin CG 57506 mentioned above, other examples include O. Strasbourg H 194 (Koenig 1997: pl. 98) and O. DeM 1077 (Posener 1938: pl. 43) The problems of identification are explainable by the similarity of this script with a large literary script: in some cases, it is difficult to know if one is dealing with one rather than the other. This suggests that literary writing and the chancery script form two gradients that should be placed close to each other on a scale of sacredness of the type [- FORMAL ------ + FORMAL]. The images of the unpublished papyrus fragments from Turin bearing chancery hieratic are accessible online via the *Turin Papyrus Online Platform-TPOP* (https://collezionepapiri.museoegizio.it/it-IT/).

81 Lopez (1984: pl. 168).

Fig. 16 O. Turin CG 57506 © Nicola Dell'Acquila and Federico Taverni, Museo Egizio

of elevating these texts from simple administrative reports to the rank of canonical texts.[82] Discursive sequences and graphic register thus constitute two complementary strategies of staging (or self-representation) of royal power. Their very presence enriches the strictly textual content with an additional layer of meaning, which in this case expresses the pervasive, imposing and sacred nature of royal authority.

This phenomenon, coupled with other clues,[83] has led P. Grandet to suggest that these papyri were perhaps intended as a form of display (he describes their writing as 'monumental hieratic'[84]). In any case, it seems that this type of document was displayed, either as a form of wall display as Grandet suggests, or as a public reading perhaps accompanied by an exhibition of the text for all to see. This is, for example, the case of the *wḫꜣ*, royal letters emanating from the Court,[85] of which P. Turin CG 1896[86] is a famous example.[87] The text on O. BM EA 50722 + O. Cairo GC 25726[88] tells that a *wḫꜣ* was officially read by the vizier before the villagers of Deir el-Medineh on the occasion of one of his visits to the Village. This underlines the very official character of the dissemination of these texts and of the ideological context for which they were designed.

4.2.3 The Non-literary Hieratic

Secular texts are mostly written in a script that is often more difficult to read than literary texts. Yet in some cases, as seen above, the non-literary nature of the content does not seem to be the determining factor in the (in)attention paid to the layout. In the corpus of letters, non-literary writing constitutes an unmarked graphic register because it is the one used by default most of the time. But this observation is not valid for all categories of texts. Sets

82 Grandet (1999: 108–10).

83 Grandet (1999: 123–24). The documents to which Grandet refers - the Judicial Papyrus of Turin, P. Lee, P. Rollin, P. Varzy, and P. Rifaud - have blank reverse sides. Furthermore, the papyrus format used corresponds to the maximum size of a papyrus sheet (Grandet 1999: 108). The use of hieratic rather than hieroglyphic writing can be explained, according to the editor of P. Harris I, by a desire that the document be read by as many people as possible.

84 See, on this designation, Ragazzoli (2017: §3.1.2), who also proposes to speak of ceremonial writing: Ragazzoli (2019: 106).

85 On the *wḫꜣ*-letters, see Bakir (1970: 15–17).

86 Bakir (1970: 24).

87 The document, moreover, refers to itself as *wḫꜣ* (P. Turin CG 1896, 7): 'Immediately the present rescript of Pharaoh VSF, your master, reaches you' (transl. *Ramses online*).

88 Demarée (2002: pl. 115).

of oppositions can emerge when we put different corpora into perspective. In this respect, the texts of the medico-magical category are opposed to the category of epistolary texts.

Texts with a magical (or medico-magical) content usually follow the tacit rules governing the writing of texts with a literary content. They are regularly written in a calibrated script, on a neat medium and employing an elaborate layout (§4.3.1). The use of punctuation in some of them testifies to their literary value.[89] Yet several documents from this category illustrate a completely opposite tendency: their layout is careless and the writing has an untidy, even illegible appearance.[90] This is notably the case with amulets on papyrus and text on execration figurines. These two types of documents, which form a sub-corpus in their own right within the category of medico-magical texts, show a sometimes neutral, sometimes meaningful use of a poorly cared-for graphic register.

The amulets on papyrus are the result of mass production; rolled up in a case worn around the neck, they were not intended to be read. The context of enunciation does not include a real addressee, and the text these objects carry were considered as performative and to function autonomously as an object providing protection.[91] This makes useless the recourse to a graphic register guaranteeing the readability of the message or any form of aestheticism.[92]

Execration figurines are ritual objects intended to symbolically annihilate Egypt's enemies. Shaped in different materials[93] and schematically representing the silhouette of a prisoner,[94] they are covered with inscriptions that mention them by name. They are attested from the Old Kingdom to the Late Period.[95] On these objects, which were broken during a ritual of execration,[96] the non-readability of the text is very probably intentional insofar as it participates in the annihilation of the enemy tribes that are mentioned by name.

4.3 Meaningful Layouts

4.3.1 Calligrammatic Layouts

A scribe could resort to layout effects to visually convey information that, in writing, would probably have required long explanations, or to increase the effectiveness of the text. The layout is then complementary to the linguistic content. One can, *mutatis mutandis*, speak about calligrams. Calligrammatic arrangements are found for example in magical texts, as on the ostracon O. Beit el-Kretleya Museum 868,[97] whose reverse bears a formula arranged in such a way that it evokes the shape of the fingers of a hand and a wrist (Fig.

89 On the material indices of the literary value given to a work, see Vernus (2010–2011: 47–48).

90 See the remarks of Gasse (1992: 69) about ostraca with a magical-religious content, in which poor care seems to have been paid to the writing.

91 See recently Donnat (2020).

92 The method of production of these types of documents, which were mass-produced, is also a factor to be considered.

93 There are figurines in terracotta, wax, wood, alabaster, see Posener (1987: 3).

94 Posener (1987: 1). More rarely, the execration text is written on pottery shards.

95 See Posener (1987).

96 Posener (1987: 11).

97 Haikal (2008).

17). The medium here also plays a role: the text is written on a fragment of stone whose shape evokes that of the hieroglyph representing the hand, 𓂧. This particular layout is undoubtedly intended to guarantee the effectiveness of the text.[98] The text asks god Amun to place his hand on the head of a sick person.[99]

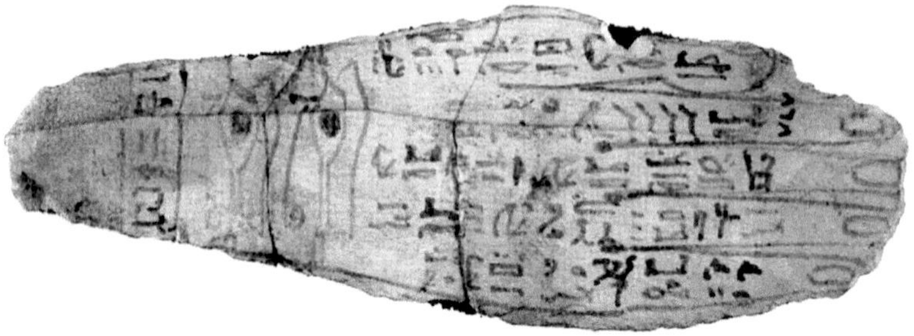

Fig. 17 O. Beit el-Kretleya Museum 868, from Haikal (2008: 246)

Another example of a particular arrangement derives from the corpus of letters, which, however, calls for a slightly different explanation. O. DeM 246[100] is a brief and hurried letter in which the sender commissions the addressee to draw a stela of a type widely used at Deir el-Medineh,[101] with instructions as to what should appear on it[102] (Fig. 18). To remove any ambiguity as to the form and function of the commissioned illustration, the scribe took care to frame his text, itself arranged in two columns of four and six lines, '*d'un trait en forme d'une petite stèle cintrée*',[103] so that the commission itself appears as a sketch:

98 This effectiveness lies in what is called 'analogy', a reasoning process typical of the magical thinking of the ancient Egyptians, see Schneider (2000). Analogical reasoning consists in finding a relationship between two situations. In New Kingdom magical texts, ancient Egyptian made large use of *historiolae*, i.e. stories of gods afflicted by sickness – as the patient is – that explain how to overcome this bad situation. In case of O. Beit el-Kretleya Museum 868, the analogy is formal: god Amun's healing power is conveyed through an object representing his hand.

99 Transl. Haikal (2008: 242): '(l. 1) *Your magic(?) caused you to be more mysterious than Seth's shadow* / (l. 2) *so that you may place 4 fingers on the head/in front(?)* / (l. 3) *of the one who hears a call for you. O Amun may you give* / (l. 4) *him strength and joy; may you give him* / (l. 5) *power and vindication and that his position be enduring…*'.

100 Černý (1939b: 2 & pl. 2).

101 Dowell (1999: 98). (col. 1, to the right) '*Please send this back to me right away today. Pay heed, pay heed!*'/ (col. 2, to the left) '*A depiction of Montu seated on a throne and a depiction of the scribe Pentawere kissing the ground before him in adoration of him – to be in outline drawing*', transl. Wente (1990: 139).

102 In another letter, O. Louvre 23554, an order for a window, the sender delivers to the recipient a sketch of the requested design with the measurements that each accompany the side of the window to which it relates. This document is not an example of calligrammatic layout, as the text, placed above the design, is not arranged in the shape of a window.

103 Černý (1939b: 2, *sub no*).

Fig. 18 O. DeM 246 © IFAO

In this case, the figurative layout provides visual information. Moreover, the scribe has separated, in his message, the description of the drawing, which makes up column 2, from the request itself, which makes up column 1. Within the description itself, he hierarchizes the data: first the god, enthroned, and below him, the prostrate human. The layout of the text reflects, voluntarily or unconsciously, the hierarchy that governs the relationship between a deity and his earthly worshipper.

4.3.2 The Use of Line Breaks in Enumerations

Enumerations are regularly found in letters, especially in those on ostraca: the sender asks for various goods to be sent to him (most often his family or a colleague), or, conversely, lists the goods he is sending. Some scribes, perhaps for the sake of clarity or out of habit, use line breaks to distinguish the list from the body of the main message, and to separate each component, as illustrated by O. DeM 122[104] (Fig. 19) and O. DeM 127[105] (Fig. 20). This layout is not systematic, nor is it the most frequent. The practice lies at the intersection of lettering and accounting.

104 Černý (1937: pl. 5).
105 Černý (1937: pl. 8).

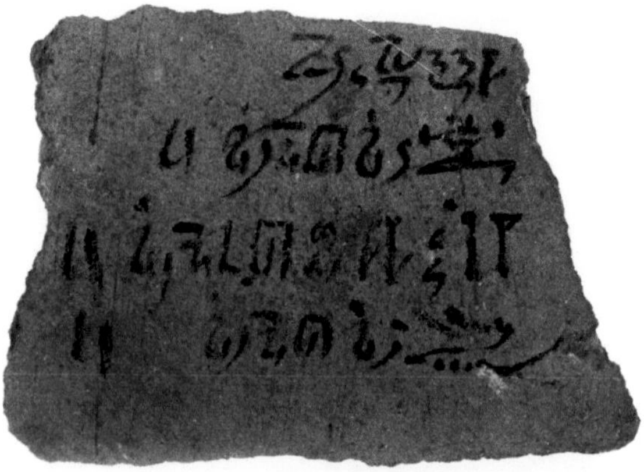

Fig. 19 O. DeM 122 © IFAO

Fig. 20 O. DeM 127 © IFAO

The next document, O. DeM 551,[106] has a hybrid layout. Here two products – *tꜥꜣ* 'a large loaf' (l. 3) and *ẖn.t 1* '1 skin' (l. 4) – are highlighted while the rest of the enumeration continues in what follows and without line breaks (the scribe uses coordinating conjunctions, *m-mἰtt* 'as well', then *ḥnꜥ* 'and, with') (Fig. 21).

106 Sauneron (1959: pl. 1).

Fig. 21 O. DeM 551 © IFAO

It is not uncommon that letters such as this, which have a particular layout, also contain paleographic similarities with other documents, indicating that they were written by the same scribe.

4.3.3 Page Layout as a Mirror of the Informational Structure: The Use of Line Breaks, Indentation and Blank Space

The use of line breaks and blank spaces are two processes used to structure written information. These graphic units[107] make it possible to distinguish different information contents, separating them into thematic blocks that are more easily identifiable to the reader. They are, naturally, more likely to be used in long documents, and thus occur in large numbers in literary, funerary or medico-magical texts copied on papyrus. Their use is very limited in epistolary ostraca, with the exception of letters with enumeration (§4.3.2), and it is most of the time difficult to ascertain whether they have a particular function or meaning such as organizing the letter or highlighting an element. Indeed, the layout of the writing seems to be usually determined by the shape of the medium. However, I have noted two letters on ostraca in which the scribe appears to make meaningful use of these layout devices.

In the letter O. Berlin P 12367,[108] a line break and an indent (or white space on the right) have been used to make the date more visible and to underline its paratextual status,

107 See Meletis (2020: 38) 'Graphetic level and units'.

108 https://dem-online.gwi.uni-muenchen.de/fragment_e.php?id=283.

i.e., to indicate that it is not part of the text itself, but delivers information about it (Fig. 22). The latter can be e.g. the moment of writing, information of reception, or reading of the text, or of the moment at which the message was followed up.[109] The paratextual status of this sequence is also marked by the use of signs larger than the text ('decalibration', see §4.1).[110]

Fig. 22 O. Berlin P 12367 © Staatliche Museen zu Berlin – Ägyptisches Museum und Papyrussammlung

In the letter O. Gardiner 125, the addressee mentioned in the incipit, Hy, is not the actual recipient of the message, but the intermediary through whom the message is to be transmitted to a certain Khaemter. The sender seems to have deliberately aligned the two addressees, first the intermediary, 'to the scribe Hy', and then the real addressee, 'to Khaemter', by having them each appear at the beginning of the line (Fig. 23).

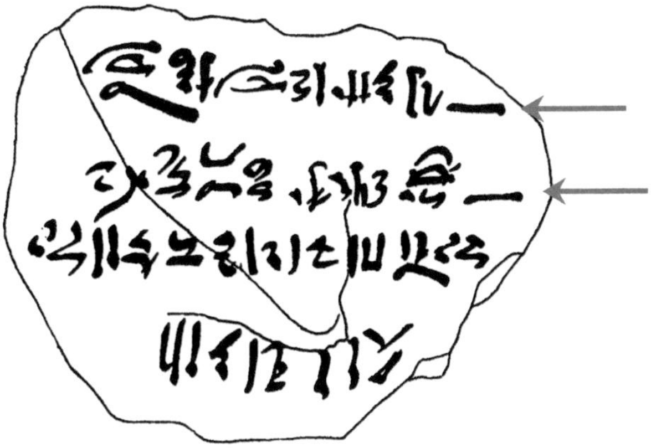

Fig. 23 O. Gardiner 125, from Černý & Gardiner (1957: pl. 32,4)

109 The writing here seems to be identical to that of the main text: the date therefore most probably refers to the time of writing.

110 For this reason, I have not included this sequence in quotation marks in the translation. I have not identified any other examples among letters of a similar treatment of the date.

These two examples suffice to show that documents as unattractive in appearance as hastily scribbled ostraca can demonstrate a thoughtful and meaningful use of layout.

Conclusion

The study of particular uses of the layout and graphics of the text in New Kingdom epistolary documents (and, for the purpose of comparison, in a few other documents) highlights a series of devices used by scribes to enrich the text with layer(s) of meaning. Defining grapheme units within a system of oppositions allows for a description of a system of variation. The use of common terms and notions such as 'registers' and 'repertoires' and of 'marked' versus 'unmarked' forms makes it possible to better compare two modes of expression, graphic and linguistic, that are of a very different nature. Following the functional approach in linguistics, in this paper I have sought to identify meaningful sets of graphic oppositions and to explain how these connote the content or scope of the message. An operative interplay between these two modes of expression is clearly seen at work within the epistolary and magical corpora, and even in documents as seemingly unpromising as small damaged shards. The relationship between graphic formalism and linguistic formalism thus appears in a new light. Often complementary, these two modes of expression can, in certain specific contexts, prove to be *a priori* antinomic; in documents with a marked layout, the appearance of the text is not so much controlled by the linguistic content, but, as we have seen, by socio-cultural practices (magico-religious or ceremonial, for example).

As specified in the methodological section, it is above all the trans-individual practices[111] that were targeted in this study. It has been observed that scribes played with the size and appearance of signs for very specific purposes (§4.1–4.2). They might bring out the informational salience and thus attract the reader's attention, to transfer a high or prestigious social status into pictorial language, endow the text with a canonical value, or to convey emotion. Some practices, such as the shifting of the preposition *n* to introduce the addressee, are already attested in earlier periods. It is also interesting to note that the use of *n* goes back to the use of a sign that was originally paratextual, which is an unusual development.[112] The coexistence of distinct graphic registers (calibrated and organized *versus* uncalibrated and unorganized) also goes back to well before the New Kingdom.[113]

The use of a calligrammatic layout (§4.3) was probably intended, in the case of the letter O. DeM 246, to facilitate the comprehension of the interlocutor. The use of line breaks, which is very common in accounting texts and is occasionally found in letters

111 See *supra*, n. 28.

112 At the time when hieratic was written in columns, a vertical line separated the name of the sender from that of the addressee. This line, which became horizontal when the scribes switched to horizontality, was later reinterpreted as *n*. Studies devoted to the paratext in ancient Egyptian sources show that normally the opposite tendency applies: most paratextual signs are originally characters of writing, see Carlig, Lescuyer, Motte & Sojic (2020).

113 Verhoeven (2015).

containing enumerations, is sometimes used for readability purposes, sometimes to structure the information, and sometimes to underline the paratextual status of a sequence.

The effects of writing and layout thus appear to have been richer than the few works devoted to the diplomatic of epistolary documents would suggest at first sight. Moreover, ostraca contribute as much as papyri to the understanding of New Kingdom scribal culture.

Bibliography

Albert, Florence, Annie Gasse & Nathalie Sojic (eds). In press. *Travaux des deuxième et troisième Académies hiératiques*.

Assmann, Jan. 1987. 'Hierotaxis: Textkonstitution und Bildkomposition in der altägyptischen Kunst und Literatur', in: Osing, Jürgen & Günter Dreyer (eds). *Form und Mass: Beiträge zur Literatur, Sprache und Kunst des alten Ägypten. Festschrift für Gerhard Fecht zum 65. Geburtstag am 6. Februar 1987*. Wiesbaden, 18–42.

Assmann, Jan. 1994. 'Die Ägyptische Schriftkultur', in: Hartmut, Günther & Otto Ludwig (eds). *Schrift Und Schriftlichkeit: Ein interdisziplinäres Handbuch internationaler Forschung 1*. Berlin; Handbücher zur Sprach- und Kommunikationswissenschaft 10, 472–91.

Bakir, 'Abd el-Moḥsen. 1970. *Egyptian Epistolography from the Eighteenth to the Twenty-first Dynasty*. Cairo; Bibliothèque d'étude 48.

Beit-Arié, Malachi. 1990. 'Stéréotypies et individualités dans les écritures des copistes hébraïques du Moyen Âge', in: Sirat Colette, Jean Irigoin & Emmanuel Poulle (eds). *L'écriture : le cerveau, l'œil et la main*. Turnhout; Bibliologia 10, 201–19.

Burkard, Günter, Maren Goecke-Bauer & Stefan Wimmer. 2002. 'Editing hieratic ostraca: some remarks for the new centennium', in: Eldamaty, Mamdouh & May Trad (eds). *Egyptian Museum Collections Around the World* 1. Cairo, 197–206.

Carlig, Nathan, Guillaume Lescuyer, Aurore Motte & Nathalie Sojic (eds). 2020. *Signes dans les textes : continuités et ruptures des pratiques scribales en Égypte pharaonique, gréco-romaine et byzantine. Actes du colloque international de Liège (2–4 juin 2016)*. Liège; Papyrologica Leodiensia 9.

Černý, Jaroslav. 1935. *Ostraca hiératiques I,2 (25501–25832)*. Cairo.

Černý, Jaroslav. 1937. *Catalogue des ostraca hiératiques non littéraires de Deir el Médineh. Tome II (nos 114 à 189)*. Cairo; Documents de fouilles de l'Institut français d'archéologie orientale 4.

Černý, Jaroslav. 1939a. *Late Ramesside Letters*. Bruxelles; Bibliotheca Aegyptiaca 9.

Černý, Jaroslav. 1939b. *Catalogue des ostraca hiératiques non littéraires de Deir el-Médineh IV (nos 242 à 339)*, Cairo; Documents de fouilles de l'Institut français d'archéologie orientale 6.

Černý, Jaroslav. 1952. *Paper & Books in Ancient Egypt: An Inaugural Lecture Delivered at University College London, 29 May 1947*. London.

Černý, Jaroslav & Alan Gardiner. 1957. *Hieratic Ostraca, Volume I*. Oxford.

Delattre, Alain & Naïm Vanthieghem. 2020. 'Les signes paratextuels dans les documents coptes. Une étude de cas : le dossier de Frangé', in: Carlig, Nathan, Guillaume Lescuyer, Aurore Motte & Nathalie Sojic (eds). *Signes dans les textes : continuités et ruptures des pratiques scribales en Égypte pharaonique, gréco-romaine et byzantine. Actes du colloque international de Liège (2–4 juin 2016)*. Liège; Papyrologica Leodiensia 9, 57–94.

Demarée, Rob J. 2002. *Ramesside Ostraca*. London.

Donnat, Sylvie. 2020. 'Les gestes rituels autour des papyrus-amulettes (Égypte, fin du IIe millénaire av. n. è.)'. *Archimède* 7, 37–50.

Dorn, Andreas. 2006. '*m33-nḫt.w=f*, ein (?) einfacher Arbeiter, schreibt Briefe', in: Dorn, Andreas & Tobias Hofmann (eds), *Living and Writing in Deir el-Medine: Socio-historical Embodiment of Deir el-Medine Texts*. Basel, 67–85.

Egberts, Arno. 1997. 'Piankh, Herihor, Dhutmose and Butehamun: A fresh look at O. Cairo CG 25744 and 25745', *Göttinger Miszellen* 160, 23–25.

Eyre, Christopher. 2013. *The Use of Documents in Pharaonic Egypt*. Oxford; Oxford Studies in Ancient Documents.

Gardiner, Alan & Kurt Sethe. 1928. *Egyptian Letters to the Dead Mainly from the Old and Middle Kingdoms*. London.

Gasse, Annie. 1992. 'Les ostraca hiératiques littéraires de Deir el-Medina : nouvelles orientations de la publication', in: Demarée, Rob J. and Arno Egberts (eds). *Village Voices: Proceedings of the Symposium "Texts from Deir el-Medîna and their interpretation", Leiden, May 31 - June 1, 1991*. Leiden, 51–70.

Goedicke, Hans. 1964. 'Diplomatical studies in the Old Kingdom', *Journal of the American Research Center in Egypt* 3, 31–41.

Grandet, Pierre. 1999. *Le Papyrus Harris I [III]: glossaire*. Cairo; Bibliothèque d'étude 129.

Grandet, Pierre. 2010. *Catalogue des ostraca hiératiques non littéraires de Deîr el-Médînéh. Tome XI: nos 10124 - 10275*. Cairo; Documents de fouilles de l'Institut français d'archéologie orientale 48.

Haikal, Faiza. 2008. 'An unusual ostracon from the Beit el Kretleya Museum', in: Gabolde, Luc (ed.). *Hommages à Jean-Claude Goyon offerts pour son 70e anniversaire Cairo; Bibliothèque d'étude 143, 241–46.*

Halleux (de), Nicolas. 1986. 'Aspects de mise en page des manuscrits de l'Égypte pharaonique', *Communications et langages* 69, 66–91.

Haring, Ben. 2018. 'Material matters: Documentary papyri and ostraca in *Late Ramesside Letters*', in: Hoogendijk, Francisca & Steffie van Gompel (eds). *The Materiality of Texts from Ancient Egypt: New Approaches to the Study of Textual Material from the Early Pharaonic to the Late Antique Period*. Leiden, 43–45.

James, Thomas. 1962. *The Ḥeḳanakhte Papers and Other Early Middle Kingdom Documents*. New York; Publications of the Metropolitan Museum of Art Egyptian Expedition 19.

Janssen, Jac. 1991. *Late Ramesside Letters and Communications*. London; Hieratic Papyri in the British Museum 6.

Klinkenberg, Jean-Marie & Stéphane Polis. 2018. 'On scripturology', *Signata. Annales des sémiotiques* 9, 57–102.

Koenig, Yvan. 1997. *Les ostraca hiératiques inédits de la Bibliothèque nationale et universitaire de Strasbourg*. Cairo; Documents de fouilles de l'Institut français d'archéologie orientale 33.

López, Jesús. 1984. *Ostraca ieratici nos 57450–57568*. Milan; Catalogo del Museo Egizio di Torino, serie seconda - collezioni 3 (1–4).

Malaise, Michel & Jean Winand. 1999. *Grammaire raisonnée de l'égyptien classique*. Liège; Ægyptiaca Leodiensia 6.

McDowell, Andrea G. 1999. *Village Life in Ancient Egypt: Laundry Lists and Love Songs*. Oxford.

Meletis Dimitrios. 2020. *The Nature of Writing. A Theory of Grapholinguistics*. Brest; Grapholinguistics and Its Applications 3.

Motte, Aurore & Nathalie Sojic. 2020. 'Paratextual signs in the New Kingdom medico-magical texts', in: Carlig, Nathan, Guillaume Lescuyer, Aurore Motte & Nathalie Sojic (eds). *Signes dans les textes : continuités et ruptures des pratiques scribales en Égypte pharaonique, gréco-romaine et byzantine. Actes du colloque international de Liège (2–4 juin 2016)*. Liège; Papyrologica Leodiensia 9, 57–94.

Parkinson, Richard. 1999. *Cracking Codes: The Rosetta Stone and Decipherment*. London.

Parkinson, Richard & Stephen Quirke. 1995. *Papyrus*. London.

Polis, Stéphane. 2020. 'Methods, tools, and perspectives of hieratic palaeography', in: Davies, Vanessa & Dimitri Laboury (eds). *The Oxford Handbook of Egyptian Epigraphy and Palaeography*. New York, 550–65.

Posener, Georges. 1938. *Catalogue des ostraca hiératiques littéraires de Deir el Médineh, I (nos 1001 à 1108)*. Cairo; Documents de fouilles de l'Institut français d'archéologie orientale 1.

Posener, Georges. 1987. *Cinq figurines d'envoûtement*. Cairo; Bibliothèque d'étude 101.

Quirke, Stephen. 2004. *Egyptian Literature 1800 BC: Questions and Readings*. London; Golden House Egyptology 2.

Ragazzoli, Chloé. 2017. *La grotte des scribes à Deir el-Bahari: la tombe MMA 504 et ses graffiti*. Cairo; Mémoires publiés par les membres de l'Institut français d'archéologie orientale 135.

Ragazzoli, Chloé. 2019. *Scribes: les artisans du texte en Égypte ancienne*. Paris.

Ragazzoli, Chloé. 2021. 'Registre graphique', in: *Abécédaire des mondes lettrés* [en ligne], available here: http://abecedaire.enssib.fr/r/registre-graphique/notices/163.

Rößler-Köhler, Ursula. 1984–1985. 'Zum Problem der Spatien in altägyptischen Texten: Versuch einer Systematik von Spatientypen', *Annales du Service des Antiquités de l'Égypte* 70, 383–408.

Rößler-Köhler, Ursula 1990. 'Die formale Aufteilung des Papyrus Jumilhac (Louvre E.17110)', *Chronique d'Égypte* 65 (129), 21–40.

Sauneron, Serge. 1959. *Catalogue des ostraca hiératiques non littéraires de Deir el-Médineh. [Tome VI] (nos 550–623)*. Cairo; Documents de fouilles de l'Institut français d'archéologie orientale 13.

Schneider, Thomas. 2000. 'Die Waffe der Analogie: Altägyptische Magie als System', in Gloy, Karen & Manuel Bachmann (eds). *Das Analogiedenken: Vorstöße in ein neues Gebiet der Rationalitätstheorie*. Freiburg, 37–85.

Simpson, William Kelly. 1966. 'The letter to the dead from the tomb of Meru (N 3737) at Nag' ed-Deir', *Journal of Egyptian Archaeology* 52, 39–52.

Sojic, Nathalie. 2019. 'Les ostraca IFAO OL 1850, 6126, 3498 et 3208. Quatres lettres relatives à des *ṯꜣy-hw*', in: Albert, Florence & Annie Gasse (eds). 2019. *Études de documents hiératiques inédits : les ostraca de Deir el-Medina en regard des productions de la Vallée des Rois et du Ramesseum. Travaux de la première Académie hiératique - Ifao (27 septembre - 1er octobre 2015)*. Cairo; Bibliothèque générale 56; Cahiers « Égypte Nilotique et Méditerranéenne » 22, 123–41.

Verhoeven, Ursula. 2015. 'Stand und Aufgaben der Erforschung des Hieratischen und der Kursivhieroglyphen', in: Verhoeven, Ursula (ed.). *Ägyptologische „Binsen"-Weisheiten I-II: Neue Forschungen und Methoden der Hieratistik. Akten zweier Tagungen in Mainz im April 2011 und März 2013*. Stuttgart, 23–63.

Vernus, Pascal. 1990a. 'Les espaces de l'écrit dans l'Égypte pharaonique'. *Bulletin de la Société Française d'Égyptologie* 119, 35–56.

Vernus, Pascal. 1990b. 'Les manuscrits de l'Égypte ancienne', in: Martin, Henri-Jean & Jean Vezin (eds). *Mise en page et mise en texte du livre manuscrit*. Paris, 16–23.

Vernus, Pascal. 2010–2011. '« Littérature », « littéraire » et supports d'écriture : contribution à une théorie de la littérature dans l'Égypte pharaonique', *Egyptian & Egyptological Documents, Archives, Libraries* 2, 19–145.

Vernus, Pascal. 2013a. 'The royal command (*wḏ-nsw*): a basic deed of executive power', in: Moreno García, Juan Carlos (ed.). *Ancient Egyptian Administration*, 259–340.

Vernus, Pascal. 2013b. 'L'acte fondamental du pouvoir dans l'Égypte pharaonique: l'ordre royal (oudj-nesou)', in: Bussi, Silvia (ed.). *Egitto dai Faraoni agli Arabi: atti del convegno Egitto: amministrazione, economia, società, cultura dai Faraoni agli Arabi. Milano, Università degliStudi, 7–9 gennaio 2013*. Pisa, Roma, 21–35.

Vernus, Pascal. 2020. 'Form, layout, and specific potentialities of the Ancient Egyptian hieroglyphic script', in: Davies Vanessa & Dimitri Laboury (eds). *The Oxford Handbook of Egyptian Epigraphy and Paleography*. Oxford.

von Bomhard, Anne-Sophie. 1998. *Paléographie du Papyrus Wilbour: l'écriture hiératique cursive dans les papyri documentaires*. Paris.

Wente, Edward. 1990. *Letters from Ancient Egypt*. Atlanta; Writings from the Ancient World 1.

Online resources

Deir el Medina Database: https://dmd.wepwawet.nl/
Deir el-Medina Online: https://dem-online.gwi.uni-muenchen.de
Ramsès: http://ramses.ulg.ac.be/
Online catalogue of the Louvre : https://collections.louvre.fr

Verbal and Lexical Suppletion in Ancient Egyptian

Jean Winand

1 Introduction

This paper is a part of a general study in ancient Egyptian linguistics at the crossroads of lexical semantics and verbal actionality. It deals more precisely with different interrelated types of semantic phenomena that are well-known in general linguistics, but still poorly investigated in ancient Egyptian: complementarity, asymmetry, and suppletion.[1]

2 Paradigmatic suppletion

Paradigmatic suppletion is a common phenomenon cross-linguistically. Suppletion is at work when a word does not have a regular morphology. Instead of taking the inflexions or endings that regularly apply to the members of their morphological class, words use different forms. In general linguistics, one usually makes a difference between weak and strong suppletion.[2] The former one applies when irregular forms related to a single root/stem are used. This is for example the case with the pair 'bring' vs. 'brought' in English. In Egyptian, a case of weak suppletion is offered by the alternation of the stems *jj* and *jw* in *jwj* 'to come'. Strong suppletion happens when a word supplies parts of its paradigm with forms from other words. This phenomenon is well-known with the so-called irregular verbs of Indo-European languages, like λέγω, εἶπον, εἴρηκα 'to say' in ancient Greek. It is also attested in nominal morphology, for instance, for expressing the degrees of comparison (ἀγαθός, ἀμείνων, ἄριστος 'good' in ancient Greek), or the plural of nouns (ребёнок vs. дети 'child', год vs. лет 'year', человек vs. люди [cf. *Leute* in German] 'person – people' in Russian). Although this does not seem frequent in ancient Egyptian, some examples suggest themselves like *z* vs. *rmṯ* 'man vs. people' in EEg.[3]

1 The following abbreviations have been adopted: EEg for Earlier Egyptian, MEg for Middle Egyptian, LEg for Late Egyptian, EgTrad for Égyptien de tradition, OK for Old Kingdom, NK for New Kingdom, SIP for Second Intermediate Period, and TIP for Third Intermediate Period. Examples are provided with the specification of date, provenance and literary genre. By provenance, one understands the provenance of the document, which does not necessarily coincide with the place of composition. I warmly thank the anonymous reviewers for their comments and suggestions for improving the quality of this paper, and Sami for his help and support. All shortcomings of course remain mine.

2 See Juge (2000).

3 In Later Egyptian, however, *z* has completely disappeared, leaving *rmṯ* as a collective but also a singulative noun (*pꜣ rmṯ* 'the man' vs. *nꜣ rmṯ* 'the men', cf. Coptic ⲣⲱⲙⲉ). The pair ⲟⲩⲁ vs. ϩⲟⲉⲓⲛⲉ (indefinite singular and plural article) in Coptic is another illustration of strong suppletion.

Sami Uljas & Andreas Dorn (eds), *Crossroads VI. Between Egyptian Linguistics and Philology*, 327–355
DOI: https://doi.org/10.37011/studmon.30.12

In this paper, I shall first produce some evidence for cases of strong suppletion in ancient Egyptian (**3**), before summing up the main arguments (**4**). I shall then enlarge the perspective by suggesting that the concept of suppletion can be extended to include other cases of what I shall here call semantic suppletion (**5**). Some words of conclusion finally wrap up the paper (**6**).[4]

3 Strong suppletion in ancient Egyptian

In this section, I review two cases of strong suppletion in ancient Egyptian, namely *šm* – *ḥn* (**3.1**) and *h3j* – *ḫr* (**3.2**).

3.1 *šm* and *ḥn* 'to go'

The basic opposition between the two generic verbs of motion ('go' vs. 'come') is expressed in EEg by the pair *šm* – *jwj*.[5] In LEg, the basic centrifugal movement was taken over by two verbs, *šm* and *ḥn*. Elaborating upon a suggestion already made by Wente, Peust suggested that these two verbs are in complementary distribution according to the grammatical tenses they are used with.[6] The verb *ḥn*, which originally meant 'to hasten, to move quickly', underwent a process of semantic bleaching, and ended up as a synonym of *šm*; it must be accordingly translated 'to go'.

When looking at the evidence more closely, the morphological patterns are not distributed between the two stems as straightforwardly as it seems, for some tenses are actually attested with both *šm* and *ḥn*. The evidence is particularly clear for the subjunctive and, to a lesser extent, the stative.[7] For the latter tense, while *ḥn* is clearly the preferred stem in LEg, *šm* sporadically occurs in conservative texts where the influence of EgTrad can still be felt. As regards the subjunctive, the distribution is rather geographically conditioned, as already suggested by Peust.[8] The relevance of the regional factor seems to be supported by the distribution of other tenses that are also worth considering, namely the imperative, the stative, and the infinitive. First, the forms used for the imperative are shown in Table 1.

---

4 To some extent, suppletion could also be advocated for explaining cases of grammatical asymmetry in the verbal predication. For instance, while there is a distinction in EEg for expressing the perfect between transitive and intransitive (*jw sḏm.n.f* 'he has heard' vs. *jw.f jw.w* 'he has come') in negative, however, the pattern *n sḏm.f* applies to both constructions (*n sḏm.f* 'he has not heard' vs. *n jj.f* 'he has not come'). The same observation can be made with respect to the subjunctive and the future (*sḏm.f* 'may he hear!' vs. *jw.f r sḏm* 'he will hear', but *nn sḏm.f* 'he will not hear'). In a more cognitively oriented approach, this might be accounted for by the phenomenon of 'radiality': see Uljas (2009), elaborating on Collier (1994).

5 See Winand (1991).

6 Wente (1959), Peust (2007). The role of *nꜥj* in this distribution appears to be limited to the expression of the stative, and is not attested in this role before later LEg, i.e. in the TIP. See the discussion below.

7 Peust (2007). For the stative, see the discussion below.

8 While *ḥn* is overwhelmingly used in the subjunctive, the predominance of *šm* after *rdj*, however, could suggest some early process of lexicalization of the causative construction.

Table 1 | Distribution of *ḥn* and *šm* in the imperative.

oDeM 1064, r° 2	unknown	
oDeM 117, 2	19th dyn.	
oPetrie 62	19th dyn.	
pDeM 39, r° 5	19th dyn.	
oDeM 10061, 19	Ramses II	
pSallier 1, 5,10	Merenptah	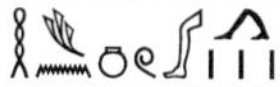
pBM 10429, v° 1	20th dyn.	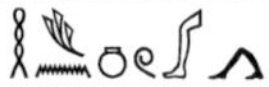
pBM 10054, r° 2,2	Ramses IX	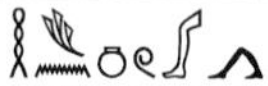
pBM 10054, r° 3,11	Ramses IX	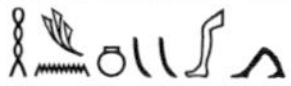
pBM 10052, r° 6,4	Ramses XI	
pBM 10403, v° 3,4	Ramses XI	
pMoscow 120 (= *Wenamun*), 1,45	21st dyn.	
pBM 10800, 5	22nd dyn.	
oDeM 1064, r° 2	unknown	
pBN 202 + pAmherst 9 (= *Astarte*), 2,x+11	18th dyn.	
pCairo CGC 58054, 4	Amenhotep III	
pDeM 01 (Ani), 3,5	19th dyn.	
pHarris 500 (= *Taking of Joppe*), 2,11	19th dyn.	
oDeM 636, r° 3	Seti I	
pOrbiney (= *Two Brothers*), 3,1	Seti II	
pAnastasi 5, 24,4	Seti II	
oCairo prov. n° 175, v° 4	20h dyn.	
pDeM 19	20th dyn.	
pTurin 1880, r° 4,21	Ramses III	
oCaire CG 25364, r° 6	Ramses IV	
pDeM 26, v° B2	Ramses III	
oGardiner 54, v° 3	Ramses III	
oChicago OIC 12074	Ramses IV	

P. Chester Beatty 1 (= *Horus & Seth*), 10,12	Ramses V	
pAbbott, 5,2	Ramses IX	
pBoulaq 4 (*Ani*), 15,16	21st dyn.	
pBoulaq 4 (*Ani*), 19,12	21st dyn.	
Inscription of Taharqa (Karnak), col. 20	Taharqa	

The data are presented in two groups, for *ḥn* and *šm* respectively, in chronological order with the spellings. As is clear enough, diachrony cannot be the governing principle for explaining the distribution of the two stems. However while *šm* is attested all across Egypt, *ḥn* is limited to texts coming from Upper Egypt, with only one isolated counter-example (courtesy of pSallier 1,5,10), which does not suffice to invalidate the hypothesis.[9] One is thus faced with the same kind of distribution as for the Future III as regards the expression of the nominal subject: while the canonical paradigm *jrj* + NP + (*r*) + infinitive is used without limitation all over Egypt, the pattern *jw* + NP + *r* + infinitive, which was fully productive in EEg, is also attested, but only in Upper Egypt.[10]

A similar line of explanation can also be suggested for the stative. It has been argued that *šm* is unusual with the stative,[11] except for some texts where some influence of EgTrad is present, like in the Poem of Qadesh. According to the data encoded in the Ramses database, there are three, possibly four, instances of the stative in texts whose core predicative system is LEg:[12]

[1] *twj* *šm.kwj* *r* *ptr* *p3* *ḫpr* *jm.s*
PRS-1SG go:RES-1SG to see:INF ART:M.SG happen:PTCP in-3SG.F
'I went to see what happened there.' (oStrasburg H 68, 2–3)
End 18th–19th dyn. – Deir el-Medineh – Letter

[2] (as for the wise men that come after the gods (…) *st* *šm*
3PL(PRS) go:RES-3PL
'They are gone.' (pChB 4 v° 2, 5–6)
19th dyn. – Deir el-Medineh – Wisdom text

[3] *sn* *šm* *r* *p3y*[ ]
brother go:RES-3SG.M to POSS:M.SG
'The brother is gone to his (?)' [ ] (oDeM 10629 r° 2)
Ramses VII – Deir el-Medineh – Non-literary

9 For other dialectal features in Deir el-Medineh, see Winand (2016, 2022, forthc. a).
10 Winand (1992, 2016, 2018).
11 Peust (2007: 74).
12 In a passage from pAnastasi 8 (K*RI* III 501, 1–2), which is unfortunately partly in lacuna, the stative is probably the best option of analysis: *mk p3j.f ḥrj-mnš* [3 c.] *šm r dj.t 3tp p3j rmṯ 2 jnn m sb.t* 'look, his captain came (?) to make these two guys of ours take charge of the cargo'.

[4]	*twj*	*šm.kwj*	*r-ḥ3.t*	*n3*	*mdw.t*	*ʿn*
	PRS-1SG	go:RES-1SG	because	ART:PL	affair-F.PL	again

‘I went again because of the “affairs”.’ (pMayer A r° 4, 5)
End 20th dyn. – Theban area – Judicial

A last example should probably be included in this small set. It is, however, methodologically better to leave the analysis undecided between a circumstantial Present I with a stative and a sequential due to the numerous lacunae of the context:

[5]	*jw*	*ns-sw-ḫnsw*	*šm*	*r*	*p3*	*ḥn*
	SBRD	Neskhons	go:RES-3SG.M	to	ART:M.SG	??

‘After Neskhons has gone to the (?) / and then Neskhons went to the (?).’ (Oracular decree for Henuttaui, l. 14)
21st dyn. – Karnak – Oracular

Finally, another candidate is probably better understood as a circumstantial Present I with (*ḥr*) + infinitive, as suggested by the spelling of the verb, although admittedly one can never draw a firm conclusion from the spelling alone:

[6]	*jw*	*p3*	*wʿw*	(*ḥr*)	*šm* ()	*ḥr*	*ʿš*
	SBRD	ART:M.SG	soldier	[PROG]	go:INF	on	call:INF
	n	*nṯr.f*					
	to	god-3SG.M					

‘While the soldier is on his way calling his god.’ (pSallier 1 7, 5–6)
Merenptah – Memphite area – Miscellanies

From this very small list, it is striking that all examples come from Upper Egypt. It is thus tempting to link them to a form typical of the southern dialect.[13] The small number should not invalidate the result. However limited in number, the examples of *šm* should not go unnoticed for the following reasons. Although the majority of the data come from Upper Egypt, *ḥn*, which is overwhelmingly the preferred stem in the stative (37 examples in the Ramses Database), provide examples from both Lower and Upper Egypt. In this distribution, the fact that the examples of *šm* are circumscribed to a geographical area that precisely belongs to the bigger subset, is clearly significant.

The case of the infinitive is also worth considering. As has been often noted, *šm* is the stem used for this tense. Nevertheless, there are a few examples of infinitives with *ḥn*:

[7]	*j3*	*jḫ*	*p3j.k*	*tm*	*ḥn*	*n*	*md3j*	*PN*
	EXLM	Q	POSS:M.SG-2SG.M	not_do	go:INF	to	medjai	PN

‘Why do not you go to the Medjai Nebmehit?’ (oDeM 554, 1)
19th dyn. – Deir el-Medineh – Letter

13 Due to its particular composition, pAnastasi 8 is better left out of the discussion as regards its geographical provenance and some possible links of its author(s) with dialectal varieties.

[8] *mtw.k* *ḥn.k* *ḥnꜥ* *mḏꜣj* *pꜣ-sr*
CORD.MOD-2SG.M go:INF-2SG.M with medjai Paser
'And you will go with the Medjai Paser.' (oDeM 558,7)[14]
19th dyn. – Deir el-Medineh – Letter

[9] *jw.f* *ḥr* *ḥn* *r* *tꜣ* *ḥw.t* *KN*
CORD-3SG.M on= go:INF to ART:F.SG temple-F KN
ꜥ.w.s. *m* *pr* *jmn*
lph in domain Amun
'And he went to the temple of KN, lph, in the domain of Amun.' (oBerlin 10633 r° 3–4)
20th dyn. – Theban area – Administrative

[10] *jw* *ṯꜣtj* *(r)* *ḥn* *n.f* *tꜣ* *wnw.t*
FUT vizier [:FUT] go:INF to-3SG.M ART:F.SG hour-F
'The vizier will leave immediately.' (oDeM 227 r° 3–4)[15]
20th dyn. – Theban area – Letter

The following example is open to discussion, for a sequential or a circumstantial Present I with a stative are both possible. Unfortunately, the context is too badly damaged to draw a definite conclusion:

[11] *jw.n* *(ḥr)* *ḥn* [ ] / *jw.n* *ḥn*
CORD-1PL [on=] go:INF / SBRD-1PL go:RES-1PL
'And we went / as we had gone.' (oDeM 227, r° 3–4)
20th dyn. – Theban area – Letter

Yet analyzing *ḥn* as a stative here is not very attractive, for one would expect either the ending *-tw* (Ex. 12) or, but less frequently attested, the conservative ending *-wjn* (Ex. 13).[16] The first ending is quite common at the end of the 20th dynasty for all persons, except for the 1st singular, where *-k(wj)* remains the default ending[17], and the 3rd masc. singular and the 3rd plural:

14 One will note here the presence of a direct object co-referenced with the subject, which is reminiscent of some uses of other verbs of motion like *ꜥn(n)* 'to return, to come back', *pnꜥ* 'to turn back', *ḥmsj* with the meaning of 'to settle'.

15 The presence of a Benefactive co-referenced with the subject is well-known with some verbs of motion, particularly with *šm* (Winand 2006: 84; 2021).

16 A zero ending is attested only once in a letter: *r-ḏd twn ḥms r-šꜣꜥ pꜣ hrw* 'we are settled (here) up to now' (*LRL* 69, 10).

17 The ending *-tw* is also possible in certain syntactic environments, and become regular during the TIP, as shown in *Wenamun* (Winand 1992: 103–49).

[12] *twn* *ḥn.tw* *m* *wḥm* *zp* *r* *nꜣ*
PRS-1PL go:RES-1PL in repeat:INF time to ART:PL
ḥtr.w *ʿn*
doorjamb-M.PL again
'We have gone back once more to the doorjambs.' (pBM 10053 v° 3, 19)
End 20th dyn. – Theban area – Judicial

[13] *jw.n* *ḥms.wjn* *ḥkr.wjn*
SBRD-1PL sit:RES-1PL be_hungry:RES-1PL
'While we continued starving.' (pBM 10403 v° 3–7)
End 20th dyn. – Theban area – Judicial

As is well known, *šm* is not found with the preposition *m* to convey the progressive.[18] This can be explained by the non-durative Aktionsart of *šm*, which properly means 'to set on (a journey)'.[19] It can take the meaning of walking by modifying its argument structure. By deleting its second argument, *šm* is recategorized as an atelic activity verb, and can consequently be used in a progressive construction with *ḥr* + infinitive. Here are three relevant examples:

[14] *jḫ* *pꜣ* *ntj* *ḥr* *šmj.t* *m-sꜣ* *pꜣ*
Q ART:M.SG REL-M.SG PROG- go:INF behind ART:M.SG
s *ʿꜣ* *ntj* *m* *jj.t* *ḥr* [*tꜣ*]
man great REL-M.SG PROG- come:INF on [ART:F.SG]
mj.t
road-F
'What is this that is walking behind the great person who is coming on the road?' (*LES* 2, 4–5)
19h dyn. – Theban area – Fiction

[15] (*j.jr.ṯ* *šmj.t*) *r* *pꜣ* [*ntj*] *twṯ*
THMZ-2SG.F go:INF to ART:M.SG REL-M.SG PRS-2SG.F
(*ḥr*) *šmj.t* *jm* *jw.j* *jrm.ṯ*
(PROG) go:INF there(ADV) MCM-1SG with-2SG.F
'When you went to the place to which you were going to, I was with you.' (pBerlin 10497 v° 5–6)
20h dyn. – Theban area – Letter

---

18 See already Vernus (1990: 157) for MEg. Examples of *m šm* in LEg must be analyzed as the full preposition *m* 'in' (i.e. the non-grammaticalized preposition *m*) followed by the noun *šm* 'expedition, enterprise, gang': *jw.k m šm wʿ jrm Kꜣr* 'you were in the same expedition as Kar (lit. in a single expedition with Kar)' (*LRL* 19, 14–15).

19 See Winand (2006: 40,112, 2021: §3.1, 4.4).

[16] *bn t3 js.t* <*n*> *p3 ẖr ḥr šmj.t*
NEG ART:F.SG gang-F of ART:M.SG Tomb PROG- go:INF
r b3k m p3 ẖr n pr-ʿ3
to work:INF in ART:M.SG tomb of Pharaoh
ʿ.w.s
lph
'The gang of the Tomb is not going to work in the Tomb of Pharaoh, lph.' (K*RI* VI 642, 5)
20th dyn. – Deir el-Medineh – Administrative

As already noted, *šm*, like other verbs of motion, could also be used as a proto-auxiliary in constructions for conveying aspectual, temporal or modal nuances, without ever reaching the full stage of a grammaticalized pattern.[20] In this respect, *šm* seems to be more frequently attested than *nʿj* for expressing the mellic aspect in LEg before the TIP:

[17] *ẖr jw.k* (*ḥr*) *šmj.t* <*r*> *wj3 rn.j*
CORD SBRD-2SG.M [PRS=] go:INF to repel:INF name-1SG
m-b3ḥ n3 rmṯ m p3 dmj ntj
in_front_of ART:PL man in ART:M.SG city REL-M.SG
twj jm.f
PRS-1SG in-3SG.M
'But you came to move away my name in front of the men in the village where I am.' (pDeM 7, v° 3–4)
20th dyn. – Deir el-Medineh – Letter

[18] *twk ḥr šmj.t* <*r*> *jrj.t jḫ*
PRS-2SG.M PROG- go:INF to do:INF Q
'What are you going to do?' (pAnastasi 5,11,6)
19th dynasty – Memphite area – Miscellanies

[19] *n3* (*j*).*wn twtn ḥr šmj.t ḥr smtr*
DEM:C was(AUX) PRS-2PL PROG- go:INF on= report:INF
ḥr.sn
on-3PL
'Those you were going to report upon.' (K*RI* III 532, 4–5)
19th dyn. – Deir el-Medineh – Letter

In the following example, the construction with two coordinated phrases *ḥr* + infinitive has a conative modal value:

[20] *sw ḥr šmj.t ḥr nḥm dḥr.w gr*
3SG.M(PRS) PROG- go:INF PRS= take:INF hide-M.PL still
š3ʿ-m p3 hrw
since ART:M.SG day
'He is still going around taking the hides up to now.' (*Urk* IV 2149, 8–9)
End 18th dyn. – Karnak – Royal decree

20 See Grossman, Lescuyer, Polis (2014: 101–05).

Finally, Peust has also suggested that the verb *nꜥj* should be integrated in the paradigm of *šm*, for supplying the latter in the construction *m* + infinitive.[21] This is, however, a different case from those studied so far. *ḥn* does indeed supply *šm* with some tenses in EEg (and it is still attested in some dialects as observed above). As regards *nꜥj*, it is actually supposed to fill a systemic gap – the expression of the progressive – since *šm*, as discussed above, is never found with this pattern. The progressive aspect does not make sense for *šm*, whose Aktionsart is non-durative. Two points are relevant here in the discussion. First, *šm* can be used in the progressive with some adaptation of its argument structure. Second, the suppletion of *šm* by *nꜥj* would entail that the latter underwent the same process of semantic bleaching as was observed for *ḥn*, which does not seem to be the case.

The case of *nꜥj*, and its relation to *šm*, should be reopened. In later LEg (i.e. at the turn of the 20th–21st dyn.), *nꜥj* was progressively used in a new pattern to express an activity about to happen.[22] In this long process that extended over several centuries, *nꜥj*, which originally means 'to navigate', underwent a process of semantic bleaching, expressing the generic activity of going before ending up as a tense-prefix in Coptic. In LEg, however, the evidence shows that *nꜥj* always retained somewhat of the idea of navigating in its meaning, not only, as expected, in texts where some influence of EgTrad can be found (Ex. 21), but also in texts written in plain LEg (Ex. 22).

[21] *pꜣ* *dj* *nꜥy* *wjꜣ* *rꜥ* *m*
ART:M.SG CAUS:PTCP navigate:SBJV bark Re with
ꜣḫ.w *nw* *tp-rꜣ.f*
magic_power-M.PL of-M.PL speech-3SG.M
'The one who makes the bark of Re navigate with the magic powers of his speech.' (oDeM 1080, 2)[23]
Ramesside – Deir el-Medineh – Hymn

[22] *ḫr* *wnn* *pꜣ* *jmw* *(ḥr)* *nꜥj,* *jw.(j)*
CORD when ART:M.SG ship [PRS=] navigate:INF CORD-1SG
ḥr *jn* *n.k* *nꜣj.k* *bꜣk.w* *ḥmw*
on= bring:INF to-2SG.M POSS:PL-2SG.M production-M.PL craftwork
'As soon as the ship will sail, I shall bring you your productions of craftwork.' (pBM 10683 v° 4–5)
19th dyn. – Deir el-Medineh – Letter

21 Peust (2007: 72). For the sake of completeness, one should also consider the use of the adverbial predicate for negating a positive activity expressed by *jwj* or *šm*: e.g. *st jw n.tn, bn st dy m-dj.n* 'they have gone to you, they are not here with us' (pLeiden I 365, 7). See also statements like *jw bn nꜣ ḫꜣstj.w jm* 'the foreigners are not here' (*KRI* VI 564, 4) or *jw mn rbw dy* 'there is no Libyan here' (*KRI* VI 564, 15) in the Journal of the Tomb, which could be the negative counterparts of *nꜣ ḫꜣstj.w jw.w* 'the foreigners have come', etc. In this respect, one can compare the role of 'to be' in Spanish as a suppletive form of 'to go' in the perfective (Pomino & Remberger 2019. 492–93), a phenomenon also known in modern French (*'j'ai été à Paris'*), without having reached the stage of grammaticalization.

22 See the extensive study on the grammaticalization paths of the construction from LEg to Coptic by Grossman, Lescuyer & Polis (2014).

23 Cf. pLeiden I 344, VI 8; oTurin N 57428 v° 3–5; oBM EA 21282 v° 3; pBerlin P 3049 IV, 5. In a different context, see also pBM 9999, 7, 5; 44, 4.

A significant part of the data deals with oracular procedures. For opposing a proposal submitted to the god, it is generally said that the god *nꜥj n-ḥꜣ.f*, i.e. moves backward.[24] The presence of *nꜥj*, instead of *šm/ḥn*, must obviously be linked to the divine portable bark carried on the priests' shoulders during the consultation:

[23]	*ꜥḥꜥ.n*	*pꜣ*	*nṯr*	*ḥr*	*nꜥj*	*n-ḥꜣ.f*
	CJVB:ANT	ART:M.SG	god	PRS=	navigate:INF	behind-3SG.M

'And then the god moved backward.' (oIFAO 1280 r° 7)[25]
20th dyn. – Deir el-Medineh – Oracular

In the same context, *nꜥj* is once used to describe the arrival of the god on the silver ground of the court of the 10th pylon in the temple of Amun-Re in Karnak, where the oracular consultation of the god used to proceed:[26]

[24]	*nꜥj*	*m*	*ḥr.f*	*ḥr*	*pꜣ*	*tꜣ*	*ḥḏ* (…)
	navigate:INF	in	face-3SG.M	on	ART:M.SG	ground	silver

'Proceeding toward him on the silver ground (…).' (pBrooklyn 47.218.3, A 2–3)
26th dyn. – Theban area – Oracular

In other texts, while the context is insufficient to decide whether a travel by boat was implied or not, there is no ground to reject it *a priori*. Or rather, there is no basis to discard what the verb seems to mean *prima facie*. In the examples I have been able to collect, it is only reasonable to assume that at least the first part of the trip was made by boat. This was then probably enough for referring to the whole trip as a *nꜥj*-journey:

[25]	*jw.f*	*m*	*nꜥj*	*r*	*ḫꜣrw,*	*jw.j*	*ḥr*
	SBRD-3SG.M	PROG-	navigate:INF	to	Syria	CORD-1SG	PRS=

pnꜥ.f	*r*	*pꜣ*	*ḫtm*
return:INF-3SG.M	to	ART:M.SG	stronghold

'(When you reported to me about my son,) as he was sailing to Syria, I had him return to the stronghold.' (pAnastasi 5 13, 6)[27]
19th dynasty – Memphite area – Miscellanies

In the Qadesh Poem, *nꜥj* is used to describe the first steps of the king's expedition northwards to Syria. There is no reason to reject the possibility that the army first sailed on the Nile before going by land for the rest of the journey. One will note that there is no other use of *nꜥj* in the Poem, which also seems relevant. The verbs for expressing the generic motion in the Poem (and the Bulletin) are *jwj* 'to come', *mšꜥ* 'to walk, to go', which is the regular verb used to describe the march of the army, and *šm* 'to go'.[28]

24 For this formula, see Černý (1930: 491–96).
25 Cf. oUC 39622 r° 6–7; Oracular text for Djehutymose, l. 14.
26 See Kruchten (1986: 167–68). In the oracular consultations of the 21st dynasty, the arrival of the god was rather expressed by *sṯꜣ* 'to draw', a verb also connected to navigation. The mention of the silver ground is also well-attested in the formula *ḥtp* (*ḥr s.t wr.t*) *ḥr pꜣ tꜣ n ḥḏ n pr jmn* for indicating the end of or a halt in the procedure (Winand 2003: passim).
27 One will note the presence of *pnꜥ* 'to return', written with the classifier P1A ().
28 One can also add *wḏꜣ* 'to proceed solemnly', which is a heritage of the Königsnovelle only found with the kings and the gods.

[26] *nꜥj* *pw* *jr.n.f* *m-ḫd*
navigate:INF DEM do:REL-ANT-3SG.M PRS=go_northwards:INF
tꜣj.f *n.t-ḥtr* *pꜣj.f* *mšꜥ* *ḥnꜥ.f*
POSS:F.SG-3SG.M chariotry POSS:M.SG-3SG.M infantry with-3SG.M
'He travelled northwards with his chariotry and his infantry.' (Qadesh Poem, §28 Sallier III)
19th dyn. – ?? – Royal narrative

In the following passage, one cannot exclude the possibility that the author of the letter had first to cross the river to fetch the men settled in Thebes.[29] The verb *nꜥj* could in this case encompass as a single activity the crossing of the Nile, the wandering in Thebes to collect the workmen, and the way back to the West Bank.

[27] *ḫr* *wnn* *twj* *<m>* *nꜥj* *m* *njw.t* *<r>*
CORD when PRS-1SG PROG- navigate:INF in city-F <to>
jn *nꜣ* *rmṯ* *nty* *ḥms.w* *jm,*
bring:INF ART:PL man-M.PL REL-M.SG sit:RES-3PL there(ADV)
jw.j *(ḥr)* *gm* *rmṯ-js.t* *PN* (…)
CORD-1SG [on=] find:INF workman PN
'As I was coming/sailing back from Ne to fetch the men who had settled there, I met the workman PN.' (pBM 10375, 14–15)
End 20th dyn. – Theban area – Letter

In the *LRL*, the verbs that are used for expressing the generic centripetal or centrifugal motion are *jwj*, *ḥn*, and *šm*. The verb *nꜥj* is attested only three times, twice in the same papyrus. In addition to Ex. 27, the second example, from pBM 10375, does in no way exclude the possibility that the garments had to be delivered (partly) by boat:

[28] *jn* *bn* *twk* *m* *nꜥj* *jrm* *nꜣ* *ḥbs.w,*
Q NEG PRS-2SG.M PROG- navigate:INF with ART:PL garment-M.PL
ḫr *mntk* *j.jr.k* *swḏ.w* *n* *pꜣj.k*
CORD 2SG.M THMZ-2SG.M deliver:INF-3PL to POSS:M.SG-2SG.M
nb
lord
'Are not you going with the garments, for it is you who should deliver them to your lord?' (pBM 10375, 26)
End 20th dyn. – Theban area – Letter

This example can be linked to a passage from a letter of 'el-Hibeh', where there is once again no obvious reason to discard the possibility that the travel was partly, and more probably in its first part, done by boat:

29 See also *KRI* II 385, 3–5 about Khaemwaset's mission to announce his father's heb-sed all across Egypt (*r nꜥj.t m-ḫt tꜣ.wj*).

[29] *st* *(m)* *nꜥj* *r* *mšꜥ* [ ] *msj* *ṯꜣj*
3PL(PRS) [PROG] navigate:INF to go:INF garment take:REL
nꜣ *rmṯ*
ART:PL man
'They are about to go [ ] garments the men have taken.' (pStrasburg 24 iv+v, v° 2–3)[30]
21st dyn. – Middle Egypt – Letter

The last example deals with the military campaign which Dhutmose was about to make with Paiankh in pursuit of Panehesy in the South. It would be awkward if the expedition, which of course would also imply some march (cf. *mšꜥ* in the same line), did not first proceed by sailing upstream as far as possible:

[30] *twk* *rḫ.tw* *pꜣj* *mšꜥ*
PRS-2SG.M know:RES-2SG.M DEM:M.SG expedition
nty *twj* *m* *nꜥj* *r* *jr.f*
REL-M.SG PRS-1SG PROG- navigate:INF to do:INF-3SG.M
'You are aware of the expedition I am about to do.' (pBN 197 V, v° 3)
End 20th dyn. – Theban area – Letter

In the *Tale of Wenamun*, *nꜥj* is used only once, to qualify the flight of the birds that are going back (lit. sailing) to cooler regions. The most reasonable explanation is that Wenamun, who is in Byblos, that is on the seaside, was watching the birds as they pass before his eyes over the sea, which is sufficient enough to explain the use of a nautical metaphor as found in other languages for describing some species of sea-birds.

[31] *ptr* *st* *jw.w* *m* *nꜥj* *r* *ḳbḥ*
look:IMP =3PL SBRD-3PL PROG- navigate:INF to cool-region
'Look at them as they are going (lit. sailing) to a cool region.' (*LES* 73, 16)
21st dyn. – el-Hibeh – Fiction

Finally in pVandier, a very late literary tale at the juncture of LEg and Demotic, one cannot exclude that the use of *nꜥj* was consciously made to describe the fatal destiny of the king. The metaphor of death as the crossing of the Nile (cf. the widespread use of *mnj* 'to moor') is well-known enough in Egypt:

[32] *j.jr(.j)* *nꜥj.kwj* *r* *pꜣ* *mwt*
THMZ-1SG navigate:RES-1SG to ART:M.SG death
'It is to death that I will sail.' (pVandier 3, 9)
25th dyn. – Theban area – Fiction

Another possible metaphorical use is provided by the following example taken from a description of the miseries of the soldier. In this passage, the charioteer is depicted losing control of his vehicle. The use of *nꜥj*, without any adverbial adjunct, is strange if it is

30 One will also note in the same papyrus the following passage where some navigation is also intended: *yꜣ wn.f (m) nꜥj smj* [ ] *n* PN *r-ḥꜥ.t.j* 'for he was about to report to PN and myself' (r° 6–7).

supposed to express the trivial idea of going. I would rather suggest that there is an intended comparison with a boat that has no direction (a well-known metaphor in the classical literature, also found in the Ramesside Letter of Menna, and, of course, previously in the *Eloquent Peasant*). In this respect, the mention in the next sentence of a slipping road, reminiscent of the river's water, makes perfect sense:

[33] *pȝj.k* *ḥtr* *nʿj.f*
POSS:M.SG-2SG.M chariot navigate:IMPF-3SG.M
{ṯȝ} *mrj.<f>* *ḥr* *tȝ* *ẖrḳ.t*
take:INF speed-3SG.M on ART:F.SG slippery_ground-F
'Your chariot is drifting away, skidding on the slippery ground.' (pAnastasi 1 25, 8–9)
19th dyn. – Memphite area – Literary letter

Finally, the verb *nʿj* can also appear in contexts where navigation was previously implied by perhaps some kind of 'semantic attraction'. This seems to be the case in the passage from *Horus and Seth*, where Isis has just crossed the lake (*dȝj*) and is now walking under the trees:

[34] *wn.jn.f* *dȝj.s* *r* *pȝ* *jw* *ḥrj-jb,*
CJVB:CNSV-3SG.M ferry:INF-3SG.F to ART:M.SG island middle
ḫr *jr* *sj* *m* *nʿj* *ẖr* *nȝ*
CORD TOPZ 3SG.F(PRS) PROG- navigate:INF under ART:PL
šn.w, *wn.jn.s* *(ḥr)* *nw* (…)
tree-M.PL CJVB:CNSV-3SG.F (on=) notice:INF
'He then ferried her to the island of the middle, and as she was walking under the trees, she noticed (…).' (*Horus & Seth* 6, 2)
20th dyn. – Memphite area – Fiction

This explanation is admittedly only half-convincing, but one has to note that this is the sole appearance of *nʿj* in the tale. The verbs usually used for expressing a generic movement are as usual *jwj*, *ḥn* and *šm*. It would thus be curious to use *nʿj* for no particular reason. In this respect, one can compare Ex. 35 with a passage from the *Tale of the Two Brothers*, in very a similar context (walking down under a tree), where *šm* has been instead used:

[35] *jw.f* *ḥr* *šm* *r* *wḫȝ* *ḥȝty* *n*
CORD-3SG.M on= go:INF to search:INF heart of
pȝj.f *sn* *šrj* *ẖr* *pȝ* *ʿš* (…)
POSS:M.SG-3SG.M brother little under ART:M.SG cedar_tree
'And he went to search the heart of his younger brother under the cedar-tree (…).' (*Two Brothers* 13, 4)
19th dyn. – Memphite area – Fiction

To sum up, the evidence provides for the following conclusions:

1) the paradigm of the verb ‘to go’ in LEg was a suppletive one, with two stems involved, *šm* and *ḥn*;
2) in this process, *ḥn* underwent a process of semantic bleaching, losing its special modality of motion (to hasten > to go);
3) the two stems are in overall distributed across different verb forms;
4) some tenses could still be expressed by either stem. This can be explained as conservative reflexes in some texts influenced by EgTrad, but one must also consider that the distribution of the two stems was partly geographically conditioned.
5) the verb *nꜥj* must be left out of the picture as far as LEg is concerned. Indeed, in most cases the notion of navigating is clearly perceptible in its meaning.[31] One has also to take into account that the respective Aktionsart of *šm* and *nꜥj* are different, for the latter behaves more as an atelic verb of activity than as a telic verb. Another point worth mentioning is that *nꜥj* is never found in LEg for expressing the stative, which is one of its main uses in Demotic and Coptic to supply *šm*. Finally, *šm* is more frequently found for expressing a mellic process (‘to be about to do something’) in Ramesside LEg than *nꜥj*, which gradually took over only from the end of the 20th dynasty onwards.
6) Of course, one should be careful not to overstate one’s point. Examples from the beginning of the 21st dynasty show that *nꜥj* progressively lost its original semantic links with the action of navigating and later of moving. But the process was precisely so, gradual. It thus seems that in LEg, including in its last phase, the action of going was still consciously felt.[32]

3.2 *hꜣj* and *ḫr* ‘to fall’

Another interesting case not previously studied is the expression of falling and lying on the ground, which illustrates another kind of process that led to a suppletive paradigm in LEg.

In EEg, *hꜣj* ‘to descend, to go down’ and *ḫr* ‘to fall’ have their respective well-defined semantic domains showing only occasional overlaps. All tenses seem to be freely open to both lexemes.[33] However, things changed dramatically in LEg, and two steps can be distinguished in the process.

First, a quick look at the data immediately shows that in LEg *ḫr* is only found in tenses expressive of resultative state, like the old perfective and the perfective participle,

---

31 The regular presence of the moving legs classifier (D54) instead of the original boat classifier (P1) is not as significant as it first seems, as this should probably be better understood as part of a more general evolution of the system of classifiers in LEg (Chantrain 2014).

32 I thank an anonymous reviewer for pointing this out to me.

33 In EEg, *hꜣj* seems to have the same Aktionsart as *šm*, i.e. a non-durative telic process with an active post-phase (Winand 2006: 40, 112; 2021) as shown by the following example: *jnk pw hꜣ.kwj r bjꜣ* ‘it happened that I was going down to the Mines’ (*ShS*, 89). It also explains why in the pattern *m* + infinitive, *hꜣj* has a mellic value while *jwj*, a durative telic process (accomplishment) has a normal progressive meaning: *mṯ wj m hꜣj r km.t …* ‘I am about to go down to Egypt’ (*Peasant* R 1, 2–3).

which are still well represented. By contrast, *hꜣj* does not seem to suffer restrictions in its capacity of combining with all grammatical tenses. Yet, as regards the respective semantic values of the two verbs, the uses of *ẖr* have been restricted to expressing the situation of a subject lying on the ground. While still retaining its historical value of descending (Ex. 36–37), *hꜣj* is increasingly used to express the idea of falling, which was previously the domain of *ẖr*, but without including the resulting post-phase, which remained expressed by *ẖr* (Ex. 38–39). One must also note that *ẖr* is overwhelmingly present in texts where some influence of EgTrad can be felt. As a second step, *hꜣj* took over the expression of the resulting state (the post-phase) of the process of falling; the two examples from the same text describing an activity and its resulting state are illustrative of this stage (Ex. 40–41). As a consequence, *ẖr* rapidly went out of use.

[36]	*pꜣj.f*	*jrj*	*ḥr*	*hꜣj*	*(r)*	*tꜣ*
	POSS:M.SG-3SG.M	companion	on=	go_down:INF	(to)	ART:F.SG
	ꜥ.t	*ḥḳt*				
	room-F	beer-F				

‘His companion went down to the beer cellar.’ (oDeM 10270, 2)
Ramesside – Deir el-Medineh – Aphorism (?)

[37]	*hn*	*jṯꜣj*	*jw*	*ns-sw*	*pꜣj.j*	*tꜣ*	*pꜣ*
	MODP	thief	SBRD	belonging_to	POSS:M.SG-1SG	country	ART:M.SG
	hꜣj	*r*	*tꜣj.k*	*br.t*			
	go_down:PTCP	to	POSS:F.SG-2SG.M	boat-F			

‘If it were a thief that belongs to my country that went down to your boat.’ (*Wenamun* 1, 18–19)
21st dyn. – el-Hibeh – Fiction

[38]	*jr*	*hꜣj*	*pꜣ*	*wḏ*	*nty*	*sw*	*ḥr.f*
	COND	fall:PROS	ART:M.SG	stela	REL-M.SG	=3SG.M	on-3SG.M

‘If the stela where it (i.e. the decree) stands falls.’ (Amarna Boundary stela A, 18)
18th dyn. – Theban area – Royal decree

[39]	*jw.w*	*ẖr.w*	*ẖr*	*rd.wj.k*	*r*	*nḥḥ*
	SBRD-3PL	fall:RES-3PL	under	leg-M:DU-2SG.M	for	eternity
	ḏ.t					
	eternity-F					

‘They have fallen at your feet for ever.’ (*Joppe*, 3, 12)
19th dyn. – Theban area – Fiction

[40]	*jw*	*tꜣ*	*ẖꜣbw.t*	*n*	*tꜣj.f*
	CORD	ART:F.SG	shadow-F	of	POSS:F.SG-3SG.M
	srp.t	*(ḥr)*	*hꜣj.t*	*r.j*	
	umbrella-F	[on=]	go_down:INF	upon-1SG	

‘And the shadow of his umbrella fell upon me.’ (*Wenamun*, 2, 45)
21st dyn. – el-Hibeh – Fiction

[41] *tꜣ ḫꜣbw.t n pr-ꜥꜣ ꜥ.w.s. pꜣj.k*
ART:F.SG shadow-F of Pharaoh lph POSS:M.SG-2SG.M
nb hꜣ r.k
lord go_down:RES-3SG.F upon-2SG.M
'The shadow of Pharaoh you lord has fallen upon you.' (*Wenamun*, 2, 46)
21st dyn. – el-Hibeh – Fiction

To complete the picture, another issue should be addressed, namely the expression of the causative. In the corpus, the older (verb with prefix *s*-) and newer (periphrastic construction *rdj* 'cause' + subjunctive) causative patterns are attested for both verbs: *sḫr* and *shꜣj*, and *dj.t ḫr.f* and *dj.t hꜣj.f* respectively. As regards the second group, the data show clear-cut results: while the combination *dj.t hꜣj.f* is attested 34 times, *dj.t ḫr.f* is absent in texts written in plain Late Egyptian, only remaining in texts where the influence of Égyptien de tradition is perceptible. The two modes of expression can be contrasted in royal eulogies, where the same type of phraseology is used:

[42] *dj.j ḫr rkj.k ḫr ṯb.tj.k*
CAUS:IAPLI-1SG fall:SBJV enemy-2SG.M under sandal-F:DU-2SG.M
'I make your enemies to fall down under your sandals.' (*Urk.* IV 612, 16)
18th dyn. – Karnak – Royal

[43] *wn.jn ḥm.f ḥr dj.t hꜣw*
CJVB:CNSV Majesty-3SG.M on= CAUS:INF fall:SBJV
pꜣ ḫr.w n nꜣ ḫr.w n ḫtꜣ ḥr ḥr.sn
ART:M.SG enemy of ART:PL enemy-M.PL of Khatti on face-3PL
'And his Majesty made the forces of the enemies of Khatti to fall on their faces.' (Qadesh Bulletin, §104 L2)
19th dyn. – Theban area – Royal narrative

In the new causative, *hꜣj* overwhelmingly keeps its core meaning of going down. In the sense of falling, except for the passages of the Qadesh texts already alluded to where *dj.t hꜣj* is used in a military context,[34] *hꜣj* is attested only once in a TIP text belonging to the Oracular Amuletic Decrees corpus (pTurin 1983, v° 74).

The two verbs are also well contrasted as regards their respective uses in the older causative. The verb *sḫr* is overwhelmingly found in military contexts, in connection with the enemies of the king, and by extension the enemies of a god (pBoulaq 17, x3). Etymologically, it expresses an action that causes the patient to move vertically downwards. Often used absolutely, it can be accompanied by an adverbial adjunct to specify the place or instrument of the action. Combined with a resultative aspect, in particular with the old perfective, its meaning can easily overlap with that of *hꜣj*, *ḫr*, or *sḏr* (Qadesh Poem, §343

34 Cf. *dj.j hꜣj.sn n mw mj hꜣj msḥ.w, jw.sn ḫr <ḥr> ḥr.sn* 'I made them descend in water as descend crocodiles, as they were lying down on their faces' (Qadesh Poem, §138 Sallier 3). The comparison made with the crocodile suggests that *hꜣj* might retain much of its core value of going down, but the presence of *ḫr* in the following sentence is indicative that the action of *hꜣj* is not at all voluntary, and very close to the one of falling.

Sallier 3). In a judicial context, it is sometimes attested to mean punishment (K*RI* I 125, 15). There is also a single example where *sẖr* is used intransitively with the meaning of crashing, in a sense again very close to *ḥꜣj* or *ẖr* (pTurin 1993 = PR 132, 3). The original meaning is still present in a passage from a hymn to Amun, about the lowering of the arm (pLeiden I 343 + 345, x13). Finally, *sẖr* is used in connection with lies or evil, or even a disease that has to be defeated (pBM EA 75025, 8–9), according to the metaphor [WIN IS TO PUT DOWN].[35] One must here underline that this is the only use of *sẖr* in a documentary text.

The causative *shꜣj*, which is unfortunately split between several entries in the *Wb.*, etymologically means 'to lower', a meaning well attested in EEg: *jw shꜣ.n(.j) bj.t jnr 300 n hrw 1* 'I brought down 300 blocks of alabaster stone in a single day' (graffito Hatnub 6, 5). From there, *shꜣj* takes on the technical sense of evacuating harmful materials in the medical papyri (*kt nt wẖꜣ ẖt shꜣj.t ẖt nb.t ḏw.tn, tt m ḥꜥ.w n z* 'Another (remedy) to empty the stomach and to evacuate any painful matter which is in the body of a man' [pEbers 7, 2–4]). The meaning of descending is undoubtedly still present in a series of three examples taken from the Myth of the celestial cow, where it is applied to an inversion of an order of presentation.[36]

In LEg, the meaning of *shꜣj* has evolved greatly. Its uses are concentrated chronologically (from the second half of the 20th dynasty to the 22nd dynasty) and geographically (the Theban region), which is perhaps, for this last point, to be related to the general distribution of the written documentation for this period. The verb *shꜣj* has by then taken on distinctly pejorative nuances. This semantic evolution follows the general metaphor that what goes down is depreciated [DOWN IS BAD]. The link with the original meaning is still perceptible in a passage from Amenemope where *shꜣj* 'to lower, to diminish' is opposed to *ꜥšꜣ* 'to inflate, to increase' (19, 2), and probably also in a metaphor involving the heart-*jb*, 'to lower the heart in the belly', for expressing that the heart is no longer in its normal place (14, 10). A small thing or a belittled person can quickly become qualitatively depreciated, a meaning that is sometimes found, in a very concrete sense or with an ethical dimension. From there, the verb receives the meaning of faking, devaluing something, defrauding; it can be used absolutely or with a direct object. When the object is a person, *shꜣj* means 'to deceive (someone)'. In this latter sense, *shꜣj* is attested twice in the Tomb Robberies,[37] in a passage with a strong flavour of slang. It will be noted here that the evolution of *shꜣj*, with an animated object, towards the meaning of 'to drop, to neglect' is already attested in EEg (Letter to the Dead, Chicago Bowl, col. 6).

---

35 This a subcategory of the generic metaphor [UP IS POSITIVE] and [DOWN IS NEGATIVE]: see Lakoff – Johnson (1980: 15–16).

36 Himmelskuh (Tomb of Sethi I, l. 49, 50, and 51), with Pupko's commentary in the *TLA* (https://aaew.bbaw.de/tla/servlet/GetCtxt?u=guest&f=0&l=0&db=0&tc=774&ws=1494&mv=3, who argues that *m shꜣj* cannot here mean 'in the reverse order' (contra the Wb).

37 It is actually the reporting of the same episode in two different documents: see Winand (2018a: 145–46), Winand (2018b: 519).

[44]	*shꜣ.k*	*wj*	*ẖr<.f>*	*m*	*wꜥ*	*n*
	con-APLI-2SG.M	=1SG	say-APLI-3SG.M	in	one	to
	pꜣj.f	*jrj*				
	POSS:M.SG-3SG.M	companion				

"'you conned me", that is what they said to each other.' (pMayer A, v° 9, 19)
20th dyn. – Theban area – Judicial

The majority of the uses of *shꜣj* are concentrated in the Wisdom of Amenemope, where it is written with the classifier 𓂽 to perhaps first express the retreat from something, before becoming a derogatory term. Here it is also noteworthy that in TIP texts the classifier 𓅪 is present (oLouvre N 698 v° 21).

[45]	*m jr*	*shꜣ*	*rmṯ*	*m*	*tꜣ*	*ḳnb.t*
	PROH	deceive:INF	man	in	ART:F.SG	court-F

'Do not fool a guy at the court.' (*Amenemope* 20, 20)
20th dyn. – Theban area – Wisdom

3.4 Suppletion is no synonym for substitution or replacement

As should be clear by now, suppletion always involves the reorganization of the tense system of a given verbal lexeme, with a mixture of the original stem with another stem (weak suppletion, *jj/jw* type) or with another verb (strong suppletion, *šm/ḥn* and *hꜣj/ẖr* type). Suppletion should then not be confused with other kinds of evolution like substitution or replacement. These latter processes can be illustrated by the history of two lexical pairs, *ẖdb* – *smꜣ*, roughly meaning 'to kill', and *pḥ* – *spr* 'to reach'.

3.4.1 The case of *ẖdb* – *smꜣ* 'to kill'

The respective meanings of the pair *ẖdb* – *smꜣ* in EEg has been the subject of a recent study by Frandsen. In a nutshell, both verbs mean 'to kill', but the latter one would do it in a special way, by implying the total destruction of the [PATIENT], its complete annihilation, and hence the impossibility of any kind of afterlife.

While this general characterisation probably retains some global value, the distribution of the two verbs in LEg is not as clear cut as suggested by Frandsen. When looking at the data, one gets the feeling that the choice of either lexeme was conditioned by time and by the type of text.

It should be noted from the onset, when considering the long time, that *ẖdb* is indisputably gaining ground.[38] Absent from the OK documentation, it is only sparingly attested in the MK, where *smꜣ* is still prevalent. In Late Egyptian, *ẖdb* is more frequently found than *smꜣ*. In Demotic *smꜣ* is still attested, but on a very limited scale, and in Coptic it has disappeared completely. Of course, *smꜣ* is still well represented in religious texts written in EgTrad until the Graeco-Roman times.

38 For a detailed study, I refer to Winand (2021).

When looking at the LEg data, the first conclusion is that both verbs could be used in the same contextual environment. The activity of killing one's enemies can be expressed by both *ẖdb* or *smꜣ*, but one must note that there are identifiable clusters where one of the two verbs is predominantly used. In the royal inscription of the 18th dynasty, *smꜣ* is found everywhere (e.g. *Urk.* IV 1297, 1). A contrastive situation – and to my opinion a very illustrative one – is offered by the texts reporting Ramses II's expedition to Qadesh (including also the Hittite treaty) and the records of Ramses III's wars in Medinet Habu. The texts composed for Ramses II almost entirely ignore *smꜣ*, which is used only twice. The reverse situation can be observed in Ramses III's inscriptions, where *smꜣ* is used 48 times whereas *ẖdb* occurs only once. Strikingly, both sub-corpora contain identical expressions where the verbs occur in variance:

[46a] *jw.j* *ḥr* *ẖdb* *jm.sn* *r* *mr.n.j*
SBRD-1SG PROG- kill:INF in-3PL as wish-APLI-1SG
'I was killing among them as I wished.' (Qadesh Poem, §140 K1)
19th dyn. – Theban area – Royal narrative

[46b] *smꜣ.k* *ntj* *jb.k* *r*
kill:IAPLI-2SG.M REL-M.SG heart-2SG.M according_to
mrr.k
desire:NMLZ-2SG.M
'You slay the one that you wish according to your desire.' (K*RI* V 97, 4)[39]
20th dyn. – Theban area – Royal narrative

[47a] *tꜣ.w* *nb.w* *ḫꜣs.wt* *nb.wt* *ẖdb.w*
land-M.PL all-M.PL foreign-country-F.PL all-F.PL kill:RES-3PL
ẖr *ṯb.tj.f* *ḏ.t*
under sandal-F:DU-3SG.M eternity-F
'All lands and all foreign countries lay killed under your sandals for ever.' (Qadesh Poem, §343 K2)
19th dyn. – Theban area – Royal narrative

[47b] *smꜣ.j* *n.k* *tꜣ* *nb* *ẖr* *ṯb.tj.k*
kill-APLI-1SG to-2SG.M land all under sandal-F:DU-2SG.M
'I slaughtered for you all lands under your soles.' (K*RI* V 97, 15)
20th dyn. – Theban area – Royal narrative

[48a] *ẖdb.k* *ḥfn.w*
kill-APLI -2SG.M hundred_thousand-M.PL
'You slaughtered hundreds of thousands.' (Qadesh Poem, §84 L1)
19th dyn. – Theban area – Royal narrative

39 The verb *smꜣ* is also used in the Bulletin of Qadesh (§101 R1) instead of *ẖdb*, which was preferred in the Poem.

[48b] *smꜣ* *ḥfn.w*
kill:PTCP hundred_thousand-M.PL
'(…) who slaughters hundreds of thousands.' (K*RI* V 44, 8)
20th dyn. – Theban area – Royal narrative

As regards the semantics of the two verbs, the difference, if any, seems to be largely blurred. There are examples where *ẖdb* was used in documentary texts in contexts where it is explicitly stated that the act of killing was actually plain murder, planned *m grg* 'wrongly' (pDeM 26, r° A,19, see also *LES* 16, 10 and 16), which matches the criteria advanced for the use of *smꜣ*.[40] This is stretched to the extreme in the oracular inscription for Henuttaui (Ex. 49) where *ẖdb* is used for punishing people whose names, as explicitly stated in the following sentence, will also be wiped out from the surface of the earth.

[49] *[m-ḏd jw.]n* *ẖdb.w,* *jw.n* *fdḳ*
COMP CORD-1PL kill:INF-3PL CORD-1PL erase:INF
rn.w *m* *pꜣ* *tꜣ*
name-M.PL-3PL from ART:M.SG earth
'We shall kill them, we shall erase their names from the earth.' (Decree for Henuttaui, l. 20)
21st dyn. – Theban area – Oracular decree

In later LEg, *ẖdb* is exclusively used in non-literary texts. This applies to people that were killed during riots as a consequence of some personal feud, but also in a judicial context, as plainly evidenced in the corpus of the Great Tomb Robberies, where a person alludes to his possible punishment as a case of *ẖdb* (K*RI* VI 785, 15, see also K*RI* VI 776, 10–11). In the same corpus, convicted robbers are said to have been pinioned (K*RI* VI 827, 6),[41] a context where in earlier times *smꜣ* would have been used. In literary texts from the 20th dynasty onward, *smꜣ* was no longer used.[42]

The reverse situation can also be observed. In a passage from the *Miscellanies*, *smꜣ* was used to describe the activity of the mosquitoes tormenting people's life (oDeM 1014, 1,14). Of course, one can postulate some metaphoric use of *smꜣ*, implying that the pain inflicted is close to total annihilation, but this seems too far-stretched. The same conclusion should be drawn from a passage of Ani *a propos* the uncontrolled activity of a mad bull (pBoulaq 23, 1).[43] Actually, when a contrast is intended, one has the feeling that *smꜣ* is preferred for describing mass murder, while *ẖdb* is more often found in reference to killing individuals. On the whole, *ẖdb* is the unmarked term.

To sum up, *smꜣ* is gradually replaced in LEg by *ẖdb*, which means 'to kill' in the wider sense of the term but also 'to annihilate' in some contexts. The evolution is chronologically

40 See the two examples given in Frandsen's study (2016: 223).

41 See also K*RI* III 530, 4–5: *jw.f sẖr dj.tw ḥr-tp ẖt* a propos someone who had to give an oath by the Lord whose power (*bꜣw*) is worse than death, a context that also would have implied *smꜣ* in MK.

42 This is largely exemplified in the *Tale of Horus and Seth* (with one exception that reproduced a fixed phraseology), the *Tale of Woe*, the *Mission of Wenamun* and the *Tale of pVandier*.

43 Probably to be connected with *smꜣ* referring to a kind of wild bull (*Wb.* IV 124, 1–7) since OK.

conditioned, as demonstrated by the use of the two verbs in war inscriptions. Interestingly enough, the choice of either verb can be a matter of personal preference as shown by the exclusive presence of *smꜣ* in Ramses III's inscriptions at a time when *ẖdb* had already become prevalent. The transition can also be seen in ritual and magical texts. As *smꜣ* was largely retained in these texts when the EgTrad idiom was used, in later LEg fluctuations are sometimes observable in the same text:

[50a] *twj* *m-sꜣ.k* *r* *smꜣ.k*
PRS-1SG after-2SG.M to kill:INF-2SG.M
'I am after you to kill you.' (pBoulaq 6 r° IV, 2)
21st dyn. – Theban area – Magical

[50b] *twk* *ẖdb* *m* *wr ḥkꜣw.j*
PRS-2SG.M kill:RES-2SG.M by magical_power-M.PL-1SG
'You have been killed by my magical powers.' (pBoulaq 6 r° IV, 3)
21st dyn. – Theban area – Magical

The history of the pair *smꜣ* – *ẖdb* in Late Egyptian illustrates a case of lexical substitution of one lexeme (*smꜣ*) by another one (*ẖdb*). The verbs never merged into a single paradigm where one of them would have supplied the other for some grammatical tenses as was the case with the pair *šm* – *ḥn*. For this to happen, one would have expected *smꜣ* to undergo a process of semantic bleaching, which did not happen. If one returns to the evidence from MK literary works where *smꜣ* dominates, one may wonder if the notion of annihilation (the second death according to Frandsen's analysis) is always present. For instance, should we really assume that Sinuhe, who has no supernatural power as the king, is inflicting total destruction to his tribe's enemies when fighting them (B 104)? Similarly, is there any particular reason to think that in medical texts the use of *smꜣ* for killing worms infesting the body implied that they were subjected to a second death (pEbers 25, 11)?

In conclusion, my impression is that *smꜣ* (and later *ẖdb*) can take this precise meaning not because it was part of its core semantics, but merely because it is suggested by the context. From the NK onward, the distribution of the two verbs *a priori* seems to lend credit to Frandsen's hypothesis. The evidence, as shown above, only partially support it. As *smꜣ* was consistently used in texts written in EgTrad (royal inscriptions, religious and magical texts, and rituals), it is only natural that he would be preferred in contexts dealing with archetypal enemies and cosmic foes for which total annihilation could only be expected.

3.4.2 The case of *pḥ* – *spr* 'to reach'

In a previous paper, I extensively examined the semantic fields of the verbs *pḥ* and *spr* as well as their mutual relations.[44] Both are well represented in the LEg corpus, but *spr* is arguably more specialized if one compares the respective core meaning of both lexemes. While *pḥ* means 'to reach, to arrive', with the implication that the actor has finally reached a destination, *spr* means more specifically 'to make a stop on a journey', a precision that is

44 Winand (2019).

rarely lexicalized cross-linguistically, if attested at all. In some context, *pḥ* also means 'to attack' someone, a sense which is more frequent when the second argument is realized as a direct object. The semantic units of *pḥ* and *spr* are presented in Table 2.[45]

Table 2 | The semantic units of *pḥ* and *spr*.

pḥ	*spr*
pḥ(1a) "arrive, reach"	*spr*(1) "arrive, reach"
pḥ(1b) "catch up"	
pḥ(1c) "achieve, succeed"	
pḥ(2) "attack, assault"	*spr*(2) "make a plea, appeal"
pḥ(3) "at last (something happened)"	*spr*(3) "succeed in doing something"

spr is no longer attested in Demotic nor in Coptic, while *pḥ* is still widely used. As the LEg corpus is drastically limited during the TIP, one cannot document the disappearance of *spr*, nor suggest any plausible clue as regards the possible triggering factors. One can of course make some plausible guesses. When two lexemes are used in parallel with small, albeit significant differences, the more generic term can absorb the more specific one. *ḥn* had to somehow lose its relation to a specific way of moving (haste) to be able to enter the paradigm of the generic verb of motion *šm*. But the reverse is not impossible either. For instance, the generic expression of the verb of seeing underwent two consecutive cycles of transformation that saw the more specific verb take over the generic sense, which twice resulted in the disappearance of the former lexeme (*mꜣꜣ* > *ptr* > *nw*).

4 Verbal suppletion in ancient Egyptian

Morphological suppletion is not the same as lexical substitution. The examples that have been discussed in the preceding sections all tell a different story. Table 3 is a summary of the questions that were addressed in this study: a) are there perceptible semantic differences between the two verbs before they began to interact?, b) can one observe a process of semantic bleaching for one member of the pair?, c) was their interaction the motor for creating a suppletive paradigm?, d) if so, are there any dialectal features at work in this process?, and finally e) what was the final outcome of the process?

Table 3 | Summary of the criteria relevant for the phenomena of suppletion or substitution.

	originally semantic differences	semantic bleaching	suppletive paradigm	dialectal features	final outcome
jj/jw	?	?	yes	?	fusion
hꜣj – ḫr	yes	yes	yes	no	> *hꜣj*
šm – ḥn – (nꜥj)	yes	yes	yes	yes	> *šm*
pḥ – spr	yes	yes	no	no	> *pḥ*
ẖdb – smꜣ	no	no	no	no	both kept

45 For lack of space, I refer to Winand (2019) for a detailed presentation.

In the discussion above, a difference was made between weak and strong suppletion. Once two (or more) forms have merged to form a suppletive paradigm, semantic differences can no longer be observed. This is of course the case for *twj jj.kwj* 'I have come' and *sw jw.w* 'he has come', a case of weak suppletion: the fluctuation between the two stems *jj-* and *jw-* has no semantic relevance. The same conclusion also applies in LEg to *twj šm.kwj* 'I have gone' and *dj.j ḥn.f* 'I let him go', a case of strong suppletion.

In case of strong suppletion, some kind of semantic bleaching is, however, to be expected in case of the donor. This can be observed with *ḥn* when it integrated the paradigm of *šm*. In this process, it lost its particular modality of motion 'to go hastily, to run' to take the generic meaning of going. The situation is also rendered more complex as the distribution of the two stems was probably conditioned along geographical lines, which probably explains why *ḥn* disappeared somewhat abruptly in Demotic and Coptic.

A suppletive paradigm can be diachronically stable, as is for instance the case for 'to go' in the Romance languages, the *locus classicus* for the study of morphological suppletion,[46] even if they adopted different solutions to solve the same original problem (the morpho-phonological instability of Latin *ire*). This also seems to be the case for *jwj* 'to come' in Egyptian. As regards *šm* and *h3j* however, the final outcome turned out to be different. For after a period of time when the paradigms of *šm* and *h3j* were partly supplied with forms coming from *ḥn* and *ẖr* respectively, the latter verbs ultimately felt out of use. In later LEg, and then in Demotic, *nꜥj* came as a new player to supply some forms of the (already much reduced) paradigm of *šm*.[47] This is also what happened for the pair *h3j* – *ẖr*; the uses of the latter were gradually reduced in LEg and were eventually absorbed by *h3j*. This case is, however, different from what can be observed for *šm* and *ḥn*. While the uses of *ẖr* were limited to the old perfective and the perfective participle, *h3j* could also be commonly found in the old perfective when meaning 'to go down'. It is only in its meaning of 'to fall' that *h3j* constituted a suppletive paradigm with *ẖr*, which took in charge the expression of the resulting phase. This situation began to fade out when *h3j* took over from *ẖr* the expression of the post-phase.

This situation bears only remote resemblance to cases like *ẖdb* and *sm3*. Indeed, *ẖdb*, which was not attested before the MK, became common only in LEg, and was still largely used in Demotic and Coptic. On the other hand, *sm3*, which largely prevailed in EEg, gradually disappeared in LEg, was still retained in Demotic in certain formulaic contexts when speaking of foes and arch-enemies, and apparently left no trace in Coptic. There is no significant semantic difference between the two verbs. The distinction that was postulated between killing and completely annihilating, i.e. inflicting a second death, which undoubtedly captures something of the anthropology of ancient Egypt, turns out to be a consequence of the context and the literary genre, and should not be integrated in

46 For French, see Aski (1995), for an overview of all Romance languages, see Pomino & Remberger (2019). The French forms can be traced back to the Latin verbs *ire*, *vadere* and *ambulare*. For interesting parallels with the Greek verb ἔρχομαι and verbs of motion in general, see Létoublon (1987).

47 As shown by the situation in Coptic where the generic expression of centrifugal motion is distributed over two verbs along dialectal lines (ϣⲉⲓ vs. ⲃⲱⲕ), one cannot exclude that some geographical forces were already at work earlier.

the core semantic meaning of *smꜣ*. As the texts susceptible to allude to such a terrible fate mainly deal with religious matters, *sensu lato*, it was only to be expected that *smꜣ*, which is the default verb in Égyptien de tradition for 'to kill', would be overwhelmingly used. In this case, *ẖdb* and *smꜣ* never formed a suppletive paradigm with dedicated forms of either verb for expressing specific TAM features as is the case for *jwj* and *šm*/*ḥn* in Egyptian, or *aller* in French.

The dilution and then suppression of a near synonym can also be observed in the case of the pair *pḥ* and *spr*, which tells another story. Both verbs share the core meaning of reaching a place or a person. The verb *spr* however had the extra-meaning of making a stop on a journey. It thus contrasted with *pḥ* whose precise meaning was to reach the final destination.[48] As both verbs were semantically very close, one could expect some kind of economic solution. A possibility could well have been an intermediary stage with a suppletive paradigm, like was the case for *hꜣj* – *ẖr*. As it turned out, this was not the option chosen in Egyptian. As the semantic range of *pḥ* was more diversified than *spr*'s, the former eventually absorbed the latter, which is no longer attested in Demotic and Coptic.

5 Semantic suppletion

It is fascinating to observe not only in Egyptian, but cross-linguistically, how activities are lexicalized. The pairs *šm* – *ḥn* and *hꜣj* – *ẖr* offer interesting cases of semantic suppletion. In this section, I would like to extend the scope of this paper by offering some general considerations on how languages classify all kind of activities, or rather states of affairs (SoA), by using lexical, but also grammatical means. As this has been recently treated, I shall here limit myself to a short presentation.[49]

A SoA prototypically has three main defining moments: a beginning, an end, and something in between.[50] Moreover, activities have commonly additional phases that immediately precede or follow, without belonging to them *stricto sensu*, but nevertheless adhering to them cognitively. Phases are mainly defined by two properties, durativity and dynamicity. Two other notions are also worth considering in this respect: gradability and, above all telicity, which is not a phasal property, strictly speaking, but a property defining a SoA globally.

The question I would like to address here is precisely what makes a SoA and why a language lexicalizes a SoA with one lexeme, while another will rather choose to have two

48 Cf. the opposition between *pḥ.wj* 'hinder part, end' and *ḥꜣ.t* 'front, begin': Polis-Winand (2015).

49 See Winand (2021). The lack of specialized lexemes in Egyptian, when compared to modern languages, is another issue that will not be treated here. Most often it is the context that suggests a specialized word in translation where Egyptian uses a generic term. For instance, *ẖꜣj* 'measure' in medical texts will be translated as 'to examine, to make a diagnosis', or *ṯꜣj* in judicial procedures will be rendered by 'to steal, to rob', although it is a generic verb meaning 'to take'. Such cases of semantic under-specification are interesting, but are not to be mingled with the issue of semantic suppletion as defined here.

50 See Winand (2006). An updated version can be found in Winand (2021: §3.4). For the concepts of pre- and post-phase in Egyptology, see Winand (2006a: 67–68).

or more lexemes. SoAs are most often complex activities made of several phases. To attach a phase to a given SoA, rather than to lexicalize it as an individual lexeme, is a matter conditioned probably by universal perceptive and cognitive means, but it also depends on cultural factors that explain differences cross-linguistically, and also chronologically in the history of individual languages.

In languages where aspect is predominant in the organisation of the predicative system, grammatical tenses are commonly used to select specific phases of a SoA. In languages where aspect is not (mainly) expressed by the grammatical system, like many modern European languages, specific phases are either left unspecified or lexicalized. The contrast between Egyptian *mwt* and French *mourir*, and between *rḫ* and *connaître, savoir* illustrates this point. In the both cases, Egyptian has only one word, which encompasses different phases related to the SoA of dying or knowing. These phases can be accessed to by dedicated tenses (progressive, perfective, and resultative perfect). The following two graphs show how grammatical aspect selects the relevant phases of a SoA:[51]

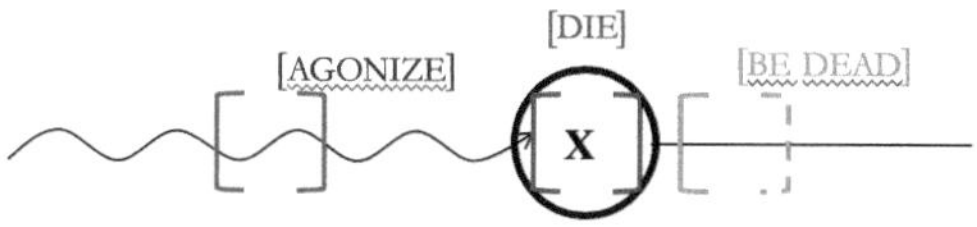

Fig. 3 | The actionality phases of *mwt* 'to die'.

As regards the expression of knowledge, Egyptian does not make a distinction between the activity of gaining knowledge of something (to learn) and the resulting state (to know).[52] Both are conceived as a single SoA. The grammatical system however leaves little doubt as regards the precise phase the speaker is referring to.[53]

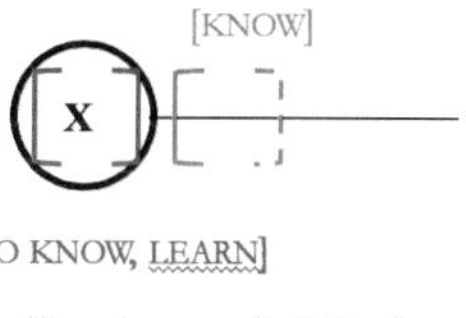

Fig. 4 | The actionality phases of *rḫ* 'to learn, to know'.

It is here important to note that *rḫ* has no pre-phase in Egyptian. When used, the progressive does not exactly express the mental activity that normally leads to the state of knowledge,

51 For mwt, cf. *Semnah Dispatches*, 4x+10 (progressive), oAshmMus. 1933.810 (perfective), and pBM 10052 4, 27 (resultative perfect). See also the opposition in Russian: Он умирал (imperfective) несколько часов … наконец он умер (perfective) 'he was dying for several hours … and finally he died'.

52 The activity of getting the knowledge of something can also be expressed by specific verbs, like *sḏm* 'to hear', which is very common, indicating how the subject receives his/her information.

53 Cf the opposition between *rḫ.n.f* (*Sinuhe*, B 31–32) and *rḫ.kwj* (pWestcar 9, 3–4). In ancient Greek and in Latin, the solution is a weak suppletive paradigm with stems coming from the same root: γιγνώσκω vs. ἔγνωκα, *cognosco* vs. *novi*.

but rather the attempt at gaining the knowledge of something (conative meaning).[54] The pre-phase is normally conveyed by verbs like *wḫ3* or *ḏʿr*.

Another way of modifying the original verbal Aktionsart is to change its argument structure.[55] While adding an argument can transform an atelic verb into a telic one (*b3k* 'to work' vs *b3k* + direct object 'to make something'),[56] suppressing an argument has the reverse effect (*jrj* + direct object 'to do something' vs. *jrj* 'to act, to have an activity'). Another strategy is to modify the grammatical expression of an argument. For instance, a transitive verb of accomplishment can be recategorized as an atelic SoA if its object is partitive.[57] This obtains in Egyptian by introducing the object with the preposition *m* 'in'.

Although the verbal predication in EEg is mainly organized with a system of aspectual oppositions, some phases of complex SoAs are sometimes lexicalized. A good illustration thereof is the case of the complex process of looking or searching that culminates in finding something. In Egyptian, there is apparently no example of *gmj* 'to find' in the progressive; verbs like *wḫ3* or *ḏʿr* are instead used to express the activity that leads to the culminating point of finding. Furthermore, the post-phase of *gmj*, its resultant phase, is more often expressed by a verb of knowing like *rḫ* than by *gmj*, which is consistent with the observation made above that *rḫ* is never found in the progressive. This contrasts with French. It is indeed possible to use *trouver* in the progressive pattern, which means that the subject is in the activity of searching that will eventually lead to the culmination event of finding. There is thus a continuum between *il est en train de trouver*, *il trouve*, and *il a trouvé*. In Egyptian such a sequence would be better expressed by three different verbs as illustrated in the last example:[58]

[61] *wḫ3.tw* | *jḳr,* | *gm.tw.k,* | *bw*
search:IAPLI-3SG.C | excellent | find-PASS-2SG.M | NEG-
jr.tw | *rḫ* | *šrj*
do:IAPLI-3SG.C | know:INF | small

'If one looks for an excellent one, one will find you, for one does know the small one.' (pChB IV v° 4, 4)

19th dyn. – Deir el-Medineh – Wisdom

54 See *Ptahhotep*, 288 P.

55 See Winand (2021: §3.4.3).

56 This also the case with some verbs of quality, like *nfr*: *nfr* + object 'make something perfect/beautiful'.

57 Another case is the verb *sḏm* 'to hear', which takes on the meaning of 'to listen to', hence 'to obey' when the second argument is obliquely expressed by being introduced by the preposition *n* 'to'. Historically, the expression *sḏm n* + NP 'to listen, to obey' was probably first to be understood as 'to listen (to something) to the benefit of someone', before being reinterpreted as 'listen to someone'.

58 Interestingly enough, in the following example, the negation of *gmj* has been expressed by *rḫ*: *j.jr.w gm.t.f jw 7 hrw p3 nty (ḥr) grḥ n p3j.f ʿḥʿw, jw bw rḫ rn n p3j.f ḥry-tp* 'one found that it is 7 days that end his lifetime, but one does know the name of his magician (…)' (pVandier 1, 7–8).

6 Conclusion

This study is a part of a larger project that aims at better understanding the ancient Egyptian lexicon. I have for a long time been interested in the relations between lexicon and grammar, particularly as regards the functioning of aspect.[59] The premises of my study rely on the intuition that SoAs are generally made of phases, which have their own semantic properties, like dynamicity, durativity, gradability, and telicity. While most SoAs are lexicalized as one single verb, it is not uncommon cross-linguistically to find cases of complementarity or suppletion. To be more precise, SoAs that historically focus on a limited and well-defined type of activity ended up merging into one single paradigm. This is what happened in several Indo-European languages where the organization of the predication was originally based on actionality rather than grammatical oppositions, with dedicated lexemes for specific types of activity, before proceeding to a system where aspect would select specific phases of a SoA, by then envisioned as a multiphased activity.[60] For instance, one can arguably show that in ancient Greek εἶμι and ἦλθον, two complementary morphological themes of the verb 'to go', were suppletive forms that stood in opposition aspectually and semantically, the former one being originally non-effective (viz. atelic), the latter effective (viz. telic).[61]

While ancient Egyptian does not seem to have been organized along the same principles, at least on such a scale, cases of suppletion can be observed. The causes are not to be searched for in a major reorganization of the predicative system as was the case in (pre-)archaic Greek, but rather in the story of particular lexemes. In the course of time, they gradually became less used and were finally reduced to a specific phase of a complex SoA. These isolated cases are thus closer to the reorganization of 'to go' in the Romance languages.[62]

In the second part of this study, I tried to show that cases of suppletion should be integrated into a larger representation of the lexical organization of ancient Egyptian. After discussing the case of multiphased SoAs whose lexical expression can be divided into several lexemes, I showed that a single lexeme could quite easily in ancient Egyptian correspond to what is conceived in European modern languages as distinct SoAs either by selecting a specific aspectual grammatical tense or by changing its argumental structure or the nature of its arguments. In other words, would it be too adventurous to suggest that EEg somehow compensated for a relative lexical paucity by its grammatical system?

Bibliography

Aksi, Janice. 1995. 'Verbal suppletion: an analysis of Italian, French, and Spanish to go', *Linguistics* 33, 403–32.

Binnick, Robert. 1991. *Time and the Verb: A Guide to Tense an Aspect*. New York & Oxford.

---

59 Winand (2006, 2021).

60 Binnick (1991).

61 See Létoublon (1987: 54–58).

62 See Aksi (1995).

Chantrain, Gaëlle. 2014. 'The use of classifiers in the New Kingdom. A global reorganization of the classifiers system?', *Lingua Aegyptia* 22, 39–59.

Collier, Mark. 1994. 'Grounding, cognition and metaphor in the grammar of Middle Egyptian', in: Allen, James (ed.). *Proceedings of the International Conference on Egyptian Grammar (Crossroads III). Yale, April 4–9, 1994*. Göttingen; *Lingua Aegyptia* 4, 57–87.

Eyre, Christopher. 2017. 'Calculated frightfulness and the display of violence', in: Bacs, Tamás & Horst Beinlich (eds), *Constructing Authority: Prestige, Reputation and the Perception of Power in Egyptian Kingship*, Wiesbaden, 89–122.

Frandsen, Paul John. 2016. 'To kill or not to kill', in: Collombert, Philippe, Dominique Lefèvre, Stéphane Polis & Jean Winand (eds). *Aere Perennius: Mélanges égyptologiques en l'honneur de Pascal Vernus*. Leuven; Orientalia Lovaniensia Analecta 242, 219–40.

Grossman, Eitan, Guillaume Lescuyer & Stéphane Polis. 2014. 'Contexts and inferences: The grammaticalization of the Later Egyptian allative future', in: Grossman, Eitan, Stéphane Polis, Andréas Stauder & Jean Winand (eds). *On Forms and Functions: Studies in Ancient Egyptian Grammar*. Hamburg; Lingua Aegyptia Studia Monographica 15, 87–136.

Juge, Matthew. 2000. 'On the rise of suppletion in verbal paradigms', in: Chang, Steve, Lily Liaw & Josef Ruppenhofer (eds). *Proceedings of the 25th Annual Meeting of the Berkeley Linguistics Society*. Berkeley, 183–94.

Kruchten, Jean-Marie. 1986. *Le grand texte oraculaire de Djéhoutymose, intendant du domaine d'Amon sous le pontificat de Pinedjem II*. Brussels; Mémoires de la Fondation Égyptologique Reine Élisabeth 5.

Lakoff, George and Mark Johnson. 1980. *Metaphors We Live by*. Chicago.

Létoublon, Françoise. 1987. *Il allait pareil à la nuit. Les verbes de mouvement en grec : supplétisme et aspect verbal*. Paris.

Peust, Carsten. 2007. 'Die Konjugation des Verbs für "gehen" im Neuägyptischen', *Göttinger Miszellen* 212, 67–80.

Polis, Stéphane & Jean Winand. 2015. 'Structuring the lexicon', in: Kousoulis, Panagiotis & Nicolaos Lazaridis (eds). *Proceedings of the Tenth International Congress of Egyptologists*. Leuven; Orientalia Lovaniensia Analecta 241, 1503–12.

Pomino, Natascha & Eva-Maria Remberger. 2019. 'Verbal suppletion in Romance synchrony and diachrony: the perspective of distributed morphology', *Transactions of the Philological Society* 117, 471–97.

Uljas, Sami. 2009. 'Radiality in Middle Egyptian grammar', in: Müller, Matthias & Sami Uljas (eds). *Proceedings of the Fourth International Conference on Egyptian Grammar (Crossroads IV). Basel, March 19–22, 2009*. Göttingen; *Lingua Aegyptia* 17, 277–90.

Wente, Edward. 1959. *The Syntax of Verbs of Motion in Egyptian*. Chicago.

Winand, Jean. 1991. '*Iy* et *iw*: unité morphologique et sémantique', *Lingua Aegyptia* 1, 357–88.

Winand, Jean. 1992. *Études de néo-égyptien*, I *La morphologie verbale*. Liège; Ægyptiaca Leodiensia 2.

Winand, Jean. 2003. 'Les décrets oraculaires pris en l'honneur d'Hénouttaouy et de Maatkarê (X^{e} et VIIe pylônes)', *Cahiers de Karnak* 11, 603–710.

Winand, Jean. 2006. *Temps et aspect en ancien égyptien. Une approche sémantique*. Boston/Leiden; Probleme der Ägyptologie 25.

Winand, Jean. 2016. 'Dialects in pre-Coptic Egyptian, with a special attention to Late Egyptian', *Lingua Aegyptia* 23, 229–69.

Winand, Jean. 2018. 'Late Egyptian', in: Stauder-Porchet, Julie, Andréas Stauder & Willeke Wendrich (eds). *UCLA Encyclopedia of Egyptology*. Los Angeles. http://digital2.library.ucla.edu/ viewItem.do?ark=21198/zz002kdgjj.

Winand, Jean. 2019. 'Did you say synonyms? The case of *pḥ* and *spr* in Late Egyptian', in: Brose, Marc, Peter Dils, Franziska Naether, Lutz Popko & Dietrich Raue (eds). *En détail – Philologie und*

Archäologie im Diskurs. Festschrift für Hans-W. Fischer-Elfert. Berlin; *Zeitschrift für Ägyptische Sprache und Altertumskunde – Beihefte 7*, 1235–75.

Winand, Jean. 2021. 'Aspect in Ancient Egyptian', in: Witte, Markus & Brinthanan Puvaneswaran (eds). *Tense and Aspect in Ancient Languages*. Waltrop; Kleine Untersuchungen zur Sprache des Alten Testament und seiner Umwelt 24, 93–260.

Winand, Jean. 2022. 'Dialects in pre-Coptic Egyptian', in: Stauder-Porchet, Julie, Andréas Stauder & Willeke Wendrich (eds). *UCLA Encyclopedia of Egyptology*. Los Angeles (https://escholarship.org/uc/item/8tr5w9nc).

Winand, Jean. forthc. a. 'Dialectal, sociolectal and idiolectal variations in the Late Egyptian texts from Deir el-Medineh and the Theban area'.

Lingua Aegyptia – Studia Monographica

ISSN: 0946-8641

1 Frank Kammerzell, *Panther, Löwe und Sprachentwicklung im Neolithikum.*
1994 (hardcover, 100 pages), out of print

2 Gerald Moers (ed.), *Definitely: Egyptian Literature: Proceedings of the symposion "Ancient Egyptian literature: history and forms", Los Angeles, March 24–26, 1995.*
1999 (hardcover, X+142 pages), out of print

3 Dörte Borchers, Frank Kammerzell & Stefan Weninger (eds.), *Hieroglyphen – Alphabete – Schriftreformen: Studien zu Multiliteralismus, Schriftwechsel und Orthographieneuregelungen.*
2001 (hardcover, VI+270 pages), ~~€ 49~~, now € 30

4 Stephan Jäger, *Altägyptische Berufstypologien.*
2004 (hardcover, X+340+xlvi+XCIV pages), out of print

5 José M. Galán, *Four Journeys in Ancient Egyptian Literature.*
2005 (hardcover, V+186 pages), out of print

6 Anthony Spalinger, *Five Views on Egypt.*
2006 (hardcover, VIII+176 pages), out of print (PDF online)

7 H.J. Polotsky, *Scripta Posteriora on Egyptian and Coptic,*
edited by Verena M. Lepper & Leo Depuydt.
2007 (hardcover, VI+230 pages), out of print

8 Petra Andrássy, Julia Budka & Frank Kammerzell (eds.), *Non-Textual Marking Systems, Writing and Pseudo Script from Prehistory to Modern Times.*
2009 (hardcover, VIII+312 pages), out of print (PDF online)

9 Eitan Grossman, Stéphane Polis & Jean Winand (eds.),
Lexical Semantics in Ancient Egyptian.
2012 (hardcover, vi+490 pages),
€ 69 (subscribers' price: € 59)
ISBN: 978-3-943955-09-5

10 R.B. Parkinson,
The Tale of the Eloquent Peasant: A Reader's Commentary.
2012 (hardcover, xii+384 pages),
€ 59 (subscribers' price: € 49)
ISBN: 978-3-943955-10-1

11 Gerald Moers, Kai Widmaier, Antonia Giewekemeyer, Arndt Lümers & Ralf Ernst (eds.),
Dating Egyptian Literary Texts.
"Dating Egyptian Literary Texts" Göttingen, 9–12 June 2010, Volume 1
2013 (hardcover, xiv+653 pages),
€ 95 (subscribers' price: € 79)
ISBN: 978-3-943955-11-8

12 Andréas Stauder,
Linguistic Dating of Middle Egyptian Literary Texts.
"Dating Egyptian Literary Texts" Göttingen, 9–12 June 2010, Volume 2
2013 (hardcover, xx+568 pages),
€ 85 (subscribers' price: € 69)
ISBN: 978-3-943955-12-5

13 Marc Brose,
Grammatik der dokumentarischen Texte des Mittleren Reiches.
2014 (cloth, xx+553 pages),
€ 85 (subscribers' price: € 69)
ISBN: 978-3-943955-13-2

14 Andréas Stauder,
The Earlier Egyptian Passive. Voice and Perspective.
2014 (cloth, xviii+448 pages),
€ 69 (subscribers' price: € 59)
ISBN: 978-3-943955-14-9

15 Eitan Grossman, Stéphane Polis, Andréas Stauder & Jean Winand (eds.),
On Forms and Functions: Studies in Ancient Egyptian Grammar.
2014 (cloth, vi+366 pages),
€ 59 (subscribers' price: € 49)
ISBN: 978-3-943955-15-6

16 Julia Budka, Frank Kammerzell & Sławomir Rzepka (eds.),
Non-Textual Marking Systems in Ancient Egypt (and Elsewhere).
2015 (cloth, x+322 pages),
€ 59 (subscribers' price: € 49)
ISBN: 978-3-943955-16-3

17 Eitan Grossman, Peter Dils, Tonio Sebastian Richter & Wolfgang Schenkel (eds.),
Greek Influence on Egyptian-Coptic: Contact-Induced Change in an Ancient African Language. DDGLC Working Papers 1.
2017 (cloth, viii+534 pages),
€ 89 (subscribers' price: € 69)
ISBN: 978-3-943955-17-0

18 Kristina Hutter,
Das sḏm=f-Paradigma im Mittelägyptischen: Eine Vergleichsstudie verschiedener Grammatiken.
2017 (paperback, x+289 pages, incl. 47 tables),
€ 49 (subscribers' price: € 39)
ISBN: 978-3-943955-18-7

19 Gaëlle Chantrain & Jean Winand (eds.),
Time and Space at Issue in Ancient Egypt.
2018 (paperback, viii+242 p.),
€ 55 (subscribers' price: € 39)
ISBN: 978-3-943955-19-4

20 Marwan Kilani,
Vocalisation in Group Writing: A New Proposal.
2019 (paperback, vi+150 pages),
€ 39 (subscribers' price: € 29)
ISBN: 978-3-943955-20-0
ISBN (OPEN ACCESS PDF): 978-3-943955-90-3 |
doi.org/10.37011/studmon.20

21 Gaëlle Chantrain,
Eléments de la terminologie du temps en égyptien ancien.
2020 (paperback, xxxiv+344 pages),
€ 59 (subscribers' price: € 49)
ISBN: 978-3-943955-21-7

22 Kathrin Gabler, Rita Gautschy, Lukas Bohnenkämper, Hanna Jenni, Clémentine Reymond, Ruth Zillhardt, Andrea Loprieno-Gnirs & Hans-Hubertus Münch (eds),
Text-Bild-Objekte im archäologischen Kontext: Festschrift für Susanne Bickel.
2020 (cloth, xxii+293 p., 23 colour, 60 b&w illustrations), € 65 (subscribers' price: € 49)
ISBN: 978-3-943955-22-4

23 Simon Thuault,
La dissemblance graphémique à l'Ancien Empire: Essai de grammatologie cognitive.
2020 (paperback, xx+376 pages, illustrations),
€ 59 (subscribers' price: € 49)
ISBN: 978-3-943955-23-1

24 Matthias Müller
Grammatik des Bohairischen.
2021 (paperback, xxiv+936 pages),
€ 49 (subscribers' price: € 45)
ISBN: 978-3-943955-24-8

25 Helmut Satzinger & Danijela Stefanović,
Egyptian Root Lexicon.
2021 (hardcover, viii+717 pages),
€ 89 (subscribers' price: € 69)
ISBN: 978-3-943955-25-5

26 Nina Speransky,
Transitivity and Aspect in Sahidic Coptic: Studies in the Morphosyntax of Native and Greek-Origin Verbs.
DDGLC Working Papers 2.
2022 (paperback, xxiv+218 pages),
€ 49 (subscribers' price: € 39)
ISBN: 978-3-943955-26-2
ISBN (OPEN ACCESS PDF): 978-3-943955-91-0 |
doi.org/10.37011/studmon.26

27 Antonia Giewekemeyer,
Wer schreibt die Geschichte(n)? Die 8. bis frühe 12. Dynastie im Licht ägyptologischer und ägyptischer Sinnbildungen.
2022 (hardcover, xxx+530 pages),
€ 89 (subscribers' price: € 69)
ISBN: 978-3-943955-27-9

28 Marc Brose,
Die Sprache der königlichen Stelen der 18. Dynastie bis einschließlich Amenophis III.
2023 (hardcover, xviii+702 pages),
€ 89 (subscribers' price: € 69)
ISBN: 978-3-943955-28-6

29 Gerald Moers (ed.)
Narrative and Narrativity in Ancient Egypt: Case Studies on Narrative Difference in Various Media.
2023 (paperback, viii+304 pages),
€ 55 (subscribers' price: € 45)
ISBN: 978-3-943955-29-3
ISBN (OPEN ACCESS PDF): 978-3-943955-92-7 |
doi.org/10.37011/studmon.29

All prices include German VAT (7%).

For orders, standing orders and further information:

www.widmaier-verlag.de
orders@widmaier-verlag.de

North American customers may also contact the official distributor ISD (for issues since volume 9):

www.isdistribution.com

9 783943 955309

LINGUA AEGYPTIA
Studia Monographica 29

Narrative and Narrativity in Ancient Egypt

Gerald Moers (ed.)

Widmaier Verlag
Hamburg